WADSWORTH
CENGAGE Learning™

RELG: World
Robert E. Van Voorst

Publisher: Clark Baxter

Senior Sponsoring Editor: Joann Kozyrev

Senior Development Editor: Sue Gleason

Assistant Editor: Joshua Duncan

Editorial Assistant: Marri Straton

Media Editor: Kimberly Apfelbaum

Marketing Program Manager: Sean P. Foy

4LTR Press Project Manager: Kelli Strieby

4LTR Press Product Development
    Manager: Steve Joos

Content Project Manager: Alison Eigel Zade

Senior Art Director: Stacy Jenkins Shirley

Production Technology Analyst: Jeff Joubert

Senior Print Buyer: Diane Gibbons

Rights Acquisition Specialist:
    Shalice Shah-Caldwell

Cover Designer: Joe Devine,
    Red Hangar Design

Text Designer: Joe Devine, Red Hangar Design

Cover Image: ©Getty Images/Gallo Images/
    Danita Dellmont

Production Service and Compositor: Integra

Inside Front Cover Images: chair and gears
    © Squared Studios/Photodisc/Getty Images;
    microscope © Siede Preis/Photodisc/
    Getty Images; dartboard and binoculars
    © Photodisc/Getty Images

Back Cover Image:
    © iStockphoto.com/René Mansi

Title Page Image: © iStockphoto.com/CostinT

For product information and technology assistance, contact us at
Cengage Learning Customer & Sales Support, 1-800-354-9706

For permission to use material from this text or product,
submit all requests online at **www.cengage.com/permissions.**
Further permissions questions can be e-mailed to
permissionrequest@cengage.com

Library of Congress Control Number: 2011926862

ISBN-13: 978-1-111-72620-1
ISBN-10: 1-111-72620-5

Wadsworth
20 Channel Center Street
Boston, MA 02210
USA

Cengage Learning is a leading provider of customized learning solutions with office locations around the globe, including Singapore, the United Kingdom, Australia, Mexico, Brazil, and Japan. Locate your local office at: **international.cengage.com/region**

Cengage Learning products are represented in Canada by Nelson Education, Ltd.

For your course and learning solutions, visit **www.cengage.com.**

Purchase any of our products at your local college store or at our preferred online store **www.cengagebrain.com**

Instructors: Please visit **login.cengage.com** and log in to access instructor-specific resources.

Printed in the United States of America
1 2 3 4 5 6 7 15 14 13 12 11

Brief Contents

Contents

© ISTOCKPHOTO/NINA SHANNON

NASA

2. ENCOUNTERING INDIGENOUS RELIGIONS: WAYS TO TRIBAL LIFE

© MARK HERREID/SHUTTERSTOCK.COM

© ISTOCKPHOTO.COM/ERIC ISSELEE

3. ENCOUNTERING HINDUISM: MANY PATHS TO LIBERATION

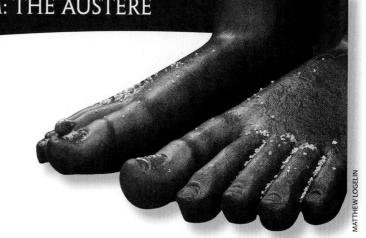

4. ENCOUNTERING JAINISM: THE AUSTERE WAY TO LIBERATION

MATTHEW LOGELIN

5. ENCOUNTERING BUDDHISM: THE MIDDLE PATH TO LIBERATION

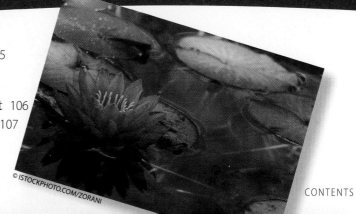

© ISTOCKPHOTO.COM/ZORANI

SARAH M. GOLONKA/BRAND X PICTURES/JUPITER IMAGES

© SERG ZASTAVKIN/SHUTTERSTOCK.COM

6. ENCOUNTERING SIKHISM: THE WAY OF GOD'S NAME

7. ENCOUNTERING DAOISM AND CONFUCIANISM: TWO VIEWS OF THE ETERNAL WAY

8. ENCOUNTERING SHINTO: THE WAY OF THE KAMI

PHOTO COURTESY PHOTOS8.COM

9. ENCOUNTERING ZOROASTRIANISM: THE WAY OF THE ONE WISE LORD

10. ENCOUNTERING JUDAISM: THE WAY OF GOD'S CHOSEN PEOPLE

© ISTOCKPHOTO.COM/GEORGE CORBIN

© ISTOCKPHOTO.COM/LUOMAN

11. ENCOUNTERING CHRISTIANITY: THE WAY OF SALVATION IN JESUS CHRIST

© ISTOCKPHOTO.COM/HAZLAN ABDUL HAKIM

© CARLOS E. SANTA MARIA/SHUTTERSTOCK.COM

12. ENCOUNTERING ISLAM: THE STRAIGHT PATH OF THE ONE GOD

PHOTO COURTESY WWW.PHOTOS8.COM

© PETE NIESEN/SHUTTERSTOCK.COM

13. ENCOUNTERING NEW RELIGIOUS MOVEMENTS: MODERN WAYS TO ALTERNATIVE MEANINGS

ANNIEGREENSPRINGS

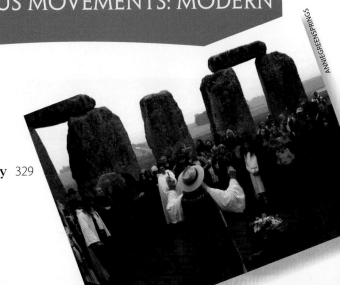

© ISTOCKPHOTO.COM/ANDREW RICH

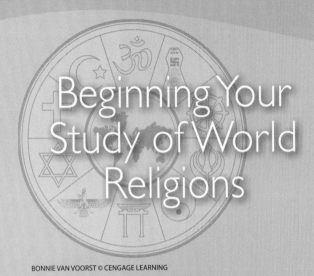

CHAPTER 1

Beginning Your Study of World Religions

BONNIE VAN VOORST © CENGAGE LEARNING

Learning Outcomes
After studying this chapter, you will be able to do the following:

LO1 State and explain the definition of *religion* used in this book.

LO2 Give your own answer to the question "Why study religion?"

LO3 List and describe the six different dimensions of religion.

LO4 Discuss how the various academic disciplines contribute to the study of religion.

LO5 Explain the special issues in the study of religion today.

LO6 State and explain your own "preunderstanding" of religion.

NASA

"Religion starts with the perception that something is wrong." —Karen Armstrong

YOUR VISIT TO THE HSI LAI TEMPLE IN SOUTHERN CALIFORNIA

Imagine that you're walking up the broad flight of stone steps to the Hsi Lai (shee lai) Buddhist temple in Hacienda Heights, California, just east of Los Angeles. Hsi Lai claims the distinction of being the largest Buddhist temple in North America, and it certainly looks like it from where you stand! When you get inside, you look around and realize that this is a religious building complex like none other you have ever seen. There seem to be no large-group ceremonies going on, at least right now. Instead, small groups of worshipers and tourists come and go, doing their own thing. Some offer incense, a few are carrying flowers to leave in the temple, others are praying and meditating in front of statues, and out in the courtyard there are people doing meditative exercise routines.

Most of the neatly dressed families coming to this temple do not seem to reflect deeply here on their faith. You see nobody reading Buddhist religious texts, nor does any monk teach or preach to a group. Rather, most worshipers come here just to sense something of the sacred and be in its presence. Their minds are calmed by the familiar architecture, by the many statues of the Buddha, by the soft smell of incense. They engage in quiet, low-key activities.

You notice people who aren't doing traditional Buddhist worship. You wonder if this means that they might come

What Do YOU Think?

Religion is mostly about finding one's way to eternal life, however that is understood.

Strongly Disagree						Strongly Agree
1	2	3	4	5	6	7

from other religious traditions. Some people you see are just tourists, a few of them mostly interested in the tasty vegetarian buffet lunch served every day. But perhaps they too have come to absorb the beauty of this place, and at least some of its religious meaning. This temple was founded not only to bridge the differences between different groups of Buddhists, but also to be a bridge between Eastern and Western religions and ways of life.

As you are introduced to the academic study of religion, you may find yourself bewildered— by the varieties of religion, by  Watch a video on the Hsi Lai temple.

distinguishing religions from other movements, by the different academic methods used to study religions, and by hot topics such as religion and gender, ecology, and violence. You may have questions about matters of fact and value: is one religion true, are different religions true, or are none of them true? What might it all mean for *you*?

Hsi Lai Buddhist temple in Southern California

< As sunlight moves over the Eastern Hemisphere, one can see the regions where most world religions were born. The new perspective of Earth from space has helped to stimulate global thinking in religions.

These issues may occur to you as well:

- Formal "separation of church and state" is strong in the United States and Canada, but religion and politics are mixed in powerful ways here and around the world. The government of China's continuous pressure on Buddhism in Tibet and on the Falun Gong movement is just one example.

Read about a law attempting to regulate reincarnation in China.

- Most people in North America affirm the importance of religion for their lives, but fewer actually practice it. For example, almost 90 percent of all North Americans believe in the existence of God or gods, but only about half regularly participate in religious services or in other religious practices such as prayer, meditation, or giving to those in need.

"Americans are by all measures a deeply religious people, but they are also deeply ignorant about religion." —Laurie Goodstein

- Despite a high level of religious belief in the United States, most Americans have surprisingly little knowledge of their faith. Stephen Prothero (PROTH-er-oh), a professor of religion at Boston University who has appeared on *The Colbert Report* and *The Daily Show*, has shown that many Americans—even many who attend services often—are "religious illiterates." As Laurie Goodstein of the *New York Times* wrote in summarizing a 2010 study of religious knowledge in the United States, "Americans are by all measures a deeply religious people, but they are also deeply ignorant about religion."[1] In Western Europe, most people don't hold formally to a religion, but they know a good deal about religion, because it is a required academic subject in the schools.

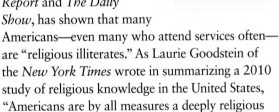

See Stephen Prothero speak on religious illiteracy.

Read a *New York Times* report on a 2010 survey of religious literacy.

- Is religion in the world shrinking, or is it growing? Actually, both. Although some parts of Christianity and Judaism are shrinking, other parts of these religions are growing, and Islam and Buddhism are also growing. The number of people in North America who formally adhere to no religion at all is growing, but certain religious practices such as prayer are stronger than ever.

- Most of the major religions of the world come from ancient times. However, every decade of the last two hundred years has seen new religious movements born around the world, some of them now powerful, some controversial. You might wonder why we still get new religions—don't we have enough already?

- Religion has evoked some of both the best and the worst in human life. Great acts of love, service, and even self-sacrifice have arisen from religious conviction. Religion has inspired some of the world's greatest music, art, and architecture, and has lifted the human spirit in countless ways. Ironically, it has also been the source of much destruction.

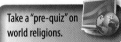

Take a "pre-quiz" on world religions.

LO1 What Is Religion?

Religion is found across all cultures and throughout the entire span of human history. Evidence of early human remains shows signs of religion, including veneration of animal spirits in art and human burials that suggest belief in a life beyond death. Most anthropologists today have concluded that Neanderthal humans who lived around 200,000 years ago may have had religious beliefs and practices, but that Cro-Magnon humans (around 35,000 years ago) definitely had religion. From the dawn of human civilizations until modern times, religion has shaped the beliefs and values of all human cultures.

DEFINING *RELIGION*

But this talk of the prevalence of religion leads us to ask: What exactly is religion? Defining academic subjects can be a boring business, but on the subject of religion, most people have something interesting to say. Grappling with this question involves both careful, objective academic thinking and personal engagement. The University of Cambridge scholar John Bowker remarks, "We all know what [religion] is until someone asks us to tell them."[2] If pressed for an answer, most people in the Western world would say first that religion is based on belief in God and obedience to God. However, do

---

[1] Laurie Goodstein, "Basic Religion Test Stumps Many Americans," *New York Times* (city edition), September 28, 2010, page A17.

[2] John Bowker, ed., *Oxford Dictionary of World Religions* (New York: Oxford University Press, 1997), xv.

they mean the God followed in a particular religion or something more general, such as "gods"? Some major religions—certain branches of Hinduism and Buddhism, for example—have relatively little teaching about gods. A few religions such as Jainism have no gods at all.

Some people around the world would give a second answer to "What is religion?"—that it is a system of morality. On first reflection, this might seem to be a more all-encompassing definition than the previous one. Karen Armstrong, a former Roman Catholic nun and now a popular writer on world religions, recently wrote that "Religion starts with the perception that something is wrong," and that the value systems in religions set out to deal with that wrong.[3] The three main Western religions—Judaism, Christianity, and Islam—have strong moral teachings. Confucianism is so centered on morality that the issue of whether it is a social philosophy or a religion is often debated. However, a few religions, such as Shinto, have little or no developed teaching about a way of life. All this shows how our prior perceptions color our answer to the question "What is religion?" Despite the difficulties of this question, many scholars from various academic fields have attempted to answer it in as objective a manner as possible.

NOTABLE DEFINITIONS OF *RELIGION*

Another way of studying the issue of what *religion* means is by looking at definitions that have been offered in the past and have had some influence on the discussion. Here is a sampling of how *religion* has been defined in the Western world, by scholars and others. Religion is …

"The feeling of absolute dependence"
—Friedrich Schleiermacher, Christian theologian (1799)

---

[3] Karen Armstrong, *A History of God* (New York: Ballantine, 1994), 1.

"The opiate of the people"
—Karl Marx, nineteenth-century founder of communism (1843)

"A set of things which the average man thinks he believes and wishes he was certain of"
—Mark Twain, American writer (1879)

"The daughter of Hope and Fear, explaining to Ignorance the nature of the Unknowable"
—Ambrose Bierce, American social critic and humorist (1911)

"A unified system of beliefs and practices … which unite into one single moral community"
—Émile Durkheim, French sociologist of religion (1915)

"What grows out of, and gives expression to, experience of the holy in its various aspects"
—Rudolf Otto, German scholar of religion (1917)

"All bunk"
—Thomas Edison, American inventor (ca. 1925)

"Something left over from the infancy of our intelligence; it will fade away as we adopt reason and science as our guidelines"
—Bertrand Russell, British philosopher (1928)

"An illusion deriving its strength from the fact that it falls in with our instinctual desires"
—Sigmund Freud, Austrian psychiatrist (1932)

"The state of being grasped by an ultimate concern, a concern … which itself contains the answer to the question of the meaning of our life"
—Paul Tillich, Christian theologian (1957)

"What the individual does with his own solitariness"
—A. N. Whitehead, British philosopher (1960)

"A set of symbolic forms and acts which relate man to the ultimate conditions of his existence"
—Robert Bellah, contemporary American sociologist

"Feeling warmer in our hearts, more connected to others, more connected to something greater, and having a sense of peace"
—Goldie Hawn, contemporary American film actress

THE DEFINITION USED IN THIS BOOK

Each student will have to wrestle personally with defining *religion*, because scholarship isn't settled on any one definition and because defining it involves some subjectivity. Here's the definition used in this book: **Religion** is a pattern of beliefs and practices that expresses and enacts what a community regards as

religion Pattern of beliefs and practices that expresses and enacts what a community regards as sacred and/or ultimate about life

sacred and/or ultimate about life.

Let's "unpack" this definition. First, religion is *a pattern of beliefs and practices*. All religions believe certain things about ultimate reality in or beyond the world. They answer existential questions most humans have:

- Why am I here?
- What does it mean to be human?
- How can what is wrong in the world—and in me—be corrected?
- Where am I—and the world—going?

They answer these questions in different ways. The different religions believe in one God (**monotheism**) or many gods (**polytheism**). They believe, with or without belief in a god, in a world soul in Hinduism, in Nirvana in Buddhism, and in the Dao (also spelled *Tao*, with both pronounced "dow") in both Daoism (Taoism) and Confucianism. They practice these beliefs in certain ways: in worship, rituals of passage at various points of the individual life cycle, meditation, and ordinary actions in daily life. Each religion has its own way of arranging these beliefs and practices into a distinctive *pattern*. Second, this pattern *expresses and enacts* what is *sacred*. *Sacred* refers to what is considered most holy and important, whether in this world, in a supernatural world that transcends this one, or both. Religions draw on their experience of the sacred, both ancient and contemporary; express the sacred in all of its aspects; and enact it by continuing to make it real for believers.

Because common Western notions of the "sacred" or "holy" often entail belief in a holy God, we add this further phrase to our definition: *ultimate about life*. This "ultimate" may be a principle, an impersonal force, or a spiritual power, hidden in the world or beyond it. Sacredness or "the ultimate" in world religions is wider than a divine being. Third, note that it is a *community* of like-minded people that forms a religion. Religions sometimes begin with an individual (Buddha, Confucius, Jesus), but they become social communities of shared belief and practice even during the lifetime or in the second generation following the life of these founders. They persist through history as communities of religion. Not all religions try to grow throughout the world, but all of them are concerned with passing themselves from generation to generation, thus becoming "traditions."

The meaning of *religion* is typically traced to the ancient Latin world *religio* (ree-LIG-ee-oh), derived from the verb *religere*, "to bind/tie fast." This verb is itself derived from the word *ligere*, "to bind" (compare our words *ligament* and *ligature*). Of course, the meaning of a word today can't be limited to what it meant thousands of years ago, but this ancient meaning shows how *religion* began and still illustrates nicely the different parts of our definition. Ancient Romans used *religio* in several senses. First, it means a supernatural constraint on behavior, doing what is good, and especially avoiding evil. It "binds" people to what is right. Second, it entails a holy awe for the gods and sacred power in general. Third, *religio* means a system of life that binds people together in a group and orients them to the gods. Finally, it entails the practices of rites and ceremonies by which the Roman people expressed and enacted their religion.[4]

Although the Romans and some other peoples used the term *religion* for their system of belief and practice, different religions of the world call themselves by different names, most of them not using the word *religion* at all. For example, Daoism is "the Way" to most Daoists; they don't refer to it as "the Daoist religion." Many Hindus call their religion "the Eternal Teaching"; Buddhists sometimes call theirs a "school"; and many Jews, Christians, and Muslims prefer the term *faith* instead of *religion*. But no matter what they call themselves, they are in fact *religions* as that term is used in scholarship and teaching. However, the definition given above doesn't rule out the necessity for world religions students to wrestle with this question on their own.

A good definition will carefully identify the subject being defined, but it can also be used to exclude other things from the definition. How does the definition given above exclude things that *aren't* religion? Here are two examples. First, the definition speaks of religion as a system based on the sacred or on ultimate value; other systems that do not view themselves as religions do not usually speak about the "sacred" or "ultimate." This is true of most political ideologies and parties such as Democrats and Republicans, academic philosophies, systems of popular psychology like that of "Dr. Phil" McGraw, and so on. (This isn't meant to demean these other groups; many people find a great deal of meaning and inspiration in them.) Therefore, people who belong to nonreligious groups can also practice a variety of religion or no religion at all. Second, a pattern of belief held by only one person can't be a religion as we define it here. Such do-it-yourself religion may be popular in Europe and North America, and it is usually sincere and important to the person who holds it, but it doesn't bring with it a social bond. Some scholars sometimes refer to this as **private religion**, but

---

[4] P. G. W. Glare, *Oxford Latin Dictionary* (New York: Oxford University Press, 1983), 1605–06.

A Closer Look:

Is *Religion* a Dirty Word?

To some religious people, *religion* is, if not a dirty word, at least a derogatory one. Some Christians, Jews, and Muslims think that "religion" is a bad thing. Many religious people want to have a strong connection with God/ultimate reality/cosmic power, but not a "religion." They call their own beliefs a "faith," "teaching," "school," or something similar, but they often call other people's belief systems, somewhat pejoratively, "religion." In his best-selling book written for Christians, *The Shack*, William Young even has Jesus say, "I'm not too big on religion."

People who don't like any religion at all also use *religion* in a negative way. An increasing number of people in North America and Europe say, "I'm spiritual, but I'm not religious." A 2008 documentary film featuring comic and social critic Bill Maher was titled not *Religious*, but *Religulous*, Maher's unflattering combination of *religion* and *ridiculous*.

> *"I'm not too big on religion."* —Jesus, in *The Shack*

To study world religions well, you have to put aside prejudice, whether pro or con, if you have it. All scholars of religion use *religion* as an academic, neutral, descriptive term, and you should, too, regardless of your own personal stance on religious belief and practice. To use an analogy, many people today, including students, often use the word *politics* prejudicially. But to study well in the academic field called "political science," one must put aside prejudice about the term *politics*. The same is true for the study of religion.

See a trailer for *Religulous*.

Read an explanation of "Sheila-ism," a private religion.

others question whether "private religion" is really religion at all.

LO2 Why Study Religion?

At first, the question "Why Study Religion?" may seem pointless to you. You might say, "I'm taking the course, aren't I?" You may go on to give your reasons for taking this course: to get course credit, to fulfill a cultural studies requirement at your school and maybe pick up some knowledge and skills along the way, and ultimately to get an academic degree. But let's explore a bit further why students today should study religion.

STUDYING THE PERSISTENCE OF RELIGION IN THE MODERN WORLD

Religion should be studied—among other reasons—to understand its persistence in the modern world, which in many ways is not hospitable to religious belief and practice. The rise of **secularism**, or life without religion, has challenged most religions for the past two hundred years. Today, the secular approach to life rejects religion

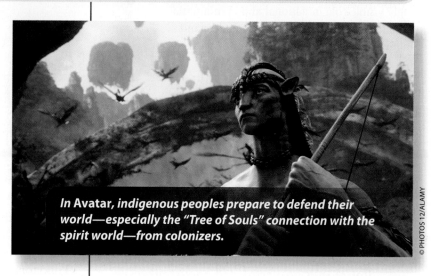

In Avatar, indigenous peoples prepare to defend their world—especially the "Tree of Souls" connection with the spirit world—from colonizers.

© PHOTOS 12/ALAMY

for the perceived evils of fundamentalism ("Look what happened on 9/11!" is commonly heard); the inappropriateness of religious training for children ("Children should be allowed to decide for themselves when they are older"); and the better view on life offered by science ("Religion is false, because we know about evolution"). Secularism has led to a lessening of religious belief and practice, and in North America to widespread illiteracy about religion. Many people, including about half of all Europeans and a growing number of North Americans, are neither especially religious nor completely irreligious; they are "in the middle" between them. They combine aspects of secular life with aspects of religious life.

secularism Life without religion

This means that reports of the death of religion are mistaken. Religion persists today and is often on the rise, even as secularism has become more widespread. More than three-quarters of the world's people identify with one or more religions. We still find religion everywhere: in high culture, in popular culture (for example, the 2009 film *Avatar* and the rock band U2), and in everyday life in North America and around the world. The religions of the world are now present in North America, and almost every religion is as close as one's keyboard, on the Internet. In the Soviet Union and China—which tried with Communist fervor in the twentieth century to suppress and even extinguish all religion—it has come back with vigor. The government of China is now bringing back Confucian texts and teachings to counteract the "money-first" mentality among so many young people there. At the beginning of the twenty-first century, religion is at or near the center of global issues and cultural conflict. Religion has an increasingly visible role in national and even international politics. One simply can't understand many of the conflicts in our world without a basic knowledge of religion. What's more, new religious movements are arising every decade, so that the number of religions in the world is increasing, not decreasing. Religion is emerging as one of the main markers of human identity in the twenty-first century, along with gender, class, and ethnicity.[5]

Read about Confucius's reentry into China's schools.

Religion is powerful and persistent, and it shows no signs of disappearing.

THE RISE OF SECULARISM HAS CHALLENGED MOST RELIGIONS FOR THE PAST TWO HUNDRED YEARS.

Why does religion keep on thriving? First, despite the challenges to religion, it continues to be a powerful resource for everyday life all around the world. Religion still provides meaning, strength, and joy to many. Another reason is that most religious traditions have proven themselves adaptable to the ever-changing situations of human life. They've changed over the thousands of years that many of them have existed, and the study of these changes forms a large part of the study of religion. (If religions can't or don't change, they usually die out.) Many religions even have some room for skepticism and for the secular, which gives them strength in our rapidly changing world. In many places, especially in central and southern Africa, indigenous religions tied to local cultures are fading, but universal religions such as Christianity and Islam have taken their place. Overall, religion is powerful and persistent, and it shows no signs of disappearing. For everyone who wants to be informed about the world, religion is an important part of understanding it.

Read "Believers Can Be Reasonable" by psychologist David Myers.

The study of religion is also a persistent part of the academic scene. Around 750,000 undergraduates take a religion course each year in the United States. Enrollment in world religion courses in the United States has grown rapidly after the religiously connected attacks on this country on September 11, 2001. Some of the students decide to make the study of religion their major or minor. Religions are taught in most liberal arts colleges, as well as in private and state universities. Leading universities that didn't have a religious studies program in the past because of a more secular orientation established one in the twentieth century, among them Harvard, Princeton, Cornell, and Stanford. In 2009 the American Historical Association reported that more historians in the U.S. now specialize in religious issues than in any others. Even the government of China, which is officially atheistic, is setting up undergraduate and graduate degree programs in religious studies in several of its most selective universities. What's more, the study of religion in U.S. K–12 public schools is growing, with new guidelines from the American Academy of Religion, an association of religion professors.[6] In sum, the academic study of religion is alive and well.

© ISTOCKPHOTO/LUKASZ KULICKI

[5] Stephen Prothero, *Religious Literacy* (San Francisco: Harper SanFrancisco, 2007), 5.

[6] "American Academy of Religion Guidelines for Teaching about Religion in K–12 Public Schools in the United States," http://www.aarweb.org/Publications/Online_Publications/Curriculum_Guidelines/AARK-12CurriculumGuidelines.pdf.

WHAT THE ACADEMIC STUDY OF RELIGION CAN OFFER YOU

Intellectual exploration to shape one's knowledge and values is one of the joys of being a student, but most students today also have valid concerns about how studying religion will help them to earn a living in today's economy. A small proportion of students in religion courses choose to make religion the center of a professional career, either as the leader of a religious community (such as a rabbi, priest, or minister) or as an academic specialist in higher education. Some students take a world religion course to clarify or strengthen their own religious knowledge and values. They realize the truth in the proverb first said by Max Müller, "Those who know only one religion know none."

Most students take a world religion course to learn more about an important aspect of the world today. This study offers students training in a unique combination of academic and everyday skills such as these:

- The ability to understand how religious thought and practice are related to particular social and cultural contexts
- The ability to understand the religious dimensions of conflicts within and between nations
- An appreciation of the complexities of religious language and values
- An ability to understand and explain important texts both critically and empathetically
- Cross-cultural understanding, or what is now becoming known academically as "cultural intelligence" or "cross-cultural competence"

Few academic fields bring together so many different forms of analysis as religion does. With this broad liberal arts background, many religion majors or minors go on to study law, business, education, and medicine in graduate school. In short, the study of religion offers a foundation for a successful and fulfilling career, in addition to growth in personal knowledge and satisfaction.

> "Those who know only one religion know none." —Max Müller

LO3 Dimensions of Religion

As we examine the varieties of religious experience, all sorts of human beliefs and practices come into view. Religion seems to be as wide as human life itself.

This was illustrated in one American publishing company's poster, which read: "Books about religion are also about love, sex, politics, AIDS, war, peace, justice, ecology, philosophy, addiction, recovery, ethics, race, gender, dissent, technology, old age, New Age, faith, heavy metal, morality, beauty, God, psychology, money, dogma, freedom, history, death, and life." To get a grip on this complexity, various scholars have organized the dimensions of religion in various ways. These patterns are somewhat artificial, but they're helpful in grasping the mass of information available about religions, for both beginning students and experienced scholars alike. The prominent scholar of comparative religion Ninian Smart first laid out five dimensions in the 1960s, but by the 1990s he had come to think there were nine. Following Smart, Rodney Stark and Charles Glock have systematized the various interlocking aspects of religion in six dimensions.[7]

THE COGNITIVE DIMENSION

Religions have cognitive (thinking) dimensions that teach their followers what it is necessary to know. Most religions teach deep knowledge about their gods and founders, often in stories. They teach about the creation of the world, the meaning of life, and ways to overcome death. They teach about human identity, both individual and social: gender, class, ethnicity, and others. They provide ways of understanding what the world is and what it should be. Often the history of religion itself is explained so that followers can know that they stand in a great tradition. The cognitive dimension of religion entails analyzing and systematizing knowledge, as well as learning it and passing it on. Its teachings are framed in stories, short statements that summarize beliefs (for example, the Four Noble Truths of Buddhism), songs, proverbs, laws, and many other forms. The cognitive dimensions of religion typically grow so comprehensive and important that religions can contain an entire worldview. However, we must keep in mind that there is often a significant gap between the official levels of religious teachings and what is believed and practiced by most people.

THE ETHICAL DIMENSION

Ethics are important in almost all religions, because, as we saw above, religions seek to correct what they perceive to be wrong in the world. Personal ethics are

---

[7] Rodney Stark and Charles Glock, *Patterns of Religious Commitment* (Berkeley: University of California Press, 1968).

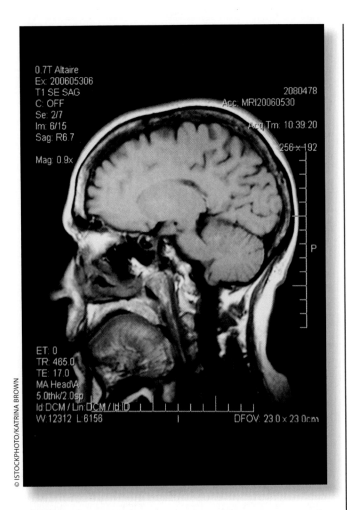

THE RITUAL DIMENSION

Ritual is symbolic action in worship, meditation, or other religious ceremonies. It's symbolic and sometimes abstract, but meant to achieve very practical goals. When most people in North America today think of religion, they think of the ritual ceremonies of worship. But ritual also includes formal and informal prayer, sacrifice, chanting of scriptures, public processions, and even pilgrimage. Pilgrimage—travel to a special destination to increase one's devotion or improve one's religious status—doesn't often come to the minds of modern North Americans as a religious ritual, but in 2009 millions of people worldwide went on a pilgrimage and spent the equivalent of 18 billion U.S. dollars on it. Ritual can be long, elaborate ceremonies performed by religious specialists or simple daily acts like such as a short prayer before eating a meal or going to sleep. Rituals are directed to one God, many gods, or to spirits or deceased ancestors. Ritual is not only symbolic, but also effective; it helps to reenact and reapply the deep truths of a religion to people in the present. Mircea Eliade (MUHR-chuh eh-lee-AH-deh), who died in 1986, advanced his influential theory of "eternal return" about myths. This theory holds that myths and rituals do not simply commemorate past acts of the gods, but actually participate in them and bring worshipers to the gods. In some religions, sacrifice of food or drink is thought to "feed" the gods or deceased ancestors and make them happy with those who offer sacrifice to them.

Within religions there is often a mixed attachment to ritual. For example, in Christianity some Protestants minimize formal rituals, whereas most Roman Catholics and the Eastern Orthodox have many elaborate rituals. Sufi Muslims emphasize pilgrimage to God "in the heart," in part to contrast with other Muslims who view

found in most religions, but the emphasis is strongly on social ethics. All religions have moral expectations for marriage, families, religious societies or congregations, social classes, and even whole nations. We may think of religious ethics as "rules" more negative than positive, but most religions have a balance of both "do this" and "don't do that." These systems of social ethics sometimes become the law of the nation where religion is not separated from the state, as in Shari'a, religion-based law in some officially Muslim countries. Values, norms, and patterns of behavior in religions are internalized with the help of moral rules. Different people and activities serve to shape religious behavior: living models such as professional religious specialists (clergy, monks, gurus, and the like); legendary models such as saviors, saints, and immortals; and behavior in the overall group. When social morality based on religion is constantly, carefully practiced, religion becomes a way of life.

ritual Symbolic action in worship, meditation, or other religious ceremonies

Ethical and ritual dimensions come together in a Hindu wedding in Ahmedabad, India.

Participating in initiation rituals, as these ten-year-old males of the Yao tribe in Malawi, binds the initiates closer to their gods and their tribe.

the pilgrimage to Mecca as the highlight of their life. Some Hindus have given up the rituals of the home and temple to seek salvation in purely solitary meditation. Although ritual may be downplayed in favor of other dimensions of religion, it never completely disappears.

THE INSTITUTIONAL DIMENSION

Because religions are social more than personal, they give an organizational structure to their religious community and (usually) the wider society. Moreover, many religions are internally diverse, with different institutional structures for each internal group. Most religions come from ancient, traditional societies, so they aren't "democratic" organizations; power in religious institutions tends to flow from the top down. This is also true of **new religious movements (NRMs)**, religious groups that have arisen since the nineteenth century and now have sufficient size and longevity to merit academic study. They are typically founded by a charismatic leader, such as L. Ron Hubbard of the Scientology movement, who wields great power. Religions typically make

a valid distinction between specialists (religious healers, priests, monks) and others, typically called "laity." This institutional dimension is so important that people often speak of "organized religion."

> **new religious movements (NRMs)**
> Religious groups that have arisen since the nineteenth century and now have sufficient size and longevity to merit academic study

THE AESTHETIC DIMENSION

The aesthetic (beauty) dimension is the sensory element of religion. Beauty appeals to the rational mind, but has a special appeal to human emotions. This dimension encompasses religion's sounds and smells, spaces, holy places, and landscapes. It also includes its main symbols (Judaism's six-pointed Star of David, Buddhism's wheel), devotional images and statuary, and all the religious items of material culture. Islamic religious art tends to be abstract, because of strong prohibitions of anything that could enable the worship of other gods. Most Hindu art, on the other hand, is fully representational, some of it even explicitly sexual. The aesthetic dimension encompasses the architecture and decoration of religious buildings, as well as works of music, poetry, and hymns. It also includes ritual gestures: hand gestures in yoga, kneeling bodies in prayer, hands pressed together in Hindu greeting and Christian prayer, and many others.

> Read about a book on religiously themed toys.

> How many religions can you name from their traditional symbols?

Dimensions of Religion

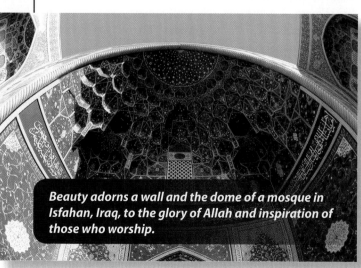

Beauty adorns a wall and the dome of a mosque in Isfahan, Iraq, to the glory of Allah and inspiration of those who worship.

WWW.CEPOLINA.COM

Sensual Hindu art put to spiritual use: a goddess in a temple sculpture

THE EMOTIONAL DIMENSION

This dimension includes the particular emotions and wider "moods" experienced in religion. They include senses of awe, fear, and love. They also include some religions' hope for life after death or other religions' hope for no more life after death. The emotional dimension includes confidence received to cope with death, suffering, and evil. The emotional self-confidence and sense of purpose that religion brings are so notable that "losing my religion" or "getting religion" about something are common expressions. The emotional dimension includes the emotions that come with belonging and personal identity, as well as with concern for others. It also includes extraordinary feelings and experiences such as isolation, feelings of union with an ultimate reality or God, and hallucinations. The emotional dimension of religion looms large today in the Western world, where belief for many is primarily a matter of emotion. In the words of the 1981 hit song

> The sense of purpose that religion brings is so notable that we speak informally of "losing my religion" or "getting religion" about something.

theology Study of a religion, based on a religious commitment to that religion, in order to promote it

by the rock group Journey, put to more recent use by such television shows as *Family Guy* and *Glee*, "Don't stop believing, hold on to that feeling."

To conclude this section, sometimes people reduce religion to one or two of these dimensions. For example, they may suppose that religion is primarily an ethical system, a system of teaching about the divine, an institution, or even a feel-good emotion. This reduction is to be expected, but it's wrong. Almost all religions are multidimensional. That the many dimensions of religion are closely related to one another was suggested by the British philosopher Alfred North Whitehead, who once wrote that the power of religion lies in its grasp of this truth: "The order of the world, the depth of reality of the world, the value of the world in its whole and in its parts, the beauty of the world, the zest for life, the peace of life, and the mastery of evil, are all bound together."[8]

> Read a review of a book on "sacred terror" in horror films.

> The Wabash Center Internet guide to religious studies underscores religion's many dimensions.

LO4 Ways of Studying Religion

The study of religion is pursued today with a wide variety of methods. These center largely on six different academic disciplines, some of which you may be studying. We'll consider the methods and the work of prominent scholars who have contributed to them, and along the way we'll encounter different theories of the origin and purpose of religion. Before we discuss these methods, however, we should deal with the important matter of the difference between theology and religious studies.

THEOLOGY AND RELIGIOUS STUDIES

The study of religion in America today is pursued in two main ways. **Theology** is the study of a religion, based on a religious commitment to that religion,

---

[8] Alfred North Whitehead, *Religion in the Making* (New York: World, 1960), 115.

in order to promote it. It is study from the "inside." Christian theology has been an important part of the Western university since the oldest universities were founded in thirteenth-century Europe. Theology is pursued today at many American schools, especially those with religious affiliations. To use the words of the eleventh-century Christian theologian Anselm (AHN-sehlm) of Canterbury, England, theology is "faith seeking understanding." This statement is true of theological study in other religions as well, in both Eastern and Western religions. The university thought to be oldest in the world still existing today— at the Al-Azhar (al-ah-ZAHR) mosque in Cairo, Egypt—was founded for theological study. Theology is older in Buddhism and Hinduism than it is in Christianity or Islam. Theology in these religions has typically relied closely on philosophy and textual studies to carry out its intellectual work.

Al-Azhar University in Cairo, founded in 972 C.E.

© AMR HASSANEIN/SHUTTERSTOCK.COM

The second branch is called **religious studies**, a relatively new field of academic study of religion that aims to understand all religious traditions, not just Christianity and Judaism, and to do so objectively, in a religiously neutral way, from the "outside." It doesn't ask students to make religious commitments or even require students to reflect on those they have. In the Enlightenment (ca. 1650–1800), the independence and separation of human reason from religion had developed to the extent that a scholarly treatment of religion independent from theology could begin. Reason, not faith, was now seeking understanding of religion. By about 1875, religious studies was emerging as an academic field. Now utilizing the tools from many other academic fields in the humanities and sciences, religious studies arises out of a broad intellectual interest in the nature of religion and the different world religions. It offers a unique, nonthreatening opportunity for students to ask important questions about religion, different world religions, and life itself.

After World War I, historians would become less naïve about their ability to be "scientifically" objective about their work.

HISTORY

History is the scholarly study of the past, whether that past is remote (the beginnings of human civilization, for example) or recent (the events of last year). It seeks to find out what really happened and why. This task is important because, as the historian Philip Jenkins has written about religion, "Virtually everybody uses the past in everyday discourse, but the historical record on which they draw is littered with myths, half-truths, and folk-history."[9] When history is applied to religion, rich and important knowledge emerges, because religions come from the past, both remote and recent. History studies the process of a religion's beginnings, growth, diversity, decline, and so on. An example is a recent volume of essays entitled *Sacred Schisms: How Religions Divide*, which carefully studies internal splits in a dozen religions and draws conclusions about the different factors and events involved in religious splits.[10] History has almost always been a main method in the study of religion.

The Oxford historian of Indian culture F. Max Müller (1823–1900), whom we already met above, is one of the founders of religious studies—some would say *the* founder. He edited a fifty-volume collection of ancient sacred scriptures from the main Asian religions,

---

[9] Philip Jenkins, "Ancient and Modern: What the History of Religion Teaches Us about Contemporary Global Trends," ARDA Guiding Paper, http://www.thearda.com/rrh/papers/guidingpapers/jenkins.asp, accessed 7/17/10.

[10] James R. Lewis and Sarah M. Lewis, *Sacred Schisms: How Religions Divide* (Cambridge, UK: Cambridge University Press, 2009).

translated for the first time into reliable English editions (the Sacred Books of the East series, 1879–1910), a foundational contribution to research and teaching in religious history. He promoted a scholarly discussion on developmental patterns in religious history and on the relation of myth, ritual, and magic to religion in the past. In his *Introduction to the Science of Religion* (1873), Müller argued that religious scholarship can be fully scientific in its methods and results. It can collect, classify, and compare religious texts just as scientifically as a botanist collects and studies plants. Müller's investigations led him and others to a supposed "oldest stage" of European and Asian culture and religion that extended from the Indians to the Germanic tribes—what he called the "Indo-Germanic" or "Aryan" stage beginning around 2000 B.C.E. By the end of the 1800s, the notion of near-steady, almost evolutionary progress often assumed in these studies (and in much of European and North American higher learning and culture at that time) started to fade, and the surprising horrors of the First World War (1914–1918) ended almost all assumptions of automatic progress in religion and culture. Müller's work was largely text-based, and based in scriptures as well. This was a necessary first step, and a part of other text-based studies in other specializations in history, but the field of history would widen in the twentieth century to social history, popular history, and even the history of material culture. It would also become less naïve about the ability of historians to be "scientifically" objective about their work.

One particular approach taken by some historians of religions is the "History of Religions School." This school of thought began in Germany in the nineteenth century, lasting with some strength into the middle of the twentieth century, and is still occasionally found today in Europe and North America. It was the first to study religion systematically as a social and cultural phenomenon. It depicted religion as evolving with human culture, from "primitive" polytheism to ethical monotheism. Religions were divided into stages of progression from simple to complex societies, especially from polytheistic to monotheistic and from informal to organized. Despite the obvious faults of such an approach, the nineteenth century saw a dramatic increase in knowledge about other religions, an increase caused by imperial expansion by European powers and the growth of a genuine interest to know about other cultures. For the first time, an

View an animated map giving "5,000 Years of Religion in 90 Seconds."

Read about current global religious trends in historical perspective.

accurate "map" of the different religions of the world emerged (see Map 1.1).

PSYCHOLOGY

Psychology deals with the structure and activity of the human mind. It is the scientific study of individual behavior, including emotions and other thoughts. Psychology has an interest in religion because of religion's role in shaping human behavior—for example in coping with the challenges of life-cycle changes and death. Psychology also focuses on how religions understand the human self, including gender. It has been particularly concerned with research in conversion, mysticism, and meditation.

Psychology sought at first to explain the origins of religion in terms of the subconscious mind. Sigmund Freud (froyd) and Carl Gustav Jung (yoong), the founders of psychoanalysis, sought in opposing ways to trace the origins from the strongest, most basic human needs and drives. Freud (1856–1939) and his school regarded religion as a neurotic condition that needed therapy when it persisted into adulthood. (See his definition of religion on page 5.) He held that religion, particularly a belief in God, derives from adults' need for a father figure when they achieve independence from their actual fathers. These ideas can be found in his books *The Future of an Illusion*, in which the "illusion" is religion, and *Moses and Monotheism*. Freud later admitted that a person could experience an "oceanic feeling" of religion in a positive way, but later Freudians would continue to be mostly negative toward religion until about the 1980s, when some change began.

Freud's pupil Jung (1875–1961), on the other hand, was appreciative of religion. In his books *Modern Man in Search of a Soul* and *Memories, Dreams, Reflections*, he held that conceptions of the divine, whether of god(s) or some other form of ultimate reality, were related to an ancient archetypal pattern that resides in the subconscious of all human minds. Religion enables each developing person to bring out and employ this archetype as the individual personality grows and achieves what Jung called "individuation," or personal maturity and wholeness. The notion of "individuation" would become important in the human potential/humanistic branch of American psychology. This positive archetype is found in all societies, Jung argued, and his theory became important for many researchers in the academic discipline of cultural anthropology.

William James (1842–1910), a professor at Harvard, was an American founder of the field of psychology. In his still-important book *The Varieties of Religious*

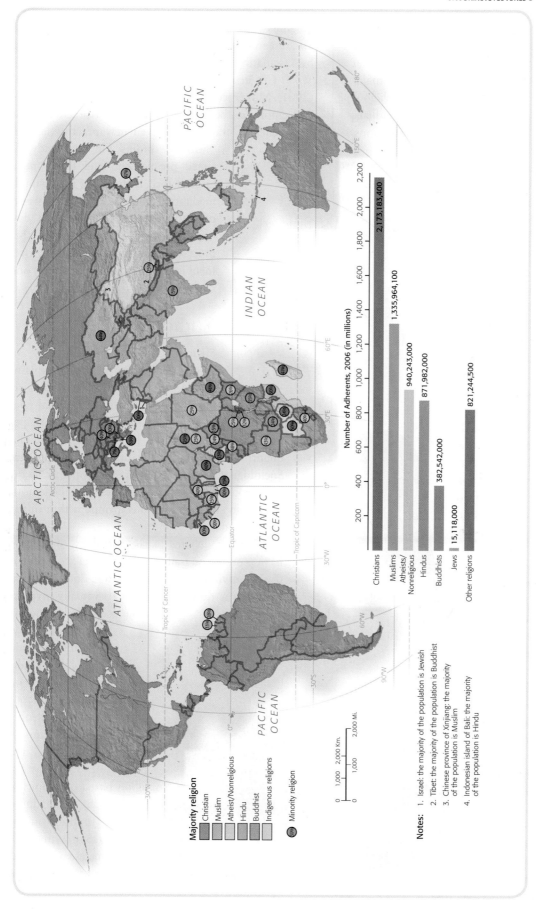

Map 1.1
Distribution of World Religions Today

Majority religion
- Christian
- Muslim
- Atheist/Nonreligious
- Hindu
- Buddhist
- Indigenous religions

◉ Minority religion

Notes: 1. Israel: the majority of the population is Jewish
2. Tibet: the majority of the population is Buddhist
3. Chinese province of Xinjiang: the majority of the population is Muslim
4. Indonesian island of Bali: the majority of the population is Hindu

Number of Adherents, 2006 (in millions)

Christians — 2,173,183,400
Muslims — 1,335,964,100
Atheists/Nonreligious — 940,243,000
Hindus — 871,982,000
Buddhists — 382,542,000
Jews — 15,118,000
Other religions — 821,244,500

Christianity has the most believers in the world today, and is the dominant faith in the Americas, Oceania, Europe, Russia, and central and southern Africa. Most people in the northern half of Africa, western Asia, and central Asia embrace Islam. Hindus are concentrated in India and Buddhists in East and Southeast Asia. Although China has been largely atheistic or nonreligious under communist rule, its main religions—Daoism, Confucianism, Buddhism, Islam, and Christianity—are espoused by about 25 percent of the population. Each is growing as the proportion of Chinese who call themselves "atheists" is now shrinking.

Experience (1902), James advanced a more pragmatic and positive view of religion than did either Freud or Jung. He maintained that the religious experience of individuals, not religious institutions, should be the primary focus of the psychology of religion and of religion itself. Intense types of religious experience in particular should be studied by psychologists, because they are the closest thing to a "microscope" into the mind. Individuals must develop certain "over-beliefs" that, while they cannot be proven, help humans live purposefully and in "harmony with the universe." After James, the psychological study of religion went into something of a decline, and scientific research into religious behavior faded.

Since the 1980s, the psychological study of religion has been advanced by neuroscience, particularly with regard to research on the human brain. (Here the psychology of religion comes very close to biology, which we will discuss on page 19.) Perhaps the most prominent researcher in this field is Andrew Newberg, a professor of psychiatry at the University of Pennsylvania. He has used scanning techniques to observe what happens in the brains of subjects while they meditate or pray—in a way, providing the "microscope into the mind" that James sought. Newberg's research used brain imaging to study Tibetan Buddhists in meditation and Roman Catholic nuns in prayer. He found that during intense sessions of these activities, areas of the brain associated with concentration and emotion are activated and areas associated with the sense of self are deactivated. Newberg hypothesizes that this may explain the sense of "otherness" and "oneness with God or ultimate reality" often reported

by people who have had intense religious experiences. Much of this research is summarized in his fascinating book *Why God Won't Go Away: Brain Science and the Biology of Belief* (2001). More recently, Newberg argued that the physical and emotional benefits of meditational practices grow over years of practice, but even new practitioners get "healthier brains." In one study, he tested people who had never meditated before, then taught them simple meditative methods. After eight weeks of meditating twelve minutes a day, brain scans and other tests show that most subjects gain significant improvement in memory, and their anxiety and anger decrease.

> Andrew Newberg has discovered that the benefits of meditational practices grow over years of practice, but even new practitioners get healthier brains.

Watch Newberg explain his research.

SOCIOLOGY

Sociology, the scientific study of groups and group behavior, explains religion's role in society. Sociologists studying religion are concerned with the mutual relationship between religion and society, how each shapes the other. They examine, by both qualitative and quantitative research, the practices of religions. Sociologists are interested in beliefs mainly as the backgrounds of social practices and behaviors. They also study the various groups within different religions.

Current debates in the sociology of religion have centered on issues such as the pace of secularization, **civil religion** (the popular, dominant religion of a nation or culture that typically involves some religious conviction about that nation or culture), and the cohesiveness of religions and religious practice in the challenges of globalization, multiculturalism, and pluralism. Sociology of religion based on empirical research is an influential tradition in the United States, in which the flagship outlet for research is the *Journal for the Scientific Study of Religion*. Quantitative sociological studies have contributed

© PIOTR MARCINSKI/SHUTTERSTOCK.COM

Yoga is one popular form of meditation.

Visit a leading website for the scientific study of religion.

greatly to our knowledge of religion, for example on current issues such as new religious movements and "fundamentalisms" in world religions.

Émile Durkheim (1858–1917), a founder of sociology, came from a long line of Jewish rabbis but studied religion from the "religious studies" approach. Many scholars today have concluded that the sociology of religion, and perhaps sociology itself, began with Durkheim's 1897 book *Suicide*, which studied among other things the rates of suicide occurrence among Catholic, Protestant, and Jewish populations in Western Europe. Durkheim theorized, especially in his essay "The Origin of Beliefs," that religion was a necessary factor in creating and sustaining a harmonious society. He saw religion as the cement that binds societies and cultures together. Through shared beliefs and practices, religion creates a sense of social identity and reinforces the moral values of society. This is true even when society is secularizing, and Durkheim argued that secularization would continue. Rites of passage are important as a means of initiating individuals into the wider society and embedding a sense of responsibility. Like Karl Marx, Durkheim recognized that religion played a role in social control of the individual, but unlike Marx, he saw this in a positive light. Religion is inevitable, just as society is inevitable when individuals live together as a group. Durkheim argued that the relationship between people and the supernatural in religion was based on the relationship between individuals and the community.

For a taste of sociology's take on religion, read the highlights of a sociological report on American religion.

His most memorable proverb in this regard is "God is society, writ large."

CULTURAL ANTHROPOLOGY

Cultural anthropology is the scientific study of human life focused on various concrete human settings. It arose in the nineteenth century, and soon after its birth it was applied to religions of the world, especially the beliefs and practices of tribal

Modern shaman, Peru

PHOTOGRAPH BY BARTHOLOMEW DEAN, 1988

"The anthropologist . . . finds in the little what eludes us in the large, stumbles upon general truths while sorting through special cases."

—Clifford Geertz

cultures. Cultural anthropology uncovers the underlying values of cultures, their answer to the question "Why are we here?" It studies such broad cultural dynamics as honor and shame, the role of kinship, and so on. It explores the role of symbols, culture, and the natural environment; the making of social boundaries; how sex is understood and gender roles are constructed; and rituals. A special focus of anthropology has been the **shaman**, a religious specialist traditionally belonging to an indigenous society who acts as a medium between this visible world and the spirit world, usually for healing and telling the future. Since the 1960s, the formal use of cultural anthropology has become more prominent in religious studies.

Cultural anthropology can study the past, especially texts, art, and other artifacts. Almost all world religions with sacred writings have had those writings subjected to some form of anthropological study. For example, in a study of early Christianity, Bruce Malina of Creighton University in Omaha, an anthropologist and New Testament scholar, has applied this method to several books of the New Testament, especially in his *The New Testament World: Insights from Cultural Anthropology*.[11] This is often called "historical anthropology." However, cultural anthropology predominantly deals with living religion. It studies current practices including pilgrimages; life-cycle rituals such as weddings and funerals; belief in miracles; festivals; and the functions of guilt, confession, punishment, and forgiveness. History, sociology, and even psychology tend to make broad analyses and conclusions, but anthropology tends to study smaller-scale aspects of human life. As Clifford Geertz wrote in his book about Islam in Morocco and

[11] Bruce Malina, *The New Testament World: Insights from Cultural Anthropology*, 3rd ed. (Louisville, KY: Westminster John Knox, 2001).

Cultural anthropology studies life through the generations, such as these young Masai women in east Africa.

© JEFF SCHULTES/SHUTTERSTOCK.COM

Indonesia, "The anthropologist is always inclined to turn toward the concrete, the particular, the microscopic.... We hope to find in the little what eludes us in the large, to stumble upon general truths while sorting through special cases."[12] For example, while historians made large studies about ancient Hindu sacred texts in the "dead language" of Sanskrit, anthropologists spent long periods of time in fieldwork in India to study the living use of contemporary oral traditions in other Indian languages.

Victor Turner (1920–1983), an influential cultural anthropologist of the last four decades, developed a powerful theory of ritual that drew the attention of scholars to religious behaviors. His conception of rituals was shaped during his fieldwork in the 1950s with the Ndembu tribe, in what today is Zambia; his personal background in Roman Catholic Christianity also forms a background for his work on ritual. He was interested in the "social drama" of ritual presentations, especially rites of passage. Ritual creates the social breaks called "marginality" and thresholds of new kinds of life called "liminality."

Watch as cultural anthropology looks at "black magic."

WOMEN'S STUDIES

When the women's liberation movement came to full bloom in the United States in the 1970s, the academic field of women's or gender studies quickly developed. It studies the social pressures, expectations, and opportunities of both genders but focuses on women with the purpose of promoting their full equality and liberation. Feminism thus has both a descriptive and a prescriptive aspect. Gender studies is flourishing in North America but is not yet strong in Europe or other parts of the world.

Feminist scholars of religion have pointed to religion as a key factor in the almost worldwide subordination of women to men. They state correctly that practically all religions stem from—and most maintain today to some extent—patriarchal (male-dominant) societies. In religions that have both male and female gods, the male gods almost always predominate; this is true of both tribal and international religions. Women's identification with female gods—for example the new goddess Santoshi Ma in Hinduism—does provide some religious strength, but this is qualified by male dominance among divine beings themselves. Predominantly masculine language is used to describe and address most gods, especially the one God of monotheistic religions.

Women's roles as professional religious specialists have been limited, even in those relatively few religious organizations that profess women's equality with men; this limitation is sometimes called in the Western world the "stained-glass ceiling." Their ambitions have often been constrained by the assertion that their primary religious duty is to obey their husbands and serve their families in the home. Some feminists have argued that a "Mother Goddess" religion centered on the earth and on women is the earliest form of human religion, but the historical basis of this is contested. Women of many religions have made other responses to the pressure of patriarchy. For example, they press for wider roles as religious specialists, trying to break the stained-glass ceiling or at least push it higher. They look for wider opportunities in the world of work, often adapting this to their religious duties in the home. In general, they interpret and live their religions in ways more congenial to women.

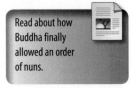

Read about how Buddha finally allowed an order of nuns.

---

[12] Clifford Geertz, *Islam Observed* (New Haven: Yale University Press, 1968) 4.

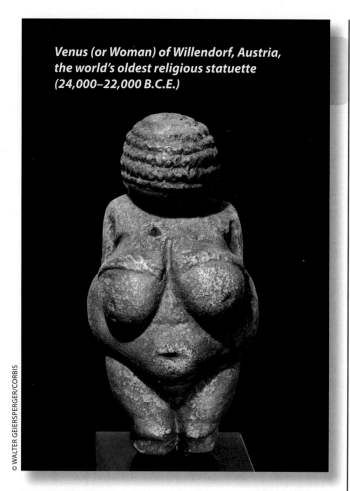

Venus (or Woman) of Willendorf, Austria, the world's oldest religious statuette (24,000–22,000 B.C.E.)

BIOLOGY

Until recently, biology (the scientific study of all life) didn't contribute much to the study of religion, aside from religious studies scholars' uncritical application of evolutionary theory to religion. Now, with the ability to study the human gene system, new possibilities are opening for understanding complex human issues in the realm of religion. Many scientists are now seeking to explain religion in genetic terms, or at least to find the genetic connections of religion. Rapidly increasing knowledge of the human genome has made this possible. Some writers have suggested that the pervasiveness of religious beliefs is due to our genetic makeup.

Supporters of the controversial theory advanced in Dean Hamer's *The God Gene: How Faith is Hardwired into Our Genes* (2005) suggest that human religious behavior is the result of, or at least made possible by, a genetic adaptation. Hamer even pointed to one gene, called *VMAT2* by the Human Genome Project, as the "God gene." However, most scientists hypothesize that the genetic background of any complex human behavior such as religion probably flows from a combination of several genes. More generally accepted is the hypothesis by some biologists and anthropologists that the development of religious belief in prehistoric peoples may have been a key factor in the development of higher-order cognitive skills. Some humans became capable of transcending themselves in thought and action, and this was passed on by natural selection.

> *Some biologists and anthropologists hold that the development of religious belief in prehistoric peoples may have given humans their higher-order cognitive skills.*

CONCLUSIONS

We'll conclude our treatment of the methods of religious studies with two observations. First, it's obvious that the study of religion, like many other branches of scholarship, is multidisciplinary. It has no "religious method" all its own, but draws from many other methods. Second, religious studies is a human, not a divine, way of knowing. Religion itself can bring divine or sacred knowledge, but our academic study of it is method related and time bound. This means that religion scholars, just like other academic experts, are part of the "concrete epistemology" (ways of knowing) of current scholarly and cultural interests and current assumptions that different generations have about life. Religion scholars' (*and* beginning students') personal development, education, and individual religious experiences, as well as their generation-specific attitudes, all affect how they adopt and use a particular method of studying religion. Religious studies as a field is always conditioned in each generation by time, a fact that is often appreciated only by a later generation, for whom temporal distance allows a better view. As we sometimes say with slight exaggeration, "Hindsight is twenty-twenty."

This conditioning can be traced through time from the beginning of religious studies until today. Religious studies first went along with nineteenth-century optimism about the progressive evolution of human religion. Then, a Protestant bias crept into religious studies from the hidden values of scholars in the field, who were predominantly Protestant Christian: the privileging of sacred texts over oral traditions; the privileging of doctrine over ritual; and the belief in the primacy of private religious experience over received traditions—all crucial elements of the Protestant branch of Christianity. Then, the religious studies "phenomenologists" of the 1920s, after the spiritual and intellectual crisis of the First World War, searched for the so-called essence of religion, devaluating differences in the process. Then, the baby-boomer generation of scholars in the 1960s through 1990s was driven by the experience and values of an alternative culture to pose provocative questions that challenged traditional methods in religious studies. The realization that each generation of scholars has characteristic limitations, which it cannot see, need not diminish the value of religious studies. Indeed, knowing the limits and biases of knowledge makes our knowledge more certain.

PHOTO BY JERRY JASPOR. COEXIST DESIGN USED WITH PERMISSION BY PEACEMONGER AT WWW.PEACEMONGER.ORG.

LO5 Special Issues in the Study of Religion Today

TOLERANCE AND INTOLERANCE

In Cambridge, Massachusetts, a controversy breaks out in the blogosphere and then in the print media over Harvard College's decision to reserve six hours a week in the college's central gymnasium for women only. The Harvard Islamic Society had petitioned for the special hours, arguing that observant female Muslim students needed these special hours in order to observe Muslim rules about modesty and coverings for women. Although many Muslim women had exercised in the gymnasium during open hours, dressed in sweatsuits and headscarves, the Harvard Islamic Society says that having hours restricted to women enables them to exercise better, in athletic shirts and shorts, without fear of male students "checking them out."

Some argue that this is a reasonable toleration of another's faith; others say that this gives Harvard's approval to practices that reinforce intolerance toward women.

The British atheist Christopher Hitchens is one of a handful of current advocates of **atheism**— the conviction that there

> "Religion is violent, irrational, intolerant, allied to racism and tribalism and bigotry, invested in ignorance . . . contemptuous of women and coercive toward children."
> —Christopher Hitchens

atheism Conviction that there is no God

agnosticism Refers to those who "do not know" if a God or gods exist

tolerance Putting up with views and actions of others opposed to your own, usually for the common good

is no God and that religion is mostly mistaken—who are making sharp public attacks on religion. (**Agnosticism**, a related term, refers to those who "do not know" if a God or gods exist; this belief is not always antireligious, and rarely combative against religion.) Hitchens recently wrote that religion is "Violent, irrational, intolerant, allied to racism and tribalism and bigotry, invested in ignorance and hostile to free inquiry, contemptuous of women and coercive toward children."[13] Although this is put in a broad, sharp way that lacks any hint of nuance, Hitchens is articulating a point of view against religion that many people share.

Tolerance means putting up with the views and actions of others that are opposed to your own, usually for the common good. We begin our discussion of tolerance and intolerance with the Western world. The modern Western idea of religious tolerance developed in Europe after brutal wars between Protestant and Catholic Christians in the sixteenth and seventeenth centuries, and has gradually been extended to people of other religions. (The murderous violence between Protestants and Catholics in Northern Ireland from about 1960 to 1998 serves to remind the modern world what was gained at the end of the seventeenth century.) The First Amendment to the U.S. Constitution guarantees tolerance in "freedom of religion." The state cannot interfere with basic religious rights and must actively protect them from restriction in law or policy. In the twentieth century, the Universal Declaration of Human Rights advocates freedom of religion for all people. Since the Enlightenment, the fostering and maintenance of tolerance, religious or otherwise, has been regarded as a duty of

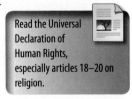

Read the Universal Declaration of Human Rights, especially articles 18–20 on religion.

---

[13] Christopher Hitchens, *God Is Not Great: How Religion Poisons Everything* (Boston: Twelve Publishing Company, 2007), 56.

 Read agnostic Gina Welch's reflections about her intolerance to evangelical Protestant Christians.

government. Tolerance and intolerance are public, social things, but they are personal and individual as well. People of one religion can be intolerant toward people of other religions, and people outside religion can be intolerant of all or some religious people and groups.

The history of world religions reveals different ideas of tolerance. In ancient China, native religions were generally tolerated, but non-Chinese religions were admitted only by government consent; this is still true of China today. Ancient Judaism was at times welcoming to other religions in its territory, at other times not. In the ancient Roman Empire, non-Roman religious groups were tolerated, with some exceptions, as long as they did not undermine the religious underpinnings of Roman imperial rule. Christianity, from the thousand years since it became the state religion until at least the Protestant Reformation, tended toward religious intolerance. (Compare the maxim from Roman Catholic history that has parallels in other religions: "Error has no rights." The Roman Catholic Church did not formally accept religious tolerance until the Second Vatican Council in the 1960s.) Islam usually granted toleration of conquered peoples of certain other religions—as a rule, but not always in practice. This toleration did not extend to Arab polytheism, which was extinguished; and over time, even tolerated religions were dramatically reduced in Muslim lands.

Hinduism has been generally tolerant to other religions but has preferred to integrate them into its own system. Hindu relations with Muslims on the Indian subcontinent have been uneasy for centuries, and mass conversions of Hindus to religions such as Christianity and Buddhism can provoke a violent reaction. The regular violence between Hindus and Muslims that has occurred since the division of India and Pakistan in 1947, and occasionally Hindu violence against Sikhs, means that the tolerance that some see in Hinduism needs some qualification.

Buddhism, which teaches tolerance, has seen intolerant periods in its history, as recently as the civil war carried on by armed Buddhists in Sri Lanka, in the violently repressive Buddhist government in Myanmar (Burma), and on a much smaller scale in bitter struggles between different Tibetan monastic groups. In sum, achieving and maintaining tolerance is no easy matter.

> **People today don't like to be called intolerant, but few people can be equally tolerant of all opposing ideas and actions.**

A difficult question involves the limits of tolerance. Few people in the world today would like to be called "intolerant," but few people can be equally tolerant of all opposing ideas and actions. If they try, some difficult questions can arise. For example, can a religious group that is itself intolerant be tolerated in the public sector? In North America, with its legal tradition of granting a maximum of freedom to intolerant groups, this isn't so much of an issue. But can a religion be tolerated by another if it grows big enough to take over a society and impose its own intolerance? In general, different religious *views* are tolerated in Western society, provided that they do not lead to *actions* that could challenge a majority consensus on religion. The line between private belief and public action isn't always easy to see, however. An example of this is the controversy in France over the public wearing of Muslim headscarves and full-body veils by women, which the government wants to forbid as an assault on the secular nature of the French state and its security. The Church of Scientology is under government pressure in Germany, in part because the post–World War II German constitution forbids "totalitarian movements," which the government suspects that Scientology is. And in China, the Falun Gong (FAH-luhn GONG)

ALAN STREVENS

Protesters against the Church of Scientology wear masks to shield their identity.

Read a discussion of limited tolerance.

Read the anti-violence "Charter for Compassion."

meditational movement is strongly repressed by the Chinese government as a "dangerous cult" that supposedly threatens public order and the health of its followers. These examples show that struggles over tolerance continue today all around the world.

VIOLENCE

Faced in April 2010 with a spreading church sexual abuse scandal in Europe, similar to one that took place in the 1990s in the United States, Pope Benedict XVI apologized in an official letter to almost 15,000 victims and their families in Ireland, expressing "shame and remorse" for what he called "sinful and criminal" acts committed by some priests over the past fifty years. Most of these acts were sexual assaults against children. "You have suffered grievously and I am truly sorry," the pope said. "Your trust has been betrayed and your dignity has been violated." But the pope didn't indicate in his letter that church leaders who looked the other way or actively covered up these crimes would be disciplined by the church, or that the whole matter would be turned over to the police, as some victims and their families were hoping. The problem of sexual predators among religious leaders isn't unique to Roman Catholics, or even to Christianity.

FABIEN DANY, WWW.FABIENDANY.COM

Violence is a difficult topic to grapple with, both emotionally and intellectually. However, this grappling is necessary. Violence is the intentional use of physical force to injure or kill people, to damage or destroy their property, or both. Violence is motivated by a variety of factors—political, economic, national, and tribal. Religiously motivated violence includes all events in which a follower of a religion is either the perpetrator or the recipient of violent behavior or both. Like most sorts of violence, religious violence can be carried out by individuals or groups. It can be by direct attack, or by indirect means such as inducing famine. It includes violence of any kind by members of one religion against people of another religion (the Crusades by medieval Christians against Islam, Muslim holy war, and occasional violence between Sikhs and Hindus), between different groups in a religion (Sunni and Shi'a Muslims, occasional violence between different Hindu castes in India), and crimes by powerful people in a religion against those with less or no power. It includes persecution of one religion by another

or by the state against its people, as in the Holocaust directed at Jews or in current Chinese prosecution of the new Falun Gong religious movement. It also includes violence against explicitly religious objects, as in attacks on religious buildings or sites or burning of holy books. Because religions have cultural, political, and other aspects, different motivations often lie behind what may appear to be purely religious violence. Sometimes violence can be inflicted on a public target in order to induce terror in a populace.

Watch a BBC report featuring former U.S. Secretary of State Madeleine Albright on religion and conflict.

Religious violence committed by groups must be understood in its cultural context—not to excuse it, but to understand it. In particular, beginning students of religions should realize that not all religious violence is the same. Some religions tend to be nonviolent, but others approve of violence in certain situations. Some religions began as explicitly nonviolent movements—Christianity and Sikhism, for example—but changed over time. Religious violence often tends to place differing emphases on the symbolic aspects of violence. For example, sometimes violence is understood as a religiously significant act with ritual aspects. In the 1990s Taliban Muslims dynamited ancient statues of the Buddha to remove "idolatry" from Afghanistan, and today they at times attack government schools for girls. Ritual violence may be directed against victims, as in human sacrifice, or it may be more or less voluntarily self-inflicted, as

In 2009, girls attend school in Afghanistan despite religiously motivated threats against them.

CAPT. JOHN SEVERNS

in self-flagellation with a whip. It may be a part of monastic practice, as for example when head monks in certain sects of Zen Buddhists beat their subordinates with sticks and rods to discipline them or try to induce sudden enlightenment. So-called "honor killings," in which family members kill another member of their family (usually female) in order to "preserve the family's honor," often have some religious motivation today, although other factors are at work there too.

Read about a book on a notorious Swedish "honor killing," *In Honor of Fadime.*

PLURALISM

Phil Jackson, the retired head coach of the Los Angeles Lakers, isn't a typical professional basketball coach. He rarely stands on the sideline and shouts at his players. Instead, he sits so serenely that he has been called "Buddha on the bench" and "Zen master," terms that apply as well to his religious approach to coaching. His teams don't play seasons; they go on "sacred quests," as in Native American religion. Jackson teaches his players short Buddhist meditations to use before they shoot free throws. He has called their main strategy on offense "five-man tai chi," and their locker room is filled with Native American religious objects. His 1995 autobiography is called *Sacred Hoops.* Raised by devout Christian parents who taught him to value both religious earnestness and compassion, he calls himself a "Zen Christian."

Nonviolent relations between religions, and between cultures and nations with different religions, are based first on toleration. Religious **pluralism**, the recognition of religious differences and the effort to deal with them constructively, goes beyond toleration. Religious

Phil Jackson

AP PHOTO/MANU FERNANDEZ, FILE

Different religions exist because religions are different. This makes dialogue between them both possible and necessary.

pluralism owes a great deal to the American and European experience of religious diversity. Chris Beneke, in his *Beyond Toleration: The Religious Origins of American Pluralism*, distinguishes carefully between tolerance and pluralism. By the 1730s, religious toleration toward minority religions was practiced in most British colonies in North America.

The policy of toleration relieved religious minorities of physical punishments and financial burdens, but it did not end prejudice and exclusion. Those "tolerated" could still be barred from holding government and military positions and from attending universities. Religious persecution had ended, but religious discrimination had not. However, colonial governments gradually expanded the policy of religious toleration, and between the 1760s and the 1780s, they replaced it with "religious liberty."[14] This was not primarily a compromise with rising Enlightenment secularism in America; it was an achievement of early American religious groups. The different Protestant Christian groups—Episcopalians, Methodists, Quakers, Presbyterians, Baptists, Lutherans, and others—saw religious liberty for everyone as in their own best interests, and for the common good. The consensus for religious liberty was so strong that when a new national constitution was adopted at

pluralism Recognition of religious differences and the effort to deal with them constructively

[14] Chris Beneke, *Beyond Toleration: The Religious Origins of American Pluralism* (New York: Oxford University Press, 2006).

A Closer Look:

Statement on Pluralism by Harvard University's Pluralism Project

First, pluralism is not diversity alone, but *the energetic engagement with diversity*.... Today, religious diversity is a given, but pluralism is not a given; it is an achievement. Mere diversity without real encounter and relationship will yield increasing tensions in our societies.

Second, pluralism is not just tolerance, but *the active seeking of understanding across lines of difference*. Tolerance is a necessary public virtue, but it does not require Christians and Muslims, Hindus, Jews, and ardent secularists to know anything about one another....

Third, pluralism is not relativism, but *the encounter of commitments*. The new paradigm of pluralism does not require us to leave our identities and our commitments

behind, for pluralism is the encounter of commitments. It means holding our deepest differences, even our religious differences, not in isolation, but in relationship to one another.

Fourth, pluralism is *based on dialogue*. Dialogue means both speaking and listening, and that process reveals both common understandings and real differences. Dialogue does not mean everyone ... will agree with one another.[15]

Visit the Pluralism Project at Harvard University.

[15] From http://www.pluralism.org/pages/pluralism/what_is_pluralism, accessed 7/17/10.

---

the end of the eighteenth century, the Bill of Rights was added almost immediately, with freedom of religion in the first amendment. The strength of religious freedom in the United States has strongly influenced the course of religious freedoms in the world.

Religious pluralism demands interfaith dialogue and some significant cooperation. Interfaith dialogue is conversation between members of different religions to reduce conflicts between them and to achieve mutually desirable goals. Dialogue calls for care to be taken with the ideas of others, without necessarily agreeing with them or assuming (as many people think) that all religions are essentially the same or could be made the same. In the words of the subtitle of Stephen Prothero's thought-provoking book, the *Eight Rival Religions That Run the World* have *Differences* that *Matter*.[16] To put it another way: Different religions exist because religions are different. These differences make dialogue between religions possible, and they make dialogue important if conflict between religions and between the cultures they shape is to be avoided. Interfaith dialogue is easier if a religion's adherents have some form of inclusivism, a belief that people in other religions may have a way to salvation or at least some significant but partial knowledge of the truth. At the far extreme, believers with a completely exclusivist

mindset—that only their religion leads to the truth—prefer to proselytize followers of other religions rather than seek an open-ended dialogue with them. In between full inclusivism and full exclusivism is a wide range of attitudes, where most believers today live.

View the World Parliament of Religions 2009 intro video.

See Ziggy Marley perform "Love Is My Religion."

RELIGION AND ECOLOGICAL CRISIS

At Windsor Castle, just outside London, representatives of nine of the world's largest religions gathered in November 2009 to discuss the ecological crisis. They'd been summoned by Prince Philip of the United Kingdom and United Nations Secretary-General Ban Ki-moon. Called "Many Heavens, One Earth," the meeting was intended to generate commitments from religious organizations and the countries in which they predominate, agreements that could reduce greenhouse gas emissions or otherwise limit human impact on the environment. In words addressed to the Christians in the delegation, but applicable to many (but not all) of the other delegates, Prince Philip remarked, "If you believe in God ... then you should feel a responsibility to care for God's creation."

Read about the "Many Heavens, One Earth" conference.

---

[16] Stephen Prothero, *God Is Not One: The Eight Rival Religions That Run the World—and Why Their Differences Matter* (New York: HarperOne, 2010).

Religion and environmentalism has emerged in the past generation as an important topic in religious studies. This isn't only because people everywhere realize that worsening pollution, especially of the air, is changing our Earth's climate rapidly and for the worse. It's also because, as the Muslim scholar Seyyed Nasr explains, "The environmental crisis is fundamentally a crisis of values."[17] Since they shape the values of cultures, religions are deeply involved in how humans treat their environment.

Historian Lynn White, Jr. argued in 1967 that Western Christianity, with its view of nature as under human control and direction, bears a substantial responsibility for the contemporary environmental crisis.[18] White's essay provoked a strong reaction, with responses ranging from complete denial of his argument to complete agreement with it. Some proposed that Eastern religions, as well as those of indigenous peoples such as Native Americans, offered more environmentally responsible worldviews than did Christianity. By the 1990s, many scholars of religion had entered the debate and begun to analyze how nature is viewed in the world's various religious systems. A series of ten conferences on religion and ecology was held at the Harvard University Center for the Study of World Religions from 1996 to 1998; the conference papers were published in a World Religions and Ecology series, one book for each of ten religions. An increasing number of courses on religion and the environment are offered in colleges and universities around the world. This topic needs careful study, because the world's religions sometimes have different views about the origin, nature, and value of the physical world. But it's probably safe to say that all religions view the world around us as significant and would view the loss of a viable home for humanity as a tragedy.

Read about pollution in Hindu India.

Visit the website of the Association for Religion and Conservation.

Religion united to nature: the Eternal Spring Temple in Taroko National Park, Taiwan

© PATRICK LIN/SHUTTERSTOCK.COM

NEW RELIGIOUS MOVEMENTS

Outside a movie premiere in Utah, crowds gather, waiting for the director, producers, and actors to arrive. Although the scene is similar to that of most premieres, the film is not. It is a feature-film adaptation of the main Mormon scripture, the *Book of Mormon*, and has been officially sanctioned by the Mormon church, formally known as the Church of Jesus Christ of Latter-day Saints. Along with its general release to theaters and then to video rental outlets, the movie would be used in the missionary activities of the church. From the birth of the Latter-day Saint Church in the 1800s, its use of the *Book of Mormon* in missionary efforts has been a key factor in making this church probably the fastest-growing religious organization in the world.

New religious movements (NRMs), as we saw above, are a widely accepted area in the field of religious studies. NRMs are religious groups that arose since the start of the nineteenth century and now have sufficient size, longevity, and cultural impact to merit academic study. We will deal with NRMs more fully in Chapter 13, but we should consider them initially here.

New religious movements is preferable in some ways to other recent terms such as alternative religious movements and marginal religious movements. It is also clearly preferable to the older terms *sects* and *cults*. Although these terms still have some validity—especially in sociology, where scholars use them objectively—they have become so loaded with value judgments that most religion scholars no longer use them for new religious movements. To judge by the dimensions of religion

[17] Seyyed Hossein Nasr, *Man and Nature: The Spiritual Crisis in Modern Man*, rev. ed. (Chicago: Kazi Publishers, 1997).

[18] Lynn White, "The Historical Roots of Our Ecologic Crisis," *Science* 155, no. 3767 (March 10, 1967).

discussed above, there is usually little or no difference between a religion and a sect or a cult. All of them have doctrines and ethics, rituals, social structures, and an aesthetic dimension, and their members typically describe powerful emotional religious experiences. The term *cult* has been used to describe many smaller, nontraditional religious groups. These groups often have new or innovative beliefs that set them apart from the prevailing religious worldviews, especially those of the religions from which they emerge. In recent times "cult" has become rather derogatory, applied to groups that are deemed to be beyond commonly accepted bounds of social behavior. In many cases, if they do not disappear, sects go on to become recognized groups within the broader context of the "parent" religion. The various Protestant churches are examples of Christian sects that eventually gained mainstream acceptance, and in Hinduism one can cite the example of the Hare Krishna (HAHR-ee KRISH-nah) movement (The International Society for

Watch Tom Cruise speak on Scientology.

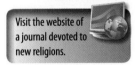

Visit the website of a journal devoted to new religions.

Krishna Consciousness, or ISKCON). Despite the intensity of its beliefs and actions that can make it look like a "cult" to some in the Western world, it is an authentically Hindu group.

Thousands of groups around the world today are NRMs, and each year sees the birth of more. Some examples are Falun Gong, the Baha'i tradition, the Church of Jesus Christ of Latter-day Saints, the Christian Science Church, the Unification Church, and the Church of Scientology. These and other movements called NRMs often don't see themselves as new religious movements, but instead as the true continuing body from an older religion now gone bad. Although scholars use the term "*new religious movements*" we must note that they usually branch off from older religions. Falun Gong is an adaptation mostly of Mahayana Buddhism and a lesser amount of Daoism. Baha'i arose in the nineteenth century from Shi'a Islam and sees itself as the successor of Islam. The Church of

Jesus Christ of Latter-Day Saints, the Christian Science Church, and the Unification Church see themselves as Christian, and most experts in comparative religions view this labeling as basically correct. That all three accept the Christian Bible is a good indication of their Christian roots. Moreover, outsiders to Christianity, such as Buddhists, would almost certainly recognize them as belonging to the stream of Christian tradition. However, one shouldn't assume that all organizations that call themselves a church self-identify as Christian. For example, the Church of Scientology does not see itself as Christian and uses *church* to mean "religious organization"; so does the Buddhist Church in America.

Some of these new religious movements are highly controversial. Many were persecuted or prosecuted in their early years by religious and civil authorities, and some still are today. However, many of the other faiths examined in this book were controversial when they were new. New religious movements can and do change, sometimes dramatically, and often much more quickly than older religions do. This often occurs when their founder dies, but later change is possible as well. Careful students of religion will want to form judgments about new religious movements that take some account of what believers say about themselves in their writings and in life. As

Read an article about change in the Christian Science Church.

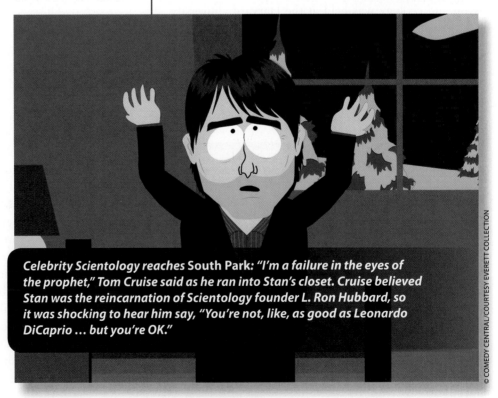

Celebrity Scientology reaches South Park: "I'm a failure in the eyes of the prophet," Tom Cruise said as he ran into Stan's closet. Cruise believed Stan was the reincarnation of Scientology founder L. Ron Hubbard, so it was shocking to hear him say, "You're not, like, as good as Leonardo DiCaprio … but you're OK."

always, our learning about a religion should precede any judgment concerning it.

LO6 Coming to Grips with Your Preunderstanding of Religion

WHAT IS PREUNDERSTANDING?

Imagine that a good friend tells you, "I've met and talked with an alien visitor from another planet." You might say to yourself, amid all the thoughts and emotions that you usually feel when you hear something strange or upsetting, "I don't believe in space aliens!" But then you might think, "Are there alien visitors to Earth after all? Maybe they're real, and maybe he *has* been talking with them."

You might think this, but probably not. Instead, your mind automatically begins to sift through your knowledge for an explanation consistent with what you already "know" to be true. Only people who are already convinced, or seriously entertaining the idea, that a set of things are true—there is life somewhat similar to ours on other planets, beings from these places travel to Earth, and they make contact with humans and talk with them—will easily accept your friend's comment. Given your prior understanding that such things probably aren't factual, you won't likely entertain these theories as a serious possibility.

We interpret all of our experience in just this way, because, as psychologists tell us, this is the way the human mind operates. Every understanding of our new experiences is made in light of an understanding that we already had going into the new experiences. **Preunderstanding** is the state of one's understanding of reality, in terms of which one makes sense of one's new experiences. It describes what we already know, whether that knowledge is correct or not. We assume that new experiences will be compatible with our prior understanding. Even if a new experience corrects our old knowledge—let's say that in this case you actually do meet a space alien with your friend—it is always understood on the basis of old knowledge. This new knowledge is then integrated into old understandings, and the preunderstanding grows. The term *preunderstanding*, therefore, describes the existing state of our understanding prior to the occurrence of some specific experience in need of interpretation. Our preunderstanding is not static, but dynamic. It changes and constantly gets modified as we alter our beliefs and convictions. Over the course of time, we as individuals reject some of our former beliefs and embrace new ones. With each change, our preunderstanding is altered.

YOUR PREUNDERSTANDING OF RELIGION

All this raises the question: What elements of your preunderstanding of religion might influence your study of world religions? Each person must examine and answer individually. In all individual encounters with new people and new ideas, our knowledge of ourselves and our knowledge of others are connected and influence each other. You should first think through your own past encounters with religion and your experiences with it, pro and con. Here are some short but thought-provoking questions to consider as you think of your own preunderstanding of religion and religions:

1. Do I have an unprejudiced view of what "religion" in general is? Or am I biased for or against it?

2. Can I "suspend my disbelief" or "suspend my belief" in order to encounter religion as a whole, or specific religions, sympathetically?

3. If I have a religious belief, can I study other religions without feeling threatened in my own?

4. Can I encounter strange, even disturbing practices without getting too upset?

5. Can I be humble and provisional in my conclusions?

Take a brief, entertaining quiz that will probe your preunderstanding of world religions.

6. Can I postpone any possible personal judgment on a religion until I've learned more about it?

You are now poised to begin your study of the world's leading religions. Like the two travelers on the front cover of this book, you are going on a journey. Your journey will encounter the lives and religions of other people. In this process, you will learn more about yourself as well. Enjoy the trip!

preunderstanding State of one's understanding of reality, in terms of which one makes sense of one's new experiences

CHAPTER 2

Encountering Indigenous Religions: Ways to Tribal Life

Learning Outcomes

After studying this chapter, you will be able to do the following:

LO1 State and evaluate the different names for indigenous religions.

LO2 Explain in your own words the challenges to the study of indigenous religions.

LO3 Discuss the common features of indigenous religions.

LO4 State and explain the main features of Lakota religion.

LO5 State and explain the main features of Yoruba religion.

LO6 State and explain the main features of Vodou religion.

MAX ARAUJO

YOUR VISIT TO THE POLYNESIAN CULTURAL CENTER, HAWAII

As you planned your trip to Hawaii, one of the things you found recommended in all the online tour sites was the Polynesian Cultural Center (PCC) on the island of Oahu. This is the world's largest and best-known cultural theme park, and the second most visited site in Hawaii. The PCC has entertained more than 37 million visitors, while presenting the culture of Polynesia to the rest of the world. So you conclude that you should check it out.

Your tour begins with eight different "villages" re-created from eight different cultures spread through the southern Pacific. In general, people from those islands appear in the villages as presenters of cultural life in them. You see different aspects of Polynesian life at each of the villages, and you're given the opportunity to interact with the village presenters. As you go along, you begin to wonder: Where is indigenous religion in these portrayals? When you ask this of your guide, or of any of the on-site interpreters, you get this answer: "Most Polynesian religions are deeply enculturated. Religion isn't evident to you as a tourist from the Western world, even if you're a beginning student of religion, unless you know what you're looking for. The few obviously religious aspects such as special ceremonies and sacred huts are often kept secret in these societies, so we keep them secret too. If you ask them, our guides will do their best to answer your questions about religion." This satisfies your curiosity for the moment, but later you begin to wonder about it again.

In the evening, after a traditional Hawaiian dinner, you attend the "Ha: Breath of Life" show at the PCC outdoor theater. With around one hundred performers and musicians, it tells the story of Polynesian culture through the life of a character named Mana. The story

What Do YOU Think?

Native American religions still have something significant to offer people of other religions or people of no religion.

Strongly Disagree   Strongly Agree
1   2   3   4   5   6   7

beings at Mana's birth and follows his journey through the universal stages of boyhood, young love, respect and responsibility of adulthood,  *Watch "Go Native at the PCC" at the website of the Polynesian Cultural Center.* and even the experience of mourning the death of friends. You notice that these events are usually marked by rites of passage with strong religious overtones. You also note that *mana* is a key concept for understanding Polynesian religions.

As you begin formal study of indigenous religions, some questions about them will occur to you. Here are some things that students often wonder about:

- Why are there so many different names for this type of religion?

- Why are they so much alike that they can be studied together, but at the same time so different from one another?

- Why are so many of their practices becoming popular among people of other religions?

- Why do they have relatively little emphasis on *teaching* when compared to other world religions, and focus so much on *rituals*?

- How much have they changed, and how much have they stayed the same, especially in the last two centuries or so?

◁ Cofan, a shaman, or tribal religious leader, from the Amazon forest, 2006.

Because of the large numbers of religions that are discussed here, this chapter has a special organization that differs from that of all other chapters (except the last, which has an organization like this chapter). First, we will discuss the variety of names scholars have given to this overall type of religion and then explain why this book calls them *indigenous* religions. Second, we'll deal with the typical challenges to the academic study of these religions, especially the kinds of challenges that students face when they begin this study. Third, we'll draw out the more common characteristics in these religions. In this section, we'll deal with history, teaching, ritual, and so on. Fourth, we'll take a closer look at just three indigenous religions: those of the Lakota (lah-KOH-tuh) tribes of North America, the Yoruba (YOHR-uh-buh) tribe of Africa, and the Vodou (VOH-doo, more widely known as *Voodoo*) of African-Caribbean peoples.

LO1 Names for This Type of Religion

Naming the overall type of religions with which we are dealing can be a challenge. But why is it necessary to name the type of religion at all, if such a comprehensive name may well distort or obscure the individual beliefs? The answer is that religious studies itself has seen this as important despite its downside, so we must grapple with the issue here. This section will deal with generic names, suggesting what is strong and weak about each one, and then we'll discuss the term settled on in this book: *indigenous religions*.

TRADITIONAL RELIGION

Traditional religion correctly implies that religions were present in various societies around the world before European and American expansion. They are *traditional* in comparison to newer, imported religions. However, as we saw in Chapter 1, all religions are traditions, because they are comprehensive ways of life that come from the past and are passed on into the

> **animism** Belief that individual spirits exist not only in people but also in all individual things in nature
>
> **totemism** [TOHT-em-iz-uhm] Religion based on the idea that the spirit of one primary source in nature provides the basis of human life

future. It has become common in scholarship to refer to Hinduism, Islam, and the rest as *traditions* as well as *religions*. Labeling only one type as *traditional* is misleading and potentially confusing.

> *Indigenous religions are often just as complex and comprehensive as other world religions.*

PRIMITIVE RELIGION

Primitive religion and the related term *primal religion* were more popular in the past, especially among cultural anthropologists who used them in a neutral, nonjudgmental way. These terms mostly describe religions that are not derived from other religions, and this is a helpful distinction. However, it's more difficult to use these terms in a neutral way in religious studies. They can imply that these religions are undeveloped, unchanging, outmoded, or simple. Research into these religions has confirmed just the opposite: They are often just as complex and comprehensive as other world religions. Most religion scholarship avoids *primitive* today, but *primal* is occasionally seen.

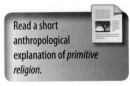

Read a short anthropological explanation of *primitive religion*.

ANIMISM AND TOTEMISM

Animism and *totemism* are popular as names for religions in some circles today. **Animism** (from the Latin *anima*, "soul, spirit") is the belief that individual spirits exist not only in people but also in all individual things in nature, whether they appear to be alive or not: individual animals, plants, rocks, thunder and lightning, and mountains, lakes and rivers. In many religions the souls of deceased humans keep a close relationship with the living, so that they are part of myth and ritual. The appearance of the sacred in dreams and visions is a key element of animism. Edward B. Tylor, a founder of the field of anthropology, argued as early as 1891 that all religion began in animism. **Totemism** is a religion based on the idea that the spirit of one primary source in nature—the land itself, a particular species of animal, or the ancestors—provides the basis of human life. Totemism is found in the Native American tribes of

Close-up of a totem pole with an eagle face

© MARK HERREID/SHUTTERSTOCK.COM

© 2009FOTOFRIENDS/SHUTTERSTOCK.COM

Totem poles

the northwest coast (with their famous totem poles) and in the beliefs of the Aborigines of Australia. It fits these totemic religions well as a comprehensive name, but it doesn't fit other religions of this type.

A Closer Look:

Totemism in the *Twilight* Series

AP PHOTO/CHRISTOPHE ENA

Kristen Stewart, Taylor Lautner, and Robert Pattinson star in The Twilight Saga.

The leader of the Quileute (KWILL-yoot) Nation of Native Americans in northwest Washington first heard about the *Twilight Saga* novels from their readers, who wanted to know more about the place where the blockbuster vampires-and-werewolves tale of teenage love is set. When the novels were made into films, interest in Quileutes exploded. "Their interest in our tribe was a good surprise," tribal president Anna Rose Counsell-Geyer said to

the press. "People are going to actually get to know the Quileute and we are going to be recognized as a people."

The Quileute's reservation on the Olympic Peninsula serves as the scenic backdrop to author Stephenie Meyer's fantasy novels, with thick woods and with rocks and cliffs rising along the Pacific Ocean. The reservation spans only one square mile. The wolf theme of *Twilight* draws on the Quileutes' own creation story, which features the transformation of an ancient wolf pack into people who became the Quileute tribe. Since that transformation, the wolf has been the tribe's totem.

In *Twilight*, the Quileute creation story is used to explain the Wolf Pack, a group of young Quileute men joined by Jacob Black (played in the film by Taylor Lautner), who shape-shift into large, powerful wolves to guard the reservation from marauding vampires. The present-day *Twilight Saga* marks a departure from Hollywood's long tradition of portraying the past, not the present, of Native Americans. It also departs from Quileute religion, which does not feature tribal members who can shape-shift into wolves; this isn't a part of totemism, but instead draws on European werewolf legends.

manaism [MAH-nah-iz-uhm] Belief in impersonal spiritual power and energy that permeates the world as a whole

shaman [SHAH-muhn] Tribal member with special abilities and the authority to act as an intermediary between the people and the world of gods and spirits (both good and evil)

MANAISM

Some cultural anthropologists held that the first stage of all human religion was **manaism**, a belief in impersonal spiritual power and energy that permeates the world as a whole. Many religions, they argued, are still based on mana. Manaism is pre-animistic, because power is not connected to spirits in individual natural things (animism) or species/groups of things (totemism). It is drawn from the Polynesian term *mana*, "spiritual power." Some see the Yoruban idea of general spiritual power that infuses the universe as an example of mana. For almost a generation at the beginning of the twentieth century, there was quite a disagreement between those who advocated manaism and those who advocated animism as the basis of all later religion. Today this argument is largely a thing of the past.

SHAMANISM

A **shaman** is a tribal member with special abilities and the authority to act as an intermediary between the people and the world of gods and spirits (both good and evil). He, or rarely she, is known by different names in different tribes; the most common are *holy man*, *medicine man*, and *healer*. Shamans are so common in this type of religion that some scholars have called their beliefs *shamanic/shamanistic religions*. But this is controversial today, especially among cultural anthropologists. Many indigenous peoples around the world, particularly in the Native American tribes, also reject this term as misleading when applied to them.

SMALL-SCALE RELIGIONS

This name, from cultural anthropology, is accurate in its implication that some of the religions to which it refers are held by a smaller number of people, but other so-called small-scale religions are actually practiced by more people than some world religions such as Judaism, Sikhism, Jainism, and Shinto. Other than the relative size of *some* of them—and there were indigenous empires in the Americas and in Africa with empire-wide religions, we must remember—there is nothing small about these religions.

> Catherine Albanese argues that "nature religion" applies to many different sorts of American beliefs, from early colonial times to the contemporary "New Age" movement.

NATURE RELIGION

Some people informally use the term *nature religions*. This correctly suggests the stronger connection to the natural environment in indigenous religions than in other world religions. But there is much more to the religion in this chapter than a connection to the natural environment. Moreover, here, "nature" itself is a Western concept that many other societies, especially the societies dealt with in this chapter, do not share. They usually have no strong distinction between the natural and supernatural that *nature religions* may imply to Westerners. Nor do they see human beings as so superior to the rest of the world that they almost stand above and apart from nature. A 1991 book by the noted religion

Doña Juanita, a Seri Indian healer in Mexico, with her supplies

TOMÁS CASTELAZO

Read the first page of Catherine Albanese's *Nature Religion in America*.

scholar Catherine Albanese, *Nature Religion in America*, argues that *nature religion* applies to many different sorts of American beliefs, from the times of pre-colonial Native American religions to the contemporary "New Age" movement.[1]

INDIGENOUS RELIGIONS

In this book we'll use the term **indigenous religions**. *Indigenous* means "native, intrinsic to an area," especially in the sense of peoples who originate and belong to a specific area. (Students should avoid a common confusion with *indigent*, which means "poor.") As we'll see shortly, *indigenous* entails a strong sense of belonging religiously to a certain place, in a way that *native* alone might not. In current usage, *indigenous* implies religions and cultures that were present in a given place for centuries, and usually millennia, before the coming of other cultures with different religions. When used in this way, it says more than the ambiguous term *native*. Strictly speaking, everyone born in North America is a "native American," but most people born in North America don't belong to continuing indigenous groups of "Native Americans." *Indigenous* today often implies a lack of political power in the wider society, when other groups of people have taken over the lands of indigenous peoples.

When considering the names for individual indigenous groups, we should ask: What names do the individual groups use, and what names are given to them by others? The European colonizers of Africa and the Americas played a large role in giving them names that Westerners know them by, so we should begin here. In general, European names for indigenous peoples and their religions have been inaccurate. Europeans did not often listen carefully to what other cultures called themselves, but instead imposed their own names or adapted the sound and spelling of indigenous names for tribes to their own languages. This reflects a colonialist mentality. In later chapters, we will see that Westerners also had a key role in the rise of names such as "Hinduism" and "Confucianism." In recent times there has been a movement to restore the original sound and spelling of these names: "Odawa" for "Ottawa" and "Algonkian" for "Algonquin," for example.

> *Calling the earliest American peoples "Indians" was one of the biggest geography bloopers of all time.*

The most famous European name for indigenous peoples is the historic Western term for peoples who inhabited the Western Hemisphere: *Indians*. In 1492 Christopher Columbus supposed that he had reached the islands off China called at the time the "Indies." However, he unknowingly had discovered a new continent between Europe and Asia, a continent that would become known as the *New World*. The name "Indians" persisted even when it became obvious that it was wrong, and it was soon used by the English and French as well. To call the indigenous peoples of the Americas "Indians" was one of the biggest geography bloopers of all time, but it has endured for centuries.

However, ideas about names do change, and sometimes in unpredictable ways. Today many native peoples in the United States happily call themselves "Indians," not "Native Americans." The latest Census Bureau Survey of terminology, done in 1995, showed that 49 percent of native peoples preferred being called "American Indian," 37 percent preferred "Native American," about 4 percent preferred "some other term," and 5 percent had no preference. "Indians" grew in approval by Native Americans at the same time as it became disapproved in wider North American culture. For example, in his highly praised memoir, *The Names*, the Kiowa writer N. Scott Momaday speaks about how his mother embraced this name: "[S]he began to see herself as an 'Indian'. That dim native heritage became a fascination and a cause for her."[2] *American Indian* is still the main term used in the U.S. Census, although it is still controversial there; many scholars use it alongside *Native American*, and we will use it occasionally here as well. The safest policy for students and scholars is to use the names indigenous peoples themselves prefer.

In general, many of the indigenous peoples of North America prefer their

indigenous religions Term for religions of peoples, usually tribes, original to an area

---

[1] Catherine L. Albanese, *Nature Religion in America: From the Algonkian Indians to the New Age* (Chicago: University of Chicago Press, 1991).

[2] N. Scott Momaday, *The Names* (Tucson: University of Arizona Press, 1976), p. 25

local group name as rendered in their language, not an English-language name or a traditional name recognized by whites. Many Sioux Nation Indians prefer to be known by the main name of "Lakota," "Dakota," or "Nakota" (each designating groupings within the same culture), and further subgroups are known as well. They use "Sioux" as a name for themselves when speaking to outsiders, but inside their group they use "Lakota" or its variants. In the 2000 U.S. census, fully 75 percent of people who identified their ethnic group as "Indian" also identified their main tribal or national group. Sometimes political differences within a tribe or nation lead to competing preferences for different names in the same group—for example "Navajos" or *Diné* ("Earth People"). In Canada the broad designation **First Nations** (note the plural) is widely accepted as a general term by native groups and wider Canadian society, but the individual tribes still use their own names. In Australia and New Zealand, **Aboriginals** (people there "from the origin") is commonly accepted as a name, although its use is lessening, with new preference being given to the specific names of the more than two hundred cultural groups that "Aboriginals" encompasses.

LO2 Challenges to Study

In Chapter 1, we dealt with some challenges to the study of religion in general. When we encounter indigenous religions, some special challenges emerge that don't apply to most other religions we will deal with in this book. We can list and explain them briefly.

LACK OF WRITTEN SOURCES

Because the cultures in which these religions are based are almost exclusively oral cultures, not writing cultures, their religions have with only a few exceptions not written down their stories, beliefs, or rituals. Where these features of religious life do exist in writing today, most of them have been written down by anthropologists. Nor do we have as much archaeological evidence for indigenous peoples as we do for other world religions. Some tribes, along with their particular religions, disappeared long before the coming of Europeans, the victims of disease, famine, and especially intertribal warfare, and we know little about them. In the first chapter of this book, we noted the importance of history as a method of studying religion, but the use of history to study the first Americans is severely limited. This restricts the scope and depth of study.

DIFFICULTY DISCERNING CONTINUITY AND DISCONTINUITY

By the time Western scholars began to study native groups in the Americas, Africa, and Australia, it was hundreds of years after the natives' first contact with European Americans. Sometimes this contact led to significant changes in indigenous belief and practices, and at other times it didn't. As a result, scholars of indigenous religions aren't certain about how far back many beliefs and practices go: Are they pre-contact or post-contact? For example, some have argued that in Yoruba religion in west Africa, the remote high god developed as an adaptive reaction to Christian and Muslim missionaries who proclaimed a religion of one God. Other scholars dispute this, arguing that indigenous religions often have belief in one high, remote deity without any question of Western religious influence.

MAINSTREAM GUILT

Many indigenous peoples have been treated brutally during the whole sweep of human history and even prehistory, whenever one group came into the territory of another group and tried to take over. Treatment that was intended to reduce their numbers and their cultures is nothing short of **genocide**, the killing of an entire racial/ethnic/religious group of people. Today we think that this should have caused second thoughts among people of European origins who took over the lands of indigenous peoples—for example in North America and Africa—but in the ethos of the times it usually didn't. Many of their present-day descendants are ashamed of the actions of their ancestors and the continued bitter legacy of prejudice and discrimination. This is probably as it should be, but sometimes guilt, powerful emotion that it is, gets in the way of understanding. It can distort the careful study of indigenous cultures and their religions. This is not to say that people shouldn't regret what happened in the past; it is to say that careful understanding of the past is a key part of knowing what to do in the present if we are to move beyond the ills of the past.

First Nations Generic term for indigenous peoples in Canada

Aboriginals [ab-oh-RIHJ-ih-nahls] Indigenous peoples there "from the origin" of Australia and New Zealand

genocide Killing of an entire racial/ethnic/religious group

MISREPRESENTATIONS IN POPULAR CULTURE

Popular culture, and especially Hollywood film that is so influential in shaping attitudes today, has distorted indigenous religions. On the one hand, films such as *Dances with Wolves* and *Avatar* have portrayed indigenous tribes as habitually moral, master ecologists, or even "noble savages." This last phrase was a theme in the influential work of Jean-Jacques Rousseau (1712–1778), who held that people are naturally good but that so-called civilization corrupts them. Such an idealized view of indigenous peoples is based on superficial knowledge; if they were in fact so noble, they would not need practices to deal with misdeeds, social disorder, and outright crimes, which they indeed have and use.

On the other hand, Hollywood has depicted some religions as dangerously exotic in order to amuse or frighten audiences, as in *Apocalypto* or the hundreds of films made about the white settlement of the American West. Negative portrayals have seeped down to the life of North American children, where playing games of "cowboys and Indians" has been popular for generations—if historically incorrect, because cowboys rarely fought Indians. Africa has frequently been depicted in film as a place of more savagery than nobility, with religions that are little more than superstitions. Popular culture's portrayal of Afro-Caribbean religions, Vodou in particular, is probably the worst misrepresentation of all. The 1973 James Bond film, *Live and Let Die*, and the more frightening *Angel Heart* portrayed Vodou as violent and dangerous. The popular *Night of the Living Dead*, originally from 1968 and remade in 1990, removed zombie lore from its Vodou context, and zombies have become increasingly popular ever since. All these misrepresentations of indigenous religions have affected how we understand them, and this makes it harder to study them today.

MISUSE OF INDIGENOUS RITUALS

In today's religious climate in North America and Europe, some people freely combine elements of indigenous religions with their own religions or other beliefs. It has become popular in some circles, for example, to use sacred objects of North American indigenous religions such as the stone pipe, medicine bundles, peyote, and sweat lodges in new religious ceremonies in non-Native American religions. This removes indigenous rituals from their deeply embedded cultural context and gives them a meaning that indigenous peoples wouldn't recognize. Some indigenous groups are offended by this and view it as detrimental to their long-term spiritual and

cultural health. For example, some Lakota leaders opposed this misuse in a controversial 1993 resolution, "Declaration of War against Exploiters of Lakota Spirituality."

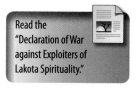

Read the "Declaration of War against Exploiters of Lakota Spirituality."

As you conclude this section, you might be wondering: With all these problems in the study of indigenous religions, how can they possibly be studied well? The answer is that they can indeed be studied well, and are. However, the first step in doing so is to recognize and deal with the obstacles to study that the past has put in your way. Now that these are in plain view, we can turn to a discussion of these religions, beginning with their most important common features.

LO3 Common Features of Indigenous Religions

Despite the terms Native American religion, African religion, or Aboriginal religion, no such things as a whole ever existed.

In this section, we will discuss the common key characteristics of indigenous religions. But we must realize up front that there are many significant differences among them. They are as diverse as the cultures and times from which they come. Africa has over three thousand ethnic and language groups, with social organizations from

Indigenous empire: Mayan temple, Chichen Itza, Mexico

© PIERDELUNE/SHUTTERSTOCK.COM

Map 2.1

Contemporary Africa

Africa contains more than forty nations. Six sub-Saharan African nations and Algeria in North Africa experienced anti-colonial revolutions, and a dozen sub-Saharan nations have been racked by civil wars since independence. In 2011, Libya, Tunisia and Egypt experienced popular revolts.

small tribes to large empires. Africa today has more than forty nations (see Map 2.1). In the Americas there have been more than two thousand tribes, some of them organized in large nations or even empires such as those of the Aztecs and Mayans. Each of the world religions that we'll consider in later chapters has some shared idea of sacred history—of the tradition's founders, sacred texts, rituals, and the like—that gives it unity. For indigenous religions around the world, diversity is the rule. Despite the terms *Native American religion*, *African religion*, or *Aboriginal religion*, no such singular things ever existed, and neither did *indigenous religion*. No single system of

A Closer Look:

Movements toward Indigenous Unity

ROLL CALL/GETTY IMAGES

Native American dancers enter the Verizon Center in Washington, D.C., as the National Powwow organized by the Smithsonian National Museum of the American Indian begins.

Smithsonian National Museum of the American Indian in Washington, D.C.

PHILLIP RITZ/GETTY IMAGES

A recent development brings a surprising "twist" to diversity within indigenous religions. Indigenous peoples around the world are realizing that they are in a common situation with regard to their dominant cultures and are beginning to act on this in ways that draw the people and the culture together.

For example, a **Pan-Indian** movement began in the early 1900s and is now prominent in North America. This movement is based on indigenous American peoples' realization that they share many social and religious concerns today. One example of this is the American Indian Movement (AIM) organization. Cross-tribal memberships, powwow (intertribal gatherings, especially of leaders) networks among tribes, and national lobbying groups, are found in contemporary Pan-Indianism. Increasingly, rituals have been shared among the tribes. Their life has

become more Pan-Indian, with wider use of ritual pipe smoking, sweat lodges, vision quests, sun dancing, and the use of peyote. Pan-Indianism is also found in universities, prisons, military forces, and urban settings where general Native American identity is more important than one's specific tribal identity. The Pan-Indian movement tries to respect local tribal identities and traditions, but some tribes object to the sharing of rituals.

Explore the AIM website.

belief or ritual unites all African, American, or Aboriginal religions. We present here the basics of indigenous religions, but this doesn't imply that all indigenous religions are the same. Nor does it imply that indigenous peoples have ever thought of their religions as the same.

Indigenous religions usually see themselves as created in their own place, despite what anthropologists think about all humans originating in Africa.

THE IMPORTANCE OF PLACE

Most anthropologists hold that the human race (*Homo sapiens*) gradually spread from one area of Africa across much of the globe beginning about 100,000 years ago (see Map 2.2). Many groups of humans have been on the move ever since, carrying their indigenous religions with them. This common origin helps to explain how modern humans are similar genetically but had some further genetic and cultural adaptations to their new environments. Despite all this movement, indigenous

Pan-Indian Movement begun in the early 1900s to bring more unity to North American tribes

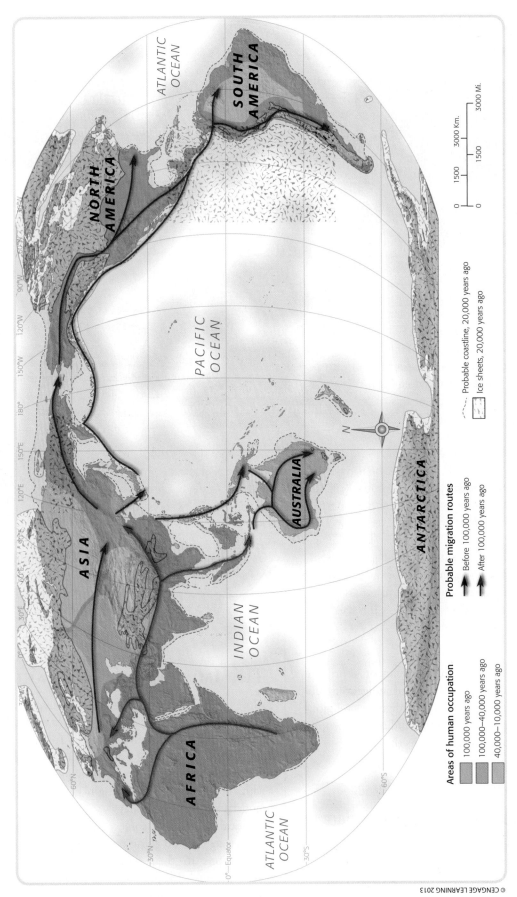

Map 2.2
Spread of Humans around the Globe

Areas of human occupation

☐ 100,000 years ago
☐ 100,000–40,000 years ago
☐ 40,000–10,000 years ago

Probable migration routes

⬆ Before 100,000 years ago
⬆ After 100,000 years ago

╌╌ Probable coastline, 20,000 years ago
☐ Ice sheets, 20,000 years ago

© CENGAGE LEARNING 2013

Chapito, a Seri Indian shaman in northwestern Mexico, points to mountain caves, a place of power.

peoples are deeply rooted in a place. Moreover, they usually see themselves as created in or from that place, despite what modern anthropologists think about all humans originating in Africa. For them *place* is much more than simply a location or even a type of geography such as forest, desert, plains, and so on. Instead, it is a matter of tribal and personal identity. Place has great practical and symbolic significance for indigenous peoples and their religious beliefs and practices. What Vine Deloria Jr. says about Native American religion is true of all other indigenous religions, "The sacredness of lands on which previous generations have lived and died is the foundation of all other sentiments."[3]

Stories about the land deal with myths of tribal origins, rituals, and patterns of everyday life. Because indigenous religions are typically rich in traditions that deal with their particular places, they often speak of being created not just from Mother Earth, but from the earth "here in this valley." They communicate with spirits not just all around them, but "in a mountain cave over there" and reverence in particular a sacred animal "in that rainforest." Sacred place has a personal status in indigenous religions. For example, at their annual intertribal gatherings in the Sweet Grass Hills of Montana, the Chippewa-Cree people pray that owners of the mines in their sacred hills will see that "these hills are just as alive as anybody, and they want to live too." People and their places are meant to live together in

Watch a preview of "Losing Sacred Ground."

a harmonious balance. Many indigenous tribes displaced from their traditional lands in the Americas, Africa, and Australia have sought to reclaim them in some religiously meaningful way, even if they cannot live on their sacred ground. Other religions we will encounter in this book all have holy places, but they are typically not connected to specific places in the ways that indigenous religions are.

GLOBAL DISTRIBUTION

Indigenous religions are found around the globe today, not just in North America and Africa. In Africa, indigenous religions are spread through most of the continent south of the Sahara Desert. In general, more-traditional forms of indigenous religions are found in central Africa; in the northern and southern thirds of Africa, indigenous religions have largely been blended into Islam and Christianity, respectively. In the Americas, indigenous religions are also widespread: Native peoples with their distinctive religions inhabit the hemisphere from the Arctic to the southern tip of Chile. Many indigenous peoples in the Americas today combine their indigenous religions with Christianity, in Central and South America particularly with Roman Catholic Christianity.

> *Indigenous religions are found around the world today, not just in North America and Africa.*

In Asia, the picture is the most complex. Indigenous religion persists almost undisturbed in some remote islands in south Asia, especially in Indonesia and Borneo. Polynesian and Micronesian cultures and religions have spread widely, so that today they are found from Hawaii to Taiwan and south. In Tibet, the ancient indigenous Bön religion persists inside and occasionally outside of Tibetan Buddhism, despite persecution in the past by the Buddhist government of Tibet. Folk religions emphasizing local spirits and gods have been common for millennia in China; sometimes these

---

[3] Vine Deloria Jr., *God Is Red: A Native View of Religion* (New York: Putnam, 1973), 278.

Aboriginal rock art, Kakadu National Park, Australia

MANY GODS AND SPIRITS

A distinctive feature of indigenous religions, especially when compared to many other world religions, is that they aren't typically focused on one deity. Some African indigenous religions claim to tend toward monotheism, usually because they have one high god, but most believe in many gods. High gods seldom figure into everyday religious life. Instead, they are remote gods, as we'll see in our treatment of Lakota and Yoruba religion. Moreover, as we saw above, when high deities are regularly invoked, some scholars suspect influence from other world religions. For example, many Native American tribes believe in a high god such as the Great Spirit but don't talk about him on a regular basis or have rituals addressed to him. Where there is more frequent talk of the Great Spirit, and where this Spirit is seen as a single personal Being, it may well be due to Native American accommodation to Christianity.

Deities or spirits are not worshiped in a detached way; they are ritually invoked and engaged as inhabitants and agents of the world itself. Some indigenous religions remember individuals from their past who were influential leaders, but none is seen as a founder of the religion. This emphasizes that native religions are less about human figures, or even gods and rituals, than they are about relationships. Relationships are shaped by prominent humans and gods and guided by morals, myth, and rituals, but they are ultimately about the people's connection to one another and the group's connection to the world around it.

INFLUENCED BY OTHER CULTURES

Many world religions have had to deal with competition and conflict with other religions, but almost all indigenous religions have had to deal with being surrounded and suppressed by alien nation–states with alien religions. In Africa, for example, centuries of colonial rule by Europeans, and the Christian missionary efforts that went with it, changed some elements of many African indigenous religions. New gods came forth, and new rituals for worshiping them. Contemporary scholarship acknowledges that culture-contact changes are central to understanding indigenous cultures and their religions today. It studies their continuities and changes, and not simply their complete destruction. Indigenous religions *as they exist today* are worthy of study and appreciation. We should not use our knowledge of post-contact indigenous religions merely to strip away perceived influences from other religions in order to arrive at

divine beings have become Daoist divinities. Japan's indigenous religion of Shinto has played such a large role in modern world history that it is often treated separately, as this book will do in Chapter 8. Islam mostly ended pre-Islamic Arab indigenous religion, but other indigenous religions have been incorporated to some degree in some areas where Islam has spread. In Australia and New Zeeland, original forms of Aboriginal religions exist alongside Christianity, although the great majority of Aboriginal people self-identify as Christians today. In Europe, Christianity gradually overwhelmed indigenous religions, but did so in part by absorbing some indigenous practices such as rituals to counteract evil elves and bringing evergreens into homes at Christmas.

Watch a *New York Times* analysis of the critically praised film on Aboriginal life, *Walkabout.*

Visit a website introducing the variety of African indigenous religions.

Watch a National Geographic video on indigenous religion and other religions in Bali.

hypothetical pre-contact religions. Scholars have little data about the past of indigenous religions that are free from non-native influence, so trying to get back to pre-contact religion is problematic. Indigenous religions themselves often erase any evidence that suggests that some of their beliefs and practices are products of a particular place and time.

BASED ON ORALITY, STORY, AND MYTH

Indigenous religious traditions are oral, not written, because the cultures in which they are based are oral cultures. Orality can open up more room for adaptive change in religion because of not being bound in a book. Most importantly, orality entails skilled, compelling storytelling. As all skilled storytellers know, audiences must be "brought into the story." In indigenous religions, this is done not just as entertainment. In the religion's stories, each person's life enters a larger group story, even a cosmic story that reaches backward and forward in time. Myths and their accompanying rituals have a critical role in maintaining good relationships between all sacred beings in the universe—human, divine, animals, and even plants.

Scholars have classified different myths according to their form and function. **Cosmogonic myths** about creation help to explain the origin of existence. They tell how the whole world was created, and especially how the particular tribe telling a myth was created. An **etiological myth** is one that explains how things have come to be as they are now, as large as why the sun travels in the sky or as small as why the beaver has no hair on its tail. The **semi-historical myth** is the elaboration of an original happening, usually involving a tribal hero such as the nineteenth-century Lakota leader Sitting Bull. Telling these myths and stories is a means of communication between humans and other beings. The religious specialist of the indigenous society is often the keeper of these stories and can perform them with power. Animals, ancestors, spirits, and gods all compose stories, and people understand the beings through the stories. Narrative is the mode that brings these indigenous traditions to life, by songs, chants, prayers, ritual dances, folktales, and genealogies. Oral tradition has not been erased by modernity and literacy, though it has taken new forms as storytellers have found modern means (including YouTube) for its expression.

Watch an explanation of African storytelling.

Painted tepee of a Plains Indian medicine man, with his granddaughter in the doorway

ORIENTED MORE TO PRACTICE THAN TO BELIEF

Indigenous traditions are not belief based, and they have no formal "teachings" on which one can do religious or theological reflection. Belief in gods and spirits is traditional and assumed, a part of the fabric of life, and children are rigorously socialized to know the moral codes of their society. These beliefs are "more caught than taught," and they are reinforced in initiation rituals as children become adults. The emphasis is on practices. Indigenous religions around the world are dedicated to maintaining personal, group, and cosmic balance through ritual actions. The purpose of this balance is that the group may thrive. The scope of rituals in indigenous religions is vast. Some mark life-cycle changes at birth, beginning of adulthood, marriage, and death. Others are designed to bless people at trying times, heal them of diseases of the mind or body, attract rain, or produce a good hunt or good crops. Still others are for purposes of putting curses on people (sometimes called *witching*) and counteracting curses (*unwitching*). The purpose of most indigenous ritual is to control the power of the world—to attract good power when needed and to turn away dangerous power.

Watch "Apache Girl's Rite of Passage."

IN-GROUP BASED

Indigenous traditions around the world are commonly in-group based. Few indigenous religions seek converts or even allow full entry by people not of their group. As we saw above, they often don't appreciate how others have recently adopted some of their beliefs and rituals or have come as "seekers" to explore their ways of life. This attitude can come as a surprise, even a shock, to well-intentioned outsiders who are on spiritual journeys that they believe lead to indigenous religions. (American popular culture sometimes portrays indigenous societies as able to be joined by outsiders, as for

cosmogonic myth Story about creation that helps to explain the origin of existence

etiological myth Story that explains how things have come to be as they are now

semi-historical myth Elaboration of an original happening, usually involving a tribal hero

example in the film *Dances with Wolves*.) Unlike religions that seek converts, indigenous religions are ethnicity based. Either one is culturally a part of the group, or one is not. If a person is inside the group, then the religion of the group pertains to that person, for his or her place in the community and the world depends upon it.

In indigenous societies, extensive life-cycle rituals are employed to bring children to fully initiated membership in the group. Apart from this initiation, the group is closed to outsiders, and much of their religious knowledge is secret, sometimes even to members of the tribe. For example, the Dogon (DOH-guhn) people of Mali, West Africa, have many rituals that are done in masks, but the meaning of the masks is known only to those initiated into a society of specialists. Tribal members may regard others outside the tribe as sincere, but they will not typically make them members of the community and give them access to religious secrets. The long oppression of indigenous peoples by others has made them even more wary of outsiders' actions and intentions.

> **trickster** God, spirit, human, or wily animal that plays tricks on people or otherwise behaves against conventional norms of behavior, often for the good of others

Indigenous religion maintains the balance of life so that the group as a whole can thrive.

THE GOODNESS OF THE WORLD

Indigenous peoples believe that each and every part of nature has a spiritual aspect that makes it live and gives direction to its life. All things in the world are related to humans in a cosmic natural balance. American and African indigenous cultures often see this balance as a circle. The Sioux imitated this natural order by setting up their camp in circles, by sitting in circles for councils and ceremonial occasions, and also by constructing circular tepees. Therefore, these traditions do not deal with "salvation," "enlightenment," or even "eternal life." Means of transcending or transforming this world aren't important to them, because the world does not need escaping. Its natural harmony needs only to be preserved and lived in. Likewise, these traditions aren't typically future oriented—for example in believing that

this world is heading toward some large religious goal. Rather, the past is privileged for them. The past contains the model for identity, behavior, and blessing in the present and the future. This desire to make the idealized past ever present makes these religions deeply "traditional." The point of indigenous religion is to maintain the balance of life so that the group as a whole can thrive in the world.

Read about the religious meaning of the painted tepee.

THE ROLE OF RELIGIOUS SPECIALISTS

Most indigenous societies have religious specialists of some sort—people selected or trained to do a variety of religious tasks at a higher level than do others. They are known by a variety of names: "holy men," "medicine men," "healers," "priests/priestesses," and others. **Tricksters** are gods, spirits, humans, or wily animals (often a coyote in North American lore) that play tricks on people or otherwise behave against conventional norms of behavior, often for the good of others. "Prophets" (a name, but not a phenomenon, drawn from contact with Christianity) arise from time to time to lead their tribes out of crisis. Perhaps the most notable religious specialist is the shaman, an intermediary or messenger between the human world and the spirit worlds. Many types of shamans exist throughout the world, often varying by tribe, although the main model for shamans comes from Siberian tribes. They are the "spiritual leaders" of their tribes. Mircea Eliade identified their main features as follows:

- The shaman communicates with the spirit world, where good and evil spirits are found.

- The shaman can treat sickness or deal with other problems caused by evil spirits.

- The shaman can employ trance-inducing techniques to leave his body and go to the spirit realm that surrounds this world, or his body can be possessed by the gods or spirits.

Watch the story of "The Shaman and the Frost."

- The shaman evokes animal spirits as message bearers to other spirits.

- The shaman can tell the future by various forms of divination.[4]

Watch "Dama," on the Dogon (African) ritual and shaman.

---

[4] Mircea Eliade, *Shamanism: Archaic Techniques of Ecstasy* (New York: Random House, 1964).

A Closer Look:

Debate on Shamanism

Some anthropologists today are critical of the recent emphasis on "shamanism" and the work of Eliade and others. Alice Kehoe, in her 2000 book *Shamans and Religion*, argues sharply that shamans are unique to each culture where they are found and cannot be generalized into a global type of religion called "shamanism."[5] She also opposes "neo-shamanism" in New Age, Wiccan, and other current Western religious movements. These not only misrepresent indigenous practices, but do so in a way that reinforces ideas such as the "noble savage," an idea Kehoe argues is racist. She is critical of the recent claim that modern-day shamanism survives from the Paleolithic period.

[5] Alice Kehoe, *Shamans and Religion: An Exploration in Critical Thinking* (Long Grove, IL: Waveland Press, 2000).

EDWARD S. CURTIS (1868–1952)

Shaman emerging from forest in a trance after an initiation ritual, 1914

CONTINUING VITALITY

The imminent death of indigenous religions has been predicted in the past by politicians, missionaries, and even scholars. If we consider the dire straits of many indigenous religions a century ago, we can understand why some observers have thought that native traditions were dying out. However, many indigenous religions can now say, with the American humorist Mark Twain, when told that his death had been announced in a newspaper, "The reports of my death are greatly exaggerated." Not only have most native cultures survived against great pressures over the last five centuries, some are now thriving in ways that would have been unthinkable until recently. Native peoples' numbers and cultural influence have risen dramatically in recent generations, in many but not all parts of the world. Improved standards of living have helped, but more important is that being "indigenous" is shifting in many places from being a social liability in wider society to being a point of pride.

> *Reports of the death of indigenous religions are, to adapt a quip by Mark Twain, greatly exaggerated.*

We can point to ways in which indigenous religions have flourished over the past half-century. In North America, many native ceremonies that were banned in earlier times are now protected by law. Native peoples have fought hard for these protections and continue to do so, and the wider society has seen the wisdom in preserving them. These include protection of peyote consumption, the use of eagle feathers in rituals, burial protections, and rights to fish and hunt. They also include the return of human remains and traditional religious and cultural objects now in museums and in private collections. Various African-Caribbean religions that combine Christianity and native African religions are regaining their voice: Santería in Cuba, Candomblé in Brazil, Rastafarianism in Jamaica, and Vodou in Haiti. In Africa, a number of indigenous religions are more prominent today than in the past two hundred years, but many continue to be hard pressed by Christianity and Islam.

Native African churches that combine Christianity with key aspects of indigenous religions are thriving, so parts of indigenous African religions survive within Christianity. The increased freedom of religion in China has led to the widespread rebirth and flourishing of suppressed folk religions that seem to have gone underground for more than fifty years. Indigenous religious traditions have persisted because they are, in a word—as the Chippewa poet Gerald Vizenor has often said about his fellow indigenous Americans—"survivors."

LO4 A Native American Religion: Lakota

More than a hundred different Native American tribes are found in North America today. (See Map 2.3 for a historical overview of major Native American tribes, 600–1500 C.E.) The one offered here for study, the Lakota group, which figures large in history and today, is meant to provide a more extensive

Explore Native American culture in Google Earth™.

look into the religious life of that tribe and also as a more definite description of what indigenous religion is.

NAME AND LOCATION

The word *Sioux* (soo) applies today to seven tribal groups organized into three main political units. It dates back to the 1600s C.E. when the people were living in the western Great Lakes area. The Ojibwa (oh-JIHB-way) tribes called the Lakota *Nadouwesou,* meaning "poisonous snakes." This term, shortened by French traders to its last syllable, became *Sioux.* They called themselves the Seven Fire Places People. The French Roman Catholic missionary Jean Nicolet first recorded the

term *Sioux* in 1640. Wars with the Chippewas and the Crees resulted in the reduction of the eastern Sioux and gradual displacement of other Sioux. The western Lakota Sioux were the first to arrive on the plains. Horses, which transformed Plains life, were obtained by the Oglala Sioux about 1750. They were not native to North America, but were introduced by the Spanish and later obtained by the Plains tribes.

Read a concise overview of current Native Americans, with blog comments.

BASIC FEATURES OF LAKOTA RELIGION

The Black Hills is the Lakota's sacred place of creation and life. For the Lakota, they are the "heart of everything that exists." A story says that the hills are like a reclining woman whose breasts gave life-giving power; the hills are a mother to the Lakota. The Sioux people were created in particular from the Bear Butte on the eastern edge of the Hills, and there the Creator first gave his sacred instructions to them. Bear Butte is the most sacred of all their holy places, and both Sioux and Cheyenne come here each year for ceremonies. It has often been said that the spirits of the Sioux dead rest in the Black Hills.

The spirit world of the Lakota is called **Wakan Tanka,** which means "all that is mysterious, sacred." This is a generic, not a personal name. Wakan Tanka is eternal. It powerfully created the universe, and paradoxically it is the universe. The sun, the moon, the stars, and the earth and everything on it (including

View from Harney Peak Trail, Black Hills, South Dakota

© JIM PARKIN/SHUTTERSTOCK.COM

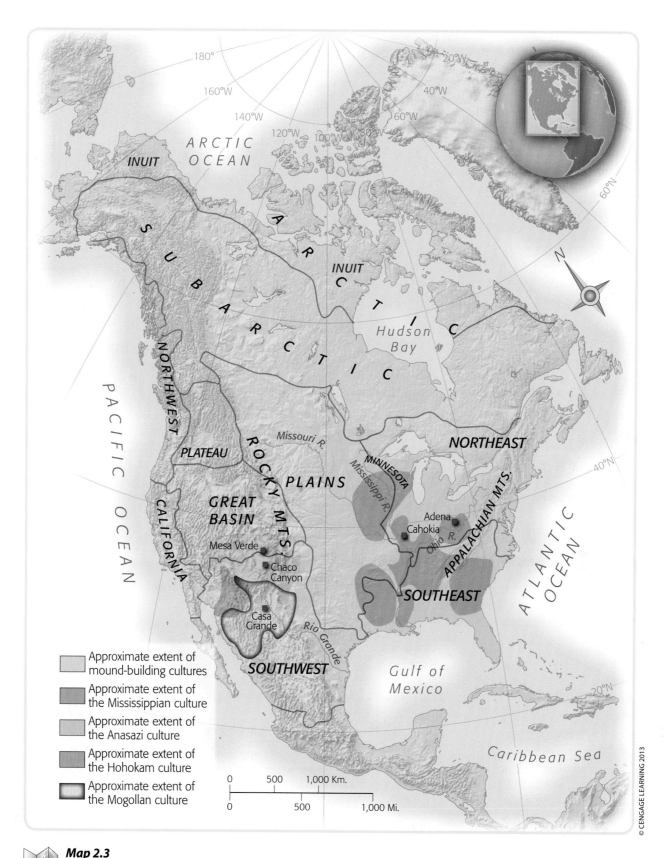

Map 2.3

Major North American Societies, 600–1500 C.E.

Farming societies were common in North America. The Pueblo peoples in the southwestern desert and the mound builders in the eastern half of the continent lived in towns. The city of Cahokia was the center of the widespread Mississippian culture and a vast trade network.

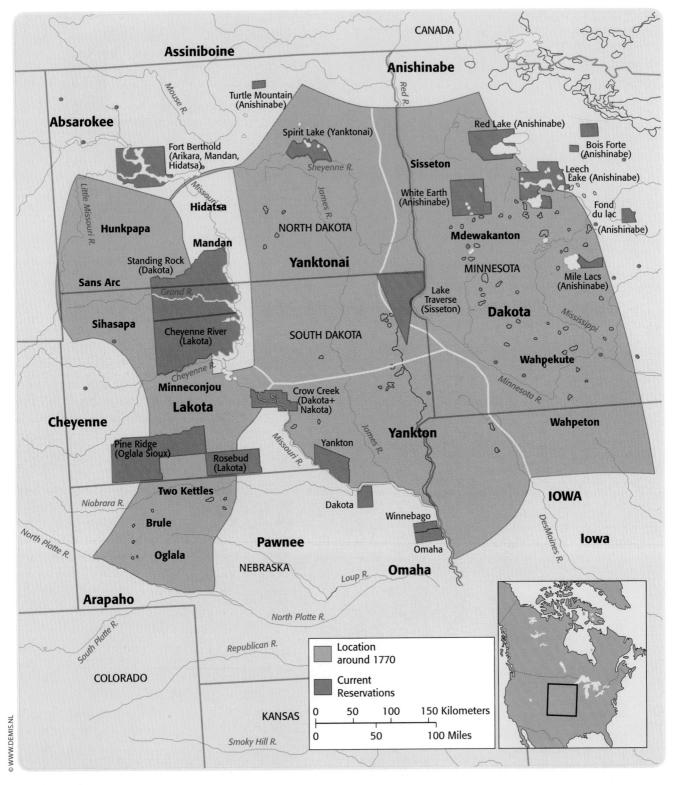

Map 2.4
Traditional Location of Sioux Tribes around 1770 and Reservations Today

Map labels:

CANADA

Assiniboine

Anishinabe

Absarokee

Turtle Mountain (Anishinabe)

Spirit Lake (Yanktonai)

Red Lake (Anishinabe)

Bois Forte (Anishinabe)

Fort Berthold (Arikara, Mandan, Hidatsa)

Sisseton

White Earth (Anishinabe)

Leech Lake (Anishinabe)

Fond du lac (Anishinabe)

Mouse R.

Sheyenne R.

Hidatsa

Hunkpapa

Missouri R.

Little Missouri R.

Mandan

James R.

NORTH DAKOTA

Yanktonai

Mdewakanton

MINNESOTA

Mile Lacs (Anishinabe)

Standing Rock (Dakota)

Sans Arc

Grand R.

Lake Traverse (Sisseton)

Dakota

Mississippi

Sihasapa

Cheyenne River (Lakota)

SOUTH DAKOTA

Cheyenne R.

Wahpekute

Minneconjou

Lakota

Crow Creek (Dakota+Nakota)

Yankton

Minnesota R.

Wahpeton

Cheyenne

Pine Ridge (Oglala Sioux)

Rosebud (Lakota)

Missouri R.

James R.

Yankton

IOWA

Two Kettles

Niobrara R.

Dakota

Winnebago

DesMoines R.

Iowa

Brule

North Platte R.

Omaha

Oglala

Pawnee

NEBRASKA

Loup R.

Omaha

Arapaho

North Platte R.

South Platte R.

COLORADO

Republican R.

KANSAS

Smoky Hill R.

Location around 1770

Current Reservations

0   50   100   150 Kilometers

0   50   100 Miles

© WWW.DEMIS.NL

humans) are all within Wakan Tanka. This term has often been translated "the Great Spirit," but this must not be understood as the one God of monotheistic religions. Wakan Tanka is remote and unapproachable, and rituals are not often performed for it. Included in Wakan Tanka are gods and spirits called *Wakanpi*, who exercise power and control over everything. Because the Wakanpi are incomprehensible to ordinary humans, they enable certain human beings to know them and deal with them. Holy men and (rarely) women have fulfilled this role. They obtain their special knowledge through direct contact with the gods and spirits through dreams and visions. They act as intermediaries through which the power of Wakan Tanka can flow.

The Sioux pass down their knowledge, rituals, and beliefs and moral code to the new generations in story form. Tribal history is also passed along orally, but it has always been guided by myths of origin so that the recent past doesn't contradict the deep past. Elders often gathered the young around the fire to impart important tales. Some of these tales, such as the stories of White Buffalo Calf Woman, can take up to seven evenings to tell and traditionally can only be told when the moon was shining.

Explore a collection of Sioux myths and other tales.

The Sioux look on death and the afterlife in the spirit world as a natural part of life. Death is painful in close-knit indigenous societies, but funeral rituals help mourners to cope with the pain of loss. The human soul is immortal; it comes from Wakan Tanka at birth and returns to Wakan Tanka at death. Because these spirits are one with Wakan Tanka, they are everywhere and in everything, even at the grave for a period after death. Before battle, Sioux warriors embraced their possible death openly, thus their famous saying "Today is a good day to die." Death in warfare was preferable to that caused by old age. This heritage of bravery in battle has continued today, and Native Americans have been for almost a century the most highly decorated ethnic group in the U.S. armed forces.

Lakotas go on a vision quest to gain a personal religious vision.

LAKOTA RITUALS

As with most religions, the Lakota believe that their rituals are given to them by the gods. Lakota myths tell of spirits such as White Buffalo Calf Woman, who brought them the sacred pipe and its ritual use. Holy men received other rituals during trance-like states. We now discuss Lakota rituals that are still regularly held.

Near the time of puberty, Sioux boys, and on occasion girls, go on a ritual of passage to adulthood called a **vision quest**, through which

Indian ceremonial pipe

they experience a symbolic death and rebirth and gain a vision of their guardian spirit. Through the vision quest, each male Lakota gains a personal religious vision that supplements the group-based religious understandings of the tribe. On returning from his vision quest, the vision seeker typically integrates his vision into the life of the community by performing it ritually in public. This integration of one's personal vision with the socially regimented roles passed down in tribal societies helps to make a good balance between individual and group life among the Lakota.

The modern healing ceremony is shortened from the traditional form. Prayer is still offered to the spirit of the stones, and spirit stones protect against danger or illness. This signifies a belief in a spiritual force in all forms of Creation. It isn't unusual to see a sacred stone at the bedside of sick or hospitalized Lakota even today.

The **sacred pipe** remains a key mediator between Wakan Tanka and humankind, reinforcing the kinship ties of the people with all spirits in the world. It has become so important as a symbol that it now unofficially stands for the whole of Lakota life; indeed, it has become a Pan-Indian ritual implement. (Sometimes it is called a "peace pipe"; although it was used for peace ceremonies, its ritual use goes far beyond this.) Black Elk reported a common belief when he said that the red stone the pipe is made from symbolizes the earth; a buffalo or other animal carved in the stone represents all animals; the pipe stem, made of wood, symbolizes all growing things; and the feathers attached to it represent the eagle and all winged creatures. All creatures in the natural world "send their voices" to Wakan Tanka when the pipe is smoked.

The **sweat lodge** is a ritual sauna meant to cleanse participants in their spirits. (It wasn't done, as our saunas today, for muscle relaxation or cleansing of the skin.) It can be a domed oblong hut or

vision quest Ritual of passage to adulthood, through which one experiences a symbolic death and rebirth and gains a vision of one's guardian spirit

sacred pipe Pipe ritually used as a key mediator between Wakan Tanka and humankind

sweat lodge Ritual sauna meant to cleanse participants in their spirits

©ISTOCKPHOTO.COM/GILL ANDRÉ

peyote [pay-YOHT-ee] Mildly hallucinogenic cactus bud used ritually in Indian ceremonies

Native American Church Church mainly composed of Native Americans, featuring a blend of indigenous North American religions and Christianity

sun dance Main festival ceremony of many Plains tribes, often featuring self-torture

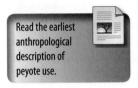

Read the earliest anthropological description of peyote use.

a hole dug into the ground and covered with planks or tree trunks. Stones are heated in an exterior fire and then placed in a central pit in the ground inside the lodge. Ritual activities inside and around the sweat lodge often include prayers, drumming, and offerings to the spirits.

The use of **peyote**, a mildly hallucinogenic but not physically addictive cactus bud, goes back for centuries among Native Americans in the Southwest. It was used as a medicine in healing ceremonies before its more-modern and wider ceremonial use. It spread beyond the Southwest at the beginning of the twentieth century, at a time when Native American culture was under much stress, and some Lakota today participate in its use. Participants reported a spiritual cleansing and experienced some physical healing as well. The peyote movement was one factor in the rise of the **Native American Church**, a blend of indigenous North American religions and Christianity that is still strong today. This group has successfully fought the U.S. legal system to get an exemption to use the cactus, which is a controlled substance, in their ceremonies. Use of peyote began to decline in about 2009, because it has been poorly grown and over-harvested during recent years.

Finally, the **sun dance** ceremony is practiced in almost twenty different North American tribes. It features dancing, singing and drumming, blowing on eagle-bone whistles, visions, and fasting. Some brave men known as *sun dance pledgers* come to the festival having already taken a vow to offer their bodies as a painful sacrifice to Wakan Tanka for the benefit of their tribe. This usually takes the form of being attached to a pole by hide thongs, which pierce one's body above each nipple on the chest with a metal hook, and then

A Native American, probably from the Lakota Sioux tribe, blows an eagle-bone whistle while participating in the sun dance during the Inter-Tribal Indian Ceremonial in the late 1940s in New Mexico.

PHOTO BY MICHAEL OCHS ARCHIVES/GETTY IMAGES

tearing oneself away from the thongs. The sun dance is ordinarily held by each tribe once a year at the height of summer when the sun is the hottest. It lasts from four to eight days, starting at the sunset of the final day of preparation and ending at sunset. It shows and promotes continuity between life and death, and offers a renewal of the life of the tribe as intertwined with the life of the earth. This ritual is still observed by many Native Americans and continues to be the most important ritual and festival for the Plains tribes.

Culture and Religion

The buffalo holds a key place in Lakota life and history. From its hide they made clothing, ropes and snowshoes, and the round, moveable homes called *tipi* (also

© ISTOCKPHOTO.COM/ERIC ISSELÉE

phonetically spelled *tepee*, the Lakota word for "dwelling"). The horns provided spoons, weapons, and ceremonial articles. The buffalo's sinew was used for bowstrings and sewing materials. The buffalo was the main friend of the Sun, and even controlled all affairs of love. Its spirit cares for the family, for the young of all beings, and for growing plants. Given the place of the buffalo in the life and thought of the Lakota, its extermination proved deadly for their traditional culture. Around 1800 there were possibly sixty million buffalo on the Plains; by 1884 the slaughter by hunters, encouraged by the federal government in part to break the power of the Plains tribes, led to less than one hundred buffalo being left. The Lakota Sioux, along with other Plains tribes, were reduced to dependence on government rations on various reservations of small size and few resources.

View a U.S. Census Bureau map of current Native American populations.

> *Given the role of the buffalo for the Lakota, its extermination proved deadly for their traditional culture.*

The sad story of gradual reduction of Native American life continued. Confinement to reservations was soon followed by a government policy to "civilize" Indian peoples by **assimilation** into mainstream white culture—by coercion if necessary. (Voluntary assimilation happened as well, but on a smaller scale.) Rapid white expansion into western North America meant that Indian conflicts had to end, and therefore much of their land granted by treaties was taken from them. Hiram Price, U.S. Commissioner of Indian Affairs in 1881, said history shows that "Savage and civilized life cannot prosper on the same ground." This was a wide conviction among Euro-Americans, and by the mid-nineteenth century it was allied to a racist theory of white superiority and the belief that it was America's "Manifest Destiny" to occupy all the lands from the Atlantic to the Pacific. Because Euro-Americans as a group assumed that they were superior to indigenous Americans, they knew what was best for them. In practice this meant the rapid elimination of native culture, language, and religion.

Much of the forced assimilation was targeted at children, because they were more changeable than their parents. In schools Indian children were prohibited from speaking their own language, living out their own culture, or having a tribal identity. Children in both the United States and Canada were separated from their families and sent far off to boarding schools if their family's influence was viewed as "negative." Some government officials did have second thoughts about this. For example, in his Indian Commissioner's report for 1934, John Collier urged an end to this assault on native culture. "The cultural history of Indians is in all respects to be considered equal to that of any non-Indian group." But this was not to become a widespread conviction until the 1960s. As late as the 1950s, it was U.S. government policy to promote assimilation toward the ultimate goal that Native American identity would disappear.

Violent conflict continued in the 1870s. In the Sioux Wars of the 1870s, the Sioux and their allies did battle with the U.S. Army in the Black Hills. This culminated on June 25–26, 1876, with a battle at **Little Big Horn** in eastern Montana. Hundreds of Sioux and Cheyenne warriors under the command of Sitting Bull, a Sioux chief and holy man, met the Seventh Cavalry Regiment of the U.S. Army, commanded by General George Custer. Custer's forces were quickly destroyed by Sitting Bull. Although Little Big Horn bolstered Native American morale, it was not to last. The federal military presence continued, as did increasing white settlement in the west, even on Native American reservations. In response to this

Ghost dance shirt
AP PHOTO/JILL KOKESH

assimilation Entry of Indian peoples into mainstream white culture, either voluntary or forced

Little Big Horn Battle on June 25–26, 1876, in eastern Montana, in which Sioux and Cheyenne warriors defeated a U.S. Army regiment

worsening situation, the **ghost dance** movement arose in the late 1880s. It would be the last militant attempt to preserve the cultural life and independence of Native Americans. The ghost dance movement was inspired by the vision of the Paiute prophet Wovoka (also known by his "white" name, Jack Wilson). Wovoka's vision spread, and reached the Sioux late in 1889. It spoke of dead native warriors coming back to life; the restoration of youth to the living; the return of the buffalo, elk, and other game; and the departure of whites.

> *"The people were crying [in the ghost dance movement] for the old ways of living and that their religion would be with them again."* –Black Elk

When reports reached the U.S. Army that the Sioux were arming themselves, wearing their ghost shirts, and acting defiantly to government agents, troops arrived at the Pine Ridge reservation on November 20, 1890, and were deployed to other Sioux areas. Sitting Bull was arrested on December 15 and killed in the process, and his followers fled. Alarmed at Sitting Bull's death and anxious at the troops' presence on their reservation, the Big Foot band of Lakota, numbering about 350, headed for Pine Ridge to confront the army. Intercepted by troops, they surrendered and were kept at Wounded Knee. On December 29, as troops sought to confiscate the weapons that some Lakota still possessed, a rifle discharged and shooting immediately broke out on both sides. Most historians conclude that what began as an accident immediately turned into a battle and then quickly intensified into what has become known as the **Massacre at Wounded Knee**. Of the U.S. Army troops, twenty-five were killed; of the Lakota, eighty-four men and boys and sixty-two women and girls were killed—virtually half the prisoners. The ghost dance movement was now over. The ghost shirts worn by the Big Foot band had failed to protect them as it was believed they would. To use the words of Black Elk, "the dream died."

Make on online visit to the Wounded Knee museum.

Native Americans then settled down to a long period of slow decline on the reservations in the United States and Canada, but over time most left the reservations to assimilate with wider American culture. In the early 1970s, a social and political protest movement arose among Native Americans. At Wounded Knee traditional Indians and members of the American Indian Movement (AIM) protested the appalling economic and social conditions on Pine Ridge reservation, which is today the poorest area in the United States. Wounded Knee was chosen for the protest because it symbolized continuity with the suffering of those who died there in 1890.

To conclude this section, the Lakotan culture involves living in a healthy, life-giving relationship with the tribe and the land. As we have seen, these relationships have been seriously damaged by forced assimilation, relocations, and government policies under a U.S. Bureau of Indian Affairs that is widely recognized as incompetent. Also, high unemployment (up to an astounding 90 percent), poverty, domestic violence, and alcohol and drug abuse continue to take a toll on the

Ancient pueblo city of Taos, New Mexico

© JOSEMARIA TOSCANO/SHUTTERSTOCK.COM

Visit the website of the White Buffalo Calf Woman Society.

Watch a news report on Native American casino gambling in Minnesota.

reservations. Some signs of hope are appearing: Tribal identities are growing, religious rituals are practiced and taught to new generations, tribal casino gambling recognized by state and federal governments is bringing in financial resources for tribal use (although some consider casinos a mixed blessing), and social ills are being more seriously attended to. Most Indian tribes are realizing that if improvement in their condition is to come, they must bring it themselves. Many Lakota organizations are dedicated to the continuation of traditional ways. The Lakota continue the struggle to hold on to the Black Hills, even refusing in 1980 a $100 million offer in return for giving up their claim to the Hills. This refusal is an indication of Sioux commitment to their traditional culture. The reestablishment of traditional Lakota ways of life requires no less than the rebuilding of the community from the family up, and much is being done to accomplish this.

LO5 An African Religion: Yoruba

To take a closer look at African indigenous religions, we will examine the Yoruba (YOHR-uh-buh) religion of west-central Africa. Not only is the Yoruba religion important in Africa today, it is also important in the Western Hemisphere, because many Yoruba were taken in slavery to the Americas, where they were instrumental in the founding of new Afro-Caribbean religions. Like most indigenous religions that cover a wide area, the religions of the Yoruba peoples vary significantly in different parts of west-central Africa today, especially in Nigeria. For example, the name of a god often has variations, or the same god may be female in one town and male in the next, and the rituals to worship them may vary as well. These differences inevitably arose as the myths were passed by word of mouth and as different tribes among the Yoruba made changes in their religion over thousands of years. When we add the influence of Christianity and Islam into the Yoruba religion—with some of these "post-contact" changes disputed by scholars—the religion becomes even more diverse and challenging to understand.

Despite this internal variety, all Yoruba religion shares a similar structure and purpose. A supreme but remote god rules the world, along with several hundred lower gods, actively worshiped, each of whom has a specific domain of rule. These gods guide believers to find their destiny in life, a destiny that was determined at the moment of reincarnation of one's soul into a new life but then forgotten. The rituals of the Yoruba identify this destiny for the individual, and this blesses the life of the Yoruba people as a whole.

Explore African culture in Google Earth™.

HIGH GOD AND OTHER GODS

The Yoruba all have a high god usually known as **Olorun** ("the ruler of the sky") or *Olodumare* (OH-loh-DOOM-ah-reh, "the all-powerful one"), but occasionally by many other names. They don't worship Olorun or make sacrifices to him, and he has no priests and no places of worship. He is a remote high god. Although the Yoruba believe that he is the creator and continual giver of life, almighty and all knowing, the Yoruba ignore him in their daily lives. He is invoked only at times of extreme need, and even then with difficulty. Some scholars argue that Olorun developed as a "post-contact" god through the influence of Islamic and Christian missionaries—as an imitation of the God of those religions, but one that could not be integrated into other Yoruba beliefs or rituals. However, belief in Olorun is widespread among the Yoruba, both in those tribes that have not had much contact with Abrahamic religions as well as those that have. Moreover, we can find other African tribes and nations with remote high gods in their traditions.

The other main Yoruba gods controlling relations between the earth and the high god are known as **orisha**. They are the gods with whom humans have contact through myth and rituals. The numbers, relationships, and names of Yoruba gods are exceedingly complex; they form a vast group of supernatural beings numbering between 401 and 601. Some Yoruba myths have a pair of gods, Orishala (also known as Obatala and Orisanla) and his wife Odudua, as the gods who created the world. This association with the creator and high god Olorun gives them a higher status than that of the other orisha. In one myth, Olorun creates the main parts of the world and then has Obatala and Odudua finish the work. They are so close that some interpreters have considered Olorun and Obatala

Olorun "Ruler of the sky," Yoruba high god

orisha Yoruban main gods who control relations between the earth and the high god, and with whom humans have contact through myth and rituals

one and the same. Obatala is often portrayed as a sculptor-god, having the responsibility to shape human bodies. The Yoruba consider physically different humans to be either his special servants or the victims of his displeasure, leaving some room for interpretation.

The Yoruba see the god Ogun as among the most important of the orisha. The god of war, hunting, and ironworking, Ogun is the patron god of blacksmiths, warriors, and all who use metals. Yoruba religion has a high regard for metal as a combination of earth, wind, and fire. Ogun also is the god of business deals and contracts. In courts in Yoruba areas of Nigeria, Yoruba swear to tell the truth by kissing a knife sacred to Ogun. The Yoruba consider Ogun fearsome and terrible in his revenge; if one breaks a pact made in his name, swift retribution will follow. One myth that illustrates Ogun's importance tells of the orisha trying to carve a road through dense jungle. Ogun was the only one with the right tools for the task and so won the right to be king of the orisha. He did not, however, care for the position, and it went to Obatala.

Shango the storm god occupies an important place among these orisha. Shango creates and controls storms by throwing "thunderstones" onto the earth. When lightning strikes, Shango's priests search for the stone, which is believed to have special powers because of its origin. As the stones are collected, they are put in Shango's shrines. A myth told about Shango provides a basis for his worship. When he was human and a king of an ancient Yoruba kingdom, he had a powerful charm that could cause lightning, but he accidentally killed his entire family with it. He hanged himself in sorrow and became deified when he entered the spirit world. He then gained more power over lightning, as well as over thunder, wind, hail, and other aspects of storms. Most scholars conclude that his popularity among the Yoruba peoples may result from a need to ward off the frequent violent storms that strike western Africa.

Shango came to the New World with newly enslaved Africans. In Annapolis, Maryland, a clay bundle about the size and shape of an American football was unearthed by University of Maryland and University of London archaeologists at an old crossroads. Dated to about 1700, it was filled with about three hundred pieces of metal and a stone axe sticking out through the clay. Archaeologists quickly identified it as African in origin, and most likely used as an object of spiritual power by African slaves recently brought to America. Although almost all slaves were baptized into Christianity, they continued to secretly observe some "spirit practices" in healing and in worship of their

CLIFFORDS PHOTOGRAPHY

Axes on this devotee's head are Shango's thunderbolts.

ancestors. The archaeologist who discovered the bundle concluded that it was connected with rites of Shango.

> *Yoruba religion has a high regard for metal as a combination of earth, wind, and fire.*

Trickster gods can blur the line between good and evil in Yoruban religion. One myth dealing with the god Eshu (EH-shoo) illustrates his trickiness. Pretending to be a merchant, Eshu sold increasingly expensive gifts to each of a man's two wives, sparking a desire in each to outdo the other in purchasing. The battle for the husband's favor after this buying spree tore the family apart. This story is told as a cautionary tale against the evils of greed and ambition. Eshu is also, but not in his trickster role, the divine guardian of houses and villages. The relationship between Eshu and many Yorubans is so close that they call him *Baba* ("father") in worship. Because tricksters often blur the lines of good and evil, Islamic and then Christian missionaries among the Yorubans attacked Eshu as a demonic figure, even as a representation of the Devil. This of course betrays a misunderstanding of a trickster's overall role to promote morality, not undermine it.

The history of Shokpona (shock-POH-nuh), the god of smallpox, is an interesting story at the intersection of religion and medicine. Shokpona became important in the smallpox plagues that arose in intertribal wars in west Africa. The Yoruba also saw Shokpona's wrath in other diseases that have similar symptoms. Shokpona's wrath is so terrifying, and worshiping him is so challenging, that the Yoruba are often afraid to say his name. Instead, they use expressions such as "Hot Earth," referring to high fever, and "One whose name must not be spoken in the dry season." Priests of Shokpona had great power; they could bring this plague down on their enemies, especially by making a ritual potion from the powdered scabs and dry skin of those who had died from smallpox. They would pour the potion in an enemy's area to spread the disease. Although this indirect contact with smallpox was less deadly than contact with living people infected by it, it worked well enough. However, because smallpox has been eradicated worldwide since about 1980, the priests of Shokpona have lost power, and his worship has all but vanished.

In the long history of the successful human battle against smallpox, African religious practice had a role at a key moment in American history. When a growing smallpox epidemic threatened the American revolutionary army encamped at Valley Forge, Pennsylvania, in 1777, George Washington ordered experimental inoculations based on an account by a famous Christian minister in Massachusetts, Cotton Mather (1663–1728). Mather detailed how his African slave named Onesimus had been protected from smallpox by vaccination, probably in a religious ritual of body marking connected with the worship of Shokpona. A small bit of smallpox scab had been put on his cuts so that, as Mather later wrote, he "had smallpox and then did not have it." Mather himself had successfully inoculated his sons with this procedure, minus the Yoruban religious elements, of course. The procedure was a success at Valley Forge, and the American army was saved.

Religious Specialists

With its many gods that must be attended to with rituals, Yoruba religion has a large place for religious specialists. These specialists don't teach or administer religious institutions; rather, they preside at the hundreds of rituals. Their skills are passed down from generation to generation.

Priests divine the future, offering advice for how to meet it. Male priests are known as a *babalawo* (buh-BAH-lah-woo), "father of secrets" or "father of the priest" and females as an *iyalawo* (ee-YAH-lah-woo), "mother of secrets/priests." They help people to understand the destinies they chose in the spirit world but lost when they were reincarnated on Earth. The priests also give people power and guidance to make their destinies come true. Seeking a priest to help with one's future is a common occurrence throughout life, but faithful Yorubas take their child to a diviner soon after birth so that the child's destiny can be made clear.

The process of divination varies by priest and region, but this is perhaps the most common method. The believer, usually under some sort of duress, makes her or his way to a diviner. Contrary to many other systems of divination and fortune-telling, the believer doesn't tell the diviner what the problem is. Instead, the diviner casts sixteen separate palm nuts or a chain of sixteen shells onto

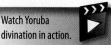

A Yoruba divination board

CLIFFORDS PHOTOGRAPHY

a divination board. Depending on the results, the diviner then chants a group of poems called *Ifa* (EE-fuh) verses, presided over by a god of the same name. The collection of Ifa verses is vast, and most diviners know several hundred of them by heart. These poems tell short stories of the gods and usually tell of some sacrifice, gift, or action the believer must take. It is then up to the believer to discern which of the poems and prescribed actions are correct in her or his situation. The Yoruba believer is very active in this process; it's not just a matter of telling one's problems to a priest and then getting some quick advice. This system of divination has worked for centuries, probably millennia, and even today many Yoruba consult an expert in the Ifa before making any important decisions. Ifa poems are now being collected and published, but this takes them out of their living context in Yoruba divination.

Watch Yoruba divination in action.

Spirits of the Ancestors

The Yoruba treat their ancestors with great respect, which is typical of indigenous societies. Anthropologists debate as to whether the rituals dealing with ancestry—prayers, sacrifices, and the like—are religious or cultural-traditional; but given the deeply enculturated nature of indigenous religion, we can safely conclude that a religious aspect is present. At least a few Yoruba groups believe that ancestors, after death, become semidivine figures. This resembles another aspect of the Yoruba faith: possession of the body by the gods. In these possessions, priests acting as mediums take on the individual characteristics of the gods. The behavioral patterns of how each god takes possession of a medium are so entrenched that mediums as far off as Haiti roll their heads and cross their legs in the same way as mediums of Shango in west Africa.

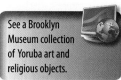

See a Brooklyn Museum collection of Yoruba art and religious objects.

LO6 An Afro-Caribbean Religion: Vodou

Those who follow the Afro-Caribbean religion of Vodou number an estimated 5 to 7 million people today. Vodou is widely referred to in North America today, but with much misunderstanding, especially in American

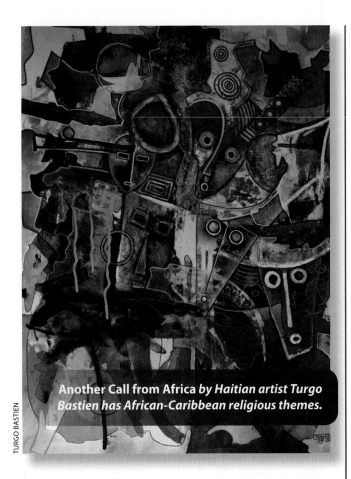

Another Call from Africa *by Haitian artist Turgo Bastien has African-Caribbean religious themes.*

TURGO BASTIEN

The word *Vodou* (or the lesser-used *Hoodoo*, which is often used on a popular level for the magical practices of Vodou) is from the Haitian Creole-French language. It is also spelled *Voudon* or *Vodun* in scholarship today. You may know it as *Voodoo*. Until recently, this was the accepted spelling of the word, but many Haitians and most modern scholars now acknowledge *Vodou* as the preferred spelling, because it is phonetically closer to the original African word. It originated in the language of the Ewe Fon west African peoples brought to Haiti as slaves from present-day Benin and Togo. Ultimately, it is from *vodú*, the Ewe Fon word for both "god" and "worship." Beginning in the seventeenth century, *Voodoo* was used in the missionary literature about the Ewe people in Africa, who called a newly initiated member of their religion a *vodúnsi* or *hunsi*, a "bride of the deity." Also, the use of *Voodoo* has too many prejudicial and exotic overtones in the Western world today. In general, Vodou in Africa is an African indigenous religion, not combined with Roman Catholic Christianity as it is in the Americas.

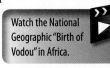

Watch the National Geographic "Birth of Vodou" in Africa.

In the Western Hemisphere, *Vodou* means various things. It most often refers to an Afro-Catholic religion that is widespread on the island of Hispaniola, especially in Haiti. It can also be applied to persons—for example, spell-workers are often called "hoodoo doctors" in the southern United States. In Haiti, Vodou is applied as an umbrella term to a large number of Haitian religious groups with roots in African religion rather than Roman Catholic Christianity. In mainstream American usage, it has become a common pejorative for "deceptive nonsense," usually with no connection to religion. For example, when George H. W. Bush and Ronald Reagan were competing in 1980 for the Republican nomination for president, Bush called Reagan's economic plan "Voodoo economics." Other uses of Vodou center on the current popularity of zombies, especially "zombie walks." Observers of American popular culture say that in 2009 zombies replaced vampires as the leading symbol of supernatural threats. To those who engage in careful academic study of Vodou, however, this interest in zombies distorts and demeans the religion.

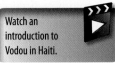

Watch an introduction to Vodou in Haiti.

popular culture. In this section, we'll put this religion in its African and New World contexts, and try to shed some light on its significance for today. An important part of our study of Vodou will be to rehabilitate the name of this religion, so that it doesn't always stir up negative emotions and misleading opinions. Although Vodou is not, strictly speaking, indigenous to Haiti, the centuries of its combination with Roman Catholicism in the setting of the New World qualifies it in the minds of most to be an indigenous religion.

LOCATION AND NAME

Like the Brazilian religions Candomblé and Umbanda, Cuban Santería, or Jamaican Rastafarianism, the Vodou religion is based on an African indigenous religion. An estimated 9 to 12 million slaves were brought to the New World between 1500 and 1850, most of them to Brazil and the Caribbean islands, and they brought their religions with them. Like other indigenous religions, Vodou is concerned mainly with bringing its followers into harmony with the gods that control the natural world, so that in this harmony their lives can be happy and blessed. These religions were brought to the New World by enslaved members of west African tribes, and there underwent an independent development to become Afro-Caribbean.

DIVINITIES

Like other Afro-Caribbean religions, Haitian Vodou has authentic African traits. Vodou is a typical example of a religion centered on different groups of gods. These gods are called **loas**, meaning "divinities" or "mysteries." The gods, or groups of gods, are called "mysteries" or more commonly "saints" (in the sense of "holy ones"). In Fon myth, there are three regions of the world, and various gods reign in each one: the sky, the earth, and, in between, the clouds. The creator god (Yoruba, *Olorun*; Creole, *Bon Dieu Bon*—literally "good God good") lives in the remote sky. Because he isn't involved with everyday life, he isn't honored in everyday rituals. Through the influence of Roman Catholicism, Vodou believers also worship the Christian God. It is not uncommon for them to worship in a Catholic church on Sunday morning and in a Vodou sanctuary on Sunday evening. They also venerate two other kinds of spiritual beings who live between the sky and the earth: souls of dead humans that have become spirits and spirits that have never been directly tied to matter. Vodou gods live on the earth: in the sea, in waterfalls, in springs, in forests, at intersections of roads, in cemeteries, and in piles of stones. Many earth gods of Vodou correspond to Catholic saints, on whose feast days the Vodou gods are also celebrated. The recognition and worship of these gods helps to bless the lives of people on earth, so that they can be happy, peaceful, and productive.

GROUPS

Gods and rites are divided into groups according to the geographical regions of their origin. The two most important groups are the *Rada* and the *Petro*, who are found especially in urban areas. *Rada* derives from the old kingdom of Arada in Africa. *Petro*, more oriented to the indigenous Creoles, comes from the name of a Vodou priest, Don Pedro, who introduced a variant of the Vodou trance dance in the eighteenth century. The Petro group

is named after him, but he did not found this Vodou group. Petro gods and spirits are invoked especially for magical or countermagical actions that we will consider below. Vodou priests may support both groups, and a believer is usually either Rada or Petro but may likewise take part in ceremonies of the other type.

loa [LOH-uh] "Divinity" or "mystery"; in west African and Vodou religions, a god or group of gods

WORSHIP

As with Candomblé in Brazil and Santería in Cuba, Vodou is a fusion of African religions with Catholicism. Some traces of Caribbean Indian religion can also be found in it. The religion of Vodou refers not to a body of belief, creeds, sacred scriptures, or the rest, but to ritual practice. Vodou is often described as a "cult religion" (*cult* here refers to a *system of ritual worship*, not to a dangerous group). In particular, it is a "possession cult" in which the gods inhabit people and speak through them, usually for a short period of time during rituals. Rituals of animal sacrifice as well as trance dances forge and maintain a bond with the gods. The rites are practiced by initiated members called *hunsi*, "brides of the gods," presided over by priests and priestesses called *hugan* and *mambo*, respectively. Initiates are introduced into the group by a complicated and spectacular ritual. Worship is held in sacred cabins or city temples, all with an altar for sacrifice of animals and other offerings. They have a central post that enables the loas to descend to believers and mount believers in trance as their "riding horses."

A few Vodou rituals tap into the power of the spirits of the dead, and cemeteries have become important places of Vodou gatherings for worship. The head loa

A Closer Look:

Rev. Pat Robertson and Vodou

On the day after an earthquake devastated Haiti on January 12, 2010, the Christian television evangelist Pat Robertson said on his U.S. television show that Haiti was struck by an earthquake and had long suffered for other reasons, because its African slaves entered a Vodou "pact with the devil" two centuries ago to overthrow the French and their system of slavery. "They have been cursed by one thing or another" ever since, he claimed. These remarks created a storm of controversy in the United States and Haiti, where Vodou has been an official religion since 2003.

On a strictly historical level, Robertson is correct on one point: Vodou followers did play a large part in slave uprisings against the French and their eventual expulsion. But whether the continuing struggles of Haiti, which has long been the poorest country in the Western Hemisphere, can be blamed on Vodou is another matter entirely. For many scholars of religion, this superficial and dismissive attitude toward Vodou is the most recent part of a long history of misrepresentation and quite literal "demonization" of Vodou in American popular culture, even in journalism.

in the cult of the dead is **Baron Samedi**, the "Lord of the Dead." His depiction and name vary, but he often wears a top hat, a black tuxedo, and cotton plugs in his nostrils, all of which are elements of a corpse prepared in a Haitian style for burial. Baron Samedi has a white, skull-like face and is regarded by all as a fearsome presence. Although dead, he is very much alive. He is charged with sexual energy and is frequently represented by phallic symbols. He is known for obscenity and debauchery, and he enjoys tobacco and rum. He is worshiped and celebrated in order to keep him at bay, so that he won't disturb the living.

Also connected to death—and the African experience of deadly slavery in Haiti—is the figure of the zombie. As we saw above, Yoruban religion has a large role for the spirits of the dead, and Vodou further blurs the distinction between the living and the dead. It believes that a human body can be revived by an especially powerful magician after the spirit of the dead has departed and used as a slave for the magician's purposes. They are the ultimate slaves, the worst possible kind of "life" for Afro-Haitian people. Zombies remain under the control of the sorcerer because they have no will, mind, or soul of their own. This is why in popular culture zombies are usually depicted as mindless, almost robotic figures that shuffle around. However, the notion that zombies eat human flesh, thus making other people into zombies, is a mistaken view that taps into revulsion against cannibalism.

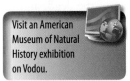
Visit an American Museum of Natural History exhibition on Vodou.

SPELL AND COUNTER-SPELL RITUALS

Like some of the world's largest religions, Vodou has a place for "magical" practices, and, also like other religions, this is found more often on a popular, not an official, level. Magic is the preferred form of Vodou

PHOTO BY TERRY O'NEILL/HULTON ARCHIVE/GETTY IMAGES

Geoffrey Holder played Baron Samedi in **Live and Let Die.** *His face paint suggests that he is both alive and dead.*

practice of the lowest social class in Haiti—the small farmers, the urban working poor, and the masses of unemployed—although today some members of the upper class are also drawn to it. People use magic to seek deliverance from all the difficulties of life, which for the lower classes in Haiti are many. Diseases, poverty, and other difficulties are seen as the effect of demonic spells, which need to be countered with magic. Probably the magical practice best known in the West is the one performed with a small doll, through which certain magical actions are seen as being able to harm someone's health or even cause death.

Also used are **gris-gris**, originally images of the gods in the shape of little dolls but now small cloth bags containing items such as herbs, oils, stones, small bones, hair and nails, and pieces of cloth soaked with perspiration, all gathered and bagged under the direction of a god for the protection of the owner. The gris-gris became traditional in New Orleans, the American headquarters for Vodou, where they were used for attracting money and love, stopping gossip, protecting the home, maintaining good health, and for many other uses. A gris-gris is ritually made at an altar containing the four elements of earth (salt), air (incense), water, and fire (a candle flame). The number of ingredients is always one, three, five, seven, nine, or thirteen. Stones and colored objects are chosen to fit the purpose for which the gris-gris is to be used. Legends of the most famous Vodou

A shop selling Vodou supplies in the French Quarter of New Orleans

JSF306

practitioner in the United States, New Orleans "Vodou Queen" Marie Laveau (1794–1881), claim her gris-gris contained bits of bone, colored stones, graveyard dust, salt, and red pepper.

Curse rituals, services of worship in cemeteries, use of snakes in worship, and zombies have made the Vodou religion a favorite subject of **exoticism**—portraying something in another culture as strange or exciting, and distorting it in the process. Ever since Spenser St. John's 1884 adventure account *Hayita or the Black Republic*, new sensations about Vodou have continually sprung up. The Vodou religion, by way of Hollywood, became an important part of the horror film genre. Filmmakers found that exotic presentations of Vodou could easily frighten and entertain audiences.

Watch a History Channel video on Marie Laveau.

POLITICAL INFLUENCE IN HAITI

Haitian Vodou has at times had an important political and social role. Its faithful were able to mobilize forces against the French colonialist rulers at the close of the 1700s; this led to the abolition of slavery and the country's independence from France in 1804. Through the years, Vodou believers opposed various Haitian regimes that were devoted to their own power as the gap between the rich and poor masses grew. The last instance of such resistance was to dictator "Papa Doc" Duvalier, who ruled from 1957 to 1971. After the devastation of Haiti in the earthquake of 2010, Vodou remains powerful on a popular level.

Socially, rural and urban forms of Vodou differ in Haiti. In rural areas, worship and belief are oriented to small farmers and are supported by extensive family alliances. Involvement with ancestors and ritual practices to induce successful farming are the center of religious practice. Vodou believers in the cities have adapted their practice to urban relationships there. They find a "second family" in the temple communities. This urban adaptation of traditional rural Vodou has found its way to the urban centers of North America.

exoticism [egg-ZOT-uh-siz-uhm] Portraying something in another culture as strange or exciting, and distorting it in the process

Widespread continuous poverty and political instability in Haiti have led to the need for a religion that can help the poor cope with their problems. Vodou offers this help; the other main religion of Haiti, Christianity, is tied in the minds of many Haitians to the social elites who oppress the common people. This dismal situation in Haiti has led to the emigration of many Haitians to North America. They have taken the Vodou religion along with them to New York City, Miami, and Montreal, but especially to New Orleans, where today there is a museum of Vodou. (New Orleans Vodou tends to be more firmly attached to Roman Catholicism than other forms are.) Vodou is starting to get a foothold in some countries of Europe, but mainly as a magical practice adapted for those who are not initiates in the religion.

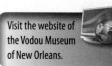
Visit the website of the Vodou Museum of New Orleans.

CHAPTER 3

Encountering Hinduism: Many Paths to Liberation

BONNIE VAN VOORST © CENGAGE LEARNING

Learning Outcomes

After studying this chapter, you will be able to do the following:

LO1 Explain what *Hinduism* means and its strengths and weaknesses as a name.

LO2 Explain how the main periods of Hinduism's history have shaped its present, especially its unity and diversity.

LO3 Outline the essentials of Hindu teachings in your own words.

LO4 Relate Hindu ethics to the essential Hindu teachings.

LO5 Outline the ways Hindus worship, at home and in temples.

LO6 State the main aspects of Hindu life in North America today.

© ISTOCKPHOTO.COM/TJASAM

"Encountering Hinduism is like your first visit to an Indian buffet. You can't sample everything, but if you choose a good variety you'll have a good introduction."

YOUR VISIT TO VARANASI, INDIA

Imagine that you're on a visit to the city of Varanasi (vuh-RAH-nuh-see) as a part of a tour of India. You know that Varanasi, located on the Ganges (GAN-jeez) River in north India, is unique among the cities of the world, but nothing can quite prepare you for its sights, sounds, and smells.

Your visit begins with a pre-dawn boat ride on the Ganges. As your rowboat glides along the river, you see Hindu pilgrims on the western shore of the river descending the wide steps—two miles of them at Varanasi—leading down to the water. They wash themselves physically and spiritually, and pray toward the rising sun. A man dressed only in a loincloth and his sacred thread fills a small copper kettle with river water and then pours it out in a small stream while saying a prayer in the ancient Sanskrit language. After the boat ride, you walk to the Golden Temple, the most sacred of the city's many shrines dedicated to Shiva (SHEE-vuh), the patron deity of Varanasi. You see Hindus making offerings of flowers to the black stone emblem of Shiva. You also visit the newer Hindu temple inaugurated by Mohandas Gandhi, the father of modern Indian independence. You return to the hotel for breakfast before taking a guided tour of Varanasi.

As you walk with your group through the narrow, twisting streets down to the river, you pass several cows wandering freely, and even a bull sacred to Shiva. You notice many small

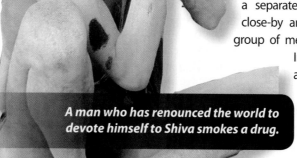

© BHUVAN TRIPATHEE

A man who has renounced the world to devote himself to Shiva smokes a drug.

What Do YOU Think?

Hinduism is mostly about escaping this material world.

Strongly Disagree   Strongly Agree

1   2   3   4   5   6   7

temples and even smaller shrines that seem to be everywhere. You also notice many old, frail people, some in the doorways of ashrams and others living on the street, who have come to die in Varanasi in the hope of achieving liberation from the cycle of endless reincarnation. You see human bodies, wrapped and propped up on rickshaws, on their way to the water. As you get close to the Ganges, you notice three men with wild hair, squatting on a stone platform overlooking the river. You can't tell if they are wearing anything at all, and your tour guide explains that their bodies are smeared with ash and dried cow dung. They are smoking hashish in a pipe, praising Shiva loudly as they draw on the pipe. (You wince when one of your tour mates makes a pun about "ganja on the Ganges.") On the right you see a large group of women bathing fully clothed in the water near the steps, and in a separate but close-by area a group of men in

Take a virtual tour of Varanasi on Google Earth™.

Indian loincloths. Both the men and the women have come to wash away their sins, and perhaps even the necessity of reincarnation. The river seems polluted to you, but this means nothing to the thousands of Hindus who worship in it.

< The Hindu god Shiva is often portrayed as the Lord of the Dance.

As you keep walking up the river, you notice a cluster of large fires and hundreds of large logs stacked up behind them, and you realize with a bit of a shock that you've reached Varanasi's open-air cremation area. In a scene that you'll remember for a long time, you see the steps of the Hindu funeral: piling wood into a pyre, laying on the wood a body that has just been dipped into the Ganges, a son lighting a pyre, priests intoning ancient scriptures as a body begins to burn, members of the Dom group gently tending a body over three hours of burning to burn it as fully as possible, and Doms pushing cremated remains into the river to float away. To die and be cremated in Varanasi is thought to bring automatic liberation from the cycle of reincarnation. Your group must stand respectfully at the top of the steps, where you happily realize that you have a better view and the odor is better, too.

In the evening, you join your guide at the shore of the Ganges to witness the happy Aarti ceremony that is part of the evening religious devotions to Shiva. The celebrative music and dancing, and small candles lit on miniature "boats" and put into the river to memorialize the dead, soothe your spirits and make for a good, inspiring end to a challenging day.

YOU REALIZE, WITH A BIT OF A SHOCK, THAT YOU'VE REACHED VARANASI'S OPEN-AIR CREMATION AREA.

IMAGE BY © ANDERS RYMAN/CORBIS

If this is your first encounter with the Hindu religion, you may become bewildered by all its varied beliefs and practices. Calling something a "religion" usually implies a unified system of belief and practice, but Hinduism has little obvious unity. It has no personal founder, defined core beliefs, common scripture that guides all Hindus, standardized worship practice, or central authority. This diversity has led to what you may consider contradictions. For example:

- Hinduism has literally millions of gods, but many Hindus typically see one god behind them all, and some see only an impersonal Oneness in and beyond the universe.

- Hindus often control their bodies to pursue a hidden spiritual reality behind all physical things, seeking liberation from the endless cycle of reincarnation and pursuing the peace that liberation brings here and now. At the same time, they joyously affirm bodily existence with a striking affirmation of sexuality, for example with erotic statues in some temples.

- Many Hindus are strict vegetarians for religious reasons, but others eat meat on occasion, and some even sacrifice animals at Hindu temples.

- Hinduism teaches personal duties tied to one's place in a rather rigid social structure but allows some people to "drop out" of ordinary life completely to pursue individual religious goals.

- Hindus number around 900 million today in India, a number that includes some 220 million Indian "outcastes." The modern Indian state now considers these 220 million as Hindus, but they are not considered as such by most other Hindu castes, nor do they often call themselves Hindus.

- Hinduism has a long history of at least three thousand years but constantly combines old traditions with new elements to produce a richer, more diverse faith and culture that bring ancient traditions into the twenty-first century.

In light of all this obvious diversity, what is the hidden unity of Hinduism that binds it together? Scholars have argued about this for more than one hundred years, and it's not an easy question to answer. The most common answer is this: Hinduism, and faithful Hindus, have a reverence for the ancient Hindu scriptures called the *Vedas* and perform their caste duties. But this may seem a bit

View a National Geographic introduction to India.

vague to you, and you should keep the question open as you study this chapter. In sum, encountering Hinduism is a bit like going to an Indian restaurant for the first time. When you see a wide variety of exotic dishes on the menu, or even if you go to an Indian buffet, you realize that you can't taste them all. But at the end of the meal, you know that your experience in the restaurant gave you a good introduction to Indian cuisine.

Religion usually implies a unified system of belief and practice, but Hinduism has little obvious unity.

LO1 The Name *Hinduism*

Like the names of a few other world religions, the formal name of *Hinduism* came from outside the faith. *Hindu* first appears around 500 B.C.E. as the ancient Persian word for the Indus River and the inhabitants of its valley. From the 1300s C.E., invading Muslim rulers of northern India used "Hindu" for all non-Muslim Indians, whatever religion they were, to distinguish them from Indian converts to Islam. Beginning in the 1500s, European colonizers coming to India used it in its current sense to mean the members of the supposedly single religion to which all Indians other than groups like Muslims, Christians, and Zoroastrians belonged. Then, from about 1800 on, *Hinduism* gradually became accepted by most Hindus in India as a valid name for their religion, especially to distinguish their religion from others. Thus, *Hinduism* is an umbrella term gradually imposed on Hindus and then accepted by them.

The approximately 2 million Hindus living in North America and the sizeable Hindu communities in other parts of south Asia (especially Bali, Indonesia), a few parts of Africa, and Great Britain also embrace this name. However, more-upper-class

Om (Aum) [OHM] Spoken syllable symbolizing the fundamental hidden reality of the universe

A Closer Look:

Symbols of Hinduism

Om

Although Hinduism has no official symbol, the religious symbol most sacred to most Hindus is the mystical syllable **Om**. You will also find the spelling "Aum," and in fact the symbol is composed of the equivalent of our letters *a*, *u*, and *m*. Although as a syllable it has no literal meaning, Om symbolizes the fundamental hidden reality of the universe and is the basic spiritual sound the universe makes, particularly the sound of the world soul. Om is written daily in formal contexts and often pronounced at the beginning of religious reading or meditation. Many Hindus wear this symbol in jewelry, and it is found in family shrines and in temples. Pronounced in a deep, lengthy way, it can resonate throughout the body and the sound of Brahman can penetrate to one's center of being.

Listen to Om.

ILLUSTRATIONS BY: BONNIE VAN VOORST © CENGAGE LEARNING

The Swastika

You may be surprised, even shocked, to encounter the swastika as a common, ancient symbol in Hinduism, Buddhism and Jainism. *Svastika* (SWAHS-tee-kuh) is an ancient Indian word meaning "sign of good fortune," and this symbol is widely used as a good-luck charm. The swastika has "crooked" arms facing in a clockwise or counterclockwise direction (both directions are common in Asia). Its arms extend in all directions, suggesting to Hindus the universal presence of the world soul. It is continually rotating like the wheel that it resembles, symbolizing the eternal nature of ultimate truth. This symbol is often found on Hindu, Jain, and Buddhist temples, and it is worn on neck pendants. In 1935, the Nazi Party of Germany adopted the swastika known in Europe, with no historical connection to the Indian svastika, as its symbol of the party and the nation—of course with no intent to endorse Hindu teachings. It is still used today by some neo-Nazi groups. So we have an odd situation: For people of many Asian religions, the swastika is a much-loved symbol; for people in the Western world, the swastika is much despised.

Hindus often refer to their religion as the "eternal teaching" or "eternal way of life." Some scholars of religion also question the adequacy of *Hinduism* as a name, preferring to speak of "Hinduisms." On the whole, it is fitting that a vague term like *Hinduism* is used today for a religious tradition that has so much internal diversity.

LO2 The Hindu Present as Shaped by Its Past

At dawn, a group of men in northern India sits around an outdoor fire pit and chants poetic hymns from memory. Nearby, outside a boundary rope that encloses the area of sacrifice, their teenage sons sit studying the sacrifice, quietly repeating the men's words and movements. Also outside the rope, women are pounding rice, cooking it, and shaping it into balls. The men occasionally pour a bit of liquefied butter from a wooden bowl onto the fire, which flares up momentarily. The men are singing ancient hymns to Agni, the Hindu god of fire, comparing him to the rising sun. After the sacrifice, the rice balls will first be offered to Agni, and then some will be eaten in turn by the priests, then by their sons, the women, and the whole community. This ceremony from more than three thousand years ago is carried out with increasing frequency in India as interest in ancient Hindu practices grows. However, some Hindus are not happy about the re-creation of ancient sacrifices, preferring instead the adaptations of these rituals that have arisen in the course of Hindu history.

History is an important tool for those who study today's religions from a Western academic standpoint. We understand the present of religions by way of their past. Although Hinduism must be understood historically as well, history itself is not an important concept in Hinduism. Most Hindus don't think of their religion in historical terms, preferring to look to the spiritual truths beyond historical events. They often look to cycles of change for individuals (for example, death and reincarnation) and for the universe itself (repeated creation and dissolution), not to the kind of linear developmental process that "history" usually implies to Westerners. Nevertheless, studying Hinduism's past is valid and helpful, particularly because in Hinduism

> Most Hindus don't think of their religion in historical terms, but look to the spiritual truths beyond historical events.

new developments reinterpret and update past practices rather than end them. In Hinduism today, we can see important beliefs and practices from the entire sweep of Indian history.

THE VEDIC PERIOD (1500–600 B.C.E.)

Around 2500 B.C.E., an Indus Valley civilization thrived in northwest India, in what is now the nation of Pakistan (see Map 3.1). It centered in two city-states on the Indus River, Harappa (huh-RAHP-uh) and Mohenjo-Daro (moh-HEN-joh-DAHR-oh). The Indus Valley inhabitants were a dark-skinned people whom most scholars connect with today's Indians called Dravidians (druh-VID-ee-uhnz). (About 25 percent of Indians today are Dravidians.) This civilization traded internationally and had a high material culture; its main cities of Harappa and Mohenjo-Daro were carefully planned and even had a sewage system connected to private houses. Their system of writing has not yet been deciphered by scholars. The religion of the Indus Valley civilization is also largely unknown to us. Many female deity figurines have been found by archaeologists, and the Indus Valley people probably worshiped goddesses of fertility in connection with their farming. The cows on their official seals—a variety of stone objects probably used in worship—and sculptures of people in seated meditation may suggest religious practices that influenced Hinduism. But until much more is known about these and other features of Indus Valley religion, its effect on Hinduism must remain uncertain.

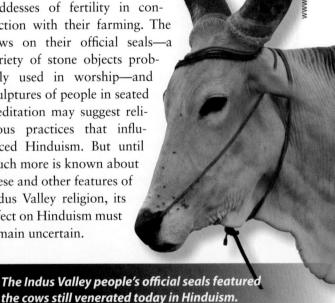

WWW.CEPOLINA.COM

The Indus Valley people's official seals featured the cows still venerated today in Hinduism.

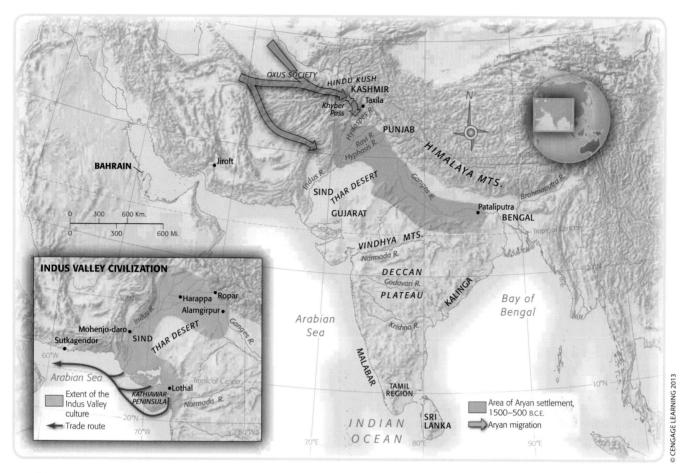

Map 3.1

Indus Valley Civilization and Aryan Migrations

The Indus Valley culture emerged in the city–states of the Indus River Basin. It was in decline when the Aryan (Indo-European) peoples began migrating into India around 1500 B.C.E.

Listen to a *Rig Veda* hymn chanted in Sanskrit.

The Indus Valley civilization was in decline around 1500 B.C.E., when nomadic tribes who called themselves Aryans (AIR-ee-unzs), or "noble ones," migrated into northwest India from their home in the Caucasus area between the Black Sea and the Caspian Sea. These *Aryans* must be distinguished from the modern Nazi misuse of this term, which was identified with Nordic-Germanic people as a claimed superior race. Moreover, many Hindus dispute this migration/invasion, so Hindu scholars sometimes refer to it as the "Aryan Invasion Theory." The Aryans were light-skinned cattle-herding and warlike tribes with horse-drawn chariots. They were a part of the migration from central Asia into both India and Europe; hence the term *Indo-Europeans* is much more common than *Aryans*. They soon took over control of the Indus Valley peoples. These Indo-Europeans spoke

Sanskrit, a language closely related to most European languages, including English. They had oral collections called the **Vedas**, which form the foundation of Hinduism. The *Vedas* represent a diversified and continuous oral tradition that extends from around 1200 to 800 B.C.E.; they were written down much later. The earliest *Vedas*, four in number, were "books of knowledge" compiling hymns to various deities, instructions for sacrifice, songs to accompany sacrifice, and spells for everyday life to bring on blessings and keep away evil.

The heart of Vedic religion was sacrifice by means of fire, accompanied by sung praises and requests to the gods. Vedic gods living in the skies or in heaven play a role in human life as forces of nature, forces that can be influenced by sacrifice. In general, Vedic sacrificial

> **Vedas** [VAY-duhs] Hindu "books of knowledge" consisting of *Rig, Yajur, Sama,* and *Atharva Vedas*

The Great Bath at Harappa

of the gods and experienced their hidden truth. He then was inspired to compose hymns in their praise, hymns which came into the *Rig Veda*. Soma even became a god, so powerful were its effects. This quest for a direct individual encounter with ultimate, hidden truth has persisted in the Hindu tradition to this day, although the encounter itself has changed. No longer is it an encounter with all the gods; it is discovery of an ultimate reality hidden in one's soul or ecstatic devotion to one's chosen god. The means of achieving it have changed (no longer a drug, but intense meditation), as have those who can achieve it (no longer limited to soma drinkers, but open to all).

rituals aim at aiding and strengthening the gods, who then strengthen the world to remain alive and strong, so that those who offer sacrifice may prosper. In this world-view the gods and humans are partners in a "circle of life" that maintains the ongoing creative processes of the world. Both need each other to thrive. The Vedic stage of Hinduism affirms the world, accepting the physical aspects of the world as good and proper. At the daily and domestic level, the simple *Agnihotra* ritual to the sun was performed by the head of most Vedic households three times each day and is still common in India. Even given its adaptations over time, it is arguably the oldest continually practiced ritual in the world. The gods to whom Agni (AHG-nee), the god of fire, carried the sacrificial offerings included Indra, the king of the gods, with traits of both a war god and a thunder god; Varuna (vah-ROON-uh), the god guaranteeing moral order; and Brahma (BRAH-muh), the god of creation. Many other gods, mostly male with some female, are also associated with physical and spiritual forces of nature.

A key person of Vedic times was the **rishi**, or "seer" of the divine, a priest who was able to commune directly with the gods. The rishis achieved an altered state of consciousness in which they could see and hear the gods. To reach this state, they drank a drug called soma, probably hallucinogenic, pressed out perhaps from a mushroom. When the rishi drank soma as a part of Vedic sacrifice, he took a trip to the realm

Read a hymn to Soma in the *Rig Veda*.

rishi [REE-shee] "Seer" of the divine, who collected the sounds of the four *Vedas*

"The sun would not rise if the priests did not sacrifice."—Famous saying of Vedic times

Near the end of the Vedic period, for reasons not clear to us, the Vedic system of sacrifice grew into a dominant power in Aryan society. The power of sacrifice was no longer dependent on the gods' favor as influenced by the humble prayer and household sacrifices of ordinary Aryans, but on the faultless priestly performance of increasingly more elaborate sacrificial rituals. At least sixteen priests, and many more assistants, were needed for the regular sacrifices. Sacrifice was no longer just a means to the attainment of blessings such as children and prosperity, but a requirement for the maintenance of the world itself. A famous saying of the time claimed that "the sun would not rise if the priest did not sacrifice" (*Satapatha Brahmana* 1.3.1). Religious and social power collected in the hands of one type of priest among many: the priests who called themselves Brahmins. The books detailing sacrifice and its power are called the *Brahmanas*, "Brahmin books." This concentration of power in the hands of the Brahmin priesthood, perhaps combined with other factors such as the influence of indigenous Indus Valley religious practices, would spark change for Hinduism in its next period of history. It would also catalyze the birth of a new religion, Buddhism, which would change religion in all of ancient Asia and, in modern times, the world.

The Upanishadic Period (600–400 B.C.E.)

In the first millennium B.C.E., Hindus added another dimension that has endured to this day. This is the quest for knowledge so deep and sacred that to know it is to bring eternal freedom from this world of appearances and constant change. The *Upanishads*, philosophical Hindu scriptures from this period, are primarily dialogues between teachers and young students who seek this sacred knowledge in a withdrawal from ordinary life. These teachers and students renounced the Vedic value put on ordinary life and pursued extraordinary truths. They criticized the Vedic rituals as unnecessary, and they rejected the rising social and economic power of the priesthood. Their criticism of Vedic sacrifice was so effective that from this period through today the only remnants of Vedic sacrifice that survive are the relatively simple ones often incorporated into newer rites, especially weddings, funerals, other traditional rites of passage, and simple daily sacrifices. The *Upanishads* urge physical and mental rigors that become increasingly important for Hindu practice. Buddhism and Jainism, which will be considered in later chapters, arose at this time in India to find a single required way to enlightenment, but each one denied key Hindu teachings and practices. Most Hindus gradually rejected these new movements in favor of Hinduism's inclusive approach.

The *Upanishads* teach that underlying reality is a spiritual essence called **Brahman**, a single "world soul" that is the foundation of all physical matter, energy, time and space, and being itself—in short, of everything in and beyond this universe. (This term is not to be confused with the Vedic creator god Brahma or the Brahmin priests.) Although it is cosmic, Brahman is present in all people in the form of the **atman**, a person's innermost self or soul. In other words, each person's innermost soul is a part of the one world soul. For most (but not all) Hindus, Brahman is not a personal being, as "world soul" might imply; it is spiritual, but it is not a spirit. The religious quest in the *Upanishads* involves understanding that Brahman and one's own atman are one and the same. The realization of this truth, which is the deepest form of self-understanding, brings freedom from ignorance and misery, and release from the endless cycle of reincarnations of one's atman. Unlike the Vedic hymns, the *Upanishads* do not affirm the physical world, but rather aim at transcending it.

This goal of liberating one's soul by perfect knowledge of it, and the use of physical and meditational techniques to achieve this knowledge, became permanent, important aspects of Hinduism. These techniques gradually coalesced into a system called **yoga**, the Sanskrit word for "yoke." Yoga is an ancient meditational practice that yokes the body and mind in the quest for religious deliverance. (You may know it as an exercise and meditation system, but it is much more than that for Hindus.) Yoga aims at removing humans from the overwhelming mental flow of the material world,

> For most Hindus, Brahman is spiritual but is not a spirit.

Statue in Bangalore, India, of the god Shiva meditating in the lotus yoga position

© DINODIA PHOTOS/BRAND X PICTURES/JUPITER IMAGES

Read an *Upanishad* praising meditation over sacrifice.

if only momentarily, in order to recapture their original spiritual purity.

THE CLASSICAL PERIOD (400 B.C.E. –600 C.E.)

A growing number of conversions to Buddhism and Jainism was a threat to Hinduism. The Mauryan (MOHR-yuhn) dynasty that governed north India was pro-Buddhist, and its most famous king, Ashoka (ah-SHOH-kuh), extended Aryan rule and Buddhist influence into all of India. Hindus dealt with this threat in a way that became typical of Hinduism through today, by integrating foreign elements into the broader Hindu tradition. The main teachings of the *Upanishads* were seen as compatible with the earlier *Vedas*—whether they were or not—and accepted into the Vedic body of scripture.

In addition, they incorporated a variety of religious practices of lower, non-Aryan classes that were converting to new religions. To put it another way, the Sanskrit tradition of the *Vedas*, for the educated upper classes and the "high" gods, took in and controlled the tradition of the lower, non-Aryan population and the "low gods" of local village and tribal deities. Local deities became a part of the village shrines and temples. The local gods were identified with the older gods, or regarded as their incarnations, or became one of their "family members." The non-Aryans were successfully taken into this system, some into the lower castes and others into the "outcastes." This development solidified Brahmin power and religious teachings, and eventually stemmed the conversions of non-Aryans to other religions. However, mass conversions to other religions, particularly Buddhism and Christianity, are still a difficult issue when they occur today among lower classes in India.

Goddess sculpture at a temple in Mathura, northern India

Bhagavad Gita [BAH-guh-vahd GEE-tuh] "Song of the Lord"; a long poem on religious duty in the *Mahabharata*

Around 400 B.C.E., as the wandering Aryans finally settled into towns and cities, they built permanent homes for themselves and temples for their gods. Before that, all sacrifice was done outdoors, with sites as nomadic as the Aryan tribes. During the Classical period the two great Hindu epics still popular today were written, the *Mahabharata* (MAH-huh-BAH-rah-tuh) and the *Ramayana* (rah-MAH-yah-nuh). Both relate royal rivalries, perhaps reflecting political turmoil during this period as different clans struggled for territorial power when they settled down. They feature a tension between the aim of upholding the world found in the *Vedas* and that of isolating a person from society in order to achieve individual liberation found in the newer Upanishadic tradition. Both epics emphasize that social and moral obligation must be maintained, and that rulers acting in the Hindu tradition have a key role in maintaining it. However, many characters in these epics have renounced the world, live alone in forests or in small settlements, and are said to possess extraordinary powers to bless or to curse. The epics' heroes almost always treat these world renouncers, or *sadhus* (SAH-doos)—of whom we will speak below—with great respect and learn much from them even as they take up their social duties.

Another solution to this tension is found in the *Mahabharata*, particularly the part of it known by the separate title of *Bhagavad Gita*, "Song of Heaven" or "Song of the Lord." In the *Gita*, the god Krishna appears to the warrior-class leader Arjuna (are-JOON-ah), to convince him to do his social duty of fighting, but in a way in which he understands and controls its effect on him. The *Gita*'s solution is a masterful blend of world-affirming action and world-denying detachment from the results of one's actions. True renunciation

> **TRUE RENUNCIATION DOES NOT MEAN RENOUNCING SOCIALLY RESPONSIBLE ACTIONS.**

does not involve renouncing socially responsible actions. Rather, it involves renouncing desire for the fruits of actions even as one fulfills one's social duty. Selfless action without desire for reward is true renunciation for the *Gita,* and no tension should exist between one's dual obligation to support the world and to seek individual liberation. The *Gita* recognizes that this is difficult and that most people must use yoga and other disciplines to accomplish it. This ingenious approach has contributed to the *Bhagavad Gita's* status as the most influential of Hindu scriptures today.

View a Kathakali performance.

A different genre of literature also concerned with society arose at this time, the law codes, particularly the *Laws of Manu* (MAH-new). What epics do in a literary way, the law codes do in a formally legal way. They carefully restrict renunciation of the world to older males. One must earn the right to renounce the world by first being in the world as a good student, then as a husband and father. Opting out of ordinary life can only be done after one has successfully engaged in it. Underlying all the law books is the strong Hindu affirmation that doing one's duty for an orderly, stable society is necessary for this world and after one's death leads to better reincarnation. This social order involves primarily the proper functioning of the main social-religious classes that arose in Vedic times, as well as the proper observance of interaction within and among these classes. Women belong to the various classes even though their social roles are not as determined by their class as their husbands' roles are. We will consider these classes more fully below.

THE DEVOTIONAL PERIOD (600 C.E.–PRESENT)

The next period in Hinduism is characterized by three developments: the rise of devotional movements, especially the main three devoted to Shiva (SHEE-vuh), Vishnu (VISH-new), and the Goddess; Tantrism; and the rise of Hindu reform movements. Of these developments, the first is so important and influential that it has given its name to the entire period.

An actor in traditional clothing and makeup performs part of an Indian epic.

WWW.CEPOLINA.COM

bhakti [BAHK-tee] Devotion, particularly in a devotional movement or group

Devotion to one's chosen god is a main way of being Hindu. Devotion, or **bhakti,** enters the Hindu tradition as early as the *Bhagavad Gita,* where devotion to Krishna brings a cognitive mental discipline to guide action in the world. Around the sixth century C.E. in southern India, advocates of devotional Hinduism led movements praising Shiva and Vishnu in emotional poetry and song. This devotional experience involves often-uncontrollable joy in one's god, sometimes with fainting, frenzy, tears of anguish, and ecstatic speech. By the seventeenth century, this devotional movement spread into most Hindu traditions, where it remains. The devotional movement gradually coalesced into three movements, one each for Shiva, Vishnu, and Shakti (SHAHK-tee), the Goddess.

Devotion is typically described in its poetry and song as deep love for one's god. Devotees are willing to sacrifice anything in order to revel with their divine lord in ecstatic bliss. The best example of this is the devotees of the cowherd Krishna, married women who leave their husbands and homes to frolic with Krishna in the woods. Women have played an important role in the rise of devotional movements. Two famous women devotees, Mahadeviyakka (MAH-huh-deh-vee-YAHK-uh) and Mirabai (MEER-uh-bigh), were both unhappy in traditional marriages and eventually left their husbands to devote themselves entirely to a god. Hinduism finds a way to balance devotion to a god and renunciation of the world. The language of love that breaks Hindu social rules is made a symbol of deep love within these rules. Even holy men who have renounced everyday life typically wear devotional marks to Vishnu or Shiva.

Hinduism finds a way to balance devotion to a god and renunciation of the world.

Tantras [TAHN-truhs]
Writings in the Tantric movement of Hinduism

mantras [MAHN-truh]
Short sacred formula used in prayer or meditation

The *Tantras*, the basis of the second major development of this period, are writings based on practices that arose outside the elite Brahmin tradition. Many Westerners today associate the *Tantras* with exotic sexual practices, but Tantrism is much broader than that. The hundreds of *Tantras* often criticize established religious practices and the upholders of those practices, especially the Brahmins. However, the *Tantras* also often express central, traditional Hindu ideas and practices. For example, an individual is a microcosm of the cosmos, and by learning the sacred "geography" and life forces of one's body one may, by means of various yogic techniques, bring about one's own spiritual fulfillment. The *Tantras* themselves distinguish between a right-handed path and a left-handed path. The right-handed path is open to most Hindus and uses **mantras** (short sacred words or sounds used in prayer or meditation), sacred diagrams called mandalas, and ritual techniques based on body geography. The left-handed path, appropriate for those with an especially adventurous, fearless temperament, centers on rituals that engage in actions strictly forbidden in Hinduism, gaining liberation by transcending the tension between good and evil. For example, by expressing lust in sexual intercourse with a forbidden woman, a man may seek to overcome lust. Left-handed Tantrism is highly controversial among many Hindus, but right-handed Tantrism is commonly approved.

We turn now to the next topic in the Devotional period: Hindu reform or revisionism. Hinduism was not, on the whole, so affected by Islam during Muslim rule in India that it had to make adaptive changes. However, with the arrival first of European colonizers and then of Christian missionaries in the nineteenth century, their interaction with Hindus led to Hindu movements for change. Attempts were made to renew Hinduism spiritually and socially, ending practices that most Hindu reformers found objectionable: the harshest features of the caste system, "superstitions" like Vedic astrology, popular blessings and curses, the worship of images, and the like.

- Rammohan (RAHM-moh-hahn) Roy (1774–1833), who was perhaps the world's first scholar of comparative religion, had watched in shock as his sister burned to death on the funeral pyre of her husband. He was dismayed at what he saw as the harmful effects of caste divisions. He founded the Society of Brahmanism in 1828. Roy claimed that the *Upanishads* reveal the one God of all people. The One was to be worshiped through meditation, quiet worship, and a moral life, not by the emotions of devotional Hinduism.

- Dayananda Sarasvati (DAH-yuh-NAN-duh SAH-rahs-VAH-tee) founded the "Noble Society" (Arya Samaj) in 1875. Dayananda found the pure, original essence of Hinduism in the *Vedas* centering on monotheism and a reasoned morality. He opposed much of devotional Hinduism and was opposed to Islam and Christianity. His movement along with Ram Roy's gained little steady acceptance from Hindus.

- Ramakrishna (RAH-muh-KRISH-nah), who lived from 1836 to 1886, taught traditional Hindu beliefs and spiritual techniques. He was a devoted temple priest of the goddess Kali, but he worshiped other Hindu deities as well—even the God of Christians and Muslims. He incorporated selected Western ideas and religions into a Hindu context and did not attempt to change Hinduism by making it conform to Western ideas of religion or rationalism. This program was widely effective and led to Ramakrishna's fame in Hinduism.

The twentieth-century Indian movement for religious reform and independence from the British Empire—particularly its religious and political leader, Mohandas K. Gandhi (moh-HAHN-dahs GAHN-dee; 1869-1948)—shows once again the persistence and adaptability of Hinduism. Gandhi is widely known by his honorific name, Mahatma ("great soul"), and he certainly was one of the great figures of the twentieth century. The civil rights movement in the United States and South Africa is heavily indebted to him for nonviolent resistance as a religious-political program. Although Gandhi drew on different religious traditions, especially nonviolence in Jainism (*ahimsa*) and Christianity (the teaching of Jesus on forgiving one's enemies while refusing to cooperate with them in evil), he was thoroughly Hindu. He emphasized Hindu teachings and practices that the masses could appreciate, such as devotion, prayer, and trust in divine grace, and combined this with strong moral reasoning and action. His favorite text was the *Bhagavad Gita*, which provided the religious foundation for his system of "persisting in the truth." This system involves expressing the truth in every action, no matter what the result, acting without regard for rewards. Acting for social good without any regard for personal

PHOTO BY KEYSTONE/GETTY IMAGES

Ben Kingsley as Gandhi, and Martin Sheen as newspaperman Vince Walker, in the acclaimed 1982 film Gandhi

reward is a main point of the *Gita*, but Gandhi chose to read the *Gita* as a text urging nonviolence, not war. He forbade violence as a tool in his political campaigns; instead, he urged self-control, negotiation and tactical compromises, and even self-sacrifice.

Gandhi's style of life drew on the renouncer tradition in Hinduism. At middle age he practiced the strict poverty of a holy man and later in life took a vow of celibacy. He wore little clothing and lived on a bare minimum of food, becoming very thin. This austere lifestyle built spiritual strength for the liberation of Hindus from caste hatred, domination by colonialists, and widespread economic poverty. The nonviolent movement he led secured independence from Great Britain in 1947, but to his sorrow this independence resulted in not one nation but two: India and the officially Muslim nation of Pakistan, to which many Muslims migrated. He was assassinated by a Hindu in 1948 after rising complaints that he was too much of a pluralist and too accommodating to Muslims—some Hindus had even mocked him as "Mohammed Gandhi." Unfortunately, his murder increased the tension between Hindus and Muslims that challenges the whole Indian subcontinent even today, but his positive legacy continues in India and throughout the world.

SOME HINDUS MOCKINGLY NICKNAMED MOHANDAS GANDHI "MOHAMMED GANDHI" BECAUSE THEY THOUGHT HE WAS TOO ACCOMMODATING TO MUSLIMS.

The government of modern India has tolerated all religions and has brought some significant improvement to the lives of the lower classes and the outcastes. This has provoked a religious-political reaction widely but controversially referred to as "Hindu fundamentalism." For the members of Hindu fundamentalist groups, Hinduism is more a symbol of national political identity than a religion. The main group to arise is the Indian People's Party, often known by its Hindi-language initials, BJP. Their principal concern is the perceived danger to the Hindu majority by conversions among untouchables and other Hindus, which they see as a threat to what they call the "Hinduness," *Hindutva* (hihn-DOOT-vah), of India. They have enacted laws restricting efforts at conversion by Muslims and Christians. In 1992, a Muslim mosque in the city of Ayodhya was destroyed by a mob of militant Hindus, and then rioting by Muslims and Hindus killed more than a thousand people.

From 1998 to 2004, the BJP was in control of the Indian government, with a leader of the BJP as prime minister. It was during this time that India openly deployed nuclear weapons, prompting Pakistan to do the same. Although they now are out of power in the national government, the BJP and its fundamentalist supporters still control a few Indian states and have a strong influence on the nation. For example, in 2007 they got the Indian government to give up a plan to build a shipping canal between India and Sri Lanka, claiming that this canal would destroy an ancient, holy "bridge" to Sri Lanka that Hindus believe was built by the gods. Most Hindus see Hindu fundamentalism as contrary to the generally inclusive, tolerant spirit of Hinduism. This will probably dampen its growth potential, but Hindu radicalism remains strong in several parts of India today.

Read about Gandhi's views on the *Bhagavad Gita*.

Read an article about Narendra Modi, current leader of the BJP.

The Taj Mahal, built in the 1600s as a Muslim tomb, has become the architectural symbol of India and is widely considered one of the most beautiful buildings in the world.

© AND INC./SHUTTERSTOCK.COM

LO3 Essential Hindu Teachings

In central India, a woman offers prayer and a sacrifice of food in a temple dedicated to Santoshi Ma (san-TOH-shee mah), or "Mother of Satisfaction." Santoshi Ma is a goddess of prosperity, especially the wife's prosperity with modern appliances in her home, and the woman in the temple is asking for a more bearable load of housework. Santoshi Ma was unknown before her existence was discerned by a few devout Hindus in the 1960s. A few temples were then built in her honor, and in 1975 she was featured in a blockbuster Hindi-language film, *Hail Santoshi Ma*. The film presented a mythology for Santoshi Ma's divine birth and growth as the daughter of Ganesha, and featured a simple devotional ritual to gain her blessing. Santoshi Ma became an important, much-loved goddess practically overnight, the first time that modern mass media have influenced the rise of a deity. Because the establishment of new deities has a strong precedent in Hinduism, Santoshi Ma is now well integrated into the pantheon of Hindu goddesses, and her many devotees see her as one with all the other goddesses.

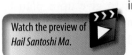

Watch the preview of *Hail Santoshi Ma.*

lingam [LING-gahm]
Symbol of erect phallus in Shiva's shrines

In this section, we will discuss the main beliefs of Hindus about the world, human society, and the individual. We will begin with a treatment of the main deities in the three devotional movements we encountered in the previous section.

MAIN DEITIES IN THE THREE DEVOTIONAL MOVEMENTS

Shiva. Shiva (SHEE-vah) is the god who meditates in his home in the Himalayas. He is a fearsome god with matted hair, with a body smeared with ashes and clothed with animal skins, and carrying snakes and human skulls. He repeatedly burns the god of love to ashes when the god tries to distract him. In the cosmic cycle of creation, destruction, and re-creation, Shiva guides and empowers destruction. However, Shiva devotees today view this destruction positively, as symbols of the removal of obstacles to salvation; destruction is a necessary part of re-creation. The destructive side of Shiva is depicted in the popular bronze statues called Shiva Nataraja (NAH-tuh-RAHJ-uh), "Shiva the Lord of the Dance" (see the photo on the opening page of this chapter). Shiva is surrounded by fire, which destroys in order to purify. He embodies the world-renouncing tendencies of Hinduism and as such provides a model for this aspect of the tradition. However, a good deal of Shiva's mythology concerns his eventual marriage to the goddess Parvati (PAHR-vah-tee), mythology in which a feminine, life-promoting side of Shiva emerges. His other consorts are Durga, the goddess of death, and Kali, the frightening destroyer of evil.

Shiva is also an appealing, attractive god. His son Ganesha (or simply Ganesh), the elephant-headed god who clears away obstacles to success, is one of the best-loved Hindu divinities. Ganesha's image is found in nearly every Hindu shop and office around the world. Shiva's most typical image in his temples is the **lingam** ("sign"). The meaning of this is disputed; it probably depicts the erect phallus, which celebrates Shiva's power, but for most Hindus this meaning is not important. Shaivites often worship Shiva by pouring milk over the lingam. Another main symbol of Shiva is the bull Nandi, whose statue outside his temples is venerated by worshipers. Shiva is also represented by the trident, and his devotees often wear horizontal

The deceptively lovely Durga, goddess of death

wife of Shiva. She is worshiped as Devi (DEH-vee), "the Goddess," who is one with Brahman. The literature of Shaktism is found in the *Tantras*; it gives a high place to women and reacts strongly against caste distinctions. In some regions of India, the Great Goddess (*Mahadevi*) is revered as the supreme divinity. Female power in the Goddess alone is seen as the ultimate cause of the creation, preservation, and end of the world.

Like Shiva, the Goddess is venerated both in her gentle, motherly aspects and in her cruel, dangerous, and erotic aspects. Accordingly, she is honored under

Watch a video on Shiva and Vishnu.

stripes painted on their forehead and display a trident.

Vishnu. Vishnu, on the other hand, is a cosmic king who lives in blissful splendor in his heavenly palace. He supervises universal order and prosperity, protecting and preserving the world. When needed, he descends to the world in various incarnations to defeat enemies of both humans and the gods. Vishnu is a royal, gracious god, revered by his devotees with loving devotion and surrender. His female counterpart is Lakshmi (LAHK-shmee), the much-loved goddess of fortune and wealth. Vishnu is often depicted with blue skin, because he once killed a five-headed snake, taking all its poison into himself; his skin then changed color due to the poison's effect. To his worshipers, this blue color is a symbol of his power.

Vishnu's most familiar incarnations are Rama, hero of the *Ramayana*, and Krishna, hero of the *Bhagavad Gita*. Both Rama and Krishna are today among the best-loved Hindu gods, which has ironically led to Vishnu himself being seen as too high to intervene directly on behalf of the individual in trouble. Devotees of Vishnu who have renounced the world typically wear two vertical markings on the forehead that come together on the bridge of the nose.

Shakti and the Goddess. The cult of Shakti and the mother aspect of the divine had its roots in the *Vedas*. The *Rig Veda* describes Shakti as the powerful upholder of the universe. She is the sister of Krishna and the

Ganesha with Om on his forehead

yoni [YOH-nee] Stone or sometimes metal representation of the human female genitalia, a symbol of the feminine power of the cosmos

dharma [DAHR-muh] Righteousness, law, duty, moral teaching, order in the universe; also, the first goal of life in Hinduism

a wide variety of divine forms. The most well known are Lakshmi, the goddess of wealth and consort of Vishnu; the black goddess Kali ("dark one"), riding on a lion; and the demon-slaying goddess Durga. The **yoni**, a stone representation of the human female genitalia usually found in Goddess temples, is a symbol of the feminine power of the cosmos. The lingam is often set within the yoni to suggest that the universe is powered by a combination of the male and the female.

With Hinduism's millions of gods—traditionally put at 330 million!—and even with these three more focused devotional movements, how do Hindus put it all together in a way that makes everyday sense for them? Whether a Hindu honors Vishnu, Shiva, or Shakti, that god is for her or him the sole and the highest, whereas other Hindu gods are lower forms. Thus, one god is thought to appear at various levels. At the "top" is a nonpersonal absolute, Brahman, the world soul that cannot be described. Brahman is so comprehensive that some Hindu scriptures describe it as encompassing everything that exists. Brahman manifests itself in various personal high divinities that create the world (Brahma), maintain it (Vishnu), and destroy it again (Shiva). In practice, however, followers of one god will attribute all three functions to him or her, as our treatment above suggests. They see all other gods as standing under their god or as further manifestations of "their" god. Although the teaching of the ultimate world soul plays little or no role in the religious everyday—it's hard to pray, sacrifice, express emotion to something that is unknowable—it has the effect that most Hindus see no problem

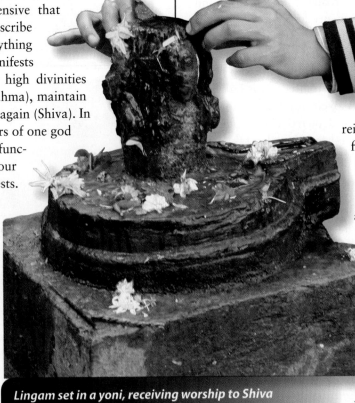

Lingam set in a yoni, receiving worship to Shiva

© GRIGORY KUBATYAN/SHUTTERSTOCK.COM

in acknowledging other Hindu traditions, and sometimes even other religions, as authentic paths to the divine.

View a gallery of the visual traits of Hindu gods.

HINDU DOCTRINAL CONCEPTS

Dharma is the most basic concept of Hinduism. It is a wide-ranging term for righteousness, law, duty, moral teachings, religion itself, or the order in the universe. Dharma is also the god who embodies and promotes right order and living. The ancient *Vedas* emphasize the order of the cosmos, and dharma builds on it by emphasizing the correct ordering of human life. Dharma is more than a set of cosmic-order ideas applying in the same way to all Hindus. It's specific to one's place in the world: one's social position or caste membership, stage of life, and gender. The dharma of a member of the warrior class is distinct from that of a laborer; the dharma of a youth is different from that of the father of a family, and a husband's dharma differs from his wife's.

A Hindu needs to conform primarily to his or her class and caste dharma. Most Hindu scripture teaches this, and it is a particular theme in the most-read Hindu scripture, the *Bhagavad Gita*. Following the social and religious rules of one's caste leads to better reincarnation; neglecting it leads to a lesser reincarnation. For a man to leave his caste for a higher one is unthinkable. Opposing the caste system itself leads to radically lesser reincarnation. One could find oneself an outcaste, a lower animal, or an insect in one's next life. This has led to a remarkably conservative social structure and explains why, even today, traditional Hindu values often frustrate attempts at social change for women and the lower castes. Hinduism divides life into four stages, each with its own particular dharma—what is seen as right for each stage. Some classes and most women do not need to observe such dharma, but the stages are an important aspect of what a Hindu would consider dharma to be. These four stages will be dealt with in more detail later.

Samsara is the cycle of reincarnation endured as a hardship by the spiritual essence of all living things. The **jiva** (individual soul) is subject to reincarnation, because it is only the jiva that earns reward or punishment in the next reincarnation (see the next paragraph). One's atman, the deeper soul identical with Brahman, is not subject to karma, but it goes along with the jiva. It travels with the jiva in reincarnation but is beyond it. Because actions in life involve choices, at every moment an individual is capable of making the choices to ensure a good situation in one's next life. The *Brihadaranyaka* (BREE-hahd-uh-RUN-yah-kuh) *Upanishad* describes this well: "An individual creates for himself his next life as a result of his desires, hopes, aspirations, failures, disappointments, achievements and actions performed during this life of his. Just as a caterpillar gets its front feet firmly on the next leaf before it leaves the one it is on, a soul creates its next life before it departs the present one." This leads us to a fuller consideration of karma.

> "Just as a caterpillar gets its front feet firmly on the next leaf before it leaves the one it is on, a soul creates its next life before it departs the present one." — *Brihadaranyaka Upanishad*

Karma is derived from the Sanskrit for "deeds" and is related to one's behavior in preceding lives. After a person's death, her or his spiritual essence is reborn in another life if any karma is attached to it. Whether one is rich or poor, healthy or sick, male or female, intelligent or not, talented or untalented, a member of a high or low caste, a Hindu or not, and endowed with many other life-defining traits depends on the karma inherited from the lives that have gone before. Karma explains and justifies all human inequalities. Although the conditions of an individual's life are determined in advance by her or his deeds in previous lives, individuals must assume personal responsibility for their present actions and their consequences.

Moksha means "liberation" from rebirth that comes with the entry of the individual soul (atman) into the highest reality (Brahman). The idea of reincarnating without end, or even attaining eternal life as an individual, is abhorrent to Hindus. The ultimate goal is to merge one's atman with Brahman, like a drop of water enters the Indian Ocean. To be liberated from samsara, one must be rid not only of bad karma but also of good karma; any karma at all causes rebirth after death. Although actions take place, if the self that does them is not egoistic, karmic results cannot attach to them. Paradoxically, one must even give up the desire to achieve liberation in order to reach it. (To illustrate this from everyday life, if you've ever had trouble falling asleep at night, you may have found that to fall asleep you must give up trying to fall asleep or even try to stay awake.) Many Hindus, however, find that complete moksha is difficult to achieve, especially in a time when many Hindus believe that their religion is in an era of

A soul, symbolized by a ray of light, travels to enlightenment through seven different lives

© ANANTASHAKTI

samsara [sahm-SAH-ruh] Cycle of reincarnation

jiva [JEE-vuh] Individual, personal soul that collects karma and is subject to reincarnation

karma [KAHR-muh] Deeds or acts as they influence reincarnation

moksha [MOHK-shuh] Liberation from rebirth and samsara

Garlands for the gods for sale outside a Hindu temple

called the *path of deeds* (karma), is doing ritual actions of worship and meditation, as well as carrying out daily conduct according to one's own dharma, but without a selfish intent that causes bad karma. Second, those on the *path of knowledge* see the central problem with human beings as their inability to realize that they are living in an unreal world and that the only thing real is the spirit. The path of knowledge brings personal merging with the ultimate unity behind the visible things of the world, particularly knowledge of the unity of the individual soul and the world soul through yoga and meditation. Third, the *path of devotion* is a loving surrender and service to one's main deity. Some who follow this path see their deity as a manifestation of the impersonal Brahman, but others see their god or goddess as the Supreme Being, with no Brahman above him or her.

decline. They are content to collect good karma and be reincarnated to a better life.

Three main paths lead to moksha, whether one finds it or not. There is a tendency among Hindus to see one chosen path as the best, but the paths are often combined as well. The way of active, obedient life,

A Closer Look:

Popular Misunderstandings of *Karma, Mantra, Guru,* and *Avatar*

Karma is not "fate," as we often hear today in North America and Europe. Fate is a random, uncontrollable power that determines human actions and events. In fact, karma is the *opposite* of what "fate" means in the Western world. In karma, each person generates her or his own reward or punishment, which comes in one's condition after reincarnation. Also, one hears muddled talk about "group" karma—for example, Hollywood actress Sharon Stone's suggestion that the 2008 earthquake in China that killed seventy thousand ordinary people was some sort of karmic retribution for the Chinese government's violent crackdown on dissent in Tibet. Stone said, "And then all this earthquake and all this stuff happened, and I thought, is that karma—when you're not nice that bad things happen to you?"

A mantra is not a slogan or proverb of "words to live by," such as "Her mantra is to enjoy life to the fullest" or "The candidate's mantra of change was very powerful."

Rather, a mantra is a short mystical utterance of great sacred power, as illustrated by the greatest of all mantras, Om.

A guru is not anyone who acquires followers in any sort of movement, or a person who has wide authority because of his or her secular knowledge or skills. Rather, a guru is a private teacher of transcendent religious truth to a student; a guru leads the student to full knowledge and release.

An avatar is not only a computer user's self-representation in a three-dimensional model for computer games or a two-dimensional icon for Internet communities. In Hinduism, an avatar is an incarnation (different, human form) of a god, as for example Krishna is an avatar of Vishnu. This understanding of *avatar* was adapted by film director James Cameron in his blockbuster 2009 film by that name, in which a human mind is projected into the body of a human-like being.

LO4 Hindu Ethics and Ways of Life

Krishnan, a thirty-year-old computer engineer in Illinois, logs onto shaadi.com to begin the process of finding a wife. This Indian website bills itself as the "world's largest matrimonial service." Some of Krishnan's friends have used it and have urged him to try it, because his parents' efforts at matchmaking haven't succeeded. (Other young Hindus rely on the more traditional means of getting a wife.) He enters the search terms "Hindu," his social-religious class, and also his birthday for a "Vedic astrology horoscope" used in traditional Hindu matchmaking. In his personal statement for the website, he writes that he is looking for a traditional Hindu young woman who can grow to love him after they are married. His parents will always come first in his life, he says, then his wife, and then his brothers and other relatives.

Explore the Indian marriage website shaadi.com.

Hindus often say that Hinduism is more a way of life than a religion. For observant Hindus today, everyday life and religious life are not separated, because Hindu ethics traditionally plays a leading role in everyday life: caste and class, marriage and children, career and retirement.

> *Hindus often say that Hinduism is more a way of life than a religion.*

THE CASTE SYSTEM

You've probably heard about the Hindu caste system, which divides people in society into economic and social groups, giving all people their occupations, level of income, and particular pattern of religious duties. India has more than six thousand castes and subcastes, and scholars have long debated the roles of color, economics, and power in the caste system. There is a long history of dissent in Hinduism from the caste system—and there are many activists working to reform it—but for the most part it has endured as one of the main features of Hinduism. Two words are used in Hindu society to refer to this social system: *varna* and *jati*.

Varna means "color" (it is related to our word *varnish*). It refers to a Hindu system of classification

of people into four classes, dating back to Vedic times. Some scholars have theorized that social classes are based on color, with the lightest at the top and the darkest on the bottom. This is probably an oversimplification, and is controversial in Hinduism, but even today in India there is a general cultural preference for the lighter skin tones found in the upper varnas. Also, class is generally related to economic standing: The lower one's class, the lower one's income. But there are many exceptions to this; some upper-caste Brahmins are of modest means, and one can find members of the common-people Vaisya class who are wealthy merchants. As a rule, outcastes are desperately poor, existing on the equivalent of a few dollars a day.

A well-known hymn in the *Rig Veda* (10.90) tells of how the four main classes arose from the sacrifice of Purusha (POOR-oo-shuh), a man as large as the universe. "The Brahmin was made from his mouth; his arms were made into the Prince; his thighs became the common people; and from his feet the servants were born." The **Brahmins** are the priests who spring from the mouth, and it is the mouth that one needs for chanting the sacred scriptures. The Purusha myth suggests that some people are born with the capabilities for leading others in important religious ritual. When Aryans first arrived in India, their scriptures were not written down but memorized by the priests, who were seen as the only class of people capable of learning, memorizing, and reciting them with precise correctness for the purpose of carrying out religious rituals that mediate between humankind and the divine.

The myth also relates that the arms formed the "Prince." This is the class of **Kshatriyas**, the people in society who are rulers, such as rajas (kings), government administrators, and, because rulership always involved protection of one's subjects and expansion of one's kingdom, warriors in particular. The strong arms of Purusha are needed for action, for an active way of life, so the myth shows us that it is the dharma of some people in life to be the protectors of others. A Brahmin could not perform this duty, because he would not have the right ingredients (of Purusha) in his personality to be a warrior. (However, Brahmins have often been advisors to rulers.)

varna [VAHR-nuh] "Color," a system of classification of people in Hinduism into four main classes

Brahmins [BRAH-munz] The top priestly class in the varna system

Kshatriyas [kshuh-TREE-yuhz] The warrior and princely varna class

The thighs of Purusha form the large class of the common people, the **Vaishyas**, who provide the necessary semiskilled labor for society to function. The thighs of the body are strong, so Vaishyas have the temperament and ability to work at manual tasks. They are merchants, small farmers, and artisans. Finally, the servant or peasant is born from the feet of Purusha. The task of the **Shudras**, people in the fourth class, is to support the rest of society by acting as a servant. Religiously, it is only men in the top three classes who are "twice-born" and are able to go through a ceremony to initiate them into the stages of Hindu religious life. Shudras and women of the top three varnas are not generally thought to have the personal qualities to be twice-born Hindus. But Shudras can do well economically, and women (not men) are allowed to marry a person of one class above them. If Shudras follow their dharma well, they can be reincarnated into a higher jati or even varna.

Dalits in northern India protesting the caste system, 2009

REUTERS/Munish Sharma

"Outcastes" are those outside the caste system, not those "cast out" of it.

Read about the four castes.

Below the class system are the *outcastes*, a term not legally accepted in India today. (Note that this term means "those outside of the caste system," not "those cast out.") The Indian government calls them "scheduled classes," but others call them Harijans (HAHR-ee-jahns), "Children of God," a positive term with an unfortunate negative connotation in that "Harijans" is also a Indian euphemism for illegitimate children. They prefer today to call themselves **Dalits**, "oppressed ones." Their sheer size—an

Vaishyas [VIGH-shuhs]
Third Varna class, the "common people"

Shudras [SHOO-druhs]
Fourth Varna class, "servants"

Dalits [DAHL-its]
"Oppressed ones," the outcastes below the four Hindu castes

jati [JAH-tee] Caste into which one is born

estimated 160,000,000—means that they can wield considerable political power in elections. Some rise to political fame, and there have been a number of cabinet ministers and even one prime minister from the Dalit class. Despite affirmative action programs for Dalits that give some a higher education and well-paid government jobs, strong discrimination against Dalits persists. In June of 2007, a group of Shudra shepherds petitioned to be officially downgraded into the Dalit class, hoping to gain access to preferential treatment afforded by the government; their attempt was met with rioting by other Hindus. Most Dalits are still confined to the most menial, ritually polluting jobs such as street cleaning, manual scavenging, and handling bodies of dead animals or humans. They cannot drink from the same water pumps as the twice-born castes or eat in restaurants with them. In some villages, occasional violence is used to keep Dalits "in their place." Hindus of the four classes do not consider them to be Hindu, and their rights and political status have been problematic in modern India. They are today the poorest of Indians.

Watch a BBC report on defections from Hinduism because of caste inequities.

Read a *National Geographic* article on the Dalits.

Jati means "birth," and this birth caste is more important than varna for Hindus because it affects so many aspects of daily life. (Modern scholars disagree about how to translate *varna* and *jati*. Here we render *varna* as "class" and *jati* as "caste." Both comprise the caste system.) Although there are only four varnas in Hinduism, there are thousands of jatis. Caste is not a religious institution as the varna system is, but is economic and geographical in origin, now

Indian wedding ceremonial plate, with a variety of foods and spices

© DINODIA PHOTOS/ BRAND X PICTURES/JUPITER IMAGES

combined with varna into an overall religious system. Most Hindus today refer to jati when they talk of caste, and it is one's jati that really dictates the life of the average Hindu. Each jati has its own special caste regulations in terms of food, occupation, marriage, social interaction, and the like. From each caste come a number of subcastes, making the whole system even more complicated. Castes may often be occupational, but this does not preclude a member of one caste working at the occupation of another, for example in agriculture, adding even more complexity to the system. The Brahmin class is subdivided into many castes, just as there are many castes in the Kshatriya, Vaisya, and Shudra classes, and even among Dalits. Just as the four varnas are hierarchically organized, so also are the various castes within a particular varna. A male is obligated to marry within his jati. Expulsion from the family and caste as a whole is likely to result should this obligation be broken, but if this and other caste obligations are kept, the individual is provided a strong network of support and protection.

THE FOUR STAGES OF A MAN'S LIFE

The life of a Hindu male is traditionally divided into four stages of time. In modern India, fewer people than in previous centuries observe the system completely and formally, but even today it is an influential pattern for a man's life. However, Shudras, Dalits, and women of all four classes rarely follow the stages. Passage through these represents the realization of the necessary stages of life, through which one travels to success in sustaining this world and to ultimate liberation from this world. Most Hindu males do not go through the four stages; many never advance beyond the second.

The first stage of life is that of a *student*. A male is taught by his elders from childhood, sometimes by a single guru as well. His education will not only fit him for a future profession appropriate to his caste, but will equip him also for family, social, and religious life in a way appropriate to his varna and jati. In older times, this period could last for twenty years or more, but today the first stage has shrunk to between twelve and fifteen years, except for those few who obtain higher education in a university.

The second is the *householder* stage, in which the Hindu male must marry and raise a family. Marriages are often arranged by parents while their children are still young—marriage is much too important to family and society to leave it up to young people! In villages "child marriages" often occur, but after the marriage the child bride and child groom are separated until puberty sets in. On average, a young man is around twenty-three at the time of marriage, a young woman around eighteen. Hindus have always felt it important to raise a family, and even today poor Hindu couples will continue to have children until a boy or two are born. During the householder stage a man works at a trade or profession appropriate to his caste, primarily to support his family, but also to contribute to the welfare of the community. He engages in public and private religious duties appropriate to his caste.

The third stage of life is that of *retirement*, traditionally called the "forest dweller." When a man's children have grown up, when he sees signs of aging like gray hair and wrinkles, his duty as a householder can end. In this third stage—if he lives to see it, which in most of Hindu history isn't a given—the man is expected to retire not only from his job, but also from family and social life and much (but not all) of his wealth and possessions. Sometimes men in this stage retreat to the forest to live a more spiritual life, either alone or in a small group of retirees, but this is rarer today than in the past. Most pleasures are renounced, although in some cases a wife could accompany her husband into retirement. His life

Watch a video of a Hindu wedding.

Two renouncers in Katmandu, Nepal

LUCA GALUZZI–WWW.GALUZZI.IT

would be that of the celibate recluse. In view of the hardships that this kind of life brings, it is not difficult to see why the stage of partial renunciation of the world has become obsolete for all but a few.

The fourth stage is that of the "renouncer" or *sannyasin* (sahn-YAH-sin), when a Hindu renounces the world and his previous life completely. This stage traditionally does not follow after the third; a man can enter it directly from the householder stage. All cares and pleasures of life are abandoned, and his concentration is devoted to achieving moksha before he dies. The renouncer engages in intense study and meditation, typically with yoga and austerities like solitude and a sparse diet. He is treated with greatest respect in Hindu lands. But this respect is mingled with a certain degree of fear and skepticism, because some holy men can be hostile, even ferocious, in their words, and some can be frauds. On taking up the life of the renouncer, men will often burn an effigy of their body to show that they have died to the world. When a renouncer has achieved moksha, at his death his fellow renouncers tie stones onto his body and throw it in a river. He needs no funeral with cremation, for the soul has already been released from the dreaded cycle of reincarnation.

> *The Kama Sutra is often seen as a sex manual, but kama is much more than that.*

THE FOUR GOALS OF LIFE

Most Hindus hold to four main goals in life and connect them roughly with the stages of life. The first goal of life, dharma, a term we have seen above, is a comprehensive religious concept that governs all stages of life. A good Hindu must know the truth of Hinduism, particularly the truth that relates to his or her caste status, and practice it. This practice includes both social morality and ritual duties. Without this first goal, the others cannot be met. The second goal of life is **artha**, material success and prosperity, especially for the sake of one's family. A householder is expected to become as prosperous as possible, while observing the bounds of proper dharma. This ties into the world-affirming side of Hindu tradition and helps to explain the entrepreneurial drive and economic success of many Indians in modern times.

The third goal of life is **kama**, aesthetic pleasure both of the mind and the body, obviously also world-affirming. This goal is restricted to the householder stage. *Kama* is a comprehensive term for all types of spiritual, intellectual, artistic, and physical pleasures. The *Kama Sutra* (SOO-trah), or *Scripture on Pleasure*, is often seen as a sex manual, but both kama and the *Kama Sutra* are much more than that. Hinduism is perhaps unique in teaching that the pursuit of pleasure and wealth is a valid and important religious goal. Though this may seem either strange or appealing to you, remember that in Hinduism the pursuit of pleasure and wealth is always subject to the retributive laws of karma. The fourth goal of life is moksha, which we defined above. It means "release" from life, particularly from the continuous cycle of death and rebirth. This goal is best practiced in the retirement and renouncer stages of life, although it can be sought in all the stages of life, particularly in the two paths of deeds and devotion.

A Closer Look:

Hindu Dress

No particular type of religious dress is required in Hinduism, as you might expect, and regional cultural styles in India differ considerably. The traditional dress for most Indian women is the sari, a piece of material five or six meters long that is wrapped and pleated around the waist and then drawn round over the shoulder so that the free end is left loose. In different parts of India, and among Jains, the sari is wrapped in different ways. Underneath the sari, an ankle-length skirt and a blouse are worn, often with a bare midriff. In northern India, women prefer light, baggy trousers called "pyjamas" (from which we get our term) and a long, loose-fitting shirt. In mixed company outside the home or when worshiping in the home or temple, women will normally cover their hair with the loose end of their saris or with a separate piece of material. Covering the head is a sign of respect to the gods as well as to other people.

Indian women of all classes typically love jewelry. Long earlobes are an ancient Indian sign of nobility, so heavy earrings are often used to stretch the earlobes slightly. The most distinctive decorative mark of a married woman is the **bindi** ("little drop") on her forehead. The bindi may be a circle of colored paste, or it may be a circle of felt with an adhesive backing, which can more easily be put on and decorated with sequins. Unmarried girls often have a small black spot on their forehead; it is not a bindi, but rather a protection against the "evil eye."

Although Hindu women most often dress in traditional Indian ways, Hindu men very often wear Western clothing, especially in Indian cities. Typical Indian village dress for men has traditionally been the *dhoti*. This single piece of usually white cloth is worn wrapped around the waist and tucked up between the legs. The *kurta* (called a "panjabi" in the U.K. and Canada) is a loose shirt coat falling around the knees and is worn by both men and women. It can be worn with a dhoti, with pants and jeans, and is both casual and formal. The wearing of a turban is usually associated with observant Sikh men (see Chapter 6), but in India some Hindu men will also wear turbans. The most important item worn is the sacred thread, a thin cotton cord worn on the body by men of the upper three classes, symbolizing full Hindu status. It is given in a special ceremony near the age of ten. The traditional garb of Hindu men, long disdained by the Indian upper classes in favor of more-Western-style clothing, is now making a strong comeback in social circles and in fashion design.

Holy men have a distinctive but not uniform look. Their hair is often wildly matted, and they sometimes cover their body in light-colored dust or powdered cow dung, giving them the look of death. Some go around only in a thong, to symbolize their full control of the senses and bodily desire. They can sometimes be seen with their sacred thread, but not wearing one shows that they have left the distinctions of once-born and twice-born behind.

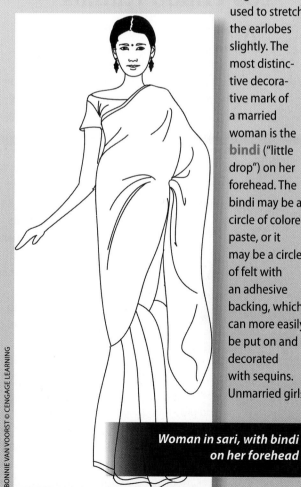

Woman in sari, with bindi on her forehead

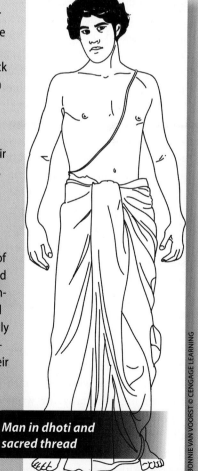

Man in dhoti and sacred thread

The Lives of Hindu Women

The vast majority of Hindu young women get married. The Hindu wife is responsible to bear children, raise them, and run the home. Motherhood is so important that a woman is considered to be a failure if she is without children, especially a son; this is true even of modern Hindu women who may work outside the home. On the other hand, being a mother of sons brings great pride and auspiciousness. The wife performs worship in the home at the household shrine, often leading worship there. However, no woman who is menstruating is traditionally allowed at the shrine or in the kitchen. She is considered ritually unclean, and her husband will not touch her during this time. After ritual bathing at the end of her menstrual period, a woman resumes normal life in the home.

> Read about the traditional life of Hindu women.

Despite the value placed on motherhood, abortion is legal and very frequent in India, even among Hindus. Prenatal testing by ultrasound is now used widely to ascertain the sex of a fetus in the womb, even though this has been outlawed in India since 1994, and if it is a female, it is often aborted. Some parents think it better to abort a female than to support a second or third daughter and pay for her expensive dowry. Contraception is encouraged by the Indian government, but having sons is necessary for economic support in one's old age because India has no national pension system. One also needs a son to perform one's funeral rites. The use of selective abortion to obtain sons has led in some parts of India to an ominous imbalance between the proportion of males and females. As a result, in 2007 the Indian government and private agencies launched a "Save the Girl Child" campaign.

Divorce for a woman is difficult to obtain, especially for women of the higher classes, despite the Hindu Marriage Act of 1955 that ostensibly made it possible for any woman to get a divorce. Although divorce and remarriage are quite common among the lower castes, there is still a general feeling in village life that a wife is to blame if divorce occurs or even if the husband dies first. The divorced or widowed woman is regarded as "unlucky" by her family and friends, and life can be difficult for her. Widows rarely remarry and are often socially ostracized. The suicide rate for widows is high, even if the ancient (if irregularly practiced) "widow burning"—when widows climbed onto their dead husband's funeral pyre to go to heaven with him, an act of great merit—is now almost unheard of. In urban areas women do have more status today; for example, they can now own property, keep their own salary, and open bank accounts in their own name. Many young Hindu women go to college, get a job, and delay marriage. Yet marriage is important, and a woman's self-esteem and social standing still have much to do with her husband. By serving him faithfully, just as she serves a god, good karma will come to her.

> Read about "Save the Girl Child" on its website.

© STEVE EVANS

IN 2007 THE INDIAN GOVERNMENT AND PRIVATE AGENCIES LAUNCHED A "SAVE THE GIRL CHILD" CAMPAIGN.

LO5 Hindu Rituals

As you drive up to the new Hindu temple in Omaha, Nebraska, you notice its traditional Indian architectural design. Inside, the richness of the Hindu tradition is reflected in the many different deities represented there. Most large temples in India are dedicated to one god, but this temple has twelve separate sanctums, or holy areas with altars, each with one or more statues representing a different god. People from various parts of India have certain deities that they honor, so Hindu immigrants from all parts of India can feel comfortable in the Omaha temple.

You are struck at once by the many colorful sights, unusual sounds, and fragrant smells of the temple. Women are dressed in traditional Indian saris; men are in Western clothing, except for the two priests, whose upper bodies are half bare and who have a sacred thread visible over the shoulder. You see different sorts of worship activities: people bowing and prostrating themselves in front of the statues and people sitting quietly in meditation, some in a yoga position. In a side room, men and women are practicing sacred songs to be sung at a service later in the week. You also notice that in some areas of the temple, men tend to be separated from women and children.

Your guide for the tour is a University of Nebraska professor, a member of the temple's leadership. As he skillfully leads you around, he tells you that the temple was built primarily as a center of worship, teaching, and Indian cultural life for people from India who live in Nebraska and Iowa. The temple is open for Hindu festivals, for a main weekly service on Sunday morning—an adaptation to American religion, he says—and for traditional ceremonies marking the life stages of Hindus, from birth to death. He adds that an important part of the temple's purpose is the education of people of other religious backgrounds, visiting or participating in prayers and rituals.

As you might expect, worship and meditation in Hinduism are diverse. Worship is a daily event for observant Hindus, whether performed at home, at a temple, at an outdoor shrine, or on a pilgrimage. Worship is most commonly called **puja**, a word suggesting "honor" and "veneration." Ritual is important to the Hindu, and much of it is ancient, although with regional and devotional-group variations.

IMAGES

Most people associate Hinduism with many gods, all of them represented by images. Westerners, especially Protestant Christians who look upon images as objects that encourage false worship, often use the term *idol*, but *image* is more appropriate. *Idol* suggests that it is the statue or picture alone that is worshiped, and it is generally a pejorative term, although one will hear Hindus using it happily. *Image* suggests something beyond the visible form that receives the worship offered to the visible form. Hindus use the term **murti** for the image of a deity, whether three-dimensional (as in a statue) or two-dimensional (as in a picture or poster). The murtis are representations of the deities, rather like a photograph represents a person. A murti draws the mind of the worshiper to the greater essence of the god. However, an image can be more than just a symbol. The power or essence of the deity is believed to be in the murti, either temporarily, as for some

An image draws the mind to the greater essence of the god.

festivals, or permanently, as in the case of some temple images that are treated as the gods themselves, with the god thought to reside inside the statue.

Shiva has both an anthropomorphic form in an image and the powerful symbols of the lingam and the trident. The female side of the divine, the Goddess, is represented by the yoni, the symbol of creative female power that is the counterpart to the lingam. Hindus of the lower castes and those Hindus outside caste do not worship the "high" gods of Hinduism, but the "low gods," especially village and localized urban deities. The high gods such as Vishnu and Shiva are generally considered to be uninterested in the daily events of the ordinary man or woman; their avatars and related lower gods do that duty for them.

WORSHIP IN THE TEMPLE AND THE HOME

Temples large and small are present in India, from great pilgrimage centers to humble huts along a side street. At many of these temples a great variety of deities are worshiped. Generally, however, the deity and the temple belong to one of three strands within the Hindu pantheon—Shaivite, Vaishnavite, and Shakta, including all their avatars and family members.

The deity, represented by a statue, picture, or other symbol, is the central part of the temple. The god is considered to be a royal guest and is treated as such throughout puja with adoration, attention, care, and entertainment. Purification is essential for the worshiper, and one usually bathes in running water and sips a little water three times to indicate purity. Washing the murti is essential, but often the washing is symbolic—a flower or a small piece of

puja [POO-juh] Devotional actions of worshiping a god or venerating a human person

murti [MUHR-tee] An image of a deity

cotton is used to touch the deity. Dressing the deity is also important, and the clothes chosen are bright, beautiful, and often embroidered with gold-colored threads. Ornaments are also placed on the murti, as well as flower garlands, perfumes, and oils. Because the deity remains at a temple, it is both woken up in the morning and put to rest at night with equal care. At many temples, sculptures help to teach about the gods and their stories, and they both shape and direct devotion. Larger temples will have priests who act as teachers.

The offering of food is also important—usually cooked rice, fruit and vegetables, liquefied butter, and sugar. The Hindu women of Bali, Indonesia, make elaborate pyramids of food (the wealthier they are, the higher the pyramids) that they carry to the temple on their head as a sacrificial offering to the deity. A cooked chicken may be put in the pyramid, surrounded by rice dishes and many kinds of fruit. The deity is believed to take the essence of the food, and the "leftovers" are given back to the worshiper as what is known as *prasad* (PRAH-sahd). Whatever the offering, both the gods and the worshipers eat the food and benefit from its richness. Fragrance and light are also offered the deity—fragrance in the form of incense sticks and light in the form of a burning lamp usually made from a burning wick placed in ghee (clarified butter), which is waved before the deity. By applying a *tilak* (TEE-lahk)—a mark made with crushed flowers sometimes mixed with another substance—to the forehead between the eyebrows of the deity, the worshiper indicates awareness of the spiritual purity and power of the deity, which in turn is passed to the worshiper. The worshiper may also entertain the deity with hymns that offer praise and of course increase the devotion of the worshipers. Groups of people—usually males, but sometimes with women, who sit separately—can be seen singing hymns informally on the temple verandas in the evening.

Bowing is the traditional way of showing respect to someone in India. The more respect one wishes to show, the lower one bows. In the case of a god or a royal person, lying flat on one's face is in order. Combined with bowing, bringing the palms together and raising them to the forehead are actions normally used in greeting in India,

South Indian bride making namaste

© DINODIA PHOTOS/BRAND X PICTURES/JUPITER IMAGES

and they are used to greet the gods as well. The Hindi word *namaste* (NAHM-ahs-tee) or its equivalent in other Indian languages, "I bow to you," are spoken as this is done. Because famous gurus are also honored with puja that sometimes approaches the worship of a god, people might touch the guru's feet in respect or remove by hand the dust from his feet before touching their own head, indicating that the dusty feet of the guru are holier than the head of the one paying respect.

For worship in the home, nearly every Hindu household has a home shrine, frequently in a special devotional room or in the kitchen, which is considered ritually pure. In this shrine, the family god, together with the gods and goddesses honored by individual family members, has the central place as images done in brass; often, photographs of a guru or saint and the family ancestors are in the shrine. To begin daily worship in the home, the believer purifies himself or herself by bathing. Then, with the help of mantras, the place of ritual is purified, and any evil spirits lurking to interfere with the puja are driven away. A small bell is rung to honor the gods and get their attention as the ritual begins. On occasion the gods are washed, clothed, fed, and given gifts, but worshipers always stand reverently with palms joined. At the climax of the ritual, a lamp is swung before the shrine: the divinity resides in the fire, and the faithful receive it within themselves by holding the palms of their hands over the flames for an instant and then touching their eyes.

PILGRIMAGE

Pilgrimage is an aspect of ritual life important for many Hindus, although most Hindus do not have the time or money to engage in it. The destination of a pilgrimage is often a river, the ocean, or a spring. But temples built on sacred mountains or in sacred cities are also places of pilgrimage. Worshiping in a place with a stronger connection to the divine brings purification from sin and ritual impurity, gains merit, fulfills vows, leads to the betterment of one's next lives in this world, and even brings deliverance from the cycle of rebirth. Millions of pilgrims come to Varanasi on the Ganges River every year to wash their sins away in the water. The largest pilgrimage event in the world is the *Kumbha Mela* (KOOM-buh MEHL-uh), held once every twelve years, when tens of millions of pilgrims gather near Allahabad, where the two sacred rivers— the Ganges and the Yamuna— merge. Pilgrimage is often "big business" in cities that host it.

Worship at a home shrine

© DINODIA PHOTOS/BRAND X PICTURES/JUPITER IMAGES

Watch a BBC report on the Kumbha Mela festival.

FUNERALS

Despite all the emphasis in Hinduism on karma and reincarnation, its death rites still emphasize the deceased happily joining dead ancestors rather than achieving a good reincarnation or release from all moksha. (A period of refreshment in heaven is often thought of as a prelude to being reincarnated.) Death is considered so ritually polluting and inauspicious that the images of deities in the home shrine are removed while the body is in the house. Unlike Western funerals, no one partakes of food or drink in any part of a Hindu funeral ritual.

The body of the deceased is washed soon after death, wrapped in a new cloth—white for men and red for women—and carried on a stretcher from the home to the cremation ground in a procession led by the eldest son. (Of course, funerals are held all over India, not just at the cities on the Ganges River, such as Varanasi.) Cremation on a wood fire is the traditional Indian method of disposing of human remains. Cremation is thought to separate the immortal soul from the body in a good way, reminiscent of fire sacrifice. At the funeral ground, Dalits of the Dom caste handle the body and incur the ritual pollution of burning it. Fresh, flowing water is usually near the cremation grounds, and the body is dipped in it for ritual purification. The body is then placed on the wood, with the feet facing south toward the home of the god who rules the dead. It is covered with a layer of wood and then clarified butter, and scriptures are chanted over the body by a priest as the family circles the body. The eldest son then lights the funeral pyre, which will burn for two to three hours. After cremation begins, the youngest son leads the procession home.

The Doms tend the fire for several hours to keep it burning hot, occasionally turning the body with long poles to consume it more fully. The ashes and remaining bones (the larger and denser bones of the human body cannot be consumed by a natural cremation alone) are finally put by the Doms into flowing water and left there, for a cooling and purifying effect. When the period of death rites is over, a Dalit is given all the household linen to wash. On the twelfth day, four balls of rice are offered to symbolize the happy union of the deceased with his or her forebears, the point of the funeral rites. Only when the house has been thoroughly cleaned can the household deities be returned.

Although cremation is the desired method of disposal of the dead, burial is not uncommon. The poorer classes usually practice burial because it is cheaper. Young children of most castes who die are buried, or sometimes put into a flowing river, rather than cremated. In the cities of India, cremation in modern crematoriums is now the norm, with ashes scattered later in sacred rivers. Customs are slightly different in North America. The body will be washed and dressed in new clothes, placed in a coffin, and surrounded by flowers. Cremation has to take place a day or two after death because of the necessary legal arrangements. At the crematorium the priest will talk about the life of the person, and after returning to the house after cremation has begun, prayers are said for the departed soul in front of the sacred fire or household shrine. The ashes of the deceased would preferably be sent to a relative in India to be scattered in the Ganges, or sent to one of the businesses recently sprung up to receive and scatter ashes, or if that is not possible cast into a fast-flowing river in North America.

Watch a video of funeral rites at Varanasi.

Visit the website of a company that scatters ashes in the Ganges.

YOGA

Yoga, with its emphasis on fitness for the body and mind, has become a main tool for achieving liberation, or at least the mental discipline that can lead to liberation. Buddhists, Christians, and people of no formal faith have adapted yogic methods to help them on their own paths to peace and freedom, or just to physical fitness. As said above, *yoga* means "yoke," which its spelling resembles. This refers to the path of union with, or yoking to, a god or Brahman. The most popular type of yoga in India and the West is *hatha yoga*, which emphasizes breathing and physical posture as a way to ultimate knowledge of Brahman in one's atman; *karma yoga* is the path of active service that breathing and postures assist; *jnana yoga* is reflective, philosophical yoga; and *bhakti yoga* is the path of devotion to a god. Bhakti yoga is the simplest form, using repeated chanting of a mantra in a fixed posture to focus on a god and offer one's life to a god.

Watch an explanation of the "Take Back Yoga" campaign to emphasize its Hindu roots.

A Bharatnatyam dancer shows yoga expertise

© PHOTOSINDIA.COM RM 4/ALAMY

6. Concentration, meaning the ability to focus on a single thing, uninterrupted by external or internal distractions

7. Meditation no longer focused on a single thing, but all encompassing

8. Finally, achieving *samadhi* or "bliss." Building on meditation, the self transcends itself through meditation and discovery of the atman that brings one to Brahman.

Read about the practice of yoga.

Watch a video about the yoga controversy in Muslim Malaysia.

> *The most popular form of yoga in the West is hatha yoga, with its emphasis on breathing and physical posture.*

Most yogic practices draw, at least in significant measure, on these eight steps.

1. First following five ethical guidelines on behavior toward others, avoiding violence, untruthfulness, stealing, lust, and covetousness

2. Following guidelines on behavior toward oneself: cleanliness of body and mind, contentment, sustained practice, self-knowledge, study, and surrender to God

3. Learning and using formal yoga postures

4. Practice of breathing exercises, coordinated with physical postures

5. Withdrawal of the senses, meaning that the exterior world is no longer a distraction from discovering the interior world within oneself, particularly the atman within

LO6 Hinduism in North America Today

Shortly before the 2008 release of the Hollywood film *The Love Guru*, written by and starring Mike Myers, self-styled North American Hindu leader Rajan Zed complains about it to mass-media outlets. Zed charges that its portrayal of Hinduism is inaccurate and insulting. The potential for damage to North American Hindus is great, Zed argues, because Hinduism is not widely understood here. Despite Zed's efforts, the consensus among Hindus living in North America seems to be that they feel comfortable laughing at themselves and even laugh at well-meaning stereotypes like Apu the convenience-store merchant on television's *The Simpsons*. However, some portrayals of Hinduism in the mass media—such as the 1984 film *Indiana Jones and the Temple of Doom*, with its false, brutal depiction of worship of the Hindu goddess Kali—have caused concern to many Hindus. Any concern over *The Love Guru*, however, fades rapidly as it is harshly reviewed in the press and then fails miserably at the box office.

Although Hinduism had moved beyond its own borders before the modern period, it was primarily a result of Indian emigration to other countries and the resulting establishment of Hindu culture in such places as Nepal, Sri Lanka, and Bali. Sometimes, as with Nepal and Sri Lanka, it was the result of Indian conquests that brought along principal aspects of Hindu culture and belief. In the main, Hinduism has been the religion of only the Indian people, and converting other peoples has not been done. However, in the last two centuries various Hindus have indeed sought to spread Hinduism outside of India, particularly in North America.

Hinduism has been viewed in widely differing ways in the West during the last two centuries. Customs such as widow burning (rarely done these days) and a caste system that resists reform have made many North Americans resistant to Hinduism until more recently. However, some Westerners were attracted by Hindu ideas of life in harmony with nature on the outside and the spirit within. Vegetarianism and Hindu philosophy, particularly Vedanta, have also attracted Westerners to Hinduism, especially in the more intellectual echelons of North America.

HINDU MOVEMENTS IN NORTH AMERICA

In the last century or so, varied expressions of Hinduism have found their way to the West in movements led by Hindu gurus. Ramakrishna's favorite disciple, Vivekananda (VIH-veh-kah-NAHN-duh; 1863–1902), was the first successful Hindu missionary to the West. In 1893 he addressed the first World Parliament of Religions at Chicago; he was enthusiastically received there and in his other travels throughout the United States. In 1906, Vivekananda established the first Hindu temple in North America, in San Francisco. He returned to India as a national hero. The Hinduism of Vivekananda was much less devotional than Ramakrishna's own piety and stressed the philosophical teachings of the *Upanishads*. Vivekananda believed that the Vedanta was the sum of all world religions, and he was one of the world's first advocates of religious pluralism. After Vivekananda came the Self-Realization Fellowship of North America, founded by Paramahansa Yogananda (PAR-uh-mah-HAN-suh YO-guh-NAN-duh) in 1920 and based in Los Angeles, where it still has its headquarters. It teaches a form of yoga to enable members to realize "the god within." The Self-Realization Fellowship has more than one hundred local meeting places in the United States and Canada today.

Two recent gurus who have gained wide popularity in North America are Maharishi Mahesh Yogi (MAH-ha-REE-shee MAH-hesh YOH-gee; 1911–2008), founder of the Spiritual Regeneration Movement better known as Transcendental Meditation (TM), and Swami A. C. Bhaktivedanta (BAHK-tee-veh-DAHN-tuh; 1896–1977), founder of the International Society for Krishna Consciousness, or ISKCON. Both movements have emphasized how their teachings align with Western science and the mental or emotional benefits obtained from them. TM is based on Vedanta, emphasizing each person's inner divine essence and the liberating powers that may be harnessed when one knows one's true identity. Yogic meditation practiced in the morning and evening is the way to tap into the transcendent and its calming, directing power. When the English musical group the Beatles took continued instruction in Great Britain and in India from the Maharishi in the late 1960s, Transcendental Meditation became even more popular. The popularity of yogic meditation today in North America, severed from its deep religious connections, is due in large part to the TM movement.

ISKCON is more commonly known as the Hare (HAHR-ee, "divine lord") Krishna movement after its main mantra. A part of the devotional movement, it emphasizes enthusiastic devotion to Lord Krishna. Many academics regard it as an authentic (true to Indian roots) form of Hinduism practiced in the West, but at times it has been dogged with charges that it is a dangerous "cult."

> Some Hindu parents in North America send their children to a Hindu summer camp.

HINDU MIGRATION AND LIFE IN NORTH AMERICA

In the past few decades, especially since a liberalization of immigration laws in the 1960s, an increasing number of Indians who practice Hinduism have moved to the United States and Canada. This Hindu "diaspora" (dee-ASS-pohr-uh), a "spreading" from its native land, has brought hundreds of thousands of Hindus to North American cities, especially on the east and west coasts. Some of these more recent immigrants are merchants, but many of them are highly skilled professionals who

A Closer Look:

Hindu Faith and Indian Food

India has considerable regional variations in food, many of which have come to North America, but the most important aspect is a preference for vegetarianism. Because all animals are sacred to Hindus due to a general reverence for life, and particularly for the souls incarnated in animals, it is most often considered wrong to kill animals for food. Vegetarianism is believed to benefit the body, the mind, and the soul. Even so, many Hindus are not strict vegetarians, and those who can afford it will eat meat occasionally. The sacrifice and subsequent eating of animals, the goat in particular, is common enough in India and Nepal. Brahmin priests are rarely involved in such sacrifices, which are done by lower-caste priests mainly in the smaller village temples.

The cow is the most sacred of all animals to Hindus, and no observant Hindu would ever eat beef. (You should never look for a beef dish at any self-respecting Indian restaurant!) Although meat from a cow is forbidden, cow's milk and the products made from it are considered very healthy. To put it in our terms today, vegetarianism is common, but a vegan diet that excludes all animal products would be unthinkable to most Hindus.

Foods high in protein are important in a basically vegetarian diet, and dal, a lentil dish, is popular throughout India. Vegetables cooked in spices are common, as are foods that are quickly fried in butter. The *Bhagavad Gita* (17:8-10) teaches that healthy foods are "tasty, soothing and nourishing." It describes unhealthy food as things that are "acidic, sour, and excessively hot." (The strong curries of Indian food often make Westerners' eyes water, but of course what makes food "excessively" hot is a matter of acculturation. The *Gita* notes foods that will give an Indian indigestion.) The particular balance of having both hot and cool foods in a meal is also important for bodily and spiritual health.

The males of the family traditionally eat first and separately from the women, and then the females eat what remains. Because all food in Hindu sacrifice is first offered to the deities and then received back by the worshiper, the practice of eating the males' leftovers as a sort of sacrificial food enables the wife to pay honor to her husband. This custom is still maintained in traditional India today, though it is not so common among Hindus living in the Western world.

---

are eager to integrate into North American civic life. They also want to preserve basic Hindu beliefs and behaviors in an environment not conducive to them. Every home of observant Hindus has a shrine to the god(s) the family serves, and worship is conducted at the shrine a few times a day. In 2001, the American Museum of Natural History in New York City opened an exhibit, "Meeting God," that documented the home and business shrines of several Hindus in the New York area.

Many Hindus join cultural organizations to keep traditions like music and cuisine alive. Some Hindu parents have started to send their children to summer camp—but camp that provides teaching and experience in Hindu life. They also build Hindu temples in which to practice Hindu worship, and at times these temples are built in authentic ways by workers brought from India. Finding Brahmin priests

View "Meeting God," an online journey through portraits of Hindu worship.

Read a *New York Times* article on Hindu summer camps.

from India to staff these temples is difficult, so activities like singing devotional songs that can be practiced by all Hindus become even more important than in India. Having many different Hindu groups worshiping under one roof, something not done in India, can be a challenge.

Hindus typically view marriage within one's caste as a necessity, and because most marriages are often still arranged to some extent, Hindu parents may network for suitable spouses living in North America or even in India. As with most immigrant groups in North America, intergenerational tension often springs up as second- and third-generation Hindu young people take on the values and practices of their non-Hindu peers. Dating and mating are often difficult for Hindu young people with Western ways; this is the theme of several films, such as Mira Nair's excellent "Monsoon Wedding" and "The Namesake." Over time, Hindus, like other religious groups, will probably reach a workable, if uneasy, compromise between their religion and life in North America.

Watch "Understanding Hinduism," produced for cross-cultural training of law enforcement officers by the Chicago Police Department.

CHAPTER **4**

Encountering Jainism: The Austere Way to Liberation

BONNIE VAN VOORST © CENGAGE LEARNING

Learning Outcomes

After studying this chapter, you will be able to do the following:

LO1 Explain the meaning of *Jainism* and related terms.

LO2 Summarize how the main periods of Jainism's history have shaped its present.

LO3 Outline the essential Jain teachings in your own words.

LO4 State the main ethical precepts of Jainism for monks/nuns and laity, and relate them to Jain teachings.

LO5 Outline the way Jains worship and practice other rituals.

LO6 Explain the main aspects of Jain life in North America today.

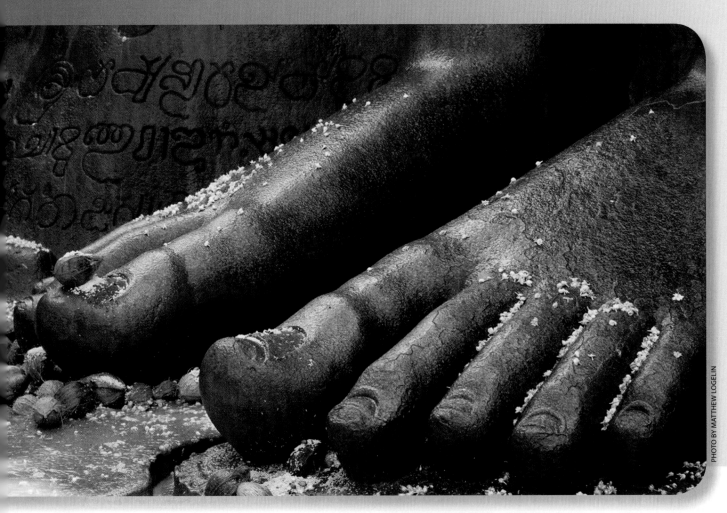

PHOTO BY MATTHEW LOGELIN

"Do no harm; let all creatures help each other."
—From the modern symbol of Jainism.

Your Visit with Jain Nuns

Imagine that you're traveling through northern India and come across a group of three Jain nuns. Like you, they're walking on the outskirts of a small town, but they walk much more slowly and deliberately than you. You notice that they're dressed all in white and have a whisk slung across the shoulder that they occasionally take down and use gently on the road in front of them.

After you greet them respectfully, they invite you to the ashram where they're currently living. You hesitate, thinking to yourself: Should I visit with nuns in their house? Is that proper? You try to hide your expression, but they're so perceptive that it makes you feel like they can read your mind. They assure you that it's okay, that they are able to receive visitors and know how to conduct themselves properly with them. So, you accompany them, keeping a respectful distance behind them as they walk.

At their house, you meet five other nuns. Led by their teacher, who is clearly in charge, they are walking around to different towns and villages in the area. You learn that a man next door is fixing their evening meal in a way that is approved by Jains, which is to do as little harm as possible to insects and other small beings, all of whom have a soul. Soon women of the town start to gather in the ashram. They greet the teacher, and she conducts a short service of prayer and meditation for them. It ends with blessings on all who have come, especially with the saying "May you attain spiritual prosperity."

After sleeping in another building, you rejoin the nuns very early the next day. They stop at a Jain temple for prayer and meditation, and you wait for them there. Then you all leave to walk to the next town, about twenty kilometers away. The progress in walking is slow, because the nuns must watch where they walk and because some of them have been fasting and have diminished physical strength. When you arrive in the town at the end of

What Do YOU Think?

The most important Jain teaching in the world today is nonviolence as a way of life.

Strongly Disagree   Strongly Agree
1   2   3   4   5   6   7

the day, you bid a fond farewell to them all. As you're about to leave, one of them startles you with the question "Why don't you become a monastic yourself?"

See photos of an actual visit with Jain nuns.

Jainism is an ancient religion of India that follows a path of doing no harm to any living being. Your introduction to Jainism will soon encounter these unique features:

- Jainism is similar in many ways to Buddhism but has been a distinct Indian religion for more than two thousand years.

- Jainism shares much vocabulary (*karma*, *nirvana*, and other terms) with Hinduism and Buddhism, but usually with a wrinkle: The Jain nuance of these words is different.

- Jainism teaches self-effort to bring one's soul to release from constant reincarnation. However, this goal can be accomplished only by those who become a monk or a nun; other Jains keep a lesser version of Jain practice, and have lesser goals.

- Jains have one of the most challenging and restrictive diets in the world, but they are remarkably healthy and prosperous.

- With an estimated 4 million followers,

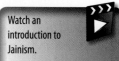
Watch an introduction to Jainism.

< Coconut offerings at the feet of the statue of Gommateshvara, a Jain hero, in Shravanabelagola, India.

Jina [JEE-nuh] "Conqueror," a person who has achieved Jain enlightenment

Jains [jines] "Followers of the Conquerors," all who follow Jain religion

ahimsa [ah-HIM-zuh] "Doing no harm" toward all the living things in this world

Mahavira [MAH-hah-VEER-ruh] "Great Hero" whose given name was Vardhamana, the twenty-fourth and last Tirthankara of this age and the founder of Jainism

Jainism is among the smallest of the faiths called "world religions." However, the contribution of Jainism, both directly and indirectly through other religions, is much more significant than what might be expected from its small numbers.

LO1 The Name *Jainism*

Jainism (JINE-ism) is commonly traced to the Sanskrit word for "conquer." This conquering refers to the battle Jains wage within themselves to gain the full knowledge that leads to enlightenment. The person who has achieved Jain enlightenment is called a **Jina**, "Conqueror," and all who follow this religion are called

Jains, "followers of the Conquerors." In particular, Jains are followers of the Jina who founded Jainism, **Mahavira** (MAH-huh-VEER-uh), but the religion was never named after Mahavira. He is the main model of how to achieve enlightenment, but he himself does not enlighten people or rescue them from error.

> *The name Jain is so important that Jains have done something unique in the religions of the world—many of them have taken Jain as their family name.*

Jainism or *Jaina Dharma* ("Teaching of the Conquerors") probably replaced a more generic name from the earliest Jain scriptures, *Nirgrantha* (neer-GRAHN-thuh) *Dharma*, "Teaching of the Bondless Ones." The name *Jain* is so important to its followers that they have done something

Read a brief overview of Indian geography.

A Closer Look:

The Symbol of Jainism

Until recently, the most commonly used symbol of Jainism has been the *swastika*, an ancient and widespread Asian religious symbol with none of the racist overtones that the swastika has for Westerners today. The Jain swastika is often seen with four dots in it. (See page 61 for more on the swastika.)

BONNIE VAN VOORST © CENGAGE LEARNING

In 1975, Jain representatives at a meeting to commemorate the 2,500th anniversary of Mahavira's death drew up an image as an official symbol for the Jain religion, one of the few world religions to have an officially adopted symbol. Since then, this symbol has become widely accepted and used. One sees it in almost all Jain official publications, religious magazines, and even in religious greeting cards and wedding announcements.

The overall shape of the image is modeled on the human torso, a shape Jains believe the universe shares. The small arc at the top symbolizes a realm above heaven. All liberated souls reside there as individual beings, forever in a blessed state, freed from the recycling of souls through life and death. The three dots just below the zone of liberation stand for the "three jewels": right belief, right knowledge,

and right conduct. By gaining these three jewels, one can achieve the liberated zone.

In the next portion, there is a swastika, which is said to have several different meanings. As a wheel, it suggests the eternal nature of the material world. It represents the four parts of the Jain community: monks, nuns, male laity, and female laity. It also represents the four infinite characteristics of the soul: knowledge, perception, happiness, and energy. (Some North American and European Jains substitute a different symbol for the swastika.) The symbol of the human right hand in the lower portion shows openness and fearlessness. The circle in the middle of the hand is a wheel with twenty-four spokes of light, symbolic of the twenty-four ancient teachers of the religion. The word in the center of the circle is **ahimsa**, "doing no harm" toward all the living things in this world. Ahimsa is the key to liberating oneself from the cycle of reincarnation, and the spokes emanate as light from this key word. A phrase at the bottom does not always appear with the use of this symbol. Sometimes it is translated as "Live and let live," but this is a cliché in contemporary English. It's better to translate it, "Let all creatures help one another."

unique in the religions of the world—many of them have proudly taken the name of their religion as their family name.

LO2 The Jain Present as Shaped by Its Past

For 30 years, the Jain monk Gurudev Shree Chitrabhanu (CHIT-ruh-BAHN-oo) was a spiritual leader for Jains in India. He walked more than 30,000 miles there, barefoot. Deciding to give up his monastic vows, he left India in 1970 to attend conferences in Switzerland and in Boston. He did so at first to raise funds and recruit volunteers to help Indians impacted by famines and floods. Then Chitrabhanu wrote educational materials from Jain scriptures that he said could apply to Jains and non-Jains alike, and he interacted with people of other religions in ways that were unusual for a Jain. Eventually, he settled in New York City, where he married, took up the life of a householder, and founded the Jain Meditation Center. In several ways, Chitrabhanu embodies the tension between the historic values of an ancient religion and the challenges of modern life, especially in the West.

Seated Tirthankara in the Jain temple, Mumbai

© OSTILL/SHUTTERSTOCK.COM

Most Jains believe that their religion has no founder and no early history. For them, Jainism has always existed and will always exist in the future, even though it goes through long cycles of decline and reform just as the world does. Historians of what Jains consider their present cycle can trace out the main lines of Jain history and point to moments of its founding, growth, and change. These moments help us to explain how Jainism got to be the way it is today.

Jains believe that their religion has always existed and will exist forever.

FOUNDING AND THE FIRST THOUSAND YEARS (600 B.C.E.–C. 400 C.E.)

Jainism arose during the sixth century B.C.E. in the Ganges (GAN-jeez) River valley of northeastern India, a time and place of intense religious activity and reform.

Jains opposed the dominant Hindu priestly groups who emphasized salvation by the sacrifices that these priests performed and interpreted. The new religious perspectives promoted **asceticism**, physical denial and mental self-discipline as a necessary part of liberation. They also promoted the abandonment of sacrificial rituals and the pursuit of enlightenment that brings freedom from **reincarnation**, the unhappy passage of the soul at death from one body to another. Jainism began as a reform movement within Hinduism, but over time it grew into a distinct religion.

Jains believe that the present era has had a series of twenty-four religious leaders. The first Jain figure for whom there is some historical evidence is the twenty-third, Parshvanatha (parsh-VAHN-ah-thuh), a religious reformer who lived in the 600s B.C.E. He rejected Hindu sacrifices and taught the abandonment of worldly attachments. Jains regard Parshvanatha as the twenty-third of the twenty-four **Tirthankaras**, "ford finders" who lead the way across fords in the rivers of constant reincarnation. Tirthankaras are not gods, but enlightened humans whose stories and teachings point the way for others. Connected with this line of ford finders are figures from the Hindu tradition, most notably Krishna, regarded by the Jains as a cousin of the twenty-second Tirthankara. By incorporating and redefining key Hindu figures in their religion, Jains kept some contact with the surrounding Hindu world—important for Jain survival and growth—and yet distinguish themselves from it.

The twenty-fourth and last Tirthankara of this age was Vardhamana (VAHR-duh-MAHN-uh), who is known to all Jains as Mahavira, meaning "Great Hero." Mahavira is seen as the last and perfect teacher of true knowledge and practice, but most Jains would not call him the "founder" of their religion, because it has always existed. Mahavira is commonly said to have lived from 599 to 527 B.C.E., although

asceticism [ah-SET-uh-SIHZ-uhm] Physical denial and mental self-discipline, a necessary part of liberation in Jainism

reincarnation Unhappy passage of the soul at death from one body to another

Tirthankaras [tuhr-TAHN-kah-ruhz] "Ford-finders" who lead the way across fords in the rivers of constant reincarnation

some put him a century later. Accounts of Mahavira's life are preserved by the Jain scriptures, but these are filled with later, legendary material. They also vary in content, depending on which of the two main Jain groups is writing his story. Despite these historical challenges, these scriptures provide an adequate basis for our historical understanding of his life and the early Jain movement.

Like the Buddha, Mahavira was born in northeast India into the Kshatriya class of rulers and warriors. When he was around thirty years old, he renounced his privileged status and took up an ascetic life. Mahavira spent the next twelve years in strict asceticism, punishing his body in order to free his soul. After pushing himself to the point of death several times, he experienced a sudden flash of enlightenment that gave him omniscience, or full knowledge of everything in the universe. He then converted eleven male disciples as the nucleus of his movement and formed a monastic community with them. They had no permanent home but instead wandered as monks from place to place. Mahavira taught his followers extensively, but many Jains believe that after his enlightenment he taught by a divine sound that emanated from his body, which his followers could interpret into human words. He was no longer hungry, thirsty, or tired, nor did he age. Unlike the Buddha, who found a "middle way" between this intense self-denial and ordinary life, Mahavira and his followers kept to intense self-denial. After more than thirty years of activity, and after starving himself at the end of his life, Mahavira's body died and his soul reached full eternal blessing, never to be reincarnated again. Two of his original eleven disciples, Indrabhuti and Sudharman, survived Mahavira and led his movement into its second generation.

According to Jain tradition, Mahavira had 14,000 monks and 36,000 nuns in his movement at the time of his death. These numbers are probably exaggerated, but they accurately suggest that the movement grew rapidly at first, especially among women. Mahavira rejected the Hindu caste system, drawing his followers from any social and economic class. Jainism also made a transition from

being a movement of only those who could renounce ordinary life to a movement that had many more lay members than monastics. Early Jainism saw some disagreements over monastic doctrine and practice, as we might expect in a religion that prizes individual accomplishment. The main disagreement to arise early and last until today was a dispute over the degree of renunciation that monks and nuns should practice. Just how much self-denial is necessary for liberation? For example, some argued that they should wear white robes and have only minimal possessions, and others claimed that a true monk should be naked and have no possessions. (This nakedness never extended to nuns; Indian cultural attitudes could permit male nakedness in public, but never female nakedness.) Another dispute is also a gender issue: whether a soul can attain liberation from a woman's body, with some arguing that a soul must be reborn in a man's body to achieve release from reincarnation.

These disagreements took time to assume the formal shape we know today, with Jainism split into two main groups. The **Shvetambar** ("white-clothed" monks and nuns) group wears clothing as allowed by their scriptures. The **Digambar** ("sky-clothed," a euphemism for naked) group advocates nakedness for monks as a symbol of complete denial of the world. Shvetambar monks and nuns own only a few possessions, such as scripture books and a whisk for clearing away small beings as they walk, but Digambar monks typically own nothing. (The sight of naked monks out in public is a striking reminder of this total renunciation.) Digambars believe that a soul in a female body cannot reach liberation, but Shvetambars affirm that it can. The details of this split remain unclear, because the later accounts of the schism

Shvetambar [shveht-AHM-bahr] Jain group with "white-clothed" monks and nuns

Digambar [die-GAM-bahr] "Sky-clothed" Jain group with naked monks

Jain monks "clothed with the sky"

were designed to justify each sect and attack the other. So today, Shvetambar texts and images of Mahavira have him clothed, and Digambar texts and images have him naked.

The Shvetambar-Digambar division was probably made permanent by a series of Jain councils held to formalize the Jain scriptures, which had existed from earliest times as oral collections of teaching and monastic practice. A council held around 455 C.E. formally adopted the Shvetambar canon that is still in use today. Digambar monks refused to attend this meeting. They denounced the Shvetambar canon, and the split between the two communities became permanent.

During these early centuries, Jainism spread westward from the Ganges River valley, settling in areas where it could enjoy royal protection in the different Hindu kingdoms of northern India. Jain tradition claims that in the first century B.C.E. a monk even led a movement to overthrow a king, replacing him with a ruler more sympathetic to the Jains. During the Gupta (GOOP-tuh) dynasty in north India (320–600 C.E.), a time of Hindu revival there, many Jains left the Ganges valley area and migrated to southern, central, and western India. Jainism became stronger in these areas than it had been in its original home, and even though Jains are still concentrated in the north and west of India, Jainism gained a more national base throughout India, which it enjoys today.

> *It might seem strange that those who have renounced the world would advise rulers, but this is a long Indian tradition.*

THE NEXT THOUSAND YEARS (600–1600)

The early part of this next period saw the flourishing of Digambar Jainism. Achieving success in the region of modern-day Karnataka, the Digambars gained the support of three Indian kingdoms. As Jain monks did earlier, Digambar monks probably influenced the succession of some kings in these dynasties, thus guaranteeing royal patronage of the new religion. Jain monks acted as spiritual

teachers and advisers to many rulers and their advisors. (It might seem strange to us that those who have completely renounced the world would advise rulers, but this is a long Indian tradition.) For centuries kings, queens, state ministers, and generals gave tax revenues to the Jain community, providing richly for their temples and monasteries and for the support of Jain writers and artists. Most prominently, in 981 a general paid for a colossal statue of the Jain hero Gommateshvara (go-MAHT-esh-VAR-uh) at Shravanabelagola (SHRAH-vahn-BEL-uh-GOHL-ah). This statue is today one of the holiest and most popular sites in Jainism.

In the time of their greatest political influence from about 500 to 1200 C.E., Jain monks of both main groups gave up wandering asceticism and took up permanent residence in Jain temples or monasteries. The causes of this are disputed, but many historians point to the influence of money, power, and prestige that came from the patronage of monks by rulers. One contemporary legacy of this change is the Digambar practice of ordaining a monk to lead a Jain institution such as a temple, school, or foundation. In this practice, a new Digambar monk doesn't wander in a naked, ascetic state, but is a settled, clothed administrator. Some Jains saw these changes as a defection from Jainism's original ideals of ending attachments to the world, but they persist today.

Take a virtual tour of Shravanabelagola on Google Earth.

Visit an exhibition of Jain art.

Pouring liquefied turmeric, as a special blessing, on the statue of Gommateshvara

The Shvetambars in the north were less prominently involved in dynastic politics than were the Digambars to the south, but they held their own there. On the whole, however, this period of Jainism's second millennium belonged to the Digambars. The Shvetambar community suffered under the occupation of western and northern India by Muslim forces in the twelfth century, and the continuing Islamic power of the Mughal (MOO-guhl) Empire there. Jains in the north were persecuted and their important shrines were destroyed. Although some Jains served Muslim rulers as political advisers or teachers, they could not use this to regain their former position. Islam was not as tolerant toward Jainism as Hinduism was. The Shvetambar community was gradually compelled to redefine itself as a reduced and marginalized group, which probably contributed to the long-term survival of Jainism in India.

During this period, sects called *gacchas* (GOTCH-uhs) arose in the Shvetambar movement. Some of the most important of these sects still exist today, such as the Kharatara Gaccha founded in the eleventh century and the Tapa Gaccha founded in the thirteenth century. They included both monks and their lay followers. They differed from one another over issues of monastic lineage, veneration of images/idols, the sacred calendar, and scripture canons. Each claimed to be the true Jainism. According to tradition, their leading teachers sought to reform lax monastic practice and participated in the conversion of Hindus in western India, who subsequently became Shvetambar Jains. A more radical group, the Lonka Gaccha, did not accept the newer Jain practices of image veneration and worship in temples. Around 1653 they emerged as the **Sthanakvasi** ("meeting-house dweller") sect of Shvetambars. This division between Jains who are "idol worshipers" and those who are not

Sthanakvasi monk reads sutras.

COURTESY OF MR. SANJAY SURANA OF SHREE DIWAKAR PRAKASHAN

Sthanakvasi [sthahn-ahk-VAH-see] "Meeting-house dweller" sect that does not accept the newer Jain practices of image veneration and worship in temples

continues today. Both Shvetambar and Digambar movements have "idol worshipers" and "non-idol worshipers" among them.

EARLY MODERN TIMES THROUGH TODAY (1600–PRESENT)

These unhappy divisions provoked a variety of reform movements among the Shvetambar and Digambar laity. The most significant Digambar reform occurred in the early 1600s, led by the layman and poet Banarsidas (bah-NAHR-sih-dahs). This reform stressed the traditional mystical, austere steps on the Jain path. It also attacked the Digambar temple ritual and what it saw as the corruption and worldly comforts of leading monks.

By the middle of the 1800s, image-venerating Shvetambar monks had almost disappeared, and control of temples passed into the hands of semimonastic leaders. Monastic life, however, experienced a revival due to charismatic monks such as Atmaramji (1837–1896), and the number of Shvetambar image-venerating monks and nuns grew to approximately 1,500 and 4,500, respectively, by about 2000. The image-venerating Tapa sect is now the largest group of Shvetambars; the non-image-venerating Shvetambar sects, the Sthanakavasis and Terapanthis, are much smaller in number. At present all the Shvetambar groups together have about 2,500 monks and 10,000 nuns, and Digambar groups have about 550 monks and 500 nuns, according to a Jain accounting in 2006. As we saw above, the total number of Jains in the world today is about 5 million, so the proportion of monastics is low indeed.

In modern times both the Shvetambars and Digambars in India have devoted much energy to preserving temples and publishing their religious texts. Modern Jains also have been involved in social and economic relief for the general public, such as drought relief in India in the 1980s. They support Jain widows and the community's poor. They maintain animal-rescue shelters to save them from slaughter as a part of their strict teachings on nonviolence and vegetarianism. A unifying movement within Jainism grew in the twentieth century. For example, in 1974 a committee

Read the *Saman Suttam*.

with representatives from every sect compiled a new common text recognized by all Jain groups, called the *Saman Suttam* (SAH-muhn SOOT-ahm). Given the divisions in Jainism, this common scripture was a significant accomplishment and has served to unify contemporary Jains.

LO3 Essential Jain Teachings

A Jain monk, after a long and fruitful life, decides to begin the process of "holy death." He has already gained the permission of his monastic order, and he has the required physical strength and soundness of mind to carry it out. He travels to a place of Jain pilgrimage and ritually "leaves his body" there. After taking vows to fulfill this ritual, he begins to eat nothing and to drink only milk and water. Then, after a week, he drinks only water on every third day. About a month after beginning this process, the monk is so physically weakened that he dies, surrounded by a large crowd of reverent witnesses. This "holy death" isn't as common among Jains today as it was centuries ago, but it ritually affirms many key teachings of Jainism. The soul of one who dies this way will find a blessed reincarnation.

Idol veneration: miniature Gommateshvara statue at the foot of the main statue

PHOTO BY MATT LOGELIN

Our survey of Jain history has introduced many of the key teachings of Jainism. In this section, we'll look at these important teachings more closely.

No Gods

Strictly speaking, Jainism has no gods, and some have called it an atheistic (or at least a nontheistic) religion. Because the world is eternal, there is no need for a divine being to create it. Also, the process of karma and reincarnation works on its own, because it is a part of the universe itself and does not need a deity to preside over it. The way to salvation is shown by human "ford finders" and must be accomplished by one's own effort, not given by any divine being. Thus, Jainism not only *has* no gods, it *needs* no gods. Sometimes one will hear Jains in the West say that all liberated souls together are the God of Jainism, but this is not a traditional Jain understanding.

Jainism is sometimes called an atheistic religion.

Although most Jains do believe in good and evil spirits and other heavenly beings, these are not considered gods. Jain lay followers worship some spirits of earth and heaven for daily protection and guidance, but not for eternal release. Ritual veneration of Tirthankaras is done mainly to dedicate oneself more fully to finding one's own release by moral and mental practice, just as they found release on their own.

Time and the World

Time is real to Jains, who compare it to a turning wheel with twelve spokes; six spokes go in an ascending direction and six in a descending direction. The ascending direction is a time of improvement. In this time, humans progress in knowledge and goodness, and liberation from reincarnation is possible. In the descending direction, all human life—including religion—deteriorates, and liberation is not possible. The two directions make one whole rotation of the wheel of time, a **kalpa** (Sanskrit for "eon"). Hindus think that a kalpa is 4.3 billion years; Jains haven't usually been that precise, but they do think that a kalpa is a very long time. Because Jains hold the universe to be eternal, without beginning or end, these kalpas repeat themselves forever, turning like an eternal wheel.

Unlike some forms of Hinduism and Buddhism, Jainism views the visible, physical world as real, not illusory. The world is eternal and uncreated. It did not come into existence, and it will not pass out of existence. The world is made up of five eternal building blocks of reality: soul, matter, space, motion, and rest. These elements are eternal, but their relationships change constantly, and their interaction makes the cosmos and everything in it "run."

kalpa [CALL-puh] Sanskrit for "eon," one whole rotation of the wheel of time

Jains divide the universe into four parts. The lowest part, hell, is subdivided into seven levels, each layer darker and more painful than the one above it. Jain depictions of hell are meant to teach about the nature of evil and warn people away from it. The middle world has many concentric continents, all with life on them, and separated by seas. At the center are the two continents where humans live, the only area where souls can achieve liberation. The heavenly world consists of twelve levels in two layers: one for the souls of those who are far from their liberation and another just above it for those who are close to their liberation. Souls become reincarnated from this heaven after a period of rest. At the top of the cosmos is the eternal home of souls who have permanently escaped the material world.

Read "The World Is Uncreated" from Jain scripture.

JIVA AND AJIVA

According to Jains, the cosmos is made up of **jiva**, a soul or a living substance, and **ajiva**, something not a soul, or an inanimate substance. The essential characteristics of jiva are consciousness, bliss, and energy. Jivas, which are infinite in number, are either immobile or mobile. Immobile souls have only one sense: touch. They inhabit tiny particles of earth, water, fire, and air, and are also found in plants of all sorts. Mobile souls inhabit bodies with between two and five sense organs.

As Jains say, just as a lamp can light up a large or small room, a jiva can fill both the smaller and the larger bodies it occupies. The soul assumes the exact dimensions of the body it occupies and causes it to live. At death it keeps this shape until it is reincarnated again. Jainism is unique among many south Asian faiths in its teaching that individual souls are not all a part of one cosmic soul that will return to it, but rather that each soul (jiva) is eternally individual.

jiva [JEE-vuh] Soul, a living substance

ajiva [AH-jee-vuh] Not a soul, an inanimate substance

karma [KAR-muh] "Deeds" and the negative result of deeds; small matter that attaches to the soul and causes it to be reborn after death

moksha [MOHK-shah] Release from reincarnation

KARMA AND LIBERATION

Each soul in itself is pure. However, the soul is made impure through time by its contact with matter, or ajiva. When this ajiva influences the chain of birth and death, it is called **karma**, "deeds" and the negative result of deeds. Karma is a form of matter so small that some modern Jains call it "fine dust" or even in modern times "atomic." If the body that a soul inhabits dies, that soul may be reborn in any of four types of living beings: humans on earth, beings in the twelve heavens, beings in the seven hells, or animals and plants.

To be free from the shackles of karma and reincarnation, a person must stop the influx of new karma and eliminate all previous karma. (Some Jains speak informally of "bad karma," but that is redundant—all karma is bad karma.) Acquired karma can be "worn away" by many different activities: fasting, restricting one's diet to approved Jain foods, controlling taste and other senses, retreating to lonely places, strict discipline of the body, modesty, service, reading Jain scriptures, meditation, and controlling one's ego. Because of karma a soul is confined in a series of bodies and must advance in spiritual development before becoming free from this confinement.

> Most Jains don't believe that anyone can reach liberation in the present period of cosmic decline.

Release from reincarnation, called—as in Hinduism—**moksha**, is the central teaching of Jainism. Liberation of the soul is prevented by the accumulation of karma. This karma attaches to the soul, making it too heavy to ascend after the death of the body to the abode of the Jinas. Because it hasn't reached this permanent home, the soul must be reincarnated. This process also has the effect of preventing the self-realization, happiness, and freedom of the soul—all elements of Jain

Sculpture of the Jain wheel adorns the roofline of a Jain temple in Rajasthan, India.

DINODIA PHOTOS/BRAND X PICTURES/JUPITERIMAGES

Three stories of the Jain cosmos

truths. Along with subjective knowledge, scripture knowledge is based on external conditions perceived by the senses and known in the mind.

3. *Unmediated knowledge* involves supersensory perception (what we might call "extrasensory perception," or "ESP" for short), reading the thoughts of others (clairvoyance), and knowing everything there is to be known about other beings and things (omniscience).

4. *Direct, immediate knowledge* is knowledge of one's soul in its pure form; this brings liberation from reincarnation. A person with this knowledge is a **kevalin**, "possessor of omniscience."

According to Jainism, yoga—the physical and meditative discipline that yokes the soul and body—is the means to attain omniscience and liberation. Yoga cultivates true knowledge of reality, faith in the teachings of the Tirthankaras, and pure conduct. It helps one to reach the goal of Jainism, to free one's soul to have its true nature.

LO4 Ethics: The Five Cardinal Virtues

A Jain blogger in Great Britain raises a question: Why do some people have extra-marital affairs, sometimes one after the other? After discussing how common it might be among her friends and acquaintances, she goes deeper to analyze the possible causes. She invites comments on this observation from her Jain belief: Marital infidelity is caused by the attraction of evil masquerading as something positive. It leads to the loss of self-control and self-esteem, and ultimately it results in the accumulation of much karma.

Liberation from the cycle of reincarnation is the ultimate goal of Jains, but this isn't accomplished only by meditation and knowledge. Jains believe that one must first practice the following five moral principles in thought, speech, and action. They aren't "rules" as such, but ways to live according to the true nature of the soul. The principles are directed against practices that harm one's *jiva*, and harm others as well, by increasing its

nirvana. Persons are called "victors" (*Jinas*) because they have achieved liberation. This is accompanied by a great inner peace. The process of liberation is difficult, because it demands a near-perfect mental, moral, and physical observance of Jainism. Most Jains don't believe that anyone can reach liberation in the present period of cosmic decline. Thus, Jain monks and nuns do not seek immediate enlightenment. Instead, they practice Jainism as well as they can to pursue a reincarnation that will bring them closer to liberation. In other words, they take "one step at a time," in one life at a time, to liberation.

THEORIES OF KNOWLEDGE

In religions that have a large role for meditation in the quest for deliverance, theories of knowledge can get complex, especially for nuns and monks. Jainism has theories of arising, change, and decay in a world of space and time that is real, as opposed to permanence based on a hidden spiritual reality (for many Hindus) and impermanence of all things (for most Buddhists). The Jains developed a complex theory of knowledge with four stages.

1. *Subjective knowledge* is ordinary observation, recognition, determination, and impression.

2. *Scripture knowledge* is based on one's reading and meditation on scriptures and general religious

nirvana [near-VAH-nuh] In Jainism, the self-realization, happiness, and freedom of the soul

kevalin [keh-VAHL-in] "Possessor of omniscience," a person who has attained liberation from reincarnation

attachment to *ajiva*. Jain scriptures call them "vows," particularly "greater vows" for monks and nuns and "lesser vows" for lay folk. As these terms imply, the degree to which the principles are practiced is usually stricter for monks and nuns than it is for the laity. Lay Jains are encouraged to practice them in a way that is appropriate to their life in the world, but monks and nuns must observe them strictly.

Watch a video about guiding principles of Jain life.

DO NO HARM; SPEAK THE TRUTH

The fundamental moral command in Jainism is *ahimsa*: "Do no harm" to any other living being, whether humans, animals, plants, or microscopic organisms. Compassion for all life, both human and nonhuman, is central to Jainism. *Ahimsa* is sometimes interpreted as not physically harming another human, but it is much larger than that. One must not injure others physically or spiritually in thought, word, or deed. Jains have a strict diet, because all animals and many plants have souls, and to kill them causes their souls to undergo reincarnation. Mohandas Gandhi, the twentieth-century Hindu who led the struggle for Indian independence from Great Britain with nonviolent opposition, was deeply influenced by the Jain practice of ahimsa. Through Gandhi, nonviolent resistance to social evils spread to South Africa and the United States in their civil rights movements, and ahimsa found a wide, deep role in the world.

Ahimsa also caused all Jains long ago to give up farming, which does harm to many souls in the soil. Jains went into commerce and finance instead, where they prospered, and today many Jains are also in the medical and engineering professions. Monks and nuns practice a strict form of ahimsa. They often wear a cloth over the mouth to avoid harming small insects near them, and they gently whisk away small insects as they walk along, and especially before they sit down. In sum, for monks and nuns, ahimsa entails taking no life at all. For laity, it prohibits taking life needlessly.

One must always speak the truth and never deceive others. This is an essential part of "doing no harm." Saying and hearing the truth often depends on one's perspective, and Jains promote "not one-sidedness," the ability to see and explain all sides of an issue. So one must see that what one says is correctly understood and that true communication takes place. One must speak the truth as long as it does no harm. If speaking truth will lead to another person's harm, one should be silent. But lying to avoid harm is not an option.

DO NOT STEAL; DO NOT BE POSSESSIVE

The commands not to steal or be possessive apply especially to Jain laity. Monks and nuns have only a few possessions (Shvetambars) or no possessions at all (Digambars). Jains must not take any object that is not willingly and fairly given. One must be satisfied with one's possessions, and then one will not steal. Also, one must labor, buy, and sell honestly. Any attempt to get the better of others financially is considered theft. Some particulars of "do not steal" are:

- Always give people a fair price for their labor or products. To use one's business power to force an unfair, harmful price is forbidden.

- Never take things that are not offered to you.

- Never take things that are left, dropped, or forgotten by others. Return them if you can, or leave them where they are.

- Never purchase things if they are made in a way that does harm to others.

Because Jains have such strict norms for truth and honesty, they have a reputation in India for being scrupulously honest businesspeople. This in turn has contributed to their prosperity.

> *Jains have a reputation in India for being scrupulously honest businesspeople.*

Possessiveness does not always result from owning things, but results from emotional attachment to a possession. When that happens, one is owned by one's possessions, and a temptation to steal may arise. Monks and nuns must be non-possessive when they enter the celibate state, having no lingering feelings for the possessions they left behind. By detaching oneself from possessions, including home and family, one takes a first step to liberation. Householders are non-possessive when they are not emotionally tied to the things they own. Householders are to relate to people and objects as their manager or steward, not as their owner. True non-possessiveness also means that one can lose one's possessions without having it affect one's inner self.

A Closer Look:

Jainism and Food

Jain vegetarianism is based on the principle of "doing no harm" to other living beings rather than on any principles of health and nutrition, is more radical than Hindu vegetarianism. Monks and nuns follow these dietary practices strictly, and the laity in a basic (but still careful) way.

Jains practice a unique concept of extended vegetarianism. Not only do they eat no meat, they also abstain from root vegetables such as potatoes, garlic, onions, mushrooms, and radishes. However, they consume rhizomes such as dried turmeric and dried ginger and prefer plantains to potatoes. The reason behind this restricted diet is that root vegetables, which are grown underground, are believed to contain far more bacteria than other vegetables, and all these bacteria are living beings with souls.

Jains refuse any food, whether from animals or plants, obtained with what they consider to be unnecessary cruelty. Many have a diet similar to veganism (no dairy products) in order to avoid harm to souls in processed dairy products such as cheese, although unpasteurized milk is a common drink. Observant Jains do not eat or drink between sunset and sunrise, when more harm is done to small living things because the fire attracts small creatures that cannot be seen. Jains drink water that is gradually boiled for purification and then cooled to room temperature, to allow tiny beings to escape in the process.

BE CHASTE

All sexual intercourse binds one to karma, so it is best to avoid it as much as possible. This includes thinking about it as well as doing it. For monks and nuns, being chaste entails complete abstinence from all sexual intercourse and any other type of sexual activity. For them, chastity means celibacy. Lay Jains must be faithful within marriage to uphold chastity in a way appropriate for them. Sex outside of marriage is seen as particularly powerful in attracting karma.

In addition to keeping their version of these five principles, lay Jains who want a better reincarnation are urged to do a variety of things. Among them are to limit their travel, limit the number and value of their possessions, guard against avoidable evils, devote specific times to meditation, and observe periods of self-denial. Bringing oneself into close contact with monks and nuns is also urged, such as spending occasional days as a monk or a nun, or giving alms in support of monks and nuns.

Read a modern Jain's reflection on root vegetables.

LO5 Jain Ritual and Worship

Near Shravanabelagola, India, at the massive statue of the Jain hero Gommateshvara carved from one piece of rock in 981 C.E., a variety of religious activities are taking place. At the foot of the statue, dozens of well-dressed Jains reverently place fruit and flowers as offerings to the hero. Coconuts are especially common. Devotees are sitting on mats, reading Jain scriptures, saying prayers and mantras, and meditating. At times they break out in song and dance, both celebratory and reverent. At the top of the statue, accessible by a flight of stairs, a group of Jain men prepare to pour buckets of colorful, fragrant liquids on the head of the statue, to venerate the statue and pay honor to the Jain ideal of finding release from reincarnation. When standing at the statue's feet, the worshipers must look up to see the inspiring vision of the Jina against the vastness of the sky. His face is designed to inspire serenity and peace in those who look on it in faith.

> Read a British Jain woman's blog on the importance of inner attitudes in worship and morality.

THE LIFE OF MONKS AND NUNS

Monks and nuns live lives of strong self-denial and self-control in order to liberate their souls at some point in their future lives. They have permanently left their families and spend days in ritual activities: study of scripture, recitation of scripture, meditation, going on "begging rounds" for their main daily meal, and occasionally teaching laity. The entire life of monks and nuns is directed toward the eternal welfare and liberation of their souls. We should now look at some of the details.

Jain nuns in meditation, focused on a wrapped scripture book

Monk and nuns always walk, and always have bare feet, no matter the weather. They don't use any vehicle—such as an automobile, ship, plane, or even a cart—for traveling, because this harms more tiny beings than walking does. (No Jain monk traveled to Europe or North America until the 1890s, and his trip by ship was controversial among Jains.) By not wearing shoes they can more easily avoid crushing the bugs or insects on the ground. As they wander, they preach the religion and provide spiritual guidance. They typically go around in groups of at least two. They don't stay more than a few days in any one place, except during the Indian rainy season, which lasts for about four months. This constant movement is intended to avoid developing attachment to material things and the people they meet.

Jain monks and nuns neither cook their food nor have others cook it for them. They go once every day to Jain households and receive from each house a little uncooked food suitable for raw consumption (householders don't have to prepare more food after the monks have departed). Unless a cook is very careful, the cooking process involves much violence to small creatures in the fire, vegetable chopping, and water consumption; monks and nuns don't want to be a part of any violence. They don't accept any food or drink outside the house, but instead go inside where the food is cooked or kept. This is out of concern for small creatures more numerous outside than inside. When they return to their religious quarters

or to their temporary home if they are wandering, they eat their food in one main meal for each day, sometimes leaving a little for a smaller, unheated meal or a snack.

Jain monks and nuns don't shave their heads or even cut their hair, nor do they go to a barber. They regularly pluck out the hair on their head, or they have others do it. This plucking is a form of self-discipline and self-denial in which one bears pain calmly.

As stated above, Digambar monks are traditionally naked at all times, but there are exceptions. Digambar nuns and all Shvetambar monks and nuns wear unstitched white clothes. For monks, a loin cloth covers the midsection and reaches below the knee, another cloth covers the upper part of the body, and another cloth passes over the left shoulder and covers the body almost to the ankles. They also carry a woolen bed sheet and a woolen mat to sit on. Those who wear clothes have a square or rectangular piece of cloth either in their hand or tied on their face, covering the mouth. They also have a small broom of soft woolen threads to clean away insects before they sit or while they are walking. Digambar monks who do not wear any clothes often have a broom and mouth cloth in their hands, but do not wear them or hang them from their bodies.

Monks and nuns give a blessing on all Jains they meet, especially the saying "May you attain spiritual prosperity." They make no distinctions between class or caste, or gender or age. Some put a little sandalwood dust on the heads of Jains as a sign of blessing. In sum, monks and nuns show and teach the path of wholesome life and of a righteous and disciplined existence to all Jains. At the end of their

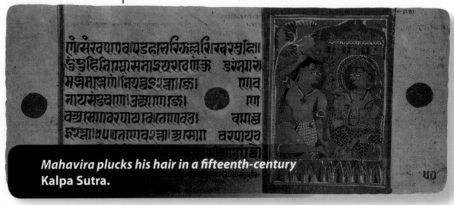

Mahavira plucks his hair in a fifteenth-century **Kalpa Sutra.**

lives, monks and nuns traditionally have the option to practice self-starvation, called "holy death," but this is no longer a common practice—if it ever was.

LIFE OF THE LAITY IN WORSHIP AND DEVOTION

Observant Jain laity have a number of daily rituals. Because Jainism arose in Hindu India and has existed mainly in India for more than two thousand years, many of these are adapted from Hinduism or formed in opposition to Hinduism. Ritual acts of compassion and ahimsa include spreading grain as food for the birds in the morning and filtering or boiling water for the next few hours' use. Worship before Jain images kept in one's home—bowing to them and lighting a lamp in front of

Jain temple in Kerala, India

© ISTOCKPHOTO.COM/TRAVELER1116

them—is an ideal way to start the day for many Jains. Some Jains oppose these rituals as no better than Hindu worship, or even as superstition. Others recognize that, while the Jain idols have no spiritual power in themselves, daily veneration of them promotes a reverent state of mind. Meditation is done early in the morning and perhaps also at noon and night. It typically lasts for forty-eight minutes (twice the number of the twenty-four Tirthankaras) and has periods of quiet recollection and spoken prayer. It involves letting go of all passions and negative attitudes and gaining a sense of purity and peace.

Some Jains oppose the veneration of images as superstitious.

The main prayer of Jainism is the **Namokar Mantra**. The term *mantra* correctly suggests that this prayer is brief. It is always repeated in its original language of Sanskrit, in which *namokar* means "I bow." In

Listen to the Namokar Mantra.

English translation, it reads: "I bow to the Prophets. I bow to the Liberated Souls. I bow to the Spiritual Leaders. I bow to the Teachers. I bow to all the Holy Ones." This prayer, if spoken in true faith, is thought to destroy sins and obstacles and help the one who prays it to move down the road to liberation.

More-elaborate worship is usually done in the temple. Jain temples in India are typically for individual worship and meditation, which can be carried out on any day at any time. In Europe and North America, the Jain community gathers for group activities. The worshiper enters the temple with the words "I bow to the Jina" and then banishes distracting thoughts about everyday affairs. Worship, or *puja*, can take many forms:

- The ritual bathing of the image. A simple, symbolic act is to touch one's forehead with the liquid used to wash the image.

- A series of prayers over three days in a temple to help remove karma that obstructs the rising of the soul to release from reincarnation.

- Paying respect to the images of the Tirthankaras. This can take the form of bowing before them, sitting reverently in prayer or meditation in their presence, or making small offerings of approved fruit and flowers.

- A ritual of prayer focused on a lotus-shaped image that has the "five praise-worthy beings": a Tirthankara, a liberated soul, a religious teacher, a religious

Namokar Mantra
[NAHM-oh-cahr MAHN-truh] Main prayer of Jainism, repeated in its original language of Sanskrit

Women worshiping in the Jain temple, Ranakpur, India

NICHOLAS DEVORE/STONE/GETTY IMAGES

Read a Jain blog on reading the *Kalpa Sutra* during Paryusana.

ceremonies are held in the temple, the most prominent being long readings of the *Kalpa Sutra*, the most important scripture for Shvetambars, to the congregation. On the final day of Paryusana, Jains seek forgiveness from family, friends, and foes for any wrong acts against them in the previous year. Shortly after Paryusana a dinner is often held, when all Jains gather and eat together, regardless of their socioeconomic status.

For Jains, **Diwali**, the Indian festival of lights, remembers Mahavira's death. The festival falls at the end of the Indian calendar year, in October or November. The eighteen kings of northern India who, according to legend, were with Mahavira when he died decided that the light of their master's knowledge would be best remembered by lighting of lamps.

leader, and a monk. This image also depicts the "four qualities" that benefit one's soul: perception, knowledge, conduct, and austerity.

As we saw above, the members of some sects of Jainism do not worship or venerate the images found in temples. They will be found there at times, but not participating in any of these rites. Instead, they engage only in meditation and silent prayer in the temple.

Two Jain Festivals

Like most other religions in India, Jainism has many festivals, and like most religious festivals, cultural and religious elements are mixed together in the celebrations. In what follows, we will deal briefly with the two most important festivals, Paryusana and Diwali.

Paryusana (also spelled *Paryushan*) is the most important festival for Jains, an eight-day period that falls in August or September. Paryusana is a time to make amends for bad acts of the prior year; one engages in austerities to shed accumulated karma. It also helps to control the desire for sensual pleasures, preventing new karma. During this period, some people abstain from eating and drinking for all eight days and some for three days, but it is obligatory to fast at least on the last day. Regular

Paryusana [PAR-yoo-SAHN-uh] Most important festival for Jains, an eight-day period of repentance and fasting

Diwali [dee-WALL-ee] Indian festival of lights; for Jains, marks the anniversary of Mahavira's death

LO6 Jainism in North America Today

In Chicago, a thirtyish computer engineer named Churinder Jain worships weekly at the Jain temple. Like other Jains around the world, he offers prayers for his blessing in this world, and especially for eventual release from endless reincarnation. He also makes small offerings to statues of Tirthankaras who have found this release. But there is another reason he comes to the temple, one not so spiritual: to talk to married Jain women who serve as unofficial matchmakers

Jains, Sikhs, and Hindus celebrate Diwali together in Coventry, England.

EVERHEARDOFASPACEBAR

in his search for a suitable Jain wife. He is looking for a young woman who is educated and cultured, one who can live with him in Chicago. Even more, he wants a wife who is a faithful Jain, meditates every day, says her prayers, and observes a Jain diet. With their connections in India, the women are able to put him in touch with a suitable partner there, to whom he soon becomes engaged.

For more than two thousand years, Jains stayed in India, faithful to their duty to minimize travel and the damage it does to other beings. It wasn't until the 1800s that Jainism became a more worldwide faith. As a result of age-old trading links, many Jains from western India settled in eastern African countries that were, like India, in the British Empire—especially Kenya, where the first Jain temple outside India was built, and Uganda. They pursued commerce and international trade. Political unrest in the 1960s forced many of them to relocate to the United Kingdom. After the U.S. Immigration Act of 1965 dropped rigid quotas on peoples from Africa and Asia and encouraged immigration of "members of the professions of exceptional ability," Jains emigrated from India and Africa to America. Many Jain students came to the United States for higher education, and most of them stayed in the West. They often distinguished themselves in their fields, as for example Anshu Jain, who in 2010 became the head of Deutsche Bank's division of corporate and investment banking.

> ### Jain temples in North America often accommodate all the different Jain groups.

In North America, Jains have continued their traditional business and professional occupations. About 30 percent are engineers and 15 percent are in medicine, with others in banking, real estate, computers, and teaching. The high point of Jain immigration to the West was in the late 1970s and 1980s. In the United States, Jains number approximately 30,000, in the United Kingdom about 30,000, and in Canada about 10,000. Because of their prosperity and because Jains in North America are concentrated in ten states in the United States and one province in Canada, the Jain community has been able to build and operate over sixty social centers, temples, and other organizations. These are often combined in one building.

Jain temples sponsor worship (often held on Sunday mornings to fit a Western weekly calendar), education, and social fellowship. Although they have strong lay leadership, Jain temples in North America typically have no monks attached to them, so they function with little of the contact between monks and laity common in India. Another distinctive feature of North American temples and social centers is that most  of them accommodate all the different Jain groups to which their members belong. In this way, they further Jain unity and survival in a North American context that makes sectarian differences less important than in India.

A desire to preserve their religious identity in North America, and the increasing challenges of passing on their faith to their second and third generations, has led Jains to form organizations such the Federation of Jain Associations in North America (JAINA), founded in 1981. Like most local Jain temples and cultural associations, JAINA crosses the lines of regional Indian customs and the different Jaina sects. English-language publications such as the *eJain Digest* (available online) and *Jain Spirit* have presented Jain ideals such as nonviolence and vegetarianism to Jains and the wider world. Most recently, Jains have been addressing issues of environmentalism. Their religious convictions that the world is eternal and that one must do no harm to all its living beings strengthen their interest in a sustainable planet.

Visit the Jain Center of America in New York.

CHAPTER 5

Encountering Buddhism: The Middle Path to Liberation

BONNIE VAN VOORST © CENGAGE LEARNING

Learning Outcomes

After studying this chapter, you will be able to do the following:

LO1 Explain the meaning of *Buddhism* and related terms.

LO2 Summarize how Buddhism was founded and developed into what it is today, especially its diversity and geographic spread.

LO3 Outline the essential Buddhist teachings.

LO4 State the main ethical precepts of Buddhism for both monastics and laypeople.

LO5 Discuss the way Buddhists worship and meditate.

LO6 State the main features of Buddhist life in North America today.

© ISTOCKPHOTO.COM/ZORANI

"I take refuge in the Buddha; I take refuge in the Dharma; I take refuge in the Sangha." —Basic Buddhist affirmation

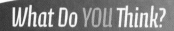

YOUR VISIT TO A ZEN RETREAT CENTER

Imagine that you're going on a weekend retreat to a Zen Buddhist temple and retreat center. You've read some popular books on Zen and can recite a few Zen riddles. The retreat will take you to Singapore in south Asia, but Zen centers in North America from Woodstock, New York, to San Diego, California, hold similar retreats.

As you walk into the temple, you notice a comfortable area where visitors can relax at a café near the entrance. You'll return there regularly during "rest time" during the retreat. It gives an impression of simplicity that is reflected in the whole retreat center. You then sign in and are required to surrender your cell phone—it will be given back when you leave, you are told. You are shown to your dormitory, where you notice about thirty woven straw mats in one large room, much like the sleeping arrangements in a Buddhist monastery. You claim one by placing on it the sleeping bag and pillow that you've brought with you.

Then you go to the main meditation hall. Meditation cushions have been neatly laid out throughout the hall, which has a white statue of the Buddha with small arrangements of flowers and small votive candles (but no incense) at one end. You also see a drum and handbell at the front. You begin each day with yoga and stretching exercises, so that the physical process of sitting in meditation won't distract your mind. Then come Buddhist prayers, both spoken and meditated, also for thirty minutes each. The center

of each day is several meditation sittings. They are only thirty minutes long and go quickly, with exercises such as yoga between them. Regular lectures and informal talks are given by the monks leading the retreat. You learn three different ways of meditation: breath meditation, self-questioning meditation, and "silent observation of the mind" meditation. You are also taught eight sitting positions and two sleeping positions.

You are awakened by the monks at 5 A.M., and lights-out is at 9:30 P.M. Three meals a day, all freshly prepared according to Buddhist dietary customs, are served buffet style. You are thankful that you don't have to go out begging for your food every morning as Buddhist monks do. You are surprised how hungry you get, and how good the food tastes, but then you remember with a little guilty feeling not to develop an attachment to the food—that's not Buddhist at all! So you quietly resolve not to go up for seconds any longer.

At the end of the retreat, you have your first and only small-group session to share experiences from the last three days. When you finally leave the retreat center with a friend, you notice that your "silent observation of the mind" meditation is continuing. You take in all the sights

Zen temple, Japan

JKT-C

< The lotus, a symbol of Buddhism, is a beautiful flower that grows over the muddy waters of this world.

Buddhism [BUHD-ihz-um] Religion of enlightenment

buddha [BUH-dah] Enlightened person; although Gautama is "the Buddha," the term applies to all individuals who attain this state

and sounds of the city, but your mind isn't affected by it. Your friend remarks, referring to the film, "It's like living in the Matrix!"

Encountering Buddhism can be a "mind-bending" experience. As you are introduced to Buddhism in this chapter, you will notice these features:

- Buddhism has many numbered lists of teachings and practices that must be learned, but Buddhism can't be known, much less lived, "by the numbers."

- Because all Buddhist teaching is said to flow from the Buddha and his carefully conceived system, we might expect it to be unified. However, Buddhism is one of the most diverse religions in the world, befitting a religion that teaches that all things are impermanent.

- Buddhists follow the life and teachings of the Buddha carefully, as the best model of the way to find liberation from suffering, the main problem with the world. But they also frequently quote the Buddha's saying "Don't believe because of what your teacher says—follow your own wisdom."

- Many Buddhists have no concept of an all-powerful god, but some Buddhists view the Buddha as a supreme heavenly being.

- Buddhism is unique among the major religions of the world in its combination of deep meditation and earnest morality, but most Buddhists who aren't monks or nuns don't meditate. Instead, they worship various buddhas and other divinities in ways that are similar to Hindu worship.

- Many people who call themselves Buddhists—especially in China, Japan, and the West—also practice other religions. They often say, "People of other religions can practice Buddhism too."

> *Buddhism is unique in its combination of deep meditation and earnest morality.*

Watch the introduction to a PBS-TV program on Buddhism.

Take a virtual tour of key Buddhist sites in India, Tibet, China, Korea, and Japan on Google Earth™.

LO1 The Name *Buddhism*

Buddhism is the religion founded by Siddhartha Gautama (sih-DAHR-tuh GOW-tah-muh), who became the Buddha. Despite the similarity of the words *Buddhism* and *Buddha*, the religion isn't named after him. **Buddhism** for most Buddhists means the religion of enlightenment, not the religion of the Buddha. The English word *Buddhism* didn't appear until the 1830s, but it expresses accurately enough the Asian Buddhist self-designations such as *Buddha Law, Buddha School,* or the *Teachings of the Buddha.* Today, *Buddhism* is happily used as the name for their religion by Buddhists in Europe and North America, and it is widely used in Asia as well. The related term the **Buddha**, or Enlightened One, usually refers to Siddhartha Gautama after his enlightenment. Both words derive from the ancient Sanskrit word *buddha*, "enlightened, awakened." *Buddhism* and *Buddha* are best pronounced BUHD-ihz-um and BUHD-ah, respectively, with first syllables that rhyme with *could*, but you will often hear BOOD-ihz-um and BOO-dah.

Buddhism teaches that anyone can become enlightened, even a buddha. Gautama is the model Buddha, but many Buddhists believe that he taught his followers to think for themselves and carefully examine the teachings of the religion to determine what is right for them. When anyone becomes fully enlightened, that person is a buddha too. So the word *Buddha* is a term, not a personal name. We'll stay true to this by referring in this chapter to *the Buddha*, with *the* and a capital *B*, when Gautama is meant. When another person who achieves the buddha nature is meant, we will omit *the* and use a lowercase *b*.

LO2 Buddhism Today As Shaped by Its Past

A layman sits in the lotus position in a temple in Busan, South Korea. He is meditating in turn on eight murals dealing with different events in the life of the Buddha. They deal with his birth through his death, but they center on the story of how he discovered the Middle Path to enlightenment and then shared it with others. As he finishes his contemplation on one picture, he shifts slightly and turns to the next until he finishes all of them. Many Buddhist temples have these series of pictures depicting the life of the Buddha. Both monks and lay folk find instruction and inspiration in them,

A Closer Look:

The Symbol of Buddhism

Buddhism is a diverse religion, and it is difficult to express in art the state of nirvana that the Buddha achieved, so Buddhism has many symbols. The swastika is one, seen often in temples and jewelry; the beautiful lotus blossom that grows out of the muck of the world is another; the deer is a third, especially used to symbolize Buddhist teaching; and the image of the Buddha in seated meditation is a fourth.

By far the most common Buddhist symbol, and perhaps the earliest, is the wheel. This is called the **dharmachakra**, "wheel of the teaching." It may look to you like the steering wheel of a ship, but it's really the wheel of a cart or chariot. Like most ancient religious symbols, it has multiple layers of meaning.

BONNIE VANVOORST © CENGAGE LEARNING

First, the Buddha "turned the wheel of the teaching" to get his movement going. Second, the wheel's implied motion is a metaphor for the rapid spiritual change created by the teachings of the Buddha. Third, the parts of the wheel summarize Buddhism. The wheel's rim represents the endless cycle of rebirth, which can only be escaped by means of Buddhist teachings. The eight spokes of the wheel symbolize the Noble Eightfold Path set out by the Buddha in his teachings. Its hub symbolizes moral discipline, which stabilizes the mind.

The wheel was a familiar symbol in early Buddhism. It stood not only for the Buddha's teachings, but for Gautama Buddha himself. Today, the dharmachakra is used in every Buddhist land. In statues of the Buddha, a wheel is sometimes on the palms of his hands and the soles of his feet. It also appears where he holds his hands in the circular dharmachakra position.

Buddhist wheel with deer on the roof of Jokhang Temple, Lhasa, Tibet

STEVE ALLEN/BRAND X PICTURES/JUPITER IMAGES

---

showing how the life of the Buddha continues to have a profound effect on Buddhists.

Today's Buddhism has a long and significant history behind it. Buddhists believe that Siddhartha Gautama discovered the "Middle Path" out of suffering, reaching the full enlightenment that rescued him from constant reincarnation into this world. This Middle Path is built on some Hindu ideas of the time and uses some similar vocabulary, but by and large Buddhism from the first was an alternative to Hinduism. The Buddha then taught his discovery to a monastic community that he founded. After his death, his teachings spread throughout the Indian subcontinent, and then over the next thousand years to most of Asia. In modern times, Buddhism has come to the West and has become the most widespread and arguably the most influential religion from Asia. With between 400 and 450 million adherents throughout the world, it is the fourth-largest religion after Christianity, Islam, and Hinduism. This section will recount Buddhism's story and introduce its diverse groups and teachings along the way.

dharmachakra [DAHR-muh-CHAHK-ruh] "Wheel of the teaching," a symbol of Buddhism

GAUTAMA'S ROAD TO ENLIGHTENMENT

Buddhism is founded on the life of Siddhartha Gautama (in the Pali language in which many Buddhist scriptures are written, *Siddhatha*

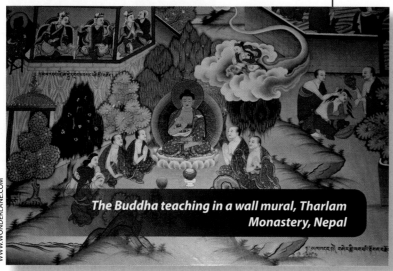

WWW.WONDERLANE.COM

The Buddha teaching in a wall mural, Tharlam Monastery, Nepal

Gotama). His life is known through scriptures written hundreds of years after his death. As Damien Keown has written, by the time it was written, the story of the Buddha's life "had become embellished with fanciful details, which makes it difficult to separate fact from legend."[1] Nevertheless, scholars have managed to discern in them a reliable outline of his life. This life is not what we would consider a modern biography, because Buddhist scriptures speak of only four key events in the Buddha's life: birth, enlightenment, first sermon, and death.

> By the time it was written down, the story of the Buddha's life "had become embellished with fanciful details, which makes it difficult to separate fact from legend."—Damien Keown

Siddhartha Gautama was born into a royal family in the northern Ganges River valley, in what is today southern Nepal, and lived for eighty years. Scholars disagree on the dating of his life. The traditional dating of his lifespan is about 566 to 486 B.C.E., but more-recent research tends toward 490 to 410 B.C.E. His family name was Gautama and his personal name was Siddhartha, but in the custom of the times his family name is used more than his personal name. In Buddhist texts he is most commonly addressed not as "Buddha" but as "Lord." Another common name for the Buddha is **Shakyamuni**, "the sage of the Shakyas," referring to the clan to which Gautama belonged.

Gautama's parents were Hindus, probably in the Kshatriya caste of warriors and rulers. An astrologer told his father, King Suddhodana, that their son would become either a powerful emperor or renounce this to become a powerful religious leader. Soon his mother, Queen Maya, dreamed that a white baby elephant entered her womb through her side. Ten lunar months later, her son was born from her right side. The whole earth reacted to his birth, and when Baby Gautama alighted by his own power on the ground, he proclaimed, "I am born for the salvation of the world; this is my last rebirth." These are probably legendary touches, of course. Gautama's early life as a prince was affluent and comfortable, protected from the ills of the world. At age sixteen he married the Princess Yashodhara, with whom he had a son. Until he was twenty-nine Gautama had a privileged, luxurious life as he waited to become king. However, this would soon change.

The story of the Buddha's enlightenment begins with a profound experience he had when he first observed the suffering of the world in the **Four Passing Sights**. On chariot rides outside the palace, Gautama saw for the first time (1) an old person, (2) a gravely ill person, (3) a human body on the way to cremation, and (4) a holy man who had renounced ordinary life. He was so shaken by the first three sights and attracted by the last sight that he renounced his wealth, his throne, and his family in order to become a holy man and answer his religious questions. During the next seven years, he received instruction from several Hindu teachers and practiced meditation with them. With five companions who were also holy men, he practiced extreme mental and physical self-denial that reduced him to "skin and bones." Eventually he passed out from weakness, and when he regained consciousness he knew that this extreme self-denial wouldn't lead to his goal. Instead, it weakened his

Chinese marketplace statues of Gautama Buddha and the jovial Maitreya Buddha flank a bust of Mao Zedong, the founder of Communist China and an implacable foe of religion.

www.cepolina.com

[1] Damien Keown, *Buddhism* (Oxford, UK: Oxford University Press, 1996), 17.

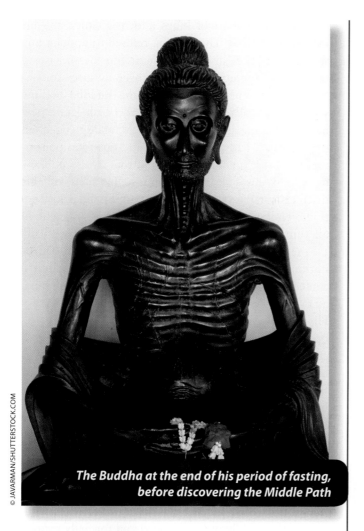

The Buddha at the end of his period of fasting, before discovering the Middle Path

© JAVARMAN/SHUTTERSTOCK.COM

tradition the "Bodhi Tree," or "Bo Tree" for short, he became *the Buddha.* Not only did he gain perfect knowledge of himself and the release this brought, but he also gained full knowledge of all his past lives. He could have passed immediately from life into full release, but he postponed this in order to help others find the way to liberation. From this point on, Buddhist scriptures call him the **Tathagata,** "one who has gone" to enlightenment, and the Buddha insisted that his followers call him by this name.

Middle Path Style of life between extreme self-denial and ordinary, indulgent life, which can lead to enlightenment

Tathagata [tah-THAH-gah-tuh] "One who has gone" to enlightenment; another honorific term of address for the Buddha

sangha [SAHN-guh] "Community" of Buddhist monks and nuns

View a film portrayal of Gautama's enlightenment.

"Decay is inherent in all things; work out your salvation with diligence!"—last words of the Buddha.

Watch a BBC presentation on the life of Gautama Buddha.

mind and even threatened his life. He then devised the **Middle Path** that could lead to enlightenment, a new way between the extreme self-denial characteristic of Hindu asceticism and the ordinary life of the Hindu householder. Hindus taught that liberation could be found in these two states, but the Buddha forged a new path between them.

ACHIEVEMENT OF ENLIGHTENMENT

Living in this Middle Path, the prince sat in long meditation under a tree in the city of Bodh Gaya (bohd GUY-uh) and achieved his own enlightenment. He reached an understanding of life that he would soon teach to his followers. Under the tree, called in Buddhist

The Buddha preached his first sermon in a deer park in Sarnath, India, announcing his discovery of the Four Noble Truths and the Eightfold Path, teaching that we'll consider below. For the next forty-five years, the Buddha taught throughout northeastern India and established an order of monks called the **sangha,** or "community."

In a scene from the film *Little Buddha, Siddhartha (played by Keanu Reeves) reaches enlightenment by the Bo Tree, accompanied by modern friends.*

© PHOTOS 12/ALAMY

Monks praying at the Bodhi Tree, Mahabodhi Temple, Bodhgaya, India.

received the support of kings and merchants, and his movement thrived. The Buddha refused to appoint any successor to guide his movement after his death, instead making the community of monks his only successor.

At about the age of eighty, the Buddha became seriously ill in Kusinara (KOO-sin-AHR-uh) and knew he would soon die. Some older scholarship suggested that he ate a bad piece of pork and got food poisoning, but most scholars now think that this is unlikely in light of his strict vegetarianism. He met with his disciples for the last time to impart his final instructions, ending with the words, "Decay is inherent in all things; work out your salvation with diligence!" He then laid down on his right side and went into meditation. He passed through several levels of meditative trance until, when he died, he passed into full nirvana, an event called his **parinirvana**.

His body was cremated on an open pyre according to Indian custom. His followers decided that the small parts of his body that remained—wood-fire cremation doesn't reduce stronger bones and teeth to ash—would be distributed as relics and enshrined in monuments.

Read a short explanation of "The Buddha in the Context of Buddhism."

Tour the Asia Society's exhibit on "Buddhist Art and Pilgrimage."

Soon after the Buddha's death, five hundred monks met at Rajagrha (rahj-AHG-ruh), India. The monastic rules and the teachings of the Buddha were finalized and formally recited. These rules, called the *Vinaya* (vihn-IGH-uh), were an oral collection for more than two centuries. The rules and teachings were recited and memorized at the council, and would soon be used in spreading the religion

In fact, Buddhism became the first of the world's religions to develop monasticism (muh-NAS-tuh-SIZ-uhm), a life of meditation, prayer, and self-control in a tightly regulated community of monks or nuns. (Sometimes lay Buddhists call their organizations a "sangha," but this is not the original or historic use of the term.) Laypeople are called upon to "take refuge" not only in the Buddha and in his teaching (dharma), but in the monastic community (sangha). These are called the **Three Refuges**, or sometimes the Three Jewels. The Buddha began the practice of going into the streets every morning on begging rounds to collect food, freeing up more time for the inner life. He

Three Refuges A basic statement of Buddhist belief and practice: "I take refuge in the Buddha; I take refuge in the dharma; I take refuge in the sangha."

parinirvana [PAHR-ee-near-VAHN-uh] The Buddha's passing into full nirvana at his death

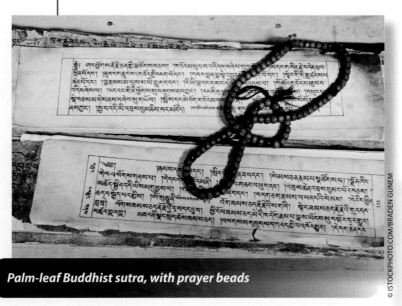

Palm-leaf Buddhist sutra, with prayer beads

to the many peoples and languages of India. Over time they would be written down and come to form the most important part of Buddhist scripture.

INDIA, SRI LANKA, AND THERAVADA

Buddhism became more diverse as it spread. The most significant split occurred after the second council, held around 375 B.C.E. After debates between those who advocated keeping strictly to what they considered the earliest practices of Buddhism and those advocating change, the second group left and called itself the "Great Sangha." This group belittled the traditionalists as **Hinayana**, or "small vehicle" Buddhists, but the traditionalists' self-designation **Theravada** eventually stuck. This name is usually translated as "tradition of the elders," but more accurately means "original/abiding teaching." Theravadins then developed a complex set of philosophical ideas beyond those elucidated by the Buddha. The Theravadins themselves experienced disagreements that led to many splinters. Over time, eighteen different Theravadin groups developed, each with its own distinctive teachings, and spread throughout India and Southeast Asia. Today, only one of these groups survives—the school stemming from the Sri Lankan Theravada.

> *Buddhism has been a "missionary religion" in ways that other Indian religions haven't.*

One of the most significant events in the development of Buddhism was the meeting of a Buddhist monk and the third-century B.C.E. Indian ruler named Ashoka (ah-SHOHK-uh). A ruler of the large Mauryan (MOHR-yuhn) Empire in India, Ashoka had expanded it until it covered most of modern-day India. But he had become deeply troubled by the bloodshed he caused in his conquests. Listening to the monk convinced Ashoka to devote himself to the peaceful message of Buddhism. Ashoka erected thousands of rock pillars all over his

Remnants of Ashoka pillars, Sarnath, India

© THERIN-WEISE/PHOTOLIBRARY.COM

kingdom, with the teachings of the Buddha carved into them, the first written evidence we have of Buddhism. He didn't make Buddhism the official religion of the Mauryan Empire, but he did support it in many ways, including building Buddhist monasteries and schools of higher learning. More importantly, Ashoka sent monks as missionaries all over India and to several foreign lands in south Asia, from which Buddhism would eventually travel to the rest of Asia and the world. Ashoka sent one of his sons and one of his daughters, both of them now Buddhist monastics, to Sri Lanka (Ceylon)—an island nation just off the southern Indian coast—around the year 240 B.C.E. Its king was converted, and his kingdom came with him into Buddhism. One of the gifts for the king Ashoka's children took with them was a cutting from the original Bodhi Tree. Trees said to have grown from this cutting can still be found in Sri Lanka. Buddhism has been a "missionary religion" in ways that other Indian religions haven't, a fact that is directly traceable to Ashoka.

Sri Lanka was the site of the fourth Buddhist council, in the first century B.C.E. For the first time, all **sutras** (scriptures) were recorded in writing, on palm leaves and in the Pali

Hinayana [HIN-ah-YAHN-uh] "Small vehicle" of southern Buddhism, a term of insult used by Mahayanists to describe Theravada

Theravada [THAIR-uh-VAHD-uh] Usually translated as "tradition of the elders," but more accurately means "original/abiding teaching"

sutra [SOO-truh; Pali: *Sutta*] Canonical scripture text

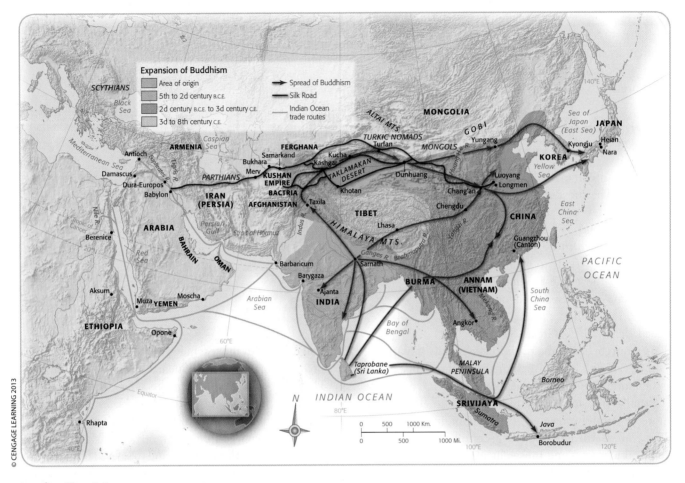

Map 5.1

Spread of Buddhism in Asia, 400 B.C.E.–800 C.E.

Buddhism originated in what is today Nepal and soon became a major religion in India. From India it spread to Sri Lanka, then to central and Southeast Asia, China, Korea, Japan, and finally Tibet.

language. This eventually became Theravada's Pali canon, from which so much of our knowledge of Buddhism stems. It is also called the **Tipitaka**, Three Baskets. The three sections of the canon are the *Vinaya Pitaka* (the monastic rules basket), the *Sutta Pitaka* (words of the Buddha basket), and the *Abhidamma* (ah-bih-DAHM-uh) *Pitaka* (the higher-teaching basket, for monks).

Historians today credit Sri Lanka's monks with saving the Theravada tradition. Although it had spread in early years to Sri Lanka and other parts of Southeast Asia, it declined in India. In fact, it nearly died out in its homeland in the northern parts of the Indian subcontinent when a revived Hinduism reduced its numbers and again when most of India was taken over by Muslims

in the 1500s C.E. Only Sri Lankan Buddhism survived, becoming the oldest form of Buddhism in the world. In more recent times, Theravada monks spread their tradition again from Sri Lanka to Myanmar (MEE-ahn-mahr, formerly called Burma), Thailand, Malaysia, Cambodia, Vietnam, and Laos (lous) (see Map 5.1).

Explore Buddhist sites in Asia.

Explore Buddhism in China and Korea after 1279.

THE RISE OF MAHAYANA: CHINA AND JAPAN

Mahayana, or the "large vehicle" branch of Buddhism found today in China, Japan, and Tibet, was a development of the split at the first Buddhist council. The monks of the Great Sangha held that Buddhism should be a large community, not just a vehicle for monks. They wanted to allow Buddhist lay folk to have a much greater participation in Buddhism than before.

Tipitaka [TIH-pee-TAH-kuh] "Three Baskets," the main internal divisions of the canon (Sanskrit: *Tripitaka*)

Mahayana [MAH-hah-YAHN-uh] "Large vehicle" branch of Buddhism in northern and eastern Asia

A Buddhist nature-spirit statue

SARAH M. GOLONKA/BRAND X PICTURES/JUPITER IMAGES

This meant that adaptation to indigenous religions was easier for Mahayanists, although Theravadins made some adaptations as well. People would convert to Mahayana Buddhism more easily if some of their gods and religious practices were a part of it. So the doctrine of *Trikaya* (trih-KIGH-yuh), the "three bodies," of the Buddha, was developed. The historical Gautama Buddha was his first body, his second body was that of various heavenly buddhas adapted from other religions, and his abstract third body was the Buddhist teaching itself.

More significant in Mahayana was the increased importance of the **bodhisattva**, or "buddha-to-be," someone who has attained enlightenment but compassionately remains in this suffering world to bring others to enlightenment. Local divinities, spirits, and heroes of other religions were often reinterpreted as bodhisattvas, and they became the object of Buddhist worship in order to bring adherents closer to nirvana. Along with new ideas came new sutras to explain them. They are attributed to the Buddha himself, even though the ideas in these scriptures are mostly new to Buddhism. One of them, the *Diamond Sutra*, defends its new teaching by having the Buddha say, "I preach with ever the same voice." However, the differences between Theravada and Mahayana teachings are unmistakable. At the root of these differences is the belief in Theravada Buddhism that individuals must find the way to nirvana on their own. Mahayana Buddhists believe that others—especially the Buddha and bodhisattvas—must help the individual find nirvana, or in some Mahayana groups simply give it to them.

"I preach with ever the same voice."—The Buddha in the *Diamond Sutra*

See a "zoomable" photo of the Chinese *Diamond Sutra*, the world's earliest printed book (868 C.E.).

China already had two main religions, Confucianism and Daoism (Taoism). Both religions, but especially Daoism, had elements of folk religions reaching back to the dawn of human life in China. Folk religion consisted of local gods and spirits, mythologies, astrology, divination, magic, folk medicine, and so on. Over time, the Mahayana that began in India became a truly "large vehicle," spreading to China and later to Korea, Japan, Nepal, and Vietnam. Most historians also consider Buddhism in Tibet to be a part of Mahayana, but it is also commonly considered a third "vehicle." So what began as a small protest by monks soon after the death of the Buddha would become—after a long period of adaptation—the dominant form of Buddhism in northern and central Asia, the third main religion of China and the first in Japan. Ultimately it would become the branch of Buddhism best known in the Western world.

Different Buddhist groups in China and Japan illustrate the diversity within Mahayana. The *Pure Land Sutra* is the most important scripture for the Pure Land Schools of Buddhism. In it, the Buddha tells about Amitabha (AH-mee-TAB-uh; in Japanese, *Amida*) Buddha and his "Pure Land," or heaven, and how one can be reborn there and then easily achieve nirvana. The people of China had for millennia worshiped gods and goddesses; venerated their ancestors; prayed for the health of their families, animals, and crops; hoped for heaven and feared hell; and so on. The Chinese found that Mahayana Buddhism's teachings met these needs and habits. The growing idea that this period of time was one of religious decline helped along the idea that people were no longer able to reach enlightenment on their own but must rely on the power of higher beings. The transcendent Buddha Amitabha and his heavenly Western Paradise ("Pure Land") fit this idea. All one has to do, Pure Land Buddhism says, is faithfully chant the name of Amida Buddha, and

bodhisattva [BOHD-hee-SAHT-vuh] Person who comes very close to achieving full Buddha nature (nirvana) but postpones it for the sake of helping others to achieve it

when that worshiper dies, he or she goes to the "Pure Land." This is not nirvana itself, but a place in which the obtaining of nirvana is easy.

Another Buddhist group that arose in China was Ch'an (chahn), better known by its Japanese name, *Zen*. The Indian monk Bodhidharma came to China around 520 C.E., bringing the "silent transmission" of secret teaching about enlightenment that supposedly reached back to the Buddha. He became the founder of the Ch'an school. Zen Buddhism focuses on developing the immediate awareness of a "Buddha mind" through meditation on emptiness. One of the methods for inducing this sudden awareness has been the **koan**, a Zen riddle meant to help reach nonrational enlightenment. Because Zen riddles and the process of administering them could be intellectually brutal, they were especially used in the Rinzai (RIHN-zigh) school of Zen that we will discuss below. Zen is also known for its dismissal of the written word and occasionally for its physically rough tactics. Rinzai abbots can and do strike monks with a stick or baton if they do not like their answers, or if they get sleepy during prolonged sitting meditation, called **zazen**. Although one of the most common pictures from Zen history is of Bodhidharma ripping up a Buddhist scripture book, Zen Buddhists do have an appreciation for the Buddhist tradition even when they are seemingly ignoring or belittling it. Zen has contributed its own literature to the Buddhist world, including the *Platform Sutra*, written by Hui Neng, the sixth Zen patriarch, around 700 C.E.; the *Blue Cliff Record* around 1000 C.E.; and *The Gateless Gate*, around 1200 C.E.

Buddhist legend says that a delegation arrived

Read the primary source "Confucian Opposition to Buddhism."

koan [KOH-an] Zen riddle meant to induce nonrational enlightenment

zazen [ZAH-zehn] Seated meditation, often for long periods, in Zen Buddhism

TAMAKISONO

Modern **Amitabha Sutra**

in Japan from Korea with gifts for the emperor of Japan in 538 C.E., including a bronze Buddha and various sutras. After rejecting Buddhism at first and even throwing these gifts into the sea, the imperial court of the 600s was drawn to the religion. Although Buddhism started as a religion of the aristocracy, in the 900s the Pure Land group became popular among the lower classes. In the 1200s, Ch'an came to Japan, where it was met an enthusiastic response by the Samurai warrior class, among others, and renamed *Zen*. Zen was introduced to Japan by two Japanese Buddhist monks who had gone to China for training. One brought the Rinzai branch of Ch'an/Zen, with its koans to punish the mind and physical blows to punish the body. The other brought the more sedate Soto (SOH-toh). Both forms of Zen have always had an artistic side; a simple, elegant style of writing, drawing, and painting developed among the monks. The tea ceremony, known for its sophisticated simplicity, also became expressive of Zen, as did the seventeen-syllable poems known as *haiku* (HIGH-koo). (Perhaps the best-known haiku is "Old Pond": "Old pond / a frog leaps in / water's sound.") Zen became more important in Japanese Buddhism than it had been in Chinese Buddhism, and from Japan, Zen would spread in the twentieth century to Europe and North America.

Watch a video on Zen and the Japanese tea ceremony.

A final Japanese innovation to be considered here was led by Nichiren (NEE-shee-rehn), a monk who lived 1222 to 1282. Trained in the White Lotus tradition, he concluded that the *Lotus Sutra* contained all that was necessary for Buddhist life. So he encouraged his students to chant the mantra "Homage to the *Lotus Sutra*"— in Sanskrit, *Om Mane Padme Hum* (ohm MAHN-ay PAD-may hoom). This practice alone would ensure enlightenment in this life. He argued that other forms of Buddhism were of little worth, a type of intolerance that earned him opposition from other Buddhists. The Nichiren School nevertheless proved to be a highly popular form of Buddhism in Japan.

TIBET AND THE DIAMOND VEHICLE

Tibet's first encounter with Buddhism occurred in the 700s C.E., when a Tantric master, Rinpoché (RIHN-poh-shay), is said in Buddhist legend to have come from India to battle the demons of Tibet for control. The demons submitted to him, but they remained as protectors of Tibetan Buddhism. This story indicates well the syncretistic

Japanese daruma doll depicting Bodhidharma

© GETTY IMAGES

Dalai Lama [DAHL-eye LAH-muh] "Ocean of wisdom," head of the Gelug(pa) School of Tibetan monks and ruler of Tibet

nature of Tibetan Buddhism—the combination of Buddhism with elements of the native animistic Bön religion. Buddhism had a difficult time getting established in Tibet; during the 800s and 900s C.E., it suffered a setback there, but in the 1000s it returned. It developed into four main schools. In 1578, the Mongol rulers of Tibet named the head of the Gelug ("Yellow Hat") School of Tibetan Buddhism the **Dalai Lama**, a title that means "ocean of wisdom" or "oceanic teacher." The fifth Dalai Lama brought all of Tibet under his religious and

A Closer Look:

Koans

In the West, koans are known as short, independent riddles employed in Rinzai Zen. Some of the more famous are:

- What did your face look like before you were born?
- What is the sound of one hand clapping?
- Why did Bodhidharma come from the West?
- If you meet the Buddha, should you not kill him?

However, in Zen, koans typically come in the context of a short story. This story does not make gaining sudden insight from the koan any easier, but it does provide a context and an opportunity for sudden insight. Here is one of these stories, centered on the koan "How many virtues does a cup have?"

> Zen master Ummon asked a head monk, "What sutra are you lecturing on?"
> "The *Nirvana Sutra*," said the monk.
> "The *Nirvana Sutra* speaks of the Four Virtues, doesn't it?"
> "Yes, it does."
> Then Ummon asked, picking up a cup, "How many virtues does this have?"
> "None at all," said the monk.

> "But ancient people said it has virtues, didn't they?" said Ummon. "What do you think about that?" He then struck the cup and asked the monk, "Do you understand?"
> "No," said the monk.
> "Then," said Ummon, "you had better go on with your lectures on the sutra."

After a Zen master poses a koan to a monk, he carefully studies the monk's reaction and his answer. He then judges how much intuitive direct insight it shows. Answers that are rational are forbidden and will sometimes result in blows from the teacher. (For example, one could answer the first koan in the list above "Like the face of my grandmother," if one resembles her. But this answer would be rational and incorrect, and might lead to blows.) Or the teacher may say nothing, respond in words, or simply walk away.

Read a story from *The Gateless Gate*, illustrating the successful answer to a koan.

political control, and the dalai lamas were from that point on the absolute rulers of Tibet. This made the country's

The present Dalai Lama, Tenzin Gyatso

demons, as well as the incarnation of a single buddha in the whole line of Dalai Lamas; organizational practices, for example the theocratic and near-absolute rule of the Dalai Lama; ritual practices such as prayer wheels, prayer flags, religious pictures made of colored sand, and oracles for telling the future; and unusual (for Buddhism) scriptures including the *Tibetan Book of the Dead*. This combination of Mahayana and indigenous religion has sometimes caused problems. For example, in 2009, the Dalai Lama said that a group of Tibetan Buddhists with whom he disagrees do not represent a true form of Buddhist religion, but "spirit worshipers" who should give up their practices. This ruling sparked large street protests against the Dalai Lama by Tibetans and others when he made public appearances in 2009 and 2010.

Read a summary of the *Tibetan Book of the Dead.*

The boy was said to have correctly claimed the possessions of the previous Dalai Lama, even exclaiming, "That's mine!" about some items.

Tenzin Gyatso (TEHN-zihn gee-YAHT-soh), who was born Lhamo Dondrub in 1935, was identified when a young boy as the reincarnation of the thirteenth Dalai Lama, a bodhisattva named Avalokitesvara (AV-uh-loh-KIT-esh-VAHR-uh), the famous "Bodhisattva of Compassion." As the Dalai Lama himself tells it, he was presented with various objects, including toys, some of which had belonged to the thirteenth Dalai Lama and some of which had not. He correctly

government a true theocracy (rule by clergy). Tibetan Buddhism also spread to Bhutan, Nepal, and Mongolia, but the direct political rule of the Dalai Lama did not extend to these areas.

Tibetan Buddhism, also known as the Diamond Vehicle or **Vajrayana**, is the most complete blend of Buddhism and an indigenous religion. (The Diamond Vehicle is also referred to as *Lamaism* for its leaders, who are called **lamas**, "gurus, teachers"; *Esoteric Buddhism* for passing its teachings secretly from guru to student; and also *Tantric Buddhism* for developing some of its doctrines from the *Tantra*.) This blending helps to explain why Tibetans have many important features unknown in the rest of Buddhism: doctrines such as many divinities and

Vajrayana [VAHJ-ruh-YAH-nuh] "Diamond Vehicle," formal name for Tibetan Buddhism

lama [LAH-muh] "Guru, teacher," leader of Tibetan Buddhism

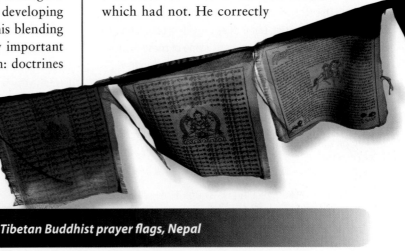

Tibetan Buddhist prayer flags, Nepal

Potala Palace, Lhasa, Tibet, traditional residence of the Dalai Lama

claimed the possessions of the previous Dalai Lama, even exclaiming about some, "That's mine!" He became the fourteenth Dalai Lama in 1950. In 1951 the Communist Chinese invaded Tibet and permanently annexed it. More than 1 million Tibetans were killed in the aftermath, including most of its monks, many of them in mass executions. Six thousand monasteries were destroyed or shuttered.

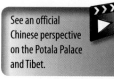

See an official Chinese perspective on the Potala Palace and Tibet.

The Dalai Lama fled in 1959 to exile in north India, where he leads a Tibetan government in exile. In 1989, he was awarded the Nobel Peace Prize for his efforts on behalf of his nation. He has travelled around the world for speaking engagements and Tibetan Buddhist rituals. Tibetan leaders in exile charge that human rights abuses continue in Tibet, including the recent moving into Tibet of tens of thousands of Chinese.

Watch a BBC report on the Dalai Lama in exile.

BUDDHISM IN MODERN ASIA

During the nineteenth and twentieth centuries, Buddhism was faced with a variety of new issues. Several countries with significant Buddhist populations came under colonial Western rule, and most other Buddhists felt the pressure of Western religions and culture. In South Korea, Christianity has converted nearly half the population from Buddhism. Even more damaging to the size and influence of Buddhism were the rise of communism in China, Mongolia, North Korea, Vietnam, Cambodia and Tibet, and the rise of secularism in Japan. Around

1800, probably one in every four people in the world was a Buddhist, but by 2000 it was down to one in every seven.

Buddhists responded in a variety of ways to these challenges. First, it adapted things it liked in Christianity. Peaceful competition between Buddhists and Christian missionaries from the West often led to Buddhist adoption of some Christian practices such as Sunday schools, mission societies, and the distribution of religious literature. Some Buddhists also promoted missionary activity modeled after Christian missions in non-Buddhist parts of Asia and in the West, with voluntary conversion of individuals. That differed from the historic Buddhist missionary method of sending monks to convert kings, with their kingdoms following them into Buddhism.

A second way that Buddhism responded to the Western, Christian challenge was to seek greater Buddhist unity. Three main societies were established to promote ecumenical cooperation between Buddhists: the Maha Bodhi Society (1891) that regained a Buddhist presence at the pilgrimage site at Bodh Gaya, India; the World Fellowship of Buddhists (1950); and the World Buddhist Sangha Council for monks and nuns (1966).

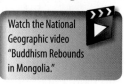

Watch the National Geographic video "Buddhism Rebounds in Mongolia."

A third type of response to modern times was Buddhists' efforts to make Buddhism more appealing in the modern world. In the late nineteenth century, some Buddhist leaders put forward a rational interpretation of Buddhism that deemphasized the supernatural and ritual aspects of the tradition and focused on connections between Buddhism and modern science. This proved appealing in the West, where Buddhism was becoming known for its psychological teachings on the human mind.

A fourth response to modernity was the development of social and political activism by monks, including a formal movement usually called Socially Engaged Buddhism founded by the South Vietnamese Zen monk Thich Nhat Hanh (tick naught hahn) in the 1960s. Some contemporary scholars of Buddhism see him as the most prominent leader of Buddhism today next to the Dalai Lama. Some Asian and Western Buddhists have developed understandings of Buddhist teachings and practice that advocate progressive political and economic changes, including ecological and feminist issues. Although they are not a part of

Monks protesting government policies in Myanmar, 2007

RACOLES

religion—something that could potentially bring reform. Until recently in Sri Lanka, some monks even participated in warfare against the Tamil rebels. The number of men who enter the monastery is declining, and it may also be true (although it's hard to prove) that the quality of monks is declining. Most monks don't behave badly, but problems with those who do have increased. Some scholars have even argued that rising illicit behavior by monks has impacted social life in Southeast Asia. But Buddhism has spiritual resources to deal with these problems, and it is in the process of doing so.

Socially Engaged Buddhism, Buddhist monks in Myanmar (Burma) have helped to organize protests against long-term dictatorships in that nation. At times they have been brutally suppressed and paid a high price for their political activism.

Read the *Newsletter for Western Socially Engaged Buddhism.*

A fifth widespread pattern of Buddhist reaction to modernity has involved the promotion of movements that give the laypeople a much stronger role than they traditionally had. In the Theravada world, traditionally very monk oriented, lay-oriented meditation movements have been successful. In East Asia, especially in Japan, this lay-oriented trend has led to a founding and rapid expansion of Buddhist groups run by lay Buddhists, a novelty in the history of Buddhism.

A final pattern of Buddhist response—the process of dealing with illicit behavior by some religious specialists (in the case of Buddhism, by monks)—is sadly too common in many world religions. In Southeast Asia, some monks are known to play violent video games in arcades, drink alcohol, and have sexual relations with lay women. At the same time, monastic authorities in Theravadin lands typically keep women from any leadership role in the

Watch a National Geographic video on Thai "body collecting."

Watch a video on Buddhism and science.

LO3 Essential Buddhist Teachings

A leading Buddhist authority in Thailand urges the country's 300,000 monks to join in the fight against AIDS. Chatsumarn Kabilsingh (CHAT-soo-mahrn KAHB-ihl-sing), the first woman to receive full ordination as a nun in Thailand, urges that monks should acquire a better understanding of Buddhist teachings to be more effective in teaching the scriptural command against adultery. She says that sex outside of marriage is a primary form of suffering caused by desire, as addressed in the Four Noble Truths. Without getting into the touchy question of whether AIDS is a retribution for sexual sins, she stresses the positive: "Sex springs from the love and care shown by two individuals, and they need to be responsible to each other. With true love, there is no need to change partners, and that is the best prevention against AIDS."

Some people in the West regard reincarnation as a happy form of eternal life, but this is not what Buddhists think.

Many religions in India in the fifth century C.E. had several basic beliefs about an unseen spiritual reality that formed a common world view. Buddhists call their version of this world view the **dharma**, "law, teaching" about the universe and release from it. The universe operates by **karma** ("actions"), the law of the cause and effect of actions done by sentient (with senses) beings. These beings have been reborn from eternity in different realms of the cosmos: in heaven, earth, and hell. This endless cycle of **samsara** ("wandering") is regarded as the cause of all suffering, and the ultimate goal is to escape from that suffering. Some in the West regard reincarnation as a happy or at least neutral form of eternal life, but this is not at all what Buddhists or traditional adherents to other Asian religions think—it is a source of never-ending suffering.

The means of escape remains unknown until, over millions of lifetimes, one gains perfection, ultimately finding the way out of constant rebirth. Those who are fully enlightened are not reborn again as humans after they die, nor do they become absorbed into the world-soul Brahman, as many Hindus have taught. Rather, they go beyond suffering into **nirvana** (literally "blowing out, extinction"). Buddhists have been unwilling to discuss what nirvana actually is, because it is indescribable, but those who come close to nirvana in this life have a deep sense of peace and calm. In short, the goal of Buddhism is a complete and definitive liberation from the painful transience of life. This can be attained through the recognition and elimination of the factors leading to endless death and rebirth.

THE FOUR NOBLE TRUTHS

A brief summary of Buddhist teaching is the **Four Noble Truths** that the Buddha taught in his first sermons. The Four Noble Truths diagnose the human problem, describe its cause, propose a cure, and prescribe a treatment.

1. *All life is suffering.* The First Noble Truth states that all thinking beings experience suffering. Suffering ranges from great physical and mental pain to mild emotional unhappiness and dissatisfaction. People suffer because they are born, get sick, age, and die. Suffering also arises from negative emotions such as anger and sadness. Even happiness is an occasion for suffering, because our happiness comes and goes. Regardless of its surface quality—long or short, happy or sad, poor or rich—this life is actually one of suffering.

> *To paraphrase the Second Noble Truth, we are addicted to life, and, like any other addiction, this one causes suffering.*

2. *The cause of suffering is desire.* Humans always want what they do not have and should not have. Insatiable desire, a craving for physical gratification, personal happiness, and even life itself is the cause of suffering. To put it another way, we are addicted to life, and, like any other addiction, this one causes suffering. Due to the impermanence of the world and the fickleness of our own minds, our sensual and emotional gratifications pass, and we find ourselves once again in the grip of desire. Craving also takes the form of pursuing wealth, power, reputation, and so on, while avoiding unpleasant and undesirable things. We want to be something other than what we are. This constant craving, which is grounded in an erroneous view of the self, is the cause of suffering.

3. *To end desire is to end suffering.* The Third Noble Truth puts together the first and the second. The means of ending our suffering is by ending the craving that causes it. This cessation of craving, which is an ending of the ignorance at its root, breaks the working of negative karma, causing one not to be reborn again. This is easier to understand than to do, and this difficulty leads to the Fourth Noble Truth.

4. *To end desire, one must follow the Noble Eightfold Path.*

---

dharma [DAHR-muh] "Law, teaching" of Buddhism

karma [KAR-muh] Law of the cause and effect of actions done by sentient (with senses) beings

samsara [sam-SAR-uh] "Wandering" through endless reincarnations, a main cause of human suffering

nirvana [neer-VAH-nuh] "Blowing out, extinction" of desire, attachment, and suffering

Four Noble Truths Basic teaching of Buddhism that (1) all is suffering, (2) suffering is caused by desire, (3) to end desire is to end suffering, and (4) to end desire one must follow the Noble Eightfold Path

Noble Eightfold Path
Right understanding, intention, speech, conduct, livelihood, effort, mindfulness, and contemplation

Three Characteristics of Existence
Impermanence, suffering, and no soul

Buddhism requires this as the path toward nirvana. Following the Eightfold Path does not *cause* nirvana, but it is a required aid in finding it. Nirvana is the state that is free from all suffering, because in it one is free from delusions and cravings about the nature of the self and reality.

THE NOBLE EIGHTFOLD PATH

The **Noble Eightfold Path** consists of eight aspects of thought and behavior that need to be cultivated on the path to nirvana. These steps on the path form the basis of Buddhist ethical teaching. Each step begins with *right*, which can be understood as "full," "skillful," or "correct." These are:

1. *Right Understanding:* developing the philosophical perspective that enables one to penetrate through one's deluded conceptions of reality and learn to see reality as it is.

2. *Right Intention:* developing a sincere commitment to embark upon the path to liberation with determination and diligence; people must *want* to change before they *can* change.

3. *Right Speech:* speaking the truth and refraining from lying, deceptive speech that adds to the suffering of the world.

4. *Right Conduct:* following the "Five Precepts" of not killing, stealing, lying, drinking intoxicants, and being sexually immoral; conduct should be without ego and self-centeredness.

5. *Right Livelihood:* doing work and living one's life in a way that does not injure others and is conducive to the attainment of liberation.

6. *Right Effort:* the development of one's consciousness so that it is free from craving; this requires a sustained effort to release consciousness from its unwholesome mental states and cultivate wholesome ones.

7. *Right Mindfulness:* the practice of meditative awareness; by mindfulness, harmful thoughts and feelings as well as their attendant cravings and ego-boosting activities may be discerned and dealt with.

8. *Right Contemplation:* the deepening of mindfulness that leads to focused states of consciousness, akin to deep concentration, in which tranquility and penetrating insight may be obtained.

THE THREE CHARACTERISTICS OF EXISTENCE

Soon after his enlightenment, the Buddha taught that all life is marked by the **Three Characteristics of Existence** (or Reality): impermanence, suffering, and no soul. These characteristics are echoed in many aspects of Buddhism, especially in its philosophical teachings.

● Impermanence, in Sanskrit *anicca* (uh-NEEK-uh), means that all things are in a constant state of flux. Only the appearance of a thing ceases as it changes from one form to another. When a bird falls to the ground and decomposes, the appearance and existence of the bird ceases, but the components that formed the bird may go on to be a part of something new.

Buddhist monks on the king's birthday, 2010, Bangkok, Thailand; collecting their daily food from others enables monks to spend more time in meditation and study.

© CHARLIE EDWARD/SHUTTERSTOCK.COM

A Closer Look:

Popular Misunderstandings of *Karma, Nirvana,* and *Zen*

Just as key Hindu terms are often misunderstood in the West, as we saw in Chapter 3, so too are some key Buddhist terms.

Karma in Buddhism isn't "fate," as we often hear today in North America and Europe. Neither is karma a system of reward and punishment worked out primarily in this present life. In fact, karma in Buddhism is the *opposite* of these ideas. In karma, each person generates her or his own reward or punishment, which comes with one's condition after reincarnation.

Nirvana is for many Western people today a state of personal bliss, where an individual has complete peace, fulfillment, and joy. This understanding aligns with some Mahayana groups, such as Socially Engaged Buddhism, but not with Theravada or Tibetan Buddhism. In these latter beliefs, it means "to become extinct," and for Buddhists it often connotes "to cool," as a flame of desire cools when it is snuffed out. As long as individual existence continues,

samsara continues. Because Mahayana traditions of Buddhism are much more prevalent in the Western world than are Theravadin traditions, Westerners tend to read all of Buddhist teaching on nirvana according to Mahayana views. This leads to distortion about the variety of Buddhist thought on this topic. Buddhists are usually unwilling to say much about nirvana, because it is indescribable, even unknowable.

Zen is the most misused in the West. Many people use *Zen* to describe any ironic or profound statement, whether or not it's meant to lead to enlightenment. *Zen* is also linked in the popular imagination to martial arts. A few Ch'an/Zen groups, especially the Chinese Shaolin (shaw-LIHN) school—of *Crouching Tiger, Hidden Dragon* film fame—use martial arts to build energy and focus the mind. But most Zen groups don't use martial arts, and most martial arts practitioners aren't Zen Buddhists.

> **Watch a BBC report on martial arts at the Shaolin Monastery.** ▶

Monks studying, Myanmar.

© LUCIANO MORTULA/ALAMY

- Suffering, *dukkha* (DUHK-uh), is the second characteristic of existence, in addition to being the first of the Four Noble Truths. Nothing found in the physical world or even the psychological realm can bring lasting deep satisfaction. Because humans are never satisfied, they form an unhealthy attachment to things, and even to life itself. This produces suffering, of which the First Noble Truth speaks.

- "No soul/self," *Anatta* (ah-NAHT-uh), is third. In contrast to Hinduism, the Buddha taught that there is no permanent "soul" or "self" (*atman*). Impermanence thus extends even to the deepest parts of human nature, and this too produces suffering. Various elements of the human mind work together to create an illusion of a permanent soul, but these elements dissolve at death. (So the self is not a "figment of our imagination"; it is a figment of the whole mind.) The task of the Buddhist is to find enlightenment before death, because enlightenment (gaining a Buddha nature) will end the cycle of reincarnation. This teaching is still carried out in much of Theravada Buddhism, but many Mahayana schools teach

Impermanence performed: monks create an intricate sand mandala, only to destroy it.

that there is in fact an essential, permanent self/soul that transmigrates in this world and lives forever when it is liberated from reincarnation.

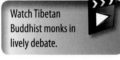

Watch Tibetan Buddhist monks in lively debate.

LO4 Buddhist Ethics for Monastics and Laypeople

As they visit a new Buddhist theme park in southern Vietnam, a family goes through an exhibit not found in most other theme parks—a tour through hell. In paintings, surround sound, and animatronics, eight rooms depict the various tortures inflicted on sinners before they are sent back to the earth for their next life. The mother and father occasionally chuckle nervously at the exhibits, but the children cling tightly to their parents. Like most depictions of punishment in the next life—and many religions have such teachings—this "Hell Pavilion" is meant to impress on people the dangers of doing wrong. Most Buddhist literary or even painted depictions of hell are not as scary as this, and some doubt whether it is wise or even possible to "scare people out of hell" by "scaring the hell out of them" in an amusement park.

precept Buddhist moral command for monastics and laypeople

The Buddhist religious life is grounded on morality. The Eightfold Path indicates that the cultivation of meditation and wisdom is dependent on morality. Meditation and reaching release cannot be done without it. Moreover, most Buddhist lay folk in their worship of the Buddha or other buddhas must build their worship on a foundation of solid moral goodness.

GENERAL BUDDHIST MORALITY

As in most religions, morality in Buddhism is well developed. If you asked Buddhists what the heart of their moral system is, most would probably say, "Show compassion to all beings." In the face of the suffering in the world, all sentient beings need compassion if they are to cope with their bad situation and finally gain liberation from it.

Aside from this general, comprehensive command, the more detailed heart of Buddhist ethical thought is *sila* (SEE-luh). This term means "virtuous behavior," "morality," "ethics," or **precept** (moral command). A precept is an action committed in a deed, a word, or in the mind. It involves a strong, intentional effort, because no precept "comes naturally." Following the precepts leads to moral purity in thought, word, and deed, as well as a proper foundation for meditative cultivation of the mind. Keeping the precepts promotes not only peace of mind in the person who obeys them, but also peace with others. Keeping the precepts itself is meritorious and brings about peaceful and happy effects for monks, nuns, and lay folk. It prevents rebirth in hell or as an animal on the earth. Breaking the precepts will certainly mean that one will not be in a position to reach release in one's next life.

Keeping the Buddhist precepts involves a strong, intentional effort, because none of them comes naturally.

© BESTWEB/SHUTTERSTOCK.COM

Besides the general command to all Buddhists to be nonviolent, moderate, and compassionate to all beings, Buddhists are urged to live moral, generous lives. The social outworking of Buddhist morality helped to differentiate it from Hinduism and aid in its spread through Asia. Two examples must suffice here. First, the Buddha didn't oppose wealth, but he also didn't make it a main goal of life as Hinduism had, and he said that wealth doesn't end suffering, but only masks it. One should develop a detachment from one's wealth and use it for the good of others. The Buddha also opposed Hinduism's caste system and the power of its priests, arguing for equality among all people. Therefore, he accepted monks from all Indian castes. Even today, when Indian "untouchables" (Dalits) have mass conversions to other religions in order to improve their social and religious conditions, they typically turn to Buddhism or to Christianity.

THE FIVE PRECEPTS

What are these precepts? As is typical of Buddhism, lay practice is based on and adapted from monastic practice. The precepts have several levels of achievement: basic morality in keeping the Five Precepts, basic morality with asceticism in following the eight precepts, novice monkhood in keeping ten precepts, full-monk status with hundreds of precepts, and even more for nuns. Lay people generally live by the Five Precepts only, which are common to all Buddhist schools. They can, at their discretion, undertake the eight precepts or even the ten precepts for a short time, which add basic asceticism. The majority of the precepts are worded in the negative, but most Buddhists realize that much positive meaning lies behind them.

The Five Precepts are ethical guidelines for a life in which one is happy, moderately self-confident without being self-absorbed in one's ego, and can meditate well. They are necessary for morality in this life and a better rebirth in the next. The precepts are considered not only imperatives, but training rules that laypeople undertake to facilitate Buddhist practice according the dharma (law). This dharma is built into the universe, governing physical things just as much as it governs living beings. Following the dharma brings happiness in this life and good karma for the next; not living according to the dharma brings endless suffering in rebirths that never end. The Five Precepts call for Buddhists to keep themselves from five different errors. They are virtually universal among Buddhists, both monastic and lay:

1. To refrain from killing sentient beings
2. To refrain from stealing
3. To refrain from sexual immorality
4. To refrain from lying
5. To refrain from intoxicants

Different Buddhist branches and groups have added to these five precepts in different ways. In the Theravada branch, lay folk wishing to practice Buddhism more fully but not able or willing to enter a monastery may adopt three precepts in addition to the Five. Some adopt them permanently, but most who take them on do so temporarily, particularly on holy days. The third of the Five Precepts is made stricter, adding the requirement of celibacy—no sexual activity at all, even within marriage. The three additional precepts are:

6. To refrain from eating between noon and the following sunrise, as monks do
7. To refrain from dancing and music, jewelry and cosmetics, or attending artistic performances
8. To refrain from using "high" (luxurious) seats and beds

OTHER PRECEPTS AND MORAL RULES

The complete list of ten precepts is a requirement for novice monks before they have taken their final vows, especially in Theravada. The seventh precept given above is made into two precepts, and a tenth added:

7. To refrain from dancing, music, singing, and shows
8. To refrain from the use of garlands, perfumes, ointments, and other things that beautify the body
9. To refrain from using high seats and beds
10. To refrain from accepting gold and silver

For monastics who are full members of an order, more than two hundred additional precepts apply to them. These now take on the character of hard-and-fast rules. If they are broken, disciplinary actions are specified in the precepts. For example, in the command of celibacy, Buddhist monks and nuns are forbidden even to think about sex. Although this may strike you as extreme, for someone who is strictly celibate, to think about sex when one never carries out one's thoughts will only increase suffering. Nuns have extra rules added to the rules for monks, most designed to keep them under the supervision of nearby monks.

These precepts seek to order monastic life for the purpose of promoting orderly morality and achievement in meditation. They are listed in the *Patimokkha* (PAH-tee-MOHK-uh), the "Monastic Disciplinary Code" in the Pali canon, and are broken into several groups. In the Mahayana canon, they are found in a three-volume book called the *Vinaya*. Monks must memorize these rules and follow them carefully.

LO5 Buddhist Ritual and Meditation

Buddhist monks gather daily in a Chinese monastery to read sutras. A low hum fills the reading room as the head monk leads them in reciting in unison. Like Buddhists everywhere, they are "making merit" by carefully reciting their key scriptures, thereby doing a deed that will wear away the effects of negative karma. This merit will enable them to be reborn after death into a better existence, perhaps eventually to achieve Nirvana and be reborn no more. If lay folk are present in the temple for this recitation, they listen reverently to the chanting, believing that this ritual will accrue to their benefit as well.

Like most aspects of Buddhism, ritual and meditation must be related to the monks and the laypeople. In some countries, many male Buddhists enter a monastic order for a temporary period at least once in their lifetime, as in Myanmar, Cambodia, Laos, and Thailand today. This temporary monasticism causes men to rise in social standing. In almost all parts of the Buddhist world, monks and laypeople live in a reciprocal relationship. Each group provides the other with an opportunity to gain merit, and thereby to make a contribution to their "karma account." For most ordinary Buddhists—monk or layperson—nirvana is far too remote and intangible a goal to be striven for immediately, so religious practice focuses on the gaining of merit. Monks recite and explain the sacred texts to laypeople, conduct protective ceremonies for them, and lead other religious rituals for them, especially funerals. The laypeople give the monks material support: food in their morning rounds outside the monastery, new garments for monks at an annual ceremony, and money for the maintenance and adornment of the monastery. Lay folk do engage in one ritual practice that monks generally do not—going on pilgrimage to sacred Buddhist sites.

Watch a video of Buddhist meditation.

Watch recitation of the scripture "Reverence to the Bodhi Tree."

TEMPLES

Inside a typical Theravada temple, you will see the following. At the front of the temple will be a statue of the Buddha, most often seated and in meditation. Sometimes a few other statues of the Buddha will also be present at the front. An altar on which worshipers place offerings of flowers and oil stands right in front of the statue. A place to set up burning incense sticks is on or near the altar, and larger temples will have places to burn incense in an open-air courtyard. Many temples contain pictures on the walls, showing the stages of the Buddha's life. As a rule, Mahayana and Tibetan temples are more elaborately decorated than Theravadin temples. Most of the main hall of the temple is open space in which worshipers sit or stand in meditation. One may see mats there, but not (in a traditional Buddhist temple) chairs or pews. Buddhist temples built in the West sometimes have a different arrangement, which we will discuss in the Buddhism in North America section on page 128.

Woman consulting a horoscope in a Japanese Buddhist temple

WWW.CEPOLINA.COM

IMAGES OF THE BUDDHA

The most prominent part of any Buddhist temple, and also found in Buddhist homes, is a statue of the Buddha. (Paintings and printed pictures of the Buddha are also seen, but not as prominently for temples or home altars. Most Buddhists do not consider them as inspiring as statues of the Buddha.) The Buddha is usually depicted as seated, mostly in the lotus meditational position. His eyes are closed or mostly closed, symbolizing that he has shut out the distractions of the world to find release within himself. He often has a circular mark on his forehead, called an *urna*, showing that he has achieved enlightenment. His large earlobes are a traditional Indian symbol of nobility. He is dressed modestly, and is physically strong and healthy but not overfed. He holds his hands, and often his arms, in one of a variety of formal positions called **mudras**, some of which are:

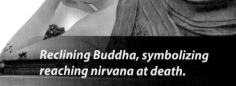

Buddha in deep meditation, Kamakura, Japan

Buddha with right hand downward, symbolizing enlightenment

- Left hand resting on thigh, right hand pointing downward or touching the ground, symbolizing the attainment of enlightenment
- Right hand held up with the palm facing forward, symbolizing a blessing of those venerating the statue
- Right hand upward with thumb and forefinger closed (our "okay" sign), symbolizing teaching the Buddhist way

Buddha in "blessing" pose

- Forming both hands into a circle, symbolizing the wheel of dharma

mudra [MOOD-ruh] Position in which the hands, and often arms, are held during meditation

One will also see statues of the Buddha reclining on his right side, symbolizing his entry into full nirvana at death. Less often, one will see statues of a standing Buddha.

PRAYER AND MEDITATION

For monks, prayer has a highly meditational dimension. For lay folk, however, Buddhist prayer

Reclining Buddha, symbolizing reaching nirvana at death.

means expressing praise and requests to a supernatural power or being. As said at the beginning of this chapter, most Buddhists don't meditate, even irregularly. Buddhism doesn't have a main deity on whom the religion centers and to whom worship and prayer are offered. But Buddhists do pray, which raises, at least for us, the question: To whom do Buddhists pray, and for what do they pray? Mostly, Buddhists pray for blessings from the Buddha, other buddhas, and bodhisattvas, and ask especially for help toward enlightenment. Some Tibetan Buddhists have "minor" gods, both male and female, to whom prayer is made for blessing and protection. They also pray for many of the same things people pray for in other religions: for health and healing, safety, spiritual strength, and for understanding.

Tibetan woman using a prayer wheel to earn good karma

indifferent to self. The meditator then begins pursuit of the higher attainments in trance meditation. Beyond the influence of perception, especially the perception of plurality of physical and mental forms, the meditator concentrates on and rests in infinite space. Transcending this stage, the meditator reaches a state of unlimited consciousness. Proceeding still further by concentrating on the nonexistence of everything, the mediator achieves a state of nothingness suggested by *nirvana*. Finally, the meditator reaches the highest level of attainment, in which there is neither perception nor nonperception. He or she has thought the way out of thinking!

Much more important than prayer for Buddhist monastics is meditation, an altered state of consciousness induced in a controlled manner. You are used to trances that come in the form of daydreams, and we even do things such as drive a car for several minutes and suddenly realize that we haven't been paying attention to driving at all. Buddhist meditation, however, is controlled and purposeful—there is no inattentive driving in a Buddhist life! Two basic forms of meditation have been widely practiced in the Theravada tradition and have also come by way of Mahayana practice to North America.

Buddhists do pray, but to whom and for what?

The first form of meditation is called "trance meditation" and has several steps. First, the meditator achieves detachment from sensual desires and impure states of mind through reflection, and enters a state of satisfaction and joy. In the second stage, intellectual activity gives way to a complete inner serenity; the mind is in a state of concentration and only mild emotional pleasantness. In the third stage, every emotion has disappeared, and the meditator is indifferent to everything. In the fourth stage any inclination toward any particular mental state, suffering, or even serenity are left behind, and the meditator becomes completely

The meditator has thought the way out of thinking!

The second type of Theravada meditation is "insight meditation." This practice also requires intense concentration, which in insight meditation leads to a complete concentration of the mind called *awareness* or *mindfulness*. This mindfulness is not an end in itself, but allows the meditator to gain insight into the saving truth that all reality is impermanent, filled with suffering, and devoid of self. This insight, from the Buddhist perspective, allows the meditator

Buddhist monk deep in contented thought

to progress toward the attainment of nirvana. In Theravada texts, both trance and insight meditation are commended, and sometimes combined. Since 1900, an emphasis on insight-meditation practices has grown, and insight movements became widespread in Mahayana and among Buddhist groups in the West. Of course, some Buddhist groups, such as Zen, have different patterns and practices of meditation. Other groups, for example Nichiren, have meditation that focuses on their main chants.

PROTECTIVE RITUALS

Buddhism has rituals designed to protect against various kinds of danger and to repel evil. In the Theravada tradition, these rituals involve the recitation of scripture texts as *parittas*, "protections." These texts are chanted in public, often with drumming and ringing of handbells, to avert collective danger. They are even more widely used privately, to protect the person paying for monks to recite scripture against illness and other difficulties. Most of these *parittas* do not speak explicitly of protections from danger; they are usually regular scripture texts, recited with the intent of using their truth and power to keep away evil.

> Scroll through a recent collection of *parittas*.

In Mahayana and in Tibet, the role taken by protective rituals is even greater than elsewhere in Buddhism, as we might expect for the branches of Buddhism that give more attention to supernatural beings and forces, including evil ones. *Dharanis* (duh-RAHN-ees), short statements of doctrine that are said to encapsulate its power, and **mantras** (a further reduction of the *dharani*, often to a single word) were widely used for this purpose. Protective rituals were important in the conversion of Tibet and East Asia to Buddhism; people there wanted to be assured that the new religion could deal with the spiritual forces that threatened them. Protective rituals have remained an integral part of the Buddhist traditions in these areas, especially in Tibet. Even today, the Buddhist Tibetan government in exile holds protective rituals for itself and will also consult traditional religious

oracles to discern the best choices when making decisions. In Japan, worshipers in Buddhist temples can get a printed horoscope-based prediction for their life. If they tie it to a special board or a designated tree in the temple area, a good fortune will come true, but a bad fortune will be thwarted. More will be said about these in Chapter 8, on Shinto.

> **mantra** [MAHN-truh]
> Short formula or single word that focuses the mind and expresses great religious meaning

FUNERAL RITUALS

Monks do not normally perform most life-cycle rituals for the laypeople. They do not lead ceremonies for newborn babies, mark passage to adulthood, or conduct weddings. These are primarily family events and more cultural than religious, although monks may bestow blessings on newborns and newlyweds in the monasteries.

Monks do participate in funerals, however. In fact, Buddhism has a leading role in funeral rituals in almost every country in which it has a presence. Because Buddhism has a strong interest in death, karma, and reincarnation, monks often lead services for the dead. Even before that, monks will visit the dying, because one's state of mind while dying impacts one's rebirth. Monks read sacred texts to the dying person to prepare the spirit for death. The elaborate

Buddhist temple in Tokyo, with predictions tied to its fence

WWW.CEPOLINA.COM

stupa [STOO-pah] Burial mound or monument, often with relics of the Buddha or famous Buddhists

procedures spelled out in the *Tibetan Book of the Dead* are the apex of this guidance for the dying and recently deceased. The soul or (if Buddhists are strict on the no-soul teaching) consciousness is thought to remain in or around the body for about three days following death. In general, Buddhist funeral observances originated in Indian customs. The cremation of the body of the Buddha and the subsequent distribution of his ashes are told in the *Sutta on the Great Parinirvana*. After simpler cremation ceremonies than for the Buddha, the ashes and bones of leading monks were also collected and **stupas**, burial mounds or monuments, built over them. The many stupas found near monasteries indicate that these funeral rites for leading monks were widely held.

Watch a BBC video on the "Temple of the Tooth."

Buddhists commonly agree that the thoughts held by a person at the moment of death are significant for his or her future.

Cremation is used for ordinary monks and laymen in Asia and the West. After cremation, typically done today in a modern crematorium, the ashes are usually buried in a cemetery. Many Buddhists will ritually honor their ancestors at their gravesites, especially in China, where the rituals are similar to those we will discuss in Chapter 7. Some regional differences should be noted here. In Sri Lanka, whole-body burial is also common. In Tibet, because of the scarcity of wood, cremation is rare. The whole bodies of great lamas are placed in rich stupas in a posture of meditation. Monks will sometimes cut apart the bodies of pious Tibetan Buddhists, both monastics and lay folk, and distribute them, piece by piece, to the waiting birds. Although this may seem revolting to Westerners—and is not easy for mourners in Tibet to watch, either—this feeding of birds with the bodies of the dead is seen as an act of compassion.

LO6 Buddhism in North America

Since 1997, a "Dharma Wheel Cutting Karma" has been turning in the Asian section of the Library of Congress in D.C. The wheel contains 208 repetitions of forty-two Tibetan scriptures, which otherwise fill fifteen Tibetan volumes. It is modeled after similar prayer wheels in Tibetan monasteries and temples. The spiritual power generated by the constant electrical turning of the wheel is said by Buddhists to generate compassion, prevent natural disasters, and promote peace in the world. Its placement in the Library of Congress is not just a recognition of Tibetan religious writings but of the increased importance of Tibetan Buddhism in modern life and international relations.

BUDDHISM COMES TO THE WESTERN WORLD

European contact with China and Japan brought knowledge of Buddhism to the West in the 1800s, and Buddhism soon became popular here even though the number of Buddhists was small. In England, societies were organized for the promotion of Buddhism, most prominently the Pali Text Society that translated and published Buddhist scriptures for wide dissemination. The Buddhist Society of Great Britain explained Buddhism in the expectation that some people would convert to it. Books appeared recommending Buddhism, for example Edwin Arnold's *The Light of Asia* (1879), a long poem telling of the life of the Buddha that was a best seller in England and America. In Germany and France as well, Buddhism captured serious attention and soon became the best known of Asian religions.

Some of this interest in Buddhism bordered on exoticism. This resulted in a one-sided view of Buddhism that emphasizes its philosophy and meditation to the exclusion of its religious practices, unfortunately still typical today of the Western approach to Buddhism. The first European conversions to Buddhism took place around 1880. In the twentieth century, the Buddhist Society of Great Britain won thousands of converts to Theravada. But the main story of Buddhism in the West begins with emigration from China, Japan, and Southeast Asia, to which we now turn.

The main story of Buddhism in the West begins with emigration from China, Japan, and Southeast Asia.

EARLY BUDDHIST IMMIGRATION TO NORTH AMERICA

In the United States and Canada, tens of thousands of Chinese immigrants with Buddhist backgrounds, usually combined with lay Daoist practices and basic Confucian social values, came to their West Coasts in the late 1800s. Like the vast majority of immigrants to North America, they came seeking a better life, not for religious reasons. Most came to provide labor for mining, fishing and farming, and especially for building the railroads. The only religious objects they had were small images of the Buddha and Chinese traditional gods for their own personal use. When the railroads were finished and these immigrants settled down in "Chinatowns" in the coastal cities, Americans began noticing their forms of Buddhism, especially when temples were built.

The size of the Chinese immigrant population grew rapidly; by 1870 one-tenth of the population of California and Montana was Chinese. Their numbers provoked a backlash in discriminatory laws and practices to keep down Chinese peoples, some of which were aimed at Chinese cultural practices (festivals, music, public funerals) that were grounded in Chinese religions. In 1882 the national Chinese Exclusion Act suspended further immigration, and in 1924 new quotas were set for all Asians. Some immigrants continued to practice their faiths. By 1900, there were hundreds of Chinese Buddhist temples and smaller shrines along the West Coast and in the Rocky Mountains. Almost all of them were founded and led by laypeople, because Chinese monks did not emigrate with them. But as discrimination persisted, and with a continued absence of monks that for thousands of years had guided lay Buddhism, many second- and third-generation Chinese began to leave Buddhist practices behind in an effort to assimilate more fully.

Japanese immigration to North America began in the 1880s. It was much smaller in scale than Chinese immigration, and was controlled and financially supported by the Japanese government. Japanese immigrants tended to be merchants and businessmen. Also, entire families immigrated, unlike the Chinese, who were predominantly males who had to leave their families behind in China. The immigrants quickly built cultural associations and temples. By 1898, the Young Men's Buddhist Association (modeled, as its name implies, on the Young Men's Christian Association, the Y.M.C.A.) had been established. By 1910, more than twenty Japanese Buddhist temples had been established on the West Coast, most of them led by ordained Buddhist monks from Japan, who had been sent by the Japanese government.

Meanwhile, on the East Coast, contact with Buddhism came from books, not immigrants. Leading intellectuals were reading about Buddhism, especially transcendentalists such as Henry Thoreau and Ralph Waldo Emerson. In 1878, the eccentric mystic Helena Blavatsky and the more conventional Henry Steel Olcott, the founders of the so-called Theosophical Society, went to Sri Lanka and formally received the Five Precepts for lay folk. Olcott was committed to Buddhism. When he became aware of how little most Asian Buddhist groups knew about each other or cooperated with each other, he worked for better relations among these groups, even publishing a *Buddhist Catechism* (CAT-uh-kihz-um) to state what he considered the main, common ideas of Buddhism.[2] (A catechism is a basic statement of faith in question-and-answer form.) He was widely known as

---

[2] Henry Steel Olcott, *Buddhist Catechism* (London: Treubner, 1882).

Seattle Buddhist Church with "Protestantizing" influences

JMABEL

"the white Buddhist," a term that would not be acceptable today but at the time was considered correct and complimentary.

During World War II, the internment of all Japanese in camps set back the religious life of the Japanese in the United States. After the war, membership in Buddhist temples declined as many Japanese Buddhists sought to assimilate by becoming Protestant Christians at a time when Protestantism was at the height of its cultural influence in America. Many Buddhist religious institutions adapted by "Protestantizing" themselves, with temples that added pews, pulpits, hymnbooks, and organs. The largest Buddhist group in the States, the Jodo Shinshu sect of Sokka Gakkai, formally changed its name to the Buddhist Churches of America, giving the Christian term *church* a Buddhist application.

A surge of interest in Zen came after the Second World War, when many Asian Buddhists—such the Zen expert D. T. Suzuki (1870–1966)—came to the U.S. to live permanently. Zen Buddhism became particularly popular in the U.S., even contributing to what was called at the time a "Zen boom." A number of Americans went to Japan and began a more serious, committed study of Zen. Many American troops based in Japan after the war gained an appreciation for Japanese ways of life in general and Buddhism in particular. In the 1950s, Zen became a part of the countercultural "Beatnik" movement, a precursor to the more diffuse "hippie" movements of the 1960s and 1970s. It was known as *Beat Zen*, and was the first time that an Asian religion became a part of American popular culture. In 1974, Zen would again appear in American pop culture, in the form of Robert Pirsig's best-selling book *Zen and the Art of Motorcycle Maintenance: An Inquiry into Values*.[3] Zen had come to be seen in North America as a way of spiritual liberation that was suited to people of Western cultures.

Some institutional dimensions of Buddhism did continue in the United States. Since the 1950s, Europeans and Americans who studied Buddhism in Asia returned to found monasteries and societies. Also, Asian Buddhist monks came to Europe and America to found meditation centers, and sometimes even monasteries. But Buddhist influence from the 1800s until about 1970 remained largely intellectual, cultural, and meditational. The full spectrum of Buddhism as a religion was yet to appear. Two main events in the rise of Buddhism in North America would soon occur: the coming of Tibetan Buddhism and Vietnamese immigration into the United States after the end of the Vietnam War.

THE NEXT WAVE OF BUDDHIST IMMIGRATION

The Tibetan Buddhist presence in North America began in the 1970s, when Tibetan meditation centers began to be established by monks who had eventually settled here after fleeing from Tibet. By 1990 almost every main Tibetan group had a center, especially on the East and West Coasts. These meditation centers mostly serve Americans of non-Tibetan backgrounds, because relatively few Tibetan laypeople live in North America.

The 1990s also saw the rise of what some have called "Hollywood" or "celebrity" Buddhism. Various films about Tibet and its form of Buddhism gained much attention, especially *Seven Years in Tibet* and *Kundun*. Film stars such as Naomi Watts, Tina Turner, Steven Segal, Uma Thurman, and Richard Gere have publicly espoused Buddhism, especially Tibetan Buddhism. Gere has become perhaps the most well known spokesman for Buddhism in the world after the Dalai Lama himself. Although the golfer Tiger Woods has not openly championed his Buddhist beliefs, the disclosure of his multiple extramarital affairs in 2009 led to a public discussion of his adherence to Buddhism. In sum, "celebrity Buddhism" has played a role in the last twenty years to shape the North American perception of Buddhism in mainly positive but sometimes superficial ways.

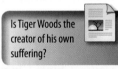

Is Tiger Woods the creator of his own suffering?

Richard Gere is honored by the Dalai Lama after the latter received the Congressional Gold Medal in 2007.

PHOTO BY STEPHANIE KUYKENDAL/GETTY IMAGES

---

[3] Robert Pirsig, *Zen and the Art of Motorcycle Maintenance* (New York: Harper, 2008; originally published in 1974).

What some have called "celebrity Buddhism" has shaped the North American perception of Buddhism in mainly positive but sometimes superficial ways.

In 1965, another Immigration Act resulted in a surge in emigration from Asia into the United States. Buddhists from Korea, Taiwan, Thailand, and Hong Kong filled old temples in the United States and established new ones. The major growth of Buddhism in the United States came in 1975, when the Vietnam War ended as Communist forces defeated the South Vietnamese army after U.S. withdrawal. The fall of South Vietnam occasioned another large wave of Buddhist immigration to the United States. When the murderous Pol Pot regime in Cambodia fell in 1979, a wave of Cambodians came. By 1990 there were approximately one million Vietnamese and Cambodians living in the United States. At first, these traumatized immigrants could only gather in their own homes to carry on the most basic forms of Buddhist worship and meditation, but by around 2000 they had made enough social and economic progress to found hundreds of temples and community centers to carry on their culture and faith for the second generation.

An American Buddhist sits in meditation.

© SUPRI SUHARJOTO/SHUTTERSTOCK.COM

A Closer Look:

Stealing Buddha's Dinner: A Memoir

In this critically praised novel, the author tells the story of her childhood as a Vietnamese Buddhist child in America. Bich Minh Nguyen (bit mihn nwin) was just eight months old when her father took her, her sister, and her grandmother out of Vietnam in 1975. They settled in Grand Rapids, Michigan, under the sponsorship of a Protestant church. Nguyen tells her story in terms of American and Vietnamese foods, as she wrestled with conflicting desires for her grandmother's native cooking and American food, much of it the "junk food" her American friends ate. She also refers often to the pop songs she heard on the radio and sang along with, and the TV shows she watched in the 1980s and early 1990s. More significantly, she traces out her complex family relationships, showing that the lives of displaced persons are often difficult for a variety of reasons.

Nguyen's short, engaging novel, published by Penguin in 2007, is an often-humorous coming-of-age tale that develops themes of loss, displacement, and new identity. The *San Francisco Chronicle* recommended it as "resonating with anyone who's ever felt like an outsider," but it makes a particular appeal to those who want to know what it's like to live as a young Buddhist immigrant in the United States. Although the author does not deal explicitly with her Buddhist background very often, the book itself is named from one short chapter that does deal with food offered to the Buddha in sacrifice: "Stealing Buddha's Dinner."

CONCLUSION

Watch a news report on the growth of Buddhism in North America.

Buddhism in North America has been constantly growing and changing. As that of other religions in North America, the Buddhist experience here has been one of adaptation and assimilation. A form of "American Buddhism" is growing, in which different people of different branches, countries, and sects of Asian Buddhism increasingly mix and cooperate with each other. In Asia, these different groups from Japan, Korea, Vietnam, Tibet, Thailand, and Taiwan seldom needed to cooperate with each other, and rarely wanted to even meet each other. The situation that Henry Olcott found there more than a century ago is still too prevalent. In North America, however, these Buddhists find themselves in a new context, where Buddhists are not numerous or socially powerful. The partly self-imposed pressure on Buddhists to secularize, to convert to Christianity, or adapt elements of their worship to Christianity has often

Read a short article about, and view pictures of, Buddhist nuns in the Theravada tradition ordained for the first time in North America.

been strong. The North American context fosters a level of inner-Buddhist dialogue and cooperation that has never yet been seen in Buddhism. At the same time, a few groups such as Zen and Tibetan monastic orders have become strong enough in North America to carry out their life on their own, without much interaction with other Buddhists.

{ Read It Your Way! }

"I really liked the 'virtual example' links throughout the chapter."
ffany Little, student, McHenry County College

"I like the idea [of the eBook]. People nowadays have their laptops verywhere and having access to the book is great."
haan Duggal, student, Boston University

Ve know that no two students read in quite the same way. Some of
ou do a lot of your reading online.

o help you take your reading **outside the covers** of **RELG,**
ach new text comes with access to the exciting learning environment
f an interactive eBook containing **live links to:**

- **Videos from YouTube, BBC, National Geographic, and others**
- **Google Earth™ explorations**
- **Interactive maps**
- **Sound clips**
- **Readings and articles**
- **Image galleries**
- **Websites**

o access the eBook and many other resources, visit CourseMate
www.cengagebrain.com

CHAPTER 6

Encountering Sikhism: The Way of God's Name

BONNIE VAN VOORST © CENGAGE LEARNING

Learning Outcomes

After studying this chapter, you will be able to do the following:

LO1 Explain the meaning of *Sikhism* and related terms.

LO2 Summarize how Sikhism developed over time into what it is today, especially its founding by the ten gurus and its life from the British Empire through the present.

LO3 Explain the essential Sikh teachings.

LO4 State and discuss the main ethical precepts of Sikhism.

LO5 Outline the way Sikhs worship and practice other rituals, especially life-cycle rituals.

LO6 Summarize the main features of Sikh life in North America today.

© MRALLEN/DREAMSTIME.COM

"There is only one God, whose name is true. Repeat his name!"—Sikh scripture

YOUR VISIT TO A SIKH TEMPLE

Visitors are welcome in any Sikh house of worship. Because all Sikh temples are run basically the same way, your experience will be mostly the same whether you visit one in India, Great Britain, Canada, or the United States. The Sikh temple you'll visit today is the spacious new house of worship in Houston, Texas, which was established by Sikh immigrants to the Houston area from northern India.

As you go in the front door of the temple at about ten o'clock on Sunday morning, you notice that the main hall is right in front of you. Like Sikh worshipers do, you must remove your shoes; they belong in a special little "shoe room" just before the main hall. Also like Sikhs, you must cover your head before entering the main hall. Because you didn't bring a head covering with you, a simple cloth is provided for you; you don't feel out of place, because many Sikhs in the main hall wear the same type of cloth. Smoking or even taking tobacco into the temple is forbidden, and if you have any alcohol on your breath you won't be admitted, even if you're completely sober.

Sikhs will bow to the big book under the canopy at the front of the main hall. This is the focal point of the temple. You also can give a slight but noticeable bow as a sign of respect, even if you don't share this religion. Sikhs go farther with their bow, and they touch the floor with their forehead after

What Do YOU Think?

Sikhism is just a combination of Hinduism and Islam.

Strongly Disagree						Strongly Agree
1	2	3	4	5	6	7

kneeling down. This shows their respect for the book, to the truths contained in it, and to God. People then walk closer to the book and place an offering of food or money in front of it. These offerings are used to run the temple and the free food kitchen attached to it. If a person has no money or food to offer, he or she may offer a flower or just some words of sincere thanks. You too should put a little money in front of the book.

Sikh worshipers at a service at the Gurdwara Sahib of Southwest Houston, Texas

DR. TEJENDRA GILL, SECRETARY, GURDWARA SAHIB OF SOUTHWEST HOUSTON

< A Sikh takes a ritual bath at the temple in Amritsar, India, the holiest site in Sikhism.

Sikh [seek] "Disciple" or "student," follower of the Sikh religion

Guru Granth [GOO-roo GRAHNTH] "The Guru Book"; the main scripture of Sikhism, also known as the *Adi Granth*, the "First Book"

About three hundred people are attending the Sunday service. You notice that everyone sits on the floor during the service; there are no cushions or seats. This is designed to make you humble in the presence of God, and it gives everyone a place of equal status to sit. However, men and women must sit on separate sides of the hall. No one sits with their feet pointing at the book at the front; this is a sign of disrespect, so be careful where your toes point. If you walk around the book itself, you must do so in a clockwise direction, the way it's done in various Sikh ceremonies.

The service consists of a few readings from the scripture book under the canopy and several songs led by musicians to the side of the canopy. The event ends with the serving of a handful of a sweet vegetarian food. You should take this in cupped hands as a gift from God. It's not really an "appetizer," but there is more food to come in about an hour; a free meal of vegetarian Indian food is offered in the adjoining hall, something Sikhs consider an important part of the service.

Sikhism is much smaller than Hinduism and Islam, but it is nonetheless important on the world stage. Today the total number of Sikhs numbers around 23 million, with estimates varying from 15 million to 25 million. Most Sikhs are ethnic Punjabis (poon-JAHB-ees) living in northwest India. Sikhism is a tenacious faith that has been able to endure under much pressure from Hinduism and Islam, and now also from the national government of India. Your study of Sikhism will soon encounter these unique features:

- Founded from 1500 to 1700 C.E., Sikhism is one of the newest major world religions, but it isn't considered one of the "new religious movements."

- Some religion scholars conclude that Sikhism was influenced by mystical, devotional movements in Hinduism and Islam, but most Sikhs view it as a direct revelation of a new religion from God.

- Sikhism began as a more-or-less pacifist religion but shifted to militancy out of self-defense early in its history.

- Sikhism is one of the smaller faiths treated as a "world religion," although Sikhs often say that their religion is the fifth largest in the world and rightly point out that it is widely spread in the world today.

Watch a music video introduction to Sikhism by Manak-E, an Indian singer based in the United Kingdom.

Watch a BBC introduction to Sikhism.

LO1 The Name *Sikhism*

Sikh means "disciple" or "student." Because the religion has always been led by a guru, or "teacher," it's appropriate that those who follow it are called "students." *Sikh* is usually pronounced "seek," but occasionally like "sick." Sikhism is the common, everyday name for the religion of the Sikhs. The early Sikh community called it the Panth, meaning "path." This name is found in their scripture but was too generic a name to last—all religions are paths, after all. The Sikhs themselves more formally call their faith *Gurmat*, "the Guru's Way."

Sikhism was established by Guru Nanak (NAHN-ahk) around 1499 C.E. and subsequently led by a succession of nine other gurus. All ten gurus, Sikhs believe, were inhabited by a single soul. When the tenth guru, Gobind Singh (GOH-bind sing), died in 1708, the soul of these gurus transferred itself to the sacred scripture of Sikhism, the ***Guru Granth*** (literally, "Guru Book"). Now this soul is believed to reside in each and every true copy of this scripture—the soul of the guru became the soul of the *Granth*.

*A reader moves a whisk over the **Guru Granth** to venerate it.*

© PIUS99/DREAMSTIME.COM

A Closer Look:

The Symbol of Sikhism

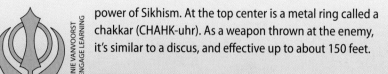

Sikhism has several unofficial symbols: the turban; the Ek Onkar (ehk ON-kahr), or "God is One" phrase from the opening of the Sikh scriptures; and the "Five Ks," all of which will be discussed below. They are dwarfed by the use of the **khanda** (literally, "double-edged sword") as the main Sikh symbol. You'll see it on the Sikh flag that flies in front of and inside many gurdwaras (Sikh houses of worship). The khanda is formed by four items, all traditional Sikh weapons. The Sikh symbol is unique among all the symbols of world religions for its military features.

The center is a vertical double-edged sword with a broad blade. On the outside are two curved single-edged swords; many Sikh men carry a small one at all times, and we'll talk more about this further on. The two swords are often said to represent both the spiritual and the political power of Sikhism. At the top center is a metal ring called a chakkar (CHAHK-uhr). As a weapon thrown at the enemy, it's similar to a discus, and effective up to about 150 feet.

> *The Sikh symbol is unique among all the symbols of world religions for its military features.*

Like most religious symbols, the khanda has also been interpreted symbolically. The circle is often said to represent the unity and eternity of God. The vertical two-edged sword symbolizes God's concern for both truth and justice, and two crossed kirpans curved around the outside signify God's all-encompassing spiritual power.

LO2 Sikhism Today as Shaped by Its Past: Two Key Periods

Regional Sikh officials in British Columbia, Canada gathered to address the 2006 arson of the Sikh temple in Williams Lake, BC. The main hall was damaged in the fire, and much repair work would need to be done before the building could be used again. In addition to calling on police to solve this case, the gathering announced plans for the ritual cremation of the "body" of the main Sikh scripture book, the *Guru Granth*, which was damaged in the arson. They called the damage done to this book "attempted murder of the living leader and teacher of the Sikhs." This startling statement reflects the long-standing Sikh devotion to their scripture as the literal embodiment of the soul of the ten founding gurus. It reflects as well the long, sad history of Sikhs having to endure persecution.

Browse a website popular among Sikhs.

THE TEN GURUS

When we think of India we tend to focus on Hinduism, but for more than a thousand years Muslims have been influential there. Sikhism arose in predominantly Hindu northern India while it was under Muslim control (see Map 6.1). During the time of the first few gurus, Muslim rulers tended to be tolerant of this new group; at the time of the later gurus, these rulers grew intolerant, and at times violent.

Around 1499 C.E., Guru Nanak (1469–1539) began teaching what many saw as a new sect within Hinduism. Nanak was raised a Hindu and eventually came to share some features of the mystical Sant (meaning "saint") tradition of northern India, a devotional movement of both Hindus and Muslims. The Sants composed songs about the divine presence and power that they saw in all things. Several of these hymns were even incorporated later into the Sikh scriptures. The Sants promoted devotion to God as essential to obeying God (important for Muslims) and liberation from the endless cycle of reincarnation (important for Hindus). However, Nanak also had differences with the Sant poets; for example, he started his own religious community and passed his teachings and leadership of this community to successors. Nanak preached a message of universal love and tolerance, downplaying the differences between religions and highlighting their

khanda [KAHN-duh]
Double-edged sword, the main symbol of Sikhism

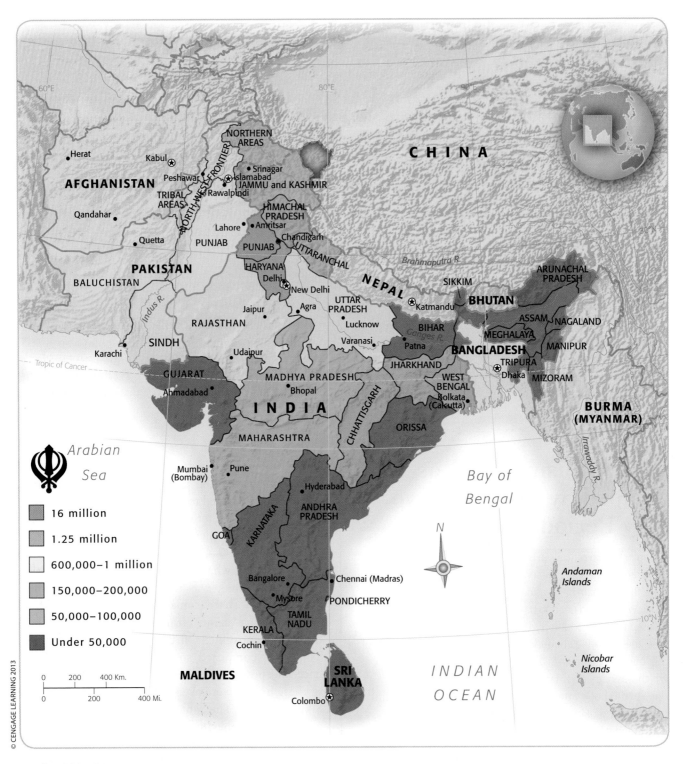

Map 6.1
Sikh Population in India and Sri Lanka, 2005

similarities. Because of the religious situation in northern India, he particularly related his movement to Hinduism and Islam. One story tells that when a Muslim awakened him from sleep and complained that his feet were pointing disrespectfully to Mecca, Nanak replied, "Show me where God is not, and I will point my feet in that direction."

Nanak collected a small number of students, and it was from this first guru–students relationship that the name *Sikhism* came. He composed many mystical hymns that were eventually collected in the Sikh scripture. He visited pilgrimage sites throughout India to spread his message of "remembering the name" of the one and only God by meditating on God constantly and devoting oneself to him. This meditation and devotion was to be done not by withdrawing from the world, but in everyday life. Moreover, like most devotional, mystical movements, Nanak's had a peaceful, even pacifistic message: God's purposes could not be advanced by coercion of violence. This message, except for pacifism, became the foundation of Sikhism through today. Beyond this very little is known for certain about Nanak. The story of his life has been expanded at length in the *janam-sakhis* ("life stories"), which were composed in the century following Nanak's death. Today scholars see most of them as legendary.

Nine gurus followed Nanak. They led the Sikh community and developed its religious beliefs and practices over the next two centuries: Angad Dev (guru from 1539 to 1552), Amar Das (1552–1574), Ram Das (1574–1581), Arjan (1581–1606), Har Gobind (1606–1644), Har Rai (1644–1661), Har Krishan (1661–1664), Tegh Bahadur (1664–1675), and Gobind Singh (1675–1708). These ten gurus are greatly revered in Sikhism today, particularly because the single soul that inhabited all of them when they were gurus has now entered the Sikh scripture.

Ram Das, the fourth guru, was the son-in-law of the third guru, Amar Das. Ram Das is best known as the founder of the city of Amritsar (uhm-RIT-suhr), which became the capital of the Sikh religion. It's the location of the **Darbar Sahib**, the "Sacred Court," also called the **Harmandir Sahib**, the "House of God." The most common of its names, the *Golden Temple*, came after it was overlaid with gold in the early 1800s, but Sikhs do not typically use this name. The Mughal (MOO-gull) emperor Akbar respected the new faith, and he granted Ram Das the land for the new temple and permission to build it. Particularly skilled in hymn singing, Ram Das stressed the importance of this practice, and it remains an important part of Sikh worship. Ram Das appointed his son Arjan (AHR-juhn) as his successor, and all the gurus after Arjan were Ram's direct descendants as well.

By the time of Arjan, the fifth guru, Sikhism was well established as a separate religious movement. Arjan made Amritsar the capital of the Sikh world, made it the religious center of Sikhism with the Harmandir Sahib, and began to compile the main book of Sikh scripture, called the *Adi Granth*, or "First Book." However, Arjan was seen as a threat by the Mughals, and he was executed in 1606 after days of continuous torture. First the emperor's agents sat him in a tank of boiling water, the next day on a plate of red-hot iron. On the third day they poured hot sand over his blisters. Arjan remained calm and peaceful throughout this ordeal, to show that people should accept the will of God; he became the first Sikh martyr in 1606. The significance of Arjan's death was not lost on the Sikhs. The sixth guru, Har Gobind, started to militarize the Sikh community so that they would be able to resist the rising persecution they encountered. Like his predecessors, Hargobind engaged in *piri*, spiritual leadership, but he now added *miri*, governmental leadership. All Sikhs gradually accepted this new dual authority of the gurus.

> **Darbar Sahib or Harmandir Sahib**
> [HAR-mahn-dear SAH-ihb]
> "House of God" temple in Amritsar, also known as the Sacred Court and (more popularly) the Golden Temple

Watch a BBC report on the *Guru Granth*.

The Guru Granth

© B P S WALIA/PHOTOLIBRARY.COM

© ERMESS/SHUTTERSTOCK.COM

The short knife carried by many Sikh men symbolizes resistance to oppression.

Guru Nanak and Gobind Singh, with the other eight gurus and the Guru Granth at the center

© ART DIRECTORS & TRIP/ALAMY

To cremate the body of guru Tegh Bahadur without raising Muslim suspicions, a Sikh brought it to his own house and then burned the house down.

The Sikhs then lived in relative peace with their Muslim overlords until a less tolerant Mughal emperor tried to force his subjects to accept Islam. In the course of this persecution, he arrested and executed the ninth guru, Tegh Bahadur (tehg BAH-hah-duhr), in 1675. A Sikh who witnessed the execution spirited away Tegh Bahadur's headless body and lodged it in his own house outside Delhi. To cremate the body without raising suspicion, he burned down his whole house.

Khalsa [KALL-suh] "The pure ones," Sikh society dedicated to strict observance

The tenth guru, Gobind Singh, who died in 1708, was the most important guru since Nanak. Portraits of him and of Guru Nanak are commonly found in Sikh homes. The son of the ninth guru, he brought Sikhism to the basic form it has today. Gobind Singh finished the compilation of the *Adi Granth*, and it was renamed the *Guru Granth*. Sikhs usually refer to it more honorifically as the "Guru Granth Sahib," the "revered" *Guru Granth*. He formed the **Khalsa** ("the pure ones") as a select society within Sikhism in 1699, with the intention that the Sikhs should be soldier-saints, able and willing to defend their faith. Current Sikh scholarship debates whether Gobind Singh intended the Khalsa to continue as a select formal group within Sikhism or to elevate gradually the whole of Sikhism to the ideals of the Khalsa. At any rate, the Khalsa has always been a select and influential society within the main body of Sikhs, but not all Sikhs have belonged to it or even desired to belong. Gobind Singh established the current Sikh rite of initiation and the distinctive dress of the Sikhs. Many of his sayings have been collected into a book called the *Dasam Granth* (DAH-sum grahnth), "Tenth Book" or "Book of the Tenth Guru." Often quoted from this book is his statement, "The temple and the mosque are one; so too are puja [Hindu worship] and prostration [Muslim worship]. All men are one though they seem to be many."

SIKHISM FROM BRITISH RULE UNTIL TODAY

Sikhs lived and mostly prospered in the Punjab in the 1700s. However, by 1757 Great Britain had begun its century-long conquest of India to make it the "jewel in the crown" of its empire. In 1845 to 1846, troops of the British Empire defeated the Sikh armies and took over most Sikh territory in the Punjab, one of India's most prosperous regions. The Sikhs, who had under Ranjit Singh founded the first

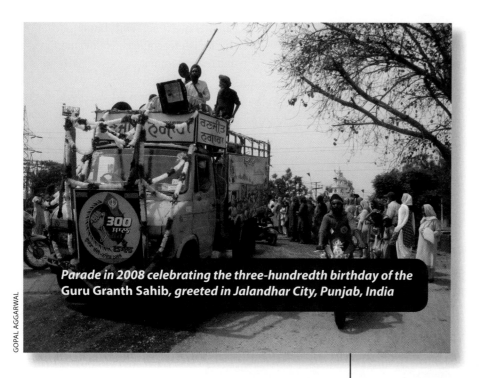

Parade in 2008 celebrating the three-hundredth birthday of the Guru Granth Sahib, greeted in Jalandhar City, Punjab, India

GOPAL AGGARWAL

and only independent Sikh nation in northern India in 1819, rebelled in an effort to regain their independence. They were soon defeated by the British. The Sikhs and the British then managed to build a good working relationship. The tradition began with Sikhs serving with great distinction in the British Army in India and in police forces in the worldwide empire. The British also got a good PR spin among most Sikhs when they were able to put pro-British Sikhs in charge of the gurdwaras. After about 1860, Sikh migration to Africa and the West began, especially to Britain and parts of the British Empire such as Canada.

The situation of most Sikhs in the world today has largely been shaped by the partition of British India. When India gained its independence in 1947, it was divided between India and the new Muslim nation of Pakistan. This partition disadvantaged the Sikhs, because it occurred right through the Punjab. Most Sikhs preferred to live in a secular state dominated by Hindus rather than in an officially Islamic state. Sikhs who suddenly found themselves in the new Pakistani areas of the Punjab fled to the Indian side, often displacing Muslims who then fled to Pakistan. Considerable violence ensued, with loss of life on both sides. When the dust had settled, the Sikhs had lost much of their land and were deeply discontented.

The Sikhs' continued desire for their own nation, which had persisted since the 1700s, was something that the new state of India refused to grant. However, in 1966, after years of Sikh demands, India did divide its Punjab state into three parts, with a new, smaller Punjab as one of them, this time with a Sikh majority with limited powers of self-rule. However, many Sikhs were not satisfied with this. As Sikh discontent grew, the political conflict suddenly became violent. Jarnail Singh Bhindranwale (JAHR-nail sing BIN-drahn-wail), a Khalsa member known for his zeal for Sikhism, became the leader of the most disaffected Sikhs. In 1983, Bhindranwale and dozens of his closest followers, heavily armed, took over the entire Sacred Court complex in Amritsar. They demanded that the Indian government set up an independent Sikh homeland, which they would call *Khalistan* (KALL-ih-stahn), "land of the Khalsa." In 1984, the Indian Army launched an assault to crush this rebellion. The fighting to retake the Sacred Court complex was fierce. Tanks had to be brought in to finally overwhelm the resistance. Over one thousand Sikh militants and Indian soldiers were killed, and the Sikh buildings were heavily damaged.

Watch BBC News anchor Sonia Deol, a Sikh, tell the story of the taking and retaking of the Sacred Court complex.

The assault shocked most Sikhs, even those who opposed Bhindranwale. They saw Prime Minister Indira Gandhi, who had ordered it, as another in the long line of Indian rulers who persecuted the Sikhs. In October 1984, Gandhi was assassinated in reprisal by two of her Sikh bodyguards. Four days of anti-Sikh rioting followed in India, with mobs roaming the Indian capital of Delhi and other cities, burning Sikh shops and even setting Sikhs on fire with gasoline. Thousands of Sikhs, perhaps as many as ten thousand, were killed.

These events are a sore point for many Sikhs today, but are only a part of the story of Sikhism since 1947. On the whole, Sikhs in India enjoyed growing prosperity and greater educational opportunities for women and men. At the start of the twenty-first century, the demands of some Sikhs for their own nation still had not been met, but the Punjab has been mostly peaceful despite some continuing tensions. The appointment of Manmohan (muhn-MOH-huhn) Singh, an Oxford-educated Sikh economist, as prime minister of India in 2004 was a source of great pride and confidence for many Sikhs around the world. It has given Sikhs a calming assurance that their concerns are heard—and spoken—at the highest levels in India.

LO3 Essential Sikh Teachings

Sikhs appeal to the city council of Cardiff, UK, for permission to scatter ashes of their deceased loved ones at a fixed site in a park along the Taff River. The scattering ceremony takes about fifteen minutes and includes prayers and recitation of Sikh scripture passages as well as the actual scattering of the ashes. Sikhs had previously obtained the permission of the regional agency in charge of environmental affairs and conducted a few scatterings. But the city council found out about it, took exception, and a follow-up request to the council ran into some opposition. The issue is a sensitive one; not only is the scattering of

Manmohan Singh, first Sikh prime minister of India

RICARDO STUCKERT/WWW.AGENCIABRASIL.GOV.BR

ashes a matter of a funeral rite, but it touches on basic Sikh teachings on reincarnation and release from it.

As we saw previously, Sikhism is often compared with Islam and Hinduism, the main religions among which it was born and grew. Sikhism does share several key beliefs with parts of Hinduism and Islam, especially with devotional Hinduism and Sufi Islam. However, it has its own beliefs and practices that make it a distinct religion. We shouldn't discount the originality of Sikh teachings and the practices built on them.

THE ONE GOD

Sikhs worship one universal God and hold that only one God actually exists, so they are rightly considered monotheists. God is one, holy, loving, and gracious. God does not have a body, nor does he become incarnated in human form, so God cannot and should not be pictured. This belief makes Sikhism a strongly aniconic (against images) religion. Neither do Sikhs have a specific name for God; the way that Guru Nanak spoke of God, "The True Name," has become the most common. Sikhs use the phrase *Waheguru* (vah-heh-GUHR-oo), meaning "praise to the Guru," for

A Closer Look:

The Mul Mantar

The first chapter of the *Adi Granth* is the *Japji* (JAHP-jee). Pious Sikhs repeat this entire lengthy poem from memory every morning during prayers. They consider it the essence of their faith. The *Japji* moves back and forth among several topics: (1) God's name, greatness, and power; (2) God's creation of the world; (3) the way of salvation by meditating on God's name; (4) good and evil; and (5) relations with Hinduism and Islam. The rich sonority of the *Japji* comes through in this translation. It

begins with the Mul Mantar (mool MAHN-tahr], the "root saying" that is a confession of faith. It's the capstone and summary of the whole composition, not just its introduction. The Mul Mantar runs:

> There is only one God, whose name is true, the Creator who has no fear or hatred. He is immortal, unborn, self-existent; [He is known] by the favor of the guru. Repeat His Name!

The Ek Onkar symbol

to cultivate and express this devotion. Sikh worship features extensive singing of passages from the *Guru Granth* to cultivate emotional and intellectual devotion to God. Salvation from the endless cycle of reincarnation comes from remembering God constantly and devoting one's life to God. Although Sikhism began as a pacifist movement, persecution by some Mughal emperors induced it to become almost militaristic in the defense of its faith, so devotion to God now means a willingness to put one's life on the line for God. Devotion to God causes traditionally observant Sikhs, especially members of the Khalsa, to dress in a way that is distinctive, both in India and in the wider world (see the "Closer Look" box on Sikh dress).

Let's look more closely now at some of these key teachings. As do other religions native to India, Sikhism teaches that all people undergo the transmigration of their soul. This cycle of reincarnation causes pain, suffering, and ignorance of God, because the world in which souls transmigrate is filled with illusion. The only way of release from the cycle of rebirth is meditation on the divine **Nam** ("Name"). According to Nanak, the Nam is centered on God and encompasses the whole of God's creation. Having heard the divine word through divine grace and knowing that there is only one true God, the Sikh believer undertakes the main practice of this religion, "meditation on the Name" or "remembering the Name." Many Sikhs use forms of yoga adapted for their religion to help in meditation. Through this devotion, the believer perceives the Nam, and the means of liberation from error and rebirth are progressively revealed. Ascending to ever-higher levels of mystical experience and devoting oneself more and more to God, the believer is blessed with increasing peace and joy. Eventually the believer reaches the "abode of truth" and enters perfect union with God. At this point, there is no more reincarnation.

God, especially in the context of worship. "Guru" in this usage refers of course to God as teacher, not any human guru. The second most important symbol of Sikhism, the Ek Onkar (ehk ON-kahr), means "One God." It is found in the Mul Mantar, the opening lines of the *Guru Granth*, and is repeated every day by observant Sikhs.

DEVOTION TO GOD

Devotion to the one God in knowledge, emotion, and behavior is central to Sikhism. As in Hindu devotional movements, music has been a key way

Sikh musicians Balbir Singh and Joginder Singh give lessons in worship music to young Sikhs at the new (2006) National Gurdwara and Sikh Cultural Center in Washington, D.C. The gurdwara serves as a national house of worship for Sikhs and hosts cultural programs.

Nam [nahm] Name of God

A Closer Look:

Sikh Dress

A Sikh who is a member of the Khalsa wears the **Five Ks**. Other Sikhs *may* wear it, but members of the Khalsa *must*. Both men and women observe the Five Ks, the men more fully. They are:

- *Kesh* (kehsh), uncut hair. Sikh men and women never cut or trim their hair anywhere on their bodies. Hair on one's head is covered with a scarf for women and a turban (a single long cloth wound around the head) for men. The turban was a common head covering for Muslim men at the time and is still used in Muslim areas such as Afghanistan.
- *Kanga* (KAHN-guh), small comb. This is used to keep one's long hair neat.
- *Kirpan* (KEER-pahn) sword. This steel sword symbolizes one's defense of the faith and of oppressed people. It's worn at all times on the outside of the body, usually in a small form similar to a knife.

- *Kara* (KAH-ruh), bracelet. This stainless steel item is worn on the right wrist, a reminder of unity with God and the Sikh community.
- *Kachha* (KAHCH-uh), underpants. These are a reminder of the duty of purity and also a reminder to Sikhs to act for the faith.

Sikhs at play; note the different dress of Khalsa and non-Khalsa members.

WASIELGALLERY

> The main practice of Sikhism is "meditation on the Name" or "remembering the Name."

LO4 Key Sikh Ethics

During the fall elections of 2010, Nikki Haley became governor of South Carolina, its first governor who is not a white male. Born Nimrata Nikki Randhawa to devout Sikh parents in Bamberg, South Carolina, she has attended with her husband and children both the local Sikh temple and a United Methodist church. She has served in the South Carolina House of Representatives and run a fashion business. Haley is known for her personal charm and political poise, and she is a rising star in the Republican Party; she was featured in a 2010 cover story in *Newsweek* magazine. But in the sometimes-nasty arena of South Carolina politics, Haley was accused in the primary campaign of having two extramarital affairs.

Sign outside a bank in Bangalore, India; note that **kirpan** *is misspelled.*

CANTONMENT BRANCH, BANGALORE

NOTICE

NO WEAPONS ARE ALLOWED INSIDE THE BANK EXCEPT FOR KRIPANS BY SIKHS

CHARLES HAYNES

Five Ks Five items of appearance and dress for Khalsa members: kesh (uncut hair), kanga (comb), kirpan (sword), kara (bracelet), and kachha (underpants)

She sharply attacked these claims of infidelity, conduct that both Christianity and Sikhism strongly forbid. She won the primary and general elections handily, becoming probably the most prominent face of Sikhism in the United States.

Sikhs have a strong sense of ethics that is closely related to their view of one God. We'll examine in particular the Sikh social ethic that rejects traditional caste distinctions, and then we'll treat personal ethics.

REJECTION OF HINDU CASTE

Sikhism from the first has strongly rejected Hindu caste distinctions, so there is usually no toleration of caste in a gurdwara. Sikhs from all caste backgrounds sit together, but with women on one side, men on the other. The gurus denounced caste as irrelevant for access to God, to God's name, and to liberation from sin, ignorance, and transmigration. Another sign of the Sikhs' rejection of caste is the food for the service, which is donated, prepared, and eaten by people of all castes. In the **langar**, the communal meal that follows every main Sikh service, everyone sits in a straight line where no one can claim a higher status. (Men and women are usually in different lines, however, just as they sit on different sides during the main service.) We'll discuss the langar at greater length below.

See a *New York Times* article and short video on the langar in the Sacred Court, Amritsar.

Although Sikhism has opposed Hindu castes, most Sikhs still have a caste. More than 60 percent of Sikhs belong to an agricultural caste. Two trading castes form a very small, albeit influential, minority within the Sikh community. Others include two Dalit castes, which are the lowest on the social scale. Sikhs have a few castes of their own in addition to Hindu castes, for example the artisans, and they also have distinctive names for several castes shared with Hinduism. This use of caste has some

bearing on how Sikhs live and worship. Sikhs typically marry within their caste. Moreover, despite what was said above about caste in gurdwaras, Sikhs of some castes have occasionally established gurdwaras intended for their caste only, particularly in the United Kingdom.

langar [LAHN-gar]
Communal meal that follows every main Sikh service

OTHER MORAL RULES

In Sikh personal ethics, the use of alcohol, drugs, or any addictive substance is forbidden. Tobacco is forbidden as well. Sikhs believe in hard work and generous charity. Members of the Khalsa are required to wear the Five Ks and to avoid four particular sins: cutting their hair, eating meat butchered according to religions' ritual rules, having sexual intercourse with anyone other than their spouse, and using tobacco or intoxicants. Sikhs who commit any of these sins must publicly confess and be reinitiated in this same ceremony. If they are known to commit these sins and don't confess, they are excluded from the faith.

Read a report on Sikh efforts to promote the Indian government's "Save the Girl Child" campaign.

Sikhs have drawn up several "codes of conduct" that enumerate the moral principles and behaviors by

Preparing the langar in the Sacred Court, Amritsar

ALICIA NIJDAM

which they are to live. Here is one of the most popular of these codes:

- There is only one God; remember, worship and pray only to Him.
- Always work hard and honestly and share with others.
- Practice truth and live a truthful life.
- Women are equal to men in God's sight and must be treated as equals.
- The whole of the human race is one, so distinctions based on caste, color, and class are wrong.
- Do not trust in superstitions or follow empty rituals; do not use idols, magic, omens, fasts, religious body markings, sacred threads, etc.
- Dress in a simple and modest way; gaudy or revealing clothes bring no credit.
- Sikh women should not wear a veil, nor should they or their husbands have body piercings.
- All persons should marry and have children, and stay in the married state; asceticism and renunciation of marriage are pointless.
- Have faith in the *Guru Granth*, not in any other book or person.
- Control the Five Evils—lust, anger, greed, attachment to material things, and arrogance.
- Practice the Five Virtues—truth, contentment, compassion, humility, and love.

LO5 Sikh Ritual and Worship

Worshipers at a Sikh temple on a weekday afternoon see three life-cycle ceremonies. First, a baby is brought in for a naming ceremony. The official reader opens the *Guru Granth* at random, and the first letter on the left-hand page becomes the first letter in the child's first name. Second, a young couple comes to be married. During the ceremony, the couple circles the *Granth* several times as musicians sing verses from its marriage hymns. Third, the relatives of a recently deceased Sikh come for the conclusion of his funeral rites. A prominent feature of the funeral is the continuous reading of the entire *Granth*, a process

Oversized turban at the Sacred Court—an obvious point of pride for this Sikh man

TXD

that takes two days, and the relatives are present for the solemn end of the reading.

> *Like most mystics, who value thought and emotion, Guru Nanak and his successors were deeply suspicious of formal ritual practices.*

Like most mystics, who place the primary value of religion on thought and emotion, Guru Nanak and his successors were deeply suspicious of formal ritual practices. He rejected the Hindu priesthood and all its ritual activities, and not just because it was connected to caste. In his new religion, he discarded priesthood, sacrifices, use of incense, religious images, pilgrimage, Muslim and Hindu dietary rules, and the like. Instead, Nanak taught that only with strong devotion shown in faith and love can one reach God. Nevertheless, like any other religion,

Read the *Guru Granth's* critique of Hindu ritual.

Sikhism has a significant ritual component. We'll begin by discussing the center of Sikh life, the Sikh temples and what happens there.

THE GURDWARA

The Punjabi word **gurdwara** means "the Guru's door," which implies that the gurdwara is the residence of the Guru. In a modern gurdwara, the Guru is not a person but the living book of Sikh scriptures, the *Guru Granth*. The gurdwara is the place of everyday worship in the morning. It's where children learn the Sikh faith, morals, traditions, and texts. Especially in the Western world, the gurdwara is also a community center for Sikhs and offers food, shelter, and companionship to those who need it. Gurdwaras are managed by a committee from their community.

There are four doors into a gurdwara, modeled after the four doors of the main temple in Amritsar. They are the Doors of Peace, Livelihood, Learning, and Grace. These doors are a symbol signifying that people from all locations and castes are welcome. Gurdwaras often fly the Sikh flag outside. There are small rooms for coats and shoes; shoes must be removed before worship. Inside the gurdwara there are no statues or even religious pictures, because Sikhs regard God as having no physical form and having no incarnation that can be pictured. Nor are there any candles, incense, or bells used in Hindu and Buddhist worship. Flowers are often used, however, especially in front of the scripture book.

The focus of attention in the gurdwara, both architecturally and in worship, is the book of Sikh scripture, the *Guru Granth*. The "Guru Book" is treated with much the same respect that would be given to a human guru. It is kept in a room of its own during the night—"put to bed"—and carried in procession to the main hall at the start of the day's worship. The book is placed on a raised platform called a "throne," under a canopy, and covered with an expensive cloth when not being read. When Sikhs enter the main hall, they bow deeply to the book, sometimes touching their head to the floor. During a service, a person with a ceremonial fan called a **chaur** waves it over the *Guru Granth*. Although Sikhs show reverence to their scripture, their reverence is to its spiritual content and the living soul of the gurus in it, not to the book itself.

Sikhs worship in a gurdwara does not follow an official form. The morning service begins with the singing of "Asa Di Var" (AH-sah dee vahr), a hymn written by Guru Nanak. Other hymns from the *Guru Granth* are then sung, accompanied by instruments. This hymn-singing, called **kirtan**, is a main part of Sikh worship.

Guru Granth *is carried on its richly decorated palanquin in Amritsar.*

MUNISH SHARMA/REUTERS/LANDOV

Many gurdwaras have a small group of musicians who lead this singing from the front. A short sermon or talk comes next, usually based on a theme from Sikh history. This is followed by the singing of "Anand Sahib," a hymn written by Guru Amar Das. The congregation then stands with eyes closed, facing the *Guru Granth* for prayer. During the prayer, the word *Waheguru* is often repeated. After the prayer, the *Guru Granth* is opened at a random page, and the passage at the top of the left-hand page is read. The text is considered to be a relevant lesson for the day.

A related memorable feature of Sikh scripture usage is **vak lao**, "taking [God's] word." In the home or in the temple, the scripture is always opened at

See scenes from worship in the Fremont, California, gurdwara.

gurdwara [guhr-DWAHR-uh] "The Guru's door," Sikh house of worship

chaur [chowr] Fan used to venerate the *Guru Granth* in the gurdwara

kirtan [KEER-tahn] Devotional singing of hymns from the *Guru Granth*

vak lao [vahk low] "Taking [God's] word" by opening the *Guru Granth* at random

granthi [GRAHN-thee] Official who cares for the *Guru Granth* and reads from it

parshad [PAHR-shahd] Simple food served at the end of a Sikh service

Read the hukam-nama for today.

random, and the reading begins from the top of the left-hand page. This reading is thought to hold special significance for the occasion, and Sikhs believe that God guides which page falls open. This is God's word for the moment, a word that must be "taken" into the believer's life. Every day in the main temple in Amritsar, the *Guru Granth* is opened at random for the "passage of the day," called the *hukamnama*, to be read out, and the passage is published on the Internet for all Sikhs around the world to read.

In India many Sikhs visit a gurdwara before work or during the day for private prayer and meditation. Sikhs do not observe a fixed day of the week as a holy day, but in the West they usually go to a gurdwara on Sunday morning, when services are regularly held. Services are also held there for the most important Sikh holy days.

As stated above, Sikhs do not have ordained priests, although sometimes high officials at Sikh gurdwaras are mistaken for priests. Any male Sikh can lead the prayers and recite the scriptures to the congregation. Each gurdwara has at least one **granthi** who cares for the *Guru Granth*, reads from it during the service, and in general organizes the daily services. A granthi must be fluent in the Gurmukhi dialect in which the *Granth* is written, and must be properly trained in looking after the *Granth*. Ganthis can be male or female, although women granthis are still rare and typically found only in the West. They are expected to be an initiated and exemplary member of the Sikh Khalsa.

Near the end of the service, food is offered to the congregation. This is **parshad**, a warm dessert-like treat made from equal quantities of wheat flour, sugar, and liquefied butter. (Visitors sometimes don't appreciate its sweet, oily taste, but it should be received to avoid giving unintended offense. Sikhs who don't like its taste ask for a small portion.) The first five portions of parshad are given to Khalsa members present, to honor them and to remember the first five members of the Khalsa. Then it is served to everyone without distinctions of rank, caste, age, or gender.

Try an easy recipe for parshad.

Most people in the service stay for the communal meal; observant Sikhs in the Western world don't go out for Sunday brunch.

THE LANGAR

Every gurdwara has a langar, a dining hall, attached to it. As we saw previously, this term is also used for the communal meal itself. An extension of the service, this meal helps to build social and spiritual solidarity in the gurdwara. Most people in the service stay for the communal meal; observant Sikhs in the Western world don't go out for Sunday brunch. The food served in the langar must be simple, to discourage wealthy Sikhs from using it to display their prosperity. Although Sikhs are not required to be vegetarian, many of them are, and only vegetarian food is served in a langar. This allows any Sikh or visitor to eat there, and it keeps the meals simple and low-cost. The meal typically includes dal, vegetables, and rice pudding; water and tea are

Communal meal in a Sikh house of worship, Spain

REINHARD KRAUSE/REUTERS/LANDOV

served as beverages. In Europe and North America, members of a gurdwara sign up to buy and prepare the food for the Sunday-noon langar, which is considered both a duty and an honor.

SIKH LIFE-CYCLE RITUALS

Sikh rituals, like rituals of all religions, have evolved over time. For example, although Gobind required that the Khalsa carry arms and never cut their hair, the wearing of the "Five Ks" didn't become an obligation of all Khalsa members until the establishment of the Singh Sabha (sing SAH-bah), a reform movement of the late 1800s and early 1900s. Other ritual reforms were also carried out then, many of them in an effort to distinguish more sharply between Sikhism and Hinduism.

> *Even though Sikhism is non-ritualistic, it does not ignore life-cycle changes.*

Even though Sikhism is non-ritualistic, it does not downplay or ignore the meaning of life-cycle changes. Sikhism recognizes four major life-cycle events with formal rites of passage. The first is a naming ceremony for newborns, held in a gurdwara when the mother has recovered from childbirth. A hymn is selected at random by an official reader from the *Guru Granth*, and as mentioned above, parents choose a traditional Sikh name for newborn children that begins with the first letter on the left-hand page. (This means that well-prepared Sikh parents have to think through possible names for all the letters of the Gurmuki alphabet.) *Singh* ("Lion") is given as a second personal name (as we say, a middle name) to all males, and *Kaur* ("Princess") to all females.

A second rite is marriage, called by Sikhs "blissful union." As a part of the ceremony, always held in a gurdwara, the bride and groom walk four times around the *Guru Granth* to the singing of one of its hymns. It's likely that this circling of the holy book was introduced around 1900 to distinguish Sikh marriage from the Hindu wedding custom of circling a sacred fire. Whatever its time of origin, this makes a dignified recognition of the importance of making the teaching of the Sikh scripture the center of one's marriage.

View highlights of an upscale Sikh wedding in Vancouver, British Columbia.

The third rite is initiation into the Khalsa, called Amrit (UHM-rith). This is often called "baptism" by outsiders, even though that term is of Christian origin. Five initiated Sikhs conduct the actual rite, while a sixth sits reverently at the *Guru Granth*. The ritual involves pouring water into a large iron bowl and then dissolving sweet powder in the water. This is stirred with a double-edged sword by one of the officiants. After the recitation of certain portions of the Sikh scriptures, the initiants drink five handfuls of the water, now called *amrit* ("nectar" of immortality). Each time this is done, the Sikh giving the water cries the main slogan of Sikhism, "Praise to the Guru's Khalsa! Praise to the Guru's victory!" Amrit is then sprinkled over the initiates' hair and eyes five times, and they drink the remainder of the amrit from the same bowl. They repeat five times the Mul Mantra (the lines that begin the *Guru Granth*), and the obligations of being a Sikh are taught to them briefly. If a candidate has not received a name from the *Guru Granth*, one is given to him or her at the

*A bride and groom follow a granthi around the **Guru Granth** at a wedding in Perth, Australia.*

THEURBANNEXUS

time of initiation. Finally, parshad is distributed, each person taking it from the same dish.

The fourth rite is the funeral ceremony. Cremation and scattering of ashes into fresh, flowing water is done soon after death. These are not done at the gurdwara, of course, but an important part of a funeral service is— the continuous reading of the entire *Guru Granth*. This is for the consolation and support of the grieving family. Relatives and friends of the deceased are expected to be in the gurdwara for the completion of the reading, at which time the funeral is considered finished. Musicians sing appropriate hymns, and short parts of the *Guru Granth* are read again. After the final prayer, parshad is given to the congregation.

OTHER FESTIVALS

> *Sikhs are serious about their religion, but Sikhism has its festive side.*

Sikhism probably seems like a serious religion to you, and Sikhs are indeed serious about their religion, but it does have its festive side. In fact, Sikhism probably has more festivals than any other world religion. There are three holidays every year for each of the ten gurus—to mark their birth, their becoming a guru, and their death. In addition to these holidays for the gurus, Sikhism has eight major festivals. Four of them mark the more important events in the lives of the gurus beside their birth, becoming a guru, and death. The remaining four are the festival of the installation of the *Guru Granth,* the New Year festival of Baisakhi (buy-SAHK-ee), the Indian winter festival of lights known as Diwali (dee-WALL-ee), and Hola Mahalla (HOH-luh ma-HALL-uh). Festivals often have processions in the streets and visits to gurdwaras, particularly to those associated with one of the gurus or with some historical event. Speeches are commonly made to crowds of worshipers.

Diwali is observed by Hindus, Sikhs, and Jains. The Sikh celebration centers on the Sacred Court, which is illuminated for the occasion. For Sikhs, Diwali has a historical connection with the happy release of Guru Hargobind from imprisonment by the Mughal emperor. Hola Mahalla, which is held the day after the Hindu festival of Holi, was established by Gobind Singh as an alternative to the Hindu holiday. It's celebrated with parades and displays of Sikh martial arts.

LO6 Sikhism in North America

A leading Sikh organization in the U.S., United Sikhs, gathers signatures on a petition. It's asking that the U.S. Census Bureau designate *Sikh* as a separate term for race in the 2010 national census. In the past, those who write *Sikh* in the "other race" space have been automatically labeled by the more general term *Asian Indian* when the forms are processed by computer. Arguing that this is incorrect, and noting that social and political power comes from census results, the organization urges American Sikhs: "Sign the petition to have Sikhs assigned a code to be counted correctly." When the Census Bureau responded to the petition, however, it said that a change could not be made for 2010, but it would be considered for the 2020 census.

Until well into the 1800s, most Sikhs who left the Punjab were traders who settled in other parts of India or in closely

A building in the Sacred Court complex in Amritsar lit up for Guru Nanak's birthday

GIRIDHAR APPAJI NAGY

neighboring countries. In the late 1800s, the posting of Sikh soldiers in the British army to stations in Malaya and Hong Kong prompted other Sikhs to migrate to those territories. This migration eventually spread to Australia, New Zealand, Fiji, and China as Sikhs discovered that their skills in commerce and trade were widely valued in Asia, and not just those of soldiers and policemen.

THE FIRST WAVE (1900–1940)

Other Sikhs sought opportunities on the West Coast of North America. The first Sikhs—usually single young men, because of immigration rules that prevented families from entering the country—arrived around 1900. Some of them worked in factories, in sawmills, and building railroad lines. Most of them worked on farms in California, Washington, and British Columbia, because they had been farmers in the Punjab, India's richest farmland. At first they were migrant farm workers, but soon many of them were so successful that they could buy their own farms and settle down. As with other immigrants from Asia, it was difficult to practice their faith here. They had left their religious institutions behind, and assimilation to North American ways of life (dress, diet, schooling, and so on) posed a direct challenge to Sikh identity.

The story of Sikh life in Canada is told well by Kamala Elizabeth Nayar in her book *The Sikh Diaspora in Vancouver: Three Generations amid Tradition, Modernity, and Multiculturalism.*[1] Most Sikh immigration to North America was to Canada, especially to British Columbia, because Indian immigration within the British Empire and the British Commonwealth was easier at most times than it was into the United States. However, many Sikhs did head for the United States. We'll focus now on Sikh life in the United States.

> By 1910, Sikhs were called "rag-heads," a term of abuse that sadly has persisted in slang until today.

The first generation of Sikh migration saw the rise of a recurring feature of Sikh life here: mistreatment by some mainstream Americans, including ignorance, intolerance, discrimination, and sometimes mob violence. Immigrant Asians were often seen as unwelcome competitors by labor unions and their (all-white) members, because they worked for low wages. By around 1910, Sikhs were called "rag-heads" on the streets and in newspapers, a term of abuse that sadly has persisted in slang until today. In 1913 the California "Alien Land Act" prohibited non-citizens from owning property, which severely disadvantaged Sikh farmers, and in 1917 the U.S. Congress choked off all immigration from India and most other Asian regions. The U.S. Justice Department even went so far as to revoke the citizenship of Sikhs who had been granted it, and the U.S. Supreme Court ruled that Sikhs did not qualify for citizenship. The Court said that even though they are from Indo-European stock, they are not "white" in the same way that mainstream Americans were. (This was before the civil rights movement for African Americans in the United States.)

For Sikhs, the most grievous effect of this racial bias was that they were now unable to bring their wives and families to America. (Then, as now, family issues in immigration are difficult matters.) Against these forces, Sikhs persisted in the process of assimilation, all the while trying to maintain the strong Sikh identity that marked their religion from its earliest years. The first gurdwara was established in the United States in 1912, in the farming town of Stockton, California; for almost two generations it was the center of the Sikh religion in the United States. From around 1910 to the 1960s, Sikhs in the United States tried to keep moving forward against occasional opposition.

All this played out against the backdrop of a rising Indian movement for independence from the British Empire. Sikhs had their troubles in North America, but they still cared deeply about events in their Punjabi homeland. In 1913, the Ghadar (GAHD-uhr, meaning "revolt") Movement was founded by Hindus, Muslims, and Sikhs—all from a Punjabi background—in California in order to raise money for resistance to British colonial rule in India, especially in the Punjab. Sikhs predominated in the Ghadar organization and gave it a militant flavor. Some Sikhs even returned to the Punjab to lead ill-fated attacks on British authorities there. Although Ghadar fortunes were set back around 1917 to 1918 during the First World War by negative publicity from court trials and the killing of one of its leaders, it reorganized in the 1920s and played a role in resistance to British rule until Indian independence was established in 1947.

---

[1] Kamala Elizabeth Nayar, *Sikh Diaspora in Vancouver: Three Generations amid Tradition, Modernity, and Multiculturalism* (Toronto: Toronto University Press, 2004).

Young Sikhs line up for a Sikh Day parade in New York City.

CATHERINE JONES/ISTOCKPHOTO

SECOND AND THIRD WAVES (1965–PRESENT)

In 1965, the Sikh situation in the United States changed significantly for the better with new federal legislation that lifted old prohibitions and quotas. A large number of Sikh immigrants, many of them educated professionals such as physicians, scientists, and educators, came to the United States looking for economic opportunity. Sikh numbers in the United States tripled in a few short years. They settled not only throughout California, but also in New York and Texas, and near major Midwestern cities such as Detroit and Chicago. The first wave of Sikh migration had settled in the countryside, but this second wave settled directly into the suburbs.

These Sikhs also brought some tensions to established gurdwaras. The newcomers were more traditionally Sikh than the more assimilated Sikhs who had been in the United States for more than three generations; some of the old-timers had married non-Sikhs and given up on distinctive Sikh dress and diet. As newcomers gradually took over, Punjabi language was heard much more frequently in worship. Chairs were removed from the main hall so people could sit on the floor before the *Guru Granth Sahib*. Shoes were taken off for worship again, music in the service became more traditional, and the langar meal was reemphasized.

A third, smaller wave of Sikh immigrants arrived from India after the violent events of 1984 in Amritsar. They were much more politicized than the second wave and brought an urgent sense of Sikh identity. Talk about "Khalistan," some of it unhappy and

divisive for Sikhs, began to be heard in American gurdwaras. This continuous reworking of Sikh identity in the United States complicated the challenging task of raising Sikh children to willingly affirm their religiously Sikh and culturally Punjabi heritage. Despite these challenges, Sikhs are thriving in North America, and not just economically. Moreover, Sikhism in North America is doing something that Sikhs in the Punjab have not tried to do—they are attracting converts to the faith and healthy lifestyle of Sikhism. This movement of young American converts is now organized into an organization called the Sikh Dharma.

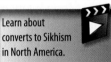

Learn about converts to Sikhism in North America.

SIKHISM IN POST-9/11 AMERICA

Some events in the aftermath of the attacks on the United States on September 11, 2001, have done "collateral damage" to Sikhs in the Western world. Al-Qaeda, the Afghanistan-based group that launched these attacks, was aligned in Afghanistan with the Taliban movement of Sunni Islam. The Taliban has a "dress code" for men nearly identical to the way members of the Khalsa dress. For almost entirely coincidental reasons, both Taliban Afghanis and observant Sikhs do not cut their hair or beards, and they both wear turbans. (Taliban members do not wear the kirpan knife, however.) Although most people in south Asia have the "cultural intelligence" to tell them apart, many residents of the United States do not. So many Sikhs in the United States have now been under suspicion and have sometimes experienced outright opposition and occasional violence, as "Muslim terrorists." Some Sikh gurdwaras have been threatened with arson. Sikh children in public schools are under particular pressure by some students who don't know the difference between Sikhs and Muslims. They are often called, or just looked at as, "terrorists." For Sikhs to be identified with Muslims is a grievous thing for them, let alone with

View "Mistaken Identity": Sikh Americans deal with the aftermath of 9/11.

Examine the "Hatred in the Hallways" report about anti-Sikh bias in the New York City school system.

Watch an introduction to Sikhism produced by the Chicago Police Department for its officers and the general public.

Listen to a rap song by young Sikhs on the possible demolition of their gurdwara in Austin, Texas.

a separatist Muslim group that carries out mass terror attacks. Most Sikhs have responded with a patient effort to educate other Americans about the differences between themselves and the Taliban.

We shouldn't end our treatment of Sikhism on this unhappy note, because that wouldn't do justice to its experience in North America. Despite the challenges of living in the Western world, Sikhs continue to live faithful lives in North America. They do struggle with issues of assimilation and discrimination, and regularly must go to court for the right to keep their distinctive appearance at their jobs. But these North American problems are much smaller than the challenges Sikhism has faced in India for the last 500 years. The Sikh community in the Western world is facing its problems resolutely and decisively. By 2000 the Sikh population of the United Kingdom was more than 300,000, and there are an estimated 150,000 to 200,000 Sikhs in both Canada and the United States. They continue to follow the Guru who proclaims, "There is only one God, whose name is true. Repeat his Name!"

CHAPTER 7

Encountering Daoism and Confucianism: Two Views of the Eternal Way

BONNIE VAN VOORST © CENGAGE LEARNING

Learning Outcomes

After studying this chapter, you will be able to do the following:

LO1 Explain the names *Daoism*, *Confucianism*, and related terms.

LO2 Outline how Daoism and Confucianism developed over time into what they are today, especially in relationship to each other.

LO3 Explain the essential teachings of Daoism and Confucianism, especially their similarities and differences.

LO4 Paraphrase in your own words the main ethical principles of Daoism and Confucianism.

LO5 Outline the way Daoists and Confucianists worship and practice other rituals.

LO6 Summarize the main features of Daoism and Confucianism in North America today.

COLIN SINCLAIR/DORLING KINDERSLEY

Like the yin and yang, Confucianists and Daoists both agreed with each other and worked against each other. Chinese culture was shaped and empowered by this dynamism.

YOUR VISIT TO THE FORBIDDEN CITY IN BEIJING, CHINA

A highlight of your tour of China is the Forbidden City, located in Beijing (bay-JING), a city formerly known as Peking. Most tourists to Beijing see at least a bit of it, but because of your interest in world religions and cultures, you are looking forward to a more in-depth view. The traditional name "Forbidden City" comes from the fact that it was formerly closed to all but the emperor, who was considered the "Son of Heaven," and his court officials. It was sacred to both Daoists and Confucianists. Now it doesn't seem at all forbidding to you, but inviting. The current official name for this complex, the Palace Museum, also seems more inviting.

View a brief introduction to Confucianism.

View a brief introduction to Daoism.

The complex consists of an astounding 980 surviving buildings spread out over an area one mile long and one-half mile wide. It covers 183 acres, which your guide puts in terms you can understand: it's the size of 166 football fields. It has two parts, both of which you can enter: the outer court, where the emperor ruled the nation, and the inner court, where he and his closest courtiers lived with their families. The complex is

What Do YOU Think?

The two main religious and ethical systems of China, Daoism and Confucianism, are trying to reach the same goal by different means.

Strongly Disagree   Strongly Agree
1   2   3   4   5   6   7

surrounded by a wide moat as well as a wall thirty feet high. As you cross into the Forbidden City through its only entrance at the Tiananmen (tee-YEN-ahn-men) or "Heavenly Peace" Gate, your guide says that it's helpful for you to understand more about the history of the area.

The Chinese have seen dragons as powerful, mostly good-natured creatures from whom people could seek favors.

< Students demonstrating their tai qi (chi) skills at the Hall of Prayer for Good Harvests in the Temple of Heaven complex, Beijing. From 1420 to 1911 C.E., emperors of China came to this temple to pray for abundant crops.

She relates the following: The Forbidden City was built in the early part of the 1400s and was home to two dynasties of China's emperors until 1912. The Ming dynasty, which ruled from 1368 to 1644, first built the palace and courtyard. The Qing (ching) dynasty then governed the area until the last emperor of China left his position in 1912. Religious ceremonies in the Forbidden City ceased in that year. It was designated a World Heritage Site in 1987 by the United Nations.

Many halls in this complex have names with religious significance, because the emperor was the intermediary between Heaven and the Chinese people. Today, these buildings are the most ancient collection of wooden buildings in the world. The Forbidden City was made fit for tourism in the 1950s, and Tiananmen Square in front of the Gate of Heavenly Peace was developed into a huge public square. For almost five hundred years imperial China had the largest palace complex in the world, and now Communist China proudly has the largest public square. You notice, however, that the guide doesn't mention how, in the spring of 1989—the year that several Communist governments in Europe fell—a pro-democracy demonstration with thousands of people took place over several weeks in this square, complete with a small replica of the Statue of Liberty, called a "goddess." In early June, Chinese army units brought in by the government opened fire on the protestors when they refused to disperse. Estimates of the dead range from five hundred to three thousand, and hundreds were imprisoned. Your knowledge of what happened here in Tiananmen Square makes your attitude about it more somber.

In your study of Daoism and Confucianism, you'll be introduced to these unique, sometimes puzzling features:

- Some scholars hold that almost all Chinese people in the world today are Confucianist in some significant sense just by virtue of being culturally Chinese, whether they self-identify as Confucianist or not. This is true, these scholars say, even if they don't think of themselves as "religious."

- Many Chinese who see themselves as either Daoists or Confucianists practice some elements of the other religion, and many are Buddhists as well, in some aspects of their lives. This makes it difficult to estimate how many followers of these faiths, the "three traditions" of China, there are today.

> Watch an introduction to the three main traditions of China.

- Confucianism is traceable with certainty to a historical founder; Daoism is not. Daoism grew out of various religious and philosophical traditions in ancient China, including shamanism and belief in the most ancient gods and spirits. This difference in beginnings has proven to be one important factor in making Confucianism a more coherent system than Daoism.

- Confucianism is a thoroughly Chinese tradition, but its influence has spread widely in East Asia beyond China, especially to Taiwan, Korea, Vietnam, and Japan. It has some influence in south Asian countries such as Malaysia and Indonesia. The reach of formal, organized Daoism hasn't been as long; it is mostly contained in China and Taiwan.

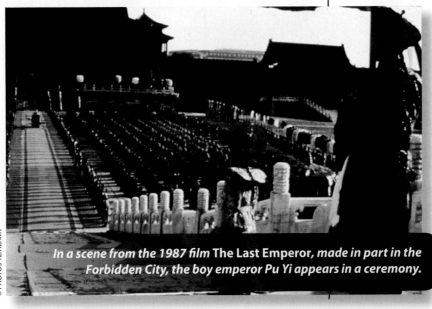

© PHOTOS 12/ALAMY

In a scene from the 1987 film **The Last Emperor**, *made in part in the Forbidden City, the boy emperor Pu Yi appears in a ceremony.*

"If you google 'Confucius,' you [get] page after page of 'Confucius says' jokes ... before you arrive at any actual quotations."
—Stephen Prothero

- Both Daoism and Confucianism have been widely misunderstood in nonacademic popular settings in the Western world, perhaps more than any other world religions. Daoism has been misrepresented as "just doing what comes naturally." The wisdom teaching of Confucius is often trivialized in popular culture, from fortune cookies to the Internet. For example, as Stephen Prothero remarks, "If you google 'Confucius,' you have to wade through page after page of 'Confucius says' jokes . . . before you arrive at any actual quotations from the man himself."[1]

In this chapter we'll make a slight change in our treatment of world religions. Since Chapter 3, we've examined one religion per chapter. Here, we'll consider together the two main religions of China: Daoism and Confucianism. The benefits of discussing them together outweigh the downsides, especially if one is careful to keep them separate. Confucianism and Daoism are similar in that they have affected, and been affected by, Chinese culture; they differ in that they have been competing formal traditions in China, with two views of the Way and how to live in it.

LO1 The Names *Daoism* and *Confucianism*

Before we discuss the names of these religions, we must explain the two common systems used for rendering Chinese into English, the older Wade-Giles and the newer Pinyin (PIN-yin). Some key Chinese words in religion are spelled the same in each system, but other words are spelled differently. For example, the Wade-Giles system spells the *d* sound in Chinese as *t*; the newer Pinyin system spells it as *d*. So the more traditional spelling is "Taoism," rather than the Pinyin system's "Daoism"; both are pronounced DOW-ihz-um.

Wade-Giles spells the Chinese word for *classic book* as "ching," but Pinyin has "jing." As a result, Wade-Giles spells the name of the main Daoist scripture "Tao Te Ching," and Pinyin spells it "Daode Jing."

For help on pronouncing Pinyin, check out a guide from Carnegie Mellon University.

Popular usage in the West stays mostly with Wade-Giles. For example, on February 20, 2011, a Google search for "Tao" returned 92 million hits, whereas a search for "Dao" returned 58 million. Nevertheless, the Pinyin system is increasingly used in scholarship. It's usually closer to the way Chinese is pronounced, which makes it easier for beginning students of Chinese religions to pronounce Chinese terms correctly. This book uses the Pinyin spelling but occasionally refers to a significant Wade-Giles spelling the first time a word appears.

Daoism, the religion of the natural Way, refers to diverse but related Chinese traditions that have influenced East Asia for more than two thousand years and have had an influence on the Western world since the nineteenth century. The word *Dao* roughly translates as "way," "path," or "road," and by extension "way of life." Scholars often divide Daoism into "religious" and "philosophical" branches. A leading scholar of Daoism, Livia Kohn, has more carefully divided it into three categories: (1) philosophical Daoism, the oldest branch, based on the texts *Daode Jing* and *Zhuangzi* (JWAHNG-zee; in Wade-Giles, *Chuang Tzu*); (2) religious Daoism, a collection of formal, organized religious movements originating from the Celestial Masters movement around 200 C.E.; and (3) folk Daoism, the widely diverse Chinese indigenous local religions taken up into Daoism after 200 C.E.[2]

Confucianism (kun-FYOO-shuhn-IHZ-um) originated as a Western term, not a Chinese term. Its first use was in the 1500s C.E. by Roman Catholic missionaries in China. They bypassed the

Confucius in a traditional pose

LIESKA/DREAMSTIME

[1] Stephen Prothero, *God is Not One: The Eight Rival Religions That Run the World—and Why Their Differences Matter* (New York: HarperOne, 2010), 101.

[2] Livia Kohn, ed., *Daoism Handbook* (Leiden: Brill, 2000), xi, xxix.

A Closer Look:

Symbols of Daoism and Confucianism

Daoism and Confucianism don't have official symbols of their faith. The Chinese character for *Dao*, "Way," is sometimes used as a symbol of both Daoism and Confucianism. Each of these two religions follows its concept of the Way. However, for people who can't read Chinese, this symbol doesn't hold a lot of meaning, so it is not widely used as a symbol of either Daoism or Confucianism.

Dao

BONNIE VANVOORST
© CENGAGE LEARNING

The most common symbol of Chinese religion is the **yin-yang**, also called the **Taiji** or "Great Ultimate," as a Chinese symbol of religion. This symbol is used mostly by Daoists and sometimes Confucianists to represent their faiths, and it is used so far beyond these two formal religions that it has become one of the most often-seen symbols in the world. The circle formed by the yin and yang represents the universe, both matter and spirit, that encircles all things and holds them together. The light and dark areas inside it represent the balance of the two opposite powers in the universe. If the line between them were straight, it would suggest motionless stability between the two areas of the circle. In fact. the line is deeply curved to show that they move and that their motion and change are constants in the cosmos. When they move with

Yin-yang

each other, not against each other, life is peaceful and productive. When they conflict with each other, confusion and disharmony result. The ideal harmony between these two is suggested in most depictions of the symbol by a small circle of light in the dark area, and vice versa. The task of life is to live according to this balance in the symbol.

What do the two parts of the yin-yang symbolize?

- Yin represents what is feminine, soft, yielding, underneath, nurturing, cool, calm, passive, and dark.
- Yang represents what is masculine, hard, powerful, above, guiding, warm, energetic, active, and bright.

Although a gender-oriented understanding of yin-yang is possible—that all aspects of yang are masculine and yin feminine—this isn't necessary, nor was it the only view in the Chinese past. Another view has the yin primarily representing aspects of the night and yang aspects of the day, which may arise from its likely original meaning of the sunny side of a hill (yang) and shadowed side (yin). Most interpretations of the yin-yang do hold that it is hierarchical, agreeing with the general Chinese cultural preference for hierarchy: the yang side and its aspects are superior to yin. One meaning it *doesn't* have is a moral dualism—it should not be understood in terms of good and evil. In the traditional Chinese view shared by both Daoism and Confucianism, life is good. Only when the balance of natural and supernatural forces symbolized by the Taiji goes into decline does evil result.

---

yin-yang [yihn yahng] Cosmic forces such as passivity and activity, darkness and light, and other opposing pairs

Taiji [TIGH-jee] The "Great Ultimate," another name for the yin-yang symbol

most common Chinese term for this tradition, "the Scholarly Tradition," a name that stresses the role of official scholars in Confucianism. The missionaries added *ism* to the Latinized form of Kong Fuzi, *Confucius* (kon-FYOO-shuhs), to make

Confucianism. Some scholars, Lionel Jensen among them, have argued that Kong Fuzi and Confucius as formal names are Western inventions and that we should keep to what Chinese tradition calls him, most commonly *Kongzi* (KONG-zhee) or *Fuzi*.[3]

---

[3] Lionel Jensen, *Manufacturing Confucianism: Chinese Traditions and Universal Civilization* (Durham: Duke University Press, 1998).

European scholars of religion in the 1800s spread the new name *Confucianism* widely. Although Confucius would almost certainly have objected to naming his movement after him, it has now "stuck" in usage. Moreover, the name *Confucianism* is accurate enough. Both Confucian and non-Confucian scholars of religion use it. More importantly, many people who follow the religion use this name. So, as in most scholarship, we will use it here.

LO2 Daoism and Confucianism Today as Shaped by Their Past

Wayne Dyer, one of North America's most prominent self-help psychologists, tapes a 2009 program on PBS television in a New York City studio. The program is titled after his new book, *Excuses Begone!* Like his earlier book, *Change Your Thoughts, Change Your Life*, this television program focuses on how people can live more-productive, happier lives by adopting the main ideas of Daoism. "Stop striving, start arriving," Dyer urges. This slogan is an excellent example of how Dyer puts complex Daoist ideas into pithy paraphrase. It's also an example of one way that Chinese religion is influencing the Western world, as a resource for psychology and personal development.

In this section, we'll briefly trace the history of Daoism and Confucianism together, from their earliest times until today. They competed with each other on an official level, especially when emperors favored one and tried to put down the other; more often they cooperated with each other on a popular level. These two religions went with each other and against each other for more than two thousand years—almost like the yin and yang—and Chinese culture was deeply affected by this movement. Before we discuss the founding of the two religions, we should look at their common background in Chinese culture and religion.

Wayne Dyer in a relaxed, non-striving pose

ANGELA WEISS/GETTY IMAGES ENTERTAINMENT/GETTY IMAGES

> *Chinese civilization is so old that the foundations of Confucianism and Daoism are as close to us as they are to the beginnings of China.*

CHINA BEFORE THE BIRTH OF CONFUCIANISM AND DAOISM (CA. 3000–500 B.C.E.)

Daoism and Confucianism arose in a civilization that was already ancient. In fact, Chinese civilization is so old that the foundations of Confucianism and Daoism are just as close to us as they are to the beginnings of civilization in China. Civilization probably began there before 3000 B.C.E., with scattered settlements along the Yellow River basin in northeast China, the "cradle of Chinese civilization." This society seems to have been highly militarized, probably because of the necessity to defend its open northern borders. Religion at this time included the worship of many gods, poetry inscribed on pottery, use of animal bones and shells in divination, and use of clay phallic statues in rituals for the fertility of crops, animals, and perhaps humans. Some of these surviving artifacts testify to religious beliefs and practices that would endure in both Confucianism and Daoism.

The earliest period in Chinese history for which there is good evidence is the Shang (shahng) dynasty period, from about 1500 to 1122 B.C.E. This society was also based in the Yellow River valley and, like other early human civilizations, centered on raising crops and animals. Powerful land-owning aristocrats controlled Shang society, enjoying luxurious homes and outfitting lavish tombs for their happiness in the next life. Almost everyone else in Shang society was a peasant or slave, with relatively few artisans. A system of writing using pictograms or ideograms as characters was developed at this time, the forerunner of the system that exists in China today. The demands of memorizing thousands of characters and acquiring the skills to draw them well limited literacy to the

© LUKAS HLAVAC/SHUTTERSTOCK.COM

Great Wall of China, built on China's northern borders beginning around 200 B.C.E. to keep out nomadic invaders. That it can be seen with the naked eye from the moon is a popular but mistaken notion.

Visit a website on Chinese history sponsored by the University of Maryland.

upper classes and professional scribes. This would help to shape the literary aspects of Chinese religions, especially their scriptures. Animal **oracle bones** inscribed with this writing were used to foretell the future and maintain good connections with ancestral spirits and nature spirits. Other methods of divination later took the place of oracle bones, but divination,

oracle bones Bones of animals inscribed with writing and used in telling the future

feng shui [FUNG shway] Literally, "wind-water"; positioning of objects to maximize the good effects of the flow of energy

Yi Jing [yee jing] "Classic of Changes," also spelled "I Ching," a diviner's manual; earliest of the Chinese classical books

Oracle bone on tortoise shell from the Shang dynasty

MUDONG/DREAMSTIME

especially fortune-telling, is still popular in Chinese religion today.

Another practice that began during the Shang has grown widely in China and is popular in the Western world today— **feng shui**, or the positioning of objects to maximize the good effects of the flow of energy. Feng shui was used at first in selecting the location of graves. When the dead are buried according to feng shui principles, the flow of energy in the earth brings yin power to their bones. This strengthens the spirits of the dead, and then blessing comes to their living families. Feng shui practices spread to altars and buildings, for the strengthening of the living. Especially in the Western world, feng shui has now been applied to furniture and decorative items. As often happens when an ancient practice is popularized commercially in the modern world, its original meaning has been altered.

Watch an explanation of feng shui today.

The rulers of the Shang dynasty led the worship of the gods, as emperors of China would continue to do. The Shang practiced human sacrifice, usually of slaves, in some of their rituals. This practice was discontinued in later periods; terracotta figures took the place of slaves in burials of kings and nobles. The final contribution of the Shang period was the writing of religious books that would become scriptures—or as the Chinese call them, *jing*, or "classics." A collection of traditional poems began to take shape; it would greatly influence later Chinese culture and religion when it became known as the *Book of Poetry*. Another classic book to influence Chinese culture and religion was the *Yi Jing* (Wade-Giles, *I Ching*), the *Book of Changes*, a collection of sixty-four mystical symbols and short explanations of them used to foretell the future. The main theme of this book is that the main forces of life are in a state of constant flux, an idea symbolized in the yin-yang. To be able to predict how flux will affect one's life is the kind of religious knowledge that this book offers to its users.

Terracotta army in the 210 B.C.E. tomb of Emperor Qin Shi Huang in Xian

© AMY NICHOLE HARRIS/SHUTTERSTOCK.COM

turbulence was not all destructive. By its end, China was the most populous society in the world, with between 20 and 40 million people. Many peasants had moved south to better farmland in the Yangzi (YAHNG-tsee) River area, and the merchant class grew in size and influence. This period was also a fertile time for Chinese thought and belief, producing many new movements seeking to restore order to a society deeply torn by continued wars and the social troubles they brought. Two of these new movements were Daoism and Confucianism.

Distinctive religious beliefs arose in Zhou times, of which the most important was about "Heaven." Heaven was not usually considered a god or set of gods, as it probably was before the Zhou, but an impersonal cosmic force working for the continuation and enrichment of life. The Zhou dynasty ended when the king of the Qin (chin; Wade-Giles, ch'in) state conquered the others and declared himself the first emperor of China, naming the whole nation after his state. The Qin was followed by the Han (hahn) dynasty, a four-hundred-year period of relatively stable rule (206 B.C.E.–220 C.E.) in which Confucianism was officially established in China.

Flux is not a negative thing, but it makes life "run." The *Yi Jing* testifies clearly to a deep Chinese cultural and religious attitude that shaped Daoism and Confucianism. The universe and the natural world in which humans live are good; human life is (or can be) basically good as well, but needs some guidance and correction in order for it to reach its full potential in the Way.

The Zhou (joh) dynasty that came next was the longest in Chinese history, from 1122 to 221 B.C.E. The king's duty was to lead the worship of the gods in order to insure a good harvest, and his power and even right to rule often depended on how those prayers were answered. The end of the Zhou dynasty is also known as the Warring States Period (481–221 B.C.E.), when the seven states of ancient China renounced their allegiance to the Zhou emperors and battled among themselves for supremacy (see Map 7.1). This prolonged period of war and social

THE ORIGINS OF DAOISM (CA. 500 B.C.E.–200 C.E.)

Daoism's origins have been traced to different periods: Chinese folk religions at the beginning of the first millennium B.C.E.; the composition of the *Daode Jing* around 350–250 B.C.E.; or the founding by Zhang Daoling (jahng dow-LING) of a movement around 150 C.E. from which would come the first main Daoist group, the Celestial Masters school. Some argue that Daoism as a religious identity only arose later, by way of contrast with the newly arrived religion of Buddhism, or with the first Daoist scripture canon in fifth-century C.E. Early religious Daoism was rooted in the religious ideas of Daoist thinkers, to which were added already-ancient local rituals and beliefs. This helped to integrate Daoism into the world views and religious life of most classes of Chinese society, but it resulted in a religion that was not as internally consistent as Confucianism or even Buddhism.

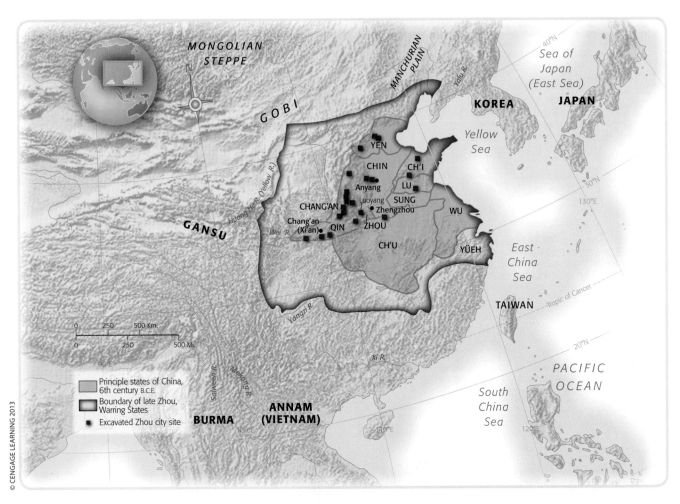

Map 7.1

China in the Sixth Century B.C.E.
During the late Zhou era, China was divided into competing, often warring states ruled only loosely by the Zhou kings. Some, such as Chiu and Wu, were large. In the third century B.C.E., the westernmost state, Qin, conquered the others and formed a unified empire.

Laozi riding an ox, in a traditional portrait

Laozi (in Wade-Giles, Lao Tzu), whose name means "Old Master," is the traditional founder of Daoism. However, many historians conclude that we have no direct, dependable evidence that he ever existed. (Some modern Daoists counter by saying that Laozi deliberately remained a shadowy figure so that others would later wonder about him.) Laozi is said to be an older contemporary of Confucius and, like Confucius, a disappointed government official who became a wandering teacher. He is also said to be the author of the *Daode Jing* and the *Zhuangzi* (in Wade-Giles, *Chuang-Tzu*), but no good literary or historical evidence supports this. It's more likely that these books were written anonymously between 300 and 200 B.C.E., and later came to be associated with Laozi.

However and whenever it originated, Daoism was widely recognized as a religious system by 300 B.C.E.

A Closer Look:

Religions or Philosophies?

At this point, a common question in the study of Chinese religions should be asked: Are Confucianism and Daoism philosophies or religions? For Confucianism, the question is livelier, because Confucius himself—and most of his followers for the past two thousand years—had much more to say about the "natural" world than the "supernatural," and his religion seems to Westerners to center on social ethics. The current Chinese government does not list Confucianism among its five officially permitted religions, even though it is reviving Confucian moral values, temples and rituals. For Daoism, this question appears in the distinction scholars often make between "religious Daoism" and "philosophical Daoism." Beginning students of world religions often encounter this question, but it's not just a question for beginners. For example, the eminent scholar Wing-tsit Chan (1901–1994) argued that Daoist religion is a "degeneration" of Daoist philosophy and that Daoist philosophy and Daoist religion are entirely different things.

Most religion scholars, even some of those who hold Chan's ideas, realize that our interest in trying to separate philosophy and religion shows a Western mindset, where philosophy and religion are separate academic disciplines. The Western inclination to separate philosophy and religion dates to the classical Greek period of philosophy and has been reinforced in early-modern and modern times. This distinction is often imposed on Chinese religion and philosophy, but this doesn't fit China. There, the closeness of what we call "philosophy" and "religion" is suggested by the commonly used words for them, *jia* and *jiao*, respectively. Daoists themselves have been uninterested in such distinctions, and today find them unhelpful.

A closer study of Confucianism and Daoism shows clearly that they are religions as commonly defined in academic study, although with strong strands of what we call "philosophy." Even "philosophical Daoism" has had distinctly religious aspects throughout its history. Philosophical Daoists have sought to increase their span of life, sometimes to the point of gaining immorality; they have interaction in various ways with supernatural forces and beings; and they order life morally according to the cosmic Dao. They practice meditation in conjunction with physical exercises, study nature for diet and health, and form monastic orders. These are all "religious" aspects of life, as Western academics define *religion*. Confucianists believe that human fulfillment comes from proper engagement in this-worldly affairs, but they also deal with matters of ultimate concern. Confucianists, as did Confucius, make room for the gods and other supernatural things but do not make them the center of their religion. As a result, Confucianism is a "humanistic" religion, but it *is* a religion as scholars generally define it.

To return to our main question: Are Daoism and Confucianism philosophies or religions? If we must answer, perhaps the best answer is that they are *both*. Of course, this book focuses on their religious aspects.

The publication of the *Daode Jing*, and other Daoist works following it, provided a focus for Daoist thinking. Daoism became a semiofficial Chinese religion during the Tang dynasty and continued during the Song dynasty. As Confucianism gained in strength, Daoism gradually returned to its roots as a popular religious tradition.

DAOISM FROM 200 C.E. TO 1664 C.E

Daoism was a broad-based movement. In its religious aspects, it developed many different monastic orders, each with its own monasteries. Because

Statue of Laozi in Quanzhou, China

Daoists looked to nature to show the way humans should live, they built many monasteries on mountain peaks and in the countryside. But they could also build monasteries near cities, the White Cloud monastery in Beijing being the most famous of these. Each monastic order tended to write its own religious literature, eventually giving rise to thousands of books in the Daoist canon, the **Daozang**.

Another product of the monasteries was martial arts. This was at first a meditational technique coupled with exercise, but

Daozang [DOW-zhahng] The Daoist canon

Zhang Ziyi (left) and Michelle Yeoh in **Crouching Tiger, Hidden Dragon (2000)**, *a blockbuster film featuring martial arts from the Wudang school of Daoism*

ideas on landscape painting contributed to a style that would last until modern times—the setting of human activities against a very large, imposing natural setting. The most well-known Daoist philosopher of this period was Ge Hong (283–343 C.E.). He pursed not only philosophical reflection, but alchemy as well, in the search for longevity (long life) and immortality. His main book, the *Inner Chapters of the Master Embracing Simplicity*, or *Baopuzi* (BOW-poo-tsee) for short, became one of the most influential Daoist scriptures through today. It has been the leading scripture for those seeking longevity by meditation, alchemy, and traditional Chinese medicines.

Read a short extract on longevity from the *Baopuzi*.

Take a brief tour of the Man Mo Daoist temple in Hong Kong.

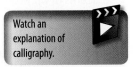
Watch an explanation of calligraphy.

developed into a sophisticated form of fighting, usually hand to hand but sometimes with weapons. Over time, the Daoist or Buddhist meditational aspects of martial arts were downplayed or lost completely. The martial arts sought to use an enemy's force against him. As this method spread beyond Daoism through Asia, it assumed many different forms: judo, karate, ju-jitsu, taekwondo. It was not widely known in the West until after World War II, when Western armed forces that had encountered it in hand-to-hand combat with Japanese troops began teaching it regularly as a part of basic military training. (The author's father learned it at that time in the U.S. Marine Corps; because he was short and slim he was often used to demonstrate its effectiveness against other Marines who were beginning to learn it, who thought they could "take him" easily.) In Daoism's philosophical movements, it developed other meditational techniques and a fuller explanation of the inner teachings. Hundreds of commentaries were written on basic Daoist scriptures such as the *Daode Jing* and *Zhuangzi*. Daoism's popular religious aspects served to integrate thousands of local gods and cults into a Daoist pantheon.

View a short video on the White Cloud Monastery.

The return of Daoism after it was suppressed in the Han dynasty is known as Neo-Daoism. Wang Bi and Guo Xiang wrote commentaries on the *Daode Jing* and the *Zhuangzi*, and became the most important figures in this movement. The "Seven Sages of the Bamboo Grove" forged a new Daoist way of life that influenced wider culture, not just remaining in mountain monasteries. This broader cultural influence of Neo-Daoism was felt in calligraphy, painting, music, and poetry. Daoist

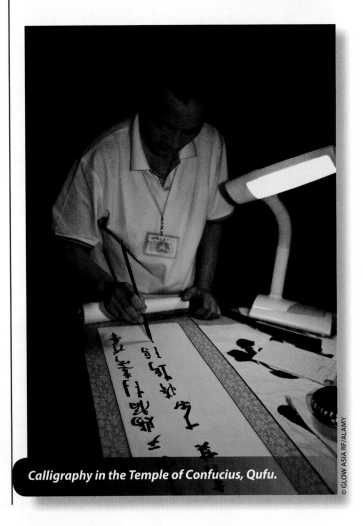

Calligraphy in the Temple of Confucius, Qufu.

A Closer Look:

The Four Editions of the Daoist Canon (*Daozang*)

A main indicator of the fortunes of a Chinese religion is the status of its sacred books. The first *Daozang* was assembled around 440 C.E. This was the first time an attempt was made to bring together religious teachings and texts from across China, and it signaled the rising strength of Daoism. It totaled around 1,200 scrolls. The second *Daozang* arose in 748 C.E., when the Tang emperor Xuan Zong, who claimed descent from Laozi, sent monks to collect further scrolls to add to the canon, which subsequently grew to about 2,000. The third *Daozang* was made around 1000 C.E. during the Song dynasty; it was revised, and many texts collected during the Tang dynasty were removed. This third version consisted of approximately 4,500 scrolls. The fourth *Daozang* was made in 1444 C.E. in the Ming dynasty; a final version was produced, consisting of approximately 1,130 titles in 5,300 scrolls.

THE NEAR-DESTRUCTION OF DAOISM (1644–1980)

The Manchurians who became rulers of China in 1644 were in the Confucian camp, and they trimmed the political and cultural power of Daoism. They removed the politically powerful head of Dragon Tiger Mountain Monastery from his position at the imperial court. Later events would prove even more detrimental. In the 1780s, Christian missionaries arrived in China and converted large numbers of Daoists. In 1849, the Hakka people of southern China, one of China's poorest ethnic groups, followed Hong Xiuquan (hoong shee-OH-chwahn), who claimed to be Jesus Christ's younger brother, in open rebellion against the emperor. Hong's movement was built on a combination of Daoism and Christianity, and sought to establish the "Heavenly Kingdom of Peace" (*taiping*). As this Taiping Rebellion conquered southeast China, it systematically destroyed Buddhist and Daoist temples and scriptures until it was finally crushed by the emperor's troops.

In the 1900s, pressure against Daoism increased. In the 1920s, the reformist "New Life" movement induced students to destroy Daoist sites and scriptures. By 1926, only two copies of the Daoist canon (*Daozang*) were left, and the Daoist heritage was in great jeopardy. But the copy of the canon kept at the White Cloud Monastery was eventually copied, and the Daoist canon was saved. There are 1,120 books in this collection, in a total of 5,305 volumes. Scholars have not yet studied much of it.

Recent times have seen an even stronger pendulum swing in the fortunes of Daoism. After the communist takeover of China in 1949,

Daoism was banned and its leaders "reeducated" and forced into other occupations. Most temples and monasteries were closed. The number of practicing Daoists fell drastically, probably 90 percent in ten years. At this time Daoism began to flourish in the greater freedom of Taiwan and also Hong Kong, a British colony then separate from China. During the "Great Proletarian Cultural Revolution" (1966–1976) instigated by the Chinese leader Mao Zedong (MOW dzuh-dong), strong attacks were made on remaining vestiges of religion and other aspects of the old order. Daoism suffered the most. Daoist monks were killed or sent to labor camps. Most Daoist monasteries and temples were destroyed, along with their texts. Before 1900 there were 300 Daoist sites in Beijing alone; by 1980 there were only a handful. After the Cultural Revolution, the Chinese government began to allow a small measure of religious freedom again. Daoism began to revive in China; many temples and some monasteries were reopened. Today,

Statue of Confucius

observant Daoists can be found throughout the country, and what was only thirty years ago called a dying religion is now growing again.

Read a *New York Times Magazine* article on the current revival of Daoism.

CONFUCIUS AND THE ORIGINS OF CONFUCIANISM (551–479 B.C.E.)

We now return to the sixth century B.C.E. to discuss the origins of Confucianism. The details of Confucius's life are sketchy, but we know its main outline. Confucius was born in or around 551 B.C.E in Qufu (choo-FOO), the capital of the small state of Lu. His real name was Kong Qiu (kong choh), but his students called him Kong Fuzi (kong foo-zhih), "Master Kong." His ancestors may have been aristocrats but brought low during a period of social instability. This would explain how someone of a relatively low social class had such a feeling for high culture from an early age. His father, who never married Confucius's mother, died when Confucius was very young, so he was taught by his mother. Confucius distinguished himself as a passionate learner in his teens. He gained a mastery of the six traditional basic arts of the time: ritual, music, archery, charioteering, calligraphy, and arithmetic. He also developed a strong attachment to Chinese history and traditional poetry that would be reflected in Confucianism and then deeply affect Chinese culture.

See a slide show of images of Confucius.

See a World Heritage Tour photographic display of the Qufu Temple.

> *Confucius was a reformer, not a revolutionary.*

As a young adult, Confucius began serving in minor posts in the government's ministry of agriculture, managing stables and granaries. He married a woman of similar social standing when he was nineteen and had children. He started his teaching career in his thirties. Confucius developed concepts about society and government that he

Mandate of Heaven
Right to rule as king or emperor, given by Heaven by means of order and prosperity in the land

hoped to put into practice in a political career. His loyalty to the king provoked opposition from the powerful landowning families, and his teaching that a ruler must set a moral example for his people did not sit well with the king's advisors, who influenced him by procuring sensuous pleasures. At the age of fifty-six, when he realized that his superiors in Lu had no interest in him, Confucius left to find another ruler who might listen to his ideas and make him an official. He gathered a growing number of students during the next twelve years, perhaps as many as 3,000. His reputation as a man of vision spread, and he was an occasional advisor to rulers. However, he was never able to get his teachings adopted in any Chinese state, or even find a steady position as a royal advisor. Confucius's own times were not right for implementing his ideas. When he was sixty-seven, Confucius returned home to continue teaching.

Watch a preview of the 2010 film *Confucius*.

Looking back on the course of his life, Confucius summarized it this way: "At the age of fifteen, I set my heart on learning; at thirty, I firmly took my stand [for what was right]; at forty, I had no delusions [about life]; at fifty, I knew the **Mandate of Heaven**; at sixty, my ear was attuned [an obscure phrase of uncertain meaning]; at seventy, I followed my heart's desire without doing wrong" (*Analects* 2:4). Despite this remarkably positive view of himself, Confucius could be a humble man. He admitted that he had not become the kind of person that he taught others to be, and at the end of his life he thought that all his teachings would perish with him. He died in 479 B.C.E. at the age of seventy-three. The fame that he brought his family is seen in the more than 100,000 of his descendants buried in the same cemetery

The Apricot Platform, where Confucius taught disciples at his home in Qufu

that he was, making it the largest family cemetery in the world and the oldest still in operation.

The story of Confucianism does not really begin with Confucius, nor was Confucius the founder of Confucianism in the way that others have been the founders of religions. Rather, Confucius was a transmitter of the best of the past, a reformer rather than a revolutionary. He retrieved the meaning of the past by breathing new life into it. Confucius's love of antiquity drove him to ask why certain rituals such as funeral ceremonies and reverence for Heaven had survived for centuries. He had faith in the power of culture to stabilize human life. Confucius's sense of history was so strong that he saw himself as a conservationist responsible for the continuity of the cultural values and social norms that had worked

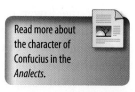

Read more about the character of Confucius in the *Analects*.

Take a video tour of Confucius's home and temple in Qufu.

so well for the civilization of China, especially in the Chou (joh) dynasty. In his system of teaching, he successfully formed a coherent system of thought and life that would shape the future of China and several other lands.

THE RISE OF CONFUCIANISM AND NEO-CONFUCIANISM (CA. 350 B.C.E.–1200 C.E.)

Mengzi (MUHNG-dzuh), who lived from about 371 to 289 B.C.E., is traditionally known in the West as Mencius (MEN-see-us). Like Confucius, he was a wandering advisor to rulers. His main work, the *Book of Mencius*, or *Mencius* for short, shows his positive view of the basic goodness of human nature. Heaven (*tian*) is found in the human heart, and the ruler need only set a good example for his people and they will follow it. Historians generally hold that

A Closer Look:

The Confucian *Four Books*

The *Four Books* of the Confucian canon are built on what Confucius and his followers saw as the main teachings of the earlier Chinese *Five Classics*. The *Analects* (*Lun yu*) of Confucius is by far the most important text in the history of Confucianism, and it gives us insight into Confucius himself. It contains sayings of Confucius, whom it calls "the Master," and occasional stories about him as remembered by his disciples and recorded after his death. The *Analects* has 12,700 characters (ideograms) in twenty short books. Like most other collections of wise sayings, the *Analects* is loosely organized. It treats, and repeatedly returns to, all the important concepts of the Confucian tradition: the virtues of humanity, propriety, and respect for parents; becoming a superior man; and proper government. Some people think that the proverbs in this book are no more helpful than proverbs that occasionally appear in fortune cookies, but they should not be atomized. In the context of the whole *Analects*, and in the living tradition of Confucianism, they are both profound and powerful.

The second of the *Four Books* is the *Mencius* (*Mengzi*), named for its author. Mencius (ca. 371–ca. 289 B.C.E.) was the most significant figure in Confucian tradition after Confucius. His disciples compiled the book of Mencius's teachings after his death. More than twice as long as the *Analects*, the *Mencius* has well-developed treatments of

several important topics, especially proper government. Mencius saw filiality as the greatest of the virtues and held strongly to the teaching of innate human goodness.

Third is the *Great Learning* (*Ta xuei*), a short book that is an excerpt on virtuous government from the *Li Ji*. Its first, short chapter is held to be the work of Confucius. The next ten chapters are a commentary on the first by one of Confucius's disciples. The *Great Learning* teaches that rulers govern by example. If the ruler is morally good, so will be his government and his subjects. If the ruler is not good, his subjects will incline to evil, and his rule, along with the Mandate of Heaven to govern, will collapse.

Fourth is the *Doctrine of the Mean* (*Chung yung*). Like most of the *Great Learning*, it was originally a chapter in the *Li Chi*. *Mean* here is better translated today as "moderation" because of the negative connotations of *mean*. "The mean" is a broad concept, embracing many aspects of virtue: moderation, right conduct, decorum, and sincerity. The good Confucianist is expected to "keep to the middle" between emotional and intellectual extremes. The superior person is formed in the middle and comes into harmony with the Dao, the cosmic "Way" of life. This book was important in the Neo-Confucian movement that arose in the twelfth century. The Harvard Confucian scholar Tu Wei-Ming has argued that the *Doctrine of the Mean* is the most explicitly "religious" of the *Four Books*.

Mencius is second only to Confucius in influence on Confucianism. Others kept Confucianism alive, but Confucius's beliefs were not influential until Dong Zhongshu (dong ZHONG-shoo) effectively promoted them in the second century B.C.E. Confucianism was then recognized as the official state religion in the Han dynasty. New religious elements including sacrifices to Confucius were then introduced. More importantly, the four main Confucian books were canonized and became the core of education and culture in China.

Despite the strong influence of Daoism and Buddhism, Confucian ethics have had the strongest influence on the moral fabric of China. A revival of Confucian thought in the Song dynasty of the twelfth century produced Neo-Confucianism, which incorporated many Daoist and Buddhist ideas, forging a sort of compromise that enabled Confucianism to continue its role as the leading influence on Chinese culture. The philosopher Zhu Xi (JOO shee, 1130–1200) believed that the ideas of Confucius had been misrepresented over the centuries. He advocated what he called a return to Confucius's original teachings, which Zhu saw as moral self-improvement largely directed by reason. Despite this emphasis on a return to Confucius, he was influenced by both Daoism and Buddhism, leading to a new and closer balance between their systems. He wrote commentaries on the classics that became "required reading" for the civil service exams. This exam system then grew in importance, and for seven hundred years it was the only way to get an official appointment in the vast imperial government, as well as the leading way for men of the lower classes to rise in rank. In time, Neo-Confucianism replaced traditional Confucianism in the higher levels of Chinese society, especially in the universities and the government.

In 1530 C.E, a Ming emperor reformed the Confucian cult to focus more on Confucius's teachings than on the sage himself. For example, images of Confucius in Confucian temples were replaced with tablets inscribed with his name and honorific titles. The ritual, worshipful veneration of Confucius declined after the founding of the Chinese Republic in 1912, but the social influence of Confucianism has continued. Neo-Confucianism was a major influence in Korea from 1392 to 1910, and it remains an important foundation of culture there. The flag of modern South Korea has the yin-yang symbol at its center.

Some Confucian scholars blamed Daoism for the fall of the Ming dynasty and the subsequent establishment of the Qing dynasty (1644–1912) by the foreign Manchus. They led a movement called "National Studies" that urged a return to traditional Confucianism. The Confucian classics came back into imperial favor, and Daoism was almost completely suppressed. For example, during the 1700s an imperial library was established, but excluded virtually all Daoist books. By the 1920s, as we saw above, Daoism had fallen so much from favor that only two copies of the *Daozang* still remained.

THE MODERN PERIOD OF DAOISM AND CONFUCIANISM (1912–PRESENT)

In 1911 to 1912, the Chinese Revolution ended the three-thousand-year-old imperial system and put a republic in its place. The Nationalist Party leaders who struggled to rule China from 1912 to 1949 embraced science, modernity, and Western culture, including some aspects of Christianity. They viewed traditional Chinese religions as mostly reactionary and parasitic. Many progressive Chinese intellectuals also rejected most of the three Chinese religions. The Nationalists confiscated some temples and monasteries for public buildings and, like the emperors of China before them, controlled traditional religious activity.

Descendants of Jeonju Lee perform 600-year-old rites to honor their ancestors in an annual ceremony in Seoul, Korea.

Basketball star Yao Ming, of the Houston Rockets, carries the Olympic torch for the 2008 Chinese Olympic team in front of the Gate of Heavenly Peace, Beijing. A portrait of Mao hangs over the gate.

世界人民大团结万岁

SHIZHAO/NPHOTO

The Communist Party of China led by Mao Zedong took power in 1949. As a Communist regime, it is officially atheistic, and initially suppressed Daoism and Confucianism with even more zeal than the Nationalist Party had. ("Religion is poison," states an old Communist propaganda saying that Mao repeated to the Dalai Lama.) Despite this suppression, most religions were able to operate at a severely reduced level. Persecution of religion, along with the Cultural Revolution as a whole, stopped when Mao died in 1976, and soon many Daoists and Confucianists began reviving their traditions. Subsequently, some of the more scenic temples and monasteries have been repaired and reopened.

The government of China now permits Daoism and Buddhism (along with Islam, Roman Catholic Christianity, and Protestant Christianity) and supervises their activities. The government considers some other religions, such as Falun Gong (which we'll discuss in Chapter 13), to be dangerous to public order, and has fiercely cracked down on them. Sensitive areas with Chinese religions include the government's relationship to the influential Zhengyi Daoist group and their leader, who lives in Taiwan, as does the current leader of the extensive descendants of Confucius. The government occasionally suppresses various traditional temple activities such as astrology and shamanism, which it calls "superstitious." It also censors films that depict popular Daoist ideas such as child vampires,

ghosts, and martial-arts cults giving supernatural abilities. But the ruling Communist Party of China has become more accommodating to religious beliefs and practices, no longer seeing them as dangerous to Communist rule or the good of the people. Daoist temples and monasteries are operating more freely, and local gods have come out of hiding.

Two recent events in Confucianism point to more Chinese openness to it. First, the education ministry is setting up programs of religious study in several selective Chinese universities, at the undergraduate and the graduate level. Students will soon be able to major in Christian, Islamic, or Chinese religion. Second, it has taken to promoting traditional Confucian values in primary and secondary schools, where students now read the *Analects* and other Confucian texts. Statues of Confucius are now seen in public places, especially in front of schools. This is being done to fill a spiritual vacuum in Chinese society. The values of communism are waning as China moves to a modified form of a free-enterprise system, and social friction, crime, and a "money-first" mentality have arisen that China's rulers see as inimical to China's well-being. Ironically, these were some of the same problems that prompted Confucius to propose his reforms more than 2,500 years ago.

> Watch a BBC report on the revival of Confucianism in China.

Performers portraying disciples of Confucius at the opening ceremonies of the 2008 Olympics in Beijing, China, recite passages from the **Analects**.

PHOTO COURTESY OF THE U.S. ARMY/TIM HIPPS

LO3 Essential Daoist and Confucian Teachings

At the giant Expo 2010 in Shanghai, China, people form lines to enter the dozens of new pavilions showcasing the theme of the Expo—how the Chinese past is shaping its desired future. Although the lines are long and a bit slow, people wait in a patient, orderly way. As an American couple just arriving at the Expo gets in the back of a line, a security agent monitoring the line asks to see identification. With some foreboding, they produce their drivers' licenses and show them to the agent. To their surprise, they are shown to the front of the line and let into the exhibit immediately, because anyone who is at least seventy-five years of age doesn't have to wait in line. The woman remarks to her husband that this policy is even better than a "senior citizen" discount, because it means that they can see much more of the Expo than they could otherwise. This preferential treatment is based on the Chinese respect for old age, a leading aspect of ethics in both Confucianism and Daoism. These practices are not monoliths and can change over time, but Daoism, with its emphasis on attaining old age, and Confucianism, with its emphasis on respect for one's parents, have contributed to the cultural heritage of honoring the elderly.

> "The Dao that can be spoken is not the eternal Dao; the name that can be named is not the eternal name." –Daode Jing

In this section we'll consider first the religious teachings that predate both Confucianism and Daoism and are important for each; then we'll examine the main Daoist and Confucian teachings that build on them.

ANCIENT TEACHINGS COMMON TO DAOISM AND CONFUCIANISM

Many of the key teachings of both Daoism and Confucianism did not originate with them around 500 B.C.E. Rather, they go back hundreds, sometimes thousands, of years in China before these religions were recognized as separate movements. Most of the gods worshiped by Daoists and by Confucianists also predate these religions. We have already considered ancient religious ideas such as yin-yang, teachings of texts such as the important *Yi Jing*, and the religious ideas behind rituals such as feng shui and divination. The other ancient teachings common to both Confucianism and Daoism are:

- **Dao** is the Way of nature that became a Way for people to walk in. This Way brings value to human culture, it shapes better relationships, and it advances health and long life. Both Daoism and Confucianism speak about the Dao, but in different ways and to different degrees. But they share a positive view of the world and Dao within it: The world is a good place, and humans must find the fullness of life within the Dao that guides the world.

- The "One" is the essence of the Dao, the energy of life. Living in this One enables things and human beings to be truly themselves. The One is often seen as operating in dualistic form, as in the yin-yang; the circle that contains the yin and yang is the One.

- *De* is typically translated "virtue," but this implies later Confucian ideas and can be confusing. Another way of looking at *de* is "power" or "working" that enables a person to follow the Dao. The meaning of *Daode Jing* suggests the relationship of de to the Dao, and not just for Daoists: "The Book of the Way (Dao) and its power/working (de)." The Dao is not a static thing with only being; it has a working power by which it reaches out to shape every living thing.

- **Qi** is the cosmic vital energy that enables beings to live and links them to the universe as a whole, and is also the basic material of all that exists. Qi gives life to the human body; its quality and movement determine human health.

> In the Abrahamic monotheisms, *Heaven* is often synonymous with *God*, but in China it means a cosmic order and principle.

- **Tian** (Wade-Giles, *T'ien*) is "heaven," an impersonal cosmic force that guides events on earth

Dao [dow] Cosmic "Way" of life

qi [chee] Cosmic vital energy that flows to and through all beings

Tian [tee-AHN] "Heaven," impersonal cosmic force working for continuation and enrichment of life and a cosmic principle that distinguishes right from wrong. In earliest times Tian was a personal god, probably the highest god among many, but in the Zhou dynasty it became an impersonal force guided by its own principle of what is right. In the Abrahamic monotheisms (Judaism, Christianity, and Islam), *Heaven* is closely tied to God; even for nonreligious people in the Western world today, it suggests a Being who lives there. In China, *Tian* does not suggest a god, but an order and principle that both transcends the world and is deeply embedded in it.

● *Ancestor veneration* or *worship* became a common practice in ancient China. Each family was expected to remember the names of its male ancestors and pay regular homage to them. Over time, their names were written on small rectangular tablets. This veneration made ancestors in the world of spirits happy, and they would bless—not haunt—their living descendants.

These ancient religious teachings and the ritual practices associated with them were established by about 750 B.C.E. They would endure throughout Chinese history, and all Chinese religions to come had to incorporate them in some way. Even foreign religions such as Buddhism, Christianity, and Islam had to make some adjustments to this religiously shaped Chinese worldview in order to grow there. Because Daoism and Confucianism drink deeply at this common well of ancient Chinese thought and practice, they share similar ideas that make it easy for Chinese people to combine them in daily life. Despite all the differences between these two religions at a high, official level, and despite the conflicts with each other that they have had in the past, Daoism and Confucianism can "fit" with each other for most Chinese.

DAOIST TEACHINGS ON THE DAO

How do Daoists understand the Dao? The first thing that Daoists say is that it cannot be described exactly in words. Human language can only sketch an outline of the Dao, not give a full picture. The most important thing about the Dao is that it works to empower,

Ancestor tablets with names of the dead are thought to be the dwelling places of the ancestors when they visit earth.

© CHUCKY/DREAMSTIME.COM

structure, and guide the world; a close second in importance is how human beings choose to relate to it. So the Dao is, broadly speaking, the way of the universe and the way of human life that ideally ties into it. The Dao is not a thing, a substance, or a being. The Dao is not a god or even a spirit, and Daoists do not worship it. Daoism does have many deities that are worshiped in Daoist temples, but they depend on the Dao like everything else. Paradoxically, the Dao gives rise to all being, but it does not have a being of its own. It is not an object of human thought or activity, but it is the hidden subject of all things. It cannot be perceived in itself, but it can be observed in the workings of the natural world.

The Dao is a Way of cosmic reality and human fulfillment. All animals and plants in the world live fully and naturally in the Dao. To some extent, humans also live naturally in the Dao, but in some aspects humans have become distant from it. To live fully in the Dao takes knowledge and intention. Despite the Dao's deep connection to the world of nature, living in the Dao isn't "naturally" easy. Moreover, living in the Dao isn't a matter of "achieving union with the Dao," as some people might put it, but rather being in complete conformity with the Dao.

The Dao includes several concepts in its one word: the source, the ultimate, the inexpressible and indefinable, the unnamable. It is the natural universe as a whole, and the principle and power within it. The most useful way to describe the Dao is found in the profound first chapter of the *Daode Jing*:

> The Dao that can be spoken is not the eternal Dao;
>
> the name that can be named is not the eternal name.
>
> Nameless, it is the origin of Heaven and Earth;
>
> named, it is the mother of all things.
>
> It is something simple and yet complex
>
> which existed before Heaven and Earth.
>
> Soundless and formless, it depends on nothing and does not change.
>
> It operates everywhere and is free from danger.
>
> It may be considered the mother of the universe.
>
> I do not know its name, so I call it *Dao*.

CHINESE TRADITIONAL DEITIES

Confucianists generally recognize the main Chinese deities, and Daoists recognize them all. The relationships among the vast numbers of gods and goddesses in China is often said to parallel, even mimic, the government bureaucracy of imperial China. Although there may be some truth to this idea, some writers argue that the reverse is true: The imperial government patterned itself after the structure of the heavenly beings. Whether this argument can ever be settled is unlikely. At any rate, it is safe to say that the imperial administration and the religious culture of the time were closely intertwined.

Westerners who know only the philosophical side of Daoism are sometimes surprised to discover that most Daoists worship gods. To Westerners, there doesn't seem to be a need for deities in Daoism. Daoism does not have a God in the way that the Abrahamic religions do, or even as Mahayana Buddhists in China have deities. In Daoism the universe constantly springs from the Dao, and the Dao impersonally guides things on their way. But the Dao itself is not God, nor is it a god, nor is it worshipped by Daoists. The Dao is much more important than that. Moreover, deities are within this universe and are themselves subject to the Dao just as much as humans are. This may seem surprising, as Daoists occasionally use what Westerners think of as language for God, for example when the Dao is called the "Venerable Lord." Some Daoists even go so far as to occasionally revere Laozi both as the first god of Daoism and as the personification of the Dao, just as some Confucianists declared Confucius a god in the early 1900s as a last-ditch effort to prop up their place in Chinese society.

In sum, China has many gods, some of them borrowed from other cultures. Many of the deities are known and worshipped by their particular role, rather than as personal divine beings; they have titles rather than names.

The Jade Emperor

The supreme ruler of heaven in Chinese tradition is popularly called the Jade Emperor, or Yu Huang. (Note how the supreme god is called an "emperor.") The Jade Emperor lives in a luxurious palace in the highest heaven, where he rules and directs all other gods. He can grant titles to the spirits of outstanding individuals and even elevate them to gods. His image and that of the gods and goddesses under his direction can be found in many Daoist temples. Most historians of Chinese religion conclude that the *Jade Emperor* was an early Daoist title for the more ancient Chinese deity called, by various names, the "Lord of Heaven."

The Earth God

We will follow the Chinese tendency in religion to think of "heaven and earth" together; after discussing the supreme god of heaven, we deal now with the main god of earth. In the countryside of Chinese lands, one can see small temples and shrines, some only a foot high, that feature a picture of a smiling, bearded old man. This is the Earth God, commonly called Tudi Gong or "Land Elder," and more formally known as Fu De Zheng Shen, "Righteous God of Good Fortune and Virtue." Tudi Gong has thousands of incarnated spirit forms who look after plots of land and the people residing on them. This guardian spirit is one of the most popular divinities in Daoism, and his image is found on many family altars.

Mazu

Mazu (MAHT-soo; Wade-Giles Ma-tsu is also common), or "Mother Ancestor," is the spirit of Lin Moniang. Lin was a young woman who lived on an island off the coast of China sometime during the Song dynasty (960–1279). Her legend says that she was a strong swimmer and employed her supernatural powers to cure the ill and save people on the sea from imminent danger. For this, she was deified after her death, and is also known as the Sea Goddess. Mazu became the most highly venerated

The Jade Emperor on his throne

Mazu, goddess of the sea, the most popular goddess in Daoism

Temple of the City God, Shanghai, China

of all female gods in Daoism, especially after an emperor of China named her the "Queen of Heaven," and she is known to Buddhists as well.

The popularity of Mazu in Taiwan is seen by the more than 400 temples dedicated to her and by the processions in communities all over the island, during which her statue is carried on a chair to spread her blessings. Tens of thousands of worshipers join in the week-long pilgrimage in her honor, and many now make a pilgrimage across the Taiwan Strait to venerate her at her grave. Mazu is widely worshiped in the provinces of China that are on the sea, and in the Chinese diaspora as well. The oldest Daoist temple in the United States, the Tin How ("Heaven's Queen") Temple built in 1852 in the Chinatown district of San Francisco, is dedicated to Mazu.

City Gods

When we think about the gods of a religion, the first thing that comes to mind are the gods that everyone in a religion knows and worships, such as the three gods we have just discussed. However, in China there are many gods who are known and worshiped only in select locales, as are the "city gods." The Jade Emperor has commanded them to guard particular cities against attack by enemies and protect their inhabitants from various evils. Most city gods were humans who served the people righteously during their lifetime, had compassion for those in danger, and protected people and good spirits from being dragged into the underworld by evil ghosts. For their demonstration of classic virtues, the righteous spirits of these people were made divine at some point after their deaths.

The City God Temple in Shanghai is dedicated to three city gods, all of whom were human beings who were deified after their deaths. Huo Guang (died 68 B.C.E.) was a famous Han dynasty chancellor. He is venerated for his role in deposing one young emperor and replacing him with another, more worthy ruler. Qin Yubo (1295–1373) was a prominent citizen of Shanghai and served in the late Yuan dynasty. When the Ming dynasty was founded, he refused two commands to serve at the court. He finally relented and served in several offices, including chief imperial examiner. Chen Huacheng (1776–1842) was a Qing-dynasty general who led the defense of Shanghai during the First Opium War. He vowed to defend China to the death, and was killed in battle against the British.

Wang Ye

Wang Ye is a generic term denoting some 360 "lords of pestilence" whose lives before becoming gods are recounted in different tales. These lords are people of great merit and exemplary lives, who after death were charged by the gods with the task of protecting mankind from evil spirits and epidemics. (They become "lords of pestilence" in the sense of controlling pestilence.) Rituals for worship of these protectors differ widely. One of the most popular rituals for driving away disease, held twice every year, is "Burning Wang Ye's Boat." A full-sized boat made of paper and wood is burned along with its spirit-money cargo. This offering is designed to make the Lords of Pestilence more inclined to do their protective work.

A "techno-neon" type of Daoist god dances at a 2010 festival in Taiwan.

KYLET/DREAMSTIME

Like most religions with many gods, Daoism can "lose" gods, add new gods, or update the portrayal of older gods. A variety of "techno-neon" portrayals of Daoist gods are popular in Chinese lands today.

DAOIST TEACHING OF WU WEI

The only method of following the Dao is by **wu wei**. This term is difficult to translate and has been rendered as "nonaction," "passive action," "uncontrived action," or "natural nonintervention." *Nonaction* wrongly implies that one does nothing at all, that one is completely passive. The *Daode Jing* might be read to support this interpretation, as in its "When nothing is done, nothing is left undone" (Chapter 48). However, wu wei is best understood as going along with nature, letting things in life take their natural, Dao-determined course.

Daoists try to live balanced and harmonious lives that are attuned to the Dao as it is seen in nature--they "act naturally." They find their way through life in the same way as breezes blow in the air, as rain falls from the sky, or as a river flows through the countryside by finding its natural course. They act, even are active, but their action is carefully attuned to their perception of the Dao, so it is easier, happier, and "natural." To use a modern analogy, most North Americans make a distinction between *work* and *pleasure*: If an activity is pleasurable, we don't think of it as work, which is supposed to be at least a little difficult. As a result, Westerners can think of the expression "act naturally" as a nonsensical self-contradiction similar to "found missing" or "minor catastrophe." But in the Daoist view, when work is done naturally—if a carpenter cuts wood with the grain, not against it, for example—it as a pleasure, and we do in fact "act naturally." This is wu wei in action. Wu wei doesn't forbid action in one's life, but it does command that one's activities fit into the natural pattern of the universe. After Buddhism entered China and made an impression on Daoism, wu wei was also understood as action that is not ego driven, but detached from individual desires. In sum, Daoism requires individuals to live on the basis that the world (outside of human life, of course) is working properly and that humans should live and "work" the same way as nature naturally follows the Dao.

DAOIST VIEWS OF QI

Daoists understand the human body to be a miniature of the universe. Like the universe, each human body has many parts, but it is filled with the Dao. The human body, as much as the larger universe, is also inhabited and ruled by a large number of gods.

The body also has spiritual energy that is cosmic, but not a part of the gods. Daoists believe that every living person has a normal, healthy amount of qi and that personal health results from the balance, harmony and smooth flow of qi. This flow is seen in several texts as a complex system analogous to the flow of water, with a sea of qi in the abdomen, its main location; rivers of qi flowing through the torso and through the arms and legs; streams of qi flowing to the wrists and ankles; and small springs of qi in the fingers and toes. A small disruption in this complex system can influence the whole and require readjustment. Overall balance and natural smoothness in the working of qi is the general goal. Daoists want to empower their qi and be empowered by it.

wu wei [woo way]
Literally, "not asserting"; going along with the true nature of the world

Image left: American man practices Tai qi

© MICHAELJUNG/SHUTTERSTOCK.COM

Tai qi is mostly known in the West as an exercise system, but this is not its significance for Daoism.

Every person receives a core of primordial qi at birth, and need to sustain it during their lifetimes. They do so by drawing qi into the body from air and food, as well as from other people through social and sexual interactions. But they also lose qi by breathing bad air, eating and drinking too much, having negative emotions, and engaging in excessive sexual or social interactions. Traditional Chinese medicines drawn from nature can be used to restore the flow of qi, and acupuncture is also commonly used to unblock qi flow. Tai qi and other movement-and-meditation systems arose to maximize the flow and presence of qi in the body. Breathing properly is key to tai qi. Although it is known in the West as an exercise system especially good for older people, this is not its significance for Daoism. Nevertheless, the medical benefits of tai qi are well established. For example, a study done by Emory University's medical school concluded that training in tai qi was highly effective in improving the balance, strength, and even self-confidence of those 70 years and older.[4]

---

[4] S. L. Wolf, M. O'Grady, K. A. Easley, Y. Guo, R. W. Kressig, M. Kutner, "The influence of intense Tai Chi training on physical performance and hemodynamic outcomes in transitionally frail, older adults," *Journal of Gerontology*, Volume 61, number 2, (2006): pp. 184–9. A summary can be found at http://www.ncbi.nlm.nih.gov/pubmed/16510864.

THE DAOIST QUEST FOR IMMORTALITY

Immortality doesn't mean escaping death by living for ever in the present physical body. This is the stuff of Western and Chinese horror stories. Most Daoists believe that all spirits are immortal in some sense—they survive the death of the body and go into the next world. The world of spirits is connected to the world of the gods. Spiritual immortality, a special goal of some Daoists, raises to a whole new level the practice of attaining immortality in this life. To attain spiritual immortality, one must change all one's qi into primordial qi and then refine it. This finer qi will gradually turn into pure spirit, enabling one to become a "spirit-person" already in this life. This process requires intense training in meditation and trances, radical forms of diet, and esoteric sexual practices. The result is a bypassing of the effects of

Daoist priest in Taiwan addresses an audience.

© YANFEI SUN/SHUTTERSTOCK.COM

A Famous Conversation Between Confucius and Laozi

The meeting of Confucius and Laozi probably never happened, but it was invented in later times to illustrate the differences between their systems, at least on an official level. Confucius, committed as he was to bringing proper order to social and political life, promotes to Laozi the value of ancient religious rituals and ideas of justice. He speaks positively about the way ancient kings ruled, especially Zhou rulers. Laozi is interested in acquiring peace and inner equilibrium. He urges Confucius in sharp words to seek wu wei, which leads to unity with the Dao.

> "Today I have seen Laozi, and I can only compare him to the dragon."
> —Confucius

Confucius asked Laozi about his opinion regarding the ancient rites and rulers. Laozi is said to have answered:

> The men about whom you talk are dead, and their bones are moldered to dust; only their words are left. When your "superior man" gets his opportunity, he succeeds; but when the time is against him, he is carried along by circumstances. I have heard that a good merchant, even if he is rich, appears as if he were poor. Likewise, the truly superior man appears outwardly unintelligent. So put away your proud airs and your many desires to change things. They are of no advantage to you; this is all I have to tell you.

In this conversation, it became clear that neither would convince the other. After their meeting, Confucius said to his disciples,

> I know how birds can fly, how fish can swim, and how animals can run. . . . But there is the dragon: I cannot tell how he mounts on the wind through the clouds and rises to heaven. Today I have seen Laozi, and I can only compare him to the dragon.

death on the spirit; the end of the body has no impact on the continuation of the spirit-person. After death, the spirit lives forever in a wonderful paradise, and the person is said to be an "immortal."

CONFUCIAN REFORMULATIONS OF ANCIENT TEACHINGS

The Confucian reworking of ancient Chinese teachings centered on ethics—what the Western tradition calls "personal ethics" and "social ethics." Confucianism is often called a system of social ethics, and from the Western perspective that is true enough, but we should remember that this distinction between "personal" and "social" is not often made in China. It doesn't make a great deal of sense in a society where the personal and the social are so fully blended, and where Western-style individualism is rejected. We'll consider Confucian ethics later in this chapter; here, however, we should state the Confucian "take" on ancient Chinese religious teachings and practices.

As stated above, Confucius and his followers were highly appreciative of Chinese tradition. His teaching reaffirms many aspects of Chinese religion before him: the role of Heaven, particularly in government;

the importance of the Way (Dao); the assumption, made explicit in Confucianism, that humans are basically good and will follow the truth when they know it; and respect for the gods and traditional rituals. On respect for ritual, Confucius once defended the sacrifice of sheep by saying to someone who objected to it, "You love the sheep, but I love the ceremony" (*Analects* 3.17) Confucius's system sought to reform traditional Chinese religious and ethical ideas, not so much by changing them as by showing people their inner meaning. Confucius believed that if people knew *why* these things are important, they would follow them more fully and carefully, and life would become what it should be.

LO4 Daoist and Confucian Ethics

Throughout North America, Amy Chua's book *Battle Hymn of the Tiger Mother* (2011) raised a storm of controversy on television, on the web, and in print. In it Chua (CHEW-ah), a law professor at Yale, details how she raised two daughters with traditional "tough love" and "Chinese mother" parenting, as opposed to what she calls the "lax" current models of American parenting. She demanded straight As from her daughters and pushed them to excel in everything they did, often using methods that seem harsh and unloving to her readers. Many Chinese American parents do take the time to guide their children in doing homework and often give them some academic work besides what is assigned; children usually respond by taking their studies seriously. This is in line with traditional Confucian values, especially the importance of self-cultivation for one's family. Chua's approach struck a nerve, as it was designed to do (notice its provocative title), but many experts on Chinese culture wonder if she hasn't misrepresented Confucian values and thereby done these values a disservice.

Confucian ethics are more fully developed, and more central to its religious system, than Daoist ethics. For example, it is often said about Confucianism that it  is a system of ethics, but this is not said about Daoism. Before we discuss Confucianism, we will consider some main moral principles from the *Daode Jing* and other early texts that have become important in Daoism.

DAOIST ETHICS

The basis of Daoist ethics is the *Daode Jing*. Although it is elusive in style and meaning, challenging the reader to figure out what it means, the main lines of Daoist moral teaching are clear. The *Daode Jing* teaches that one must follow the way of the Dao in order to live a good life. Other living beings in nature, plants, and animals and the system of nature as a whole follow the Dao automatically; they can't do otherwise.

But human beings do not follow the Dao naturally. The *Daode Jing* suggests that human distinctions such as good and evil, beauty and ugliness generate the troubles and problems of existence (Chapter 3). Humans impose such things on the Dao; they aren't really there. Persons following the Dao must not live according to human-made distinctions (Chapter 19). Indeed, these distinctions emerge only when people aren't following the Dao (Chapters 18, 38); they are a form of disease (Chapter 74). Daoists believe that the Dao unties the knots of life, blunts the sharp edges of relationships and problems, and soothes painful occurrences (Chapter 4). So it is best to practice wu wei in all endeavors, to act naturally, and not to oppose or tamper with how life is flowing.

All this can seem very abstract, but Daoism carries out these ideas in everyday practice. For example, many Daoists have a preference for vegetarianism, which they see as more "natural" than meat-eating. This Daoist moral practice, along with the Buddhist promotion of vegetarianism, explains why Chinese restaurants have so many vegetarian dishes on their menus.

This passage from Chapter 7 of the *Zhuangzi* explains the key points of wu wei:

> Wu-wei makes the person who practices it the lord of all fame. It serves him as the treasury of all plans. It fits him for the burden of all offices. It makes him the lord of all wisdom. The range of his action is inexhaustible, but there is nowhere any trace of his presence. He fulfills all that he has received from Heaven, but he does not see that he was the recipient of anything. . . . When the perfect man employs his mind, it is a mirror. It does nothing and anticipates nothing. It responds to what is before it, but does not retain it. Thus he is able to deal successfully with all things and injures nothing.

CONFUCIAN ETHICS

Filial Piety

Although Confucianism has not often ranked its moral virtues, filial piety, **xiao**, is traditionally considered among the most important and has had a powerful effect on Chinese culture. As a phrase, "filial piety" is a bit unwieldy and old-fashioned, but no other term has taken its place. *Filial* means "of a child" (*filius* is the Latin word for "son"), and *piety* means "inner devotion" and "outward obedience," both bordering on religious reverence. So *filial piety* is first of all the honor and obedience that children owe their parents.

The *Book of Filial Piety* is our main source for this topic, attributed traditionally to Confucius and one of his sons but almost certainly written anonymously in the 200s B.C.E. Filial piety must be shown towards both living parents and dead ancestors, and this leads to ancestor worship. It binds families into an almost-eternal bond. This relationship was extended by analogy to the Five Relationships: (1) ruler and subject; (2) father and son; (3) husband and wife; (4) elder brother and younger brother; (5) older friend and younger friend. Each person in these sets of relationships had specific duties; the first person in the relationship must lead with honor and kindness, and the second person must faithfully obey. Duties extended to the dead, who were expected to bless descendants that honored them and lived well, and withhold blessing from descendants who didn't. The only relationship where respect for elders did not apply was the friend to friend. In all other relationships, high reverence was held for the older person of the two.

> **xiao** [show; rhymes with *now*] Filial piety; honor and obedience to one's parents and deceased ancestors

Read a short explanation of the Five Relationships from the *Classic of Rites* (*Li Jing*).

All this was traditional in Chinese culture by the time Confucius came onto the scene. He stressed not only the duty to perform the actions of filial piety, but much more the inner attitude of these acts. Only when inner attitude empowers and guides the outer acts will filial piety "work" to improve society. One must have the genuine reverence that xiao, piety toward parents, implies. Confucius taught, "Filial piety nowadays means the support of one's parents. But dogs and horses are also able to do something in the way of support [for the dogs and horses that gave them birth]. Without reverence, what is there to distinguish the one support from the other?" (*Analects* 2.7).

Even for those outside the Chinese cultural and religious system, Confucius's teaching on relationships has a great deal of wisdom. For example, he said that filial piety can be illustrated by "Not making your parents anxious about anything else than your being sick." To those with aging parents he said, "The age of one's parents should always be remembered, as a reason for joy and for fear" (*Analects* 2.6, 21).

One's family name is traditionally put first, then one's personal name—family is more important than an individual member of it.

Note how family relationships are the center and key to the five relationships. When people in the West speak of "family values" in wider society, their ideas pale in comparison with China's emphasis on family values. The importance of one's family is shown by traditional Chinese names. The family name is traditionally put first, then the personal name—family is more important than the individual members of it. In general, the individual lives for the family, not vice versa. (When Chinese people in the West put their personal name first, it can get a little confusing for non-Chinese to tell the personal name from the family name. The family name typically has one syllable and the personal name has two. In the traditionally-ordered name of the scholar Tu Weiming, *Tu* is the family name, *Weiming* the personal name; with a scholar who Westernized his name, Wing-tsit Chan, his two-syllable personal name is first.) Filial piety has continued to play a central role in Confucian thinking, and in Chinese culture, to the present day.

Reciprocity

Ren, variously translated "humaneness, reciprocity, virtue," is a basic Confucian value, second only to filial piety in its importance. Despite the hierarchical and authoritarian structure of life that Confucianism encourages, the more powerful people in every relationship must act with humane, gentle reciprocity toward the less powerful in the relationship. Confucius himself once said that *ren* is the key moral teaching, and summarized it by saying, "What you don't want done to yourself, don't do to others."

Loyalty

Loyalty (zhong) is closely related to filial piety. Loyalty is an extension of one's duties to friend and family, and is carried out in the Five Relationships. Loyalty to one's father was first, then one's spouse, then to one's ruler, and lastly to one's friends. Like filial piety, Confucius' teaching on loyalty was often subverted by the autocratic social structure of China. More emphasis was put on the obligations of the subjects to their ruler, and less on the ruler's obligations to his subjects, whether that ruler was an emperor, a father, or a husband. Nevertheless, loyalty was always considered one of the greater human virtues.

The "Perfect Man"

The term **junzi** (Wade-Giles, *chun-tzu*) literally "a prince's or lord's child," is crucial to Confucianism. More than any other Confucian concept, it expresses the process of self-cultivation and self-improvement. A succinct description of the junzi is one who, in the Anglo-American phrase, is a "scholar and a gentleman." In ancient times, the masculine gender of the phrase

Statue of Confucius in Berlin, Germany. An inscription on the base of the statue is from Analects 15.23, on reciprocity: "What you don't want done to yourself, don't do to others."

SIEGFRIED GRASSEGGER/PHOTOLIBRARY.COM

was intentional—only males could become a junzi. In modern times the masculine translation in English is still frequently used, although women are also urged in some parts of the Confucian world toward self-cultivation.

In addition to the charge of sexism, this term has also been linked with elitism. The junzi is seen as a better person than others, and he is expected to act as a moral guide to the rest of society. Indeed, *junzi* has often been translated "exemplary person." However, becoming a junzi by education and then experience was open to every class. Confucius would take on as a student anyone who could pay him even the smallest amount, and later Confucianism was in many respects a meritocracy of learning and virtue, not an aristocracy of automatic privilege for the high-born.

For Confucianists, the great example of the "perfect man" is Confucius himself. Perhaps the biggest disappointment of his life was that he was never awarded the high official position that he desired, from which he wished to demonstrate the social blessings that would ensue if humane, wise persons ruled and administered the state. Despite this disappointment, the continued to teach his system, even when he thought that it would die out when he did. His students carried on his teachings for hundreds of years before his system took root in Chinese life.

Watch a student-made instructional video on business manners in China.

LO5 Ritual and Worship

A solitary sage studies ancient Chinese poems in Hong Kong. He pauses to reflect on their meaning, especially on how they relate to his Confucian beliefs. After reflecting, he writes out the passage calligraphically; his artistic brush stokes as he draws the Chinese word-characters show the inner meaning of the text and the results of his meditation. This simple ritual helps him improve his character toward becoming a "superior man," the highest goal of the Confucian tradition, and his study of the ancient classics is a key ingredient in this self-cultivation. Daoists also use the drawing of key words and passages to live more deeply in the Dao.

DAOIST TEMPLES AND WORSHIP

Daoist temples are more colorful and elaborate than those of other religions in China. They are ornately decorated on the exteriors and interiors. Those who visit and worship there often add brightly colored flowers and streamers to decorate the temple. Color, particularly red, is seen as bringing blessing and good luck. Vendors outside most temples sell small statues for taking home, as well as incense and flowers to use in the temple. Inside is an altar at the front, on which flowers can be placed and incense burned. Worshipers may kneel in reverence in front of this altar. Behind the altar, the focal point of the temple, are statues of the gods honored in that temple.

Sometimes there are group ceremonies in the temple, such as continuous reading of a scripture text to earn merit or monastic worship on holy days, and people in the temple are welcome to look on. But most people come to the temples for individual experiences, to seek the favor and blessing of the god(s) for a particular need. One of the oldest needs of worshipers is to gain direction for their future. In ancient times, various divination rituals were used, going all the way back to oracle bones inscribed with writings; the bones would be put into the fire, and how they cracked would indicate the future. Other methods arose over time, and the most common one used today in or just outside Daoist temples is casting yarrow sticks to select a passage from the *Yi Jing*, which a diviner will then interpret.

Stone lion covered with good-luck streamers at a Buddhist temple in Shanghai, China

© ISTOCKPHOTO.COM/PEGGY DE MEUE

Influence of Daoism on Buddhism: tourists visiting a Buddhist temple have their fortunes told by a nun.

CONFUCIAN TEMPLES AND WORSHIP

In China before the twentieth century C.E., every county had one official temple to Confucius. Most of these temples were next to Confucian schools. The front portal of the temple was an ornamental gate. Inside, there are usually three courtyards, two in smaller temple complexes. The main building on the inner courtyard was the "Hall of Great Achievement" or "Hall of Great Perfection." This housed the ancestral tablet of Confucius and the tablets of other important masters and sages, usually the first main disciples of Confucius. A second significant temple building was the "Shrine of the Great Wise Men," which honored the ancestors of Confucius.

Unlike Daoist or Buddhist temples, Confucian temples do not normally have images. In early years, Confucius and his disciples were probably represented with wall paintings and statues. However, there was rising opposition to this practice, which over time was seen as Buddhist. In the 1500s C.E., all existing images of Confucius were replaced with memorial tablets

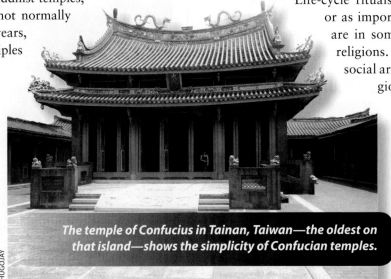

The temple of Confucius in Tainan, Taiwan—the oldest on that island—shows the simplicity of Confucian temples.

in imperial temples in the capital and other bureaucratic locations. However, statues are still found in temples controlled by Confucius's family descendants, such as that in Qufu. The point of almost all Confucian temples was to honor and promote Confucius's teachings, not Confucius himself. Confucius was a human example, not a god.

The state-mandated worship of Confucius centered upon offering sacrifices to Confucius's spirit in the Confucian temple. A dance known as the "Eight-Row Dance," consisting of eight columns of eight dancers each, sometimes carrying feathers or a weapon, was also performed. This is performed on Confucius's birthday and is accompanied by musical performances and prayers. Animal sacrifices (the animals are killed before the service, not as a part of it) and incense are offered to the spirit of Confucius.

In addition to honoring Confucius, Confucian temples also honored other disciples and Confucian scholars through history. The composition and number of figures venerated changed and grew through time. Because temples were a statement of official Confucian teaching, which Confucians to enshrine was often a difficult issue. Today, a total of 162 figures are venerated in Confucian temples.

THE TRADITIONAL CHINESE FUNERAL

Life-cycle rituals are not as plentiful or as important in China as they are in some other cultures and religions. Marriage is more a social arrangement than a religious one, for example. But the traditional Chinese funeral is well developed and has great religious and cultural significance. It still reflects some of the most ancient Chinese beliefs about life, death and life after death.

> *Cremation is rare, even unthinkable, for Daoists and Confucianists, because it destroys the qi that remains in the bones of the dead.*

Cremation is rare, even unthinkable, for Daoists and Confucianists, because it destroys the qi that remains in the bones of the dead. This qi is important for the spirit of the deceased in the next world. In-ground burial of the whole body is the rule. For Chinese Buddhists, however, cremation is common. Male heads of the family receive the most elaborate funerals, infants or children very simple funerals, with rites for people in between on a sliding scale.

Funerals take place in the home and the cemetery, not in a temple or mortuary business. An undertaker is hired to oversee all funeral rites, especially actions involving physical contact with the corpse, because this contact is defiling to the family. When the family prepares to receive visitors come to pay their respects, all statues of gods in the house are covered so that they will not be exposed to the body or coffin. All mirrors are removed or covered, because seeing a body in a mirror is thought to be inauspicious. When the body of the deceased is cleaned and dressed in the deceased's best clothing, it is put in the open coffin and placed inside the house or in its courtyard. Flowers, gifts, food, and a portrait of the deceased are placed near the coffin as an offering to the deceased and as a comfort to the bereaved family. The immediate family is now ready to receive visitors from their wider family, neighbors and friends.

Various activities take place in the home during the period of visitation. Relatives typically cry or even wail during mourning, both out of genuine emotion and as a sign of respect and loyalty to the deceased. The spirit of the dead will see this grief and be pleased by it. A small altar with burning incense and a candle is put at the foot of the coffin. These honor the dead, and help to keep the smell of death at bay. Symbolic paper money is burned continuously outside to provide the deceased with income in the afterlife. Visitors light incense for the deceased and bow to the family out of respect. A monk reads aloud verses from Buddhist or Daoist scriptures. (Confucianists generally rely on Buddhism and Daoism for funeral rites.) The souls of the dead face many troubles and even torment for the sins they have committed in life before they can enter the happier afterlife. Chanting by the monks eases the passage of the deceased's soul into heaven. These prayers are accompanied by music, and the family arranges for as much scripture and music performance as it can afford.

A solemn procession then goes from the home to the cemetery. Chinese cemeteries are traditionally located on hillsides, where feng shui is best. (As we saw earlier in this chapter [p. 160], feng shui began with burials, and its influence on burial is still strong.) When the coffin is removed from the hearse and lowered into the ground, the mourners look away. Then family members throw a handful of earth into the grave before it is filled. As they depart, the keeper of the cemetery offers other prayers for the deceased.

After the burial, the ritual continues. All clothes worn by the mourners are burned to avoid bad fortune associated with death. Special prayers to the deceased will be offered by the family at home, especially directed at the ancestral tablet that now has the deceased's name on it. The family's mourning period continues for one hundred days, signified by a piece of colored cloth worn on their sleeves. From this time on, for as long as the family endures, the dead will be venerated in the home (and in a family temple if the family is wealthy), and imitation paper money will be sent to them by burning it at their graves.

Read about Chinese American teens' views on ancestor worship today.

Watch the burning of possessions being sent to the deceased's spirit.

Watch a National Geographic video on "second burial."

In Gansu Province, China, mourners in white shrouds burn symbolic paper money at a Daoist funeral.

EYE UBIQUITOUS/PHOTOLIBRARY.COM

A Final Comparison of Daoism and Confucianism

Before we turn to the topic of Daoism and Confucianism in the Western world, it may be helpful to sketch a final comparison of Daoism and Confucianism. Daoism shared some emphases with classical Confucianism, such as the necessity of self-cultivation and a concern for the concrete details of life, not abstractions (the latter seen, for example, in Buddhism). Both Daoism and Confucianism are world-affirming religions, and religions that also affirm the ancient cultural and spiritual life of China. Despite these similarities, Daoism and Confucianism have been competing alternative religions—in main teachings, ethics, and ritual.

As we saw previously, Daoism teaches that human distinctions such as morality and beauty generate the troubles and problems of existence. They are imposed on the world by the human mind; they do not exist in the world itself. The person following the Dao must cease living by human distinctions. Daoists believe that the Dao naturally makes human life full and right. So it is best to practice wu wei, to act naturally, and not to oppose or tamper with how nature or even human reality is moving. Daoism teaches that it is better to be passive rather than active, yielding rather than assertive, quiet rather than vocal. In terms of the yin-yang, Daoism is the yin of China.

> *Daoists take their hands off life, but Confucianists put their hands on everything.*

Confucius and his followers, on the other hand, have viewed themselves as the yang, the active and assertive side of life. They have been "proactive," to use a current term, in setting human life straight. They study current life in the light of Confucian thought, plan changes, educate people to be active, and develop solutions to China's problems. Daoists take their hands off life and let it go its own way; Confucianists put their hands on everything they can to guide and shape people. To use another illustration, Daoists let life shape them like a piece of rock or wood is shaped by natural forces; Confucianists try to carve themselves into a sculpture.

LO6 Daoism and Confucianism in North America

Daoism first came to the West when its main works were translated into European languages. The *Daode Jing* has been consistently popular for more than two centuries and is one of the most translated books in the world. From 1927 to 1944 the chief advocate of Daoism for the Western World was Professor Henri Maspero in Paris. More recently, Michael Saso (born 1930), an academic expert in Daoism and author of several leading books on it, has advanced Daoism in the West. He was the first Westerner to become a Daoist priest. He also served as coeditor of *Taoist Resources*, a major academic journal to be devoted entirely to Daoism; it ceased publication in 1997. Today, many Daoist organizations have been established throughout the West. Confucianism also came to the West by means of its writings. The *Analects* and the *Mencius* were among the first books translated in Max Müller's *Sacred Books of the East* project in the 1800s, and dozens of translations have been made since that time into almost every European language.

Chinese religions have been spread to North America not primarily from China itself, but from neighboring lands in which these religions have long been present: Taiwan and Korea in particular, and also to a lesser degree Japan, Vietnam, and Indonesia. In Taiwan, despite the modernizations that have made the country a thriving democracy and economic powerhouse, traditional Chinese religions remain stronger than on the mainland. Nine out of ten residents of Taiwan call themselves Buddhists, Daoists, Confucianists, or a mix of the three. In Korea, almost half the population is Christian, but the other half is devoted to Buddhism, Confucianism, and/or the service of local gods.

> *Confucianism is probably the only world religion to come to North America that doesn't have formal temples here.*

Confucianists and Daoists came to North America from these lands as well as from China. We will deal with Confucianism first. Because Confucianism is a moral system that is built on elements of traditional Chinese religion found in much of Daoism, and because

Confucian temples in Chinese lands were almost all state sponsored, Confucian temples couldn't be transplanted in North America as Daoist or Buddhist temples could. The temples to Confucius, with their associated schools—from primary schools in every county to the imperial university in Beijing—that anchored Confucianism in Asia could not be built in North America. Indeed, they wouldn't make sense here, in a society that isn't Confucian and doesn't establish any religion as the national faith. Chinese people did eventually build social and educational associations that had an appreciation for Confucianism, sometimes even a room or two dedicated to the veneration of Confucius and his main disciples. But they couldn't, and didn't, build temples such as one finds in China and lands in the Chinese cultural orbit. Confucianism is probably the only world religion to come to North America  that doesn't have formal temples here. Chinese cultural centers often must host Confucian ceremonies.

A much more recent feature is the establishment of "Confucius Centers" or "Confucius Institutes" in major American cities, usually connected with universities, by the government of the People's Republic of China. Dozens of these centers have been set up since about 1990; in Chicago alone, there are several. These centers and institutes are an effort at "public diplomacy" by the Chinese government, an outreach especially to secondary schools and higher education. The main Chicago Confucius Center describes itself this way: "The Confucius Center is a non-profit institute aiming to enhance intercultural understanding in the world by sponsoring courses of Chinese language and culture, so as to promote a better understanding of the Chinese language and culture among the people of the world; develop friendly relationships between China and other countries; accelerate the development of multiculturalism at the international level; and help bring about global peace and harmony." So it's clear that, despite the name "Confucius Centers," the spread of Confucianism itself isn't what they are primarily about. But there is something traditionally Chinese about this arrangement—Chinese culture and Confucian values are so deeply intertwined that to deal with the first is necessarily to deal with the second. As a result, Confucianism is found at these centers and institutes not only in the plentiful Confucian scriptures that are there, but even more in the promotion of Confucian values in Chinese life and learning.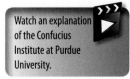

Daoism came to North America with the first Chinese, who arrived to participate in California's gold rush. The new settlers established several temples in San Francisco. One of these, the Tin How Temple, was built in 1852 and still stands today. It was built out of gratitude to Mazu as the Queen of Heaven, for protecting the settlers on their long sea voyage. In the next decades, statues and name tablets of other gods were installed in the temple. By 1890, dozens of Chinese temples were found along the West Coast of the United States and Canada. Together they served a multitude of gods, just as their temples in China had. They were usually staffed by a trusted caretaker who acted as a janitor for the building, supervised the worship and sacrifices, and organized festivals. Daoist priests were not yet to be found in the New World, and neither were monks. Despite the hard pressure on Daoism in China during the 1800s, priests and monks did not make the perilous trek to a non-Chinese culture in the New World.

Should these be considered *Daoist* temples? This depends on how one understands Daoism. To use the three-fold understanding of Daoism advanced by Livia Kohn, they certainly were not temples of "philosophical Daoism." They can make a good claim for "religious Daoism," and certainly they were "folk Daoist" temples. But most gods worshiped in these temples were not the main Daoist deities, with the exception of the Jade Emperor. Rather, they were local gods that Chinese Americans could still look to for help, but these gods had long ago been taken up into the vast Daoist collection of gods.

The ups and downs of Daoism in the United States varied with immigration policies, just as all other religions of immigrants did. The federal Chinese Exclusion Act of 1882 effectively stopped all new Chinese immigration, and Daoist temples suffered. When the Immigration Act of 1965 was passed, a good level of Chinese immigration resumed. Temples revived, and many other Daoist organizations have been founded. The largest of these is the network of "Healing Tao" centers in the United States and Canada, a movement that combines Western and Daoist healing arts. These new associations and temples typically have well-educated members from the middle and upper classes of Chinese immigrants. They have also drawn a strong following of non-Chinese and non-Daoists who are attracted to various aspects of Daoist thought and practice. Probably the greatest "draw" is the practice of tai qi, which is most often promoted as a system of physical, mental, and spiritual exercise and health, not as a system that depends deeply, as we saw previously, on Daoist beliefs about the cosmos and its relationship to the human body and soul.

The greatest influence of Daoism on the Western world continues to be its foundational teachings. The *Daode Jing* influences life and thought far beyond the lives of Daoists in the West. It continues to be the most translated book from Asia, and its elusive style and challenging wisdom have never ceased to fascinate North Americans. The appeal of this book is echoed in the titles of more than fifty recent books, such as *The Tao of [Winnie the] Pooh*, *The Tao of Parenting*, *The Tao of Love and Sex*, *The Tao of Spycraft*, *The Tao of*

Take a tour of the Daoist Temple of Original Simplicity in Boston.

Coaching, *The Tao of Sales*, and even *The Tao of Jesus* and *The Tao of Islam*. Of course, many of these books are Westernized adaptations of vaguely Daoist ideas—*The Tao of Golf* doesn't have many authentic Daoist teachings to help the author's game—and bear little resemblance to the rich Daoist understandings of the Dao. In a different category is the use of Daoism in psychology and psychotherapy, in which Wayne Dyer is the leading figure. All this adaptation of Daoism may raise questions in some minds, but it is probably exactly what we should expect—a wide-ranging but wu-wei attempt to tap into the elusive, all-encompassing Dao.

Watch American psychologist Wayne Dyer explain the *Daode Jing* in his work.

{ Test coming up? Now what? }

81% of students surveyed found that 4LTR Press Solutions, like RELG, made it easy to study for course exams.

With **RELG** you have a multitude of study aids at your fingertips. After reading the chapters at least once, check out these ideas for further help:

Chapter in Review cards include all learning outcomes, definitions, and a timeline for each chapter.

Online flashcards give you additional ways to check your comprehension of key concepts.

Other great tools to help you study include **online quizzes**.

You'll find it all when you visit CourseMate at **www.cengagebrain.com**.

CHAPTER **8**

Encountering Shinto: The Way of the Kami

BONNIE VAN VOORST © CENGAGE LEARNING

Learning Outcomes

After studying this chapter, you will be able to do the following:

LO1 Explain the meaning of *Shinto* and *Kami no michi*.

LO2 Summarize how the four main periods of Shinto's history have shaped its present.

LO3 Outline essential Shinto teachings in your own words.

LO4 Describe the main features of Shinto ethics.

LO5 Outline Shinto worship and other rituals, and explain why they play a leading role in Shinto.

LO6 Explain why the practice of Shinto in North America is so small.

PHOTO COURTESY PHOTOS8.COM

YOUR VISIT TO THE TSUBAKI SHINTO SHRINE IN GRANITE FALLS, WASHINGTON

When you meet your guide to the Tsubaki (tsoo-BAH-kee) shrine just outside the gate, he says, "Please remember what we talked about on the telephone. The shrine grounds are a sacred place, so correct behavior is very important. No food, drink, or smoking is allowed. Keep a quiet, hushed voice. You may make a formal prayer and personal prayer at any time. If you wish to talk to the priest or have him do a ceremony for you, you must not be barefoot or wearing shorts or a sleeveless shirt. And no cell phone use, please."

First you visit the hand water station to purify yourself, because purity is important in Shinto. You follow the actions of your Shinto guide, using a dipper to pour water on your left hand. You lean back slightly from the basin as you pour, so water from your hands doesn't mix with the pure water. You pour water on your right hand and then into your left palm to rinse your mouth, not spitting the water back into the basin. You pour water again onto your left hand. Last, you let the small amount of water still in the dipper run back down its handle, and you place the wooden dipper back in the basin.

Next, you approach the shrine building. Continuing to follow your guide's actions, you bow slightly at the inner shrine gate and then walk on. The centerline is reserved for the kami, whom you know to be the gods and spirits of Shinto, to walk on, so you carefully avoid walking on it. As you get farther in, you offer a prayer to the gods and spirits of the shrine with two bows, then two claps, then one bow. Inside the shrine, you move to the offertory box, where you drop in an offering of money. Standing next on the centerline, you grip the bell rope tightly and

What Do YOU Think?

The Shinto religion explains the Japanese "love affair" with robots and robotics.

Strongly Disagree						Strongly Agree
1	2	3	4	5	6	7

pull it to ring the bell. You fix your gaze toward the mirror in the inner shrine and then bow deeply twice. You clap twice and pray while keeping your hands together at the

A follower of Shinto ceremonially washes her hands outside a Shinto shrine.

© PNC/JUPITER IMAGES.COM

< Famous "floating gate" of the Itsukushima Shrine, Miyajima Island, Japan, showing that the sea around Japan is considered sacred.

center of your chest. When your short, quiet prayers are done, you bow once again.

You guide doesn't know if you have any specific questions or religious issues, so he says, "If you have an appointment with a priest, please enter the shrine building. If you have a question for shrine staff, please ring the buzzer." You don't, so you keep looking around, and you see little shops where you can buy small prayer plaques and slips of paper for fortune-telling. You buy a plaque, write your wish/prayer on it, and hang it up with the others nearby for the gods to read. Then you draw at random a fortune-telling slip; these slips of paper contain several predictions ranging from "great good luck" to "great bad luck." By tying your slip to a rope where others have tied theirs, good fortune will come true or bad fortune can be averted. As it happens, you drew a good fortune, making for a happy conclusion of your visit to the shrine.

Visit the Tsubaki shrine by way of its website.

> *Shinto is an indigenous religion with origins in ancient times, but it has succeeded in a starkly modern nation.*

Shinto is a religion of formal rituals and inner feelings more than of doctrines, ethics, and organization. Its sentiments and rituals are directed especially to the natural world of the Japanese islands and secondarily to the history of the Japanese state. Shinto connects the people of Japan and their land, as well as Japan's present and its past. In your study of Shinto, you'll encounter these unique features:

- Some scholars hold that all Japanese are Shinto just by virtue of being culturally Japanese, whether they practice Shinto or not. Many Japanese who see themselves as Shintoists also practice elements of other religions, especially Buddhism. This makes it difficult to know how many Japanese practice Shinto, and estimates vary widely—between 2 million and 127 million, the current estimated population of Japan.

- Shinto has no founder, no creed, and (for most of its history) no central authority. It didn't even have a name until the sixth century C.E., when it was necessary to distinguish it from Buddhism once that religion reached Japan from China.

- Shinto has no scripture. In fact, Shinto is the only religion based in a literate culture that hasn't developed a scripture. It does have mythological books of ancient Japanese history written in the eighth century, but these don't function in an authoritative way in the religion.

- Shinto has been a major part of Japanese life and culture throughout the country's history, but for more than a thousand years it has shared its spiritual, social, and political roles with Buddhism and Confucianism. This mirrors the religious situation in China, where Daoism, Buddhism, and Confucianism are combined in some way by most believers.

- Shinto is an indigenous religion with origins in ancient times, but it has succeeded in a starkly modern nation. Although it could be treated with other indigenous religions, Shinto's unique features as an indigenous religion and its role in the modern world merit separate treatment.

LO1 Names

Shinto means "the way of the gods." It derives from the Chinese *shen dao*, combining two words: *shin*, "gods," particularly the higher gods, and *tao/dao*, the "way" of thought and life. After the coming of Buddhism to Japan in the sixth century C.E., *Shinto* was invented to counter the Japanese term *butsudo*, "the way of the Buddha." A more-Japanese way to express this name, but not more prevalent in scholarship, is *Kami no michi* (KAH-mee noh MEE-chee), "the way of the kami." This name is more accurate than

Prayer placard with an image of Colonel Sanders posted in a Tokyo KFC restaurant.

CHRIS GLADIS

Shinto, because the typical notions of "gods" in most religions treated in this book don't fit this religion very well. **Kami** are spirits, deities, or essences of something notable. They can be humanlike, animistic, or natural features or forces in the world (for example, mountains, rivers, trees, rocks, lightning, and wind). Most kami are morally good, but a few of them are unpredictable or downright dangerous. Kami and people exist within the same world and are interrelated in it.

REUTERS/YURIKO NAKAO

Official shrine maidens perform a Shinto ritual dance for purification at the Meiji Shrine, Tokyo.

LO2 The Shinto Present As Shaped by Its Past

When the present Emperor Akihito (ah-kih-HEE-toh) became the 125th emperor of Japan in 1989, he spent a night with the Sun Goddess as a dinner guest, something every emperor is required to do shortly after ascending to the throne. First recorded in 712 C.E., the ritual takes place at night because the Sun Goddess is in the sky during the day; she comes down on this special occasion to be present with the new emperor. After a bath for purification, the emperor carries out the ritual called the Great Food Offering. It takes place in two log huts specially-constructed at the Imperial Palace in Tokyo. During the rite, the emperor receives some of the Sun Goddess's spirit and thus become with her a kind of living ancestor of the entire Japanese family. The pre–World War II belief that the emperor was a living god was reinforced by this ritual. No one but the emperor has ever witnessed the ceremony or knows its details, and Akihito's continuation of it was controversial among some Japanese.

Explore Japanese culture and religion at Google Earth™.

Shinto history can be presented in four major periods: before the arrival of Buddhism in Japan in the 600s; Shinto and Buddhism together in Japan from 600 until about 1850; the Meiji (MAY-jee) reinterpretation of Shinto from 1850 to the end of the Second World War in 1945; and Shinto from 1945 until today.

BEFORE THE ARRIVAL OF BUDDHISM (TO 600 C.E.)

Before Buddhism came to Japan in the sixth century C.E., there probably was no religion that we would recognize as Shinto, but rather many local gods and shrines that are now grouped under Shinto. The first, aboriginal inhabitants of Japan were animists, devoted to powers of nature that they saw in every living thing. These were the kami that were found in all significant natural things: plants and animals, mountains and fertile plains, rivers and seas, earthquakes, storms in the air and the seas, and even powerful human beings. Shrines began to be built in places where these kami were thought to be particularly present. At these shrines, simple worship would be offered to the kami of the place, and the blessings offered to the kami would result in the kami's blessings on the people. Some of these shrines had women called **miko** who acted as shamans. With the passing of time and the coming of more-patriarchal Chinese religions and culture, the miko became the "shrine maidens" of today, unmarried young women who assist the male priests in rituals but who no longer act as shamans.

Like other indigenous peoples, the early Japanese developed myths that enabled them to make sense of life in their place, as well as rituals to bless it. For example, the myth relating the creation of the Japanese islands probably arose at this time, telling how the husband-and-wife gods **Izanagi** and **Izanami** made Japan. Other religious groups arrived from Korea to settle in Japan in late

kami [KAH-mee] Spirits, deities, or essences found in both animate and inanimate objects

miko [MEE-koh] "Shrine maidens" who assist male priests

Izanagi [EE-zah-NAH-gee (hard g)] "Male who invites," the male deity who created the Japanese islands, according to Shinto mythology

Izanami [EE-zah-NAH-mee] "Female who invites," the female deity who assisted her husband, Izanagi, in creating Japan, according to Shinto mythology

The "Wedded Rocks" of Futami, Japan, tied together by a one-ton rope of rice straw, represent the union of Izanagi and Izanami and celebrate the marriage of male and female.

CYRIL BELE

prehistoric times; they were absorbed into Shinto long ago. The realms of earth and the supernatural, as well as the realms of the common and the sacred, were closely related in the worldview of the early Japanese. Things that modern people regard as "supernatural" were just another part of the natural world, although with great power. The oldest Shinto ceremonies were dedicated to agriculture and emphasized obtaining ritual purity that would lead to the blessing of fields and flocks. Worship took place outdoors, at sites thought to be sacred to the kami of the place. In time, the ancient Japanese built permanent structures to honor their gods. Shrines were usually built on or near mountains, at the edge of forests, or in rural areas.

SHINTO AND BUDDHISM TOGETHER IN JAPAN (600–1850)

The second stage in Shinto history is the long sweep of time from about 600 to 1850, when Shinto coexisted with Buddhism and Confucianism, religions that arrived at the beginning of this period from China. The introduction of the Buddhist religion and Confucian social values from China and Korea brought a different way of life for the Japanese,

Kojiki [koh-JEE-kee] *Records of Ancient Matters,* Japan's earliest history

Nihongi [nih-HAWN-gee (hard g)] *Chronicles of Japan,* Japan's second-earliest history

including changes to their religion. (Daoism, the third main religion of China, made little effort to enter Japan, perhaps because Shinto already had a full complement of gods and spirits.) Japan established close connections with the Chinese and Korean courts that would last for four hundred years and adopted a more sophisticated culture. This new culture was essentially Chinese and included, in addition to Confucianism and Buddhism, literature, philosophy, art, architecture, science, medicine, and government. Most important was the introduction of the Chinese writing system, revolutionizing Japan, which had no system of its own. The *Kojiki* (*Records of Ancient Matters*) and *Nihongi* (*Chronicles of Japan*), Japan's earliest histories, were written in the early 700s, soon after the introduction of Chinese writing. Ever since that time, the relationship of Shinto with Chinese religions in Japan has been complicated—sometimes peaceful, sometimes conflicted. Indeed, the name *Shinto* arose then to distinguish indigenous Japanese religion from the new Buddhist beliefs coming from China. Many Shinto shrines were completely changed into Buddhist temples, made a part of Buddhist temples, or kept as Shinto shrines and led by Buddhist priests. Separate new Buddhist temples were built as well. From this time comes the distinction in names still used today: Buddhist houses of worship are called "temples," but Shinto houses of worship are called "shrines."

> The rising combination of Shinto, Buddhism, and Confucianism made for religious and cultural unity, important in a land undergoing rapid change.

In general, the emperors and ruling aristocracy approved this rising combination of Shinto,

Buddhism, and Confucianism. It made for religious and cultural unity, important in a relatively small land undergoing rapid change—and still true in Japan today. The rulers took a role in religions by establishing a government office to oversee them, something that persisted until 1946. Shinto was the native religion of Japan and had a richer feeling for the natural environment than did Buddhism and Confucianism. Shinto had a disadvantage compared to Buddhism and Confucianism in its lack of complex teachings. Unlike the other religions, Shinto had no sacred scriptures in which doctrine was formulated and by which it could be passed along. This meant that the doctrinal development of Japanese religion and philosophy inevitably drew on the comparative intellectual richness of Buddhism and Confucianism. But Shinto had found its niche in Japanese life, one that continues through today.

As the Japanese nation was formed, the idea grew that humans should follow the will of the gods in political and social life. The emperor and the court had clear religious obligations, particularly the meticulous rituals that ensured that the powerful kami looked favorably on Japan and its people. These annual ceremonies for purification and blessing, which soon included many Buddhist and Confucian elements, became a regular part of the Japanese government. As time went on, the Japanese became more accustomed to integrating Shinto and Buddhism. For example, they accepted the Buddhist idea that the kami were incarnations of the Buddha, manifested in Japan to save all sentient beings. During the seventh and eighth centuries, the spiritual status of the emperor as the descendant of the Sun Goddess **Amaterasu**, the chief deity worshiped in Shinto, became official doctrine when it was written up in the *Kojiki* and *Nihongi*. This was buttressed by rituals and the establishment of the important Ise (EE-sah) shrine of the imperial household.

> **Amaterasu** [ah-MAH-tehr-AH-soo] Sun goddess, the chief deity worshiped in Shinto

From 800 to about 1800, Buddhist influence in government grew steadily stronger. Japan was in the hands of three power blocs: the emperor, the aristocracy, and the leaders of Buddhism and Shinto. Throughout most of Japanese history up until the end of World War II, the aristocracy had more power than the emperor, despite what the creation myths implied about him. Religion became more controversial when Roman Catholic Christian missionaries arrived in Japan in the 1500s and started making converts from Shinto and Buddhism. Over time, Christianity came to be seen as a political threat—it was a foreign religion, didn't allow converts to blend Christianity formally with other religions, and was beginning to convert the aristocracy. Various rulers ruthlessly tried to stamp it out from the 1500s until 1640. Most notably, in 1597 dozens of Japanese Christians were crucified in a macabre memory of the death of Jesus Christ; and more than forty thousand died in the persecutions. Surviving Christians were driven underground for hundreds of years. The seventeenth century was dominated by Buddhism, partly because an anti-Christian measure forced every Japanese person to register as a Buddhist at a Buddhist temple and pay a tax.

Japanese civic religion still included many elements of Confucianism in its ideas

The Seven Lucky Gods are a mixed group of Shinto and other deities popular in Japan, all thought to bring good luck, including a happy buddha (left).

JTB PHOTO/PHOTOLIBRARY

A Closer Look:

The Symbol of Shinto

A **torii** is a traditional Japanese gate or portal at the entrance of, and often within, a Shinto shrine. (Its original meaning is "bird perch.") It consists of two upright wooden posts connected at the top by two horizontal crosspieces, the top one often curved up slightly at the ends. The outer gate is often said to separate the "ordinary" area from a sacred area, but in view of the strong Shinto belief that *all* Japan is sacred, it's probably more accurate to say that the outer gate marks ordinary sacred space from extraordinarily sacred space. Seeing a torii at the entrance is usually the easiest way to determine if it is a Shinto shrine. Smaller torii are also found occasionally inside the grounds of Japanese Buddhist temples.

The first mention of torii is in 922. Torii were commonly made from wood or stone, but today they can also be made of metal, stainless steel, or other modern materials. They are

usually either unpainted or painted a striking vermilion, with black tops. A person who has been successful in business often donates a torii to the shrine in gratitude. The Fushimi Inari (foo-SHEE-mee in-AHR-ee) shrine near Kyoto has some forty thousand torii, each bearing its donor's name, along paths that lead three miles up a mountainside.

Torii formed into a sacred walkway at the Fushimi Inari shrine

about government, but popular Japanese religion was a pragmatic fusion of Shinto rituals and myths with a hefty dose of Buddhism. Confucianism provided social ethics; Shinto provided everyday rituals and a feeling for the nation; Buddhism provided philosophy and (because it was Mahayana Buddhism) a hope for life after death. Just as China had "Three Traditions" in Daoism, Confucianism, and Buddhism, so too Japan had its three traditions of Shinto, Buddhism, and Confucianism.

After this long period of powerful influence of Buddhism on Shinto, Shinto pushed back. Around 1700 there was a movement toward what was considered a purer form of Shinto, with particular emphasis on the Japanese people as the descendants of the gods and therefore superior to other races. (This, of course, is something that most Japanese Buddhists denied.) Buddhist and other influences were filtered out of institutions and rituals. Historians generally hold that this

torii [TOH-ree-ee] Traditional Japanese gate or portal at the entrance of, and often within, a Shinto shrine

wasn't so much a return to something that had once existed as it was the creation of a more unified religion from a group of many different Shinto rituals and beliefs. During this period Shinto acquired a stronger intellectual tradition than it previously had. A part of the Shinto revival entailed the renewed study of archaic Japanese texts. Just as Shinto myths were written down in the eighth century for national political reasons, so now they were reinterpreted for nationalistic purposes.

> *"From the divine descent of the Japanese people proceeds their immeasurable superiority to the natives of other countries in courage and intelligence."*
> —Hirata, nationalistic Shinto scholar, 1836

As Japan encountered the world beyond East Asia that it had avoided for a thousand years, it drew on its indigenous religion to buttress its national claims. A leading Shinto scholar during this period, Hirata (hih-RAH-tah), wrote in 1836, "The two foundational doctrines of Shinto are that Japan is the country of the gods, and her inhabitants are the descendants of the gods. Between the Japanese people and other peoples . . . there is a difference of kind, rather than of degree. The Emperor is the true Son of Heaven, who is entitled to reign over the four seas and the ten thousand countries. From the divine descent of the Japanese people proceeds their immeasurable superiority to the natives of other countries in courage and intelligence."[1] This growing, religiously oriented nationalism contributed to rapid "modernization" of Japan in the 1800s (see Map 8.1). It would prove damaging to East Asia as Japan began to build an empire around 1900, and it would prove near-disastrous to many Pacific Rim nations from China to the United States in World War II.

The main hall of the Yasukuni Shrine

THE MEIJI PERIOD (1850–1945)

The third major period of Shinto began with the Meiji (MAY-jee) Restoration in 1868, so called because Emperor Meiji was restored to his powers after a rebellion by warlords. (The emperor was still dominated by the aristocracy, however.) The Meiji Restoration accelerated the revival of Shinto that had been going on for two centuries and launched Japan on a path that would change its history and the history of the world. Japan had been modernizing rapidly; the Industrial Revolution that took almost two hundred years in Europe and North America was accomplished in Japan in less than a century. The aim of the new religious climate was to provide a sacred foundation and a religious rationale for the new Japan and its national ethos. Emperor worship became a leading mark of "state Shinto" during this period.

In the Meiji period, Shinto was reorganized, completely separated from Buddhism, and brought under the power of the state. The state made a distinction between the new "state Shinto," "shrine Shinto" of the traditional past, and "sect Shinto" comprising mostly new movements in popular religion. Many historians

of religion consider these new Shinto sects a result of the "culture shock" that Japan experienced after opening to the West. Between 1882 and 1908, the government recognized thirteen Shinto sects, and their number constantly increased. They are forerunners of many of Japan's new religious movements today. A new shrine was set up at Yasukuni (YAS-soo-KOO-nee) to honor Japanese war dead. Amaterasu, who until then had not been a major divinity, was brought to center stage and used to validate the role of the emperor, not only as ruler but also as the high priest of Shinto.

One result of this change was the separation of Buddhism from Shinto. The kami could no longer be explained as incarnations of the Buddha or various bodhisattvas. Ritual was also affected. All Shinto shrines were purged of every trace of Buddhist imagery (for example, statues of the Buddha) and ritual (chanting scriptures). Buddhist priests were stripped of their status, and new Shinto priests were appointed to shrines. Shinto was enthusiastically promoted by Japan's militaristic aristocracy, who stressed that the emperor was a divine being, directly descended from the gods who had given birth to the Japanese islands. Japanese children were taught at school that the emperors were descendants of Sun Goddess Amaterasu, and every classroom had a small shrine to the emperor on the wall. Shinto bound the Japanese people together with a powerful mix of devotion to kami, ancestor worship, and group loyalty to family and nation; Buddhism with its more pacifist and international tendencies was demoted. This separation of Buddhism and Shinto continues today, with both religions having different shrines, priests, and rites.

---

[1] *Transactions of the Asiatic Society of Japan*, Vol. 3 (Yokohama, Japan: Asiatic Society Press, 1873), 36.

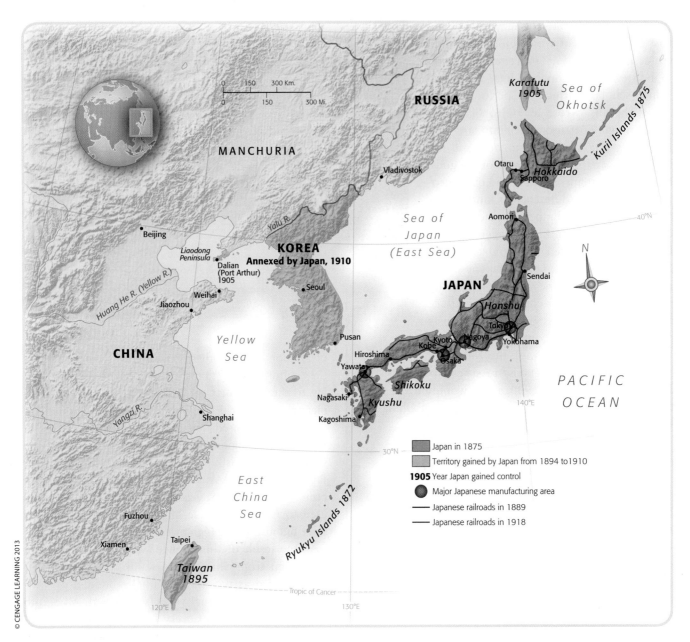

Map 8.1

Japanese Modernization and Expansion, 1868–1918
Japan undertook a crash modernization in the later 1800s. This modernization coincided with the rise of state Shinto. By 1910 its military power had increased and it had won a war with Russia and colonized Korea, Taiwan, and Sakhalin (then known as Karafutu).

Map legend:
- Japan in 1875
- Territory gained by Japan from 1894 to 1910
- **1905** Year Japan gained control
- Major Japanese manufacturing area
- Japanese railroads in 1889
- Japanese railroads in 1918

Despite the religious devotion of Japanese warriors in World War II, the Divine Wind did not come, and the emperor's rule as a god would soon end.

Shinto played a significant role in World War II, which started in Asia with the Japanese invasion of northern China in 1937. Since the 1870s, it had been fueling a strong nationalism among the Japanese, a force that would inevitably lead to war. Service in the military was a religious as well as a civic obligation, and the spirits of those who died were honored as kami. **Kamikaze** pilots intentionally crashed their planes into American warships at the end of the war in a last-ditch effort to stave off an invasion of Japan. *Kamikaze* is often used popularly today as meaning "reckless to the point of suicide," but it really means "Divine (*kami*) Wind (*kaze*)." The Divine Wind was a typhoon that destroyed a Chinese fleet threatening Japan in the 1200s, and the modern Divine Wind was meant to reproduce that deliverance. Another well-known feature of that war was the Japanese shout "Banzai!" (bahn-ZIGH)—"ten thousand years!"—and was understood to mean "May the emperor live ten thousand years!" This was frequently used as a cry of attack by Japanese forces. Despite the religiously motivated self-sacrifice of Japanese warriors, the Divine Wind did not come, and the emperor's rule as a god would soon end, falling far short of ten thousand years.

> *Banzai* literally means "ten thousand years" and was understood to mean "May the emperor live ten thousand years!"

SHINTO IN RECENT TIMES (1945–PRESENT)

The last and current stage of Shinto history begins when the victorious Allied powers ended the status of Shinto as the state religion in 1946. Japan was allowed to keep Hirohito (HEER-oh-HEE-toh, who lived from 1901 to 1989) as emperor, but he lost his claim to divine status as part of the Allied reforms in Japan. He went on the radio to tell his people that Japan was surrendering (although such direct language was not used), the first time that ordinary Japanese had heard an emperor's voice. He later wrote in a message to the nation, "The ties between Us and Our people have always stood on mutual trust and affection. They do not depend upon legends and myths. They are not predicated on the false conception that the Tenno [emperor] is

A Japanese commander prepares a young pilot for battle in World War II, tying on a white cloth with the sun used to honor kamikaze pilots.

© GETTY IMAGES

kamikaze [KAHM-ih-KAHZ-ee] "Divine Wind" that saved Japan

divine, and that the Japanese people are superior to other races and destined to rule the world." Then he affirmed that the Japanese people still had an important role to play in the world: "By [the Japanese people's] supreme efforts . . . they will be able to make a substantial contribution to the welfare and advancement of mankind." This contribution did indeed come in the postwar revival of Japan, when Japan became a model of economic development, democracy, and peace in Asia. Since about 1990, however, Japan has been in a prolonged economic slump that has dispirited many of its people and lessened the appeal of Japanese ways of business to other nations. The dwindling attendance at many Shinto shrines is probably related to this economic downturn.

Japan's postwar constitution separates religion and state. Although the constitution of modern Japan had guaranteed freedom of religion since 1873, it finally came true. No religion receives support from the Japanese state. No citizen has to take part in any religious act, celebration, rite, or practice. Many (but not all) governmental ceremonies were stripped of their explicitly religious aspects. Despite the loss of its official status, Shinto retains a significant influence in Japanese spirituality and culture. Considerable Shinto religious meaning still surrounds some regular imperial ceremonies, and a few well-attended Shinto shrines honor those who died in World War II.

In sum, Japan is today both a secular and a religious society. Industrialization and urbanization have led to the declining influence of Shinto, which has accelerated since the end of World War II. Continuing controversy over the Japanese role in that war has diminished Shinto influence among the younger generation, many of whom see Shinto myths as outmoded. Most young people go to Shinto shrine only as tourists or to pray for success in school exams. Some Japanese, especially the older generation, still frequent Shinto shrines regularly, and all generations have a strong, even spiritual feeling for the physical beauty of Japan that is a heritage of Shinto. New religious movements have combined Buddhism, Shinto, and other religions to address contemporary

A Closer Look:

The Yasukuni Shrine Today

The Yasukuni Shrine was founded in 1869 under the orders of Emperor Meiji and is dedicated to the souls of all Japanese military personnel who have fallen in battle since that time. Most controversially to some (to Japan's enemies in World War II, at least), it does not distinguish between honored dead and dishonorable dead. For example, it honors fourteen men such as Prime Minister Hideki Tojo (hee-DECK-ee TOH-joh) who were convicted of war crimes, including the killing of prisoners of war and civilians, and hanged for them after the war. Within the shrine the dead are worshiped rather than just remembered. They willingly sacrificed their lives for Japan, and this has made them kami. Surrounded by war banners and military regalia, they are venerated by the hundreds of thousands of visitors who attend the shrine each year. Some come as tourists to this site and are not interested in venerating the dead, but others come to worship them, some even believing that the souls of the war dead live in the shrine.

Junichiro Koizumi (joo-NEE-chee-roh koh-ee-ZOO-mee), who was the prime minister of Japan from 2001 to 2006, sparked international protest when he visited the Yasukuni Shrine in person every year. He refused to explain his reason for these visits, which caused tension with China and South Korea. Tensions have lifted a bit as subsequent prime ministers haven't gone in person to the shrine, but public controversy continues in East Asia over this. When Shinto appears in the news, it is usually in connection with visits to the Yasukuni Shrine.

Visit the Yasukuni Shrine website.

Read a *New York Times* article on the controversy aroused in 2010 when the Japanese prime minister decided that no government official would attend the annual ceremonies at Yasukuni.

Read a CNN report on how the Japanese drew on their religions to cope with the 2011 disasters.

Japanese issues such as family finances, environmental pollution, and family solidarity. The widespread destruction visited on northeastern Japan in the 2011 earthquake and tsunami caused many Japanese, even the younger generations, to draw upon both traditional and newer religions for comfort and strength.

However, on the whole the Japanese people are becoming more secular. In a 2000 census, although most Japanese called themselves Buddhists or Shintoists or both, not even 15 percent reported a formal religious membership or regular religious practice. Remarkably, this rising secularization hasn't had significant negative social effects, and Japan continues to be the most peaceful, law-abiding society in the developed world. (Even after the 2011 tsunami, there was virtually no increase in crime.) Sociologists say that this is due to a desire to honor one's living relatives or other social group and an even stronger reluctance to shame them, rather than from a connection to the spirits of one's ancestors or other aspects of Shinto or Buddhist religion. To many students of Japan, the strongest religious influence today may be that of Confucianism. It has virtually no formal presence in Japan, but the system of

Confucian social values that arrived in Japan 1,400 years ago still influences the lives of most Japanese today.

Read the Allied powers' "Directive for the Disestablishment of State Shinto."

LO3 Shinto Teachings

A September 13, 2010, blog in the *New York Times* has a discussion about a writer's remarkable claim that Shinto religion explains the Japanese "love affair" with robots and robotics. He claims that Shinto's blurring of the boundaries between the animate and the inanimate has shaped the positive Japanese view of robots as "helpers" and not as the rebellious, violent machines portrayed in Western stories and films. These helpers even include the recent invention of a female robotic companion for men. As one writer said of Japan, "A humanoid and sentient robot may simply not feel as creepy or threatening as it does in other cultures."[2]

The *Kojiki* and *Nihongi*, Japan's earliest histories, were compiled on the orders of the imperial family in the

---

[2] Hiroko Tabuchi, "Robot Invasion Welcomed in Japan," *New York Times*, accessed September 23, 2010, http://lens.blogs.nytimes.com/2010/09/13/robot-invasion-welcomed-in-japan/?scp=3&sq=shinto&st=cse.

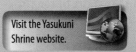

early 700s C.E. Although there was an obvious political aim to unite all the regional and clan deities under the authority of Sun Goddess Amaterasu, who was the clan deity of the emperor's family, these legends provide an explanation for the basic ideas in Shinto teachings, ideas that endure even today. We begin with three basic concepts that emerge in Shinto teachings about the kami.

THE KAMI

First, the kami are not "gods" as Westerners understand them or even as Mahayana Buddhists understand them, but should be understood as powerful natural forces with a spiritual dimension. No clear distinction exists between what is alive and not living, natural and what is socially constructed, or human and divine. The kami are identified with natural features but are spirits in and beyond those features. One well-placed rock can have a kami just as much as Mount Fuji can. The whole world, including human life, is an expression of spiritual powers. Spiritual power is not found evenly throughout the world, but is especially powerful in particular things, including humans.

Second, the kami are virtually countless. Shinto focuses on the kami that are important to people and influence human life directly. Most kami are identified with places—especially forests, mountains, or waterfalls—that seem especially spiritual to the Japanese. They are also identified with natural phenomena that are awe inspiring, such as wind, thunder and lightning, and with destructive phenomena such as the earthquakes that regularly shake Japan and tsunamis that sometime follow them. Particular kami are also identified with ordinary places and activities in human life, such as the kitchen, safety on the roads, education, and other things. Living individuals who have a special charisma or are very successful in business, politics, or life might be called kami. Other spiritual forces are recognized as kami, for example mischievous elements such as fox spirits or tree spirits. On special occasions, a kami may possess a human medium to send a message.

Third, individuals should know and venerate the kami most important to them. Not only is the kami's goodwill required, but the spirits are said to respond to an individual's

Watch a National Geographic video about Mount Fuji.

Offerings to the kami, marked by paper streamers, are made by farmers at a humble Shinto shrine in preparation for trimming the trees.

JOI ITO

concern. They are not all-knowing, because their identity and activity are restricted mostly to special objects in nature. They want to be informed about significant events that involve their activities, so prayer to the kami will sometimes contain these reports.

CHARACTERISTICS OF OTHER SHINTO TEACHINGS

The main thing to be said about Shinto teachings is that Shinto has no developed teachings about either this world or the next. It doesn't speak about the original creation of the whole universe, only of Japan. Nor is there anything about a future end of the world. Likewise, there is no clear description of any afterlife. Some Shintoists believe that after a person dies, he or she becomes deeply related to their ancestral kami and has no individual soul in the afterlife, as in much of Mahayana Buddhism. Others believe that their souls go to a shadowy, gloomy underworld; this was probably the original Shinto thought. The dead are honored by the living as individuals, but they are not individuals as they were in this life.

> *The main thing to be said about Shinto teachings is that Shinto has no developed teachings.*

LO4 Shinto Ethics

Afollower of Shinto goes to a shrine in Kyoto. She has committed a bad act; it's weighing on her mind, and she wants to deal with it. So she goes to her local shrine and there undergoes a simple ritual of purification. She washes at the cleansing station before entering and then contacts one of the shrine priests to pray with her in front of the shrine gods. She leaves, at peace with herself and determined that she will do better. Shinto teaches that humans are born pure. Evil actions and impurity are things that come later in life and can usually be dealt with by simple cleansing or purifying rituals.

General Characteristics

To identify the distinctly Shinto elements in Japanese ethics isn't easy. Confucian values have inspired much of Japanese social ethics, supplemented by more individual ethics derived from Buddhist monastic rules. In general, Shinto ethics are based not on a set of commands or of virtues that tells one how to behave, but on following the general will of the kami, understood through myth and ritual. The "way" implied in the word *Shinto* is primarily a ritual way, to keep the relationship with the kami on a proper footing. Good moral practice flows from this relationship.

However, the kami aren't always perfect, so they don't serve as moral examples. Shinto texts tell many stories of kami behaving badly. As we saw above, some of them are mischief makers and therefore wouldn't serve well as role models in such an orderly, proper populace. This clear difference with religions whose gods are morally perfect and can serve as moral examples is probably a main reason why Shinto ethics avoids absolute moral rules.

Purity

Purity is essential to pleasing the kami, bringing a happy life, and turning back disappointment or disease. Many rituals feature the exorcism of sins in order to restore purity. Cleanliness in particular signifies a good character and freedom from bad external influences. In Western societies one hears the proverb "Cleanliness is next to godliness." In traditional Japanese society cleanliness—of body, mind, and spirit, both ritual and practical—*is* godliness. To be in harmony with the kami, one must keep one's person, home, and business clean. The Japanese emphasis on

freshness and purity in food and drink brings a high quality to the diet, and practically it means that shopping for food is often done every day. Purity in relationships entails being honest, sincere, and thoughtful about how other people feel; therefore, apologies for unintended affronts are very common. The kami particularly dislike blood and death. Therefore, women traditionally were excluded from shrine events during menstruation, as were people who worked with the bodies of dead animals, such as leather makers. Soldiers require special purification after battle, and people helping at funerals need to purify themselves as well.

> *In Western societies one sometimes hears the proverb "Cleanliness is next to godliness." In traditional Japanese society cleanliness* is *godliness.*

The overall aims of Shinto ethics are to promote harmony and purity in all spheres of life. Purity isn't just spiritual purity, but also moral purity—having

Read a Shinto statement on ecology.

a pure and sincere heart, leading to good conduct. It has a connection with ritual purity—doing things in a certain way, in a certain state, with a certain attitude. Shinto views both human beings and the world as morally good. Evil enters from outside the world of nature and human society, usually by the agency of evil spirits. This affects humans similar to a physical disease. When people do wrong, they bring ritual pollution and moral fault upon themselves. This blocks the blessings of life as they flow from the kami, and must be dealt with in ceremonies of cleansing.

LO5 Shinto Ritual

Most Shinto rituals are tied to the life cycle of humans and the seasonal cycles of nature. Life-cycle rituals include naming ceremonies for children and ceremonies for blessing children as they grow. The time of taking university entrance exams is particularly trying for Japanese young people, and going to the shrine to pray for success is important for them and their parents. We'll consider the

© ISTOCKPHOTO.COM/MATTHEW RAGEN

Incense sticks burn down in a Shinto shrine.

Shinto wedding ritual more fully below. Although Shinto does have a funeral ritual and although the emperor always receives a Shinto service, for more than a thousand years most Japanese have preferred Buddhist funerals. This will be treated below as well.

Visit a photo and video blog on a 2010 festival honoring the dead.

THE SHINTO SHRINE

Rituals at Shinto shrines mark one's entry into a different world, the world of the kami. Even in a bustling city, shrines offer a quiet atmosphere removed from the busy noise of modern Japanese life. Surrounded by evergreen trees and approached on a gravel path, they hush everyday conversation before one enters. The silence is broken only by ritual hand claps or the sounds of nature. Shinto ritual, including music and dance, is remarkably simple and brief, much like the Japanese tea ceremony, quite unlike complex Buddhist ritual. It has a slow, measured pace thought to be pleasing to the kami and quite different from daily life outside. However, at special festivals in and around the shrine this changes dramatically. A mass of local people will be crowded together in noisy festivity, "letting themselves go" in front of the kami in ways they would never dream of doing outside the shrine. Sometimes this includes enough consumption of alcohol to get worshipers slightly drunk. This religious carousing serves as a temporary release from a society that prizes almost-constant orderliness and properness.

Take an interactive tour of a Shinto shrine.

The shrines are built to blend in with the environment chosen by the kami of the place. The main sanctuary building of each shrine is the **honden**, in which symbolic sacred objects such as a mirror or a sword are kept at the center front, where they receive worship. Traditionally built from wood and usually left unpainted, the buildings need regular repair or rebuilding by the local community. This is still the tradition of one of Japan's most famous shrines, the Grand Shrine of Ise, which is reconstructed in traditional style every twenty years.

honden [HAHN-dahn] Main sanctuary building of a Shinto shrine

See the activities surrounding the ritual rebuilding of the Ise Shrine.

The kami dwell near, not in, the shrines and must be invited politely. As we saw above, at least one torii marks the entrance to a shrine, and a basin is just inside to rinse one's hands and mouth. A shrine is usually dedicated to one particular kami but may host any number of smaller shrines representing other kami that local people should also venerate. Sacred places, such as particular trees and rocks, will be marked off by ropes of elaborately plaited straw, or by streamers of plain paper. The kami are summoned by a series of brief actions: ringing a bell outside the shrine, making a money offering, clapping hands twice, saying a short silent prayer, and bowing twice.

THE SHINTO PRIESTHOOD

The work of Shinto priests is located largely in the shrine. Most new Shinto priests, like most Japanese Buddhist monks, must now be university graduates. Women priests can be found, but they aren't nearly as numerous as men, because traditional Japanese society is still strongly patriarchal. Most priests are "volunteers" who have their main jobs outside the shrines. They are almost always married and have families.

"The contemporary miko is typically a university student collecting a modest wage in this part-time position." —Lisa Kuly

The Shinto priesthood exists mainly to carry out Shinto rituals and run the shrines, and duties such as

ema [AY-muh] Wooden plaque inscribed with prayers and wishes

omikuji [OH-mee-KOO-jee] Fortunes on preprinted slips of paper

teaching, religious counseling, etc., are minor activities for the priests. Traditionally, the priesthood was limited to the great shrines, and it rotated among the able men of the community. But now the priesthood has been opened up to many shrines, and it has grown to about twenty thousand, including two thousand women. All but the smallest shrines are staffed by a team of priests of various ranks, assisted by a team of shrine maidens, the miko discussed above. These miko assist with shrine functions, assist priests in ceremonies, perform ceremonial dances, sell souvenirs, and distribute omikuji. Lisa Kuly writes that today's miko is typically "a university student collecting a modest wage in this part-time position."[3] A miko is traditionally dressed in red trousers, a white kimono jacket, and white or red hair ribbons. Shinto has no overall leader in Japan, and each shrine is self-governed and self-supporting through offerings and donations by worshipers. Most shrines are associated through a national shrine organization.

Emas posted at the Izumo Grand Shrine

AMY NAKAZAWA

WISH PLAQUES AND FORTUNES

In Shinto shrines, it's common to see **emas**, small wooden plaques, hung in prominent places. Worshipers buy an ema, write personal wishes and hopes on the reverse, and then hang it near a sacred tree together with emas made by others. The kami then read them and help make them come true. This ritual is understood more as "asking for wishes" or "making hopes" than as praying, although prayers can also be written on an ema.

Next, we should discuss the **omikuji**, literally "sacred drawing/lottery." They are fortunes on preprinted slips of paper. For an offering of about 100 yen (approximately one dollar), worshipers can obtain an omikuji from a person at a shrine desk, or even from a vending machine. Opening the paper allows one to see a fortune that has several items on it. The first deals with the general category of "blessing" and ranges from "great blessing" to "great curse." Then it states fortunes for various aspects of life, for example business, schooling, the stock market, falling in love, and others. (No matter the general category of blessing, in the area of schooling almost every omikuji advises one to study

Shinto priest officiates at a shrine altar in Tokyo.

JOI ITO

Women in traditional dress tie omikuji on ropes at the Shinto shrine in Kamakura, Japan.

JESSLEE CUIZON

[3] Lisa Kuly, "Locating Transcendence in Japanese Minzoku Geino," *Ethnologies* 25 (2003), 201.

Draw an electronic omikuji for yourself.

more, study harder, and the like!) If the prediction is bad, the paper is folded up and attached to a tree, to ropes, or to wires. If the prediction is favorable, one can either take it home or tie it up in the shrine; the latter is more common.

You are very expressive in word, action and feeling.

MICHELLE TRIBE

We connect the fortune cookie with China, but some think that it comes from the Japanese omikuji.

The Shinto priesthood exists mainly to carry out Shinto rituals and run the shrines, and duties such as teaching and religious counseling are minor activities for the priests.

THE WEDDING CEREMONY

The wedding ceremony is conducted by the Shinto priest (or priests) and the mikos at the front of a Shinto shrine after a formal procession. The families are present in the room. The groom and bride typically wear formal Japanese clothes. After ritual purification, the priest offers prayers for the couple's good fortune and happiness, as well as for the protection and guidance of the kami. Then the miko serves three sips of purified rice wine to the wedding couple. Brief words are spoken before the kami and rings are exchanged, followed by the offering of a small sacred evergreen branch. One more sip of rice wine is shared, and the ritual is complete.

A wedding procession at the Meiji Shrine, Tokyo: main priest, assistant priest, temple maidens, bride (with white cloth on head), groom (in a black gown), and family members

UPENDRA KANDA

A Closer Look:

A Shinto Prayer for the Blessing of the Crops

This Shinto prayer found in the *Yengishiki* prayer book clearly demonstrates the Shinto feeling for kami and the natural world.

I declare in the great presence of Amaterasu who sits in Ise:

Because the sovereign great goddess bestows on him [the emperor] the countries of the four quarters over which her glance extends—

As far as the limit where Heaven stands up like a wall,

As far as the bounds where the country stands up distant,

As far as the limit where the blue clouds spread flat,

As far as the bounds where the white clouds lie away fallen—

The blue sea plain as far as the limit, where come the prows of the ships,

The ships which continuously crowd on the great sea plain,

And the roads which men travel by land,

as far as the limit whither come the horses' hoofs,

with the baggage cords tied tightly,

treading the uneven rocks and tree roots,

and lining up continuously in a long path without a break.

Making the narrow countries wide and the hilly countries plain,

And drawing together the distant countries by throwing, so to speak, many ropes over them,

He will pile up his crops like a range of hills in the great presence of the sovereign great goddess, and will peacefully enjoy the remainder.

THE HOME SHRINE

Traditional Japanese show respect for the kami by having a small shrine or worship space in their house or outdoors. They also have a **kamidana**, a "kami shelf" on which small statues of the kami are placed, sometimes along with small memorial tablets containing the names of ancestors. The kamidana is typically placed so high on a wall that it is near the ceiling, It holds several different items, at the center of which is a small circular mirror, a stone, or a jewel. Worship at the kamidana includes placing flowers, offering food such as rice, fruit, and water, and saying short prayers. Family members carefully cleanse their hands with water before they perform these daily rituals.

See a video of a kamidana for sale.

THE SHINTO FUNERAL

As we saw above, Japan is a land of multiple religions, which affects how the Japanese deal with death and how they believe in an afterlife. Keeping memorial tablets with the names of one's ancestors in household shrines and offering food and drink to them is Confucian in origin. In ritual matters of entering the afterlife, such as funerals and memorial services for deceased relatives, a Buddhist priest officiates with basically Buddhist rites.

The basic lines of the historic funeral rite are still discernible in villages. It particularly applies to men who are heads of households; in what follows, we will describe this sort of funeral. In towns and cities today, the rite has been adapted or lost, especially as the burial of cremated remains has replaced full-body burial for reasons of space and cost. The immediate family members keep themselves in their houses. The men of the neighborhood gather near the family home to make the items required for the funeral, including paper flags containing prayers, paper processional lanterns, and a wooden candlestick. The women prepare the food required for the feast given before the burial. One woman of the neighborhood has the special honor of sewing a white pilgrim's cloak that will shroud the body for its journey to the land of the dead. Meanwhile, the men who will be pallbearers dig a grave in the cemetery.

The spirit of the dead is thought to still be present and listening, so as the relatives shroud the body, they politely describe out loud the tasks they are performing. To mask the odor of death, burning incense is kept nearby. So that the spirit may pay the ferryman for passage into eternity, a bag with a few coins is put near the

kamidana [KAH-mee-DAH-nuh] "Kami shelf" found in most private homes

body, and meditation beads are entwined in the dead man's hand. A fan is laid in the coffin, together with some small favorite object belonging to the deceased. The Buddhist priest tells the spirit of the dead to begin its journey to the land of the dead, and other ancient formulas are recited. On completing their task, the family members wash their hands in salt water.

The funeral procession reaches the cemetery with a lot of noise. For the grave, a round hole has been made, just big enough to pass the body through. The hole widens continuously as it goes deeper, until it is much wider at the usual depth of six feet. At the bottom, to one side, a large compartment, approximately six feet long and four feet wide, has been excavated. The body is taken out of the coffin and laid into the grave on straw floor mats along with the objects put earlier into the coffin. The oldest son praises his father for his honorable life as his mother continues to pray for the soul of her husband.

A few days after the burial, the family holds a "feast of consecration," at which time they feed and entertain numerous guests. This feast ends with a procession in which relatives, friends, and neighbors wear sackcloth. The property of the deceased is then divided, with the oldest son receiving most of it. In older times a small "memorial house" was built over the grave; more commonly today, a tombstone is erected. At each of these events a Buddhist priest recites prayers before the deceased's portrait. Although the number of commemorative meals varies, they are still common in Japan today as the conclusion of the funeral ritual. Life is then expected to return to normal.

LO6 Shinto in North America Today

Shinto has a very small presence outside of Japan. Shintoists do not seek or even encourage converts, so almost all followers of Shinto are Japanese. Because the kami are tied so closely to the land of Japan, Japanese people living in the wider world often have a lessened

Entrance to the Tsubaki Shinto Shrine in Granite Falls, Washington

connection with Shinto. Although the people of and in Japan combine Shinto with Buddhism, people of Japanese descent living in North America typically see themselves only as Buddhists if they keep to one of the traditional Japanese religions. One estimate of Shintoists in North America has them at only one thousand people. In the most recent Canadian census, fewer than 1% of the approximately 100,000 Japanese Canadians called themselves Shintoists. In the United States, most of those who practice Shinto are found on the West Coast. They are served by a small number of Shinto shrines, including the Tsubaki Shinto Shrine in Granite Falls, Washington. Of course, Shintoists in North America can and do have kamidanas in their homes, at which the simple, regular home rituals can take place.

Even though the formal presence of Shinto in North America is remarkably small, it has a certain appeal to some Westerners today. Its reverence for nature, feeling for ritual, and open acknowledgment of pluralism (at least in a Buddhist and Confucian context) have attracted some independent-minded religious seekers. Small movements to practice Shinto have arisen here and there in North America. Whether or not Shinto will have a larger role in North America, it will almost certainly continue to be an important feature of life in Japan.

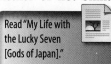

Read "My Life with the Lucky Seven [Gods of Japan]."

CHAPTER 9

Encountering Zoroastrianism: The Way of the One Wise Lord

Learning Outcomes

After studying this chapter, you will be able to do the following:

LO1 Explain the meaning of *Zoroastrianism* and related terms.

LO2 Outline how Zoroastrianism developed over time into what it is today.

LO3 Explain the essential Zoroastrian teachings of monotheism and moral dualism.

LO4 State the main ethical precepts of Zoroastrianism.

LO5 Outline the way Zoroastrians worship and observe rituals.

LO6 State the main features of Zoroastrian life in North America today.

"I acknowledge my faith in Good Thoughts, Good Words, and Good Deeds, the Good Religion of Ahura Mazda." —from the Zoroastrian declaration of faith

YOUR VISIT TO YAZD, IRAN

For more than a year you've planned and prepared for a hiking trip through Iran. You've been careful to get the correct visas and learn about cultural ways. Now that you're hiking there, you come across fascinating remains of the past as you approach the ancient city of Yazd (yahzd) on the ancient Silk Road. You already know about the importance of Silk Road caravan trade routes that ran from China to the Mediterranean Sea. Now you see the remains of a stone way station on the Silk Road, one of hundreds, each every thirty kilometers. They had lodging and food for humans and animals—even running water. It occurs to you that they were like full-service rest stops along this ancient highway.

Yazd is the historic center of Zoroastrianism (ZOHR-oh-ASS-tree-uh-NIHZ-uhm) in present-day Iran, although most Iranian Zoroastrians now live in the capital city, Tehran. Yazd has an active Zoroastrian temple, one of the most beautiful in the world, housing a fire that Zoroastrians believe has burned for more than a thousand years. Zoroastrians are not "fire worshipers," as you may have heard some Iranians say, but use fire as a symbol of the spiritual essence of God.

You hoped to hike out into the desert to Chak-Chak, an important pilgrimage site for Zoroastrians about 110 kilometers north of Yazd, to see a four-day festival that was about to start. But then you hear that only the faithful can attend the festival and that the temple will be closed at that time to non-Zoroastrians, so you travel out there right away before the festival starts. Chak-Chak, literally "drip-drip" in Persian, is a small group of buildings built onto the side of a mountain cliff. According to legend, a Zoroastrian princess who was fleeing the invading Muslim Arab armies escaped from Yazd into the desert. She arrived at this cliff and was

cornered, with the army closing in on her. She prayed to God to be spared, and the cliff opened and she disappeared inside forever. From that time on, dripping water from a spring has marked the place of her rescue. Legends such as this one have helped Zoroastrians cope with the predominantly Muslim nation in which they find themselves.

Back in Yazd the next day, you hike out of town to the round stone "towers of silence" built on the hills, used as the funeral buildings for Zoroastrians until recent times. After climbing to the top of a tower, you think about the somber scene. For more than two thousand years, Zoroastrians didn't bury or cremate their dead, believing that this would contaminate the earth. Instead, they left dead bodies in these towers to be eaten there by vultures until only clean bones remained to be bleached white by the sun. The bones were then swept into a central depository within the tower, but you can't see them any longer. On the plains of Yazd below, you see partially ruined temples and buildings used for funeral rites. Beyond the ruins, you can see the well-maintained, modern Zoroastrian cemetery where Zoroastrians now bury their dead inside concrete-lined graves. You take in the whole scene from the tower, amazed by how this site is so peaceful now. The towers are indeed silent.

Visit Chak-Chak and Yazd in an ABC Australia video.

Explore Zoroastrianism in Iran in Google Earth™.

◁ A Zoroastrian priest lights candles to begin the Zoroastrians' New Year festival of Nowruz at their temple in Suffern, New York. Pictures of Zarathustra, the founder of the faith, are on the table and the rear wall.

Begun thousands of years ago by Zarathustra, the prophet known to the Greeks as Zoroaster, Zoroastrianism became the state religion of the ancient Persian and Sassanid empires. Some historians estimate that it had as many as 40 million followers, making it one of the largest religions in the ancient world. Today, its numbers are severely reduced, for reasons we will explore in this chapter. About 150,000 adherents, almost all of them ethnic Persians, are clustered in eastern Iran and Mumbai (Bombay), India, and about another 50,000 are scattered in twenty-three nations of the world, including 20,000 in North America. These numbers are estimates, because exact numbers are hard to come by.

> "Zoroastrianism has probably had more influence on human life, directly and indirectly, than any other single faith."
> —Mary Boyce

Despite these reduced numbers, the study of Zoroastrianism has an appeal all its own. Any religion from so long ago that is still present today deserves to be studied carefully. Scholars also study Zoroastrianism today for a wider reason, to discern the possible influence of Zoroastrianism on other Western religions. Most scholars conclude that Zoroastrianism had some direct influence on ancient Judaism and then some indirect influence (mostly through Judaism) on Christianity and Islam. The exact extent of this influence is sharply debated. On the one hand, a leading scholar of Zoroastrianism, Mary Boyce, argues for a maximum influence: "Zoroastrianism has probably had more influence on human life, directly and indirectly, than any other single faith." She also argues that Zoroastrianism's teachings on judgment, heaven and hell, the resurrection of the body, and life everlasting were borrowed by Judaism, Christianity, and Islam.[1] This position is frequently seen on the Web. On the other hand, Hebrew Bible scholar James Barr and others have argued that significant borrowing of Zoroastrian ideas, directly or indirectly, cannot be demonstrated in early Judaism, aside from a few small points of contact. Barr argues as well that later Christian and Islamic beliefs cannot be shown to have drawn from Zoroastrianism.[2] This debate continues today.

In your study of Zoroastrianism, these unique, initially puzzling features may appear:

- Zoroastrians place a strong emphasis on morality in thought, word, and deed. But unlike many other religions that stress moral purity, Zoroastrianism gives emphasis to dealing with hundreds of ritual impurities, because they can ruin the effect of moral deeds.

- Zoroastrianism is a monotheistic religion, teaching that only one God exists. But it also features dozens of other spirits good and bad, most of them named, who have large roles in human life. Sometimes they are even called "divinities," as for example on the opening page of a matchmaking website for Zoroastrians, which invokes the power of Ava Ardvisur, the "Divinity of fertility and childbirth."

- Christians throughout the world, and many people who aren't Christians, know about the Bible's story of "wise men from the east" visiting the newborn Jesus to honor him and bring him gifts. Two of these gifts, frankincense and myrrh, have been offered in Zoroastrian worship for more than 2,500 years now. And most Christians don't realize that the term the Bible uses for the wise men, *magi* (MAJ-igh), is a special Zoroastrian word for their priests.

> View an introduction to Zoroastrianism.

LO1 Names for Zoroastrianism and Zoroastrians

Zoroastrianism is the most common designation of the ancient Persian monotheistic religion. This name is built from the Greek form of the name of its founder, Zoroaster (ZOHR-oh-ASS-ter). The founder is known as Zarathustra (ZAHR-uh-THUHS-truh) in the religion's most ancient writings. *Zoroastrianism* was originally a European name for the faith and reflects the European tendency to name religions after their founders whether the religions themselves do so or not. Zarathustra would probably not have been pleased with this name. But *Zoroastrianism* "stuck," and most followers of the faith use it happily today.

---

[1] Mary Boyce, *Zoroastrians: Their Religious Beliefs and Practices* (London: Routledge and Kegan Paul, 1979), 1, 29.

[2] James Barr, "The Question of Religious Influence: The Case of Zoroastrianism, Judaism, and Christianity." *Journal of the American Academy of Religion* 53 (1985): 201–35.

> *Zoroastrianism was originally a European name for the faith and reflects the European tendency to name religions after their founders.*

Ancient Zoroastrian sources called it the "Good Religion," not in a generic sense (after all, what religion doesn't think of itself as good?) but as pointing especially to the key role of struggle for good in Zoroastrianism. This moral dimension of the faith is richly reflected in its symbol, the **faravahar** (or farohar), which means "Divine glory." More specifically, Zoroastrians have called their faith the "Mazda-worshiping" or "Mazdayasnian" (MAHZ-duh-YAHZ-nee-uhn) religion. The latter name refers to **Ahura Mazda**, the "Wise Lord," who is the only God. He created the universe as a place in which good will eventually prevail. This book will follow the current scholarly convention of referring to the name of the religion as Zoroastrianism and the name of its founder as Zarathustra.

One other name for Zoroastrians has become important. Zoroastrians who moved to India from Iran in the 900s C.E. are called **Parsis** (sometimes spelled "Parsees"), a name derived from *Persians*. The Zoroastrian communities in east Africa, Great Britain, and North America descend largely from this group, so it has spread beyond India. *Parsis* is often used as a synonym of *Zoroastrians*.

faravahar [fahr-uh-VAH-har] "Divine glory," winged symbol of Zoroastrianism stressing morality

Ahura Mazda [ah-HOOR-uh MAHZ-duh] "Wise Lord," the single, all-powerful god worshiped by Zoroastrians

Parsis [PAR-seez] Name for Zoroastrians in India, also spelled "Parsees"

LO2 Zoroastrianism As Shaped by Its Past

A prominent Zoroastrian of the twentieth century was the rock star Freddie Mercury (1946–1991), the lead singer in the British band Queen. Born as Farrokh Bulsara to a Zoroastrian family in what is now Tanzania, he was raised as a devout Zoroastrian and was initiated into the faith as a teenager.

A Closer Look:

The Symbol of Zoroastrianism

Zoroastrianism has had a few different symbols throughout its history. One ancient symbol still seen today is

BONNIE VAN VOORST
© CENGAGE LEARNING

a sacrificial fire burning in a ritual urn. But the symbol most associated with Zoroastrianism for more than 2,500 years is the faravahar, the figure of a human being with eagle's wings. Its origins are debated. Some think that it originally represented Ahura Mazda, because it seems to draw some elements from the symbols of gods in Assyrian religion. However, Zoroastrians have always considered God to be an undepictable spirit.

The central human figure represents the individual Zoroastrian believer. The figure is obviously a male, with the long beard that Persian men wore, but this hasn't prevented

Zoroastrian women from identifying with the symbol. He is aged in appearance, so the soul is wise. He wears a traditional Persian hat, suggesting respect for culture. One hand is open and lifted upward, symbolic of faith in and obedience to the goodness of Ahura Mazda. The other hand holds a ring, which may represent loyalty and faithfulness. The circle around the center of the human figure represents the immortality of the soul or the eternal significance of human actions in the here and now.

The two wings have three main rows of feathers, representing good thoughts, good words, and good deeds. Doing these things lifts up one's soul as on powerful wings. The tail below also has three rows of feathers, said to represent bad thoughts, bad words, and bad deeds. The two streamers below the human figure represent the spirits of good and evil. Every person must constantly choose between the two, so the figure is facing the good and turning his back on evil.

Mercury sang many hit songs, including "Bohemian Rhapsody," "We Are the Champions," and "Crazy Little Thing Called Love." Although he hadn't formally observed his ancestral Zoroastrian religion as an adult, his funeral in London was led at Mercury's wishes by Zoroastrian priests. It was conducted entirely in the Avestan language and included prayers and hymns from the Zoroastrian scriptures. After the service, his body was cremated. The debate over Mercury's legacy indicates a divide in modern Zoroastrianism: Can it be followed by keeping just its main moral commands, as some argue Mercury tried to do, or is it necessary to keep the full, traditional way of life of Zoroastrianism, as he did not?

Read an article on Freddie Mercury and Zoroastrianism.

The early history of Zoroastrianism is still shrouded in the mists of antiquity. We aren't certain of many key details about its beginnings, because most of its earliest writings were destroyed in persecutions. But as it moved closer to our time, Zoroastrianism emerged from the mists and became a key religion in the world. It can be divided into three main periods: birth and formation (ca. 630–550 B.C.E.); growth into the official religion of the Persian Empire, decline under Greek and Parthian rule, and revival and renewed official status in the Sassanian Empire (550 B.C.E.–650 C.E.); and slow, steady decline under Islamic rulers and in the modern world (650 C.E.–today).

> *As it moved closer to our time, Zoroastrianism emerged from the mists and became a key religion in the world.*

THE BIRTH OF ZOROASTRIANISM (CA. 630–550 B.C.E.)

The question of when Zarathustra lived isn't easy to answer. A few scholars and many traditional Zoroastrians date it all the way back to 7500 B.C.E., at what they consider the dawn of human civilization; others hold to a time between 1400 and 900 B.C.E. Most commonly today, historians put his birth around 630 B.C.E., at the beginning of the **Axial Age** in Europe and Asia. This term was given by philosopher Karl Jaspers to the

Axial Age Name given by philosopher Karl Jaspers to the period from 600 to 400 B.C.E. when many religions and value (axial) systems were founded

period from 600 to 400 B.C.E. when many religions and value (axial) systems were founded. This wide chronological range, so unusual for dating the founder of a major religion, shows that firm evidence for the life of Zarathustra is lacking. The Zoroastrian scriptures that he is thought to have authored, the central chapters of the *Gathas*, do not locate him chronologically. No historical sources outside of Zoroastrianism give reliable information that can be used in dating his life. Moreover, most Zoroastrian scriptures weren't written down until about 400 C.E., at least a thousand years after the events they relate.

The birth of Zarathustra was said by some sacred writings to be prepared by prophecies and accompanied by miraculous signs. For example, the glory of Ahura Mazda descended on Zarathustra's mother, resulting in a virginal conception, and the newborn Zoroaster was said to have laughed when he was born. The main outline of Zarathustra's teaching, which he gave to disciples and at the court of the Persian kings, can be reliably traced, although the details are sketchy. The ancient Persians were polytheistic, as were all other Indo-European peoples. The basic structure of Persian polytheism was probably the same as that of Vedic Hinduism. For example, both religions worshiped many gods in nature, sacrificed animals whose souls were thought to join the gods, and used a hallucinogenic drug in some sacrifices.

Zarathustra saw this religion as mistaken. He had a revolutionary monotheistic vision that only one God existed, Ahura Mazda. He also had a vision of an evil figure (supernatural but not divine), named Angra Mainyu, who opposed God. Zarathustra taught that all people had to choose which of these two moral forces they would follow, a choice that would either improve the world or make it worse. This choice determined their judgment by God to heaven or hell when they died, but Zarathustra taught that a final restoration would come when Ahura Mazda completely defeated the forces of evil. In this restoration, even hell would come to an end, and all people would be resurrected with a re-created body to an eternal, blessed life. Despite the up-and-down fortunes of this faith, Zarathustra's powerful teaching has endured through today.

THE SPREAD OF ZOROASTRIANISM IN THE PERSIAN AND SASSANIAN EMPIRES (550 B.C.E.–650 C.E.)

The first certain date in Zoroastrian history is its establishment in Persia during the reign of the Persian kings, beginning in 550 B.C.E. These kings created and ruled over the largest empire the world had yet seen, and

Zoroastrianism spread with it (see Map 9.1). Some Persian kings drew explicitly on Zoroastrianism for the legitimacy of their empire, claiming that Ahura Mazda wanted his fame and goodness spread throughout the world. However, the Persians never attempted to impose Zoroastrianism on subject peoples with other religions. Given Zoroastrianism's monotheism and moral rigor based on individual choice, religious ideas not widely shared in the ancient Middle East, this was a wise policy. Persian rule was autocratic but tolerant and efficient, respecting and even embracing cultural and religious differences in its subject peoples. As the ancient Greek historian Herodotus wrote, "No nation so readily adopts foreign customs as the Persians do."[3]

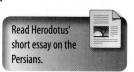
Read Herodotus' short essay on the Persians.

"No nation so readily adopts foreign customs as the Persians."—Herodotus, ancient Greek historian

Cyrus (SY-rus) II, later called Cyrus the Great, ruled the small Persia homeland from 550 to 530 B.C.E. He began the expansion of Persia by overthrowing the king of Media to the north, and he kept on marching. Within ten years he had conquered much of the Middle East. He was a faithful Zoroastrian, as were the emperors of Persia who came after him, but tolerant toward other religions in his empire. When he captured Babylon, he rebuilt the temple of its main god, Marduk (MAHR-dook). He released many captive peoples held in Babylonia, allowing them to return to their homes and pursue their religions. For example, Cyrus allowed the thousands of Jews taken to Babylon in 586 B.C.E. to return to Jerusalem in 539, to rebuild their temple and land as a loyal part of the Persian

Miniature relief carving of Cyrus the Great

© ISTOCKPHOTO.COM/GRAEME GILMOUR

Empire. Historians who argue for a large influence of Zoroastrianism on Judaism typically point to this "Persian period" in Jewish history as the time when it occurred.

Darius (dah-RY-us) I, called "Darius the Great," ruled from 521 to 486 B.C.E. He is known mainly for his great building projects, such as a spectacular new capital at Persepolis. He was adept at managing his empire and expanded Persian rule to its greatest extent. Darius referred to Ahura Mazda in his royal inscriptions as the source of his successes, and he had monumental faravahars carved on many walls in Persepolis and in older cities. He attempted to conquer Greece, but wasn't successful.

Darius's son Xerxes (ZUHRK-seez), who ruled from 486–465 B.C.E., also tried to conquer Greece, this time with a massive effort. Like his father, he failed. Several relatively small Greek city-states turned back the mighty Persian Empire, marking a turning point in Persian fortunes. (This story is told in historical-fantasy form by the much-mocked 2006 film *300*, with its false depiction of the Persians and of Xerxes.) Xerxes and his successors changed the policy of tolerating different religions and ethnic groups as their predecessors had, betraying Zoroastrian values. Local and regional imperial officials were now drawn only from Persian ranks, not as before from local national and ethnic groups. Over the next hundred years, the empire suffered from various revolts and struggles over the throne. It was greatly reduced in size and splendor by the time Alexander the Great of Macedon, a nation that had once been a part of the Persian Empire, easily toppled it in 334 B.C.E.

Zoroastrians today see much to be proud of in this period, including the birth and early growth of their faith. But they view the accomplishments as short-lived due to the onslaught of Alexander. They blame Alexander for many of the troubles of later Zoroastrianism. They have so hated Alexander that they have called him not "Alexander the Great" but "Alexander the Accursed." They cursed him for murdering priests and scholars, extinguishing ritual fires, destroying temples, and carrying off sacred writings and having them burned or (worse) translated for non-Zoroastrians. Some of these charges are no doubt

---

[3] William Stearns Davis, *Readings in Ancient History: Illustrative Extracts from the Sources*, Vol. 2: *Greece and the East* (Boston: Allyn and Bacon, 1912), 60.

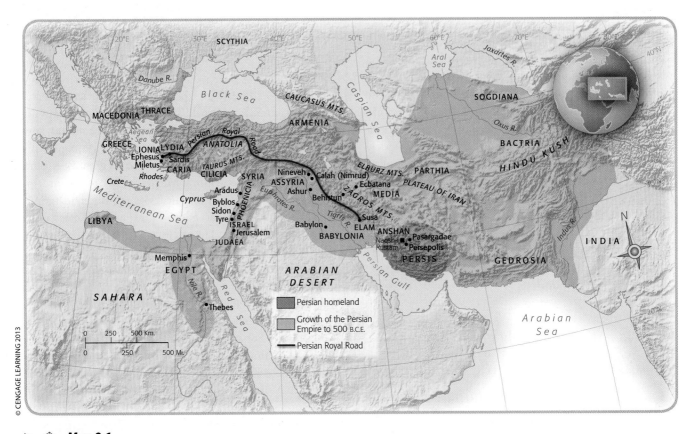

Map 9.1

The Zoroastrian Persian Empire, ca. 500 B.C.E.

At its height around 500 B.C.E., the Persians controlled a huge empire that included northern Greece, Egypt, and most of western Asia, from the Mediterranean coast to the Indus River in India.

Avesta [ah-VEHS-tuh]
First and basic Zoroastrian scripture

tower of silence Stone funeral structure where the Zoroastrian dead were placed and bones stored; no longer used in most locations

exaggerated; Alexander, like the Persians, tended to be basically tolerant of other religions. But the fact remains that Alexander overthrew the empire to which Zoroastrianism had become closely connected, and Zoroastrianism was greatly damaged in the process. In particular, the loss of much of the sacred literature at this time and in later book burnings means that we are no longer able to reconstruct the history of Zoroastrian teachings.

Zoroastrianism struggled under Hellenistic, Roman, and Parthian rule that controlled parts of its homeland from 334 B.C.E. until 224 C.E. Zoroastrian religious leaders praised the kings of

Coin of Sassanian King Shahpur II (309–379 C.E.), with a fire altar and priests

the Sassanian Empire (224–651 C.E.; also known as "Sassanid") for powerfully reestablishing the religion. For the second time, Zoroastrianism was the official religion of a large empire (see Map 9.2). This was the "golden age" of Zoroastrianism. Several Sassanian rulers featured Zoroastrian symbols in official inscriptions and coins. Their patronage enabled the establishment of many Zoroastrian temples and the rise of a professional Zoroastrian priesthood to staff them. The *Avesta*, the first and basic Zoroastrian scripture, was collected. **Towers of silence**, stone funeral structures for the Zoroastrian dead, were built throughout the land. In the Sassanian period, Zoroastrianism reached the basic form that it would keep through today.

The Sassanians presented themselves as pious Zoroastrians, putting religious images on their coins and buildings. Later sources celebrated some Sassanian kings as a blessing to Zoroastrianism. Zoroastrians still use the date of

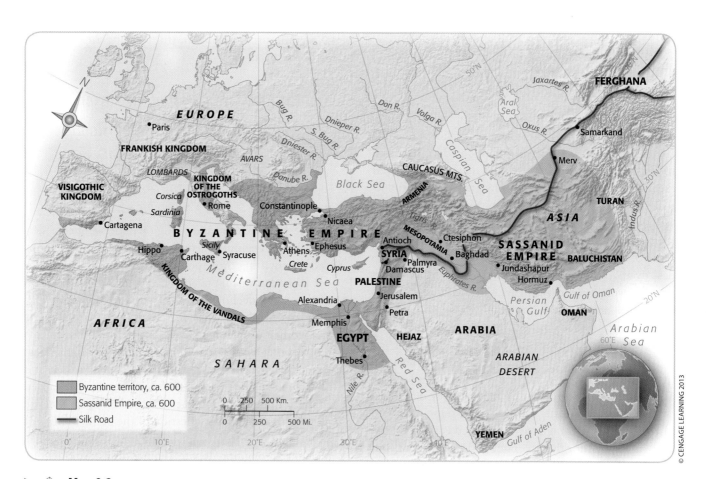

Map 9.2

The Sassanian and Byzantine Empires, 600 C.E.

By 600 C.E., the Christian Byzantine Empire controlled much of the eastern Mediterranean. The neighboring Zoroastrian Sassanian Empire dominated most of western Asia. It was centered in the older Persian homeland, which today is in southern Iran.

the coronation of the last Sassanian king, Yazdgird, in 631 C.E. as the first year of their calendar (for example, 2011 C.E. = 1380 Y.). However, modern Iranian Zoroastrians blame the Sassanians for beginning the decline of their religion, saying that its misuse for political purposes led to the downfall of the empire. Zoroastrian religion had been too closely tied to imperial rule, they say, and the strong moral essence of the religion was compromised. The Sassanian Empire was conquered by Arabic Muslim forces around 650 C.E. As happened earlier with Alexander's conquest of the Persian Empire, the brutal Muslim conquest of the Sassanian Empire caused great damage to the state-sponsored Zoroastrian religion and to most Zoroastrians. They found themselves in a Muslim empire that would, over time, further reduce their numbers and influence.

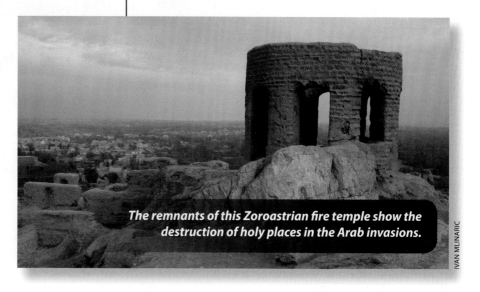

The remnants of this Zoroastrian fire temple show the destruction of holy places in the Arab invasions.

THE COMING OF ISLAM AND THE ZOROASTRIAN DISPERSION (650 C.E.–PRESENT)

The Arabic conquest of the Sassanian Empire began a process of Islamic growth and Zoroastrian decline that would last for centuries. Muslim rulers considered Zoroastrians to be "People of the Book" and did not forcibly convert them, but most Zoroastrians converted to Islam nonetheless, probably drawn by its rigorous monotheism and strict morality. Those who remained Zoroastrians had their religious liberty restricted, and they were often persecuted. Up to three-quarters of their sacred literature was destroyed. A few times, various Zoroastrian communities openly revolted against their Muslim overlords, only to be crushed and decimated. By 900 C.E. the Zoroastrians were reduced to such a small minority that they were concentrated in a few areas of Iran.

These pressures on the Iranian Zoroastrians led many to flee to the western coast of India, in the Gujarat area, in 936 C.E. In the course of time, they developed a specific ethnic identity with a strong sense of shared history, and even a language they named Parsi-Gujarati. The Hindu authorities tolerated Zoroastrianism, but did not allow conversions of Hindus to Zoroastrianism (which Zoroastrians prohibited as well) or even Hindu visits to Zoroastrian temples. For centuries, Zoroastrians in India had their own dress and diet codes. These have now mostly disappeared in everyday life but are carefully observed on important occasions such as initiations, feasts, weddings, and funerals. Thus began the development of two different communities of Zoroastrians, Iranians and Parsis, a split that would last through today. An effort in the early twenty-first century to found an organization for all Zoroastrians failed to overcome the old differences.

The Parsi communities blossomed during Mughal (Islamic) and British rule in India. These latter groups were more tolerant of Zoroastrianism than were the rulers of Iran. Many Parsis today regard these times as a high point of their community's history, in material wealth, social prestige, cultural achievements, and political influence. Zoroastrians in India prospered economically in commerce and the professions. An unprecedented number of temples were built, most of them in urban Mumbai, still the modern stronghold of Zoroastrianism.

> *The Arabic conquest of the Sassanian Empire began a process of Islamic growth and Zoroastrian decline that would last for centuries.*

At the same time, their religion underwent considerable change beginning around 1800. The fear of demons and of unwitting ritual pollution that characterized earlier Zoroastrianism ended. The socioreligious position of the clergy declined, and lay participation in leadership was firmly established, along with certain rights for women. Social and religious reform movements representing a minority of Parsis started to fight against what they regarded as Zoroastrian "superstitions" and advocated a return to what their members regarded as the original teachings of Zarathustra. Since the late nineteenth century, the question of the permissibility of conversion to Zoroastrianism and mixed marriages has brought an ongoing debate about Zoroastrian identity. Parsis did not permit conversion to Zoroastrianism, and although intermarriage with people of other faiths happens in many Zoroastrian families, it is still regarded as taboo. The religious status of persons of other religions who marry Zoroastrians, and the children born of such marriages, is still a matter of difficult dispute today almost everywhere Zoroastrians are found.

One of the several Zoroastrian fire temples in Mumbai

© FRÉDÉRIC SOLTAN/CORBIS

Indian independence in 1949 was a mixed blessing for the Parsis. It brought a greater measure of freedom, but it also brought the challenge of numerical decline. Parsis now number fewer than 70,000, down from more than 100,000 a century ago. Part of this decline is due to a reluctance to procreate that is typical of modern groups with upper-class social standing such as that of the Parsis, but this is clearly at odds with the exhortations to bear children that can be found throughout Zoroastrian religious literature. Migration has also contributed to dwindling numbers in India. Starting with the late 1700s, Parsis settled in distant parts of the British Empire, including in Chinese port cities, Burma, Ceylon, and parts of Africa, but mostly in Britain itself. Since the 1960s, new waves of immigration brought Parsis to North America, Australia, New Zealand, and the Persian Gulf nations.

Read a 2004 interview with the leader of India's Zoroastrians.

In Iran, Zoroastrianism had been reduced to a tiny minority of fewer than 10,000 by 1900. These Zoroastrians had to bear a wide range of harsh discriminatory practices from the dominant Muslim population. Help from Zoroastrians in India and substantial political and legal changes improved the lot of the Iranian Zoroastrians and led to a tripling of their numbers. Many Zoroastrians left agriculture, migrated to the modern capital of Tehran (which is now the main stronghold of the Iranian Zoroastrians), and went into the new middle-class professions. As the Parsis did in India, some Iranian Zoroastrians found great success in commerce.

Modern Iranian Zoroastrianism has undergone fundamental changes. When Zoroastrians were freed during secular Iranian rule from many restrictions in much of the twentieth century until 1979, the religion has been reconceived as a message of moral freedom. Iranian Zoroastrians have claimed that this was the essence of Zarathustra's message. The ceremonial ritual system has been deliberately neglected, and many rules and rituals that are still carefully upheld by Indian priests have been all but abandoned in Iran. The *Yasna* (YAHZ-nuh) ceremony, for example, which the Parsis regard as an important liturgy (it takes a pair of trained priests several hours to perform it), is celebrated only rarely nowadays, and in a drastically reduced format, by some Iranian priests. Most of the purification rituals have been abandoned. The professional priesthood has seen a sharp decline, and the leading priests have joined the social and intellectual elite in a crusade to uproot ancient "superstition" in the faith, including some rituals for women, devotion to "lesser" divinities

such as Mithra, and animal sacrifice. The fear of being called "fire worshipers" led the community to emphasize the symbolic role of fire in their worship; some new temples even house gas fires. Consecrated wood fires are still kept burning but aren't tended according to past ritual.

Zarathushtrian Assembly International group based in California advocating the modernized form of Zoroastrianism and accepting people willing to convert

Zoroastrianism in Iran gradually transformed itself into a religion of freedom and morality, representing the splendor of ancient Iran. For most of the 1800s and 1900s, Zoroastrianism became an appealing alternative to Shi'a Islam for many Iranians, where pride in Iran's Persian heritage is deeply felt by many. Some even converted to Zoroastrianism. This more liberal form of Zoroastrianism is today also represented by an international organization based in California called the **Zarathushtrian Assembly**. This group advocates the modernized form of their religion and accepts people willing to convert. However, it is strongly opposed by other Zoroastrian organizations, including a traditionalist organization based in Mumbai called the Zoroastrian Studies Association. When the Islamic Republic of Iran was established in 1979, conversion to Zoroastrianism or any other religion became almost impossible. The New Year festival, which is widely shared among Iranians who are Muslims, is among the few accepted occasions for celebration that include both Zoroastrians and Muslims.

LO3 Essential Zoroastrian Teachings: Monotheism and Moral Dualism

On the crowded streets of Mumbai, India, a young Zoroastrian woman sees an automobile with a familiar name: Mazda. The auto company's logo she sees on this car looks like the wings of a bird, suggesting to her the main symbol of her faith, the faravahar. This causes her both wonder and consternation: Is it really connected to Zoroastrianism? Why should a car company abuse the name of God? So, like most young people today, she goes on the Internet and finds the website of the Mazda automotive company in Japan. The company website states that the name derives from Ahura Mazda, "a god of the earliest civilizations in West Asia, the god of wisdom, intelligence and harmony." The company website further notes that the company name also comes from a shortening of *Matsuda*, the last name of its Japanese founder.

The teachings of Zoroastrianism stress belief in one God and moral dualism. Zoroastrianism was probably the first faith to put these two features together, and most Zoroastrian teachings are connected to them.

THE ONE GOD, AHURA MAZDA

Zoroastrianism's foundational teaching is that there is only one supreme God, Ahura Mazda, a name that means "Wise Lord" or "Lord of Wisdom." Ahura Mazda is the source of all light, truth, goodness, and life. He is infinite, and infinitely good. Zarathustra emphasized the central importance of Ahura Mazda by portraying him as the one God, accompanied by many spirit-lords, all the other older Indo-Aryan gods who were "demoted" in the new religion. In later Zoroastrianism, the name Ahura Mazda was compacted into a single-word form, Ormazd. As the first verse in the ancient *Avesta* scripture proclaims, "Ahura Mazda is the creator, radiant, glorious and best; the most beautiful, firm, wise, perfect and bounteous Spirit!" Zoroastrians look to Ahura Mazda as the source of all created things that are good, the one who sustains goodness and life in the present, and the one who at the end of time will defeat all evil and give eternal life to all people.

> *"Ahura Mazda is the creator, radiant, glorious and best; the most beautiful, firm, wise, perfect and bounteous Spirit!"*
> —The *Avesta*

For Zoroastrians, only Ahura Mazda is a true God; only he is to be worshiped. All the other "lords," ahuras, and demons are beneath him and are not gods. They form an entourage of spirits that accompany the forces of either good or evil. In sum, Zoroastrianism is properly called monotheistic because it teaches the existence of one God. However, it was never as assertively monotheistic against other faiths as Judaism, Islam, or Christianity tended to be. It lacks a clear denial of the existence of other gods, characteristic of the more radical monotheisms. This may be connected to its historic tolerance toward other creeds.

THE SPIRIT OF DESTRUCTION, ANGRA MAINYU

Opposition to the evil and impurities in the world was also a fundamental feature of Zoroastrianism from its beginning. Because Ahura Mazda is good and made the world to be a good place, he desires the people in his creation to be morally good as well. This entails a positive effort to do what is right and a negative effort to engage in a real fight with evils of all sorts. People who think, say, and do evil on earth are deceivers and liars who turn others against the one true, good God by promoting all sorts of evils. Evil doesn't always look like evil, nor is it always easily recognized. Instead, it disguises itself as good, hence one of the main figures of evil is known as the Druj (drooj), the "Spirit of Deceit" or the "Spirit of the Lie." The supreme evil spirit, Zarathustra taught, is **Angra Mainyu**, the "Spirit of Destruction." Zarathustra seems to have used this as only a title, to judge from the oldest parts of Zoroastrian scriptures, but later it became a proper name and was shortened to Ahriman (AH-rih-mun).

A Closer Look:

The Zoroastrian Creed

At key moments in a Zoroastrian's life, the Fravarane is recited. This declaration of faith is a shortened version of the full creed from the Zoroastrian scriptures.

"Come to my help, Ahura Mazda. I am a Mazdayasnian according to [the way of] Zarathustra. I firmly declare my faith. I acknowledge my faith in Good Thoughts well conceived. I acknowledge my faith in Good Words well spoken. I acknowledge my faith in Good Deeds well done.

I acknowledge my acceptance of the Good Religion of Mazda, which ends strife and disarms violence, which makes us righteous and self-reliant. It is the religion of those who have been, and shall be, the noblest, the best, and most sublime. The religion of Ahura Mazda was brought to us by Zarathustra. All good derives from Ahura Mazda. This is the declaration of the Mazdayasnian religion."

MORAL DUALISM

Another foundational feature of Zoroastrianism is **dualism**, the notion that the cosmos is composed of two competing forces. This opposition between good and evil is also found in early Vedic Hindu sources, so it must have been some part of pre-Zoroastrian Persian religion, but Zarathustra developed it significantly. From the beginning of the world, the Zoroastrian scriptures say, there have been two incompatible, antagonistic spirits in the world. One is the good God, Ahura Mazda; the other is a devil-like figure, Angra Mainyu. The **Twin Spirits** under Ahura Mazda made an ominous choice: The Bounteous Spirit chose to be truthful in thoughts, words, and deeds, but the Deceitful Spirit chose to be a follower of evil. When the Zoroastrian scriptures teach this dualism, it is always with a command to follow the good; for example, "Let those who act wisely choose correctly between these two, not as evil-doers choose" (*Yasna* 30.3).

Then it was the turn of the old gods of pre-Zoroastrian Persian religion to choose between good and evil; these gods, called daevas (DIGH-vuhs), all chose badly. Ever since, the daevas have tried to corrupt people's choices also. The two powers of good and evil are roughly equal to each other in this world, so the fight between good and evil is real. The two powers draw all people into their service as they fight this cosmic moral battle, as people decide which spirit to follow. These two forces will continue to limit and challenge each other until the end of time, when evil will finally be defeated.

Zoroastrianism's form of moral dualism was never understood in an absolute fashion where good and evil are exactly equal, because it was qualified by monotheism. If there is only one God, and this God is both good and has supreme power, evil at the end of the day doesn't have much of a chance to win. Instead, the forces of good are assured of eventual triumph. Ahura Mazda limits the exercise of his supreme power as this struggle plays out. Humans should join this cosmic war because of their capacity of free choice.

The dualism is moral, but it isn't physical dualism, the idea that matter is evil and spirit is good. Humans serve either good or evil with both their souls and bodies, because both the human soul and the human body participate in the divine nature. For example, fasting and celibacy—important practices in many religions to control the body and its supposed impulse to do or think wrong—are almost unknown in Zoroastrianism. The fight has a ritual aspect as well: Humans must keep themselves pure in body and soul by avoiding defilement by contact with dead humans and animals, treating fire with great respect, avoiding demons in their dreams, and so forth. There are short but necessary rituals for cleansing oneself after cutting hair or nails, sneezing, eliminating bodily wastes, and using toothpicks. Thus, traditional Zoroastrianism has ritual aspects that are just as all-pervading as its ethical aspects.

dualism Notion that the cosmos is composed of two competing forces

Twin Spirits The Bounteous Spirit and the Deceitful Spirit, two supernatural beings under Ahura Mazda

Fire, such as this one in Yazd said to be burning for more than a thousand years, symbolizes the purity and power of good.

ALEXANDER NITZSCHE

SUPERNATURAL INTERMEDIARIES

Zoroastrianism's strong moral dualism is buttressed by supernatural intermediaries that personify and promote what is morally good. Between Ahura Mazda and human beings there are six intermediary beings called **Amesha Spentas,** or benevolent immortals. They are Good Thoughts, Perfect Truth, Desirable Lordship, Beneficial Devotion, Plenty, and Immortality. These immortals are the entourage of personified virtues that constantly surround Ahura Mazda. They are individual divine beings and at the same time cosmic moral virtues. Humans who choose to follow Ahura Mazda take on the moral characteristics of these immortals, and they progress from Good Thoughts to Immortality.

JUDGMENT AND THE FINAL VICTORY OF AHURA MAZDA

In Zoroastrian belief, the soul hovers above the body for three days after death. On the fourth day, it takes a rapid journey to the next world and faces judgment on the **Chinvat Bridge.** The deeds of the soul during all of life are weighed. If its good deeds outweigh evil ones, the soul ascends to the stars (representing good thoughts) then to the moon (good words), to the sun (good deeds), and finally to paradise, where eternal lights shine. There the soul is led to the golden throne of Ahura Mazda by the Good Mind. However, if evil outweighs good, the soul is dragged off to hell, to be punished there until the end of time.

Read a description of judgment on the Chinvat Bridge.

At the end of time, hell will be emptied of souls and sealed forever, and Angra Mainyu and all his forces will be annihilated.

In the last great struggle near the end of time, the armies of good and evil will battle to the death, and Ahura Mazda's soldiers will defeat their evil enemies. Then a final judgment comes at the end of the world,

after all bodies of the dead are resurrected and reunited with their souls, whether they have been in heaven or hell. A final cleansing of fire purifies the souls and bodies of evil human beings, so that all people are fit to live in paradise. This will restore the goodness of the world at the time of creation. The personified Spirit of Fire and Angra Mainyu will cause the metals of the mountains to melt and to flow down as a river of fire. All resurrected humans must walk through this valley of trial. The fire will burn off the sins of the wicked for three painful days, but to the righteous it will be as delicious and restorative as warm milk. Then all people will enjoy happiness and divine blessing forever. On the renewed earth, men and women will have no shadow because they are sinless. Hell will be emptied of souls and sealed forever, and Angra Mainyu and all his forces will be annihilated.

LO4 Zoroastrian Ethics

A young Zoroastrian man in California logs onto a Zoroastrian matchmaking website. Because his religion is important to him and because it commands marriage within the faith, he is now looking for a suitable Zoroastrian who could possibly become his wife. He has tried to find a possible mate in San Francisco, but the Zoroastrian community there is too small, and the website gives him worldwide possibilities, especially in India, where his family came from generations ago. Some of his friends, both male and female, have married non-Zoroastrians, and his religious community has refused to welcome them or recognize their children as Zoroastrians. The young man would like to avoid these difficult problems.

As we have seen previously, the two main doctrinal teachings of Zoroastrianism are monotheism and morality. These are deeply intertwined. In a culture that rarely thought of its gods as morally good, Zarathustra proclaimed that the one God, Ahura Mazda, was infinitely good and was attended by six spirits who personify his righteousness and mediate it to humankind. Ahura Mazda fights a cosmic battle against evil, a force that is strong and real (*Gathas, Yasna* 44:10; 53:1).

Because Ahura Mazda does what is good, he expects all people to follow him in doing what is right and putting away evil. In this way, they join the ongoing cosmic spiritual and physical battle for righteousness, a battle that Ahura Mazda will certainly win. Zoroastrians do not simply fight against evil in themselves or society around them, but by their good actions they fight against demons and Angra Mainyu himself. People have the freedom to know right from wrong and choose what is right, and Ahura Mazda holds them responsible for these choices. Most Zoroastrians have a lively sense of the heavenly reward for doing right and the hellish punishment for doing wrong.

ZOROASTRIAN GENERAL MORALITY

Zoroastrian ethics focus on the maintenance of life and the fight against evil, but this abstract ideal is carried out in very concrete ways. The most ancient scriptures of Zoroastrianism relate that one must earn an honest living by means of cattle raising and agriculture. This wasn't just a cultural given—it was a religious norm. Over time, many Zoroastrians went into commerce and prospered in it, in part because they had a reputation for being honest with all people, not just those of their faith or ethnic group. At one time, Zoroastrians in Mumbai owned more businesses than did Hindus, who vastly outnumbered them.

Zoroastrians hold to values of saying and doing the truth, being faithful to Ahura Mazda, and doing what is good in the world. Goodness in one's individual life can be attained only by living a balanced, morally healthy life of good thoughts, good words, and good deeds. In the Avestan language, these three have the same beginning sound, suggesting they go together: Humata (hoo-MAHT-uh), Hukhta (HOOK-tuh), and Huvereshta (HOO-vuh-RESH-tuh). This threefold statement of morality is so important in the faith that it is a key part of the Zoroastrian confession of faith, as we saw previously. It is inscribed over many a door to Zoroastrian temples and community centers. In the past few centuries, generous giving to Zoroastrian philanthropies has become a hallmark of Zoroastrian moral effort. The steady work of Zoroastrians to spread good in the world has improved the education of girls and the social status of women in India, Iran, and other countries.

> *At one time, Zoroastrians in Mumbai owned more businesses than did Hindus, who vastly outnumbered them.*

Traditional Zoroastrians live their lives in this world with a view of their individual judgment after death. Their future life in the next world, at least from the time of their death to the end of the world, is determined by the total balance of good and evil deeds, words, and thoughts. This principle, however, is flexible enough to allow for human weakness. Zoroastrians don't believe that all their sins must be weighed on the scales. There are two means of erasing now their negative effects at one's personal judgment. The first of these is confession of one's sins, which brings forgiveness and lightens the weight of sin at the judgment. The second means is the transfer of merits from the Zoroastrian saints, whose good thoughts, words, and deeds are far more than what the saints need to pass judgment and enter heaven. This is the rationale for Zoroastrian funeral prayers and rituals asking Ahura Mazda for mercy on and forgiveness of the souls of the dead.

A CURRENT ETHICAL AND SOCIAL ISSUE: MARRIAGE AND CHILDREN

Another key moral command in Zoroastrianism is the duty to marry and have children. To Zoroastrians, the world is a good place even though evil has marred it. Marriage and children are good things for every Zoroastrian; in contrast with some other religions among whom Zoroastrians have lived (for instance, Hinduism and Jainism), one won't see any form of celibacy at any stage in life. Moreover, marriage must be to another Zoroastrian, preferably a member in a clan relationship, although avoiding incest. In other words, marriage must be close, but not too close. Zoroastrians have even called their religion the "faith of kindred marriage."

The fact that many Zoroastrians in India and the Western world have only one or at most two children, and others marry outside the faith, means that these ancient values are threatened. Unless marriage takes place more often within the faith, and unless Zoroastrian couples have more children on average than one or two, Zoroastrians may all but disappear in a few centuries. Many Zoroastrians are apprehensive about the future of their faith. Some other Zoroastrian groups that call themselves "reformist" accept children of mixed marriages into the faith, but this is strongly rejected by the main body of Zoroastrians.

LO5 Zoroastrian Rituals

As he sits on the floor in a Zoroastrian temple in a Chicago suburb, a priest offers sacrifice for the souls of the dead. In his secular occupation, Kersey Antia is a clinical psychologist

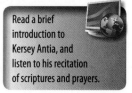

Read a brief introduction to Kersey Antia, and listen to his recitation of scriptures and prayers.

specializing in panic disorders. As a Zoroastrian priest, he officiates at fire ceremonies, feeding sandalwood and frankincense into a blazing fire in a large urn. He recites prayers that he learned to pronounce by special training in the Avestan language at a school in India. Although Zoroastrians today understand only a few Avestan words, the Zoroastrian god Ahura Mazda does speak Avesta, so the words are still effective.

FIRES IN THE FIRE TEMPLE

The Zoroastrian house of worship, in which all worship takes place, is the **fire temple**. In the Western world an "eternal flame" is a symbol of honored memory; in Zoroastrianism every temple has an eternal flame for the worship of Ahura Mazda. Fire temples and their activities center on the fire within them, and they are named by three types of fires.

> *In the Western world an "eternal flame" is in memory of an honored person; in Zoroastrianism every temple has an eternal flame for the worship of Ahura Mazda.*

The Appointed Place Fire is the first classification of sacred fire. It can be consecrated in a few hours by two priests, who recite scriptures as they light and tend the fire. An approved layperson may tend the fire when no services are in progress. The smallest and most humble Zoroastrian temples have only this sort of fire. It is also found with the two greater fires in more impressive temples, where priests celebrate the main rituals of the faith and believers invoke blessings in front of the fire.

The next level is the Fire of Fires. It requires a gathering and mingling in one sacrificial urn of fires from representatives of the four main social groups: priests, soldiers and civil servants, farmers and herdsmen, and artisans and laborers. These are the traditional classes in Zoroastrian society from ancient times. Eight priests must consecrate this fire in a ritual that takes up to three weeks.

The highest level is the Fire of Victory. Its consecration involves the gathering of sixteen different fires from sixteen different sources, including from lightning and a metal-molding furnace. Each of the sixteen fires goes through a purification ritual before it joins the others in a common fire. Thirty-two priests are required for the ceremony, which takes up to a year. Veneration of the Fire of Victory and the Fire of Fires is addressed only to the fire itself, using the songs of praise in the Zoroastrian scriptures. Priests and believers don't ordinarily make requests of Ahura Mazda before these two higher fires.

INTERIOR PLAN OF THE FIRE TEMPLE

When they enter a fire temple, both men and women must wear a head covering. First, one goes through a large hall where ceremonies take place. The faithful then enter an anteroom smaller than the main hall. Connected to this anteroom, but not visible from the hall to ensure a sense of holiness and quiet, is the "place of the fire" in which the actual fire altars stand. These fire altars are usually large urns that sit on the floor; priests sit or stand in front of them as they offer sacrifices of spices and incense in the constantly burning flame. Lay Zoroastrians stand before the fire to offer their prayers to God.

Zoroastrian temple in Kolkata (Calcutta), India, showing Indian influence

R BARRAEZ D'LUCCA

Only priests enter the inner, most sacred room, which has a double-domed roof. The double dome has vents to allow the smoke to escape, but the vents of the outer dome are offset from the inner dome's vents, preventing debris or rain from entering the room and potentially desecrating the holy flame. The walls of the inner room are almost always tiled or of marble but otherwise undecorated. The only lights are those of the fire itself in the inner room, an arrangement that is powerfully symbolic to Zoroastrians.

In one corner of the main fire-room hangs a bell, which is rung five times a day to mark each new "watch" period. The fire is usually fed at this time with dried sandalwood or other sweet-smelling wood. Tools for maintaining the wood fire are hung on the wall or stored in an adjoining room. In Parsi temples, non-Zoroastrians are prohibited from entering any space from which one could see the fires. This typically means no entry into a temple at all, and many Parsi temples in India have "Parsis Only" signs at their front door. If non-Zoroastrians are permitted to enter them during ordinary times, they are closed during feasts and holy days. Traditionalist Zoroastrians insist that these restrictions aren't meant to offend non-Zoroastrians and point to similar practices in other religions. Iranian and "Reformist" Zoroastrians more often open their temples to non-Zoroastrians.

WORSHIP

When the adherent enters the room where the fire burns, he or she will offer wood for the fire. The person making an offering doesn't put the wood directly into the fire, but gives it to the priest. At the proper time, the priest places the offering in the fire, using silver tongs. He wears a cloth mask over nostrils and mouth to prevent his breath from polluting the flame. The priest then uses a special ladle to give some holy ashes to the layperson, who in turn dabs them on his or her forehead and eyelids; the layperson may take some home after an initiation ceremony.

A Zoroastrian priest doesn't preach or teach, but tends to the sacrificial fire, offering prayer and sacrifice there. Fire temple attendance is particularly high during seasonal festivals, and especially for the New Year's festival. There is no instrumental music or group singing in Zoroastrian worship, only the musical chanting of the scriptures and prayers by the priests. Social events may occur in the main hall, especially at festivals and initiations, but rarely as a part of regular worship.

PRIESTHOOD

The **magi**, an order of priests not originally Zoroastrian, apparently became acquainted with the prophet Zarathustra's teachings before 400 B.C.E. and converted to the faith. The priests rose to power quickly and had a monopoly on priestly power at the Persian court. Under the Sassanians, a three-level hierarchy of priests developed among the magi. Admission to the priesthood is hereditary, but all priests have to go through one or more ceremonies of ordination over and above those practiced by all the faithful. In 2010, a violent confrontation broke out in India when a group of more liberal Zoroastrians unsuccessfully tried to ordain a Russian convert to Zoroastrianism as a priest. Training for the priesthood has always centered on performing the ceremonies, especially the ritual words and actions.

The chief ceremony, the *Yasna*, is essentially a sacrifice of haoma (HO-mah), the sacred liquid. The sacrifice is celebrated before the sacred fire with recitation of large parts of the *Avesta*. There are also offerings of bread and milk, which replace the former offerings of meat or animal fat. The sacred fire must be kept burning continually and is fed at least five times a day, at the beginning of each watch. Prayers are also offered five times a day in the presence of the fire.

> *A Zoroastrian priest doesn't often preach or even teach, but rather tends the sacrificial fires.*

OTHER RITUALS

All young Zoroastrians must be initiated in the **navjote** ceremony when they reach the age of seven (in India, Africa, Europe, and North America) or ten (in Iran). The ceremony is led by a priest, and the young people must receive instruction before the navjote. They receive the shirt and the sacred cord (kusti), which they are to wear their whole life. The kusti is tied around the waist and symbolizes a lifelong commitment to keeping the tenets of the religion.

In a religion that stresses ritual purity, Zoroastrian rituals of purification are particularly important. There are three types of purification, in order of increasing

magi [MA-jigh] An order of priests not originally Zoroastrian

navjote [nahv-JOH-tee] Initiation ceremony when young Zoroastrians reach the age of seven or ten

A Parsi woman weaves a kusti, the sacred thread given in the navjote.

importance: the ablution, ordinary washing for the smallest compromises of one's purity; the full-body bath, for medium-sized impurities; and the fullest purification ritual—the *bareshnum* (ba-RESH-num)—a complicated ritual performed at special places and lasting several days.

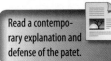

Read a contemporary explanation and defense of the patet.

It includes the participation of a dog, whose left ear is touched by the person seeking cleansing and whose gaze makes evil spirits flee.

Penance for sins is necessary to keep the accumulation of one's sins from resulting in condemnation after death. It entails reciting the *patet* (PAH-teht), the firm resolve not to sin again. The patet also calls for one to confess one's sins to a priest.

Festivals are an important aspect of Zoroastrianism, and full of happy celebration. There are six seasonal festivals throughout the year. and at year's end a few days are dedicated to the memory of the dead. The New Year feast, **Nowruz**

Watch a PBS video on Nowruz.

Nowruz or **Noruz**
[NOH-rooz] Iranian New Year festival celebrated by both Zoroastrians and Muslims

(often spelled **Noruz)** is the most joyous of all Zoroastrian festivals.

FUNERAL RITUALS

The following traditional funeral ritual isn't fully followed in most of the Zoroastrian world today. After death, the body is washed and clothed in a simple white garment. A dog is then brought before the body—preferably a "four-eyed" dog with a spot above each eye. This indicates its ability to frighten evil spirits into fleeing and not posing a threat to the soul of the dead person, which hovers above the body for three days. The ritual is repeated five times a day. On the second day after death, fire is brought into the room and burns there until three days after the corpse is moved to the tower of silence. This placement in the tower had to be done during the daytime.

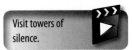

Visit towers of silence.

The interior of the tower of silence was originally built in three concentric circles (one each for men, women, and children), with a large central well in the center of the tower. The clothing on the body was then removed, and after it was exposed, naked, the mourners left the tower. The vultures descended from their circling flight and took only about an hour to strip the flesh off the bones.

Priests at a contemporary sacrifice

Tower of silence in Yazd, Iran

LAURA AND FULVIO'S PHOTOS

next to the temple property worries that the temple, which will include a parking lot for fifty cars and its own water and septic system, will limit the already-declining water supply for residents. Others say the worship center will bring an unwanted influx of traffic. Most of the complaints, government officials say, have nothing to do with the religious nature of the project, but are about allowing the temple in a residentially zoned area. But the Zoroastrian community has all its permits for construction in order. The leader of the Zoroastrian community has said, "We are a very small religion," adding that only three hundred Zoroastrians live in the Washington, D.C., area. "Our finances aren't good. We have no home for gathering together for worship."

Dried by the sun for a few days, the bones were swept into a large stone box in the central well to preserve them reverently until the resurrection. The morning of the fourth day after death is the most solemn in the death ritual; on that morning the soul goes into the presence of Ahura Mazda and is judged. Special prayers are offered for souls of the dead on this day.

Zoroastrian funeral practice changed in Iran. In its role as a religion in a modernizing country, Zoroastrianism replaced the towers of silence during the twentieth century with cemeteries. By the 1960s, the towers in Iran had fallen into complete disuse. In the new cemeteries, care was taken to protect the earth from direct contact with bodies of the dead, a key Zoroastrian value. The towers of silence are still used in Mumbai, India, despite the fact that there are no more vultures there to devour the corpses. Bodies are put in the towers to decay in the sun and open air, a practice that has led to some inner Zoroastrian controversy and conflict with local officials over health issues.

> Watch a BBC report on Zoroastrian burial.

LO6 Zoroastrianism in North America

Residents of a rural area outside Washington, D.C., are upset about the construction of a Zoroastrian temple in their community. One man who lives

> Watch an audio slide show, "A Religion in Decline," featuring Chicago-area Zoroastrians.

Most Zoroastrians in North America are from India; they speak English and their own dialect of Gujarati. More recent Zoroastrian immigrants are from Iran; they speak Farsi. Because these two communities were separated in Asia for more than a thousand years, they developed some differences in their rituals and festivals that are still reflected in North America today.

Zoroastrians began to arrive in North America in the 1860s, in very small numbers, settling on the East and West coasts. They engaged in a variety of professions, from gold prospecting to farming and commerce. The first Zoroastrian "congregation," formed by seven Zoroastrians in New York City in 1929, met in private homes. As with other people of Asian origin, Zoroastrians were largely prohibited by U.S. immigration laws from entering the country from about 1900 until the 1960s. Then, when the laws were liberalized, many Zoroastrians came to North America seeking a more prosperous life, and more Zoroastrian organizations were founded. The main goal of these organizations, like those of almost all other Asian religions that came to North America, was to establish the faith in the New World so that it would be successfully passed down to the Zoroastrians' children. Maintaining Zoroastrian culture—language, dress, food, and festivals—through the generations is also important in North America. Many Zoroastrian temples have cultural centers attached to them where these cultural values are emphasized.

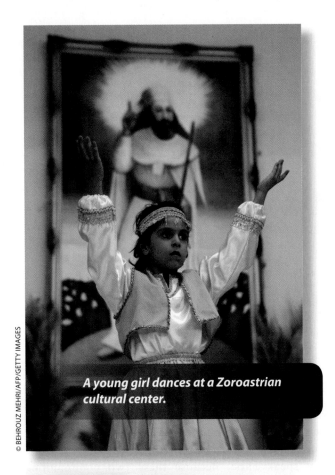

A young girl dances at a Zoroastrian cultural center.

© BEHROUZ MEHRI/AFP/GETTY IMAGES

"Marry inside our community, and SAVE our religion."—from a Zoroastrian website

After the 1979 Islamic Revolution in Iran toppled the more religiously tolerant regime of the Shah, many Iranian Zoroastrians no longer felt safe there. Thousands fled their ancient ancestral homeland, and most came to North America. The numbers of Zoroastrians there quickly doubled, but some tensions arose between Indian and Iranian Zoroastrians. For the most part, they manage to coexist, if only because their small numbers force them to get along. In a few larger Zoroastrian communities, worship services are held separately for each group, with only some important festivals celebrated by Iranians and Indians together. In 2010 it was estimated that the entire population of Zoroastrians in North America was around twenty thousand. Zoroastrians have taken to cyberspace, with many websites to promote the common faith of all Zoroastrians and also some of the distinct groups such as the "reformist" Zarathushtrian Assembly and the traditionalist Mazdayasni Zoroastrian Anjuman. Many observers of North American Zoroastrianism expect these differences to soften over time—especially when the second and third generations take over—and an "American Zoroastrianism" to be established. Some of these sites have matchmaking areas to encourage Zoroastrians to marry each other; as one pleads, "Marry inside our community, and SAVE our religion." This will help to keep alive into a new millennium one of the world's most ancient faiths.

Visit the website of the Zarathushtrian Assembly in the United States.

A Closer Look:

Thus Spoke Zarathustra

The most influential work on Zarathustra in North America today—*Thus Spoke Zarathustra* by the German philosopher Friedrich Nietzsche (FREED-rik NEE-chuh)—is, ironically, not about Zoroastrianism at all. This book is widely regarded as a literary masterpiece and has had a wide cultural impact in the arts and in philosophy. It uses Zarathustra to express Nietzsche's views, including the introduction of the controversial doctrine of the "Superman," a term later twisted by Nazi propagandists to connote racial supremacy. (The comic-book and film hero known today by the same name isn't drawn from Nietzsche's book; that Superman is traditional in moral matters.) A passionate, semi-biblical style is employed to inspire readers to transcend conventional morality. This work remains a standard on college reading lists.

However, *Thus Spoke Zarathustra* has been disavowed by almost all Zoroastrians from the time of its publication, because its theme of an individual getting beyond conventional morality, and then even beyond morality itself, contradicts one of the main beliefs of Zoroastrianism. The universe is deeply moral, because it is based on Ahura Mazda's goodness, and people must follow the way of Zarathustra to live out Ahura Mazda's morality, not invent their own.

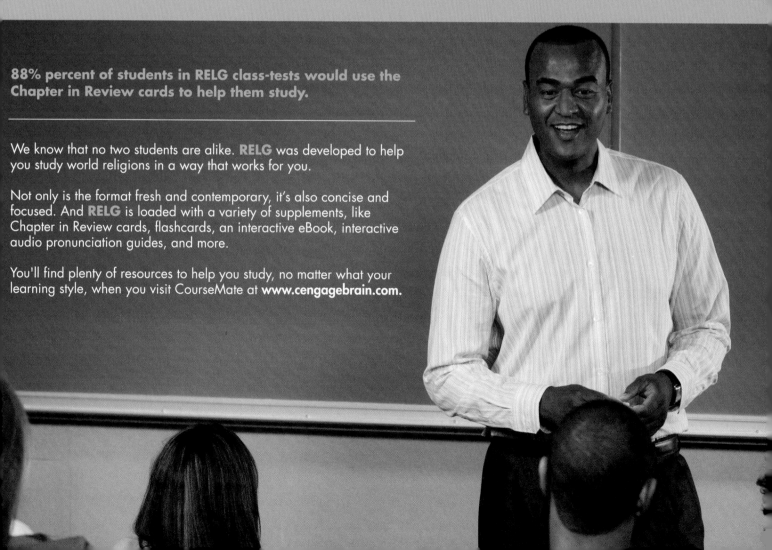

{ Learning Your Way }

88% percent of students in RELG class-tests would use the Chapter in Review cards to help them study.

We know that no two students are alike. **RELG** was developed to help you study world religions in a way that works for you.

Not only is the format fresh and contemporary, it's also concise and focused. And **RELG** is loaded with a variety of supplements, like Chapter in Review cards, flashcards, an interactive eBook, interactive audio pronunciation guides, and more.

You'll find plenty of resources to help you study, no matter what your learning style, when you visit CourseMate at **www.cengagebrain.com**.

CHAPTER 10

Encountering Judaism: The Way of God's Chosen People

BONNIE VAN VOORST © CENGAGE LEARNING

Learning Outcomes

After studying this chapter, you will be able to do the following:

LO1 Explain the meaning of *Judaism* and related terms.

LO2 Summarize how the main periods of Judaism's history have shaped its present.

LO3 Outline the essential teachings of Judaism in your own words.

LO4 Describe the main features of Jewish ethics.

LO5 Summarize Jewish worship, the Sabbath and major festivals, life-cycle rituals, and the Kabbalah.

LO6 Outline the main features of Judaism in North America today.

© ISTOCKPHOTO.COM/MOTIMEIRI

"Hear, O Israel: The Lord our God is One." —The Shema

YOUR VISIT TO THE WESTERN WALL IN JERUSALEM

In your hotel the evening before you visit the Western Wall, your tour guide gives you instructions for the next day's events. "Everyone is welcome at the Wall," she says. "But you must wear modest clothing—no one in shorts, sleeveless tops, or jeans is allowed. Men must wear a hat or other head covering. Women must wear clothing that covers their shoulders and knees; they can borrow shawls at the entrance. Proper behavior is a must—be respectful of others." All this is pretty standard stuff, you think, and applies to most important religious sites around the world. But there's one item that's unique to a visit to the Western Wall: People are allowed to put a paper note with a prayer written on it into a seam between the stones, where (many Jews believe) God will pay special attention to one's prayer. Most people write out their prayer before coming to the wall.

Almost everyone in Israel calls this place simply "the Wall." But your guide gives you a warning: Don't call it "the Wailing Wall." This term is often used today, but many residents of Jerusalem find it offensive. "Wailing" is supposed to refer to mourning for the destruction of the temple in 70 C.E. There is typically no wailing here, so the term is indeed misleading.

Despite the preparation you've done for visiting the Wall, some things still surprise you during your visit. First, long-established Jewish rules apply here, so women must go to their own section and not stand with the men and boys. Even in the women's section, they may not read aloud from Jewish scriptures or wear Jewish prayer shawls. There's some murmuring in your tour group over

this, but the women do have access to the wall itself and can place prayer notes in it. Second, when you ask an official about what happens to your prayer, you learn something surprising. More than a million notes are left in the Wall each year, and you see that the cracks between the stones are jammed with papers. Twice a year the notes are collected and buried on Jerusalem's Mount of Olives. Third, most surprising of all is how emotionally moved you are. The closer you get to the Wall, the more it towers over you. The prayerful piety of others at the site impresses you

Jews praying at the Western Wall in Jerusalem

‹ A Jewish man wearing a prayer shawl blows a ram's horn to herald the Jewish New Year holy day.

Watch a video about the Western Wall.

and helps to explain why this is for most Jews the holiest place in the world.

Judaism is a monotheistic religion that believes that the world was created by an all-knowing, all-powerful God and that all things in the world were designed to have meaning and purpose as part of a divine order. God called the Israelites to be a chosen, special people and follow God's law, thus becoming the means by which divine blessing would flow to the world. God's law guides humans in every area of life; it is a gift from God so that people might live according to God's will.

The main influence of Judaism stems directly from its strong devotion to God over more than 2,500 years. Some of the impact of Judaism has been lost in the modern world, and Judaism itself is more fragmented in the modern world than ever before. Its deep influence on everyday life and on patterns of Western culture is still clearly visible, however. The belief that there is only one God, now self-evident for believers in all Western religions, is the main gift of Judaism. The idea that the world is a real and mostly good (or at least redeemable) place has shaped Western religion and thought. Our seven-day week with its rest on the weekend originates in Judaism as well. The convictions that all people are equally human before God, each other, and the law; that the human race is one family; and that each individual can fully realize the meaning of life regardless of social or economic class have also come to the Western world from Judaism.

Key teachings and values of Judaism have spread in Christianity and Islam to over half of all the people of the world.

In your study of Judaism, you'll encounter and study in some depth these unique features:

- For a relatively small religion, about fifteen million adherents today, it has had a big impact. The teachings and values of Judaism have spread in Christianity and Islam, which are closely related to Judaism, to over half the people of the world. However, Islam and

Judaism [JOO-dee-ihz-um] Historic religion of the Jewish people

Christianity have often been rivals of Judaism as well.

- The world has had a mixed attitude to Judaism for more than two thousand years. The Jews' strong, clear monotheism and morality have been influential, but Jews have drawn near-constant opposition as well. Prejudice against them, often leading to violent persecution, has sadly been a recurrent feature in Jewish life.

- Judaism is both geographically scattered and centered. Since about 300 B.C.E., most Jewish people haven't lived in the traditional Jewish area now in modern Israel. Instead, they've lived in the wider Middle East, Europe, and North America. In fact, more Jews now live in the United States (about 5.2 million) than live in Israel (about 4.9 million). Still, Israel is an essential part of Judaism for most Jews today.

LO1 The Name *Judaism* and Related Terms

Judaism is commonly and correctly defined as the historic religion of the Jewish people. This name comes from the ancient tribe of Judah, one of the original twelve tribes of Israel. When the leaders of the southern kingdom of Israel came back from exile in Babylon in the 530s B.C.E., the name of their larger tribe became the name of the political area (Judah) and the people who lived there became the *Judahites* (JOO-duh-ights), or *Jews* (jooz) for short. In time their religion became known as *Judaism*, a term derived from the ancient Greek language. For most of the history of the Jewish people, to be Jewish was to practice Judaism in some way. But around 1800 C.E., it became possible in Europe to give up Judaism and still call oneself Jewish. Jewishness then became for many Jews a matter of ethnic status and cultural identity, not of religion. Other Jews replied

that only by keeping Judaism do Jews stay Jewish. Although these two positions cannot be completely separated, this chapter will focus on Judaism as a religion.

Before 500 B.C.E., the ancestors of the Jews went by other names. The first was **Hebrews** (HEE-brewz), the name of the people during patriarchal times through the Exodus (1800–1200 B.C.E.). This name is from *Habiru* (ha-BEE-roo; also spelled "Hapiru"), a word for nomads that is found in many languages in the ancient Fertile Crescent and seems to have been attached to the descendants of Abraham while they lived in Egypt. When they settled in Palestine after the Exodus and became a nation there, they became known as **Israelites** (IS-ray-ehl-ights), a name derived from the ancient patriarch Israel (whose original name was Jacob). Historians speak generically of their religions during this period as "Hebrew religion" and "Israelite religion," not as "Judaism." A more recent twist adds some confusion to these names. The modern nation of Israel, founded in 1948, calls itself by the same name as that of ancient Israel, but the people of modern Israel (whether Jewish by religion or not) are called **Israelis** (ihz-RAIL-eez), not Israelites.

A Closer Look:

Symbols of Judaism

Several symbols have served Judaism over time, and we will begin with the lesser-used ones.

Chai

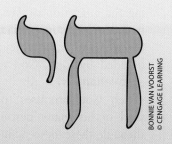

Chai (chigh, with a throat-clearing initial sound), a symbol of modern origin, popular and fashionable in jewelry today, is the Hebrew word for "living." Some say that it refers to God, who alone is perfectly alive; others think it comes from the common Jewish toast "Le chaim" (leh CHIGH-ihm), "To life!" More likely, it reflects Judaism's general focus on the importance of life. It is a symbol of their Jewish faith for many people who wear it.

BONNIE VAN VOORST © CENGAGE LEARNING

Menorah

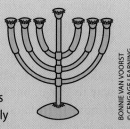

The oldest symbol of the Jewish faith is the **menorah**, a large usually seven-branched candelabra. It was a prominent accessory in the Jerusalem temple, and one sees it today in many Jewish homes and houses of worship. It's especially

BONNIE VAN VOORST © CENGAGE LEARNING

prominent during the celebration of Hanukkah, when a nine-branched menorah is used for the nine days of this festival. For many Jews, the menorah is a symbol of Israel's mission to be "a light to the nations" (Isaiah 42:6). It is featured today on the coat of arms of the state of Israel.

Star of David

The six-pointed Star of David is the symbol most commonly associated with Judaism today, but it isn't nearly as old as the menorah. A symbol of two overlaid equilateral triangles was a common symbol of good fortune in the ancient Near East and in North Africa. It appears occasionally in early Jewish artwork from as far back as the first century C.E., but not as a symbol of Judaism. In the 1600s it began to be used to mark as Jewish the exteriors of some Jewish houses of worship in Europe and then began to be associated with the ancient King David. The Star of David gained popularity as a symbol of Judaism when it was adopted in 1897 as the emblem of the Zionist movement to resettle Palestine. Today it is a well-recognized symbol of Judaism, particularly because it appears on the flag of the modern state of Israel.

BONNIE VAN VOORST © CENGAGE LEARNING

LO2 The Jewish Present As Shaped by Its Past

An American college professor leads his class on European religious history through the Dachau (DAHK-ow) concentration camp outside Munich, Germany. They walk through the gate, and the professor explains the macabre meaning of its inscription, *Arbeit macht frei* ("Work makes [you] free"). He explains, as they walk by, the barracks for prisoners and the other buildings around the site. They see the gas chamber disguised as a shower room and then inspect the crematorium. This is all a somber experience, but the full horror of this site doesn't really register on the students until they go into its museum, with exhibits of what went on here. A suspicion and hatred of "alien" groups, especially the long history of hatred of the Jewish people, reached a horrific outcome in dozens of camps such as this. Everyone in the class is in tears as they leave, including the professor, who has been here before and isn't an emotional person. He brings his students here for this searing experience so that they'll never forget the evil humans can do, and the courage it takes for persecuted groups to continue on in life.

The Jewish people have a long, storied history that includes both tragedy and triumph. In Judaism today we can see important beliefs and practices from the entire four-thousand-year sweep of Jewish history. The periods of this history that we will consider here are: from the creation of the world to Abraham (ca. 2000 B.C.E.); the emergence of Israel (ca. 1200–950 B.C.E.); the First Temple Period (950–586 B.C.E.); the Second Temple Period (539 B.C.E.–70 C.E.); revolts and rabbis (70 C.E.–ca. 650 C.E.); Jews under Islamic and Christian rule (ca. 650–1800 C.E.); emancipation and change (1800–1932); and the Holocaust and its aftermath (1932–present).

patriarchs Hebrew founding family of the later Israelites and Jews: Abraham and Sarah, their son Isaac and his wife Rebekah, their son Jacob (Israel) and his wives Rachel and Leah, and Jacob's twelve sons who founded the twelve tribes of the nation of Israel

covenant Agreement God made with Abraham in which God promised to be with Abraham and be the God of his many descendants and Abraham promised to follow God

circumcision Ritual of the covenant, removing the foreskin of the penis

FROM THE CREATION TO ABRAHAM (CA. 2000 B.C.E.)

Chapters one through eleven of the first book of the Bible, Genesis, span the creation of the universe to the time of Abraham, father of the Jewish people (ca. 2000 B.C.E.). It narrates and provides a religious perspective on the creation of the world, the rebellion of the first humans against God and their expulsion from the Garden of Eden, the wide dispersal of people, Noah and the flood, and other topics. These stories echo the earlier mythology of Mesopotamia and provide an Israelite alternative to them. The rest of Genesis (Chapters 12–50) covers just four generations of one family of the **patriarchs** and their wives: Abraham and Sarah, their son Isaac and his wife Rebekah, their son Jacob (Israel) and his wives Rachel and Leah, and Jacob's twelve sons who founded the twelve tribes of the nation of Israel. The Israelite and then the Jewish people emerged from these tribes. Scholars debate the meaning and historical accuracy of the early biblical story, but they don't doubt the role that it played in shaping Judaism.

> *Scholars debate the early biblical story, but not the role that it played in shaping Judaism.*

Genesis 12 begins by narrating the migration of Abraham from Ur in Mesopotamia to the land of Canaan, a journey commanded by God. God makes a **covenant** with Abraham in which God promises to be with Abraham, be the God of his many descendants, and bless the world through these descendants. In return, God demands that Abraham follow him faithfully. Abraham then carries out, on himself and all the males in his clan, the ritual of **circumcision**, cutting off the foreskin of the penis, which is the perpetual sign of the covenant. Abraham's son Isaac marries Rebekah; she secures the line of succession for her younger son Jacob. Jacob's simultaneous marriages to Leah and Rachel produce twelve sons, who are the origins of the twelve tribes. Genesis 37 to 50 tells the story of Joseph, the youngest of Jacob's twelve sons. Joseph is betrayed by his jealous brothers, who sell him to slave traders on their way to Egypt, but Joseph rises to great power under a sympathetic pharaoh. All Abraham's descendants then move to Egypt and prosper there until a later pharaoh enslaves the Israelites.

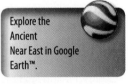
Explore the Ancient Near East in Google Earth™.

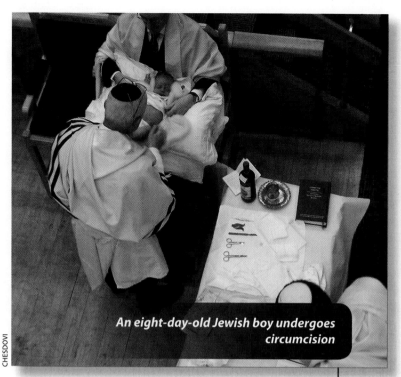

An eight-day-old Jewish boy undergoes circumcision

THE EMERGENCE OF ISRAEL (CA. 1200–950 B.C.E.)

The book of Exodus contains the story of Israel's enslavement in Egypt, God's call to Moses to lead his people out of Egypt, Pharaoh's stubborn resistance, and the Israelites' escape through the parted waters of the Red Sea. Moses leads the Israelites to Sinai, a mountain in the wilderness where they enter into a covenant relationship with God. The Israelites agree to live by all the teachings and commandments, the **Torah**, conveyed to them by Moses. In keeping the Torah, they will live out their calling to be God's chosen people. After a forty-year journey through the wilderness, a new generation of Israelites arrives at the Jordan River, where they prepare to cross over and occupy the land promised to them. The books of *Joshua* and *Judges* relate the story of the Israelites' conquest of Palestine, its division among the tribes, and the first hundred years of settlement.

The focal center of early Israelite religion during this period was the movable tent-shrine housing the **Ark of the Covenant,** a sacred box containing two tablets inscribed with the Ten Commandments, Moses' staff, and a pot of manna, with angels on the top. This tent, called the *tabernacle,* is where the first formal worship of ancient Israel took place, with sacrifice, prayer, and praise to God. Unlike the nations around it, Israel had no national government; the twelve tribes were bound together in a tribal confederacy under their covenant with God. When Israel's enemies threatened, the tribes would act together under charismatic leaders, some of them women. Israel changed its form of government from a tribal confederacy to a monarchy. Saul was anointed king around 1025 B.C.E. Israel's second monarch, David, consolidated the monarchy over all Israel. The Bible celebrates the reigns of David and his son Solomon as a golden age, but it doesn't gloss over their considerable failings.

THE FIRST TEMPLE PERIOD (950–586 B.C.E.)

Solomon's construction of a temple to God in Jerusalem (ca. 950) inaugurated the **First Temple Period,** which lasted until the temple was destroyed in 586. The royal

> **Torah** [TOHR-uh]
> Teachings and commandments conveyed by Moses, particularly in the first five books of the Bible
>
> **Ark of the Covenant**
> Sacred box in the tabernacle and then the Temple
>
> **First Temple Period**
> Era of Israelite history from ca. 950 B.C.E. until the destruction of Jerusalem in 586

Read another, revisionist explanation of the origin of ancient Israel.

Watch a trailer for Steven Spielberg's animated film on Moses and the Exodus, *The Prince of Egypt.*

Modern replica of the Ark of the Covenant, the holiest object in ancient Israel

prophets Mostly men and some women who spoke for God to ancient Israel to call them to greater obedience

Judean captives from the town of Lachish on their way into exile in Assyria; a relief from the palace of King Sennacherib, Nineveh

ERICH LESSING/ART RESOURCE, NY

court became increasingly lavish as the power and size of the state increased. So did the tax burden on the lower classes. Many viewed the increasing social and economic divisions, with "the rich getting richer and the poor getting poorer," as a violation of God's will. Over the next centuries, a line of **prophets**, mostly men and some women who spoke for God, denounced the leaders of Israel for their greed, exploitation of the poor, and other social injustices and immoralities. They also criticized the leaders' faith in alliances with other nations and not in God's power to protect the nation. Today, prophets are those who can see the future, but prophets in Israel were much more "forth-tellers" of God's will than foretellers of the future. The importance of prophets to Israelite and Jewish religion is indicated by the fact that the books of the prophets are the largest section of the Bible. (We'll consider the formation and use of the Bible below, at the beginning of "Essential Teachings of Judaism.") As contemporary Jewish scholar Abraham Heschel wrote, the prophets portray the righteousness of God and God's "pathos" (anguish) over Israel's disobedience.[1] The prophetic tradition that demands justice in God's name for the poor and oppressed is one of the great gifts of Judaism to the world.

> *Today prophets are said to see the future, but prophets in Israel were much more "forth-tellers" of God's will than foretellers of the future.*

When Solomon died in 922 B.C.E., the people of God divided into two different nations—Israel, comprised of ten tribes in the north, and Judah, comprised of the tribes of Judah and Benjamin in the south, each with its own king (see Map 10.1). Each

---

[1] Abraham Heschel, *The Prophets*, study edition (Peabody, MA: Hendricksen, 2007).

nation claimed to be the true successor of the united kingdom of Saul, David and Solomon. Sometimes the two kingdoms warred with each other, and at other times they cooperated against common enemies. But two centuries later the northern kingdom of Israel was wiped out by the Assyrian Empire in 722. Its ten tribes would never appear again, becoming in Jewish lore the "ten lost tribes." The southern kingdom of Judah was crippled at the same time by the Assyrians, who conquered several Judean cities and deported their citizens. Judah was finally conquered in 586 by the Babylonian Empire. The temple in Jerusalem was destroyed and the population decimated by death and exile. The First Temple Period had ended with a disaster, and Israelite religion was poised to disappear into the mists of time like the religions of so many other conquered peoples.

Exile and return provides "the structure of all Judaism."—Jacob Neusner

The exiles carried off to Babylon were mostly members of the Judean ruling class and skilled craftsmen. Although some exiles probably assimilated into Babylonian religion, others viewed recent events as confirmation rather than disproof of the sovereignty of Israel's God. The warnings of the prophets, remembered in the exile, helped Israel interpret what had happened to them as God's punishment for repeated violations of the covenant. In the ancient world, military defeat and

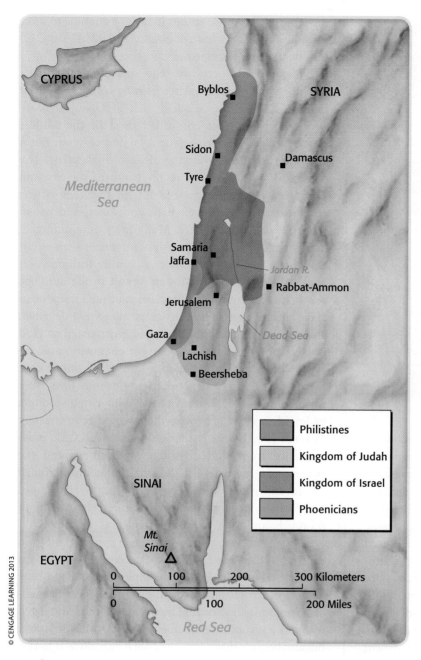

Map 10.1

The Monarchies of Israel and Judah, 924–722 B.C.E.

The northern kingdom of Israel and the southern kingdom of Judah had expanded beyond the traditional areas of the twelve tribes, especially at times when neighboring kingdoms and empires were relatively weak. The kingdom of Israel fell to the Assyrian Empire in 722 to 721 B.C.E.

exile usually spelled the end of a particular ethnic group, as it already had for the northern kingdom of Israel. Despite the disaster of 586 B.C.E. and even larger disasters to come, Israelite religion survived and emerged from the ancient world into the medieval and modern periods with a continuous religious identity now called

Judaism. The pattern of exile and return would provide a historical and religious pattern that a leading scholar of Judaism, Jacob Neusner, calls "the structure of all Judaism."[2]

THE SECOND TEMPLE PERIOD (539 B.C.E.–70 C.E.)

In 539 B.C.E. the Babylonians were defeated by Cyrus (SIGH-rus) of Persia, a Zoroastrian whose empire covered almost the whole Near East (see Chapter 9). Cyrus authorized the rebuilding of the Jewish temple of Jerusalem. The exiles would be allowed to return to Judea and live as a subject state in the Persian Empire. In Judea, the new leaders Ezra and Nehemiah zealously promoted a renewed commitment to the Mosaic covenant. Increasingly, community life was organized around the Torah, which was now in written form as the first five books of the Bible. The Second Temple was completed between 521 and 515, and the **Second Temple Period** would extend until 70 C.E., when the Romans destroyed the Second Temple. During this time another permanent feature of Jewish life arose: the **Diaspora**, or "dispersion," of Jews outside the ancient territory of Israel. Many, perhaps most, of the Jews in Babylon stayed there when others returned to Jerusalem in the 530s. Within a hundred years or so, there would be more Jews living outside the territory of Israel than inside it. Large Jewish communities could be found in Alexandria, Egypt, and in Antioch, Syria, and smaller ones in hundreds of cities in what would become the Roman Empire. This Diaspora situation became permanent in Judaism and endures even today.

Take a 3-D tour of the Second Temple.

---

[2] Jacob Neusner, "Judaism," in Arvind Sharma, ed., *Our Religions* (New York: HarperOne, 1994), 314.

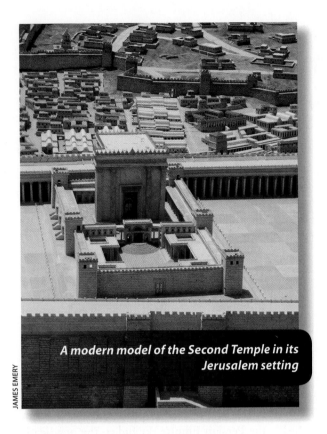

A modern model of the Second Temple in its Jerusalem setting

In the 330s B.C.E., Alexander of Macedon (in northern Greece) began conquering and amassing the largest empire yet seen, taking Israel in his conquest. In Alexander's time tens of thousands of Greeks migrated to all parts of his vast empire. Greek culture in Palestine extended until the rise of Islam in the 600s C.E., because many Jews in Palestine were significantly Hellenized in culture while keeping to Judaism. The two centuries after Alexander's conquests saw the formation of Jewish movements with diverse understandings of Judaism. The Sadducees were a priestly movement who accepted only the earliest books of the *Bible* as authoritative and cooperated with the Romans. The **Pharisees** were a lay movement of Torah teachers who later became religious leaders and developed the oral traditions of the Torah. The Essenes (ESS-eenz) probably began the separatist ultra-Torah-observant community at Qumran on the Dead Sea. Various prophetic or messianic movements also arose within Judaism from time to time, including one led by Jesus of Nazareth (4 B.C.E.–30 C.E.) that would later become the Christian religion.

Alexander's successors had a significant impact on Judea and Judaism. After gaining control of Judea in 198 B.C.E., the Seleucid (sell-YOO-sid) dynasty of Greek rulers that controlled most of the Middle East rewarded the pro-Seleucid faction of Jews. But a struggle soon arose over the office of high priest. The Seleucid king suspected a revolt, captured the city, and plundered the Temple in 168 B.C.E. The Temple was rededicated to the Greek high god Zeus, and pagan sacrifices were made there. Many Jews were outraged, and when foundational Jewish observances such as circumcision and Sabbath observance were forbidden on pain of death, the **Maccabean Revolt** broke out. The revolt was led by Judas Maccabeus, of the Hasmonean clan, and his sons. The Seleucid armies were defeated, and the Temple was liberated and rededicated to God in December, 164 B.C.E., an event commemorated by Jews to this day in the winter festival of **Hanukkah**. Before and during the revolt, many devout Jews were tortured and killed, leading to the first written accounts of Jewish martyrs. Their example would echo strongly through Jewish history until now. In 142 B.C.E., independence from the Seleucids was secured, and the Hasmonean family ruled the small kingdom of Judea for several generations. The Hasmoneans ruled until the Roman general Pompey captured Jerusalem in 63 B.C.E. and took Judea into the Roman Empire.

King Herod ruled Israel by Roman appointment from 37 to 4 B.C.E. He undertook extensive and ambitious building projects, including a complete rebuilding of the Temple in Jerusalem, making it one of the most magnificent temples in the Roman Empire. However, he was hated by many Jews not only for cruelty and his loyalty to Rome, but also because many Jews doubted if he really was Jewish by birth. Relations between the Jews and their Roman overlords steadily deteriorated, and Rome appointed its own governors of the area after Herod died.

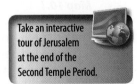

Take an interactive tour of Jerusalem at the end of the Second Temple Period.

REVOLTS AND RABBIS (70 C.E.–CA. 650)

In 66 C.E., a full-scale Jewish revolt broke out against Rome. Although it began well, with the Romans being chased out, it ended very differently than the Maccabean Revolt. Rome summoned all its military

Pharisees [FAIR-uh-seez] Lay movement of Torah teachers who later became religious leaders and developed the oral traditions of the Torah

Maccabean Revolt Rebellion against Hellenistic Greek rulers led by Judas Maccabeus and his sons

Hanukkah [HAHN-uh-kuh] Winter festival commemorating the rededication of the Temple in 164 B.C.E.

Arch of Titus in the Roman Forum, showing trophies from the Jewish temple

When Christianity became the official faith of the Roman Empire around 400 C.E., Jews were allowed to survive but not thrive. From about 100 to 400 C.E., Christianity and Judaism had been in the process of separation, and mutual hostility was often strong. The Code of Justinian in 527 C.E. contained discriminatory legislation against the Jews and Judaism that was to influence European legal systems for centuries and contribute to **anti-Semitism**, prejudice and discrimination against the Jewish people. Anti-Semitism isn't Christian or even European in origin or expression. Its oldest forms can be traced to 500 B.C.E. in Egypt, and today the strongest forms of it are found in the Muslim Middle East. Despite these hardships, or perhaps because of them, many Jews chose to form their communities around synagogues. The local synagogue became the chief organization of Jewish life in late antiquity and remained so until the modern period.

The single most important Jewish community from about 600 to 1500 C.E. was in Babylonia, outside the sphere of Greek, Roman, and then Christian power. As we've seen, Israelites arrived in Babylonia during the time of their exile in 586 B.C.E. In later periods there was some immigration from Palestine, but scholars didn't made their way to Babylonia and establish a home there until the persecutions after the Bar Kochba revolt in the 130s C.E. Over the next centuries the status of the Babylonian Jewish community grew in prestige, and immigration increased. Although the Babylonian Jewish community confronted problems and occasional persecution, its freedom from Christian government and from the hardships that prevailed in Palestine enabled it to

might to crush the revolt, engaging in massive slaughter of combatants and noncombatants alike. It destroyed the Temple in 70 C.E., and a permanent transformation of Judaism resulted. The Temple had been the only place that represented the whole nation to God and was the location of great religious events such as Jewish festivals and the Day of Atonement. It was also the only place where sacrifices could be offered to God. In addition, the Temple was a forum for Jewish teachers and the location of the high council of religious leaders that governed Judaism. The destruction of the Temple was a disaster for Judaism, and the end of the revolt against Rome brought the end of every group in Judaism except the Pharisees, who would eventually take over the religion's leadership.

Take a Google Earth™ tour of the Arch of Titus.

Jewish hopes for independence and Roman heavy-handed tactics continued in the ensuing decades, climaxing in a revolt in 130 led by messianic claimant Simon Bar Kochba. This revolt was also crushed by Rome. The Jewish population had now been hit hard by two wars of their own making in only sixty years. Yet during this period a small and peripheral group connected to pre-70 C.E. scribes and Pharisees preserved a Torah-centered, lay-led Judaism. It would be at least two centuries before these teachers, or **rabbis**, would begin to win broader influence and judicial authority over Judaism. In the 300s and 400s, the rabbis gradually became spiritual leaders in local Jewish communities, the **synagogues**.

rabbis [RAB-ighz] Teachers of the law and successors of the Pharisees who eventually gained influence and judicial authority over Judaism

synagogue [SIN-uh-gawg] "Gathering" of local Jews in a congregation for worship and community life, a term later applied to a building

anti-Semitism [SEHM-ih-tihz-um] Prejudice and discrimination against the Jewish people

develop into a vibrant center of Jewish intellectual and cultural life. By 600, it had surpassed the Palestinian community in its leadership of world Judaism.

> **All modern forms of Judaism are built on, or react to, the foundation of the Babylonian Talmud.**

The work of the rabbinic academy in Babylon centered first on the *Mishnah*, a collection of primarily legal traditions on all aspects of the Torah—what we today would call civil, criminal, and religious law—produced in Palestine and brought to Babylonia in the early third century C.E. Generations of Babylonian rabbis discussed the *Mishnah* and related teachings, adding to them and ultimately producing a huge legal work known as the **Babylonian Talmud**. Rabbinic Judaism is the Torah-centered way of life that finds expression in the vast sea of materials produced by Palestinian and Babylonian rabbis from 70 to 630 C.E., most prominently the Babylonian Talmud. The Talmud achieved a remarkable degree of power in Jewish communities worldwide, a power that withstood serious challenges well into the early modern period. Almost all forms of Judaism in the medieval and modern ages are built on, or react to, this foundation of the Talmud as interpreted by the rabbis.

Examine an interactive sample page of the Babylonian Talmud.

JEWS UNDER ISLAMIC AND CHRISTIAN RULE (CA. 650–1800)

Jews in the medieval period lived under either Muslim or Christian rule. Muslims guaranteed religious toleration as long as the Jews recognized the supremacy of the Islamic rule. They had a second-class but protected status. On the whole, Jews adapted well to the Islamic regime and the political, economic, and social changes that it brought. They lived predominantly in major Arab cities; worked in commerce, banking, and the learned professions; and participated in cultural life, even adopting Arabic as their everyday language.

Some rabbis from these **Sephardic** Jewish communities, which centered in the Middle East, North Africa, and Spain, were interested in the philosophical clarification of religious beliefs and the systematic presentation of their faith, just as Muslim and Christian theologians were doing. The most prominent medieval Jewish philosopher was Rabbi Moses ben Maimon (1135–1204), known as Maimonides (my-MAHN-uh-deez). He addressed his *Guide for the Perplexed* to a student whose education in philosophy left him confused about his religious faith—a common situation for many students from a religious background! Maimonides was a brilliant legal scholar whose fourteen-volume work on Jewish law became almost instantly authoritative. In modern editions of the Talmud, his views are often cited.

Jews were outsiders in medieval Christian society in western, central, and eastern Europe where they called themselves **Ashkenazi** Jews, as distinguished from Sephardic. Rulers granted them permission to live in specified neighborhoods. In these neighborhoods, Jews ran their own affairs and maintained their own institutions, such as social-relief funds, schools, a synagogue led by a rabbi, a council and court for religious affairs, a bathhouse for ritual cleansing, kosher meat shops, and so on. They developed their own language, Yiddish, a combination of Hebrew and German that originated in Germany but spread to almost all European Jews. Most Jews in Western and Central Europe lived in cities. Many of those in Eastern Europe (Poland and Russia) lived in small villages centered on farming, the kind of society depicted in an 1894 collection of short stories by Sholem Aleichem (SHOH-luhm uh-LIGHK-uhm), which became the basis of the Broadway musical and film *Fiddler on the Roof*.

Watch Rabbi Jonathan Ginsburg's explanation of Yiddish and some of its terms.

In the 1200s, decrees by the Roman Catholic Church after the Fourth Lateran Council altered the life of European Jews. Christians were now forbidden to lend money at interest, so Jews were free to move into banking, which they did with great success. Direct restrictions on Jews arose at this time: wearing distinctive clothing (especially hats) or a yellow badge alerting others to their presence; exclusion from most crafts and trades by guilds that controlled access to training and jobs; exclusion from the new universities being

Babylonian Talmud [TALL-mood] Jewish law code, a compilation of the "oral Torah"

Sephardic [seh-FAR-dik] Jews in medieval and modern times living in the Middle East, North Africa, and Spain

Ashkenazi [ash-kuh-NAHZ-ee] Jews in medieval and modern times living in Western, Central, and Eastern Europe

Street scene in the medieval Jewish quarter of Lublin, Poland

founded in Europe; restriction to Jewish neighborhoods called *ghettos*; and special permission required to work outside the ghetto. The rising view of Jews as dangerous was fueled by envy, irrational suspicions, and even hatred, which led to repeated expulsions and massacres. Jews were expelled from France in 1182 and 1306 and from England in 1290. The most devastating massacres were in Germany in 1298, wiping out 140 Jewish communities, and in 1348 to 1349 when the Black Plague was falsely attributed to Jews poisoning wells. In 1492 Spain expelled all Jews, estimated to be between 100,000 and 150,000. Many of them fled to temporary safety in Portugal, some of whom eventually went to The Netherlands—one of the few relatively safe havens for Jews in Europe. One reaction of European Jews to this continued persecution was the development of Jewish mystical piety, particularly the Kabbalah (kah-BAHL-uh), which we will consider below in the section "Jewish Worship and Ritual." The Protestant Reformation in the 1500s was a mixed blessing to the Jews of northern Europe. In some places such as The Netherlands and England, Protestant reformers treated them with some tolerance. But in Germany, the Protestant reformer Martin Luther continued some aspects of anti-Jewish sentiment, in ways that would echo through later German history.

EMANCIPATION AND DIVERSITY (1800–1932)

Around 1800, mostly under the influence of the Enlightenment, many Western European nations began to drop their restrictions on Jews. No longer did Jews have to live in their own neighborhood, be subject to the local rabbi, or dress and talk like Jews had in Europe for more than a thousand years. In less than a century, many Jews rose to become some of the leading figures in science, medicine, education, commerce, and banking. (This astonishing level of achievement continued in the twentieth century, when one-quarter of all Nobel Prize winners were Jewish.) Their **emancipation** prompted many nineteenth-century Jews to wonder why they should continue to be Jews when they could be citizens of European states. Many modern Jews chose to assimilate, which sometimes included conversion to Christianity. Some—for example, Sigmund Freud and Karl Marx—even began systems of thought, science, and government that rationalized God out of existence and opposed religion in general and particularly Judaism.

Many other Jews responded that Jewish identity was not primarily ethnic or national, but religious. One could be a loyal citizen of a European nation, but still keep the Jewish religion. They urged not assimilation, but *acculturation*, that is, taking on the culture of one's nation while retaining Jewish religious faith. Just as Christians could practice their religion as citizens of different nations, so too should Jews. The German-Jewish intellectual Moses Mendelssohn (MEN-dul-sohn; 1729–1786) was an influential example of those who made embraced modernity while staying Jewish. He urged Jews to participate in European culture and to continue in Judaism, what he called the "double yoke" placed on them by God.

> *Many Jews questioned why they should shoulder a "double yoke" of being both Jewish and European—why not just assimilate completely?*

However, many Jews in the early 1800s began to question why they should shoulder this "double yoke"— why not just assimilate completely? This questioning, and doubts about some elements of traditional Judaism that looked increasingly odd to many modern Jews, sparked controversies among mostly German Jews in the mid-1800s that eventually led

emancipation Jewish freedom from Christian and state control in Europe after 1800

to the three main branches of Judaism today: Reform, Orthodox, and Conservative. The Reform movement, led by Abraham Geiger (GIGH-gehr; 1820-1874), was the first new form of Judaism to arise. Geiger wanted to change Judaism into a modern religion with patterns of worship and devotion similar to German Protestant Christianity. Synagogues were renamed "temples," and services were no longer conducted in Hebrew, but German. Sermons by the rabbi and music by trained choirs were introduced; candles were put at the front of remodeled synagogues that now resembled Christian churches; and the ethnic and national aspects of Judaism were no longer mentioned. Reform Judaism gave up kosher food regulations, Jewish dress and hair codes, the Yiddish language, and most other traditional aspects. It ended beliefs and practices it considered not a part of the spiritual essence of Judaism. Of course, this entailed an almost complete rejection of the Talmud. The Reform movement quickly spread through much of Europe and North America.

Traditionalist Jews condemned these reforms as a betrayal of Judaism. They viewed their form of Judaism as the only legitimate continuation of Rabbinic Judaism and biblical Israel. The leader of modern Orthodoxy was Samson Raphael Hirsch (hersh; 1808–1888). Hirsch urged a combination of most traditional Jewish religious practices and selective appreciation of European civilization. He criticized the Reform movement for diminishing Judaism for the convenience and contentment of modern Jews. Instead, he urged the Orthodox movement to elevate Jews to classical Judaism in a fresh and vigorous way. The Orthodox movement has several different internal groups, some of them now called (especially in Israel) the "ultra-Orthodox." Because of their high birthrate and ability to keep their children in the faith, the Orthodox continue to grow in numbers in Europe and North America.

A third main branch of Judaism, originally called "Positive-Historical" in Germany, came to be known in North America as Conservative Judaism. It was led by the German-Bohemian rabbi and scholar Zecharias Frankel (FRAHN-kul; 1801–1875). It claimed the middle ground between Reform and Orthodoxy. In that sense, "moderate Judaism" would be a better name for it than "Conservative Judaism," but the latter name stuck. (In Israel and Europe today, this movement is known as *Masorti* [mah-SOHR-tee], "traditionalist.") It opposed Reform's sweeping changes by affirming the positive value of much of past Judaism in which the voice of God could be discerned. It opposed the Orthodox movement by asserting the historical evolution of the Judaic tradition, which Orthodoxy denied with its claim that the whole Law of God—the written form that became the Bible and the oral form that became the Talmud—was revealed to Moses on Mount Sinai.

Although many European Jews modernized rapidly in the 1800s and were optimistic about the future of Judaism, a wide outbreak of hostility toward the Jews in the 1870s and 1880s cast a dark shadow on their sunny optimism. For example, in France the Dreyfuss affair, in which a Jewish army officer was falsely accused of crimes, stirred up wide anti-Jewish feelings. In Russia, the czar's secret police authored a vile book entitled the *Protocols of the Elders of Zion* that purported to relate how rich and powerful Jews were plotting to take over the world. Modern anti-Semitism was a backlash against Jewish success in Europe, a sign that Jews were still considered outsiders. In earlier times, anti-Semitism had a mostly religious basis, but in modern Europe it was mainly based on ethnicity.

In the light of this revived anti-Semitism, and in a time of rising European nationalistic movements that formed new nations such as Germany and Italy, Jewish movements sprang up emphasizing newfound Jewish nationalism. Most important was **Zionism**, so called after an ancient Hebrew name for Jerusalem, which aimed for large Jewish emigration from Europe to Palestine. In 1897, Theodor Herzl (HURT-zuhl;

A modern Reform synagogue

© RON ZMIRI/SHUTTERSTOCK.COM

1860–1904) organized the First Zionist Congress in Basel, Switzerland, which called for an internationally recognized Jewish national home in Palestine. The Zionist movement was largely secular in orientation. With continued anti-Semitism in Europe, increasing numbers of Jewish immigrants settled in Palestine and began to set up the social infrastructure of a modern nation. The quest for a Jewish nation free from the threats of anti-Semitism was well on its way. In 1917 the British government issued the Balfour Declaration giving British support for a national home for the Jewish people in Palestine.

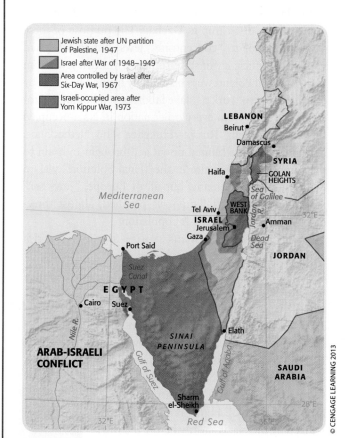

Badge worn by all Jews in Nazi Germany. Jude (pronounced YOO-deh) is German for Jew.

> *The Zionist slogan was "a land without a people for a people without a land."*

The Zionist slogan was "a land without a people for a people without a land," but the Jewish settlers there found that Palestine wasn't really a land without a people. Palestinian Arabs in the tens of thousands, both Muslims and Christians, had been living in that small territory for more than a thousand years. Moreover, Palestinians were among the most culturally advanced Arabs in the Middle East, and still are today. As the numbers of Jewish settlers increased, friction grew with the Arab population. Freedom for European Jews would come at the expense of a future conflict between Israeli Jews and Arabs, in which they would be locked in a long struggle for a land they both considered holy. Islam had been tolerant of Judaism for 1,300 years but now became mostly intolerant, largely because of Muslim resistance to non-Muslims taking their holy land. Several wars were fought between Israel and its Arab neighbors from 1948 through today, all of them won by Israel, sometimes at a high cost (see Map 10.2). A few peace treaties have been signed, but the conflict continues. Jewish settlement in Israel grew quickly after the events of World War II, especially after Germany's extermination of most European Jews. We now turn to a brief examination of this horrific story.

THE HOLOCAUST AND ITS AFTERMATH (1932–PRESENT)

Adolf Hitler and his Nazi Party won office in the 1932 German national elections, and in 1933 Hitler quickly moved toward totalitarian power with a variety of repressive measures. Some of them pursued Nazi ideology to "purify" Germany in a series of anti-Semitic laws gradually introduced between 1933 and 1938. Germans who had just one grandparent who was Jewish by ethnicity—on a synagogue roll, for example, or a member of a secular Jewish organization—were deemed to be Jewish, whether or not they thought of themselves as Jewish. Jews had to wear a yellow star in public for identification. Marriage and sexual relations between Jews and so-called Aryan Germans were banned, and by 1938 all German Jews had been stripped of their citizenship, most civil rights, and some from their professional jobs. Some Jews fled as these laws were passed, but most stayed, hoping that each new law would be the last.

Map 10.2
Arab-Israeli Conflict, 1947–Present
By Egyptian-Israeli agreements of 1975 and 1979, Israel withdrew from the Sinai in 1982. By 1981 Israel annexed the Golan Heights in Syria. Through negotiations between Israel and the PLO, Jericho and the Gaza Strip were placed under Palestinian self-rule, and Israeli troops were withdrawn in 1994. In 1994 Israel and Jordan signed an agreement opening their borders and normalizing their relations.

> *The Nazi aim in the "Final Solution" was to make not only Germany, but all of Europe, "Jew-free."*

These hopes were in vain. When World War II began, Hitler ordered a "Final Solution" of the "Jewish Question." The term **Holocaust** (literally, a "completely burned" sacrifice) came after the war, used to describe the Nazi genocide of Jews and other groups; the Hebrew term *Shoah* (SHOW-uh, "destruction") is also used. When the war in the East broke out, "special assignment groups" of German troops held mass executions of hundreds of thousands of Jews who lived in villages and towns in newly conquered territory. But this soon proved "inefficient." In 1942, the German government erected concentration camps in western Germany and occupied Poland, after the model of the first camp in Dachau. The purpose of these camps was not to "concentrate" Jews, but to kill them with all the efficiency of state-run mass murder. Jews from Germany and Poland were brought by train to be killed by poison gas or to work as slave laborers in adjoining factories. Then Jews from every other nation in Nazi-occupied Europe—especially Russia, Hungary, The Netherlands, and France—were hunted down and brought by train to the camps. The Nazi aim in the "Final Solution" was to make not only Germany, but all of Europe, "Jew-free." Approximately six million Jews perished, almost three-quarters of Europe's Jewish population.

Relatively few Germans dared—or cared—to risk almost certain death by opposing the actions of their government. Among the most famous examples of those that did are the Roman Catholic industrialist Oskar Schindler, who protected 1,200 Jewish workers from death, and the Protestant theologian Dietrich Bonhoeffer (BAHN-haw-fuhr), who spoke out against anti-Semitism and Nazi control of the German churches. He also participated in a failed plot to kill Hitler. Bonhoeffer was hanged by the Nazis shortly before the war ended; when Schindler died in 1974, he was buried with great honors in Jerusalem.

Holocaust [HAUL-oh-caust] Nazi genocide of Jews and other groups in World War II

Visit a website devoted to Oskar Schindler.

The Holocaust brought a crisis of faith to Judaism like no event before it. To adapt Jacob Neusner's phrase, it was an "exile" from which "return" was extremely difficult. Orthodox Jews in general explained the Holocaust as punishment for recent Jewish sins, as a test of faith, or even as an opportunity to die for the faith. For many other Jews, it shook the foundations of Judaism. Some Jews, such as Richard Rubenstein, said that the only possible valid response to the Holocaust was the rejection of God. If God could allow the Holocaust, then there was no God. Many Jews agreed with this, and the abandonment of traditional beliefs and practices of Jewish religion begun in the Jewish emancipation accelerated. On the other hand, Emil Fackenheim and others insisted that the Holocaust did *not* show that God was dead. To reject Judaism's God, Fackenheim said, was to aid Hitler in the accomplishment of his evil, even demonic goal to destroy Judaism.

Whatever the best response to the Holocaust—not yet a settled question in Judaism—the field of religious studies has given it a large and important place in teaching and research. Holocaust museums have sprung up in several major North American cities. Popular literature and film have also dealt extensively with the Holocaust. *The Diary of Anne Frank*, authored by the Dutch Jewish teenager who wrote about her life in hiding, has become required reading in secondary schools all over the world. The works of Holocaust survivors such as Elie Wiesel (EHL-ee vee-ZEHL), particularly his moving novel *Night*, are widely read. Hollywood films on the Holocaust—*Schindler's List*, *Sophie's Choice*, *Life Is Beautiful*, and many others—have portrayed it in especially powerful ways.

Liam Neeson (center) as Oskar Schindler in Schindler's List, walking through lines of his Jewish workers, whom he saved

© UNIVERSAL/COURTESY EVERETT COLLECTION

Watch an interview with Elie Wiesel on the relationship of the Holocaust to other genocides.

Watch an introduction to Yad Vashem, the Israeli national museum of the Holocaust.

We should close this section with a consideration of Judaism in Israel today. The Orthodox movement is the only movement legally recognized in Israel. Until about 2000, only Orthodox Jews could serve on religious councils. Today, only Orthodox rabbis may perform marriage and conversion and grant divorce in Israel. Orthodox men are exempt from military service, and some of them receive lifelong stipends from the government in order to devote themselves to full-time Torah study. Some non-Orthodox Israelis bristle at this preferential treatment.

Most Israelis today don't formally identify with the three movements known in North America. Instead, they describe themselves in terms of their degree of observance. More than half of all Israelis call themselves "secular." About 15 to 20 percent describe themselves as "Orthodox." Most of the rest in the wide middle are "traditionally observant." However, the secular and the traditionalists (*Masorti*) of Israel tend to be more observant than are their counterparts in Europe and North America. For example, many secularists in Israel observe some traditional practices, such as lighting Sabbath candles on Friday evening, limiting their activities on the Sabbath day of rest, having a full Passover home ritual, or keeping some Jewish dietary laws (avoiding pork, for example). These practices are almost nonexistent among American Jews who call themselves "secular." An Israeli quip on this combination of secularism and observance runs, "Most Israelis don't belong to a synagogue, but the synagogue they don't belong to is Orthodox."

LO3 Essential Teachings of Judaism

A Jewish woman enters her home in Los Angeles. Just before she goes through her front door, she looks at a small box fastened to the right frame of the door. It contains a small scroll with three short passages from the Hebrew Bible, especially the key words of Deuteronomy 6:4–9: "Take to heart these instructions. . . . Recite them when you stay at home and when you are away, when you lie down and when you get up. . . . Inscribe them on the doorposts of your house and on your gates." She touches this box reverently as a reminder to remember God and keep God's teachings within her home. This little ritual act displays a key characteristic of Judaism: that it is a religion of action more than a religion of reflection.

Judaism as a whole has no official statement of its essential teachings. Unlike many other religions, it has rarely argued over doctrine to the point of division. The closest it came to a confession was the *Thirteen Articles* of Maimonides, but this was never widely accepted as a formal statement of Jewish teaching, in its time or later. Persons are Jewish whether they hold a system of traditional Jewish teachings, have simple beliefs associated with rituals such as the Passover meal, or even don't hold to any traditional Jewish teachings at all. This situation arises largely because actions in accordance with the Torah, not beliefs, are the most important aspect of Jewish religious life. Today, *Jewish* describes a people and a culture as well as a religion, so some who call themselves Jewish have little interest in any Jewish religious practices and even less in the teachings of Judaism.

Read the *Thirteen Articles* of Maimonides.

FOUNDATION OF JEWISH TEACHINGS: THE TANAK

The foundation of Jewish teaching and ethics is the Jewish Bible, commonly called the **Tanak**. This name is an acronym formed from the first letters of the three divisions of the Bible: the Torah (instruction, law); the second division, called the Nevi'im (prophets); and the third, the Kethuvim (writings). The Jewish scriptures arose over a period of more than a thousand years, and the Tanak was finalized only at the beginning of the first century C.E. Around the second century B.C.E., a translation into Greek was made in Egypt for Jews who had lived so long in the Diaspora that they had lost their knowledge of the Hebrew language. In the consolidation of Judaism that occurred after the Jewish revolt, the status of this Greek translation, called the *Septuagint* (sep-TOO-uh-jint), fell. Soon only the Hebrew Bible

Tanak [TAH-nahk] Name for the Hebrew Bible, an acronym formed from the first letters of Torah (the law), Nevi'im (the prophets), and Kethuvim (the writings)

was used in synagogues, even though many Jews could not understand it.

Even more important than the particular documents of the Bible is the authority that most Jews have invested in the biblical canon. These documents are said to be the written revelation of God—they are God's very words. The Bible is especially authoritative in expressing what God expects the Jewish people to do in response to the divine self-revelation. They express and shape the faith and action of Jews through all times. Jews have debated the meaning of the Bible, have often strongly disagreed about it, and in modern times have studied it with modern scholarly methods, but most Jews accept the Bible as their special book in some sig-

Examine a chart of the structure of the Hebrew Bible.

nificant sense. The Jewish use of their scriptural canon has deeply influenced the formation, contents, and use of scripture in Christianity and Islam.

Despite this lack of primary emphasis on teaching, the Bible and Talmud contain a great deal of teaching about God, humanity, and the meaning of life. Jewish history has seen significant theological and mystical inquiry into religious concepts. We'll consider three main teachings: one God, the chosen people, and life after death. (We'll consider other foundational teachings, the notions of obedience to God's will in the Torah and the concept of *ethical monotheism*, below in the section "Essential Jewish Ethics.")

ONE GOD

Judaism is a monotheistic faith, meaning that Jews believe that only one God exists. Hebrew and Israelite religion acknowledged the possible existence of other gods, but only one God for Israel. This *henotheism*—the belief in one God while accepting that other gods may exist—seems to have been prevalent in ancient Israel. For example, Canaanite gods were worshiped at Israelite holy places shortly after Israelite settlement in their promised land, King David named some of his children after Canaanite gods, and Solomon built a shrine to a Canaanite fertility goddess outside Jerusalem.

Full, formal monotheism seems to have come in the Babylonian exile in the 500s B.C.E. As we saw above, the return from Babylon featured a strict enforcement of monotheism, and Judaism has continued in it ever since.

Shema [sheh-MAH, or shmah] Basic statement of faith from Deuteronomy 6 that begins "Hear, O Israel, the Lord our God is One"

Israel's God is eternal, holy, all-knowing, all-present, all-powerful. God is a divine being, not a principle or a force. God guides not only those who know him, but also the nations and human history. God is transcendent, far above the world and human ability to comprehend God; but God is immanent as well, present in the world and in each human being. Because God is holy and just, God punishes humans for their disobedience, particularly those who know the Torah; but because God is merciful, God forgives and renews relationships.

How individual Jews choose to relate to God has varied in different times and places. Some have related to God by studying and keeping the Torah, by formal worship in the two Temples and in synagogues, with piety and emotion, even with mysticism such as the Kabbalah. An important part of Jewish piety relating to monotheism is the **Shema**, a basic statement of faith from Deuteronomy 6 that begins "Hear, O Israel: The Lord our God is One." Some Jews today even relate to God by denying God's existence, but ironically this too has become a Jewish option.

Listen to a recitation of the Shema.

Judaism's names for God are an important aspect of its teaching about God. The most sacred name of God, as God revealed to Moses in the book of Exodus, is YHWH. This name seems to be built on the Hebrew verb *to be* and means either "I am" or "I will be." YHWH is sometimes referred to as the *tetragrammaton* (TEH-trah-GRAM-mah-tahn), from the Greek for "four lettered." When vowels were added to Hebrew in the Middle Ages, this name was considered too holy to be changed, so we don't know its original pronunciation. The common word *Jehovah* (jeh-HOH-vuh), however, is incorrect as a vocalization. A more grammatically correct spelling and pronunciation, one used by scholars, is *Yahweh* (YAH-weh). Nevertheless, this discussion is irrelevant to most Jews, because they don't pronounce God's name. When

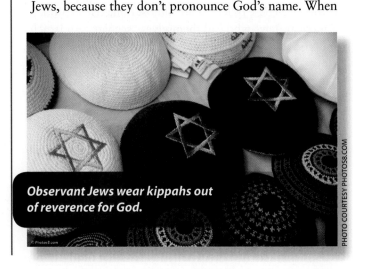

Observant Jews wear kippahs out of reverence for God.

PHOTO COURTESY PHOTOS8.COM

יהוה

The tetragrammaton, or name for God in Hebrew, YHWH (Hebrew reads from right to left)

the Torah is read aloud, *Adonai* (ad-oh-NAI), meaning "Lord," is read in place of YHWH. This practice is reflected in most English translations, including in the Christian Bible, in which YHWH is rendered as "Lord."

Many traditionalist Jews also refer to God as *Hashem* (hah-SHEHM), "the Name," understanding that God, not just God's name, is meant. The prohibition against pronouncing God's name expresses a profound human reverence for God. Some modern Orthodox Jews carry this reverence for God's name one step further. They refrain from writing the word *God*, replacing it instead with *G-d*. Other branches of modern Judaism do not follow them in this practice, saying that *God* is a generic noun, not a biblical name.

THE JEWS AS GOD'S CHOSEN PEOPLE

Most religions that believe in gods have seen themselves as having a special relationship with their gods, a relationship that makes them "chosen" or otherwise special. The Jews believe that they are God's "chosen people," chosen to be in a covenant with God. They didn't choose God; God chose them. The Jewish idea of being chosen is first found in the Torah and is elaborated in later books of the Tanak. This status carries both responsibilities and blessings, as described in the biblical accounts of the covenants with God.

According to the Tanak, Israel's character as the chosen people goes all the way back to Abraham and the eternal covenant God made with him: "I will establish my covenant between me and you and your descendants after you in their generations, for an everlasting covenant, to be God to you and your descendants after you" (Genesis 17:7). Being chosen as God's people brings a call to be holy and a realization of how amazing this is: "For you are a holy people to YHWH your God, and God has chosen you to be his treasured people

from all the nations that are on the face of the earth" (Deuteronomy 14:2). This choice is grounded in God's love and faithfulness to the covenant promises made to Abraham, not on Israel's own qualities: "The Lord did not set his love upon you or choose you because you were more in number than any people, for you were the fewest of all people. It was because the Lord loved you, and because he would keep the oath which he had sworn unto your ancestors" (Deuteronomy 7:7–8).

> *Jews throughout history have found that being God's chosen people is mostly a blessing, but sometimes a mixed blessing that brings trouble.*

The "flip side" of this chosen status is demanding, even ominous at times. Alongside the positive things said about being chosen, there is the necessity of obedience: "If you will obey my voice indeed, and keep my covenant, then you shall be a peculiar treasure unto me above all people" (Exodus 19:5). The obligation, even

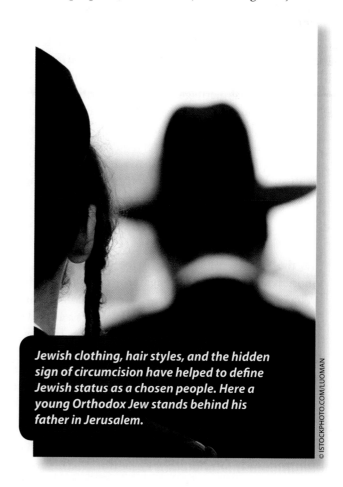

Jewish clothing, hair styles, and the hidden sign of circumcision have helped to define Jewish status as a chosen people. Here a young Orthodox Jew stands behind his father in Jerusalem.

© ISTOCKPHOTO.COM/LUOMAN

threat, that this demand for obedience entails is emphasized by the prophet Amos: "You only have I singled out of all the families of the earth; therefore will I punish you for all your iniquities" (Amos 3:2). Despite their status as a part of the chosen people, the ten tribes of the chosen people were wiped away in 721 B.C.E. because they disobeyed God continually. Jews throughout history have found their belief in being God's chosen people mostly a blessing, but sometimes a mixed blessing that brings troubles with both God and other people. One of the most wry expressions of this mixed blessing is in the musical *Fiddler on the Roof*, when Tevye, the main character beset by difficulties, prays, "I know we are the chosen people. But once in a while, can't you choose someone else?"

Throughout its history, Judaism has usually linked being the "chosen people" with a mission or purpose, such as being a "light to the nations," a "blessing to the nations," or a "kingdom of priests" between God and the world. This special duty derives from the covenant God made with Abraham and was renewed at the giving of the Torah on Mount Sinai. Through the long history of Judaism and Israelite religion before it, the idea of being God's chosen people sustained many Jews throughout military defeat and exile, discrimination, persecution, even the Holocaust. In modern times, more secular Jews have understood it to mean that their human abilities should be put to use for the good of all humankind. Even among secularized Jews there is a continuing feeling for the special status in having a Jewish heritage. In sum, the British historian Paul Johnson once wrote that historians cannot deal well with the religious claim that God actually chose the Jews and guided their history, but it can be affirmed that "The Jews believed that they were a special people with such unanimity and passion, and over so long a span, that they became one." [3]

LIFE AFTER DEATH?

As the Hebrew Bible book of Job (johb) puts it, "If mortals die, will they live again?" (Job 14:14). Most religions of the world address this question, because clarity on the issues of life after death means a great deal to how they think about life *before* death. However, the Tanak has little to say about what happens after death, and Judaism as a whole today doesn't dwell on it. This may seem surprising to non-Jews, because the sacred texts of Christianity and Islam, both of which have their foundations in Judaism, speak often about life after death. But with Judaism's focus on actions more than beliefs, it is actually to be expected that it not speculate about the world to come. Because many religions, including Judaism's sister faiths of Christianity and Islam, rely in part on fear of the fires of hell and the hope of heaven to motivate good conduct in their adherents, it is remarkable that Judaism, with its strong emphasis on morality, hasn't usually done the same.

An early common theme in the Bible is that death means joining one's ancestors in the land of the dead—being "gathered to one's people" (Genesis 25:8, 25:17, 35:29, 49:33; Deuteronomy 42:50). Another image emphasizes the reality of mortality. God made humans from the dust of the ground, and because of their sins they die and return to dust (Genesis 3:19). Most Jews take this literally—they regularly today use wooden coffins that over time allow the body to rejoin the ground. The most common biblical image of the afterlife is as a shadowy place called *Sheol* (SHEE-ohl), which is similar to the Greek conception of Hades. Sheol is a shadowy underworld, a place of darkness (Psalms 88:13; Job 10:21, 22) and silence (Psalms 115:17). Good and evil people alike go there, and God isn't present there. These early biblical descriptions of death indicate a belief that the person continues to exist in some way after death, but not with a full or happy life. Much later in the biblical tradition the concept arises of the resurrection of the dead and a final judgment leading to either a blessed or a damned life. Daniel 12:2 declares, "And many of them that sleep in the dust of the earth shall awake, some to everlasting life and some to reproaches and everlasting abhorrence."

Fully developed concepts of the resurrection of the dead and eternal life came into much of Judaism around 200 B.C.E. When rabbinical Judaism—based largely on the earlier Pharisees—took over, belief in resurrection was near-universal in Judaism all the way to the Jewish Enlightenment in 1800. The resurrection of the dead is one of the *Thirteen Articles* by Maimonides, and a prayer said regularly in traditionalist synagogues from medieval times through today affirms the resurrection. One early rabbi, Hiyya ben Joseph, suggested that the dead will travel through the ground and rise up in Jerusalem; the unrighteous will arise naked and ashamed, and the righteous will rise up clothed and happy (Babylonian Talmud, Ketubot 111b). The hope of being raised in Jerusalem has led to large cemeteries there, especially on the Mount of Olives. Despite belief in a divine judgment that separates those whose deeds are on balance good from those whose deeds are not, some rabbis held that a middle group of people of more mixed accomplishments

---

[3] Paul Johnson, *A History of the Jews* (New York: Harper and Row, 1987), 587.

ALAN KOTOK

Jewish cemetery on the Mount of Olives facing the former site of the Temple, now occupied by the Dome of the Rock mosque

will go into hell for an eleven-month period of purification and then enter heaven (Babylonian Talmud, Rosh Hashanah 16b-17a, Eduyot 2.10). This belief is probably connected to the Jewish practice of eleven months of mourning deceased loved ones.

Most Jews have believed that one need not be Jewish to enter heaven. Because God judges actions and not beliefs, those who do what God commands will be rewarded. Maimonides, for example, wrote that all good people of the world have a portion in the next world. Those who are "righteous among the Gentiles" (non-Jews) by virtue of their deeds, even if they belong to a different religion, will enter heaven. Heaven is typically called the "Garden of Eden," a place of joy and peace that recaptures the original home of humanity on earth. The Babylonian Talmud's imagery of heaven includes sitting at banquet tables (Taanit 25a), enjoying lavish banquets (Baba Batra 75a), and even enjoying heavenly sex with spouses (Berachot 57b). A few rabbis didn't like this imagery and held that there will be no eating, drinking, or sex in heaven—or if there is, they won't be so enjoyable. Instead, the blessed will enjoy heaven in a purely spiritual way (Babylonian Talmud, Berachot 17a). For example, despite his affirmation of

the resurrection in the *Thirteen Articles*, Maimonides held that there is no material substance in heaven at all, only souls of the righteous without bodies (Mishneh Torah, Repentance 8). This purely spiritual view of heaven never became a mainstream Jewish teaching, because Judaism had long held that "soul" and "body" belong together. Both Islam and Christianity give much more importance to the teaching of resurrection and eternal life.

> *"I don't believe in [an afterlife]. I believe this is it, and I believe it's the best way to live."—Natalie Portman*

As stated above, this Talmudic teaching on the afterlife prevailed in virtually all of Judaism from about 400 to 1800 C.E. Today, Orthodox Jewish movements still teach the resurrection of the dead, judgment by God, and life in heaven or hell. Reform Judaism, on the other hand, rejected these doctrines as binding. Instead, its members are allowed to form their own opinions on life after death. The general view in Reform, drawn from Enlightenment ideas, is that even if there is a life after death, we can't know much about it here, so it shouldn't play a large role in how people live. Human immortality, Reform Jews hold, is mostly in one's children and the spiritual legacy one leaves behind. As a result, many Reform Jews and secular Jews have no belief in life after death. For example, when the Israeli-American actress Natalie Portman, who was raised "Jewish but not religious," was asked about her concept of the afterlife, she said, "I don't believe in that. I believe this [life] is it, and I believe it's the best way to live." The Conservative movement, between Orthodoxy and Reform on most teachings, holds to the continued importance of the main lines of traditional teachings on this topic, but notes its historical conditioning and interprets its more vivid imagery as symbolic.

LO4 Essential Jewish Ethics

In Grand Rapids, Michigan, a short controversy breaks out in the press over the religious implications of a museum exhibit called "Bodies Revealed." This exhibit, which has played in several other North American cities, shows fourteen full human bodies and "hundreds of organs" in various states of dissection. The museum's website says it has anticipated the controversy that has followed this exhibit as it travels, so it has consulted ethical and religious experts on bringing the exhibit to town. Although it's a popular exhibit with excellent ticket sales, some controversy does break out in the open. The most articulate examination is in a newspaper column by a local rabbi, David Krishef, leader of the local Conservative synagogue. Rabbi Krishev examines the good that can come from the exhibit but, he asks, at what cost? He raises the traditional Jewish moral command to honor the bodies of the dead, not to display them to the public for profit, entertainment, or even education.

Read about the "Bodies Revealed" exhibit.

The moral life of the Jewish people, of all branches today, rests on biblical foundations. God created the world as a good place, to reflect God's own glory and goodness. God created the world as a place for human culture in all its fullness. When human beings rebelled against God, God went in search of them, calling Abraham to live in covenant with God. But God not only searches and redeems humans; God also commands them to follow his way. For the rabbis of antiquity and the Middle Ages, and for Orthodox and most Conservatives today, the moral code of the Bible is composed of laws that demand obedience—they are indeed commandments, not general moral guidelines. In their understanding, God didn't give the "Ten Suggestions."

God didn't give the "Ten Suggestions."

ETHICS IN THE IMAGE OF GOD

Jewish morality and ethics rest on the foundation of *ethical monotheism*. Not only is God one and the only God, but God is perfectly right and righteous. Holiness is at the center of God's nature; God is good, just, and compassionate. The good world that God made, especially the people in it, are created to live in conformity with God's nature and will. The Torah given by God enables people to know more exactly what God's will is, but a basic notion of God's will is written in every human heart. In contrast with other religions of the ancient Near East, evil is not built into the structure of the universe but is the product of human choices. Humans are free moral agents.

A fundamental Jewish teaching shared by almost all Jews today (except those who reject the existence of God, of course) is that human beings are created in the "image of God." Israelites and Jews never took this to mean that humans somehow physically look like God, because God is a spirit and invisible to the human eye. Although the Bible doesn't explain the "image of God" in detail, Jews have interpreted it to mean that humans can think rationally and have a moral sense to know what is right. Because humans are created in God's image, humans have the ability to know and even act like God. The "image of God" is related to the human mind and spirit, but it means that humans are like God, not that a part of them *is* God.

The good impulse and the evil impulse are like having an angel on one shoulder and a devil on the other, each urging a particular course of action.

The early rabbis taught that God built two moral impulses into each human being: the "good impulse" called the *yetzer hatov* (YAY-tser ha-TOHV) and the "evil impulse," the *yetzer hara* (YAY-tser ha-RAH). The good impulse is the moral conscience that reminds a person of God's law and creates an urge to follow it. The evil impulse is the urge to satisfy one's own needs and desires. Despite its name, there's nothing intrinsically evil about the evil impulse, because it was created by God and is natural to humankind. The "evil" impulse, acting with the good impulse, drives us to eat, drink, procreate, and make a living—all necessary and good things. However, it can easily lead to sin when not held in check and balanced by the good impulse, and this is why it is called "evil." Eating, drinking, procreating, and making a living can be taken to extremes and destroy human life. The good impulse and the evil impulse are like the modern image of a person who has an angel on one shoulder and a devil on the other, each urging a particular course of action. Some rabbis have been uncomfortable about talk of a created "evil" impulse and have preferred to speak of one impulse that can be used in two different ways.

THE TORAH

The Torah, the first five books of the Bible but in a wider sense the whole teaching and law of Judaism, is this religion's most important text. It contains stories and commandments that teach about life and death. The rabbis enumerated 613 commandments (*mitzvot*): 248 positive commandments ("You shalls") and 365 negative commandments ("You shall nots"). Moreover, all the commandments are held to be binding and more or less equal. Some Jews in the modern age would make a distinction between the "moral law" and the "ceremonial" and "ritual law." This isn't found in the Bible and Talmud, but history seems to have ratified it, because some of the 613 commands cannot be fulfilled now that the Jewish temple is gone. All commandments come from God, the ancient and medieval rabbis said, so all are binding forever. Today, all Jews consider the Ten Commandments to be the most important commandments in the Torah, though not all Jews adhere to the 613 mitzvot, forming one of the main differences between the different branches of Judaism.

The Ten Commandments in Hebrew, in their shorter form. Writing on stone suggests the permanence and seriousness of the commandments.

© ISTOCKPHOTO.COM/JAMES STEIDL

The Ten Commandments run as follows, with short explanations in brackets:

1. I am the Lord your God [not a commandment in grammatical form, but the basis of the people's relationship with God].

2. You shall not recognize any as god beside Me [the root of monotheism].

3. You shall not take the Name of the Lord your God in vain [God's name, symbolic of God's essence, must be respected].

4. Remember the day of Sabbath, to keep it holy [the Sabbath is a day of rest and rededication to God].

5. Honor your father and your mother [parents are to be respected as long as they live].

6. You shall not murder [not all killing is murder, but unlawful killing is].

7. You shall not commit adultery [breaking marriage vows breaks marriage].

8. You shall not steal [other people's property is to be respected].

9. Do not give false testimony against your neighbor [lying in legal settings undermines justice].

10. You shall not covet the possessions of others [desiring to have things that others have].

The rest of the Torah's legal material is based on these Ten Commandments. The rabbis of the ancient world compiled the *Mishnah* and the *Gemara*, finally combining them into the Talmud, expanding on these commandments and bringing them into every aspect of the life of the Jewish people. Judaism's emphasis on justice and love in community, rather than on just the letter of the law, has enabled it to keep to its moral tradition while adapting to changing circumstances in life.

GENERAL JEWISH ETHICS

Beside these Torah-based commands that originate with the Hebrew Bible, the biblical tradition also has broad legal injunctions, wisdom narratives with moral lessons, and prophetic teachings. These other teachings became important in the first millennium B.C.E., although the Torah commands remain central and foundational. In modern times, as the Torah commands became problematic for many Jews, the more-general ethical principles became paramount for them.

The biblical prophets exhorted their audiences to lead a life that honored their covenant with God. They pointed primarily to obedience to the Torah, but they also spoke of more-general moral duties: kindness to the needy, benevolence, faith, relief for the suffering, a peace-loving disposition, and a humble spirit. Civic loyalty and obedience, even to a foreign ruler, is urged as a duty (Jeremiah 29:7). This was also important in later times, as Jews lived under non-Jewish governments. What the prophets viewed as the end-time is uncertain, but the moral vision was clear: the end-time will be one of peace and righteousness (Isaiah 2:2).

In early rabbinic Judaism, the oral Torah both interpreted the Bible and delved afresh into many other ethical topics. Jewish morality, encompassing both commandments and general ethics, is known to Jews today as **halakhah**, literally "walk" of life. God has a way for the chosen people to walk in.

The best-loved and most influential rabbinic text on ethics is the Mishnah tractate of Pirke Avot (PEER-kay ah-VOHT), the "Sayings of the Fathers," often translated as "Ethics

halakhah [hah-luh-KAH] "Walk" of life, the way of moral obedience to God

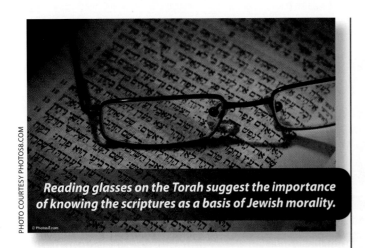

Read a selection from the Pirke Avot.

Read about how the different Jewish branches approach the moral issues relating to homosexuality.

Watch a video on Jewish rabbis working for greater Israeli justice on the West Bank.

Reading glasses on the Torah suggest the importance of knowing the scriptures as a basis of Jewish morality.

of the Fathers." The Pirke Avot traces the transmission of the oral Torah from Moses to the second century C.E., when the Mishnah was compiled. Throughout this work, the word Torah refers especially to the oral Torah, a "fence around the [written] law," the body of legal opinions developed by the rabbis and codified in the Mishnah. The idea behind this "fence" is that by keeping it one would also be keeping the written Torah that it protects.

MODERN JEWISH ETHICS

In the modern period, Jewish ethics sprouted many offshoots, due to developments in modern secular ethics and to the formation of Jewish branches, each needing clarity on ethical teachings. The nineteenth-century and early twentieth-century Reform movement promoted the idea of Judaism as pure ethical monotheism. Since about 1900, liberal Reform and Reconstructionist rabbis have fostered novel approaches to Jewish ethics—in the work of Eugene Borowitz, for example. Also in these centuries, Orthodox rabbis have often engaged in applied ethics by interpreting the Talmud for bioethics: end-of-life issues, in vitro fertilization, genetic therapy, and other topics.

Perhaps the most influential work of Jewish social ethics is *I and Thou* by Martin Buber (BOO-buhr; 1878–1965). In this profound work, which is reputed to have changed the lives of many of its readers, Buber uses two pairs of words to describe two fundamentally different types of relationship between one's self and the world: "I-It" and "I-Thou." For I-It relationships, the "It" refers to other people as objects. It objectifies and devalues them. In other words, the "I" looks upon others as "Its," not as people like oneself. Buber held that most human problems are caused by I-It attitudes. By contrast, the "I" in an I-Thou relationship doesn't objectify

any "It" but has a living, mature relationship with others. It recognizes that the "Thou" is a whole world of experience within one person, just as one's "I" is. Buber taught that God is the "eternal Thou" known by direct encounter with God and indirect encounter with God as one develops I-Thou relationships with other people.

LO5 Jewish Worship and Ritual

In London, a prominent Jewish rabbi criticizes pop singer Madonna's practice of Jewish mysticism known as the Kabbalah. Rabbi Yitzchak Schochet of London's Mill Hill Synagogue strongly objects to Madonna's use of the Kabbalah, arguing that it tarnishes Judaism when people who don't observe Jewish law engage in Jewish mysticism. Rabbi Schochet and many other traditional, observant Jews are particularly upset by the tattoo on Madonna's right shoulder of the ancient Hebrew name for God, which most Jews regard as so holy that they don't use it. (They forbid permanent tattoos as well, so this is a double fault.) Madonna's interest in the Kabbalah began with her 1998 *Ray of Light* album, was strengthened by her 2007 visit to the Kabbalah center in Jerusalem, and continues today. Public fascination with her use of the Kabbalah also remains strong, and she has become the leading celebrity voice of the Kabbalah.

Watch an interview with Madonna on the Kabbalah.

Because Judaism is a religion of practice, it has a full set of rituals for synagogue worship, home practices, and community-based religious festivals. We'll begin with synagogue worship, then consider the Sabbath and the main festivals; the major life-cycle rituals of circumcision, bar/bat mitzvah, and funerals; and finally the Kabbalah.

WORSHIP IN THE SYNAGOGUE

The main synagogue service takes place on either Friday evening or Saturday morning, both of which fall on the Sabbath day. In Orthodox synagogues, males and females sit separately; in Conservative and Reform, they may sit together. A *minyan* (MIHN-yahn), or minimum number of men to have a service (usually ten), is necessary. We've already discussed, in "The Jewish Present As Shaped by Its Past," language and music differences between these three branches. But the three branches all share the same basic structure of service: gathering into the main synagogue room; hymns and prayers often lead by a cantor, or singer; and readings from scripture.

In synagogue worship, the readings themselves are very musical. The worship leader chants the words in Hebrew, guided by marks written in the Hebrew text and also employing traditional Hebrew melodies. The place where the Torah scrolls are kept is the *ark*, a reference to the Ark of the Covenant. It is a special closet or recess in the synagogue wall on the side nearest Jerusalem and is usually the focal point of the synagogue. The scrolls themselves are typically covered with richly embroidered cloth, and the upper ends of the wooden rollers are adorned with gold and silver decorations. Their use follows a prescribed ritual:

- When a scroll is removed from the ark during the service, everyone in the synagogue stands and a special song is often sung.

- The scroll is placed on a reading desk.

- The readers use a special pointer, often made of solid silver, to keep track of their place in the text and avoid touching it with their hands.

Reading the Torah scroll in a synagogue

- When the reading is complete, the scroll is rolled up, its covers are put back on, and it is returned to the ark with great solemnity.

Then the rabbi sometimes preaches a short sermon based on the texts that were read, especially the Torah reading.

THE SABBATH

One of the Ten Commandments orders that the "Sabbath" (seventh) day of the week be kept holy. This day begins at sunset on Friday and concludes on sunset on Saturday. Sabbath usually begins at home, with a festive meal for which the whole family is present. The meal leads off with the lighting of the Sabbath candles. At least eighteen minutes before sundown on Friday, the mother and daughters light candles, usually on the dining table, to welcome the Sabbath. In many modern Jewish households the candle blessing is performed together as a family. After the candles are lit, this blessing is recited over them: "Blessed are You, Eternal One our God, Ruler of the Universe, who makes us holy with mitzvot [commandments] and gives us this mitzvah of lighting the Sabbath lights."

The command goes on to say that no work may be done on the Sabbath. This rest from work is connected to both the creation of the world and the giving of the Torah. The Talmud interprets this strictly; that is why traditional Jews have tended to live within walking distance

A Jewish mother and daughter light the Sabbath candles.

Seder plate with special Passover foods; the Hebrew word is **Pesach,** *meaning "Passover"*

SLGCKGC

of the synagogue, because to walk too far is considered work.

JEWISH ANNUAL FESTIVALS

The Jewish year has several annual festivals. Most of them have both a historical reference and a contemporary meaning to build faith and obedience in those who celebrate them. We can deal with them quickly here. *Rosh Hashanah* (rohsh ha-SHAH-nah) is the Jewish New Year, in September or October, depending on how the Jewish lunar calendar matches the solar calendar. It begins a ten-day solemn period of repentance and self-examination. This period ends on *Yom Kippur* (yohm kip-PUHR), the "Day of Atonement" that is the holiest day in the year. *Sukkot* (SOOK-koht) is the festival of "tabernacles" or "booths," a seven-day harvest celebration linked to the wandering of the Hebrews after the Exodus; people often live in special outdoor huts during this time. *Passover* celebrates the escape of the Hebrews from Egyptian slavery. A special meal, called the *seder* (SAY-duhr), with various foods including unleavened bread (*matzoh*), is the highlight. Hanukkah we have explained above. *Purim* (POOR-eem), "lots," recalls the Queen Esther story in which Persian Jews were saved from genocide when the drawing of lots exposed that evil plan. Costumes and plays, as well as special foods, are featured. Finally, *Shavuot* (SHAHV-oo-oht), meaning "weeks," comes fifty days after Passover; it celebrates the giving of the Torah.

KOSHER FOOD

Kosher means "fitting or proper," not (as is often read) "pure or clean." A body of ritual Jewish law deals with kosher: what foods can and cannot be eaten, and how those foods must be prepared and consumed. Contrary to popular opinion, rabbis don't "bless" food to make it kosher, but they do inspect it and its processing to assure kosher consumers that the

food is kosher. All sorts of ethnic foods can be kosher; in fact, kosher Chinese restaurants can often be found in Jewish neighborhoods.

Leviticus 11 gives a list of clean and unclean foods, and the Talmud treats them in detail. The types of unclean animals specified are (1) four-footed animals that do not chew the cud and have a split hoof (pigs, for example); (2) meat-eating birds; (3) insects with wings; (4) water animals without fins and scales, for example shrimp; and (5) small creeping ("swarming") animals. In order to be kosher, acceptable animals must be butchered in a humane way and prepared for sale in a clean way. Also, kosher food must be served and eaten according to kosher regulations (for example, no mixing of dairy products and meat in cooking or serving). In general, raw vegetables are always kosher, and so are cooked vegetables as long as they are cooked and eaten correctly.

Kosher rules are observed at all times, but additional kosher restrictions come during Passover. Some foods that are kosher for year-round use are not kosher for Passover, because they have leaven in them. A bagel, for example, can be kosher for regular use but is certainly not kosher for Passover.

Kosher food is so closely linked with Jewish identity that the misconception has arisen that it's only for Jews. In fact, in 2009 almost 85 percent of kosher meat sales were to non-Jews, who appreciate the quality of the meat and its general healthfulness. (If you like hot dogs, for example, and are concerned more about taste and health than about price, a kosher hot dog is for you.) In 2010, kosher food was served for the first time at the Super Bowl, and it almost sold out.

Even though its beef may be kosher, the cheese on this burger makes it not kosher.

Read an article about the rising popularity of kosher food among non-Jews in the U.S.

EVAN SWIGART

CIRCUMCISION, THE SIGN OF THE COVENANT

Circumcision is the most important life-cycle ritual in Judaism and probably the one most universally observed among Jews. Its most common name is the *bris milah* (brihs MIL-luh), Yiddish for "covenant of circumcision" and usually called "bris" for short. Most secular Jews who observe no other part of Judaism regularly practice this rite; to be Jewish is to be circumcised. Orthodox Jews affirm the Talmudic view that a person of Jewish descent who is not circumcised will not enter heaven. A few Reform and Reconstructionist leaders oppose circumcision today, but they're in the extreme minority.

As we have already seen, the commandment to circumcise is given first in Genesis 17:10–14 as an essential part of God's covenant with Abraham. According to God's command to Abraham, circumcision is performed only on males as the sign of the covenant and membership in God's people. (Some Reform Jews argue that circumcision is sexist, so they have a "naming ceremony" for baby girls, with most of a circumcision ritual except for the actual cutting.) Circumcision is often perceived by Reform and Conservative Jews to be a hygienic measure. Orthodox Jews disagree and correctly point out that this rationale isn't found in the Torah. Instead, circumcision is a religious measure: It is an outward physical sign of the eternal covenant between God and the Jewish people. It is done not for any health benefits, but because God commands it.

Circumcision is performed on the eighth day of a child's life. If this falls on the Sabbath, circumcision is still done then, even though the drawing of blood is ordinarily forbidden as work. Circumcision (from the Latin for "cut around") involves surgically removing the foreskin of the penis. The circumcision is performed in a home or synagogue by a **mohel**, a respected Jewish man educated in the relevant Jewish laws, skilled in hygienic practices, and possessed of a steady hand. While the cutting is done, an honored man holds the baby still on his lap. Blessings of God are recited, and a drop of wine is placed in the baby's mouth. He is then given a formal Hebrew name. As with most Jewish rituals, circumcision is a joyous, celebrative occasion (except for the baby, of course) and is followed by refreshments or more often a festive meal.

Bar Mitzvah and Bat Mitzvah

A Jewish young man in a coming-of-age ceremony becomes a **bar mitzvah**, which literally means "son of the commandment." A young woman becomes a **bat** (or **bas**) **mitzvah**, "daughter of the commandment." The singular *mitzvah* ("commandment") is used here even though the Torah as a whole is meant. Although these terms literally refer only to adult standing in the Jewish community, they are also commonly taken to mean the ceremonies themselves, for example in the

At a bar mizvah ceremony, a young man carries the Torah scroll with pride and joy.

expression that someone is "having a bar mitzvah." In Reform and Conservative Judaism, the ritual for females is the same as for males. In all Orthodox practice, women are not permitted to participate in rituals such as these, so a ceremony is usually little more than a modest party to mark a female's thirteenth birthday, if it is held at all.

What does it mean to become a bar/bat mitzvah? In Jewish law, children are not obligated to obey the Torah, although they are encouraged to do so. (Like any religion passed through the generations, Judaism raises its children in the faith, as the Shema commands. Moreover, historic Jewish teaching knows nothing of the modern concept of "teenage" years between childhood and adulthood; when one comes near to puberty, one is an adult.) When they are

mohel [MOI-uhl, rhymes with *oil*] Jewish man who officiates at a circumcision

bar mitzvah [bahr MITZ-vuh] "Son of the commandment," the assumption of responsibility before God for keeping the Torah

bat (bas) mitzvah [baht (bahs) MITZ-vuh] "Daughter of the commandment," the assumption of responsibility before God for keeping the Torah at an "age of understanding" to know the difference between right and wrong and choose between them—traditionally thirteen for boys and twelve for girls—children become obligated in God's sight to obey the Torah. The bar/bat mitzvah ceremony marks the beginning of that obligation, but it doesn't create it. Now the young people gradually begin to assume the privileges and responsibilities of Jewish adults. They help to lead religious services, count in a minyan, enter binding contracts, and may even marry (although most marriages are not carried out until later).

The bar/bat mitzvah is an innovation of the last few centuries, to mark the passage into Jewish adulthood in a ritual way. In its earliest, most basic form, it is the celebrant's first participation in leading a service. During a Sabbath service or a weekday service, the young person is called up to the Torah scroll to recite a blessing over the weekly reading. The common practice today for one becoming a bar/bat mitzvah is to do more than the blessing. The celebrant learns the entire Torah reading for the day in its chanted form and recites it during the service. He or she sometimes reads the entire weekly Torah portion, leads part of the service, or leads the congregation in certain important prayers. The celebrant is also generally required to make a short speech, which traditionally begins, "Today I am a man/woman." All this requires a good deal of training by the rabbi, often over some months. The father traditionally recites a blessing thanking God that his child has become an adult. The often-elaborate post-ceremony parties that are commonplace today in North America arose around 1900 among more-prosperous Jews.

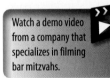

Listen to an example of a chanted blessing at a bar mitzvah.

Watch a demo video from a company that specializes in filming bar mitzvahs.

MARRIAGE

Judaism strongly encourages marriage and family life. If asked what the first commandment in the Torah is, an observant Jew will reply, "Be fruitful and multiply" (Genesis 1:28), which is indeed God's first command to the human race. Among Ashkenazi Jews, monogamy has been the rule since the 900s C.E. Among Sephardic Jews, whose rules reflect the Bible and Talmud more closely on this point and have been influenced by the Muslim context, polygamy was permitted until the 1950s, but still wasn't common. For both groups, Jews married only Jews. But in the last century, intermarriage has become more common. This has posed a problem for Reform and Conservative Jews, because Jewish identity is traced through the mother, not the father, and intermarriage leads more often to assimilation of the Jewish spouse to the Gentile world than it does to the conversion of the non-Jewish spouse to Judaism. Lately, Reform Jews have urged, and sometimes instituted, either matrilineal or patrilineal descent for membership in the Jewish people.

Jewish marriage has engagement (sometimes preceded by the work of matchmakers), rings, a vow or a document certifying marriage obligations, and a grand celebration to follow. Ceremonies are often held outdoors or in hotels, not in the synagogue, as long as there is a rabbi to officiate and a canopy called a *chuppa* (CHUP-uh, with a guttural *ch*). But the Jewish ceremony has something unique. As the last part of the wedding, the groom crushes under his foot a glass wrapped in a cloth, a reminder in a time of great joy of the sorrow that came to Judaism when the Temple of Jerusalem was destroyed in 70 C.E. Then there are loud cries of "Mazel tov!" (MA-zul tahv)—literally "Good luck," but in celebratory situations with more a nuance of "Congratulations"—and the wedding reception begins.

FUNERAL RITUALS

Jewish practices relating to death and mourning have had two purposes, primarily to comfort the mourners and secondarily to help, as much as possible and appropriate, the deceased into the next world. In what follows, we will deal with long-established Jewish practices that go back hundreds, sometimes thousands, of years. Some variations to this pattern will be found among Conservative/Masorti Jews today, and more among the Reform.

After a person dies, burial must be carried out in less than forty-eight hours. The body is never left alone. In the past, most Jewish communities had an organization to care for the dead; these societies are now making something of a comeback as a replacement for more-conventional funeral home arrangements. Autopsies are forbidden as a desecration of the body, but they are permitted where civil authorities require it. Embalming of the body is strictly forbidden as desecration, and organ donation is likewise not done. However, some contemporary Jewish ethicists have argued that organ donation is permitted, even meritorious, if the recipient's body is buried at death.

Both the dress of the body and the coffin are simple, so

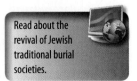

Read about the revival of Jewish traditional burial societies.

that all people are equal in death. The upper body is wrapped in a prayer shawl with its fringes cut short. The body is never viewed at funerals; open-casket ceremonies are forbidden by Jewish law. The body must not be cremated, but buried in the earth. If coffins are used, which is common in the Western world, they must be made of wood, and must rest directly in the earth. Some Orthodox groups go so far as to poke holes in the bottom of coffins to facilitate the process of "dust to dust."

Jewish mourning practices have periods of decreasing intensity. When a person first hears of the death of a close relative, it is traditional to express the initial grief by tearing one's clothing, or sometimes a piece of cloth that is then worn on one's clothing. During the first two days after death, the family is usually left alone to allow for the full expression of their grief. The next period of mourning is known as *shiva* (SHIHV-uh), the Hebrew word for "seven," because it lasts seven days, beginning on the day of burial. This process is often called "sitting shiva." Shiva is observed by the entire family of the deceased in the deceased's home. They wear the clothing they had on when they tore it in mourning. Mourners sit on low stools or the floor. They don't wear leather shoes, shave their faces or cut their hair, wear cosmetics, work, or do things for comfort, entertainment, or pleasure.

After shiva, lighter mourning of eleven months continues for the immediate family. *Kaddish*, a prayer of faith and petition, is to be said every day. After the period is complete, the family of the deceased is not permitted to continue formal mourning. Jewish law requires that a tombstone be prepared. Many Jewish communities delay putting it up until the end of the twelve-month mourning period. Where this custom is followed, a formal unveiling ceremony for the tombstone is usually held at the cemetery.

Read suggestions for making a good shiva visit.

THE KABBALAH

While official rabbinic Judaism preoccupied many middle- and upper-class Jews who had the leisure to study the Talmud, unofficial folk religion grew in the medieval period to become a permanent feature of Judaism. The intense rationalism of medieval Jewish philosophy and Talmudic studies was countered by the rise of Jewish mysticism, emphasizing the immediate, personal, and nonrational experience of God. In twelfth-century France and thirteenth-century Spain, mystical forms of Jewish religiosity would combine with mainstream Judaism to produce the Kabbalah. The rabbis strongly condemned such practices, but they grew nonetheless.

The Kabbalah pictured God not as a simple unity but as a structured Being with an inner configuration of ten attributes. Evil is believed to be provoked by human sin and set right by good deeds, fulfillment of the commandments, prayer, and mystical contemplation. Other Kabbalistic beliefs have included the transmigration of souls and the practice of sexual intercourse as a mirror of the union among the divine attributes. Many of these ideas are found in the *Zohar*, the leading book on Kabbalah by Moses de Leon (1250–1305). The Kabbalah spread quickly, and in the sixteenth century, Rabbi Isaac Luria (1534–1572 C.E.) reformulated this esoteric system in a manner that emphasized messianic redemption. Another offshoot of Kabbalah arose around an itinerant folk healer named Israel ben Eleazar (1700–1760)—known as Baal Shem Tov (bah-AHL shehm tohv), or "Master of the Good Name." This was **Hasidism**, a Jewish mystical movement that stresses joyful emotion. Hasidism soon attracted Jews in Russia, Poland, Hungary, and Romania. The message of the Hasidic masters was that God is present and directly accessible in the world, that God is best experienced and worshiped in joy, that even the most evil persons and events are capable of redemption, and that each Jew has an essential role to play in making the world holy. The new Hasidic pietism drew on the Kabbalah in a way that overcame its esoteric character.

Rabbinic authorities opposed Hasidic movements, criticizing their fervor and their ecstatically emotional worship. They disliked the Hasidic figure of the charismatic man holding strong religious authority in his movement. But Hasidism soon became established in the Jewish communities of Poland and the Ukraine. It split into smaller groups, and by the early 1800s Hasidic dynasties had formed that still exist today. In Lithuania, Lubavich (LOOB-uh-vich) Hasidism emphasized a distinctive blend of Kabbalistic speculation and rabbinic learning. Despite Hasidism's anti-traditionalist origins and history, it has ironically come to represent orthodoxy, even so-called "ultra-orthodoxy," in the modern world, especially to non-Jews. Hasidism is strong in North America and Israel.

At the end of the twentieth century, the Kabbalah was popularized and spread beyond Judaism. Its psychological and social aspects were emphasized, and its Torah-related

Hasidism a Jewish mystical movement that stresses joyful emotion that arose in the 1700s

In 2004, pop star Madonna and then husband Guy Ritchie visit the grave of Kabbalist author Rabbi Jehuda Ashlag.

wine, and then all leave the table to wash their hands ritually. Gathered around the table again, they recite a blessing of God for the gift of food. Each receives a slice of the bread to eat, and the main meal begins. At the end of the meal, special Sabbath songs are sung by all, and the meal is concluded with a prayer. This Sabbath ritual is so meaningful in Judaism that it is practiced in much the same way by Orthodox and Conservative families in North America. It is even making something of a comeback in Reform Judaism.

Jews have been in North America as early as the 1600s, settling first in New Amsterdam (modern New York City). For almost two hundred years, most North American Jews were Sephardics of Spanish and Portuguese ancestry. The first American synagogue was established in 1677 in Touro, Rhode Island, a colony that was a center of religious toleration. Although they couldn't hold office or even vote in most colonies, Sephardic Jews became active in their civic communities in the 1790s. Until 1830, Charleston, South Carolina, had the largest Jewish community in North America. Large-scale Jewish immigration, however, didn't take place until the mid-1800s, when Ashkenazi Jews from Germany, many of them secularized, arrived in the United States, primarily becoming merchants and shop owners. There were approximately 250,000 Jews in the United States by 1880.

Jewish immigration to North America increased sharply in the early 1880s, mainly as a result of persecution in Russia and Eastern Europe. Most of the new immigrants were Yiddish-speaking and religiously observant Ashkenazis from the poor rural areas of these lands. They came to America seeking freedom and a better life. Over 2 million Jews arrived between about 1880 and 1924, when the U.S. Immigration Act of 1924 and National Origins Quota of 1924 all but ended immigration from Eastern Europe. Many settled in the New York metropolitan area, particularly the Lower East Side of Manhattan, establishing what became one of the world's major Jewish population centers.

Around 1900, newly arrived Jews began to build many synagogues and community associations. American Jewish leaders urged speedy integration into the wider American culture, which most Jews quickly accomplished. After World War II, in which almost half a million American Jewish men fought against Germany and Japan, younger Jewish families joined the

and messianic elements were muted. This is controversial among many observant Jews, but today there are hundreds of Kabbalah centers, conferences, books, and other sources of information about Kabbalah practice, almost all of them catering to non-Jews.

Read a 2008 newspaper article on controversy over the Kabbalah in British schools.

LO6 Judaism in North America Today

On a Friday night in Chicago, a Jewish family gathers in their home to welcome the Sabbath with a traditional ritual meal. As the sun is just about to set, the wife, assisted by her daughter, lights two Sabbath candles on the dining room table. It has been set for dinner, and on its white tablecloth are a wine cup and two loaves of challah (soft braided bread), covered with a special cloth. The father blesses each of his children and then recites a prayer of blessing over the wine, remembering how God rested on the seventh day of creation and hallowed the Sabbath day. Everyone around the table has a sip of the

American trend of settling in new suburbs. There they became increasingly assimilated as previous anti-Semitic discrimination began to lessen. For example, in the 1950s many leading American universities and colleges began to drop their quota systems that held Jewish enrollment to very small levels. Enrollment in Jewish religious schools doubled between 1945 and 1955, and synagogue affiliation jumped from only 20 percent of Jews in 1930 to 60 percent in 1960. Reform and Conservative congregations experienced the most rapid growth. In the 1970s and 1980s, waves of Jewish immigration from Russia largely joined the mainstream American Jewish community. However, most of these immigrants had been secularized by generations of Soviet Communist rule and anti-Semitic pressures.

Today, approximately 5.5 million of the world's 15 million Jews live in North America. Three major movements are found in North America: Reform, Conservative, and Orthodox. A fourth movement, the Reconstructionist movement, is more liberal than Reform and is substantially smaller than the other three. Orthodoxy has several different groups: the modern Orthodox, who have integrated into modern North American society while strictly keeping the Jewish law from the Talmud; Hasidic Jews, who live in their own, separate neighborhoods and dress distinctively; and the Yeshiva Orthodox. They all believe that God gave Moses the whole Torah at Mount Sinai, including both the "written Torah" that became the first five books of the Bible and the "oral Torah," an oral tradition interpreting the written Torah that became the basis of the Talmud. The Orthodox believe that the Torah contains 613 mitzvoth (commands), binding upon Jews but not upon non-Jews. A survey of American Jews in 2000 found that 10 percent identify themselves as Orthodox. The Orthodox tend to have large families and resist assimilation, so their overall numbers are growing.

Reform Judaism doesn't believe that the Torah is divinely written or inspired. It views the entire Bible as a record of Jewish religious experience.

The oldest synagogue in America, the Sephardic congregation in Touro, Rhode Island; the building dates to 1763.

DAVID KING

Reform Jews don't believe in observance of most traditional commandments, but they attempt to preserve much of what they consider the spiritual essentials of Judaism, along with some selected Jewish practices and culture. A recent survey found that 35 percent of American Jews identify themselves as Reform. Approximately nine hundred Reform synagogues are found in the United States and Canada.

Conservative Judaism grew out of the tension between Orthodoxy and Reform at the end of the 1800s, and its efforts to mediate between them is an American impulse. Conservative Judaism maintains that the truths found in Jewish scriptures and the Talmud come from God but were transmitted by humans and contain a human component. It generally accepts the binding nature of Jewish law but believes that law should change and adapt, absorbing aspects of the predominant culture while remaining true to Judaism's values. Because Conservative Judaism occupies the large middle ground between Orthodoxy and Reform, there's a great deal of variation among Conservative synagogues. This flexibility is deeply rooted in Conservative Judaism. Twenty-six percent of American Jews identify themselves as Conservative. There are approximately 750 Conservative synagogues in the world today, most of them in North America.

All told, the varieties of Judaism in North America all attempt, in their widely diverse ways, to continue the mission of God's chosen people to be a "light to the nations."

Hear a lighthearted take on American Jewish identity, "The Chanuka Song" by Adam Sandler.

Visit the website of Reform Judaism.

Visit the website of Conservative/ Masorti Judaism.

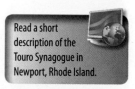

Read a short description of the Touro Synagogue in Newport, Rhode Island.

Read an editorial on the American Jewish debate about Israel.

CHAPTER 11

Encountering Christianity: The Way of Salvation in Jesus Christ

BONNIE VAN VOORST © CENGAGE LEARNING

Learning Outcomes

After studying this chapter, you will be able to do the following:

LO1 Explain the meaning of *Christianity* and related terms.

LO2 Trace how the main periods of Christianity's history have shaped its present.

LO3 Outline in your own words essential Christian teachings as found in the Nicene Creed.

LO4 Describe the main features of Christian ethics.

LO5 Summarize Christian worship and other rituals.

LO6 Explain the variety of Christianity in North America today.

© ISTOCKPHOTO.COM/HAZLAN ABDUL HAKIM

"I am the Way, the Truth, and the Life." —Jesus Christ, in the Gospel of John

BONNIE VAN VOORST © CENGAGE LEARNING

YOUR VISIT TO ST. PETER'S IN ROME

As a part of your visit to Italy, you spend a day in Vatican City, the world's smallest nation, which serves as the headquarters of the Roman Catholic Church. The center of Vatican City is St. Peter's Basilica. You've seen pictures of this building, and you've seen snippets of religious services there on television, so you're eager to see it for yourself.

Your tour guide gives you some advice the night before your visit: "You should expect the church to be full of visitors today, as it is almost every day. Not only is St. Peter's the center of the Roman Catholic faith, it's also a historical building and an important part of art history. Neither men nor women can wear anything that shows their shoulders, stomach, or any leg above the knees. There are guards at the church entrance, and they're experts at spotting the tricks that some people use to enter without appropriate clothing."

Stepping inside St. Peter's Basilica, the grandness of the church itself is stunning. Seeing it from the outside gives no indication of how large and impressive it really is. Like many of the world's most important religious sites, the grandeur of this place and what it means to believers—in this case Roman Catholic Christians—brings you a deep sense of respect. Many people pause after entering the front door to take it all in. On the right you see Michelangelo's life-size sculpture of Mary the mother of Jesus holding the body of her dead son in her arms after his crucifixion. So many people want to see it that it takes a few

minutes to work your way to the front of the group. It shows an artistic genius that can only be marveled at, but it also shows the profound Christian faith of Michelangelo.

The natural light coming from above illuminates the church and spreads a subdued radiance all around, especially under the dome. Looking up at the dome, you see the large Latin letters giving the words of Jesus in the Gospel of Matthew 16:18–19, which the Catholic Church has always considered the foundation of its organization: "You are Peter, and on this rock I will build my church. I will give you the keys of the kingdom of heaven."

After you go up to the outside of the dome to take in the magnificent view of Rome, you take a guided tour of the tomb of St. Peter, led by a priest from the Vatican archaeology office. It's a few stories below the main altar of the church, what in the first century C.E. was a cemetery on Vatican Hill, outside the city limits of Rome. You walk down an excavated street, past expensive mausoleums, toward the traditional grave of Peter. When you reach it, your guide shows pictures of what it used to look like—very simple, even humble. You realize that, for all the grandeur of the building above, the foundation of it all is the grave of a humble fisherman who was killed near this spot for his faith in Jesus Christ.

RANDY OHC

Front of St. Peter's Basilica, Rome

< Mosaic portrait in Hagia Sophia Church, Istanbul, Turkey, of Jesus Christ enthroned in heaven. His halo contains a cross, and the Greek lettering is an abbreviation of "Jesus Christ."

Explore St. Peter's Basilica by way of Google Earth™.

Watch an introduction to St. Peter's and other Roman churches.

Christianity is a monotheistic religion based on the first-century C.E. life, death, and resurrection of Jesus of Nazareth in Galilee. Christians believe that Jesus is the Son of God and the savior of the world, and his teaching shows how to live for God and others. Christianity began as a prophetic reform movement within Judaism, led by Jesus, in the first century C.E., but it quickly moved out into the wider world after Jesus' departure. It has been from the first a strongly missionary faith, eager to spread itself and make converts, and it has become the largest religion in the world. Geographically the most widely diffused of all faiths—the only religion to be found on all continents and in every nation, for example—it has about 2.2 billion adherents today. Christianity has been a major influence in the shaping of Western civilization, and since around 1500 it has increasingly shaped the rest of the world. Its three largest groups are the Roman Catholic Church (which is larger than the two other groups together), the Eastern Orthodox churches, and the Protestant churches. In your study of Christianity, you'll encounter these unique features:

- Christianity is centered on a person, Jesus Christ. But it is also strongly concerned with teaching and doctrine—more than Judaism and Islam, the other Abrahamic monotheisms, have typically been.

- Because Christianity is centered on Jesus, it takes seriously his teachings as recorded in the New Testament. But Christianity is also shaped by the church's later teaching about Jesus, which raises the question: What is the relationship of the teaching *of* Jesus to Christian teaching *about* Jesus?

- Christianity shares much with Judaism and Islam, but with some key differences. It teaches that the one God exists in three persons—the Father, the Son, and the Holy Spirit—a mystery and a paradox. However, modern scholars have located Christianity firmly among the monotheistic religions of the world.

- When seen from the outside, Christianity appears to be quite unified. However, when seen from the inside, it seems very diverse, even fragmented, with an estimated nine thousand different church groups. We'll discuss the variety of Christianity throughout this chapter, but especially in the last section, "Christianity in North America Today."

Christ Literally, "anointed one," or prophet

Christianity The religion based on Jesus Christ's life and teaching

LO1 Names

The name **Christ** originated in the ancient Greek word *Christos* (KRIHS-toss), literally "anointed one." This word is in turn the Greek equivalent of the Hebrew word *messiah* (meh-SIGH-uh), one anointed as a king or prophet. The earliest Christians came to believe that Jesus was the promised messiah who would bring God's blessings to Israel. When the church moved into the Greek-speaking world, the term *Christ* was attached to the personal name *Jesus* to produce the longer name by which he is known to Christians, *Jesus Christ*. It's a common misunderstanding that *Jesus* is his first name and *Christ* is something of a last name, but that's incorrect.

Christians was a name given by others, most likely as a derogatory term that can be paraphrased "those Christ people."

Christianity, the religion based on Jesus Christ's life and teaching, is built from *Christians*, those who belong to the religious movement based on Christ. As related by the first-century book of early church history, the Acts of the Apostles, the first Christians themselves had called their movement within Judaism "the Way," by which they probably meant the "Way of Jesus"; they called themselves "followers of the Way." *Christians* was a name given to them by others, most likely as a derogatory term that can be paraphrased "those Christ people." But they soon accepted *Christians* as accurate and meaningful. They transformed this put-down into an honorable name used by Christians in every time and place since then.

The term *Christendom* is sometimes used in connection with Christianity. Most often it refers today to those nations of the world in which Christianity is the recognized, predominant religion, whether it is the official religion of these nations or not. This term has now fallen into disuse, and in some circles even disfavor, so it will be seen mostly in older literature.

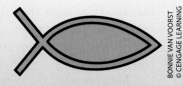

Symbols of Christianity

The fish was an early informal symbol of Christianity. It was connected to one of Jesus' miracles, multiplying bread and fish to feed a crowd. Later, the five letters in the Greek word for *fish*, transliterated into English as *ichthus* (ick-THOOS), became an acronym for "Jesus Christ, God's Son, Savior." The fish is still popular today as a symbol of Christianity, especially among Protestants; one can often see it in jewelry and on bumper stickers.

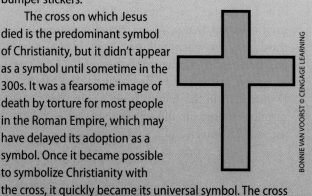

BONNIE VAN VOORST © CENGAGE LEARNING

The cross on which Jesus died is the predominant symbol of Christianity, but it didn't appear as a symbol until sometime in the 300s. It was a fearsome image of death by torture for most people in the Roman Empire, which may have delayed its adoption as a symbol. Once it became possible to symbolize Christianity with the cross, it quickly became its universal symbol. The cross

BONNIE VAN VOORST © CENGAGE LEARNING

symbolizes the whole of the faith, but it specifically represents Jesus' death, which most Christians have believed is the sacrificial basis of their salvation from sin. Many kinds of symbolic crosses have developed over time. Some have specific religious meaning, and others are culturally associated with certain groups—the Celtic cross in Irish Roman Catholic Christianity, for example, or the Russian cross for Orthodox Christianity there.

The simplest and most-common Christian cross is the Latin cross with its extended vertical beam. The empty Latin cross, usually favored by most Protestants, suggests the **resurrection** of the crucified Jesus, when his dead body was made eternally alive by the power of God. The **crucifix**, a Latin cross with a representation of the body of Jesus on it, favored by Catholic and Orthodox churches and a few Protestants, is a reminder of Christ's sacrifice. The Greek cross, with arms of equal length, is just as ancient as the Latin cross and is found particularly in Eastern Orthodox Christianity. The ritual action of making the sign of the cross on one's head and torso in prayer and formal worship is one of the most common ritual acts for a majority of Christians.

LO2 The Christian Present As Shaped by Its Past

In New York City, a college student who wants to train for the priesthood in the Orthodox Church in North America visits his bishop, the regional leader of this church, to inquire about education and expectations for ordination. After a pleasant conversation about his background and intent, the bishop offers the requirements. The student is surprised by the first and last items mentioned: grow a beard, finish college, and get married—preferably in that order. With these things accomplished, the student can enter a theological seminary (graduate school) to prepare more fully for the priesthood. As the student will soon learn as he travels toward becoming a priest, these expectations are a part of the ancient tradition for almost all Eastern Orthodox clergy.

Today's Christianity has been shaped by a long and significant history. Christianity is built on the foundation of Judaism and uses Jewish words and concepts, but over the first few centuries C.E. it became a separate religion and started drawing on Greek vocabulary to

express its more complex teachings. From Jesus' death and resurrection until today, his teachings have spread throughout the world. This section will tell the high points of this story and introduce the teachings, rituals, and diverse groups of Christianity along the way.

THE LIFE, DEATH, AND RESURRECTION OF JESUS CHRIST (CA. 4 B.C.E.–30 C.E.)

The primary sources for knowledge of Jesus are the four canonical **Gospels**—Matthew, Mark, Luke, and John—in the **New Testament**. A number of noncanonical sources written in the early 100s,

resurrection Dead body made eternally alive by the power of God

crucifix Latin cross with a representation of the body of Jesus on it

Gospel (GAHS-puhl) "Good news" of salvation, the Christian message; early Christian book telling the story of Jesus

New Testament The Christian scriptural canon consisting of twenty-seven documents

notably the Gospel of Thomas, contain a few stories about him and many more sayings attributed to him. The material about Jesus in ancient non-Christian sources, both Jewish and Roman, does not add substantially to our knowledge of Jesus.

The chronology of the life of Jesus is slightly uncertain in its details. Matthew places the birth of Jesus at least two years before Herod the Great's death late in 5 to 4 B.C.E. Luke connects Jesus' birth with a Roman census that probably occurred in 6 to 7 C.E. Most historians incline to Matthew's dating and place Jesus' birth around 4 B.C.E. The church, following the Gospel of John, usually supposes that Jesus had a public ministry of three years, but the other canonical Gospels may portray a one-year ministry. Jesus' death during the rule of Pontius Pilate, the Roman governor of Judaea from 26 to 36 C.E., is most often placed around the years 29 to 30.

Explore the PBS site "From Jesus to Christ."

Jesus' encounter with John the Baptizer, the fiery Jewish prophet who preached repentance and baptism in view of God's coming kingdom or kingly rule, marked the beginning of Jesus' career. Jesus taught in vivid *parables* (short stories about some aspect of life in the rule of God) and performed miraculous healings. He traveled through Galilee and became a popular prophetic figure. He gathered twelve male Jewish followers whom he called disciples, or "students"; the church later called them **apostles**, those "sent out" by Christ to be missionary leaders in the church. Women, both married and unmarried, were also a prominent part of his movement, highly unusual for the time. Jesus' attitude toward some aspects of the observance of Jewish law—especially as the strict law-keeping groups understood it—generated some conflict with groups such as the Pharisees. The Pharisees believed in strict Sabbath rest and not associating closely with "sinners" or with women not one's wife. The ruling Jewish authorities also began to suspect Jesus, but he probably didn't reach the attention of the Roman rulers.

Watch a clip from Jesus of Nazareth, *showing Jesus giving controversial teaching and healing in a synagogue.*

A triumphal entry to Jerusalem at Passover time was the prelude to a final crisis. After a last supper with his twelve closest disciples, he was betrayed by one of them, Judas Iscariot. Jesus was arrested by the Jewish temple authorities and tried by the Sanhedrin (Jewish council) and then by Pilate, who condemned

apostles Those "sent out" by Christ to be missionary leaders in the church

him to death by crucifixion, being nailed to a cross to die an agonizing death. Christians everywhere believe that three days after Jesus' death, God raised him from the dead to live eternally. The earliest church believed that sometime after the resurrection—the Gospels differ on the precise timing—the risen Jesus ascended to heaven, there to stay in power until his return at the end of time.

Jesus preached the imminent coming of God's kingdom (or full rule) to the earth and said that it has both a future and a present reality. His teachings and miracles pointed to and explained this kingdom. His disciples recognized him at some point in his ministry or shortly after it as the Messiah, although the Gospels indicate that Jesus did not often call himself that. He was mainly called "prophet" and "teacher." Jesus characteristically used the term *Son of Man* (though mysteriously in the third person) when talking about his own suffering and death, and at other times his role as God's agent of judgment at the end of time. This title is derived from Daniel 7:13 in the Jewish Bible, where "one like a son of man" represents the oppressed people of God, then ascends to heaven to be vindicated by God.

Jesus called social and religious outcastes to repentance and faith, healed their diseases, and restored them to membership in the people of Israel.

Jesus' teaching was critical of both Jewish and (implicitly) Greco-Roman society, saying that they fell far short of God's rule. Jesus encouraged the poor and oppressed, but rejected violent revolution. To Jesus, the social and religious outcastes of society (lepers, criminals, prostitutes, Jews who collected taxes for Rome, and others) were the special objects of God's love. He called them to repentance and faith, healed their diseases of mind and body, and restored them to membership in the people of Israel. Jesus taught that God desires the salvation (divine forgiveness leading to restored relationship with God and the people of God) of the marginalized more than the righteousness of those who constantly obey God, a teaching that has proved a continual challenge for the church. Jesus' embrace of outsiders also seems to have included the Samaritans, whom most other Jews regarded as terrible people. (We'll consider Jesus' teaching more fully later, in "Christian Ethics.")

Modern scholarship has delved fully into the Gospel accounts. Christianity has attracted a good deal of scholarly analysis by a variety of academic methods, and scholars have made research into the historical Jesus the largest single enterprise in religious scholarship. What scholars call "the quest for the historical Jesus" has been going strong for more than two centuries and shows no sign of lessening. In general, scholars agree on the main lines of Jesus' life and teaching. They are divided over other issues:

- *Did Jesus intend to found a church?* Jesus gathered a community of followers around himself. This community continued after his time, regarding itself as the special gathering of God's people. But many scholars doubt that Jesus intended to begin the organization that was later called the "church," with its formal organization.

- *Did Jesus intend his gospel to be addressed to Jews only?* In the Gospels, Gentiles (the Jewish term for non-Jews) appear only occasionally, but often in a positive light. Jesus' choice of twelve Jewish men as his closest disciples is an indication that his movement was mainly an inner-Jewish thing. Because welcoming Gentiles into the church caused such intense debate less than ten years after Jesus' departure, it's clear that Jesus didn't speak about this matter.

- *How did Jesus understand his relation to the coming of the kingdom of God?* Scholars disagree about whether Jesus merely proclaimed the kingdom/rule of God, whether he embodied it, or something in between. To what extent did the events of his life, death, and resurrection make the kingdom/rule of God a reality for his followers?

THE EARLIEST CHURCH (30 C.E.–100 C.E.)

The earliest church in Jerusalem was initially composed of those Jews who had followed Jesus during his ministry, perhaps one hundred people in all. They saw

Pilgrims at the Stone of Unction, the place where tradition says the body of Jesus was washed before his burial, in the Church of the Holy Sepulcher (tomb) in Jerusalem

themselves as a continuing reform movement within Judaism. In a few days after Jesus' departure from earth, the early church experienced on the Jewish feast of Pentecost an outpouring of the Spirit of God to empower it for its continued ministry.

Paul is criticized today by some Christians for his socially conservative statements, but in his own time he was criticized for being too liberal.

"Garden Tomb" in Jerusalem, a favorite location believed by some Protestants to be the tomb of Jesus

UPYERNOZ

Saul—or as he was known after his conversion, Paul—was a Pharisee who zealously and violently persecuted the earliest church. Born at Tarsus (TAR-suhs) in southern Asia Minor (present-day Turkey), he had come to Jerusalem as a student of the famous Rabbi Gamaliel and had tried to suppress a Christian group called by Luke the "Hellenists," who were led by Stephen, the first Christian to be killed for the faith. While on the road to Damascus to persecute the followers of Jesus, Paul was suddenly, dramatically converted to faith in Christ. In this conversion, or soon afterward, he came to a conviction that the Gospel must be spread among the Gentiles without a requirement that they become Jews as well. Paul was a controversial figure throughout his career. Although he is criticized today by some for his conservative statements about women and slaves, in his own time he was criticized for being far too inclusivist, even liberal. He gained recognition in the Jerusalem church for Gentile converts. He saw clearly that the universal mission of the church to all humanity, implicit in the coming of Christ, meant a radical break with many of the rabbinical traditions in which he had previously lived. Paul worked tirelessly as a missionary, founded dozens of churches in strategically located cities, and became known as "the Apostle to the Gentiles."

Because of the preservation of several of his letters to his churches, we know a good deal about Paul. He didn't write so much about Jesus' earthly life and teaching, but made the death and resurrection of Jesus the center of his proclamation. The crucifixion of Jesus was the supreme redemptive act, a self-sacrifice for the sin of humankind. Salvation is a gift of grace, and in baptism the Holy Spirit comes to transform the new Christian. Paul linked this doctrine of **justification** with his strong view that the Gospel brings liberation from the Mosaic Law, especially for Gentiles. Justification brings freedom, not from parts of the Mosaic Law such as the Ten Commandments as a whole, but from parts that particularly mark Jewish identity—for example, keeping Jewish food regulations, observing the last day of the week for mandatory rest, and especially by being circumcised. This created difficulties at Jerusalem, where many followers of Jesus wanted to see the heritage of Judaism continued. Once this struggle was settled, the radical character of

justification Salvation as being made right with God, for Paul a gift of God

Paul's doctrine of justification began to be forgotten in the church, where salvation became a matter of both faith and obedience to God's law.

See an introduction to Paul produced by travel expert Rick Steves.

All the Gospels record a special commission of Jesus to Peter as the leader among the twelve disciples, but Peter's life can only be partially reconstructed. He was a key leader in the earliest Jerusalem church until James, a close relative of Jesus, became its leader. We know from Paul's letters that Peter did missionary work in the Gentile world. Two letters in the New Testament bear his name, but many scholars are doubtful about their authorship by Peter, especially the second letter. According to early tradition, Peter died in Nero's persecution in 64 C.E., probably at the same time when Paul was killed. Later traditions say that he was crucified, at his request, upside down, because he wasn't worthy to die the same way that Jesus did. Peter was probably buried in a cemetery on the Vatican Hill across the Tiber River in the outskirts of Rome; later, Constantine would build a large church on the site, a church that was replaced by the present St. Peter's Basilica. Rome had gotten the bones of Peter and Paul, which helped to ensure its leading role in the Western church.

THE ANCIENT PERIOD (100–500 C.E.)

Although Christian tradition focuses on Peter and Paul, it is certain that many other missionaries also contributed to the growth of Christianity by planting churches. Some churches, most prominently that at Rome, seem to have begun without any formal mission effort. By 100 C.E., Christianity had established itself in every large and mid-sized city in the eastern half of the Roman Empire (see Map 11.1). In the next two centuries, Christian churches were founded throughout the whole Roman Empire and even beyond it. These were all *house churches*, groups of Christians who met in private homes ("church" here refers an association of people, not a building). Ancient Christianity experienced rapid growth for a variety of reasons:

● The struggle over whether to allow Gentiles to join the church without converting to Judaism was quickly settled for most members of the earliest churches.

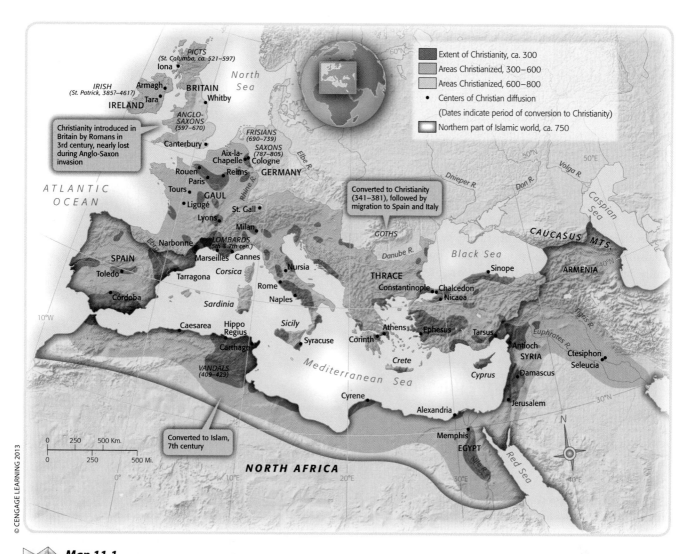

Map 11.1

The Spread of Christianity to about 800 C.E.

Christianity arose in Palestine in the first century C.E. and gradually gained footholds in parts of western Asia, North Africa, and southern Europe by 300 C.E. Over the next five centuries, Christianity became the dominant religion in much of Western and Central Europe, and expanded its influence in western Asia and North Africa. By about 750, Islam had conquered much of the Middle East and all of North Africa and Spain, and Christian populations in most of these areas were reduced.

- Much of church life was dedicated to making converts and assimilating them into the close-knit social structure of the Christian community.

- Christianity offered things that many people in the ancient world were seeking: a meaning for life and purpose for living greater than what Roman religion and philosophy could provide, happiness in this world, the promise of eternal life, a higher religious standing for women and slaves, and a loving social-support network.

- Unlike other religions in the Roman world, Christianity made a broad appeal to people of all ethnicities, classes, and genders, which gave it a wide field for conversion and growth.

As Christianity spread among Gentiles, it continued to grow out of its early status as a Jewish group. By the end of the first century, many Jewish leaders began to decree that Jews confessing Jesus to be Messiah should be expelled from synagogues. As Christians began to outnumber Jews in some cities, Christian pressure on Jews began, only to increase

Take a tour of the oldest house-church in the world, in Dura-Europos, Syria.

in 313 when the state persecution of Christianity ended. Thus began a bitter legacy of Christian **anti-Semitism**, prejudice against the Jewish people that has haunted the Western world through our own time. Christianity did not invent anti-Semitism—it was hundreds of years old by the time Christianity was born—but it added its own twist to it. The church understood itself, and was understood by most Jews, to be Gentile. By around 400 C.E., historians generally agree today, the separation between Judaism and Christianity was complete. Judaism and Christianity are sister faiths, but like most family feuds, their conflict has been intense and sad. However, Christianity remains built on the foundation of Judaism. They share much of the same Bible, monotheism, a moral code, and similar patterns of worship.

> *Judaism and Christianity are sister faiths, but like most family feuds, their ongoing conflict has been intense and sad.*

As Christianity grew, it also challenged the Roman Empire. During the first century, this challenge was muted. But at the end of the first century, with the outbreak of imperial persecutions of Christians, Christianity challenged the legitimacy of the empire and the Roman religious ideology with which it was allied. Christians believed—and acted on the belief—that Jesus, not Caesar, is the Lord of this world. This led to even more Roman persecutions and the **martyrdom** of Christians. Persecution was sporadic but often fierce, especially in the late 200s, in an effort at times to kill off all Christians. Romans also countered Christianity in an informal, popular way by charging that Christians practiced secret cannibalism, were sexually immoral, and were intolerant of others, among other claims. However, Roman persecution didn't stem the rise of

anti-Semitism
Prejudice against the Jewish people

martyrdom Death of Christians for the faith, especially as an act of witness to others

heresy The church's characterization of organized internal opposition

Gnosticism Religious movement that believed this world is evil because it is material

Graffito of a Christian youth in Rome saluting a crucified figure with a human body and an ass's head. The Greek inscription reads, "Alexamenos worships God." This anti-Christian drawing from about 200 C.E. may be the earliest depiction of the crucifixion of Jesus.

Christianity. As one church leader at this time remarked, "The blood of the martyrs is the seed of the church."

Read Celsus's comments on the person of Jesus.

> *Some groups in the church were labeled "heretical" because they were too doctrinally conservative and morally rigorous—almost too "Christian" for other Christians.*

The church was also challenged from within by **heresy**, the church's characterization of organized internal opposition. Like most new religions, it took time for diversity to arise and become controversial. Some alternative churches arose in the second century, and in some areas they outnumbered what was becoming mainstream Christianity. The movement known as **Gnosticism** or Gnostic Christianity believed that this material world is evil and hostile to the good. As Christianity defined itself in the second century against Judaism, Roman imperial religion, Gnosticism, and other movements, **orthodoxy** gradually arose, with its emphasis on correct teaching of the essentials of the faith and (to a lesser extent) correct moral practice. This effort to achieve and preserve correct teaching has characterized much of Christianity ever since. Gnosticism and other dissenting groups within ancient Christianity used to be viewed and studied as corruptions of divine truths, but today historians study them more objectively as alternative forms of Christianity. Some "heretics" were given this label because they were more doctrinally conservative and morally rigorous than the mainstream church—almost too "Christian" for other Christians. The most able opponent of heresy was Irenaeus, the second-century bishop of Lyon, in modern-day France. Irenaeus defined heresy as a significant departure from the Bible and the rule of faith, a move away from the center of the faith in Jesus Christ.

Read a selection of Irenaeus' attack on Gnosticism.

Emperor Constantine's toleration of Christianity in 312 ushered in a new era in the faith, one that many historians view as lasting until the twentieth century. This era featured the close association of church and state, often called **Constantinianism.** Constantine and later emperors saw religious unity and peace as important for their rule; there was one God, one Church, and one Emperor. By moving his capital to Constantinople in northern Asia Minor, Emperor Constantine created a new culture that attempted to preserve the best of ancient Greece and Rome and yet transform it through the

The head of a statue of Constantine, more than four feet tall, suggests his importance in Roman history.

© ISTOCKPHOTO.COM/PIXELBARON

Nun in traditional clothing, praying the rosary

© ISTOCKPHOTO.COM/RAPIDEYE

Christian faith. The Eastern Orthodox branch of Christianity, and the many nations it has shaped, is the continuation of this effort.

Finally, this period saw the beginnings of Christian **monasticism** in the 200s. It was modeled on scriptural examples and ideals, including the life of Jesus, but monasticism isn't mentioned in the Bible or based on a direct Jewish precedent. Those living the monastic life are known by the generic terms *monks* and *nuns*. Monks began by living alone, at first in the Egyptian desert. As more people took on the lives of monks, they started to come together and form communities, usually living by the threefold vow of poverty, chastity, and obedience. When the great persecutions ceased with Constantine, the rigorous self-denials of monasticism, such as celibacy (no sexual activity), were seen as a substitute for martyrdom. Monastics generally dwell in a monastery (monks) or a convent (nuns). Monks became the bearers of civilization in the Western church. They preserved the Christian Bible and the literary and some of the scientific heritage of Rome, which would have perished for lack of manuscript copying and study. Unlike the first Christian monks, they worked in their monasteries and convents as a part of their monastic calling to support themselves. By the Middle Ages, many Catholic monasteries enjoyed vast properties, wealth, and social power.

Explore Christianity in late antiquity.

orthodoxy Emphasis on correct teaching of the essentials of the faith and (to a lesser extent) moral practice

Constantinianism (CON-stan-TIN-ee-uhn-iz-uhm) Close association of church and state, named after Constantine, for the promotion of religious and civil unity

monasticism Christian monks and nuns living in community

BYZANTINE, MEDIEVAL, AND RENAISSANCE CHRISTIANITY (500–1500)

The Eastern Roman Empire, also called the Byzantine Empire, with its capital of Constantinople, lasted for more than a thousand years from its creation by Constantine in 330 to the Turkish Muslim conquest in 1453. The traditional power of Byzantine emperors over the church was curtailed after the **Iconoclastic Controversy** that began in 726. This controversy was caused by the attempt of some emperors to remove the two-dimensional pictures of Jesus and the saints from churches, ending the veneration of these *icons* during worship. The emperors' iconoclasm was in part an effort to cope with Islam's attack on Christianity for what it called idolatrous use of images. In both Eastern Orthodox and Roman Catholic Christianity, worship is offered only to God, with veneration for the saints. Muslims did not agree with this distinction. Leading monks and several empresses resisted the emperors and their allies in the church, and icons were eventually restored. The controversy over images cemented their place as an essential element of the Eastern Orthodox identity. Today, every Orthodox church has an **iconostasis**, a screen or wall of icons, between the people and the altar. To the Orthodox, icons represent the reality of God's presence in the person of Jesus Christ and the importance for the church of the saints in heaven. When the controversy ended in 843, the power of the church to direct its own doctrine and worship was strengthened. The controversy also strengthened the tendency of Eastern Orthodoxy to define itself by its worship and devotion rather than, as in Western Christianity (both Roman Catholicism and the Protestantism to arise later), by institution and doctrine.

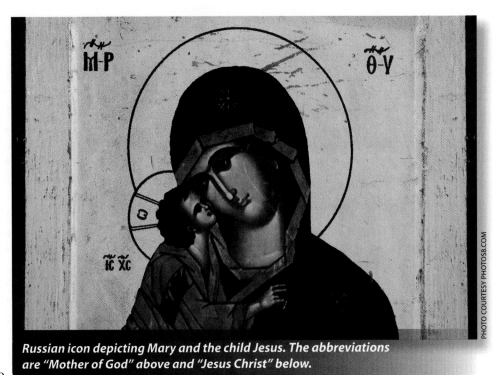

Russian icon depicting Mary and the child Jesus. The abbreviations are "Mother of God" above and "Jesus Christ" below.

> *Eastern Orthodox missionaries preserved indigenous cultures to a degree that Roman Catholic missionaries didn't.*

Byzantine Christianity also carried out missionary activity, especially to its north. The peoples of what are now Bulgaria, Russia, and Moravia were converted to Christianity in the 800s, Hungary in the 900s, and Poland in the 900s to the 1100s. Orthodox missions tried to preserve indigenous cultures. Missionaries translated the Bible and the rituals of the church into the language of the peoples. In the Catholic West, Latin was the main language of the church and the only language of the Bible. Slavic Orthodoxy, particularly in Russia, which thought of itself as "the third Rome," was to carry on the Christian heritage of Byzantium when the eastern Roman Empire finally fell to Muslim forces in 1453.

In the Latin West, the bishop of Rome, the **pope**, set the tone for the continuing development of Christianity. By the end of the ancient period of Christianity, the popes had already asserted their leadership over much

---

Iconoclastic Controversy (eye-con-oh-CLASS-tick) Struggle in Eastern Orthodoxy over removing pictures of Jesus and the saints from churches

iconostasis (eye-con-oh-STAH-sis) Screen or wall of icons at the front of Eastern Orthodox churches, between the people and the altar

pope Bishop of Rome, the head of the Roman Catholic Church

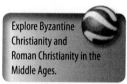

WWW.KREMLIN.RU.

The 2008 inauguration of Dmitry Medvedev (in background with his wife) as president of Russia included a ceremony at a Russian Orthodox Church.

of Christianity. When the western Roman Empire fell in the fifth century, the pope came to be the main embodiment of faith and cultural unity for Western Europe. Over time the pope extended his spiritual and even political power over many of the European states. Gradually, the influence of Rome spread across the entire western half of the European continent. At the same time, the Western church's relations with the Eastern Orthodox churches worsened, until the two formally split in 1054 over doctrinal, cultural, and political issues. This division still endures today. Many Christians suppose that the Catholic-Protestant split in Western Christianity is the most problematic, but the split between East and West is earlier and in many ways more difficult to overcome.

Read about the reasons why the East and West split.

Medieval Christianity in the West expressed itself not only through the pope, bishop, and priest, but also through the monk and friar. Medieval reformers within the Catholic Church, such as Bernard of Clairvaux and Pope Gregory VII, were **friars** (members of the new monastic orders that arose in the twelfth century, as opposed to the monks in the older monastic orders). Most of the theologians who systematized and developed Christian doctrine in the high Middle Ages, such as Anselm of Canterbury, England, and Thomas Aquinas (ah-QUIGH-nahs), were monastics. In his major work from 1265 to 1273, Aquinas made a comprehensive overview of Christian theology from the vantage point of the ancient Greek philosopher Aristotle's newly rediscovered thinking and became the most influential theologian in Roman Catholicism from that point on. Some of the new movements preached the Gospel to the people in churches and outdoors. Through this reform,

the life of the whole Catholic Church was enriched and renewed. Another feature of the later Middle Ages was the building of cathedrals, usually one in each large city throughout Europe, in the new Gothic style that seemed to soar to heaven.

Both Eastern and Western Christianity were forced during this period to come to grips with the rising power of Islam. From its beginning in 622, Islam spread rapidly in the Middle East (see pages 295–299). Soon, almost all the Middle East and North Africa was Islamic. Christian minorities lived somewhat peaceably under Islamic rule, protected by Islamic law, but they dwindled in number. Islam continued to press on the Byzantine Empire until, in 1453, Constantinople itself became a Muslim city and its cathedral, the Church of Holy Wisdom (Greek: *Hagia Sophia*), became a mosque. The main confrontation of Western Christianity with Islam was to be in the long period of the Crusades (1095–1350), when Christian forces from all over Europe retook Palestine from the Muslims, an effort that eventually failed and damaged Muslim-Christian relations through today.

Explore Byzantine Christianity and Roman Christianity in the Middle Ages.

At the end of the Middle Ages, beginning around 1400, life in Western Christianity began to be renewed in the Renaissance, the "rebirth" of classical Greco-Roman cultural ideals in art, architecture, philosophy, and literature. Some Renaissance scholars called the church back "to the foundations" in the New Testament and the ancient church. The Renaissance examined received institutions and teachings, not trusting in tradition for tradition's sake or authority for authority's sake, as had largely been the case in the Middle Ages. It promoted a more human-centered view of life—usually a Christian humanism, but sometimes not—in place of the medieval heaven-centered view. Renaissance art, for example, more realistically portrayed saints and ordinary people on earth. The Christian humanism of Desiderius Erasmus (DEH-sih-DAIR-ee-uhs er-ASS-muhs) of Rotterdam (1466–1536), the leading figure of the Northern Renaissance, prodded the church (both Protestant and Catholic) into self-examination and eventual reform. But not every

friar Member of the new monastic orders that arose in the twelfth century, as opposed to the monks in the older monastic orders

aspect of the Renaissance would prove to be positive. For example, it hastened the rise of nationalism and ended the medieval Catholic ideal of a Europe united by a common faith.

REFORMATION IN THE WESTERN CHURCH (1500–1600)

Movements for the reform of church teaching and practice were prevalent in the later Middle Ages. This reform usually expressed itself *through* the other traditional structures of the Catholic Church. Where occasionally reform expressed itself *outside of* or even *against* the Catholic Church, as for example in the cases of John Wycliffe (WIHK-liff; 1329–1384) and his movement in England and John Hus (1373–1415) in Bohemia, it was declared heretical and stamped out by force.

The **Magisterial Reformation**, or mainstream reform, began with Martin Luther (LOO-thur). He led an effective reform movement against the structure of the traditional church. Luther (1483–1546) was an Augustinian friar, a priest, and a professor at Wittenberg University in east-central Germany. Like all would-be reformers before him, Luther initially saw himself as a loyal son of the Church. In 1517, he called for a public debate over reform issues by posting his Ninety-Five Theses (propositions) on the door of the castle church in Wittenberg. The immediate complaint Luther had was the selling of indulgences, certificates securing the forgiveness of punishment in the next world, to raise funds for the present St. Peter's Basilica in Rome. He found the idea of buying and selling salvation unbiblical, corrupt, and even ludicrous.

Luther soon found himself so at odds with the Roman Catholic Church that he moved to create an alternative church that he called the Evangelical (characterized by the Gospel of Christ) Church; after his death, others began to call it the Lutheran Church. Popes, bishops, monks, and nuns were done away with in this church. He envisioned Germany, and probably other nations as well, as having its own more indigenous forms of Christianity. He translated the Bible into German, put hymns and worship into the language of the people, and reformed the Mass. Evangelical

Magisterial Reformation
Mainstream Protestant reform that began with Martin Luther

Radical Reformation
Branch of the Protestant Reformation that wanted radical reforms to restore "New Testament Christianity"

Christians were urged to receive Holy Communion every week, in contrast to the once-a-year Catholic practice in the Middle Ages. Luther and his followers moved to put the Gospel, the essential religious message of Jesus Christ, at the center of Christianity. Luther saw the center of the Gospel in the doctrine of salvation by faith alone. He also stressed the central role of God's love and grace; the sole authority of the Bible over the Church; and the role of the individual Christian's conscience. Over time, faith took precedence over moral activity in Protestantism and still has precedence today. Reformers devalued the role of the saints and their power to intercede with God for Christians on earth. When Luther and his movement were protected and then promoted by the rulers of several German states, Protestantism gained a foothold that would enable it to endure and spread to other parts of Germany. By 1600, the Lutheran reform had taken over much of Germany and all of Scandinavia (see Map 11.2).

Watch a preview of the 2003 film *Luther.*

What historians call the **Radical Reformation** arose in tandem with the Magisterial Reformation, during the 1520s in Zurich, Switzerland. Conrad Grebel (GRAY-buhl) and the Swiss Brethren movement insisted that the mainstream reform of Luther

Martin Luther

1483–1983 USA 20c

© MARKAUMARK/SHUTTERSTOCK.COM

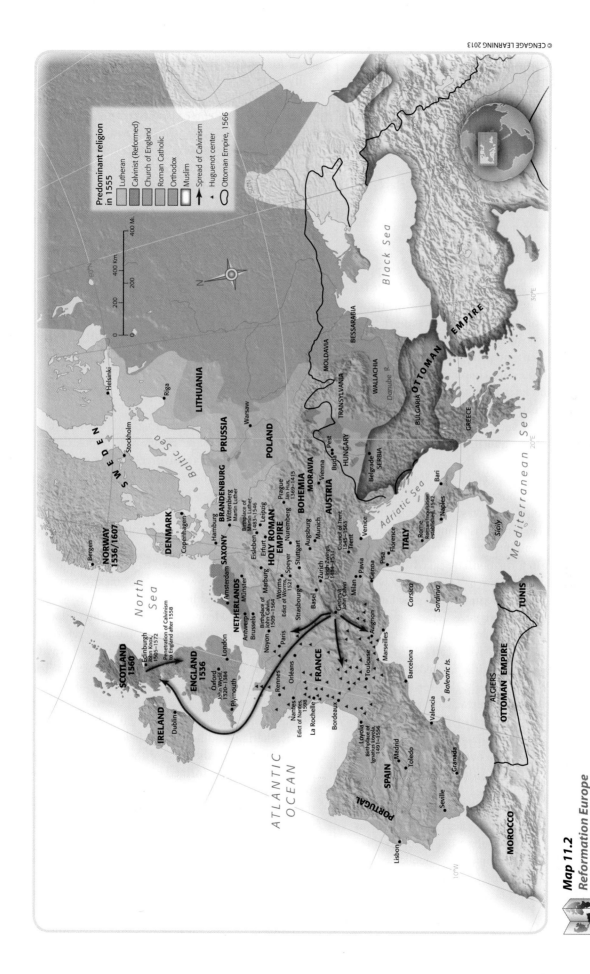

© CENGAGE LEARNING 2013

Predominant religion in 1555
- Lutheran
- Calvinist (Reformed)
- Church of England
- Roman Catholic
- Orthodox
- Muslim
- → Spread of Calvinism
- ▲ Huguenot center
- ◯ Ottoman Empire, 1566

Map 11.2
Reformation Europe

The Protestant Reformation reshaped Europe's religious landscape in the 1500s and early 1600s. By the mid-1550s, some form of Protestantism had become dominant in much of northern Europe, England, and Scotland. Catholicism remained predominant in the southern half of western Europe and parts of eastern Europe. Catholic lands in eastern Europe felt pressure from the Islamic Ottoman Empire.

and others was inconsistent and halfhearted. They argued for what they saw as pure "New Testament Christianity," including:

- Baptism of adult believers only, after a conversion experience
- Complete separation of the church from the civil government
- Pacifism, with refusal to be drafted for warfare
- Common ownership of some property
- Strict church enforcement of Christian morality among church members

They soon became known as **Anabaptists**, "rebaptizers," but over time the name was simplified to *Baptists*. In the 1520s, the movement spread through Switzerland and later found a home in many Protestant lands. Eventually, the Baptists became the most widespread Protestant church, even spreading to lands such as Russia, where other Protestant churches could not penetrate. Anabaptists and later Baptists kept their leading emphasis on the baptism of believing adults only, but other Anabaptist groups such as the Mennonites and Amish preserved pacifism and detachment from civil authority until today.

The Reformed (Calvinist) branch of Protestantism was, like the Anabaptists, born in the political world of the Swiss city-republics. (All Protestant churches were "reformed" from Roman Catholicism, and the movement is called the Reformation, but the churches born of the Calvinist branch of the Reformation have called themselves in particular the "Reformed Church.") Huldreich Zwingli (HUHLD-righk TSVING-lee) began the Reformed movement in Zurich, but in the next three decades it shifted to Berne, Basel, and especially French-speaking Geneva. There, the Frenchman John Calvin (1509–1564), who had studied law and theology at the University of Paris, reformed the city to Protestant ideals. He stressed (in addition to Luther's main ideas) such teachings as the sovereignty of God over all life and human responsibility to live out one's Christian calling in everyday life. Calvin carried out social reforms that became common in the Western world, such as levying a tax to support free compulsory public education for all children. Geneva became a haven for persecuted Protestants from many places in Europe.

Like Luther, Calvin wrote prolifically, and soon his ideas for reform spread widely. He was known especially as a systematizer and promoter of Protestant Christianity. His book *The Institutes [Foundations] of the Christian Religion* soon became the most influential book of Protestantism. Calvin's influence in the Reformed movement was so great that it also became known in later centuries as *Calvinism*. Calvinist churches were found by the end of the century not only in Switzerland, but also in France (where Calvinists were called Huguenots [HYOO-guh-nots]), the Netherlands, Germany, Hungary, and Scotland.

> **The name *Puritan* has come to mean "killjoy" or even "self-righteous," but Puritanism wasn't like this.**

Reformation came to England by way of politics. In the 1520s, King Henry VIII opposed the pope over the king's right to divorce and remarry. In 1529, Henry began forming a Church of England under his control, which was to become a "middle way" between Catholics and Protestants, especially in worship and organization. Its doctrine eventually was closer to the teaching of the Reformers than to that of Rome. Henry's daughter Mary tried to bring England back to the Roman Church by a variety of means, some so violent that they earned her the name "Bloody Mary," but by the reign of Henry's younger daughter Elizabeth I, one of the most important monarchs ever to sit on the English throne, the Church of England was firmly established. English monarchs were made the head of the Church of England and "Defender of the Faith," which explains why in 2011 the wedding of Prince William (the presumptive eventual heir to the throne) and Katherine Middleton was held in formal Anglican style, officiated by the head of the Anglican Church.

In 1620, the Reformed movement came to America via the English Protestants called **Puritans**, because they wanted to purify the Church of England from its continuing Roman Catholic elements. The name *Puritan* has come to mean "killjoy" or even "self-righteous," but Puritanism wasn't like this. Of all religious groups, the Puritans were to have the largest influence on the development of American government. As David Hall says in his 2011 book, *A Reforming People*, Puritanism was the most daring and successful reform

Anabaptists
"Rebaptizers," members of the Radical Reformation group that accepted only adult baptism

Puritans English Protestants who wanted to purify the Church of England from its continuing Roman Catholic elements

movement in the English-speaking world during early modern times.[1]

The **Catholic Reform** was in the past called the Counter-Reformation, and that term is still used by some. When his initial measures against Protestants didn't prove effective, the pope finally called a council of bishops and theologians in 1545 at Trent, Italy, to consider church reform. Widespread reforms

Spanish mission in Santa Barbara, California. Today, an active parish church meets in its chapel (right), and the mission is one of the largest tourist attractions in Santa Barbara.

© ISTOCKPHOTO.COM/SANTA BARBARA MISSION

of Catholic Church life emerged from Trent, and many of the more-glaring abuses were removed. With the help of the new Jesuit order, these reforms were carried out in nations and regions that were still predominantly Roman Catholic. Even there the reforms of Trent were subject to national policy; for example, France rejected them as too conservative and intrusive, and Spain—which often viewed itself as more Catholic than the pope—resisted them as too liberal. For areas that had already become mostly Protestant, about half of Europe above the Alps, the reforms of Trent were "too little, too late." Once nations became Protestant, they didn't return to Rome. Other parts of the Catholic Reformation were a revival of mysticism, especially in Spain, and a new focus on the system of Thomas Aquinas as a mighty fortress against Protestant thought. In all, the Roman Church emerged from the 1500s severely chastened in numbers and political influence, but strengthened in spirit.

Meanwhile, events in the New World were proving a bright spot in the fortunes of Roman Catholicism. When Spain and later Portugal explored and then colonized the New World in the Western Hemisphere, Roman Catholic missionaries accompanied them. They conquered

Take a virtual tour of the Santa Barbara mission.

See a preview of the Hollywood film *The Mission.*

[1] David D. Hall, *A Reforming People: Puritanism and the Transformation of Public Life in New England* (New York: Knopf, 2011).

together "for God and for gold." The indigenous peoples of Central and South America were quickly brought into the Christian faith. Spanish cultural, military, and religious outposts called *missions* were constructed; then thousands of churches were built for the indigenous peoples; and eventually monasteries and nunneries were established for them. A few priests and bishops protested the high cost of colonization to the indigenous peoples, even founding a "Jesuit state" in what is now Peru (a story told in the acclaimed 1985 film *The Mission*), but to no avail. Although the Roman Church lost many lands in Europe in the 1500s, it gained much in the Americas, where Roman Catholicism is still strong.

THE EARLY MODERN PERIOD (1600–1900)

Because of the settled and more tolerant situation after the "wars of religion" ended around 1648, each Protestant church and the Roman Catholic Church occupied its own parts of Europe, and Protestant teachings were articulated more fully. *Confessionalism,* named for the doctrinal statements called "confessions" issued by the various Reformation churches, brought a drive for doctrinal correctness as the most important aspect of church life. *Scholasticism* stressed the rational explanation and defense of the various Protestant belief systems.

The reaction against arid confessionalism and scholasticism wasn't slow in coming. When the several dimensions of religion that we saw in Chapter 1 are reduced to just a few, reaction will set in. **Pietism** arose in the last half of the seventeenth century, born with Philip Jakob Spener's (SPAY-ner) *Pious Considerations* in 1675. Spener rebelled against the Protestant

Catholic Reform
Movement that was in the past called the Counter-Reformation, spurred on by the 1545 Council of Trent

Pietism (PIGH-uh-tiz-um) Protestant movement stressing individual piety, in knowledge and emotion

orthodoxy of his day, which he viewed as sterile and lifeless. He proposed a continuing Reformation to bring the goals of Luther to fulfillment: personal Bible study, mutual correction and encouragement in Christian living, spiritual growth for all laity, and stress on emotional dimensions of faith. Pietists formed separate churches in many Lutheran and Reformed nations. The leadership of the Lutheran churches tried to suppress Pietism, but it soon became a major movement. Like Anabaptist churches before them, Pietism lead to *gathered churches*, not state churches to which all citizens belonged. English Puritanism also had its Pietist aspects, and the Methodist movement that emerged from the Church of England was Pietist as well. Even in the Roman Catholic Church, the Jansenist movement in France and then in North America promoted personal piety and holy living among the laity.

In the 1700s, Pietism took on the major goal of counteracting the influence on Christianity of the Enlightenment, the period of secularization of culture led by reason and not faith. The Enlightenment's rationalism and "free thinking" were easier for the church to deal with when they were aggressively atheistic, as in the French Revolution. But when the Enlightenment led to more-subtle changes in the church itself, such as the introduction of modern historical sciences and their application to the Bible and theology, the effect on Christianity was more profound. Especially in Protestant faculties of German universities, the acceptance of these new methods of scholarship led some to question the Christian faith. The concurrent discovery of other religions, especially the ancient religions of Asia, led to a questioning of the uniqueness and absoluteness of Christianity, a questioning that continues today. The Enlightenment's effort to separate church and state, and the ideas of religious toleration and the freedom associated with it, would succeed throughout Western and Northern Europe, but most fully in the United States. Constantinianism was rapidly losing ground.

The nineteenth century saw the challenge of secular reason continue. Historical scholarship, particularly the historical study of the Bible, continued to chip away at some of the old certainties of the Christian faith. Even more challenging to traditional belief were discoveries in natural science. The work of the evolutionary biologist Charles Darwin called into question the ancient Christian beliefs in the special creation of humanity in the image of God. Although Protestant churches were more directly and immediately affected by the Enlightenment and its heirs, which produced both secularism outside the church and doctrinal change inside, Roman Catholicism later saw its effects in the Catholic *Modernist* movement. Not until the twentieth century would Catholic, Protestant, and (to a lesser extent) Eastern Orthodox churches come to grips with the challenges of modern knowledge.

Despite these challenges, nineteenth-century Christianity was broadly optimistic about the prospects of the Christian religion. The largest cause for optimism was the powerful missionary movement that flourished in the 1800s and continues somewhat lessened today. Most of the churches of the West set out to evangelize the entire world, or at least the large parts of it not yet exposed to the gospel. (The Orthodox churches didn't participate significantly in this missionary movement.) In 1800, fewer than one in four people in the world were Christian; by 1900, one in three were Christian. Although the missionary and the colonial/commercial agents marched together, as they had often done in the past, especially in the New World, the nineteenth century saw the beginning of their separation. Christianity finally became the global religion that "catholic" implies.

Read a selection from the 1898 *Women's Bible* by Elizabeth Cady Stanton, an influential early feminist.

Watch a preview of *Amazing Grace*, the story of Anglican evangelical William Wilberforce's attack on slavery in the British Empire.

MODERN CHRISTIANITY (1900–PRESENT)

The optimistic hope present in Western culture and the church at the end of the 1800s went largely unfulfilled. The new era was one of severe crisis and challenge. The carnage of World War I (1914–1918), the worldwide pandemic of influenza, and then global economic depression began the movement away from cultural optimism. Then the rise of aggressive, totalitarian regimes, first in Russia and then in Italy and Germany, led to the horrors of World War II (1939–1945), with its massive civilian casualties and the Holocaust. Even the end of the war brought with it the new uncertainties of nuclear weapons and the Cold War. All these events were to shake to its roots Christian optimism in much of Protestantism and in parts of Catholicism. The result for some was a loss of faith, but for most a rethinking of the essence of Christianity. In the United States, **fundamentalism** arose to oppose

fundamentalism
Movement in reaction to Protestant liberalism featuring strictly literal interpretation of the Bible and an insistence on the truth of certain "fundamental" Christian teachings

liberalization of church doctrine. Fundamentalism features a strictly literal interpretation of the Bible, an insistence on the truth of certain key Christian teachings (the "fundamentals" from which the movement takes its name), and an aggressive attitude toward Christian liberalism specifically and toward unbelief generally.

This impulse against liberalism in the 1900s was shared by others who were in no way fundamentalist. The Swiss theologian Karl Barth (bart), who was to become the most influential Christian theologian of the century, turned away from liberal, optimistic Protestantism to reassert the transcendent power of a faith that cannot be shaped by human culture. The movement that Barth (1886–1968) sparked came to be called "neoorthodoxy," a new assertion in modern times of traditional Christian theology, especially in its Protestant form. (It has no formal relationship with Eastern Orthodoxy, however.) After World War II, this movement came to the English-speaking world and had a direct effect on its theology and life, as it still has today. Liberal, progressive theology has continued in some parts of Protestantism, especially in the mainstream *denominations* (Protestant churches united in a single name and organization, such as the Episcopal Church or the United Methodist Church), although reduced in size and chastened in spirit from its heyday around 1900.

While the theological reassessment occurred, a movement for greater unity among the churches came into prominence. **Ecumenism**, a movement for greater understanding and cooperation among Christian churches, had been planted and nurtured in the mission fields of the various Protestant churches, where missionaries learned to minimize their denominational differences and cooperate together in the face of a non-Christian environment. In the twentieth century, the National Council of Churches in the United States and a World Council of Churches would be the institutional bearers of this movement. Ecumenism has changed how theologians conceptualize the faith, how the different Christian churches relate to each other, and how grassroots Christians live out their faith in worship and daily life. This spirit of ecumenism also affected the Eastern Orthodox churches throughout the world; they've participated fully in the ecumenical movement from the start.

Read the ecumenical agreement on Christian teaching between the Roman Catholic Church and the Lutheran churches.

> *Never before had any church changed itself so quickly and so deeply as the Roman Catholic Church did after Vatican II.*

At the same time, a new movement for reform was gathering in the Roman Catholic Church that would prove to be the most important Christian event of the twentieth century. Catholicism had been insulated from dealing with modern challenges (science, secularism, religious toleration, and so on) by its sheer size and its church structure. But when Pope John XXIII convened the Second Vatican Council from 1962 to 1966, fresh, strong winds of reform blew through the church. In Vatican II, the Catholic Church:

- Recognized the status and role of the laity as essential to the church.
- Reformed worship by putting masses in national languages and increasing lay participation.
- Moved the altar from the front wall of the church and had the priest face the people as the Mass was said.
- Opened ecumenical dialogue with

ecumenism (eh-KYOO-men-iz-uhm) Movement for greater understanding and cooperation among Christian churches

Assertive, even confrontational, efforts to spread the faith are typical of fundamentalism, as shown by this street preacher outside a football game at Michigan State University.

SARAWARE

Protestants and the Orthodox, affirming that they were in some way legitimate Christians.

- Affirmed for the first time religious liberty and toleration for all people.

- Took a new, more balanced view of non-Christian faiths.

Never before had any church changed itself so quickly and so deeply as the Roman Catholic Church did after Vatican II. Most Roman Catholics today don't remember the way the Church was before Vatican II, and it's hard for them to imagine a form of Catholic Church life that had existed since the Council of Trent in the 1500s.

Two liberation movements in North American Christianity have become increasingly important in the modern period. (We'll deal with the charismatic movement, the "Global South" phenomenon, and evangelicalism on pages 285–288.) First, *feminism* has stressed the full emancipation of women. It recognizes that the church by its teaching and practice has held women down and tried to make second-class Christians of them. Some feminists have urged rejection of Christianity, arguing that it is hopelessly patriarchal. Most feminists in Christianity take a more moderate approach, trying to recover the biblical roots of feminism, stressing the (admittedly few) women who have played significant roles in Christian tradition, and working toward full liberation of women within the various Christian churches. This latter approach is still the mainstream of Christian feminism, and it will continue to be a potent force for years to come, in culture in general and in the church specifically. As the movement progresses, it is loosening its European-North American orientation and will likely make more of an impact in the churches of Asia, Africa, and Latin America.

Read about the debate over women bishops in the Church of England.

Read a *New York Times Magazine* article on feminism in the American Protestant Church.

liberation theology
Movement that stresses the active Christian mission of delivering the oppressed from evil social structures and situations

Pope Benedict XVI, on a trip to Brazil in 2007
FABIO POZZEBOM/AGÊNCIA BRASIL

A second current movement is **liberation theology.** The heart of liberation theology is not theology but practice. This movement stresses the active Christian mission of delivering the oppressed from evil social structures and situations. Using a combination of Marxist social analysis and the Christian Gospel, this movement was born in Roman Catholic theological circles in Latin America. Some trace its roots all the way back to the "Jesuit state" in Peru, mentioned earlier on page 269. But it has spread widely and been applied to several different situations: women's liberation, black liberation, Hispanic liberation, and now gay liberation. The latter has been particularly problematic in mainline Protestant churches and in the worldwide Anglican communion, which many observers think may be breaking apart over it. (The African American civil rights movement in the 1950s and 1960s came before black liberation theology, but much of the Christian aspect of this continuing movement is now related to liberation theology.) These new applications of liberation theology are still powerful influences in much of world Christianity, especially in the West, but the original form of political-social liberation theology in South America is waning.

LO3 Christian Teachings as Reflected in the Nicene Creed

Christian believers in Seoul, South Korea, gather at the Yoido Full Gospel Church, at 1 million members the largest single Christian congregation in the world. This church, which belongs to the Assemblies of God denomination, has back-to-back services held from dawn to dusk to accommodate the numbers. Protestant Christianity—both mainstream and independent—has grown so strong in South Korea that the church has begun to send Korean missionaries to other parts of the world. The congregation's size is emblematic of the world-wide growth and power of Pentecostal, Holy Spirit-centered Christianity.

Christian teaching is founded on the doctrine of the **Trinity**, one God in three Persons, the Father, Son, and Holy Spirit. Christians believe that Jesus was the incarnation of the eternal Son of God. He suffered, died, was buried, and was resurrected from the dead to open heaven to those who believe in him. Jesus founded a community of his followers; after his bodily ascension to heaven, the church carried on the organized, human dimensions of Jesus' work by the power and direction of the Holy Spirit. Jesus rules and reigns with God the Father until he will return to defeat evil, judge all humans (living and dead), and grant eternal life to his followers.

The Nicene Creed, known by its revised form completed in 381, is the most influential of all Christian statements of belief. **Creeds** (from the Latin *credo*, "I believe") are formal statements of belief meant to be binding on the church. All Roman Catholic and Eastern Orthodox doctrine is formally rooted in creeds, as well as that of most churches originating in the Protestant Reformation. Even more-independent and fundamental Protestant denominations that reject the idea of creeds believe the doctrines taught in the Nicene Creed. Moreover, changes in Christian teaching in the history of the church are changes *from* the Nicene Creed. In what follows, we'll discuss Christian teaching in terms of this creed, under the main headings of Father, Son, and Holy Spirit. In this discussion, we'll also deal briefly with later Christian formulation and use of these teachings.

Trinity Christian teaching of one God in three equal persons, the Father, Son, and Holy Spirit

creed Formal statement of belief meant to be binding on the church

The Trinity Knot, of Celtic Christian origin, symbolizes the Father, Son, and Holy Spirit as one. The crown of thorns tied into it is a symbol of the suffering of Christ.

© ISTOCKPHOTO.COM/RICHARD SEARS

A Closer Look:

The Nicene-Constantinopolitan Creed, 381 C.E.

Several English versions of the Nicene-Constantinopolitan Creed have been used in the last fifty years or so. He is the "Ecumenical Version" of 1975, the form used by most Protestant churches and the Roman Catholic Church.

> We believe in one God, the Father, the Almighty maker of heaven and earth, of all that is, seen and unseen.
> We believe in one Lord, Jesus Christ, the only Son of God, eternally begotten of the Father,
> God from God, Light from Light, true God from true God, begotten, not made, of one Being with the Father.
> Through him all things were made.
> For us men and for our salvation
> he came down from heaven:
> by the power of the Holy Spirit
> he became incarnate from the Virgin Mary, and was made man.
> For our sake he was crucified under Pontius Pilate;
> he suffered death and was buried.

> On the third day he rose again in accordance with the Scriptures;
> he ascended into heaven and is seated at the right hand of the Father.
> He will come again in glory to judge the living and the dead, and his kingdom will have no end.
> We believe in the Holy Spirit, the Lord, the giver of Life, who proceeds from the Father and the Son.
> With the Father and the Son he is worshipped and glorified.
> He has spoken through the Prophets.
> We believe in one holy catholic and apostolic Church.
> We acknowledge one baptism for the forgiveness of sins.
> We look for the resurrection of the dead, and the life of the world to come. Amen.

GOD THE FATHER

Christianity's teaching about God the Father is unproblematic, and the Christian tradition has rarely had to debate it. Most of the first article of the Nicene Creed is drawn directly from Jewish belief about God that was settled long before Jesus. God is all powerful ("Almighty") in heaven and on earth. God is the creator ("maker") of heaven and earth, not only of "all things seen" on the earth, but also all things "unseen" to humans (in heaven). Nothing is outside of God's power. That God is the creator of all physical and spiritual reality—and that God would become human in Jesus—strongly implies that the world is a good, or at least a redeemable, place. Behind this teaching about God lie other key Jewish ideas. God is a living being, the "I am who I am" in Exodus 3:14, not a force or a principle. Christians believe that God the Father is a personal being just as fully as Jesus is a person. The decisive aspect of creation is that God fashioned humans in God's own image. This special position of humans in the creation makes them coworkers with God in the continuation and care of creation. The incarnation of God in the human being Jesus is the ultimate validation of the worth of human life.

What's new in the Christian teaching about God lies in the first thing the Nicene Creed says about God: that God is *the Father*. God was known metaphorically as a father to Israel in Judaism, but this wasn't a main understanding of God. In Christianity, God is first and foremost the Christian's *Father*, but this relationship derives from and is built on Jesus' special relationship to God. Jesus regularly calls God "Father," especially in the prayer that he taught his disciples, known variously as the "Our Father" or the "Lord's Prayer." Jesus used the Aramaic word *abba* (AH-bah) for God; it was usually employed by children for their earthly father and expresses childlike trust in, and intimacy with, one's father. This father-son relationship that Jesus had with God became a model for the relationship of Christians to God.

According to the account of Jesus' baptism, Jesus understood his sonship when a voice from heaven said: "This is my beloved Son, with whom I am well pleased" (Matthew 3:17). In the Gospel of John, this sonship constitutes the basis for the self-awareness of Jesus: "I and the Father are one" (John 10:30). Although scholars disagree on whether Jesus actually said things like this, Christians believe it is an authentic insight into who Jesus really is. In Jesus Christ, God the Father was revealed more fully to humans, and worked in and through Jesus for the salvation of the world. Some Christians today dislike the term *Father* for its apparent gender reference and its use of human fathers—who are often flawed and sometimes abusive—to explain God. However, the fact that Christian teaching understands the human relationship with God to be based on Jesus' relationship with God helps to ameliorate the weakness of this metaphor.

GOD THE SON

The fullest section of the Nicene Creed, as with most Christian statements of belief, is the center section that deals with Jesus Christ, the Son of God. Teachings about Jesus Christ go back to the faith experiences of the first disciples. The early church experienced and recognized the incarnated Son of God in the person of Jesus, although the Gospels are clear that his disciples didn't fully recognize this, much less spread this message on their own, until after Jesus' resurrection. Jesus is the crucified and exalted Lord, and the Son of God. He sits at the right hand of the Father and will return in glory to bring in the Father's rule. Jesus has become the center of belief and devotion for most Christians. However, as we saw above, Jesus is an enigmatic figure,

Piety toward the death of Jesus: kissing his hand wounded by crucifixion

and the church's teaching about him can't easily be reduced to a series of simple sentences.

From the beginning of the church, different interpretations of Jesus have existed, and it took several centuries for the church to fully articulate its understanding of Jesus. The author of the Gospel of Mark, for example, seems to understand Jesus as the man upon whom the Holy Spirit descends when he is baptized in the Jordan River and about whom the voice of God declares from the heavens, "You are my beloved son" (Mark 1:11). In Matthew and Luke, Jesus' special identity begins at his conception in the womb of the Virgin Mary. The teaching in Mark's Gospel, and to a lesser extent in Matthew and Luke, provided the foundation for one of two early schools of thought concerning the person of Christ.

Two "schools," or types of theology, dominated the ancient church's teaching on Jesus Christ. Approaches to that derived from the theological school of Antioch in Syria start from the humanity of Jesus and view his divinity as joined to him by God through the Holy Spirit. In other words, Jesus' status as God's Son is founded on his humanity. This view is common among many modern Christians—both Protestants and Roman Catholics—in the Western world, who stress Jesus' humanity while also affirming that God was in him in a special way. Another view, adopted by the school of Alexandria, is a leading theme of the Gospel of John. This Gospel regards Jesus Christ primarily as the eternal Son of God become human. Here, his divinity is first and foundational, and the humanity of Jesus is joined to it. The divinity of Jesus is understood as the result of the descent of the divine Logos—a preexistent heavenly being who is the Son of God—into the world. This view is common today among traditional Roman Catholics, doctrinally conservative Protestants, and most Eastern Orthodox. Both the Antiochene and Alexandrian schools had a wide sphere of influence in the ancient church, not only among the clergy, but also among the monks and the laity. They were a factor in the Christological controversies of the 300s and 400s.

The Nicene Creed affirms that Jesus Christ is "the only Son of God, eternally begotten of the Father." In other words, the divine nature in Jesus is God's eternal Son. The Creed stresses this divine nature in Jesus by poetic repetitions: Jesus Christ is "God from God, Light from Light, true God from true God." In his divine being, he is "of one Being with the Father," not a different, lesser kind of god "made" (created) by the Father. The Creed then ties the Son of God to God the Father by stating the Son's role in creation—"Through him all

Jesus as the Good Shepherd is a common image of salvation and spiritual direction in Christ.

SHARON MOLLERUS

things were made"—just as it affirmed earlier that the Father made all things. Then the Creed talks at more length about the incarnation: "For us men [humans] and for our salvation, he came down from heaven, by the power of the Holy Spirit he became incarnate from the Virgin Mary, and was made man." Eastern Orthodoxy has stressed more than Western Christianity the meaning of the incarnation for the salvation of humankind; Western Christians stress the meaning of the death and resurrection of Jesus for salvation.

Then the Creed skips to the end of Jesus' life and emphasizes the reality of his redemptive suffering: "For our sake he was crucified under Pontius Pilate; He suffered death and was buried. On the third day He rose again in accordance with the Scriptures." Exactly *how* Jesus' death saves humans is often debated: Is it a sacrifice, a defeat of evil (Christ as victor), a moral example, or all of these and more? Without belief that Jesus "rose again" in resurrection, it is clear from the New Testament accounts, his movement would have ended and Jesus would soon have disappeared into the mists of time. The final part of the Creed's section on Jesus speaks about his present and future: "He ascended into heaven and is seated on the right hand of the Father; He will come again in glory to judge the living and the dead, and his kingdom will have no end." That Jesus sits on the Father's "right hand" refers to his present reign with God the Father. The rest of this section affirms the standard Christian expectation that Jesus will return "in glory" at the end of human history to bring God's eternal reign to earth.

A Closer Look:

The Doctrine of the Virgin Mary

The teaching that the Virgin Mary is the "mother/bearer of God," or **Theotokos**, is closely connected to the incarnation. As the church wrestled with articulating its belief in the identity of Jesus, the mother of the Son of God gained a special place within the church. To a significant degree, this was in an effort to understand the nature of Jesus, not to "promote" his mother.

The expansion of the veneration of the Virgin Mary as the "Mother of God" and the formation of doctrines explaining this are known to historians as one of the most remarkable occurrences in the ancient church after about 100 C.E. The New Testament offers only scanty points of departure for this development. Although she has a prominent place in the narratives of the Nativity, Mary soon disappears behind the figure of Jesus. Jesus' ministry was opposed by his family, including his mother, who thought he was mentally disturbed (Mark 3:21). All the Gospels stress the fact that Jesus separated himself from his family, and only the Gospels of Matthew and Luke mention the virginal conception. The Gospel of John mentions the "mother of Jesus" in a positive light, but not by name. Both Roman Catholics and the Orthodox believe that Mary was a life-long virgin; this serves as example of dedication to God, even of celibacy. Most Protestants believe that she was virginal only until the birth of Jesus, and then had other children with Joseph by natural means.

Despite her earlier doubts, Mary was present as a believer in the earliest Church, and in the early 200s the doctrine of the virginal conception of Jesus spread widely in the church, where it was put together with the doctrine of the incarnation. The doctrine of the virginal conception found its way into all Christian creeds, as did mention of the Virgin Mary herself. Veneration of Mary (not worship) spread widely in the West and the East, and by medieval times many churches had special chapels dedicated to the Virgin Mary. (In England they can still be found in many Anglican churches, where they are known as the "Lady Chapel.") Mary became the chief intercessor for the church on earth and the Queen of Heaven. She received increasing prayer (the "Hail Mary") and devotion, especially in times of great distress such as the Black Plague in the 1400s. Devotion to Mary was "throttled back" somewhat after the Catholic Reform, and it was never as strong in the Orthodox churches as in Roman Catholicism. In recent times, veneration of Mary has been promoted by certain popes, especially John Paul II (pope from 1978 to 2005).

In sum, Christian devotion to Mary has been steady and persistent for most Roman Catholic and Eastern Orthodox Christians, and many Anglicans as well. For most Protestants, however, this devotion to the Virgin ended at Reformation times, and many liberal Protestants today no longer believe in the virginal conception of Jesus.

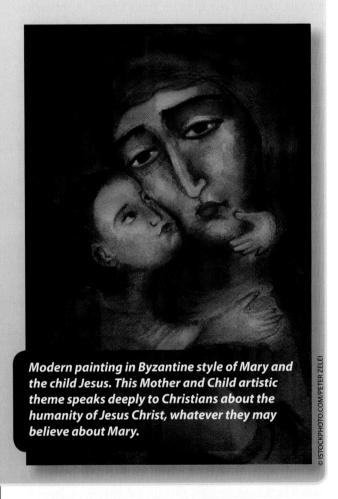

Modern painting in Byzantine style of Mary and the child Jesus. This Mother and Child artistic theme speaks deeply to Christians about the humanity of Jesus Christ, whatever they may believe about Mary.

© ISTOCKPHOTO.COM/PETER ZELEI

Theotokos (thee-AH-toh-koss) Virgin Mary as the "mother/bearer of God"

GOD THE HOLY SPIRIT

The Holy Spirit is one of the most challenging topics in Christian teaching. To begin with, the name "Holy Spirit" doesn't evoke meanings such as "Father" and "Son" do. It has been harder for Christians to conceive of the Holy Spirit as a divine person in the same way as they think of the Father and the Son. (Feminists, however, hold that this is a good thing and point to the feminine aspects of the Spirit.) The foundational view of the Holy Spirit is sketched in the next section of the Nicene Creed: "We believe in the Holy Spirit, the Lord, the giver of Life, who proceeds from the Father and the Son. With the Father and the Son he is worshipped and glorified. He has spoken through the Prophets." (Historians are divided about whether the wording that follows this—about the church, baptism, and the rest—is a part of the section on the Holy Spirit.)

The Creed ties the Spirit to God the Father and God the Son in a variety of ways. The Spirit is called "Lord," the term Christians regularly use for the Father and the Son. Next, the Spirit is called "the giver of Life," which refers not only to

God the Father, Son, and Holy Spirit in the St. Nicholas Church, Amsterdam, The Netherlands

© ISTOCKPHOTO.COM/ICTOR

a role at creation, but especially to giving life to believers now and eternally. The next phrase has been problematic between the Eastern and Western churches. Originally, the Creed said that the Spirit "proceeds from the Father," just as Jesus (in parallel) is "begotten" by the Father, but in the Middle Ages the Catholic Church added "and the Son," which most Protestant churches then shared. This was a huge point of contention between the East and the West, and one of the causes for their formal split in 1054. Some Western churches omit it today, or put it in brackets. Next, the Creed says that the Spirit is "worshipped and glorified," a sign of certain divine status.

The last thing said about the Holy Spirit, that the Spirit "has spoken through the prophets," is the most powerful and problematic of the Nicene Creed's statements about the Spirit. Although the Holy Spirit is said in the New Testament to mediate the presence of Jesus to the church and explain his words, essentially a conserving task, the Spirit also is powerful, uncontrollable, and unpredictable. Prophetic speech in the Spirit is challenging to the church. Every movement for change in church history has appealed to the authority and leading of the Holy Spirit. Opposition to the mainstream church—through appeal to the Holy Spirit—was found in Montanism (MAHN-tuh-NIHZ-um) around 150 C.E. This movement saw itself as the fulfillment of the promise of the coming of the Spirit on the first church. In the 1200s, a movement against the institutional church was begun by Joachim of Fiore in Italy. He promised

the beginning of the period of the Holy Spirit, in which the institutional papal church would be replaced by a community of charismatic figures, all filled with the Spirit. This was put down, but it stimulated a number of revolutionary movements in the medieval church. The sixteenth-century reformer, Thomas Müntzer (MOONT-zer), defended his revolution against the princes and church officials with a new coming of the Spirit. In the twentieth century through today, the widespread charismatic movement has centered on the recovery of the experience of the Holy Spirit.

THE CONCLUSION OF THE NICENE CREED: CHURCH, BAPTISM, AND CHRISTIAN HOPE

Finally, the Nicene Creed affirms, "We believe in one holy catholic and apostolic Church. We acknowledge one baptism for the forgiveness of sins. We look for the resurrection of the dead, and the life of the world to come." Belief "in the Church" affirms that the Church, which is holy, catholic (universal), and apostolic, is a divine part of God's plan for human salvation. Ancient Christians believed that it is the continuing body founded by Jesus. The Creed then mentions the importance of "one baptism" for salvation but makes no mention of the Eucharist or any other church ritual. Baptism has from the first Christian generation been

Chalcedon (KAL-seh-don) Council in 451 that defined the relationship of the human and divine natures of Christ

the ritual of initiation into the Christian faith; the experience of baptism and the instruction that surrounds it gives guidance for the moral and spiritual life of the Christian. The Creed closes with an affirmation of "the resurrection of the dead, and the life of the world to come." Although the Creed doesn't mention him explicitly at this point, Jesus is the center of resurrection and life, just as he was the first to rise from the dead. He will return in glory to fully bring in God's reign, and the "world to come" will be present with its full life. This traditional Christian teaching about the end of the world—the return of Christ, resurrection, and judgment with eternal reward and eternal punishment—has been widely believed in the history of Christianity, but in modern times many Protestants and some Roman Catholics have called it into doubt, preferring to think of an open human future.

Getting back now to the continuing controversy over Christ's nature that the Nicene Council did not fully settle, a new council at **Chalcedon** (451) finally ended the dispute between Antioch and Alexandria by drawing from each. It declared: "We all unanimously teach . . . one and the same Son, our Lord Jesus Christ, perfect in deity and perfect in humanity . . . in two natures, without being mixed, transmuted, divided, or separated. . . . The identity of each nature is preserved and concurs into one person and being." At Nicea and Chalcedon, the church affirmed a paradox, and continues today to affirm it: Jesus is fully human and fully divine, God and humanity perfectly present in one person. Second, Jesus Christ is completely human, not only in his historical life, but after his resurrection and through all eternity. As Paul wrote, "The whole fullness of deity dwells bodily" in him (Colossians 2:9). The genius of the Nicene and Chalcedonian Creeds is that they hold that the mystery of the person of Jesus Christ could be grasped in a decisive, authoritative formula: two natures in one person.

LO4 Christian Ethics: Following the Way of Jesus Christ

A new translation of the New Testament published by the American branch of Oxford University Press causes a stir around the world. Titled the *Inclusive Bible*, it features "thoroughly non-sexist" wording. Some critics deride it as the "politically correct version" and a dangerous innovation. However, students of Christianity recognize that this type of translation has a rich pedigree in America. It can trace its roots to the influential, and even more controversial, *Women's Bible* of 1898, a seminal work in the foundation of the feminist movement. The publication of the *Inclusive Bible* touches an important contemporary moral theme in Christianity: the place of women in the faith.

As an "ethical monotheism," Christianity's moral teaching is based on its view of God. God's self-revelation shows God to be both radically good and radically loving. Christians must worship God but also must live their entire lives according to God's will. Being God's people means following God's law, which in turn means walking in the way of God's truth (Psalms 25:4–5) and obeying it (Romans 2:8; 1 Peter 1:22). Jesus affirmed that the main point of this obedience is to love God and to love one's neighbor (Matthew 22:37–39).

FOUNDATIONS IN THE TEN COMMANDMENTS, THE SERMON ON THE MOUNT, AND THE LETTERS OF PAUL

Christian ethical teaching has two main biblical foundations: the Ten Commandments (Exodus 20:1–17; Deuteronomy 5:6–21) and the Sermon on the Mount (Matthew 5–7). The Ten Commandments (see above, page 245) remain valid for Christians, although God's laws have been broadened by Jesus Christ. The "first table" of the Law calls on Christians to worship only God, not to worship images, and keep the Sabbath day holy. This Sabbath was changed to Sunday, the day of the Lord's resurrection, when Christians around the world gather in the morning for worship. The "second table" of the Law tells Christians to honor parents and abstain from murder, adultery, theft, false witness, and coveting.

The Sermon on the Mount opens with the Beatitudes (or statements of blessings), which contain implicit moral directions (Matthew 5:1–12). Jesus declared that the powers of the imminent Kingdom of God would enable his followers to witness to this kingdom before the world, even to be the "light of the world" (5:14–16). Jesus upheld the value of the Law of Moses for his followers, but radicalized it in a variety of ways. He pointed to the necessity of controlling one's thoughts and emotions, not just one's actions; Jesus called anger murderous and lust adulterous

(5:21–22, 27–28). Doing what is right proceeds from the inner person, and thus is not a sham or hypocritical action. The repeated warnings against hypocrisy in the Sermon on the Mount are primarily warnings to Jesus' followers, not attacks on others. Jesus commanded his followers to "be perfect, as your heavenly Father is perfect" (5:48). Human perfection is expressed in what Christian tradition calls the "Golden Rule," a summary of the ethics of the whole Jewish Bible: "In everything do to others as you would have them do to you." Christians have believed that taking the "hard way" (7:13–14)

In a scene from the 2003 film **The Passion of the Christ,** *the dead Jesus is lowered from the cross. Identification with the death of Jesus is foundational in Christian ethics.*

© PICTORIAL PRESS LTD/ALAMY

is possible by virtue of the divine gift of the Holy Spirit. Jesus knew that this "hard way" would not be easy for his followers, and that they would fail in parts of it every day, as indicated in the daily prayer that he taught them in the Sermon on the Mount, which contains a request for divine forgiveness for one's sins (6:12).

Watch a film re-creation of the Sermon on the Mount.

Jesus affirmed the summary of God's will given in Judaism, to "love the Lord your God" with all your being and to "love your neighbor as yourself." This love is possible because of Jesus' life, death, and resurrection. When the Christian commandment of love was connected to Christ's person and work, the demand of love for the neighbor becomes a "new commandment": "A new commandment I give to you, that you love one another; even as I have loved you, that you also love one another" (John 13:34). The followers of Jesus are to have this love: "By this all men will know that you are my disciples, if you have love for one another" (John 13:35). All this might imply that Christian love is given only or mostly to other Christians, but the Christian commandment of love has never been limited to fellow Christians. On the contrary, the Christian ethic crossed social and religious barriers and saw a neighbor in every suffering human being, especially the innocent and helpless. This is why, for example, Christians in the ancient world rescued infants left in remote places or garbage dumps to die. Jesus himself explicated his understanding of the commandment of love in the parable of the Good Samaritan, who followed the commandment of

love and helped a person in need whom a priest and a Levite had chosen to ignore (Luke 10:29–37).

The Apostle Paul often drew on the Ten Commandments to shape the moral life of Christians. Because his churches were made up mostly of Gentiles, they needed basic instruction in the Jewish basis of morality. Paul's letters also stress the moral virtues of the Christian life: trust in God, hope in the future God will bring, peace in one's heart and in the church, and especially love for all people. More than any other New Testament author, Paul grounds the ethical life of the Christian in the life, death, and resurrection of Jesus. For Paul, the *indicative* (who Christians are by virtue of God's action) serves to ground the *imperatives* of moral attitude and behavior. The believer has "died with Christ" in baptism and will be "raised with Christ" at the end of time, and in the meantime must "walk in newness of life." The moral dimension of the Christian faith is a struggle; in an image drawn from clothing, one must constantly "put on Christ" and "put off" sin and self-centeredness. The presence of the Spirit in the individual and in the church gives both direction and empowerment for spiritual living. Summing up his ethic, Paul says, "I appeal to you therefore, brothers and sisters, by the mercies of God to present your bodies as a living sacrifice, holy and acceptable to God, which is your reasonable service. Do not be conformed to this world, but be transformed by the renewal of your mind, that you may prove what is the will of God, what is good, and acceptable, and perfect" (Romans 12:1–2).

THE ENACTMENT OF MORAL LIFE IN THE CHURCH

Christian social ethics are foundational for the community of the faithful. As the church took in all sorts of people, certain occupations were deemed incompatible with a Christian life of love toward others. Thieves, brothel-keepers and prostitutes, workers in pagan temples, actors, charioteers, gladiators, soldiers, magicians, astrologers, and fortune-tellers could not keep their trades when they became Christians. (Slave owning, however, was still mostly tolerated, and the church often allowed slaves who were forced to engage in these forbidden trades to be church members.) Moral instruction for **catechumens**, those preparing for baptism, and many ancient sermons reveal that preachers regularly explained Christian morality and urged their audiences to keep it. In the Middle Ages and Byzantine times, moral instruction centered on the Ten Commandments, the Beatitudes, and the lists of virtues and vices drawn from the New Testament. The ritual act of reconciliation (as it is now called), in which individuals confessed their sins in the "confessional" to a priest in order to receive direction and assurance of forgiveness, helped to shape individual character and conduct. At least in the West, people leaving church in the Middle Ages would typically see a painting of the Last Judgment over the doors, to remind them of the rewards of doing good and the penalty for evil.

Watch an explanation of the Roman Catholic confessional.

Beside this inner-church sphere of morality the "conversion of the empire" in the 300s permitted bishops to begin influencing the personal and political affairs of government and the wider life of society. Soon **canon law**, the legal system that codifies ethical and other matters in the Roman Catholic Church, arose to guide the overall moral life of the church. Canon law is still today an important foundation of moral reflection and decision making by priests and

catechumen (KAT-uh-kyoo-men) Individual preparing for baptism in a period of doctrinal and moral instruction

canon law Legal system that codifies ethical, organizational, and other matters in the Roman Catholic Church

© ISTOCKPHOTO.COM/AMANDA ROHDE

bishops in the Church of Rome. In the Protestant churches, different patterns of social ethics emerged based more directly on the Bible. One of the most powerful and controversial explanations of Protestant ethics is Max Weber's book *The Protestant Ethic and the Spirit of Capitalism*, which argued for a strong relationship between Protestant (specifically, Calvinist) morality and the development of capitalism in the West.

Read a summary of *The Protestant Ethic and the Spirit of Capitalism* by Max Weber.

Modern times have seen a decline in the direct institutional role of the churches in society, as church leaders can no longer directly influence rulers with whom they share authority. Instead, church leaders advise the shaping of public laws and policies, seeking to guide not only the members of their churches but also the whole common life of nations. In Roman Catholicism, this has occurred at the global level through the so-called social encyclicals of popes, from Leo XIII in 1891 to today. These teaching documents deal with a variety of topics in social ethics, and almost every pope has issued them. At times, these encyclicals have been highly controversial, as when Pope Paul VI in 1968 used one (*Humanae Vitae*, "On Human Life") to forbid the use of all artificial birth control among Roman Catholics. In Eastern Orthodoxy, the fall of communist rule has presented particular problems and opportunities to help guide public life. Protestant denominations have typically made pronouncements and initiated programs on their own and through ecumenical agencies to which they belong.

The World Council of Churches, a fellowship of Christian churches founded in 1948, has created "middle axioms" (the notion of a "just society," for example, or "the care of creation"), which were intended as common ground on which Christian churches and governments could meet for thought and action. Now, they are common ground for cooperating with people of other religions, especially today on environmental issues. The rise of Christian social organizations such as Church World Service, Catholic Relief Services, Bread for the World, World Vision, Habitat for Humanity, and many others is particularly notable. In the developing world, Christian organizations are among the largest

ROBERT SCOBLE

Bono and former U.S. Vice President Al Gore speak at a conference on poverty and climate change.

In this section, we'll discuss the rise of Christian worship in history. Christian worship emerged from, and then gradually separated from, the worship practices of Judaism. The Acts of the Apostles relates that the first Christian believers worshiped in the Jerusalem Temple, as Jesus had. They worshiped in synagogues as well. But the church also had from the first its own meetings for worship that drew on Jewish precedents, especially the kind of worship in the synagogue. After Constantine, worship and the church buildings in which it was held became more formal. The Roman Catholic Church built itself around seven **sacraments**, rituals believed to be a special means of grace, and the Eastern Orthodox Churches made its worship in its various branches more unified. In the Protestant Reformation and Catholic Reform, and again in Vatican II, worship was reformed by being made more the work of the people, the **liturgy**. Since around 1950, the ecumenical movement has brought a consensus of worship style and content.

Read a 2011 social pronouncement by the Roman Catholic bishops of Great Britain urging the recovery of "public virtue."

Watch an interview with Bono on Christianity's role in combating AIDS in Africa.

nongovernmental organizations working for human and social development. Individual Christians have also had an impact here—for example, the lead singer of the rock band U2, Bono, advocates tirelessly for justice for Africa. He has become known almost as much for his advocacy of justice as his music.

LO5 Christian Worship and Ritual

In Rome, the Congregation for Divine Worship, the Roman Catholic department responsible for guiding the Church's religious services, presents to Pope John Paul II a report entitled "Authentic Liturgy." It states that language used in the Mass is to avoid many of the features of inclusive language, because they obscure the meaning of the text. For example, where the original language of Scripture or the Mass book says "brothers," expressions such as "brothers and sisters" or "friends" may not be used. This document stirs up a controversy in European and North American Catholic churches, which have gotten used to more-inclusive language. This controversy shows how issues of inclusive/exclusive language have become an important issue in the contemporary churches, both Roman Catholic and Protestant.

Read "Authentic Liturgy."

CHRISTIAN WORSHIP BEFORE CONSTANTINE

Christian worship and ritual varies widely throughout the world, but its common foundation can be traced to the first centuries of the church and before this to the Jewish synagogues. As in the worship of the synagogue, public prayer and praise to God are a constant in the church. So too are the reading and explanation of a portion of Scripture. Christian churches, especially in the eastern half of the Roman Empire, adapted the **lectionary** system of the Jewish synagogues and added readings from the New Testament. Changes from synagogue worship were introduced as well. The weekly day for worship went from the Jewish Sabbath on the last day of the week to Sunday.

sacrament Ritual believed to be a special means of grace

liturgy Literally, "work of the people" in worship; pattern of worship in Christian churches

lectionary Systemic schedule of reading the Bible in worship

A Closer Look:

An Ancient Christian Service

As a part of his defense of Christianity in sections 65–66 of his *Apology,* Justin briefly describes a Christian service from about 150. This is the earliest description of Christian worship that we have. It has the same basic elements and almost exactly the same order as almost all Christian worship since: gathering as a community, reading of scripture, prayer, sermon, Holy Communion, and dismissal. Singing hymns isn't mentioned here, but we know from other sources that it was common.

> After thus washing [baptizing] the one who has been convinced and signified his assent, we lead him to those who are called brothers, where they are assembled. The memoirs of the apostles or the writings of the apostles are read, as long as time permits. When the reader has ceased, the presiding leader instructs and exhorts us to imitate these good things. Then we rise together

and pray. We pray that we may be made worthy, having learned the truth, to be found good citizens and keepers of what is commanded, so that we may be saved with eternal salvation. On finishing the prayers we greet each other with a kiss.

> Then bread and a cup of wine mixed with water are brought to the one presiding. Taking them, he gives praise and glory to the Father of the universe through the name of the Son and the Holy Spirit, and offers thanksgiving at some length that we have been deemed worthy to receive these things from him. When he has finished the prayers and the thanksgiving, the whole congregation assents by saying, "Amen." Those whom we call deacons [assistants] then give a portion of the consecrated bread and wine to all those present, and they take it to the absent.

Baptism replaced circumcision as the main rite of initiation into the faith, and it was preceded by instruction and fasting. Persons about to be baptized renounced evil, and after they declared their faith, they went into the water. They then received by anointing with oil and by the laying on of hands the gift of the Holy Spirit, just as the Spirit had descended on Jesus at his baptism. Only the baptized were admitted to the Eucharist, and weekly participation is this ritual meal took the place of both the Passover meal and Jewish sacrifices. Baptism has been the rite of entry, but the Eucharist is the regular ritual of food for the body and soul.

WORSHIP AFTER CONSTANTINE

After Christianity became permitted and then official in the 300s, almost every element of worship became more elaborate. Formal church buildings were erected, and church officials dressed for worship in special vestments modeled after Roman government garb. The church developed a liturgical calendar with seasons of self-denial, such as Advent and Lent, and seasons of celebration, such as Christmas and Easter.

basilica Building with a long rectangular area for the congregation and a semicircular area at the front for clergy, adapted by early Christians from Roman courts for Christian church architecture

> *The basilica type of building was used by Christians for the first church buildings, and has been the most common pattern of churches since.*

Before about 350 C.E, almost all worship was in private homes. (A religion almost constantly persecuted by the government isn't able to put up its own buildings.) The service was held in the largest room of the house, usually the central atrium in a middle- or upper-class house. When church buildings became common around 350, they were designed for the community. The rectangular **basilica** with a long nave (main area for the congregation) and an apse (semicircular area at the front), which had been used for Roman law courts, was particularly suitable for Christian worship. This architectural layout of the church building has been the most common pattern of church buildings ever since. Many Byzantine churches had mosaic pictures on their floors. Old Testament/Jewish heroes of faith also appear in the earliest Christian art in both the East and West. The artists adapted conventional pagan forms: the shepherd carrying a sheep, the praying person with

Iconostasis inside a Greek Orthodox church

hands uplifted, various birds and animals. Symbols of the Eucharist and baptism were especially common. The exteriors of these churches were simple, but inside they were often richly ornamented with marble and mosaic. The decoration was designed to represent the angels and saints in heaven with whom the church on earth was joining for worship, saints whose presence was suggested by icons in the East and statues, paintings, and then stained glass in the West. The oldest church buildings to survive largely intact are from early medieval and early Byzantine times: Hagia Sophia at Constantinople (which became a mosque and is now a museum) and San Vitale at Ravenna in Italy. Worship in churches became more impressive and formal for a greatly enlarged and now official religion, but much of the earlier intimacy that was a part of house churches was necessarily lost.

In the early Middle Ages, Catholic worship became centered on the sacraments and has stayed centered on them ever since. These are, the *Catholic Catechism* says, "efficacious signs of grace, instituted by Christ and entrusted to the Church, by which divine life is dispensed." The sacraments are necessary for salvation, because they were instituted by Christ as the means through which God communicates grace. Christ bestows a particular grace through each sacrament, such as

baptism's joining one to Christ and the Church, confession/reconciliation's forgiveness of sins and amendment of life, and the Eucharist's feeding body and soul with the mystical food of Jesus' body and blood. A sacrament works *ex opere operato* (ehks OH-puh-reh OH-puh-RAH-toh), Latin for "by the working of the work." In other words, they are effective just by being administered, regardless of the personal holiness of the one administering them. However, the holiness of the recipient does make a difference; lack of a proper spiritual attitude can thwart the effectiveness of the sacrament. These seven sacraments are known today as baptism, confirmation, the Eucharist, reconciliation, anointing of the sick, ordination (to holy orders), and marriage. The Eastern Orthodox Church also has seven sacraments but hasn't organized its worship so fully around them.

Other worship practices also began in post-Constantinian times. One of the more significant was the **cult of the saints**, the veneration of saints in shrines, churches, and other places (This "cult" has no connection with the more modern use of the word to designate some new religious movements.) Shrines were erected in honor of local

> **cult of the saints**
> Veneration of saints in shrines, churches, and other places

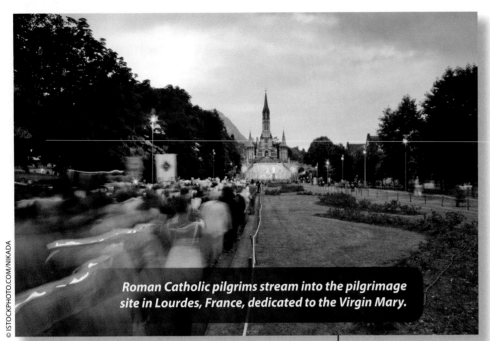

Roman Catholic pilgrims stream into the pilgrimage site in Lourdes, France, dedicated to the Virgin Mary.

from the Roman Catholic version.) Earlier beliefs that Jesus Christ was somehow present in the celebration of Holy Communion, especially in the bread and wine, were greatly developed in the Middle Ages. The Roman church officially adopted the teaching of *transubstantiation*, that the bread and wine were changed in all but appearance into the substance of Christ's body. Music also became elaborate after Constantine, with chanting in Gregorian style of Psalms, hymns, and service music, and plainsong with several voices unaccompanied by instruments. Eastern Orthodox chanting, like the liturgy in general, was richer, more sonorous and soaring than Gregorian plainsong.

holy men and women, especially those Christians who had worked miracles and those who had suffered for the faith. Usually shrines were found in churches and contained a relic or the entire body of the saint. Until modern times, most Christian saints weren't recognized by the whole church but were known and venerated regionally. The saints were recognized as intercessors with God for the faithful on earth and were thought to be vehicles for God's miraculous power. The shrines became the focus of religious pilgrimage. Some of the most popular shrines today are dedicated to the Virgin Mary, particularly the places where she is believed to have appeared: Lourdes, France; Medjugorje in Bosnia and Herzegovina, and Guadalupe, Mexico.

The pattern of the Eucharistic liturgy was basically set by the year 400, but different forms existed in different areas. Especially varied was the main, long prayer of Holy Communion, which the Orthodox called *anaphora* (uh-NAH-fohr-uh), or "offering," and the Romans called *canon*, "prescribed form." The canon of the Latin Mass in the 500s was basically similar to the form it has kept through today. (Most Protestant forms for Holy Communion were adapted

The Protestant Reformation carried out an immediate reform of worship along with theology. In general, the Lutheran churches kept some distinctly Roman Catholic features such as crucifixes and altars, the Calvinist churches kept a few (kneeling in services, baptismal fonts), and the Anabaptist churches discarded everything they didn't find in the Bible. In general, the worship of churches in the Baptist tradition is *non-liturgical*, not bound to a set form of

See a presentation of Gregorian chant by Cistercian monks in Austria.

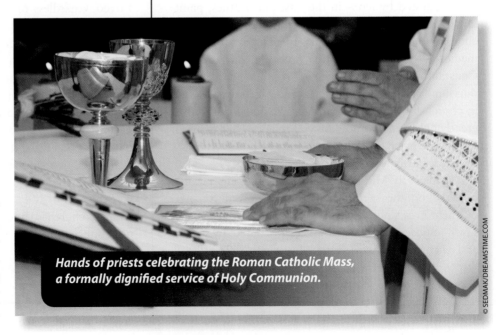

Hands of priests celebrating the Roman Catholic Mass, a formally dignified service of Holy Communion.

worship or rituals—embracing spontaneous, informal prayer rather than written prayer, for example—but other Protestant churches tend to be *liturgical*, with set forms. Worship in the Church of England remained the most Catholic of all the breakaway churches.

All Protestant churches shared a few important new features of worship. First, the Bible was restored to what the Reformers considered a more central place. Preaching the Bible in sermons was emphasized, as was private reading of the Bible in homes. Second, the sacraments were generally reduced to the two that had been founded by Jesus: baptism and Holy Communion. Most Reformers made frequent communion the rule for all laity, and denied the Roman Catholic doctrine of transubstantiation in favor of other understandings of the spiritual meaning of communion. Third, all services were put completely into the language of the people, and the liturgy became literally the "work of the people" again. Music, especially hymn singing, was done by the people as well as trained musicians. The Catholic Reform in the 1500s and Vatican II in the 1960s brought the Roman church into line with many of these changes, but its theology remained the same.

Read an analysis of contemporary Protestant worship trends by leading liturgical expert James White.

> **Some observers have estimated that between one-fourth and one-third of all Christians today "speak in tongues."**

In the years since the Reformation, Christian worship has become more diverse. The strongest impact on worship has been the **charismatic movement** stressing supernatural "gifts of the Holy Spirit," a movement also known as **Pentecostalism**. These two names are a bit tricky—*charismatic* usually refers to groups inside the Roman Catholic, Orthodox, and mainline Protestant churches. *Pentecostal* usually refers to Protestant churches such as the Assemblies of God where these practices

are the norm, whether these churches have "Pentecostal" in their formal name or not. "Gifts of the Holy Spirit" are called in Greek *charismata*. These gifts are used primarily in worship. The Pentecostal movement began in 1906 in an African American church in Los Angeles. Over time it has moved into mainstream Protestantism and Roman Catholicism as well. Today, the charismatic movement has spread throughout the Christian world. "Speaking in tongues," an emotional outpouring of prayer in human sounds but in no human language, is its primary activity, but others are often seen as well: interpretation of tongues, prophecy, healing, and so forth. The charismatic movement has often been divisive and controversial when it appears in non-Pentecostalist denominations, but it has brought new life and an emphasis on spirituality. Some observers have estimated that between one-fourth and one-third of all Christians—about 600 million people—are charismatics.

Reading the Bible regularly is a distinctive practice for many Christians.

© CARLOS E. SANTA MARIA/SHUTTERSTOCK.COM

Watch an ABC News report on speaking in tongues.

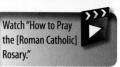
Watch "How to Pray the [Roman Catholic] Rosary."

LO6 Christianity in North America Today

A group of Old Order Amish has met in a home for worship in Lancaster County, Pennsylvania. As their horses and buggies wait outside, they conduct a two-hour service of hymns, prayers, scripture readings, and sermon, all in their own "Pennsylvania Dutch" language, which is actually a Swiss dialect of German. No cleric conducts

charismatic movement (Pentecostalism)
Modern Christian movement stressing use of supernatural "gifts of the Holy Spirit," a movement also known as *Pentecostalism*

the service, for in their religious life the men are all equal. Their worship and lifestyle continues the same pattern of "coming out from the world and being separate" that their Anabaptist ancestors practiced at the dawn of the Reformation. The Amish have been oppressed in many parts of the world, but they've found a happy haven in the United States and Canada, where they are widely respected for their consistent witness for peace.

Christianity is the largest and most popular religion in the United States, with 78 percent of those polled identifying themselves as Christian in 2009. About 62 percent of those polled reported that they were members of a church congregation. With around 240 million Christians, the United States has the largest Christian population on earth. In Canada, the church has slightly less of a presence, but more than 60 percent of Canadians identify themselves as Christians. As a result of immigration, widespread importation of European (and now African and Asian) churches, and new denominations springing up in the United States, Christianity is more internally diverse—for better and for worse—in North America than anywhere else in the world. This poses a challenge and an opportunity for the study of Christianity.

OVERVIEW

Protestant denominations account for about 50 percent of North Americans, Roman Catholicism about 25 percent, and Eastern Orthodox less than 1 percent. Roman Catholics are by far the largest single church group, and the Roman Catholic Church in the United States is growing in size with Hispanic immigration. The Eastern Orthodox population is relatively tiny, making up only about 0.04 percent of North Americans, due largely to smaller immigration from most Orthodox nations, recent difficulties in "Americanization," and the persistence of twenty-six different ethnic-based denominations within Orthodoxy.

Read a summary of the Hartford Institute for Religion Research's study of Orthodoxy in America.

Christianity came to the Americas when it was first colonized by Europeans beginning in the 1500s. The vast majority of colonists were Christians, and over time a majority of Native Americans became Christians as well. Today, most Christian denominations and congregations are mainline Protestant, evangelical Protestant, or Roman Catholic, or the various denominations of Eastern Orthodoxy. Sociologists of religion distinguish the *mainline* Protestant churches from the *evangelical* Protestant churches. The authoritative Association of

Religion Data Archives (ARDA) estimates 26 million members of mainline churches versus about 40 million members of evangelical Protestant churches. Good evidence suggests a sizeable shift in membership from mainline denominations to evangelical churches since about 1950. Then, most Protestant Christians belonged to mainline churches, and evangelical churches were comparatively smaller.

THE DIFFERENT CHURCHES: ROMAN CATHOLIC AND PROTESTANT

At the time the United States was founded, only a small fraction of the U.S. population were Catholics, mostly in Maryland. As we saw above, the number of Roman Catholics has grown dramatically in recent years. The United States now has the fourth-largest Catholic population in the world. The Church's main national body is the United States Conference of Catholic Bishops, made up of all bishops and archbishops of the United States, although each bishop has independent power in his own diocese, responsible only to the pope. Although many other nations have a Roman Catholic *primate*, or lead bishop, there is no primate for the United States.

Although Protestantism is divided into mainline and evangelical groups, as we saw above, the distinction between them is not easy to maintain. Mainline Protestant denominations are those brought to North America by its historic immigrant groups. The largest are the Episcopal (English, from the Anglican Church), Presbyterian (Scottish), Methodist (English and Welsh), and Lutheran (Scandinavian and German) denominations. They are generally more open to new ideas and social changes than are evangelical Protestants and Roman Catholics. For example, they've been increasingly open to the ordination of women and equality in church and society for gay and lesbian persons. Mainline churches belong to organizations such as the National Council of Churches and the World Council of Churches. Mainline Protestant groups were dominant in North America for more than two centuries, up until the 1960s.

> The experience of conversion that most evangelicals see as necessary for salvation is called being "born again."

Evangelicalism is the modern movement that seeks to spread the gospel of Jesus Christ, giving people an opportunity to convert. The experience of conversion that most evangelicals see as necessary for salvation is called being "born again." Although it became strong in the past two centuries, it has roots that reach into the earliest decades of the Reformation. It arose with the Anabaptist movement in the 1500s, moved into the mainstream Reformation with Pietism in the 1700s, and became stronger in the late 1800s, especially as a result of the world mission movement of the time. The most famous evangelical of the twentieth century was the Southern Baptist (U.S.) evangelist Billy Graham, who held mass meetings that ended with a call to come forward to "accept Christ as your personal Lord and Savior" and be "born again." There is a good deal of variety in evangelicalism. Most evangelicals tend to be politically conservative, but an increasing number today—especially younger evangelicals—are politically moderate or liberal. Probably the most influential modern voice in the evangelical movement was C. S. Lewis (1898–1963), the University of Oxford professor of medieval literature and a traditionalist Anglican who ironically did not call himself an "evangelical." Lewis wrote popular religious works such as *Mere Christianity* and *The Screwtape Letters*, which are still best sellers for their clear, creative presentation of the faith. He also wrote the popular children's novels *The Chronicles of Narnia*, which are full of traditional Christian themes but not overtly Christian.

The *black church*—or, more commonly today, *African American church*—in North America are those churches that are mainly African American in membership. Most African American congregations belong to African American denominations such as the National Baptist Convention or a variety of other Baptist or Methodist groups, although many black congregations belong to predominantly white denominations. The first black congregations and churches were formed before 1800 by freed slaves in the South and especially in the North. After slavery ended, African Americans continued in separate congregations and denominations, creating communities and styles of worship that were culturally distinct from those of their white counterparts. They continued a unique, powerful form of Christianity that adapted African religious practices in preaching, music, and congregational life. For example, matriarchal traditions from Africa have led to some women having a much higher status, even authority, in African American churches than in white churches. Many African American congregations have "mother boards" composed of older women who are real power-brokers in their churches. Segregation of the races discouraged and, especially in the South, prevented African Americans from belonging to the same churches as whites, thus helping to preserve the distinctive patterns of African American Christianity.

African Americans continued to form separate congregations and denominations during the 1900s. This separation continues today despite the decline of segregation and the rising occurrence of integrated worship. African American churches are usually the centers of their communities, opening schools in the early years after the Civil War, and pursuing other social welfare efforts. As a result, they have founded strong community organizations and provided spiritual and political leadership, especially during the civil rights movement, seen most clearly in its leadership by the African American Baptist pastor Martin Luther King Jr.

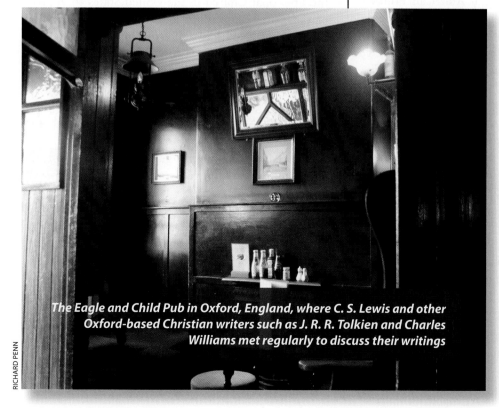

The Eagle and Child Pub in Oxford, England, where C. S. Lewis and other Oxford-based Christian writers such as J. R. R. Tolkien and Charles Williams met regularly to discuss their writings

RICHARD PENN

Choir singing is an important part of worship in African American churches, as here in Jacksonville, Florida.

Church founded by Joseph Smith, more commonly called the Mormons, is the most notable. Visitors to the Mormon headquarters in Salt Lake City, Utah, can view the hour-long movie *Joseph Smith: Prophet of the Restoration*. Another major Restorationist religion is that of the Jehovah's Witnesses. It's estimated that in the United States, 1.9 million adults identify themselves as Jehovah's Witnesses. Like the L.D.S. Church, the Jehovah's Witnesses reject many teachings of the Nicene Creed and view themselves as the only true church.

Finally, perhaps the single most important factor in the present and future of Christianity in North America comes from outside North America. For most of its history, Christianity has been strongest in the Northern Hemisphere, especially in Europe and North America. Now, Christianity is shifting to the Southern Hemisphere, where most Christians live and where Christianity is growing quickly as the number of Christians in the Northern Hemisphere declines. These "Global South" Christians with their more traditional interpretations of the Bible and the creeds sometimes present a challenge to older churches. For example, the African Independent Churches, a dynamic adaptation of Christianity by European mission churches in Africa, is now spreading to North America. To cite another example, the Anglican churches in Africa, where more people in Uganda or Nigeria attend Anglican religious services on a typical Sunday than in all of Great Britain, strongly oppose efforts in the Church of England and the Episcopal Church in the United States to approve of same-sex relationships and ordain gay and lesbian clergy. Mark Noll has written in his 2009 book, *The New Shape of World Christianity: How American Experience Reflects Global Faith*, that Global South Christians are less concerned about historic patterns of church government and doctrine, things important in the North, as they are about spiritual warfare between good and evil today and the continuing gulf between the wealthy North and the "Majority World."[2] The future of Christianity in North America may well be shaped by Christianity from outside it.

Visit the website of the Redeemed Christian Church of God, an African Independent Church now found in several U.S. cities.

Another broad trend in North American Protestantism is *Restorationism*. This refers to the belief held by various religious groups in that the Christianity of the first century C.E. is the purest form of the faith; it can and should be restored. (It was a strong impulse in the United States in the 1800s.) Such groups typically claim that their group is that restoration. They teach that restoration is necessary because other Christians before them introduced defects into Christian faith or lost a vital element of genuine Christianity. Restorationist denominations include the Christian Church (Disciples of Christ) and the Churches of Christ. Several groups that emerged in the Restorationist impulse from American Protestant denominations eventually became new religious movements. The Latter-day Saints

Examine the results of a recent survey that analyzes North American Christians by types and levels of belief and practice.

---

[2] Mark Noll, *The New Shape of World Christianity* (Downers Grove, IL: IVP Academic, 2009).

© JIM WEST/ALAMY

{ Speak Up! }

"With the aesthetics of the textbook, the limited programme, it was very easy to focus on what I was reading and obtain from distraction as opposed to many hundred textbooks that are filled cover to cover with black and white... textbook offers colorful pictures on almost every page... the text itself is written in an easy-to-read format. A person reading from this is engaged with the information. It almost does not even look like something that would fall under the classification of 'work.'"

Crystal Wells, student, University of West Florida

RELG was built on a simple principle: to create a new teaching and learning solution that reflects the way today's faculty teach and the way you learn.

Through conversations, focus groups, surveys, and interviews, we collected data that drove the creation of the version of RELG that you are using today. But it doesn't stop there—in order to make RELG an even better learning experience, we'd like you to SPEAK UP and tell us how RELG worked for you. What did you like about it? What would you change? Are there additional ideas you have that would help us build better tools for next semester's world religions students?

Speak Up! Go to **www.cengagebrain.com**

CHAPTER 12

Encountering Islam: The Straight Path of the One God

BONNIE VAN VOORST © CENGAGE LEARNING

Learning Outcomes

After studying this chapter, you will be able to do the following:

LO1 Explain the terms *Islam* and *Muslim*.

LO2 Know how the main periods of Islamic history have shaped its present, especially different Muslim groups.

LO3 Give the essential elements of Islamic teachings in your own words.

LO4 Explain Muslim ethics, especially in diet, dress, and marriage.

LO5 Explain the ways Muslims worship, especially the Five Pillars.

LO6 Explain the main aspects of Muslim life in North America today.

SPECTRUMPHOTOFILE

"There is no god but God, and Muhammad is God's prophet."
—Main statement of belief in Islam

Your Visit to Mecca

Imagine, if you will, your visit to Mecca (MEHK-uh), Saudi Arabia, during the Month of Pilgrimage. Your emotions run high as you come within sight of Mecca. You've looked forward to this trip as long as you can remember, and now you're there, at the very center—geographically and spiritually—of Islam. With Muslims all participating in the pilgrimage together, you feel a strong sense of Muslim unity.

Before you enter Mecca, you must be physically and spiritually clean. If you're a man, you shave your head, take off your outer clothes, and put on over your underwear two large triangular pieces of linen. Everyone dresses in these, whether rich or poor, royal or commoner. If you're a woman, you bathe and wear a traditional Muslim full-body veil, but you don't shave your hair. You also stay in women's groups apart from men for most of your activities on the pilgrimage. From now on, until you begin the journey home, you'll strictly observe all ritual restrictions in how you dress, act, speak, and eat. But you know all this beforehand, and you're still looking forward to it. In fact, these rules heighten your appreciation of how special this trip is.

Next, you walk seven times around the cube-shaped shrine at the open-air center of the Grand Mosque. This walking gets closer to the shrine with each circle, so the walk isn't at all tiring for you. It ends when you touch the sacred stone, a meteorite embedded in the shrine by Abraham himself about three thousand years ago. As you circle, you notice all the different races and nationalities present.

After you touch the sacred stone, you run seven times back and forth between two hills, just as Abraham's wife Hagar ran between them until an angel gave her water from the Zamzam well. These two hills are now inside the Grand Mosque and are connected by a long hallway. You know that this area has been the site of a few deadly stampedes in the past, but you realize that you have no fear of one as you pass through, because all is in the hands of God. Then you drink water from Zamzam before leaving this area.

Next, you move with all the other pilgrims out of the city of Mecca. You gather on the Plain of Arafat near the Mount of Mercy. From the afternoon prayer until the sunset prayer, the pilgrims "stand in the presence of Allah" by praying, meditating, and reading the Qur'an, the holy scripture of Islam. An older friend told you that this afternoon would be the high point of your pilgrimage, and he was right. That evening, you walk back to the village of Mina, where all of the pilgrims live in a huge tent city for three days. In the evening, sheep and goats are slaughtered as offerings to God, then roasted and eaten in happy feasts. These sacrifices commemorate Abraham's sacrificing an animal to God instead of his son Ishmael.

The next day, you throw small stones at three pillars representing the devil. Every pilgrim is supposed to do this, symbolizing your rejection of evil, a life-long task. Then you go back into Mecca and walk in the Grand Mosque one more time; your pilgrimage is complete. You return home to find that some of your friends half-teasingly call you *Hajji*, the new name given informally to people who make the pilgrimage, called *Hajj* in Arabic. This makes you smile, but you know that this new name points to a deeper truth: No one who goes on the pilgrimage will ever be the same again.

Visit Mecca by way of Google Earth™.

What Do YOU Think?

Islam is mostly a religion of peace.

Strongly Disagree						Strongly Agree
1	2	3	4	5	6	7

< Pilgrim praying during the Month of Pilgrimage at the Grand Mosque in Mecca

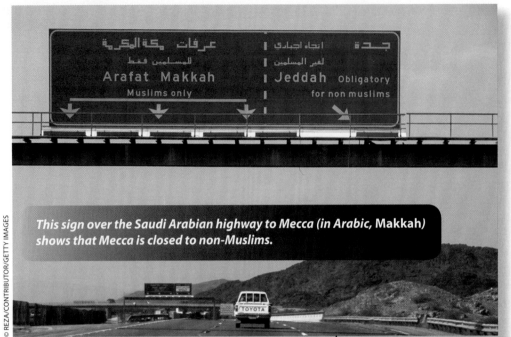

This sign over the Saudi Arabian highway to Mecca (in Arabic, Makkah) shows that Mecca is closed to non-Muslims.

View a PBS video on Islam in contemporary Indonesia.

Islam is the world's second-most populous religion, after Christianity. It has almost 1.3 billion followers, almost one out of every five people. Islam is now present in virtually every part of the world. About 8 million Muslims live in North America and 12 to 15 million in Western Europe. Although Islam is traditionally associated with the Middle East, the largest Muslim populations are in south Asia: Indonesia, Malaysia, Bangladesh, Pakistan, and India. Indonesia has the largest number of Muslims—around 200 million—of any country in the world. Large Muslim populations are also found in central Asia, including China. In the aftermath of recent events involving violence done in the name of Islam, careful and unbiased study of Islam has become more challenging for North American students than in the past. However, it is all the more necessary. As you begin your study of Islam, these particular puzzlements may emerge:

- Islam seems to be centered on Muhammad (moo-HAHM-id) and his teaching. Whenever Muslims mention his name they say, "Peace be upon him," and "Muhammad" is now the most common first name in the world. Muslims honor Muhammad and are usually quick to defend him. However, Muhammad isn't at the heart of Muslim devotion, or even near it. Muslims believe that he was only the human conduit of God's revelations.

- Islam is a deeply spiritual religion centered on the one God, but it is equally a religiously shaped way of life for a community of people. From its founding, Islam has preferred to function as both a religion and a state, and in twenty-five nations of the world—in the Middle East, North Africa, and south Asia—it is the official state religion.

- Islam has spread throughout the world and has adapted to many cultures, but wherever it goes it still carries on key elements of its Arab origins. For example, all Muslims who own a Qur'an are expected to have one with the Arabic text alongside a modern translation if they can't read Arabic, and most Muslims typically have an Arabic first name.

- Some Muslims today seem to speak for all of Islam, but no one really can because of its diversity. For example, Muslim leaders in some nations enforce laws in the name of Islam that

This mosque in Singapore shows a combination of Arab and south Asian styles.

all women wear a veil in public that covers their whole body, but Muslim women in other nations are free to go out in regular clothing, with their hair covered by a scarf and their face fully visible.

- Many non-Muslims today think that Islam is a violent religion, but the vast majority of Muslims don't engage in violence for their faith today—nor did they in the past. This misconception is especially prevalent in nations that have been the objects of recent attacks by terrorists acting in the name of Islam.

Read an introduction to Islam for Westerners by the Saudi Arabian government.

Muslims understand the name of their religion as submission to God, not peace with God.

LO1 The Name *Islam*

Muhammad and his first followers referred to their movement as **Islam**, "submission," always understood as submission to God and his will. They came to be known as *Muslims* (MUHZ-limz), which means "submitters." (The older spelling *Moslem* is still found, and is not incorrect, but *Muslim* is now preferred.) Explanations of the word *Islam* today, even by some Muslims, sometimes imply that it comes from the Arabic word for "peace," *salam* (sah-LAHM). *Salam* is indeed related to

Islam, but it is a different word. Although Muslims see peace as coming from submission to God, the great majority of Muslims understand the name of their religion as *submission* to God, not *peace* with God.

Islam [ihz-LAHM] "Submission" to God

The term *Mohammedanism* for Islam came about when Christians wrongly supposed that followers of Muhammad named themselves after him, just as Christians were named after Jesus Christ. You may see this term in older literature, but you should avoid using it. You may also see the current term *Islamist* for Muslim radicals, particularly those who espouse violence in the name of Islam. We'll consider the validity of this term later this chapter, but for now you should know that it covers only a very small proportion of Muslims.

Read a geographic sketch of the Arabian Peninsula.

LO2 Islam Today As Shaped by Its Past

A film depicting the life of the Prophet Muhammad began production in 2009. In keeping with Muslim tradition, however, the face and voice of the Prophet won't be seen or heard on screen. *The Messenger of Peace* is a remake of *The Message* from 1977. Producer Oscar Zoghbi, who worked on *The Message*, said that his team had great respect for the original film and that this latest project will employ modern film techniques in its renewal of the original film's message. The mistaken belief that actor Anthony Quinn was portraying

A Closer Look:

The Symbol of Islam?

This chapter opens with a representation of the crescent and star, said by many to be a symbol of Islam. Because Islam is typically against religious images and pictures, whether worshiped or not, it hasn't officially adopted pictorial symbols for itself. The crescent and star symbol is featured prominently on the flags of several countries in the Islamic world. It's often thought to be an Islamic symbol from the first centuries of Islam, but it first appeared as the symbol of the Ottoman Empire that governed much of Islam from about 1300 to 1920, not of Islam as a

BONNIE VAN VOORST © CENGAGE LEARNING

whole. Thus, it's no more than five hundred years old. The Ottoman flag had the crescent and star symbol, and has since become associated with Islam itself.

Crescents without a star are often found at the top of mosques, where they remind Muslims of God's rule over creation, and in particular of the importance of the moon in the Muslim religious calendar—which is based on the phases of the moon, not the sun. Also, the crescent and star are carved as a symbol of Islam into the gravestones of Muslims in the U.S. armed forces buried in U.S. military cemeteries. But on the whole, Islam has no official symbol.

Muhammad in the 1977 film sparked protests by Muslims in the West, some of them violent, and harmed the commercial prospects for the film. With the risk of similar misunderstandings lessened by careful publicity in the Muslim world, work on the new film goes forward, but slowly and carefully.

Read a newspaper account of planning for the film *The Messenger of Peace*.

ARABIA AT THE TIME OF MUHAMMAD (500S C.E.)

Arabian religion of the sixth century C.E. had many gods, and Muslims refer to it as the "age of ignorance." Mecca, the largest city in the Arabian Peninsula, was a regional center of this religion, and many pilgrims visited its shrines. Pilgrims entering Mecca first saw statues of the three beautiful daughters of Allah, one of the high gods of traditional Arab religion. They visited a cube-shaped shrine dedicated to the god Hubal and drank from a sacred well. Although religious practices were important in Mecca, social life in the tribes shaped the key values of pre-Islamic Arabia much more than did religion. One scholar has called pre-Islamic Arabia's way of life a "tribal humanism."[1] Pre-Islamic Arabia honored loyalty to one's kin, bravery in battle, and protection of the weak. But it had no strong religious values that could go against the grain of tribal values and little belief in any meaningful afterlife.

Pre-Islamic Arabia had no religious or social resources to deal with rising social inequities. In the generation before the beginning of Islam, unprecedented wealth from international commerce was pouring into Mecca, which had come to control international trade that passed through the Arabian Peninsula. This new wealth produced new social divisions, and it brought more cross-cultural interaction throughout the peninsula. Jews, Christians, and Zoroastrians lived there in significant numbers along with the Arab majority, particularly in the north. A small group of Arab monotheists, the *hanifs*, or "pious ones," was devoted to the worship of Allah, the one and only God.

THE LIFE AND WORK OF MUHAMMAD (CA. 570–632)

Muhammad Ibn ("son of") Abdullah was the founder of Islam. Historians disagree about how much his ideas arose out of older religions, as well as about the factors that contributed to the rapid expansion of Arab rule and Islamic religion. But what follows here is mostly agreed on. Muhammad was born around 570 C.E. in Mecca, into a relatively humble family of the Quraysh (KUR-aish) tribe that controlled Mecca. He was orphaned as a boy and raised by relatives. They couldn't afford schooling for Muhammad, so he worked as a camel driver and then a caravan manager. His scant financial resources meant that he wasn't able to marry at the usual age.

Eventually, he came to work for a wealthy widow engaged in trade, Khadija (kah-DEE-juh). When she suggested marriage to him, he agreed, even though she was fifteen years older than he. Muhammad and Khadija were devoted exclusively to each other; while she lived, he didn't take another wife. They had six children together, four girls and two boys, but the boys died in childhood, a situation that has influenced Islam through today, as we'll see later this chapter. Muhammad prospered and became a wealthy merchant, and his extensive travel for business brought him into contact with Jews, Christians and Zoroastrians as well as hanifs and believers in many gods. Much current scholarship suggests that this contact likely helped shape his own faith as he began to doubt his own inherited religion, although traditional Muslim teaching maintains that Muhammad obtained monotheism from Allah. His humble origins as the son of a poor widow, then an orphan, and finally as a happy husband to Khadija are no doubt related to Muhammad's strong concern, as expressed in the Qur'an, that the treatment of widows, orphans, and wives be significantly improved.

In 610 C.E., Muhammad was meditating continually for days and nights in a cave outside Mecca. There he saw visions that came in a dream-like state and revealed the word of God to him. When he fell into a trance, the angel Gabriel, known to Jews and Christians from the Bible, spoke to him. Muhammad heard Gabriel's voice outside himself and sometimes inside. "Recite!" the angel commanded (Qur'an 96), and Muhammad submitted to this command, reciting Gabriel's words to others. In a short time, the uncertain seeker of truth became a bold prophet. He had been transformed by submitting to the one true God who spoke to him, and in his submission he found freedom and courage. According to Islamic tradition, Muhammad received his first revelation from Gabriel the night of the twenty-seventh day of the month of Ramadan (RAHM-uh-dahn), and the month-long fast all Muslims undertake for Ramadan celebrates the giving of the revelations.

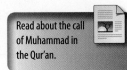

Read about the call of Muhammad in the Qur'an.

---

[1] W. Montgomery Watt, *Muhammad: Prophet and Statesman* (New York: Oxford University Press, 1974), 51.

Muhammad's early prophetic message to the Meccans had two main themes. First, only one God exists, **Allah**, Arabic for "the God," who commands people to believe in this one God and to submit to God's holy will. Second, a day of judgment will certainly come, when those who have submitted to God will be rewarded forever, and those who haven't submitted will be punished eternally. Other themes of the early revelations include generosity to the poor, widows, and orphans; the presence and goodness of God in the natural world; and the prophetic call of Muhammad himself. This message shows clearly that Islam from its beginning is in the line of the Abrahamic monotheisms, Judaism and Christianity.

Khadija and other members of Muhammad's immediate family believed him, but as Muhammad began his public proclamations (probably around 613), some Meccans became hostile to him. However, Muhammad did gain some followers outside his family, and in ten years of growth the number of Muslims numbered in the thousands. Most of them were relatively young and of lower social status. The tribal leaders in Mecca looked on Muslims as social deviants whose denial of the traditional gods and growing numbers threatened the economic foundations of the city. They ridiculed Muhammad as a lunatic, "only a poet" inventing his own revelations (Qur'an 52:30–49). They pointed out that Muhammad worked no miracles or offered other supernatural signs of his prophetic calling. Muhammad responded by saying that the revelations themselves were a supernatural sign. His "Night Journey" to Jerusalem later on was a supernatural event that served to bolster his credibility, and his ascent into heaven from the rock on the Jewish Temple Mount would lead to the building of the Dome of the Rock mosque on that site. But

Read about the Night Journey.

persecution escalated, and after the death of both his uncle and Khadija in 619, Muhammad's position in Mecca deteriorated.

> *"In Medinah, Muhammad became a prophet-statesman, the founder of a political order ... that would change the world."* —Daniel Peterson.

In 622 C.E., the prophet and most of his followers fled Mecca for Medina (then called Yathrib), about two hundred miles to the north. This relocation is called the **Hijra**, "flight," and is used to mark year 1 A.H. ("in the year of the flight") on the Islamic calendar, much as Christians traditionally use A.D., "in the year of our Lord (Jesus)." The Muslims were welcomed in Medina, and Muhammad was soon in charge of the fractious town. Muhammad would live in Medina for the rest of his life. In Medina, Islam developed into a well organized religious-political community called the **umma**, a complete way of life for its followers. As Daniel Peterson remarks, "Muhammad became a prophet-statesman, the founder of a political order and eventually of an empire that would change the history of the world. And Islam took on a political dimension that it has never abandoned."[2] Principles of a legal system came in divine revelations given at Medina, as did details about prayer, fasting, charity, and pilgrimage, key practices that would later become the "pillars" of Islam. Muhammad made a pact with the Jews of Medina; they didn't need to become Muslims and would have a rich measure of religious freedom.

The Muslims organized armed raids on Meccan caravans to punish them for their hostility. These raids continued until the Muslim military victory over Mecca in the Battle of Badr (BAHD-er) in 624 C.E. The booty from this battle greatly increased the financial strength of the Muslims, and Muhammad gained great respect in Arabia; the battle proved to be a turning point in the fortunes of Islam. The gradual decline of Judaism in Medina, culminating in the killing of hundreds of Medinan Jews and the expulsion of the rest between 624 and 627 after a failed Jewish attempt to assassinate Muhammad, led to a more powerful dependence on Arabian religious practices reformed for Islamic use, particularly the religious system of the Quraysh tribe. For example, Muslims were no longer to pray facing Jerusalem, but rather toward Mecca (see Qur'an 2:142). The first Muslim pilgrimage to Mecca occurred in 629; pilgrimage to Jerusalem fell in importance. And the month-long Ramadan fast replaced the ten-day fast connected with the Jewish Day of Atonement.

Many Arab tribes in the region came into Islam while Muhammad controlled Medina, acknowledging his leadership. When the army he commanded got Mecca to surrender without a fight in 630, Muhammad immediately removed all idolatrous images from the city. He left only the sacred cubic building and its holy stone that was believed to have come directly from God. He kept Mecca as

Allah [AHL-lah] "The God" in Arabic

Hijra [HIHJ-ruh] "Flight" of Muslims to Mecca in 622 C.E.

umma [OOM-uh] Organized Muslim community

---

[2] Daniel Peterson, *Muhammad, Prophet of God* (Grand Rapids, MI: Eerdmans, 2007), 91.

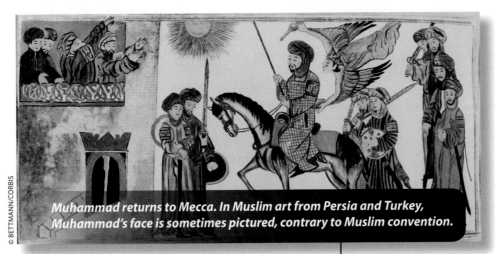

Muhammad returns to Mecca. In Muslim art from Persia and Turkey, Muhammad's face is sometimes pictured, contrary to Muslim convention.

the destination for Muslim pilgrimage and maintained some of its religious sites, for example the sacred well. Muhammad raised armies to conquer the important northern regions of the Arabian Peninsula, taking on the Christian Byzantine Empire in the process. By the time Muhammad died in Medinah two years later, in 632, he ruled most of the Arabian Peninsula. Islam had established itself permanently in this area, and it had become a rapidly growing religion (see Map 12.1).

ISLAM IMMEDIATELY FOLLOWING THE DEATH OF MUHAMMAD (632–661)

The most pressing issue at Muhammad's death was who would succeed him as leader of the Islamic movement, and the way it was settled affects Islam through today. For whatever reason, Muhammad hadn't publicly designated a successor. Muslims needed to select a leader of the faith who would be the **caliph**, the "representative" or "successor" of Muhammad. This successor would not receive new revelations from Gabriel or change Islam in major ways, but would lead the community in its political and religious life. In the Arab culture of the times such leadership would usually stay in the family, but Muhammad had no surviving son, so the leading choice from his family was his cousin Ali (ah-LEE), who was also his son-in-law due to his marriage to Muhammad's daughter Fatima (FAH-tih-muh). Ali had always been

caliph [kah-LEEF] "Representative" or "successor" of Muhammad; ruler of Muslim community

Shi'as [SHEE-uhs] or **Shi'ites** [SHEE-ites] "Party" or "followers" of Ali, the group that hold that Muhammad's true successors descended from his son-in-law Ali

Sunnis [SOON-eez] "People of the tradition," the majority of Muslims

enthusiastic for Islam, and Ali claimed that Muhammad had privately designated him as his successor. However, Ali's fitness to rule was contested by many.

A majority consensus arose among Muhammad's most powerful followers that Abu Bakr (AB-oo BAHK-uhr), Muhammad's father-in-law, would be Muhammad's successor. He was an early believer and one of Islam's main military leaders. Abu Bakr soon took over the leadership of Islam, due to three factors: his power base in the Muslim military forces; the need to squelch defections from Islam by several Arab tribes when Muhammad died; and his connection to the Prophet by way of Muhammad's favorite wife, A'isha (AH-ee-shah), who was Abu Bakr's daughter. Naturally, Ali's supporters objected to this, and the seeds of division were sown. The groups that grew from these seeds are the **Shi'as** or **Shi'ites**, "followers" or "party" (of Ali), and the **Sunnis**, the "people of the tradition" who formed the majority of Muslims. We'll discuss these two groups in more depth at the end of this history section.

> The most pressing issue at Muhammad's death was who would succeed him, and how it was settled affects Islam through today.

The rejection of Ali's leadership happened two more times, once when Abu Bakr died and was replaced as caliph by Umar in 634 and again when Uthman, a member of the Ummayad tribe, became caliph in 644 when Umar was assassinated. Ali's supporters grew increasingly bitter about these rejections. The caliphate seemed to be moving further and further from Muhammad's family. Despite this conflict, Islam continued to spread by Arab military conquest and follow-up Muslim missionary activity. In an action that would influence all of Islam to come, Uthman gathered all of Muhammad's revelations and issued an authoritative edition of the Qur'an. Muhammad himself had not committed any of the revelations to writing, much less oversaw that process. Instead, his followers had recorded his prophetic

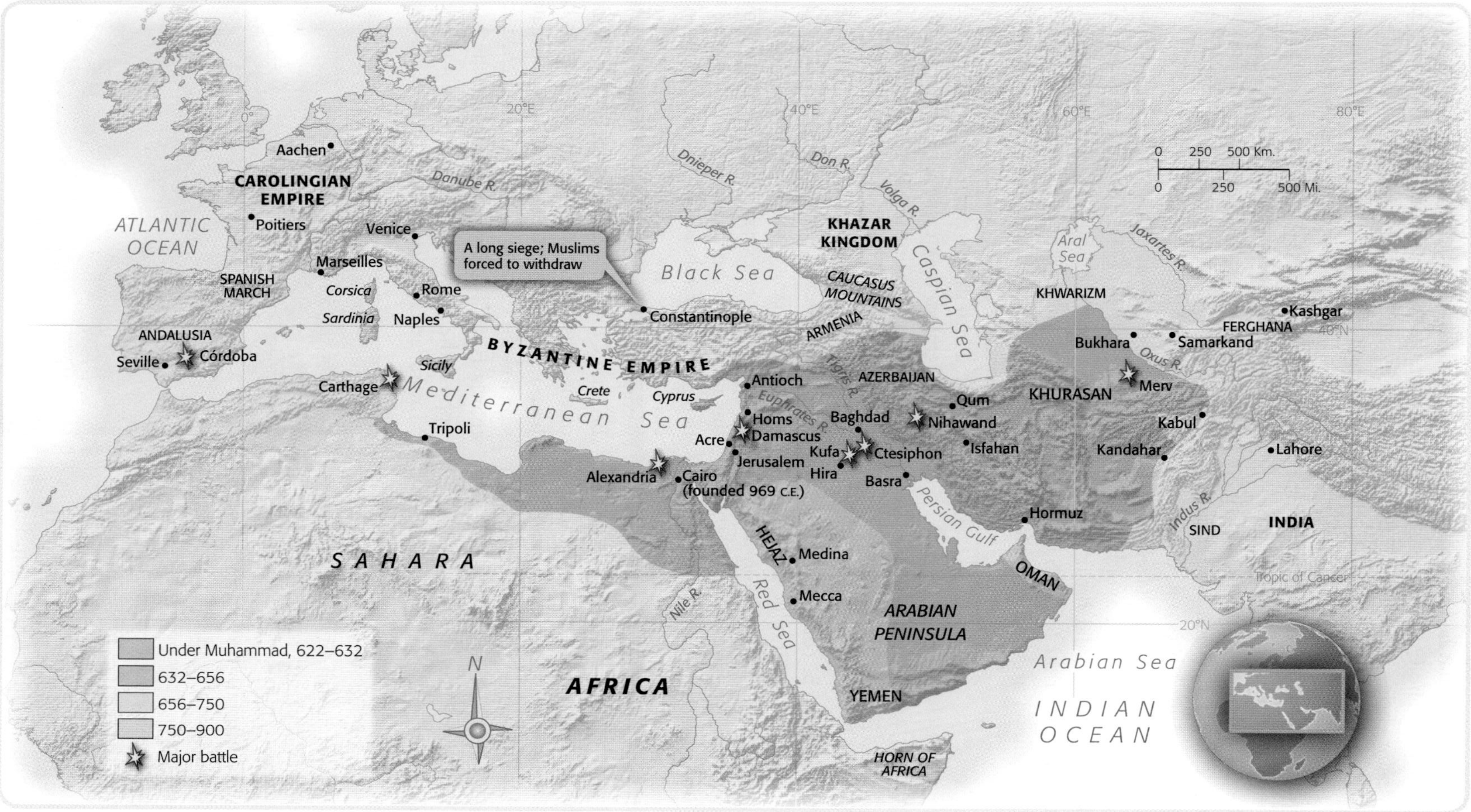

Map 12.1

Expansion of Islam to 900 C.E.

The Arabs rapidly conquered much of western Asia, North Africa, and Spain, in the process expanding Islam into the conquered territories. By 900 their empire included all the Mediterranean islands, and stretched from Morocco and Spain in the west to western India and central Asia.

Map labels:

© CENGAGE LEARNING 2013

Kashgar
FERGHANA
Samarkand
Joxartes R.
Bukhara
KHWARIZM
Merv
KHURASAN
Oxus R.
Kabul
Lahore
Kandahar
INDIA
SIND
Indus R.
Aral Sea
Hormuz
OMAN
Isfahan
Qum
Nihawand
Ctesiphon
Persian Gulf
Arabian Sea
INDIAN OCEAN
HORN OF AFRICA
Caspian Sea
Volga R.
KHAZAR KINGDOM
CAUCASUS MOUNTAINS
Don R.
Dnieper R.
AZERBAIJAN
ARMENIA
Baghdad
Tigris R.
Kufa
Basra
Hira
Euphrates R.
Antioch
Homs
Damascus
ARABIAN PENINSULA
YEMEN
Red Sea
Medina
Mecca
HEJAZ
Jerusalem
Acre
Cairo (founded 969 C.E.)
Black Sea
Constantinople
BYZANTINE EMPIRE
Cyprus
Crete
Alexandria
Nile R.
Mediterranean Sea
AFRICA
SAHARA
Tripoli
Sicily
Naples
Rome
Venice
Marseilles
Corsica
Sardinia
Danube R.
CAROLINGIAN EMPIRE
Aachen
Poitiers
SPANISH MARCH
Córdoba
Seville
ANDALUSIA
Carthage
ATLANTIC OCEAN
Tropic of Cancer
20°N
20°E
60°E
80°E

A long siege; Muslims forced to withdraw

Scale: 0 250 500 Km. / 0 250 500 Mi.

Legend:
Under Muhammad, 622–632
632–656
656–750
750–900
★ Major battle

recitations on parchment, palm leaves, or even pieces of wood. Uthman gathered these, along with the collections that already existed. He kept what he knew to be authentic and destroyed the rest. The Qur'an emerged as we have it today, and Muslims believe that it perfectly reflects Gabriel's revelations to Muhammad.

After Uthman was assassinated by rebels in 656, Ali finally became caliph, the last of what Muslims call the four "Rightly Guided Caliphs," that is, caliphs whom God directed to be faithful in ways other caliphs have not been. However, a leader of the Ummayad tribe soon claimed the caliphate. Hostilities between Ali and the Ummayads increased, and their armies faced off in 661. When Ali tried to compromise and avoid war, some of his followers killed him. War did break out, and the Sunnis were triumphant over the Shi'as. Sunnis had become the majority tradition of Muslims, in fact as well as in name.

ISLAM FROM THE UMMAYADS UNTIL TODAY (661–PRESENT)

The subsequent history of Islam can be concisely traced by means of its dynasties and its geographic growth. Sunni leadership belonged to the Umayyad (oo-MY-ahd) tribe for about one hundred years (661–750). The Umayyad Islamic Empire included almost all the Middle East, Persia (modern-day Iran), Egypt, North Africa, and Spain. The largest of the empires this area had seen since the fall of Rome in the fifth century C.E., it remained largely united for two centuries after Muhammad's death. However, the Ummayad rulers and their courts were lax in devotion to Islam, and their drinking of alcohol and their marital infidelities offended pious Muslims, who often revolted.

They were replaced by the Abbasid (ah-BASS-id) dynasty, which had a long rule from 750 to 1258. Islam spread farther into Africa and Asia; this was the second main period in the expansion of Islam. Many Muslims consider the Abbasid period to be the high point of Islamic history, particularly in such fields as art, science, philosophy, and Muslim theology. Muslim lands enjoyed a higher civilization than that of most Europeans during Abbasid times. They preserved much of the science, medicine, and mathematics of the ancient Mediterranean world, and they made important contributions of their own to these fields. Abbasid rule saw Islam strengthen as a religion, with greater equality between Arab and non-Arab Muslims. Muslim belief and practices grew wider and deeper in the Arab empire. By the 900s, religious schools known as madrasas (muh-DRAH-suhz) began to appear, usually headed by a well-known scholar of religion or religious law. Thousands of these schools can be found today all over the Muslim world. In 1285, Abbasid rule was ended by the invading Mongols, who had recently been converted from Buddhism to Islam. Arab control of Islam was permanently ended, and Islam was hurt both politically and culturally. Islamic law and philosophy, for example, were never the same again. However, between 1285 and 1550, Muslim territory doubled in size.

Read a BBC article on Muslim Spain.

In Egypt, Abassid rule yielded to the Shi'a Fatimid kingdom (919–1171). The end of wider Abbasid rule started when the Seljuk (SEL-jook) Turks took power in the eleventh century. The Turks—a name for a wide family of tribes and peoples—had long been residents of central Asia, but around 900 C.E. some of them migrated into the northern parts of the Middle East. As they migrated, they came into contact with Islam and converted to it. The Turks took over Arab Muslim rule as they moved. They lost possession of Palestine during the Crusades, when Christian military forces from Europe invaded to take control of the "Holy Land" where Christianity was born. *Crusade* comes from the Latin word for "cross," and Crusaders typically wore this symbol of Christianity on their clothing and shields to replace the symbols of their own European states. The Crusader state was never large and was ended by the second dynasty of Turks, the Mamluks (MAM-luhks). Because Christian nations were able to hold a key part of the Muslim homeland—including their holy city of Jerusalem—for more than a century, a negative impression toward Christianity was strengthened in Islam, one that lasts until today. This explains why Muslims who oppose the presence of Western military personnel in Muslim lands sometimes call them "Crusaders."

© 20TH CENTURY FOX FILM CORP

Film depiction of Crusaders in battle: Orlando Bloom starring in **Kingdom of Heaven** *(2005)*

In 1453, Muslims finally conquered Constantinople and renamed it Istanbul; the last Christian empire in the Middle East had finally fallen, and many of its churches were converted to mosques. For example, the former Christian Church of Holy Wisdom (Hagia Sophia) in Istanbul, Turkey, was made into a mosque. Turkish Muslim control spread eastward into India, where from 1526 until 1858 the Mughal (MOO-gahl) dynasty of Turkish Muslims ruled most of the Indian subcontinent. (Our word *mogul*, a powerful leader such as a Hollywood "movie mogul," comes from *Mughal*.) When the modern age began to dawn in the 1600s, Islam reached the height of its power in three main empires: the Sunni Ottoman Turks in the Middle East, North Africa, and much of southeastern Europe; the Shi'a Safavids in Iran; and the Sunni Mughals in India.

> "The most persistent mistake Westerners make about Islam today is to think of it as monolithic." —Rodney Stark

After the Mamluks lost their rule, the Ottoman Turks took over a vast empire of Islam and became the longest Islamic dynasty (1300–1923). It collapsed after its defeat in World War I, when it was on the side of Germany and Austria-Hungary. For the first time, the main Muslim empire had fallen to external powers. Something new to Islam was imposed on it by the victors: Instead of one Islamic empire, there were now many Muslim nation-states, almost all of them officially Muslim. Turkey, under its leader Mustafa Kemal (muh-STAHF-uh keh-MAHL), known as Ataturk (which means "Father of the Turks"), became the first and still today only officially secular nation with a predominantly Muslim population. It remains so today not without some difficulties, as some religiously conservative Muslims attempt to make it officially Muslim. Since 1918, Muslims in these nation-states have struggled to preserve Islam as an umma within their borders. They have also struggled with democratization, as European colonization after World War I held back that process. The popular uprisings in several Arab nations in 2011 demanded an end to autocratic rule and a measure of democracy. Despite these challenges, Islam is firmly established throughout North Africa, the Middle East, and both central and south Asia (see Map 12.2).

DIVERSE MUSLIM GROUPS TODAY: MAINSTREAM, ZEALOUS, AND MODERATE

The noted sociologist of religion Rodney Stark wrote in 2008, "The most persistent mistake Westerners make about Islam today is to think of it as monolithic."[3] In fact, Islam has a good deal of internal diversity, and often strongly opposing factions. We begin discussion of contemporary factions with the mainstream groups: Sunnis, Shi'as (whom we met above, but who are so important that they require fuller treatment here), and Sufis. Then we'll consider the more zealous groups in Sunni Islam: the Wahhabis, the Muslim Brotherhood, and the Taliban. Finally, we'll consider moderate Muslim movements. Along the way, we'll take a closer look at the term *Islamic fundamentalism*.

> Read a National Geographic report on unity and diversity in Islam.

Sunnis and Shi'as. The most important diversity within Islam is the split between Sunnis and Shi'as. As we saw above, the roots of this split go back to the death of Muhammad. When Caliph Ali died in 661, a lasting formal split developed between the rival Sunni and

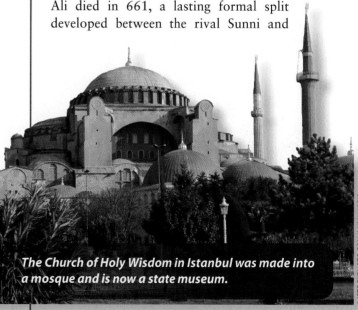

The Church of Holy Wisdom in Istanbul was made into a mosque and is now a state museum.

© ISTOCKPHOTO.COM/AMY HARRIS

---

[3] Rodney Stark, *Discovering God: The Origins of the Great Religions and the Evolution of Belief* (New York: HarperOne, 2008), 378.

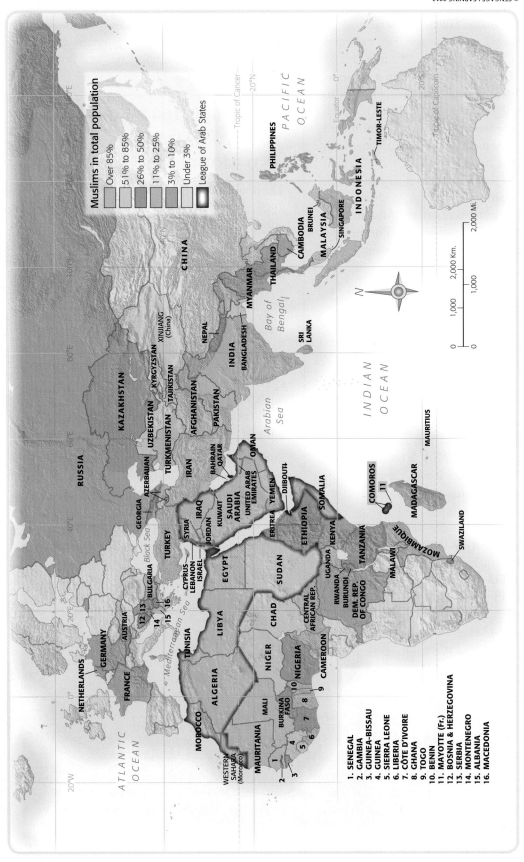

Map 12.2

The Islamic World Today

The Islamic world includes not only the Middle East—western Asia and North Africa—but also countries with Muslim majorities in sub-Saharan Africa, central Asia, and south and Southeast Asia. Sunnis predominate in most of the Islamic world; Shi'as predominate in Iran and form sizeable minorities in Iraq and Lebanon. In addition, Muslims live in most other Eastern Hemisphere nations and in the Americas, all under 3 percent of the population.

Muslims in total population

- Over 85%
- 51% to 85%
- 26% to 50%
- 11% to 25%
- 3% to 10%
- Under 3%
- League of Arab States

1. SENEGAL
2. GAMBIA
3. GUINEA-BISSAU
4. GUINEA
5. SIERRA LEONE
6. LIBERIA
7. CÔTE D'IVOIRE
8. GHANA
9. TOGO
10. BENIN
11. MAYOTTE (Fr.)
12. BOSNIA & HERZEGOVINA
13. SERBIA
14. MONTENEGRO
15. ALBANIA
16. MACEDONIA

Shi'a groups. Ali had two sons, Hassan and Husain, who were of course the grandsons of Muhammad. Shi'as claimed then, and still do today, that this descent made them the rightful caliphs. Hassan gave up his claim due to illness and died soon afterwards. In 680, Husain's army battled the Sunnis near the town of Karbala in present-day Iraq. But the Sunnis cut off the Shi'a army from its water supply and then destroyed the Shi'as. When Husain's severed head was thrown over the wall of Karbala, his supporters in the town put it on a lance and reverently carried it around with deep mourning. Shi'a would continue in Islam as a separate group averaging about 10 to 15 percent of all Muslims, but never again would Shi'as challenge Sunnis for control of Islam as a whole.

The day of Husain's death, the tenth of Muharram, is observed by Shi'as as a day of mourning—called *Ashura* (uh-SHOOR-uh), "the tenth." Husain's death is now viewed as martyrdom, a holy death, for the true form of Islam; commitment to martyrdom for Islam became a leading part of Shi'a. In mass processions still held on this day, many Shi'a men connect with Husain's martyrdom by lashing themselves with chains and whips until their blood flows. It was on Ashura in 1979 that Shi'a radicals in the capital of Iran stormed the American embassy and held its personnel hostage in violation of international law for more than a year, an event that still casts a dark shadow on U.S.-Iranian relations.

> *Shi'as and Sunnis have typically lived, worked, and worshipped apart from each other.*

As we saw above, Shi'as believe that the line of Islamic leadership continues through Ali and Husain, that is, through the family of Muhammad. Each leader receives, as Shi'as claim Ali received from Muhammad, a direct designation of succession from his predecessor and a supernatural knowledge of Islam to be an effective leader. The Arabic term for "leader" is **imam**, a general term that carries different (and sometimes confusing) meanings; for example, it is also the term for the leader of a

MR.MINOQUE
Ruholla Khomeini, head Shi'a imam and leader of the Iranian Revolution in 1979

Sunni mosque. Shi'as typically view their imam's interpretation of Islam as perfect and fully authoritative. Sometimes they even view the imam as unusually holy, even saintly; this is especially true for regional or national imams. All this makes for powerful religious leaders in Shi'a, more so than in Sunni groups. Shi'as revere and make pilgrimage to other holy places in addition to Mecca, such as the tombs of the imams, particularly those of Ali and Husain.

Shi'as and Sunnis have typically lived, worked, and worshipped apart from each other. Shi'as have their own territories where they predominate, and beyond this they tend to be minorities in many Sunni nations. Where Sunnis and Shi'as are found in the same cities, they prefer to live in different neighborhoods. They usually don't intermarry or go into business with each other, and they have their own mosques and leaders. Shi'as have five additional pillars—besides the Five Pillars common to all Muslims that we'll consider below—stressing Shi'a doctrines and practices, and slight differences in their formal prayers.

Shi'a history is a story of almost continual internal splits. Shi'a sects are still wary of one another. (One of the features of splinter groups in religion is that they're often beset by internal splintering; in other words, splitters keep splitting.) Three main groups account for most Shi'as today, but each has its own subgroups. The three groups are named by how many original imams they recognize.

- The *Twelvers*, also known as *Imamites*, recognize twelve imams in the line of succession from Muhammad. The twelfth imam vanished when he was five years old and is still living in a hidden cave. Some day he'll return as the Mahdi (MAH-dee; "the one guided" by God) near the end of time and establish worldwide Shi'a rule. Twelvers are the majority of Shi'as today; they make up most of Iranian and Iraqi Shi'as, and they are present in Lebanon as well.

- The *Seveners*, or *Ismailites*, are found today in India, Pakistan, and east Africa. Some Seveners believe that the seventh imam, Ismail, was Allah in human form, a notion that all other Muslims regard as heretical. Ismailites claim that Ismail will return as the Mahdi. The Fatimid dynasty in Egypt was from the Seveners. The current leader of the largest group of Seveners is Prince Karim Aga Khan IV, the forty-ninth Ismaili imam, who traces his lineage to Muhammad through Fatima.

- The *Fivers*, or *Zaidites*, are a small sect of Shi'as found mostly in Yemen. Their fifth imam is Zaid, who began a different line of succession that eventually died out. He is now living in concealment. Fivers tend to be less hostile to Sunnis, but in the past decade they've engaged in armed rebellion against the Sunni government of Yemen.

The Sunnis and Shi'as comprise the two main divisions in Islam, but other Muslim groups have brought further Muslim diversity. Despite their relatively small size, they've exerted a significant influence within Islam and are still important in Islam today. We'll consider them in chronological order.

Sufis. Islam typically emphasizes the practice of religion, not thinking or feeling it. Submitting to God's will in one's actions is most important. However, Islam developed a mystical tradition to find deeper spiritual power within its religious teachings and practices. Islamic mystics are **Sufis**, a word for the woolen garments worn by the first Muslim mystics. Sufism arose in the 700s and is still found among both Sunnis and Shi'as. It has spread Islam on the peripheries of the Muslim world. Within Islamic lands it has spread deeper religious commitment among the lower classes, particularly in "folk Islam" in Africa and central Asia. Sufism is also very popular today in Pakistan. In its long history, it has organized into several "orders" or "brotherhoods," among whom are the Medlevi (mehd-LEHV-ee) order. Sometimes connected to Sufis, but in fact related to Ismailites, are the Hashishin (ha-SHEESH-een), who used hashish to induce visions of the divine and then became hired killers. (Our word *assassin* comes from this group.)

Explore Islamic religion and culture.

Sufis pursue a mystical quest for a direct, ecstatic experience of God.

Sufis pursue a direct, loving, and ecstatic experience of God, usually to narrow the gap between God and humans. Poetry, music, and dancing are important in this mystical quest. At first Muslim authorities viewed Sufism with suspicion, until it became apparent that Sufis did indeed follow key Muslim practices. Sufism was allowed to continue, but many Muslims viewed the notion of human beings becoming literally one with God as idolatrous. (A factor in this suspicion, beyond the doctrinal element, could have been the influence of passages in the Qur'an about Muhammad's struggle with religious poets in Medina and Mecca.) All Muslims expect to be close to God after the final judgment, but most except the Sufis see achieving a mystical closeness—not to mention oneness—with God in this life as difficult and dangerous. The most influential Sufi by far is Jalal al-Din Rumi (jah-LAL al-DIHN ROO-mee), the thirteenth-century Persian poet of mystical love who has been called the most popular poet in America today, even among non-Muslims. Sufism produced the "whirling dervishes" who seek ecstasy in their dance; they have attained religious and cultural fame today.

According to some proponents of Sufism in the Western world, Sufi ideas developed prior to our modern "organized" religions and are universal in nature, a system of mysticism that is employable by people of many faiths. They point to verses in Rumi's poetry, such as this one from "One Song":

> All religions, all this singing, one song
> The differences are just illusion and vanity.
> Sunlight looks different on this wall than it does on
>   that wall
> and different on this other one,
> but it is still one light.

However, Sufis themselves typically reject the notion of Sufism without Islam. Despite the words of Rumi, "I am neither Christian, nor Jew, nor Zoroastrian, nor Muslim," Sufism has been, and probably will remain, an inner-Islamic movement.

Wahhabis. From its very beginnings, Islam has seen movements that strive for strict purity and zeal. In more recent times, one such group, the **Wahhabi** reform movement in Sunni Islam was begun by Muhammad al-Wahhab (al-wah-HAHB) in the late 1700s. Wahhab was shocked by what he regarded as widespread corruption in Islam. He despised Sufism because he thought that it mixed Islam and Hindu pantheism, and he disapproved of many Shi'a popular practices as well. For example, the tombs of prominent Muslims in Shi'a and Sufi circles became places to venerate them in order to gain spiritual power. Wahhab considered this idolatry, the most serious sin in Islam. His message of reform was summed up in the cry "Back to the

Sufi dancers, "whirling dervishes," of the Medlevi order

strong convictions are carried out not in religious thought or theory (Sunni, Shi'a), or even in emotional dimensions of submission to God (Sufi), but in daily practice. Most Sunnis in the world today don't live under Wahhabi requirements. However, Saudi Arabia is the most influential nation in the Muslim world for its holy cities of Mecca and Medina and its vast oil wealth, so the way it practices Islam has become widely known and influential.

The Muslim Brotherhood.

When the Ottoman Empire collapsed around 1920, the Muslim world was left for the first time without a caliph. This vacuum in religious leadership, coupled with new colonial control of many Middle Eastern nations by European powers under the direction of the League of Nations, led to a rise of conservative movements in several large Muslim nations. One of the earliest and most influential—the Muslim Brotherhood—was launched in Egypt by the charismatic Hassan al-Banna in 1929. Opposed to corruption, the lax practice of Islam, and Westernization in Egyptian government and life, the Brotherhood worked for purely Islamic legal systems in Egypt. Since then, the movement has spread to several other Sunni Muslim countries.

Sometimes the Brotherhood's actions are violent, and many Arab governments view it as undermining their rule. The Muslim Brotherhood is often said to be the beginning of organized "Islamic fundamentalism" with "political" dimensions, but that distinction should probably belong to Wahhabism. Muslim Brotherhood members have taken very conservative stances; for example, in Kuwait they have recently opposed laws giving women the right to vote. In early 2011, Muslim Brotherhood members played a key role in toppling the rule of Egyptian president Hosni Mubarak (HOHS-nee moo-BAHR-ahk), and observers have been anticipating their continued role in political change in other Middle Eastern nations.

Book [the Qur'an] and the Tradition [sunna] of the Prophet!" He adhered to the most conservative method of Quranic interpretation.

In time, Wahhab gained the support of the powerful tribal ruler Ibn Sa'ud (EE-bin sah-OOD). They began to cleanse the Arabian Peninsula of anything they considered detrimental to pure Islam. They sacked the Shi'a shrines in what is today Iraq and destroyed Sufi settlements in the Arabian Peninsula. (The 2009 destruction of a historic Sufi shrine in Peshawar, Pakistan, by militant Sunnis is an echo of Wahhabi opposition to Sufism.) After Wahhab's death in 1792, his movement made uncertain progress in the 1800s, because the Ottoman rulers occasionally cracked down on new religious groups that they saw as a challenge to their authority and religious moderation.

A Wahhabi state was finally established in the 1920s when the Sa'ud family became rulers of the new nation of Saudi Arabia. Practices that Wahhabis considered idolatrous were strongly punished: consumption of any alcohol, veneration of saints at their tombs, playing of secular music, possession of anything deemed pornographic, or the formal presence of any other religions. Muslim religious law became the law of Saudi Arabia, and is strictly enforced. The so-called religious police, formally called the "Commission for the Promotion of Virtue and the Prevention of Vices," patrol public areas to enforce this law, particularly on women's dress and conduct, but this has been easing a bit since 2001. The Western press often calls Wahhabism "puritanical," but that's a term from Protestant Christian history that ill fits this Islamic movement. Wahhabism's

The Taliban.

The latest movement important for understanding Islam today is the **Taliban**, "students" of the Qur'an. (We'll consider a related group, al-Qaeda,

Taliban [TAHL-ih-bahn] "Students" of the Qur'an, a radical Sunni group that came to power in Afghanistan

A Closer Look:

"Islamic Fundamentalism"?

Deciding what to call the phenomenon commonly known as "Islamic fundamentalism" isn't easy. This term became popular after the Iranian Revolution in 1979 as a description of the resurgent Shi'a movement. It was used first by Westerners, especially American journalists, often unaware that they were applying a term for certain American Protestant Christians to Muslims. Sometimes other contemporary groups are labeled "Islamic fundamentalists," for example the Taliban, al-Qaeda, the Wahhabis, and the Muslim Brotherhood.

Islamism is found today in the press and in scholarly writing. It avoids the weaknesses of *Islamic fundamentalism* and has the appeal of one-word simplicity. However, *Islamism* is an oddly constructed word, and the suffix *-ism* can be pejorative. Some groups labeled "Islamists" maintain that they are simply faithful Muslims—that they follow Islam, not "Islamism"—and that their political convictions are an expression of their religious belief in the Islamic way of life.

Political Islam is occasionally used today for this movement's effort to reunite the "political" and the "religious," but as we've seen, Islam traditionally strives to do this and has in fact done so in most of its history. *Activist Islam* is accurate enough but is vague and wrongly implies that mainstream Islam isn't really "active." In *militant Islam*, we must distinguish between those who use violence and those who don't. Even among the first, a distinction must be drawn between those who use violence according to traditional rules of jihad and those who use it outside of jihad (a term discussed in an upcoming section).

Radical Islam is perhaps the best of these options, although it isn't without its own problems. *Radical* is vaguer than the terms above, and it can have a pejorative connotation. On the positive side, it has the connotation of both "going to the root" and going all the way with what "radicals" believe God wants.

below.) They draw members from many Sunni Islamic countries. The Taliban was influenced by the Wahhabi movement during the successful Muslim struggle to drive the Soviet Union out of the Muslim nation of Afghanistan in the 1980s. In the 1990s, the Taliban was able to gain control of Afghanistan. The first Taliban home page on the World Wide Web invited Muslims to contribute money to what they called the "first truly Islamic state in history." They gained opposition in the West for repressive measures against Afghani women, such as ending all education except homeschooling for females of any age and prohibiting women from working outside their homes. Like some Muslims before them who were also zealous for Islam, the Taliban considers those Muslims who don't adhere to their strict attitudes and standards of behavior to be false Muslims and enemies of Islam. Their means for bringing about their ideals were often brutally violent, and as of this writing they continue their military struggle to regain rule in Afghanistan. Their strong belief has made them tenacious fighters.

Moderate Muslim Movements. It might seem to you from this treatment of Muslim groups that Islam has only gotten more conservative in the last century or so. This would be a mistake. In recent times, Muslim modernism tried to revive the most ancient forms of Islam and reform it by determining the meaning of the Qur'an. Some historical methods new to Islam but

well known in Europe were introduced to attempt to recover the original meaning of the Qur'an. For example, the Indian Muslim scholar M. Azad (1888-1958) argued that one must study Arabian culture at the time of Muhammad to understand what the Qur'an originally meant. This liberalizing movement was generally confined to the more Westernized upper classes, and it didn't get much traction.

After 2001, a small but vocal group of Muslims has been trying to move Islam to the center, and some even call themselves "Progressives." Omid Safi, a professor in the University of North Carolina at Chapel Hill who wrote *Progressive Muslims: On Justice, Gender, and Pluralism*, opposes (along with moderates) Wahhabism, the Taliban, and all other radical Islamic groups.[4] Another example of progressive Islam is Sisters in Islam, a Malaysian group founded in the 1980s by the politically connected professor Zainab Anwar. Sisters in Islam promotes an Islamic vision of freedom, justice, and equality for women. Taking their cues from the ministry of Muhammad, who reformed the conditions of the poor and women, they urge further reform. Progressive Muslims typically claim that after Muhammad died, a conservative wave

---

[4] Omid Safi, *Progressive Muslims: On Justice, Gender, and Pluralism* (New York: OneWorld, 2003).

swept over Islam, and his reforms were effectively frozen when they should have continued. They view themselves as carrying on in the spirit and message of Muhammad.

An important part of this moderating movement is the liberation of Muslim women. The status of Muslim women has been a persistently difficult issue, both within Islam and in the wider world. Traditionally, Islam sees gender differences as given by God. The Qur'an says, "Men have authority over women because God has made the one superior to the other, and because men spend their wealth to maintain women" (4:34). It also affirms that "Women shall with justice have rights similar to those exercised against them, although men have a status above women" (2:228). Moderates and progressives struggle to give women a greater measure of freedom: to wear a head covering or not; to have an opportunity at a full education equal to that of men; to vote and participate in politics; and in several other ways. Their progress is slow, and they encounter opposition in parts of the Muslim world, but they are not discouraged.

Watch a video on Irshad Manji, a prominent Muslim feminist.

LO3 Essential Teachings

California's Orange County has a thriving mosque. Yassir Fazaga keeps an eye on the American calendar to provide a connection for his weekly Friday sermon as the imam. Around Valentine's Day, he talks about how the Qur'an endorses romantic love within certain moral boundaries. "My main objective is to make Islam relevant," said Fazaga, thirty-four, who was born in east Africa, went to high school in Orange County, and attended college and a religious training school in Virginia. As the first generation of American-born Muslims begins to graduate from American colleges in significant numbers, some mosques are beginning to seek native-born leaders who can teach not just about the main central teachings of Islam, but also about religious and social issues that are relevant to Muslim young people here, such as dating, marriage, and drugs. One of the challenges facing Islam in North America is to obtain imams who can lead Muslim communities in the North American context.

GOD IS ONE

Because Muslims forbid anything that encourages idolatry, they don't make images or pictures of God or even Muhammad.

Muslims consider the teaching that there is only one God to be the basis and the center of their religion. The Arabic word *Allah* doesn't refer only to the God of Islam. It is the common, generic Arabic word for God—any God—and when Muslims talk in Arabic about the God of Jews, Christians and Zoroastrians, *Allah* is the word they use.

The roots of Muhammad's understanding of Allah lie in monotheism. God is an eternal, spiritual being; God is not a force but a divine person. The Qur'an sees Islam as carrying on this true monotheistic religion that Judaism and Christianity have mostly abandoned. Islam has a strict, absolute form of monotheism, because God is seen as one and one only. Therefore, Muslims reject all forms of polytheism as false religions, and other gods as false. Like Muhammad, they urge others to follow only the one God. Muhammad considered the "fatherhood" of Allah—which he associated with the sexual procreation of a son or the "daughters of Allah," taught in pre-Islamic Arabian religion—as idolatrous. Muslim monotheism led to opposing the

Allah *written artistically*

© ISTOCKPHOTO.COM/QUTAIBA

Read the Qur'an on God's oneness.

Christian doctrine of Jesus as the Son of God. The Qur'an says, "God is One, the eternal God. He begot no one, nor was He begotten" (112:1–3). In Islam, idolatry (*shirk*), acknowledging other gods beside the one and only God, is considered the worst sin.

Muslims forbid idolatry so strongly that they forbid anything that encourages it or even makes it possible. Therefore, they don't make images or pictures of God. If Muhammad is depicted at all, his face is omitted. (A few schools of Muslim art in the past have ignored this.) Strict Muslims today object to any representational art forms as a temptation to idolatry. This has led to mosques being decorated only with colorful geometric patterns, which are said to reflect the order and beauty of the creation as a whole, not of God. These patterns can be strikingly beautiful and inspiring. When the author of this book went for the first time into the Dome of the Rock mosque in Jerusalem, it impressed

Non-iconic art in a mosque in Isfahan, Iran

© ISTOCKPHOTO.COM/JAVARMAN3

him as one of the most beautiful buildings he had ever seen. Verses from the Qur'an are also used in decorating mosques and homes.

God is unique in essence and attributes, infinite, and the creator and sustainer of all that exists. "His are the beautiful names," ninety-nine in all; most of these names are scattered in the Qur'an, but they are compiled in a later tradition. Moreover, God is beyond all human thought and understanding. God can be described, but not known in any comprehensive way. God is all-powerful, and Muslims typically believe that all that happens in the world, good or evil, happens within the plan and control of God. The phrase *enshallah* (en-SHAHL-ah), "if God wills it," is used by Muslims whenever they talk about the future; in fact, it's probably the most commonly used Arabic expression.

ANGELS AND SPIRITS

God created angels and spirits to serve God and the human beings created later. Muhammad received the Qur'an through the archangel Gabriel. Islam recognizes three other archangels and a large company of ordinary angels. As in Judaism and Christianity, angels are the messengers carrying divine revelation to humans. There are also many **jinn**, "spirits" (related to our word *genie*). In the Qur'an they say about themselves, "Some of us are Muslims and some are wrongdoers" (72:14). Evil jinn are led by the devil, a spirit who rebelled against God when humans were created. Muslims must be on guard against the jinn, because they can cause not only physical harm but also spiritual harm by luring believers away from Allah.

Many Muslim believers have a lively sense of the good and evil forces of the jinn. Although the Qur'an and official Muslim teachings focus on belief and practices that draw the believer's focus to God alone, some Muslims practice Islam primarily to keep evil spirits at bay and bring the blessing of good spirits. Many Islamic teachers are laboring today, as Sufis did in the past, to raise all Muslims to a fuller understanding of monotheism: The focus of one's faith should not be on spirits, but on the God who controls good and evil spirits.

THE QUR'AN

Muslims believe that the angel Gabriel divinely revealed to Muhammad the Qur'an, the perfect copy of an eternal, heavenly book. The name *Qur'an* means "recitation," which indicates the main origin and use of this scripture in oral communication, first from Gabriel to Muhammad, then from Muhammad to his followers.

CRYSTALINA

Even mass-produced modern Qur'an covers suggest the high regard Muslims have for their scripture.

Televised contests of Qur'anic recitation are as popular in Muslim lands as shows such as American Idol are in North America.

The Qur'an is divided into 114 chapters called *surahs*, and each chapter is divided into verses. Because it is viewed by Muslims as the successor and fulfillment of the Jewish and Christian scriptures, it is legitimate to compare their relative sizes: The Qur'an is about two-thirds the size of the New Testament and half the size of the Jewish Bible. The chapters are arranged by length, from longer chapters to shorter ones. The shorter, older chapters focus on the basic themes of one God and future judgment; the longer, later ones contain many detailed instructions for the Islamic community as well as references to biblical history. Unlike the Jewish and Christian Bibles, the Qur'an tells virtually no historical narratives; it's almost all teaching and commands. It begins with **al-Fatihah**, "the Opening," Chapter 1, a beautifully resonant prayer that is recited at most prayer times. This chapter comes close to providing a summary of Islam:

> In the name of God, the Most Gracious, the Most Merciful. All praise and thanks be to God, the Lord of the Worlds, the Most Gracious, the Most Merciful, the only Lord of the Day of Judgment. You alone we worship, and You alone we ask for help. Guide us on the Straight Way, the Way of those on whom you have bestowed your grace, not of those who incur your anger or those who have gone astray.

The Qur'an itself is said to exist only in Arabic, the language in which it was revealed by Muhammad to others. (Whether Gabriel communicated it in Arabic or in a more supernatural way to Muhammad, who then understood it in Arabic, has been an open question to many Muslim leaders; most Muslims assume it was spoken by Gabriel in Arabic.) Muslims believe that all translations of the Qur'an involve some distortion of meaning, so no translation can be the authentic, perfect Qur'an. Where translations are used, most printed Qur'ans have the original Arabic text on facing pages. Muslim schoolchildren memorize large sections of the Qur'an in Arabic, even if Arabic isn't their main language. Imams are required to memorize all of it. Recitation of the Qur'an is an art form, with fame and sometimes riches going to those who are talented in recitation. Many Muslim nations televise contests of this recitation, and the level of excitement for these television shows approaches that in North America for shows such as *American Idol*.

al-Fatihah [fah-TEE-huh] "Opening," the first chapter of the Qur'an, used as a prayer in Islam

View a Qur'an contest recitation by a young girl.

The Qur'an contains many references to people and stories in the Jewish and Christian Bibles. We meet in the Qur'an figures such as Adam and Eve, Noah, Abraham, Moses, Jesus, and Mary, all of whom are considered Muslims and "prophets" in the prophetic line that culminates in Muhammad. Muslims believe that Gabriel spoke these biblical references to Muhammad during the revelations of Qur'anic content, thus accounting for the differences in these materials between the Bible and the Qur'an. However, non-Muslim scholars typically hold that Muhammad probably heard these materials first from his Jewish and Christian contacts.

Read the Qur'an on the Qur'an.

PROPHETS

The Qur'an states that God has revealed the divine will at key points in human history through prophets. All the prophets, including Muhammad, call for the same response: submission to the will of God and preparation for an impending judgment. Most of the twenty-five prophets mentioned in the Qur'an are the well-known figures in Judaism and Christianity mentioned above. The Qur'an also names three other prophets—Hud, Shu'aib, and Salih (7:66-93)—who may have been leading figures in the tradition. Although Jews and Christians claim many of these prophets as their own, Muslims view them as Islamic prophets who

Wooden placards decorated with Qur'anic verses for sale in a Moroccan bazaar

the law, and David composed the Psalms, for the Jews; Jesus taught the Gospels to Christians. Muslim call these groups "people of the book." This expression doesn't refer, as is sometimes said, to all people who have sacred books in their religions—after all, many religions have sacred books—but only to people whose sacred book(s) Muslims view in a line of religious development with *the* Book, the Qur'an. Some passages in the Qur'an even suggest that "people of the book" who follow their religions carefully will enter heaven along with Muslims.

Muhammad gave these "people of the book" privileges not available to others under his rule. After Muslim forces conquered their nations—their status didn't protect them from attack—they weren't forced to choose between conversion to Islam and death, as people of other religions usually were. They had to pay an extra tax and were subject to greater government oversight, but they were allowed to practice their religion among themselves. As long as they respected Muslim rule in their lands, these communities were tolerated; but if they didn't obey, especially if they turned rebellious, they were subject to annihilation. They didn't have the right to seek or even accept converts from Islam, build new houses of worship, or sometimes even repair old ones. They didn't have what most North Americans would call "freedom of religion," but they weren't a violently persecuted minority either.

teach submission to God. They didn't come to found Judaism, Christianity, or the hanif tradition as different religions—Muhammad is the culmination and conclusion of the entire line of prophets.

Despite this emphasis on Muhammad as the culmination of the prophets, some Muslims look for one more prophetic figure to come, the Mahdi. As stated above, Shi'as expect the last in the line of imams to be the Mahdi. He will come shortly before the end of time and the final judgment; his work is to rid the world of injustice as a preparation for the end. In the early 2000s, the main Shi'a paramilitary force in Iraq was called the Mahdi Army, but without any direct implication that the powerful Shi'a imam leading it was the Mahdi. The Mahdi idea has even appeared in Sunni circles at times, which is a bit odd, because the Sunni view is that Muhammad was the final prophet, a view that leaves no room for a Mahdi.

"PEOPLE OF THE BOOK": JEWS, CHRISTIANS, AND ZOROASTRIANS

Some in the line of Muslim prophets gave books to their people: Zoroaster wrote down his revelations; Moses recorded

Arab Muslim man reads the Qur'an

Over time, most of the Jewish, Christian, and Zoroastrian communities shrank to shadows of their earlier sizes in the Middle East and North Africa, as second-class status, pressure for conversion to Islam, and migration out of the Islamic empire took their tolls. In the past sixty years or so, there has been a great migration to Israel of Jews living in Arab

Read the Qur'an on
Jews and Christians.

lands and, in the past twenty years, a steady migration of Arab Christians from Palestine and Iraq to the United States.

FINAL JUDGMENT

The Qur'an's teaching on the judgment is simple and sobering (20:100–127; 18:101–104; 23:105–115). On a day known only to God, a heavenly trumpet will sound, and all the dead will rise from their graves with eternal bodies to meet their Maker. Everyone will be given a book in which is recorded all the deeds he or she has done in life. Angels will put the books of the wicked in their left hand, a symbol of divine disapproval, but the righteous will receive their book in their right hand. The righteous can then enter heaven, but the wicked go straight to hell.

God will judge people by how they submitted to God's will. Saying that one is a follower of Islam won't save anyone at the judgment; living in an obedient way is the important thing. In fact, the Qur'an states that severe punishments are in store for hypocrites who claim to be Muslims but haven't lived by Islam. To other Muslims who sincerely believe in God and try to do what God has revealed, God is "most gracious" and "most merciful." God gives special consideration to those who die in warfare or other struggle for Islam; they go to heaven, with great blessings. Literalist interpretation of this belief is used by a few radical Muslim groups today to recruit young men—those who seem to have little prospect for blessings on earth—for suicide missions as "martyrs." Most Muslims trust that God will forgive the occasional sins of mostly obedient people. For hypocrites and unbelievers, including those of other religions who know of God but haven't submitted to God, there is no forgiveness.

Islam focused from the first on heaven as an eternal reward for those who submit to God's will and on hell as an eternal punishment for those who don't. Heaven and hell are pictured in the Qur'an as places with physical and spiritual aspects (56:1–56). Heaven is a place of beautiful gardens, cool waters, plentiful food, wine that doesn't intoxicate, and the beautiful virginal women called *houris* (HOO-rees) whom God has created as rewards for righteous men. Hell is a place of physical and spiritual pain, complete with darkness, fire, and boiling filth. Although Muslims differ on how these descriptions of heaven and hell are to be interpreted—and most interpret them quite

literally—all observant Muslims believe that heaven and hell are real. Muslims are motivated to submit to God by the attractive promises about heaven and fearsome warnings about hell that reach all the way back to Muhammad.

LO4 Islamic Ethics

A young married woman in Jiddah, Saudi Arabia tunes into a twice-weekly broadcast of the *Oprah Winfrey Show*. "I feel that Oprah truly understands me," she tells an American visitor. "She gives me energy and hope for my life." This Saudi woman isn't alone; Saudi women under thirty watch *Oprah* more than any other television show. They are drawn by Oprah's welcoming personality, modest dress, and helpfulness in dealing with personal and family issues similar to some of those faced by Muslim women in Saudi Arabia. Government censors usually see nothing subversive in the *Oprah* show, but its segments dealing with forbidden practices, such as drinking alcohol or same-sex love, are not allowed to enter the nation.

A Muslim's whole life is a submitting to God's revealed way of behavior. Muslims believe that every person is born with an equal inclination toward God and doing what is good. Faith is a matter of knowing God and submitting to God's way. According to Muslim moral thought, all actions fall into one of three categories. *Fard* are good actions that are required, such as the Five Pillars of Islam that we'll consider in the next section. *Haram* (hah-RAHM) are evil actions explicitly prohibited, such as idolatry, immorality, and theft. *Halal* (hah-LAHL) are neutral matters that are permitted and

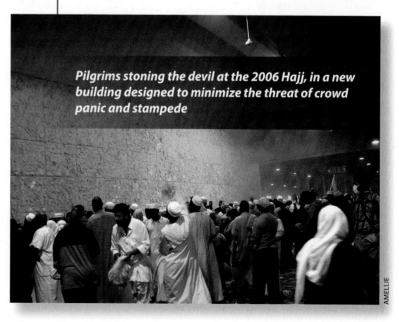
Pilgrims stoning the devil at the 2006 Hajj, in a new building designed to minimize the threat of crowd panic and stampede

left up to the discretion of the believer. Before considering the Five Pillars, we must first discuss a variety of other Muslim practices: foundations in the Hadith and the Shari'a; modesty in dress; marriage and gender relations; and jihad, struggle for the faith.

> *Muslims are obligated to commend what is good and reprimand evil.*

THE HADITH

The Qur'an is the main source of Muslim practices by which believers submit to God. For any issues that are undefined in the Qur'an, the prophet's life and informal sayings are the authoritative sources. These traditions are called the **hadith**, and they were vigorously collected and evaluated in the first generations of Islam after Muhammad's death. The hadith point to Muhammad's life and teaching—as distinct from God's teaching through Muhammad as found in the Qur'an—as indications of how Muslims should act. The Qur'an itself says relatively little about the actions of Muhammad, so this further interpretive aid came to be viewed as necessary as a context in which to interpret the more difficult or undeveloped material in the Qur'an.

The hadith include many sayings that are attributed to Muhammad. These may be used to clarify the revelation of the Qur'an, and thus their authority comes close to that of the Qur'an itself. Among the hadith are various stories, including Muhammad's important Night Journey from Mecca to Jerusalem and back to Mecca as well as his ascent to heaven, while in Jerusalem, for receiving revelations.

Read a hadith.

SHARI'A

If you've already heard of the **Shari'a**, traditional Islamic law enforced in many Muslim lands, it was probably in reports about the stoning of women convicted of adultery or the cutting off of thieves' hands. These sensationalist reports give a misleading impression of Muslim law. Shari'a developed to guide the implementation of Qur'anic and

hadith [huh-DEETH]
"Traditions," a traditional report recording a saying or action of Muhammad

Shari'a [shah-REE-uh]
"Way, path," formal system of law in Islam

hadith interpretation. Two hundred years after Islam's founding, its central institution was Shari'a law, guiding the implementation of the Qur'an and the hadith. Shari'a deals with many aspects of day-to-day life, including politics, business, family life, sexuality, hygiene, and social issues. Many people today might consider it a civil and criminal law shaped by a religion, but Muslims don't make that distinction. They believe that Shari'a is simply God's law for the regulation of all Muslim life. Four different schools of Shari'a arose in Sunni Islam between 750 and 850, and still exist today. These aren't schools of theology that differ in belief or practice, because the four Sunni schools hold to the same basic Muslim beliefs and practices. Rather, they are distinct ways of defining morals and practices in precise and technical legal terms. A part of Muslim law is the *fatwa*, a religious ruling by an imam trained in Shari'a, urging a particular course of action for Muslims that may or may not be binding on them.

Shari'a is now the most widely used religious law system in the world. It is fully used in a few Muslim nations, is used more selectively in many other Muslim nations, and even seeks to make an entry in some Western and Asian nations. In 2008, the head of the Church of England, Archbishop Rowan Williams, stirred up a controversy when he urged publicly that Muslims in Great Britain should be given more latitude to judge themselves according to Shari'a. Informal Shari'a courts already operate in the Muslim communities of Great Britain, dealing mostly with marital conflicts and divorce. That same year in France, where relations between the secular government and observant French Muslims can be difficult, a nationwide political dispute broke out when a French court upheld a Shari'a-based annulment of the marriage of two Muslims after the groom discovered on their wedding night that his bride wasn't a virgin.

DIET AND OTHER REGULATIONS

Only halal ("permitted") foods may be eaten by Muslims. One can see restaurants and fast-food outlets in the Muslim world that advertise this concept, for example the popular Halal Fried Chicken chain, HFC for short. Foods that are haram, "forbidden," may not be eaten. Consuming pork or products with even a small amount of pork mixed in them is particularly forbidden. The Qur'an also prohibits the drinking of wine (2:219); this is taken to mean prohibiting all alcoholic drinks and even food cooked with alcohol.

Other behaviors and practices are haram as well. Muslims must not gamble or charge interest on loans.

Halal restaurant and bakery in Brooklyn, NY

PAUL LOWRY

Banks in more moderate Muslim nations don't observe this prohibition on interest; banks in stricter Muslim nations do. An interesting case on haram is the current controversy over whether smoking tobacco—a widespread practice in the Arab part of the Muslim world—should now be forbidden. Some Muslims argue that it should be forbidden as something that is harmful to the body that God has created. Others argue that what the Qur'an, hadith, and Shari'a don't expressly prohibit should be accepted. "Islam has so few permitted vices," some of them say with a smile, "so the ones it has should be kept." In general, Muslims must "commend what is good and reprimand evil." This applies to matters of dress for both men and women (see "A Closer Look").

MARRIAGE AND THE STATUS OF WOMEN

The status of women in Islam is determined by its view of marriage, not by its view of gender or gender relationships in themselves. Marriage is customary for all Muslims; parents typically arrange it while children are young, although women often can refuse engagements to men they don't like. Some Muslim parents living in North America will travel back to their Middle Eastern homelands in order to find suitable matches for their children. The Qur'an says that a man may have up to four wives at one time as long as he provides for them equally and with separate living quarters, but the vast majority of Muslim men have only one wife.

The Qur'an also says that the limitation on the number of wives didn't apply to Muhammad (33:50–52). His multiple marriages, to nine wives after the death of Khadija and the move to Mecca, are thought to be a part of his special calling as the Prophet. Some were entered for political reasons, but an effort to obtain a son may have figured into these multiple marriages as well. Muhammad's marriage to A'isha, Abu Bakr's nine-year-old daughter whom we already met, was controversial because of her young age, and his marriage to Zainab, the ex-wife of Muhammad's adopted son Zaid, was controversial because of the closeness of the family relation. Because the life of Muhammad can be viewed as normative for Muslims, the Qur'an and later Muslim tradition are careful to say that these practices do not apply to other Muslims.

Read an Amazon.com description of Sherry Jones's controversial novel about A'isha.

Divorce is relatively simple for a man to obtain in most Muslim nations today; women can divorce their husbands only with difficulty. The Shari'a states that a man can divorce his wife by saying, "I divorce you" in front of other male witnesses at three different times, usually over a period of three months. Divorce is not to be undertaken trivially. A hadith states that divorce is "hateful in the sight of God." However, the Qur'an fully and carefully provides for it (2:228–242; 115:1–7). Of course, Muslim nations that don't follow the Shari'a fully have other procedures for divorce that follow Muslim tradition more loosely. If there are children in the marriage, they are typically in the main custody of the man after the divorce. Early Islamic law gave Muslim women significant new rights in marriage and divorce. A man must provide adequate alimony for his ex-wife as long as she lives, but there is usually no expectation that an ex-wife must be supported in "the manner to which she has become accustomed," as divorce laws in the Western world sometimes say.

Read "Thinking through Western Questions about Islam and Women."

A Closer Look:

Muslim Dress for Women and Men

No specific types of clothing are prescribed for Muslims. No requirements were laid down in the Qur'an or hadith, probably because Arab ways of dress were a given in the first decades of Islam. In line with Semitic cultures, all Muslims are required to dress modestly. You may have encountered the view of Muslim modesty common in the West: women in robes and veils with only their eyes visible. In some Middle Eastern cultures such a covering over other clothes is the required Islamic mode of dress for women. For example, in the 1980s the Shi'a government of Iran required full-body veiling of Muslim women out in public. This garment, called *chador* (shah-DOHR) in Iran, is referred to as the *burkah* (BUR-kuh) in most places. In the 1990s, the Taliban government of Afghanistan imposed it on all Muslim women there, and some Afghani women still wear it today.

Many Muslims argue correctly that the Qur'an, hadith, and Shari'a don't say that a woman must be completely shrouded, and they disagree with this added requirement. The Qur'an does require that a woman should dress in a way that conceals her physical beauty from men (24:31). Most Muslims interpret this requirement by saying that a woman's body, including her arms and legs, should be fully clothed. Her face may be visible, but her hair needs to be covered at least with a *hijab* (hih-JAHB), a scarf placed around the head that is the most common form of modest dress in the Muslim world. These rules don't apply in the home; among her immediate family a woman is unveiled and with no hijab, but still modest. They also don't apply where only women are present, such as in all-female areas. For example, Egypt's Mediterranean coast has some all-female beaches for Muslim women who want to follow religious expectations and still wear Western-style swimming suits, to "have fun and not sin."

Muslim men must dress modestly as well. Most of their body must be clothed in a way that doesn't draw attention to their shape. In general, Muslim men don't expose their skin above their elbows or knees, and they're usually clothed to their ankles. (You'd rarely, if ever, see a Muslim man shirtless in public.) A head covering for men, such as a turban or cap, is a part of men's dress in many Islamic lands, but this is more cultural than religious.

Woman in burkah

BONNIE VAN VOORST © CENGAGE LEARNING

The hijab

BONNIE VAN VOORST © CENGAGE LEARNING

Muslim man in cap

BONNIE VAN VOORST © CENGAGE LEARNING

---

jihad [jee-HAHD] "Struggle," both personal, inner struggle and armed struggle for Islam

JIHAD

Jihad means "struggle" for God and Islam. Islam seems to most Westerners today to have expanded in its first centuries through methods that were mostly military struggle, not religious. Recent activities by terrorists ostensibly acting in the name of Islam have reinforced this stereotype. On the other hand, many Muslims and non-Muslims say that "Islam is a religion of peace" and that jihad refers mostly to peaceful struggle to be better Muslims. As Stephen Prothero remarks, "This crucial conversation rarely advances beyond a ping-pong match of clichés."[5] So let's go deeper into this difficult issue.

---

[5] Stephen Prothero, *God Is Not One* (New York: HarperOne, 2010), 26.

Most Muslims today want to be seen as tolerant toward others. "There must be no compulsion in religion," says an often-quoted verse in the Qur'an (2:256). Muslims frequently—and correctly—point out that many Qur'anic passages about jihad refer to spiritual striving within individual Muslims. The basic meaning of jihad for most Muslims is the struggle against one's own evil to fully submit to Allah. It also refers to groups of Muslims who struggle to improve the state of Islam. Nevertheless, jihad as military action is important in the Qur'an. Muslim scripture repeatedly commands Muslims to take up arms and fight when necessary on behalf of the Islamic community (for example, 2:190; 8:38; 9:29; 22:39–41), and it treats jihad as military struggle more often than nonmilitary. Muhammad himself strongly criticized those who implied that spiritual struggle substituted for military struggle. Military action is "prescribed ... even though it may be hateful to you" (2:216). This struggle is directed most often against opposing military forces, but it includes deadly action against people of other religions in Islamic lands when they resist Muslim rule. Muslim warriors in conflicts with a religious dimension are often called *mujahedeen* [moo-JAH-huh-DEEN], "those who engage in jihad." Today in the West they are frequently called "jihadists," but this is usually pejorative.

> *"This crucial conversation [about war and peace in Islam] rarely advances beyond a ping-pong match of clichés."*
> —Stephen Prothero

The basic principles of the military aspect of jihad were drawn up by Abu Bakr from the Qur'an and the practice of Muhammad, and expanded later by others. Although the "rules for jihad" vary somewhat in history and today, here are the main common points:

- Violence shouldn't be used to advance the cause of Islam. An Islamic country may never initiate conflict against another state or people for religious reasons only.

- Suicide in warfare is often seen as evil. It usurps the power of God alone to determine life and death, even in battle. The Qur'an makes a blanket prohibition of suicide (4:29) but doesn't explicitly apply it to warfare, so some Muslims disagree with its application there.

- If another nation acts aggressively against an Islamic country, that country is justified in using military force to defend itself. Muslims must publicly and formally declare war in a *fatwa* (ruling by a recognized Muslim leader) before any military action can commence.

- All noncombatants—women and children, the sick and the elderly, and enemy soldiers who surrender—are to be spared and treated well.

- If a Muslim or non-Muslim country uses physical or legal force to repress the free exercise of Islam, those actions constitute hostility to Islam. It would then be appropriate, even a requirement, for Islamic nations to liberate the oppressed Muslims by force of arms.

- Jihad can be waged against other Muslim nations who are thought to have departed from the faith. For example, Ayatollah Khomeini, the Shi'a religious leader of Iran, declared its 1980s war against Sunni-ruled Iraq to be a jihad and Iranian soldiers who died in it martyrs.

- Once a country is Islamic, it may not be allowed to go back into non-Muslim rule, as this would be an action against Islam. Jihad must be waged to bring it back to Islam. This is why many Muslims today don't recognize the nation of Israel as legitimate.

Usually there was little resistance to the spread of Islam in its first centuries, due to the strength of the Muslim forces and the cultural conditions in the lands they conquered. Whole regions welcomed the advancing Muslims, eager for them to replace the hated Byzantine rulers. Most Christians and Jews welcomed the Muslim armies, expecting and receiving basically respectful treatment. In several Muslim areas, a sizeable Christian and Jewish population continued for centuries; for example, in Egypt the Coptic Christian group was a majority of the population for more than a thousand years until in modern times the Copts were reduced to a small minority. They are still the occasional targets of violence today. As we saw above, peoples not "of the book" were converted to Islam by force if necessary. The Muslim armies marched on, annexing an enormous amount of territory in a very short time. Almost the entire Middle East came into the Islamic rule in about thirty years, and by one hundred years it stretched from the Atlantic coast of North Africa to modern Afghanistan. This was one of the fastest imperial expansions in history.

We should end our discussion of this challenging topic by saying this: Despite all the attention

Mujahedeen family inside their home, Arghandab, Afghanistan

justifiably paid to it today in some parts of Islam and especially in the Western world, jihad is not one of Islam's central practices. It isn't a pillar, nor is it one of the key doctrinal teachings. But to understand Islam in the world today, one must understand jihad well.

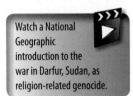

Watch a National Geographic introduction to the war in Darfur, Sudan, as religion-related genocide.

LO5 Worship: The Five Pillars of Islam

In Dearborn, Michigan, home to one of the largest Muslim populations in North America, Hussein Elhaf prepares for the annual month-long fast observed by Muslims around the world. Hussein's family owns a restaurant with a mostly Muslim clientele, so he works around food during the month of Ramadan, but he will eat and drink only between sunset and sunrise, when eating and drinking are permitted. The restaurant serves food during daylight hours in Ramadan for non-Muslim customers, and it is crowded with Muslims taking their main meal of the day from sunset until 11:00 p.m. Fasting while working with food and drink all day won't be a struggle for him, he says; in fact, "it strengthens my faith and brings me closer to God."

The study and practice of religion in our time have reaffirmed the importance of core religious practices of worship: stating one's beliefs, prayer, giving of one's wealth, occasional fasting, and others. The core practices of Islam are all related to worship and form what Muslims call the "Five Pillars of

shahada [shah-hah-DAH] Fundamental confession of faith: "There is no god but God, and Muhammad is the apostle of God."

Islam." (Most Shi'as recognize ten pillars, with particularly Shi'a additions in the second group of five.) The notion that Islam has "pillars" is not in the Qur'an or the hadith, although Muslims view it as faithful to what the Qur'an and hadith say about these five obligations. The pillars—of the worship of God on which Islam is built—are essential but not exhaustive.

CONFESSION OF FAITH

The first part of the Islamic confession can be said sincerely by a monotheist in any religion; the second, only by Muslims.

The first pillar is built on the foundational rock of Islam. Although we've said that Islam is primarily a religion of action, not of belief, the first pillar is indeed a statement of belief. The **shahada** is the "confession" of Islam; here, "confession" means a formal statement of faith, not a confession of sin. It runs: "There is no god but God, and Muhammad is the apostle of God." Its Arabic form is resonantly poetic: *La ilaha illa Allah, Muhammad rasul Allah* (lah ih-LAH-ha ihl-lah AHL-lah, moo-HAHM-id rah-SOOL AHL-lah). This confession is among the shortest of any world religion that has formal confessions. The shahada isn't found in the Qur'an in this exact form, but its two parts are often repeated there separately. Sometimes the shahada is translated "There is no god but Allah." But in Arabic, its second and fourth words are *Allah*, so "There is no god but God" is a better translation.

The first part of the confession can be said sincerely by a monotheist in any religion. The second part connects monotheism to the Islamic faith. Saying "Muhammad is the apostle of God" entails submission to all God's commandments as given through Muhammad. He is the *rasul*, the final prophet who speaks God's words definitively. The shahada encompasses the key point of a Muslim's life. Newborn babies hear it whispered to them. Those who convert to Islam repeat this confession as their own. Those who say the formal prayers repeat it every time they pray. The last words of dying Muslims are the shahada; if they are unable to speak, someone else says it for them.

PRAYER

Prayer is the main, regular form of Muslim worship, so we will treat it more fully than the other pillars. Each observant Muslim says the ritual prayers called **salat** five times a day: at sunrise, at noon, in mid-afternoon, at sunset, and one hour after sunset. Prayers must be performed wherever one finds oneself at the hours of prayer. A **mosque** (from *masjid*, "place of prostration") is a building for prayer. Each mosque typically has towers called minarets. These minarets traditionally have balconies from which the *muezzin*, or "caller," summons the people to prayer. Today in Muslim lands, this task is often done through loudspeakers on the minaret. The most common pattern of the call to prayer goes like this:

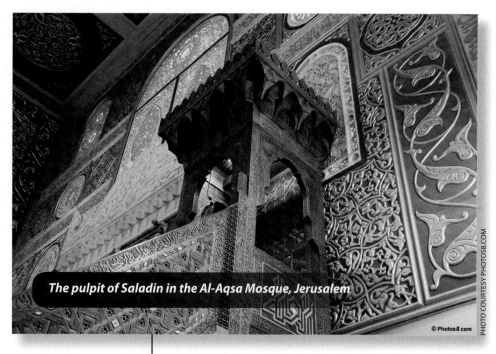

The pulpit of Saladin in the Al-Aqsa Mosque, Jerusalem

> God is great [said 4 times].
> I bear witness that there is no god but God [2 times].
> I bear witness that Muhammad is the messenger of God [2 times].
> Make haste to prayer [2 times].
> Make haste to success [2 times].
> God is great [2 times].
> There is no god but God [1 time].

The main part of the mosque is the prayer hall, an open room often with abstract decoration on the ceiling or walls. It has no pictures, statuary, incense, altars, or marked-off areas as are found in the sanctuaries of other world religions. To enter a prayer hall, worshipers must remove their shoes and wash. Then they get in straight lines facing the *mihrab*, a niche at the front of the prayer hall that indicates the direction toward Mecca, called the **qiblah**, to which prayer and the whole service is oriented. These straight rows also signify to Muslims the equality of all people before God. Most mosques have a pulpit at which the imam preaches a sermon at the Friday noon service, and one often sees a few copies of the Qur'an on wooden stands for reading.

The prayer itself then begins. The sequence of salat is tightly structured in both words and actions; personal, spontaneous prayer is not a part of salat. Just before the prayer time, the muezzin or his recorded voice gives the official call to prayer in a

Inside a mosque in Morocco

salat [sah-LAHT] Ritual Muslim prayers done five times a day

mosque [mahsk] Building for formal Muslim worship

qiblah [KIB-luh] Direction toward which Muslims face during prayer

melodic chant that can be heard throughout the neighborhood. Visitors in Muslim countries often notice the public call to prayer. (When the author was studying in Amman, Jordan, as a college student, he was startled awake by the dawn call to prayer on a loudspeaker next door to the rooftop where he was sleeping.)

As stated above, Muslims prepare for prayer by ritual washing. Hands, feet, eyes, ears, nose, and mouth are rinsed three times with water. When women pray in the mosque, they are out of the men's sight, in back of them, or in a separate room. The reason for the segregation of the sexes is said to be preserving the dignity of women. Because a part of the prayer ritual is to bow and prostrate oneself, it would be unseemly in traditional Muslim cultures for men to line up alongside or behind women in this position. If one were to touch a woman in the mosque, even accidentally, one would have to then go out and ritually wash again.

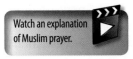
Watch an explanation of Muslim prayer.

Salat is a formal ritual with both postures and recitation. All the people in the prayer hall do the words and actions together, giving a sense of unity. The imam at the front leads the process. People begin the prayer standing upright and cup their ears with their hands, showing God that they are present and listening. The first chapter of the Qur'an is spoken as a prayer, followed by other prescribed words. One's body is active in prayer: bowing, standing, kneeling, prostration while kneeling with one's forehead to the ground, kneeling, prostration, and standing again. These actions remind Muslims in a physical way of their submission to God. The prayers are uttered in a quiet, humble voice, but in contrast the changes of posture are indicated by the leader's louder call of "Allah." Depending on the number of repetitions, daily prayers take approximately five to ten minutes to perform. On Friday afternoons, special prayer services in the mosque feature a sermon preached by the imam. This whole service, which is typically the best-attended service of the week, lasts between thirty and sixty minutes. It was after Friday noon prayers in the first months of 2011 that worshipers poured out into the streets to demand change from unresponsive, authoritarian governments in many Arab nations.

FASTING

In commemoration of Muhammad receiving the Qur'an, Muslims are required to observe fasting, called in Arabic **sawm**, during daylight hours throughout the month of Ramadan. This is designed to cultivate greater submission to God. Not a bit of food or drink may be taken for the entire daylight hours. (Some particularly pious Muslims won't even swallow their own saliva.) Sexual intercourse during the daylight is also forbidden, as are some types of amusement. Eating, drinking, and sex are permissible in the morning while it is still dark and after sunset. Because leap days are not inserted into the Muslim lunar calendar, Ramadan moves through the seasons. When it falls in winter, fasting is comparatively easy. But when Ramadan falls in the longer, hot days of summer—and most Muslims live in tropical or subtropical lands—it calls for much more effort.

Fasting in Ramadan is done in a humane way, as are all Muslim pillars. Infants and young children are excused from the fast, but many students in school keep it. The hunger produced can be a challenge to learning. People who are sick, those infirm from old age, and soldiers on active duty may fast when they are better able to do so. When it is impossible to make up the fast, one may substitute a significant act of mercy or charity. When the month of Ramadan is finished, Muslims celebrate the Eid-al-Fitr festival with a special service in the mosque. Families feast together during the day and exchange gifts in decorated homes.

Imam Murtza Alidina preaches a Friday sermon in a mosque in Dar es Salaam, Tanzania.

MUHAMMAD MAHDI

ALMSGIVING

The Qur'an urges all Muslims to give generously to the poor, such as orphans and widows (e.g., 2:43), but as with the other four items that became traditional pillars, it doesn't lay down specific requirements. The Shari'a made this generosity a formal obligation with specific rules, and it has become so important that it is the fourth pillar of Islam, called **zakat,** "almsgiving" or "charity." Although it is an obligation, Muslims are expected to be generous from the heart, out of liberality. In most Islamic lands it is a monetary obligation collected by a representative of the umma, often a department of the government. It is then distributed to poor families, widows and orphans, stranded travelers, and others in need. In addition, it can be used in jihad for defense and support of Muslims under threat.

> ## Muslims are expected to be generous from the heart, out of liberality.

In places such as Europe and North America, zakat is based on voluntary giving to the mosque or an Islamic charity. The rate for zakat in all parts of the world is not large, especially when compared to the system of tithing (10 percent of income) that it resembles, laid down in the Jewish Bible. Zakat is one-fortieth (2.5 percent) of the value of one's assets, not counting necessary personal possessions such as homes, animals, vehicles, or clothing. Because every observant Muslim gives zakat, it generates large sums of money in the international Muslim community. Zakat has provided Islamic countries with the resources for comprehensive programs of social support and development that are unique among world religions and reinforce solidarity among Muslims of different classes. It is the principal way in which Muslim lands promote a fuller measure of social justice.

PILGRIMAGE

The last of the Five Pillars of Islam is pilgrimage to Mecca. A Muslim is required to participate in the official pilgrimage, called the **hajj,** to Mecca at least once in his or her lifetime. This requirement applies to both men and women, but traditionally the great majority of pilgrims are men. As with the other pillars, it is imposed humanely: In this case, one who is unable to make the pilgrimage may designate someone else do it on his or her behalf. The last month of the Muslim calendar, called al-Hajj, is the official period of pilgrimage. Muslims can go to Mecca at other times when it isn't so crowded, but these visits are not considered a hajj. Muhammad at first had his followers pray facing Jerusalem, and some Muslims did pilgrimages to Jerusalem as well. After his conflict with the Jews of Medina, he made Mecca, and particularly the Kaba in the Grand Mosque there, the geographic center of Islam. (For an account of activities during the hajj, see the section that begins this chapter, "Your Visit to Mecca.")

> **zakat** [zah-KAHT] "Almsgiving" or "charity"; mandatory contribution of one-fortieth of one's income to support Islam
>
> **hajj** [hahj] Pilgrimage to Mecca

> ## "Creating a global community seems less daunting after making a pilgrimage, especially one that stirs us—physically and spiritually—in a single pot with all humanity." —Robert Bianchi

Dome of the Rock mosque in Jerusalem, the third-holiest Muslim site

PHOTO COURTESY PHOTOS8.COM

Tents for Hajj pilgrims on the Plains of Mina outside Mecca

MUBEEN RAHMAN

LO6 Islam in North America

Chicago's Mosque Maryam is host to Louis Farrakhan, leader of the Nation of Islam. He strongly defends the Libyan leader Muammar Qaddafi against military attacks begun in 2011 by the United States and other NATO nations in support of a rebellion against Qaddafi. The Nation of Islam is one of North America's oldest African American Muslim groups. Calling him a brother in Islam who has been supportive of the cause of the Nation of Islam, Farrakhan asks, "What kind of brother would I be if a man has been that way to me, and to us, and when he's in trouble I refuse to raise my voice in his defense?" Although this is greeted with cheers by his followers in the mosque, other observers wonder if these controversial, attention-grabbing statements are not an effort to regain strength for Farrakhan's faltering movement. The Nation of Islam has, according to many experts, lost about half of its membership to more traditional Muslim groups since around 1995, when it was able to rally a huge crowd for its Million Man March on Washington, D.C.

Other cities are centers of other pilgrimage for some Muslims. Medina is the second-holiest city in Islam, especially because it was the home of Muhammad for the second part of his prophetic career and the place where he is buried. The Dome of the Rock mosque in Jerusalem, which Muslims call the "Noble Sanctuary," was built in the seventh century. Muhammad made his ascent to heaven during his lifetime from a prominent rock now inside the mosque. The first mosque on this temple hill was built slightly before the Dome of the Rock and was known as Al-Aqsa (ahl-AHK-suh), "the farthest" mosque from Mecca at the time it was built. Shi'as have their own holy places of pilgrimage, including Qom in Iran and Karbala in Iraq. They also make the hajj to Mecca, but sometimes violence has erupted between Sunnis and Shi'as during the hajj. Muslims have designated other centers of pilgrimage, but no other place comes close to Mecca in importance. A man who has journeyed to Mecca on the hajj receives an additional, honorary personal name, Hajji. The importance of the hajj for Islam and the world has been well summarized by Robert Bianchi, who as a Muslim made the hajj himself: "Creating a global community seems less daunting after making a pilgrimage, especially one that stirs us—physically and spiritually—in a single pot with all humanity."[6]

Watch a CNN introduction to the hajj.

Islam has typically been spread by near-continuous, intentional movement from Arabia and other historic points to the farthest reaches of the world. In North America, however, the picture is more mixed. Some slaves brought here from Africa were probably Muslims—estimates range from 5 percent to almost 50 percent—but they were unable to maintain their faith through the generations due to the harsh conditions of slavery and their owners' insistence that slaves share their masters' Christian religion. In the early twentieth century, a new "Black Muslim" movement grew in North American soil.

THE NATION OF ISLAM AND THE AMERICAN MUSLIM MISSION

About one-third of North American Muslims today are African Americans who have joined either mainstream Islam or a sectarian Islamic movement. The largest sectarian group is the Black Muslim movement. In 1930, Elijah Poole, an African American living in Detroit, met W. D. Fard, a man of either Iranian or Turkish descent who preached Islam as the only true religion for

---

[6] Robert R. Bianchi, *Guests of God: Pilgrimage and Politics in the Islamic World* (New York: Oxford University Press, 2004), 272.

A Closer Look:

Difficulties of the Hajj for Muslims in Western China

In the province of Xinjiang (zin-JYANG) in northwestern China, practicing Muslims from the Uighur (WEE-guhr) ethnic group of Turkic peoples have a challenging time participating in the pilgrimage to Mecca. Communist Party authorities there want to discourage Muslims from going to Mecca, thinking that they may be exposed to more radical forms of Islam and would return to form separatist movements in Xinjiang.

Uighur Muslims are prohibited from arranging their own trips for the hajj, either individually or in groups. The government has confiscated their passports, although they can obtain them for short business trips. To be among the fortunate few who receive passports for a government-approved hajj, one must pay a deposit of $6,000, to be refunded upon one's return, and about $4,000 for the trip (plus an occasional bribe). Most Chinese Muslims in the province can't afford such an expense; the large cost ensures that only a few thousand who can afford

it will go on the hajj. Communist Party rules also state that applicants must be fifty to seventy years old, have a clean criminal record, and "love the country." The trips are led by imams deemed most loyal to the Chinese government.

The regional Communist Party restricts Islam in other ways as well. All students and government workers are required to eat and drink during the daylight hours of Ramadan; fasting is prohibited. Prayer in public is also forbidden. Workers in government and government-controlled businesses aren't allowed to attend services in mosques; women in businesses are forbidden to wear head scarves. No Muslims may teach the faith in private, Arabic is taught only in government schools, and all Qur'ans must be the government-approved version. Although this government control is ostensibly to keep down religious opposition to Communist rule, many people are convinced that it is doing exactly the opposite. Western human-rights groups and some Muslim nations have been sharply critical of these policies.

Uighurs at Friday noon prayers

African Americans. Poole converted to this movement, changing his name to Elijah Muhammad. He effectively spread Fard's teachings, and their movement grew rapidly. Fard disappeared in 1934, and Elijah Muhammad took over. The movement then became known as "The Lost-Found Nation of Islam in the Wilderness of North America," or the **Nation of Islam** for short, and spread to many urban areas in the northern United States. Its appeal to prisoners was especially potent, and still is today. It has five main teachings:

- W. D. Fard is an incarnation of God, and Elijah Muhammad is God's prophet.

- African Americans are descended from a tribe called Shabazz, the ancient pre-Islamic inhabitants of Mecca; they are by nature good.

- White people are evil and oppressive, the creation of an evil scientist named Yakub.

- Black people ought to recapture their African Muslim roots by submitting to the Five Pillars of Islam and opposing white oppression.

- Black people who submit to God will rule the world, and white people will get the punishment they so richly deserve.

Several obvious differences exist between these Nation of Islam teachings and the teachings of most other Muslims. Other Muslims sharply reject the ideas of an incarnation of God in any human and also reject a new prophet equal to Muhammad; they view both as idolatry. Moreover, race-based beliefs are not a legitimate part of Islam. On the other hand, the Nation of Islam appreciates Islamic practices such as the Five Pillars. Despite being largely ignored—or considered heretical—for most of

its history by the rest of the Islamic world, the Nation of Islam became a potent force in the African American community in the United States. It gave hope for a better life to many oppressed people, with resources to fight against drug abuse, poverty, and racism. But it had a race-based message that was problematic for fellow North Americans and for the rest of Islam.

In 1960, a black Muslim led a significant change in the Nation of Islam. Malcolm X (born Malcolm Little) went to Mecca on pilgrimage and saw a harmony between peoples of different races. This experience, along with his growing disillusionment with Elijah Muhammad, gave him a new vision for African American Muslims: God did not want one race to rule another race, but for all races to live together in harmony. He began a new organization of Muslims not based on racial hostility. Malcolm's new message was appealing to many African American Muslims, and it survived his death in 1965 at the hands of two disgruntled members of the Nation of Islam.

Warith Muhammad, Elijah's son, then led the Nation of Islam until his death in 2008, taking the black Muslim movement in the direction that Malcolm X had begun. He brought the Black Muslim movement into mainstream Sunni Islam. He renounced all beliefs that Sunnis considered heretical, adopting authentically Muslim beliefs and practices. He began cooperating with worldwide Islam. He permitted American Muslims in his movement to participate in politics and vote, and he abolished the paramilitary wing of the Nation of Islam. He renamed the movement the American Muslim Mission. These changes resulted in his movement receiving large amounts of Arab financial support. Islamic centers then spread throughout the United States, serving new immigrants from the Arab world and African American Muslims.

This reform produced an almost-immediate reaction. In 1978, Louis Farrakhan (FAIR-uh-kahn) moved some African

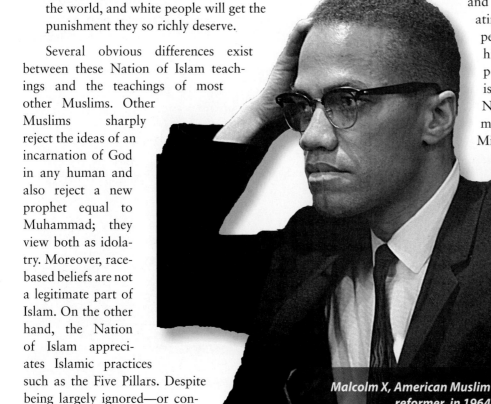

Malcolm X, American Muslim reformer, in 1964

American Muslims back to a revived Nation of Islam. Farrakhan occasionally used strong rhetoric, especially against Jews. He continued the efforts to free African Americans from white economic power, as well as educational and private-policing activities to keep their neighborhoods free from

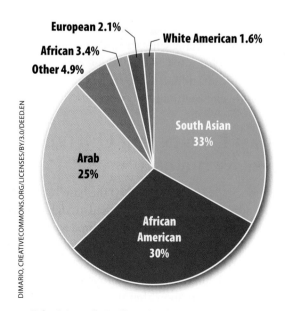

An issue of Louis Farrakhan's newspaper, The Final Call

© JEFFREY BLACKLER/ALAMY

drugs and drug-related crimes. Farrakhan's movement is based in Chicago, but three other groups claiming to be the authentic Nation of Islam are based in Baltimore, Detroit, and Atlanta. Today, most African American Muslims belong not to these Nation of Islam groups but to the American Muslim Mission, where they are mainstream Sunnis. Despite its small size relative to the American Muslim Mission and the fact that it is much smaller now than before 1960, the Nation of Islam is an active and occasionally vocal part of American religious life today.

MUSLIM MIGRATION TO NORTH AMERICA

From about 1950, millions of Muslims immigrated to North America from various nations in the Middle East, and some from British Commonwealth lands in south Asia have come to Canada. Some smaller immigration had occurred before 1950, but most Muslim families entered after that year. Muslims can be found in virtually every city in North America, with more substantial numbers in large cities on the East and West coasts. The proportion of Sunnis and Shi'as in North America is about the same as in the wider Muslim world—about 85 percent to 15 percent. Dearborn, Michigan, a suburb of Detroit, has the largest population of Muslims outside metropolitan New York City. Canada has Muslims in every major city, with larger numbers in the cities in Ontario, Alberta, and British Columbia. Today there are 6 to 7 million Muslims in

North America with origins in other nations, most from the Middle East. The majority of them have no formal affiliation to a mosque (in lands that are officially Muslim, one doesn't "belong to a mosque"), but they are nonetheless practicing Muslims.

Our knowledge of Muslims in the United States is a bit imprecise, because the U.S. Census does not collect information about religious affiliation. However, scientific surveys have filled in much of this gap. A 2007 Pew Research Center survey of Muslim Americans found that about two-thirds are foreign born, and most of these have immigrated since 1980. A second generation of Muslims is now arising in the United States, facing the same sort of intergenerational issues that other immigrant groups have faced. Of the one-third of Muslim Americans born in the United States, the majority are converts and African American. In 2005, almost 100,000 people from Islamic countries—most of them Muslims—became permanent residents of the U.S., more than in any single year since 1980. Most of them are on a path to citizenship. As a

European 2.1%
African 3.4%
Other 4.9%
White American 1.6%
South Asian 33%
Arab 25%
African American 30%

DIMARIO, CREATIVECOMMONS.ORG/LICENSES/BY/3.0/DEED.EN

Ethnicity of Muslims in the United States, 2008

result of immigration since the 1950s, Islam in North America now more closely reflects the global diversity of Islam than at any time in the past.

> *Muslims in North America are significantly more educated and affluent than the average American and the average Muslim worldwide.*

See an interview with Imam Zaid Shakir, a leading U.S. Muslim.

A recent survey by the Zogby polling company showed that Muslims are prospering in the United States. They are significantly more educated than the national average, with incomes to match. Some 60 percent of them hold at least one academic degree, and about 40 percent have an income over $75,000. Compared to most Muslims in Europe, North American Muslims are more assimilated into wider cultural life. The United States and Canada have largely extended the same extensive rights to practice religion to Muslims as they have extended to others. In some European nations, this isn't the case; the French prohibition of Muslim head scarves in schools and other public buildings is particularly controversial. U.S. Muslims practice the pillars of Islam with little need for adaptation, although observing afternoon prayers has occasionally been problematic for Muslims working in businesses and factories. Some have worked for improved relations between Muslim and non-Muslim Americans. Many scholars have held out the hope that North American Muslims may show other Muslims how they can lead faithful religious lives in a predominantly non-Muslim environment.

MUSLIM LIFE IN THE UNITED STATES AFTER 9/11

On September 11, 2001, **al-Qaeda** ("the base" of jihad), an organization of radical Muslims based in Afghanistan, launched coordinated attacks on the United States. That morning, nineteen members of al-Qaeda from various Middle Eastern nations who had been living in "sleeper cells" in the United States hijacked four large commercial passenger airliners soon after they took off from airports in the eastern United States. The hijackers crashed two of the airplanes into the main towers of the World Trade Center in New York City, causing both towers to collapse unexpectedly about two hours later. They crashed a third airplane into the Pentagon, the U.S. military headquarters in Washington, D.C. The fourth plane crashed into a field in western Pennsylvania when its passengers and crew bravely tried to retake control of the plane as it was heading east, probably to another prominent target in Washington, D.C. Excluding the hijackers, 2,974 people died; another 24 are missing and presumed dead; and several thousand were injured. The great majority of deaths and injuries were of civilians, including citizens of over ninety different nations who worked in the World Trade Center.

> *Osama Bin Laden recorded messages in the cadences of the Qur'an, and liked to be photographed living in caves as Muhammad once did.*

What is this al-Qaeda organization? Osama bin Laden (oh-SAM-uh bin LAHD-en, 1957–2011) founded it to oppose with violence those he saw as a threat to true Islam. A Saudi Arabian banished from his land for extremism, he took up residence with the other leaders of his movement in Afghanistan, where al-Qaeda secretly bankrolled the Taliban government. He mounted first verbal and then physical attacks against a variety of targets, with strong religiously based opposition to the influence of Western nations in Muslim nations and opposition to the presence of the Jewish state of Israel. Bin Laden typically spoke in taped addresses in the poetic cadences of the Qur'an, and he liked to be photographed living in caves as Muhammad once did while hiding from his enemies. Al-Qaeda brought something new to Islam: continual attacks on non-Muslims. Al-Qaeda and its splinter groups have carried out dozens of other attacks from the 1990s until today on civilian targets in both Western and Muslim nations (especially England, Spain, Saudi Arabia, India, Indonesia, and various east African countries), attacks designed to terrorize their people and influence government policy. Most of their victims have been Muslims. As a predominantly Sunni movement, however, al-Qaeda has gathered only a little support from Shi'as, and even the majority of Sunnis in the world do not approve of it.

The attacks on September 11, 2001, deeply shocked not only the United States but most other

Demonstrators at a pro-Taliban demonstration on September 28, 2001, in Peshawar, Pakistan. The poster has an image of Osama bin Laden.

nations of the world. The United States responded by leading a broad coalition of international military forces in invading Afghanistan to depose the Taliban and destroy the home base of the al-Qaeda network. The hunt for Osama bin Laden lasted for ten years after that, ending with his 2011 death in a U.S. military raid on his hideout in Pakistan. The 2001 federal "Patriot Act" gave the U.S. government far greater powers than previously permitted in gathering intelligence on suspected terrorists in America and around the world. Many other nations also increased their antiterrorism efforts and stepped up military preparations. Muslim organizations in the United States were swift to condemn the attacks on 9/11 and called upon Muslim Americans to help the victims. In addition to large donations of funds, many Islamic organizations held blood drives and provided medical assistance, food, and housing for victims of 9/11. Some Muslim groups in the United States have even worked effectively with law enforcement agencies to identify North American Muslims who may be fostering violence.

One result of 9/11 has been a rise in anti-Muslim prejudice and actions by some American citizens who suppose that many or all Muslims are active or potential terrorists, or aid terrorists. (Other Western nations—including Germany, France, and Britain—have significantly stronger popular prejudice against Muslims.) This is upsetting to American Muslims, particularly because the 9/11 attacks were the work of foreign Muslims who came to this country to carry out attacks. The al-Qaeda network has sometimes obtained help from ordinary Muslims in Europe. Also, the latest worrisome trend in

Europe and Asia is that some Muslims born and raised in non-Muslim nations are now launching their own terror attacks in looser connection with al-Qaeda, as they did in the 2005 attacks by suicide bombers on the London mass-transport system. India is particularly plagued with violence from native Muslim groups, some related to al-Qaeda and some not.

So far, there have been only a few cases of this home-grown violence in North America, although 2009 did see a worrying uptick with at least two dozen U.S. residents charged with terrorism-related crimes. More widely troubling to many American Muslims has been the systematic monitoring of Muslim individuals and institutions. The U.S. government has especially investigated those Muslim charitable organizations that distribute abroad the funds raised from American Muslims, some of it from zakat. Although some funds have indeed gone into the shadowy network of terror, the vast majority of funds do not, and many American Muslims are disturbed over this perceived interference in their exercise of a pillar of their religion. However, Muslims in the United States and Canada are increasingly working with other religious and civic organizations for better Muslim relations with the wider public. They are hopeful that relations are in fact improving, although the progress isn't always steady. (A setback of sorts came in 2010 with the conflict over building a mosque near the site of the al-Qaeda attacks on New York City and threats by a few non-Muslim Americans to burn the Qur'an in opposition to Islam.) Another constructive reaction to the 9/11 attacks and their aftermath has been an increase in the study of Islam in colleges and universities all over the world—of which you are now a part.

Read a widely reprinted *New York Times* story, "American Muslims Ask, Will We Ever Belong?"

Read the story of a young Arab American man from Alabama who became a "jihadist."

Watch a video about the conversion of Hispanics in Los Angeles to Islam.

CHAPTER 13

Encountering New Religious Movements: Modern Ways to Alternative Meanings

Learning Outcomes

After studying this chapter, you will be able to do the following:

LO1 Evaluate the different names for new religious movements.

LO2 Summarize the common features of new religious movements.

LO3 Survey the distribution of new religious movements in the world today.

LO4 State and explain the teachings and practices of Falun Gong.

LO5 State and explain the history, teachings, and practices of the Church of Jesus Christ of Latter-day Saints.

LO6 State and explain the teachings and practices of Scientology.

© ISTOCKPHOTO.COM/STEVE GEER

YOUR VISIT TO TEMPLE SQUARE, SALT LAKE CITY, UTAH

The Church of Jesus Christ of Latter-day Saints (LDS), popularly called the Mormons, has its world headquarters in downtown Salt Lake City. Temple Square is named for the main LDS temple that stands majestically there. The other buildings are designed to be impressive as well. Most other church sites are within walking distance.

You can't miss the six-spire granite temple towering in the city's center. Only members of the LDS church can go inside an LDS temple, and this lends a mysterious air to it. This is the high point of any saint's visit to Salt Lake City, but there is still plenty to do for non-Mormons. The LDS church has always spread its faith, so it has built several other impressive buildings for non-Mormons to enter and learn more about the LDS church. You can see exhibits at the two visitor centers; take a tour of the Mormon Tabernacle Building, built as a concert hall for the Mormon Tabernacle Choir; attend a concert at the gothic-style Assembly Hall; and take a walk around the formal gardens. A short walk north of Temple Square is the Conference Center. This is where the General Conference of the LDS church is held twice a year. Most non-Mormons come away from Salt Lake City with the feeling that the LDS church is both secretive and open.

Because you're interested in your genealogy, you've been looking forward to seeing the Family History Library just west of Temple Square. Even though you're only visiting, you can research your ancestral roots in the world's largest genealogical library housed there. Staff members and volunteers are available to help guests through the researching process. All research is done on computers.

What Do YOU Think?

New religious movements are often dangerous organizations.

Strongly Disagree   Strongly Agree
1   2   3   4   5   6   7

It's a little unnerving to you to hear that the LDS church has collected genealogical information from every corner of the world, perhaps for every person who has ever lived and left behind a record. But you're happy for it too, because it makes for the best genealogical searching in the world.

Finally, you walk nearby to see the Beehive House. Built in 1855, this is the residence of Brigham Young, second president of the Church of Jesus Christ of Latter-day Saints, for whom Brigham Young University, the largest LDS university, is named. Free tours are available to go through the home and see how Brigham Young and his family lived.

Take a Google Earth™ tour of LDS sites in Salt Lake City.

The academic term **new religious movements (NRMs)** generally denotes religious groups that arose in modern times and now have sufficient size, longevity, and cultural impact to merit academic study. (*Modern* here doesn't mean "contemporary" or even "recent," but in the modern age of history.) These movements have been studied for decades, especially by

> **new religious movements (NRMs)**
> Religious groups that arose in modern times and now have sufficient size, longevity, and cultural impact to merit academic study

◁ Baha'i temple in Wilmette, Illinois. Baha'i arose from Islam in the 1800s, and its temples resemble mosques.

Temple Square in Salt Lake City, Utah

Watch an introduction to a new religious movement with Christian origins.

sociologists, but *new religious movements* is a recent term in the field of religious studies. Most recently published encyclopedias, handbooks, and textbooks on religion use this term and provide information about the groups to which it refers.[1] More than five hundred groups around the world today have been identified as NRMs. Each year sees the birth of dozens more, and also the death of some. This chapter will first give a general description of NRMs and briefly discuss several of them to illustrate the description. Then it will focus in more detail on three NRMs that have become significant worldwide. These three are treated here to illustrate the general description offered, which students can subsequently apply to other NRMs.

Some things that students often wonder about NRMs can be listed quickly here to stir thought and imagination:

- The inclusion of these groups in this chapter isn't intended to imply that they see themselves as new religious movements. Often they don't, and some even view this term as uncomplimentary. They often see themselves as restorations of the traditions from

which they arose, not as something new.

- Some of these NRMs are highly controversial. Many were persecuted, or prosecuted, in their early years by religious and civil authorities. However, several world religions were controversial when they were new too—some still are!

- Other world religions examined in this book go back so far in human history that scholars can't fully know about their origins. Because the study of NRMs shows us religions as they are born and begin to grow, they are fertile fields of study for scholars and students alike. As Eileen Barker said, NRMs are "interesting because you can see a whole lot of social processes going on: conversion, leaving, bureaucratization, leadership squabbles, ways in which authority is used, [and] ways in which people can change."[2]

- Because these NRMs are contemporary, a lot of detail is available on many of them. Some of this detail will be dealt with later in this chapter. But students should keep their focus on the general features of NRMs as discussed and illustrated here.

The study of NRMs often proves to be a strong test of a student's impartiality and objectivity. Some of these movements are in the news and on the Web today, and not always for complimentary reasons. Careful students of religion will want to recognize any preconceived notions they may have about NRMs, and deal with them. You can make evaluations of NRMs, as of older religions, but you must earn the right to evaluate an NRM by studying it carefully first. In other words, before you conclude, "That's a weird group," you should learn about it and then try to think like one of its "insiders": What is it about this movement that makes it appealing to some?

---

[1] For a concise overview of new religious movements, see W. H. Swatus Jr., ed., *Encyclopedia of Religion and Society* (Walnut Creek, CA: AltaMira, 1998), 328–333. For an excellent anthology of primary sources, see Michael Ashcraft and Dereck Daschke, eds., *New Religious Movements: A Documentary Reader* (New York: NYU Press, 2005).

[2] Quoted in Toby Lester, "Oh, Gods!" *The Atlantic* (February, 2002), http://www.theatlantic.com/magazine/archive/2002/02/oh-gods/2412/, accessed 4/25/2011.

> With NRMs, "You can see a whole lot of social processes going on: conversion, leaving, bureaucratization, leadership squabbles, ways in which authority is used, [and] ways in which people can change." — Eileen Barker

Because of the many religions treated in this chapter, it has a special organization that differs from most previous chapters. First, we'll discuss the variety of names that scholars have given to this overall type of religion, and then we'll explain why this book calls them "new religious movements." Second, we'll draw out the most important common characteristics of the religions. Third, we'll examine the world distribution of new religious movements. Finally, we'll look in some detail at three important NRMs.

LO1 Names for This Type of Religion

Naming the overall type of the religions we're dealing with in this chapter has been a challenging task for scholarship. Some have even asked: Why it is necessary at all to group them together and give them one name, if such a comprehensive name may well distort or obscure them? The answer is that religious studies itself has seen the label as important to research and teaching in these religions, so therefore we must deal with this issue in our discussion here.

The first names that were given to this type of religion are *cults* and *sects*. These two terms overlap to some extent. **Sect** derives from the Latin term for "cut off" and refers to a new, small group that has emerged from within an established religion. Many of today's world religions began as sects within a larger religion and only later grew separate. **Cult** refers to a religious group that is extreme in its dedication to its beliefs, often living communally or semi-communally under the control of an authoritarian leader. It often carries the connotation of a false, even dangerous religion. Up until about 1980, these two names were commonly used in Christian churches and scholarship to denote controversial groups that had separated

from Protestant churches. Although the terms have some validity, they have become so prejudicial that most religious studies scholars no longer use them to characterize new religious groups. Other recent terms such as *alternative religious movements* are used, sometimes by those who apply the term to more long-standing NRMs (for example, the LDS church), to keep *new religious movements* for more-recent groups such as Scientology and Falun Gong. The term *marginal religious movements* is also sometimes used with reference to all new groups. But this prompts some to ask: Marginal to what? Some of these movements are so significant that they can't be considered marginal (the LDS church, for example, which is perhaps the fastest-growing religion in the world). A final term for this type of religion is *emergent religions*, which highlights their contemporary origin and initial development.

Gradually, scholars of religion and sociologists settled on the term *new religious movements*. Although it has gained wide use and been accepted by most religion scholars, it has been criticized by some for three reasons. First, how does this term distinguish NRMs from reform movements in established religions (as Buddhism and Christianity started), especially before the reform movements become a separate religion? Second, even though it is neutral, the term can be used with a polemical tone. Third, to call them *religious movements* may imply that they are not full-fledged religions, which most are.

Despite these questions, the term *new religious movements* is widely accepted and used today. *New* is ambiguous, of course, but a general consensus among religion scholars takes it to mean within the last two centuries or so. For example, *Nova Religio*, a scholarly journal on NRMs, covers as "new religions" those from about 1800 to the present. It recognizes the recent origin of these movements, and most scholars use it to mean that these movements are not just "religious," but religions. The term *new religious movement* holds out the nuanced understanding that, with the passage of time, some of today's NRMs may become regarded as established religions, as for example many scholars hold that the Church of Jesus Christ of Latter-day Saints is becoming.

Examine the home page of *Nova Religio*.

---

sect New, small group within a whole religion

cult Religion or religious sect that is extremist and under the control of an authoritarian leader

LO2 Common Features of New Religious Movements

Many NRMs are rooted in ancient traditions, but they arise in the modern world and address modern concerns.

Although there's a great deal of diversity among NRMs, they have a number of common features. First, NRMs are *religious responses to the modern world*. Most world religions come from the past, often from ancient times. NRMs are not only *new* in the sense of *recent*. Although many NRMs represent themselves as rooted in ancient traditions, they arise in the modern world and address modern concerns, often in new ways. For example, NRMs are often more comfortable using electronic media than established world religions are. The Church of Scientology has all its scriptures in electronic form. Many of them incorporate scientific (real or claimed) understandings into their teachings and practices that older religions do not.

Second, NRMs are usually *countercultural*. They move against the mainstream currents of society, especially as those cultures have been shaped by the dominant historic religions. This countercultural quality often makes them controversial in a whole culture, not just with established or traditional religions in that culture. For example, the Unification Church and Scientology have been blamed for disrupting traditional North American family ties. The Latter-day Saints movement encountered wide cultural opposition in the 1800s for its espousal of polygamy, and pockets of polygamy among sectarian Mormons still make headlines today.

Third, NRMs are almost always *founded by a single magnetic, powerful leader*. This is true of all the NRMs mentioned in this chapter. The founder is often believed to have extraordinary, even supernatural, powers or insights. He or she is skilled at organizing and guiding a new religious movement. If the NRM is based in a literate culture, leaders typically write authoritative literature that almost immediately guides the movement as its sacred scripture. Because they are founded by a single person, they arise quickly, in contrast to older religions that typically developed over generations, even centuries, under multiple leaders.

Fourth, NRMs *can spring up quickly, but they can disappear quickly as well*. Sociologists estimate that

Bill Paxton, Chloë Sevigny, Ginnifer Goodwin and Jeanne Tripplehorn (clockwise from top right) star as husband and wives in the HBO series Big Love, *about Mormon polygamy in a Utah suburb today.*

HBO/PHOTOFEST

more than thirty NRMs begin in the United States annually, but many of them don't last for more than a decade, some of them even less. At times NRMs disappear in violent tragedy, as with the Branch Davidian, Heaven's Gate, and People's Temple movements that we'll discuss below. Those that survive often face another threat to their continuity or even their existence when their founder dies. When an NRM is able to last for centuries, it loses *new* and *movement* and becomes known simply as a *religion*.

Fifth, most NRMs are *tightly organized with high intensity*. In light of their self-understanding as outsider, countercultural movements, these groups often make strong demands on the loyalty and commitment of their followers. Many—but not all—are what sociologists of religion call "high-intensity" organizations, in which members live for the group and the group directs individual life. (Established religions can be high-intensity as well, but in general NRMs are more "intense" than the older, established religions.) For example, many NRMs become substitutes for the family and other conventional social groupings. This sort of high-intensity religious life with different views of family life is the main reason why some NRMs are popularly known as "cults." When NRMs encounter opposition, this usually serves to solidify their tight organization.

Sixth, NRMs *start small but can become international movements.* Established world religions usually started small as well, but this is the rule with all NRMs. Some NRMs from the 1800s that survived are strong in numbers today: the Church of Jesus Christ of Latter-day Saints, the Jehovah's Witness church, the Baha'i movement from Islam, and others. Even a few more recent movements such as Falun Gong can quickly gain an international following and become "world religious movements." No study of world religions is complete without a consideration of NRMs.

Finally, NRMs *address specific needs* that many people seemingly cannot satisfy through more-traditional religious organizations or through modern secularism. They are products of and responses to aspects of modern life, religious and cultural pluralism, and the scientific worldview. Because the overall number of NRMs and the numbers of believers in them is increasing, NRMs are obviously making an effective appeal in the modern world.

LO3 New Religious Movements in the World Today: A Survey

Many people in the Western world suppose that new religious movements are primarily a Western thing and aren't found in other areas of the world. Nothing could be further from the truth. As this section will show, NRMs are spread throughout the world as widely as the older, established religions are.

NRMS IN THE WESTERN WORLD

The history, teachings, and practices of NRMs in the West are widely diverse. Most of them come from Christianity, the dominant religion in the West, but many

don't. The following overview organizes this diversity into certain categories, but many NRMs could be classified under more than one, and other groupings could be used as well.

Some NRMs are shaped by **apocalyptic** belief about the end of time, that the end of the world is near and that a new earth with a new, perfect society will replace the old one. Many world religions have apocalyptic features. However, modern Christian apocalyptic, especially **millenarianism**—a belief in some forms of Protestantism that Christ will establish and lead a thousand-year reign of peace on earth—has formed a particular backdrop for the development of many of the NRMs in the West. Even in Asia, a millenarian impulse for a golden age on this earth occasionally surfaces, sometimes with Christian influence but usually without it.

Among the first significant NRMs in the United States were the Seventh-Day Adventists and the Jehovah's Witnesses, both the products of apocalyptic, millenarian teaching. William Miller (1782–1849) predicted that Christ would return to earth to establish his kingdom sometime in 1843 or 1844. The failure of Miller's prophecy didn't deter many of his followers, who still believe in the imminent return of Jesus. The Seventh-Day Adventists formed under the leadership of one of Miller's followers, the prophet Ellen G. White (1827–1915). As their name implies, they keep to Saturday as their day of worship and rest, and look forward to the coming (advent) of Christ. The Jehovah's Witnesses, founded by Charles Taze Russell (1852–1916), continue to believe in the imminent return of Christ and the end of time. Members of this international movement recognize no human government, and are in other ways aggressively countercultural. They suffered greatly in World War II, when Jehovah's Witnesses were systematically killed in the Holocaust. The Latter-day Saints ("saints living in the latter days" of human history) movement begun by Joseph Smith also drew some of its energy from apocalyptic. These three NRMs have actively spread their message and are spread throughout the world today.

apocalyptic [uh-POC-uh-LIP-tick] Belief that the end of this world is near and that a new earth with a new, perfect society will replace the old one

millenarianism [MILL-en-AIR-ee-uhn-iz-uhm] Belief that Christ will establish a thousand-year reign of peace on earth

© ISTOCKPHOTO/MESHAPHOTO

A statue of the Angel Moroni is found on LDS temples. An angel blowing a trumpet to the world is common apocalyptic imagery in Christianity.

> *The aim of most New Age groups is to bring the individual to a state of higher consciousness.*

The utopian impulse in millenarianism also underlies a movement largely outside the Christian tradition, with touches of various Asian and indigenous religions, which arose in the 1970s and 1980s. The **New Age** movement is an eclectic, often unrelated grouping of beliefs and practices that includes crystal healing, "channeling" with spirits, new versions of shamanism, veneration of the Earth, and a variety of therapies and techniques. The aim of most New Age groups is to bring the individual to a state of higher consciousness. The movement as a whole presumes that the world has entered, or is about to enter, a new age of more-fulfilling spiritual life. Scholars disagree about whether it is a genuine movement, largely because it is so eclectic.

Apocalyptic movements can sometimes turn violent, and this happened with a prominent NRM in the 1970s. A magnetic Christian minister named Jim Jones moved many members of his large, prominent congregation (called the People's Temple) from San Francisco to Guyana, in South America. He attempted to build a utopian community based on what he called "apostolic socialism," a version of Christianity influenced by liberation theology (see page 272), which was strong in South America at the time. Jones became increasingly autocratic and grandiose, even naming his settlement Jonestown. In 1978, a group of concerned family members led by a U.S. congressman from San Francisco visited the group's commune and began to leave with an unfavorable report. Jones then induced most of his followers to kill themselves by drinking Kool-Aid laced with cyanide rather than see their community broken up. (This is the origin of the expression "drink the Kool-Aid," meaning to accept something unthinkingly, to one's own detriment. In light of the tragedy from which it comes, this expression is insensitive, to say the least.) Those who didn't willingly take the poison were forced to drink it or were killed by other means. In all, 913 persons— about equal numbers of men, women, and children— died at Jonestown.

A tragedy also befell the Branch Davidian (dah-VID-ee-uhn) NRM in 1993. The group, originating in the Seventh-Day Adventist Church but independent from its control, first settled in a compound near Waco, Texas, in 1935. Vernon Howell, who later took the name David Koresh (ko-REHSH), became leader of the group in 1987. He identified himself as an apocalyptic figure from the New Testament book of Revelation. Allegations of sexual abuse of children and the launching of a gun business in the compound attracted the attention of state and federal authorities. This led to an armed standoff with the FBI. When federal authorities assaulted the compound to end the standoff, a resulting fire killed Koresh and some eighty members of the group, and the Branch Davidian movement ended.

Read more about the Jonestown tragedy.

Watch news coverage of Jonestown.

New Age Eclectic, often unrelated group of beliefs and practices that aim to bring the individual to a state of higher consciousness

ASIAN NRMs IN THE WEST

As we saw in our study of Hinduism (page 85) and Buddhism (pages 128-129), the teachings of these religions appeared in Europe and the United States in the 1800s and began to influence Western intellectuals. The most influential of the doctrines were Hindu Vedantic beliefs, especially the idea that the cosmos participates in a single divine spiritual reality. A few NRMs with Vedantic teachings were started in the 1800s by North Americans, especially the Theosophical Society founded by Helena Petrovna Blavatsky. These groups brought Hindu concepts into a combination with traditional and nontraditional Western religious teachings and practices.

By the end of the nineteenth century, the first Hindu groups took root in the United States when Indian gurus brought them over. Because their beliefs were presented in language Westerners would appreciate, these NRMs were stronger in the West than in India, where they were often marginalized. Vivekananda (VIV-uh-kah-NAHN-duh), a prominent Indian philosopher, founded the Vedanta Society in New York City. Based on the teachings of one of Hinduism's main philosophical schools as interpreted by Vivekananda's teacher, Ramakrishna (RAM-uh-KRISH-nuh; 1836–1886), the Vedanta Society attracted the attention of many prominent members of the artistic community. With centers in India and throughout the world, the Vedanta Society (also known as the Ramakrishna Mission) claims that all world religions teach fundamentally the same truth but maintains that Vedanta is uniquely capable of articulating this truth.

Another teacher from India, Paramahansa Yogananda (PAR-uh-mah-HAN-suh YOH-guh-NAHN-duh; 1893–1952), established the Self-Realization Fellowship in Los Angeles and was the first to teach yoga to Americans. Adapting Hindu practices of mental, physical and spiritual self-control and self-realization, Yogananda explained yoga in scientific terms that appealed to his audience. Like Vivekananda, Yogananda promoted an inclusive approach, maintaining that other religious teachers, including Jesus and Paul, had preached the same message. Self-Realization Fellowship societies are found today in most large American cities.

Although these Hindu movements introduced Hinduism to North America, it was only in the 1960s and 1970s that NRMs based on Eastern religions became widely attractive here. In 1959, Maharishi Mahesh Yogi (1914–2008) founded the Transcendental Meditation movement, or TM, in North America. Like Hindu movements in the West before him, TM was represented as a scientifically sound method for obtaining both personal and social peace. TM's system of so-called Vedantic science featured concentration on an individualized mantra imparted to the initiate by the guru. This is similar to long-standing Hindu practice. The Maharishi and his teachings gained great fame and attracted millions of practitioners to TM, even though most of them didn't formally join his movement. Its fame increased when it attracted celebrities such as American film star Mia Farrow and director David Lynch, American architect R. Buckminster Fuller, and especially the English rock group the Beatles and other pop stars.

The Rajneesh International Foundation is another NRM from India. This group was founded by Bhagwan Shree Rajneesh (1931–1990), who taught a Westernized form of Tantrism that stressed its psychological and sexual aspects. Also called Acharya Rajneesh and Osho, and more informally the "sex guru," Rajneesh urged his Western followers to overcome their problems by what he called "dynamic meditation." Unlike other meditation, which is quiet and still, "dynamic meditation" featured screaming and dancing, even physical violence and sexual intercourse, the latter sometimes in public settings. Of all Indian groups that came to North America, this one was most widely known as a "cult" for its strong countercultural practices and the flamboyant lifestyle of its founder.

This isn't to imply that the only presence of Hinduism and Buddhism in North America is by way of NRMs. As we saw in the concluding sections of the chapters on these two religions, they've also been introduced into North America and Europe with little change in their traditional forms, particularly by the immigration of Hindus and Buddhists. The forms of these religions in North American NRMs can depart significantly from those of the religions in Asia. For example, in India one would not often see the emphasis many Hindu-based NRMs place on leadership of a mass movement by a guru, explicit religious universalism as a key teaching,

In 1968, the Beatles and their wives studied in India with the Maharishi Mahesh Yogi (center background). Seated left to right on the red platform are Ringo Starr and Maureen Starkey, Jane Asher and Paul McCartney, George Harrison and Patti Boyd, and Cynthia and John Lennon.

and the "scientific" nature of religious teachings and techniques. The modern appeal of science leads us to the next group of NRMs.

"Scientific" NRMs: Christian Science, UFO Groups, and Scientology

Many NRMs claim to reveal "scientific truths" that haven't yet been acknowledged by the public or even discovered by the official scientific community. These NRMs draw on a powerful form of legitimization in the modern world: science. Some groups have claimed that science has proven their truth and value, and other NRMs have developed in the West with self-proclaimed scientific validity of their main teachings and practices.

The founder of Christian Science, Mary Baker Eddy (1821–1910), was a prolific writer, like many founders of NRMs. Although NRMs sometimes consider everything their founders wrote to be scriptural, the Christian Science Church has named only one of Eddy's writings scriptural: *Science and Health with Key to the Scriptures* (first published in 1875). The title of the book accurately suggests its content: a "science" that uses prayer, Christian scripture, and Eddy's book itself to heal body, mind, and spirit. This science involves a view that the mind is the source of health and sickness; to cure the mind leads to cures in the body. Until recently, the Christian Science Church has completely rejected medical science and treatment. It is still headquartered in Boston today, and its local churches spread throughout North America have "reading rooms" for the general public.

> *UFO groups developed teachings of space aliens who will bring advanced knowledge and spiritual wisdom.*

UFO groups, also more recently called the "contact [with space aliens] movement," represent another type of a scientific NRM, although one quite different from Christian Science. That they sometimes look to outsiders more like "science fiction" than "science" is largely unimportant. Adapting religious stories of the coming of supernatural or superhuman beings from the heavens, UFO groups developed teachings of space aliens who will bring advanced knowledge and spiritual wisdom. Beginning in the 1950s, groups such as Understanding, Inc., argued that UFOs carried beings who would promote world peace and personal development. The Amalgamated Flying Saucer Clubs of America and the Aetherius Society believed that space aliens hold the key to the salvation both of the planet as a whole and of every human. Usually this key consisted of superior technical and psychological knowledge that would bring in a blessed age, not the revelation of more-traditional religious truths. These movements from the 1950s and 1960s came at a time when most North American popular culture feared the thought of space aliens coming to earth, a fear many believe to be related to the threat of nuclear war that was widely felt at the time.

The Raëlians (rye-EHL-ee-uhnz) is a UFO-oriented movement now headquartered in Quebec, Canada, with about 55,000 members worldwide. It was founded in 1973 by Raël, a French journalist whose given name was Claude Vorilhon (b. 1946). Raël states that in December of 1973 he was taken onto a flying saucer, where he met a four-foot-tall humanoid extraterrestrial. Raël had conversations for one week with this extraterrestrial. He learned that the human race was begun by genetic manipulation by beings known as Elohim—a word that the Bible mistranslates as "God" and actually means "those who came from the sky." Humans are descended from these beings from the sky, and knowledge of this leads to enlightenment. Raël has also formed Clonaid, a company devoted to efforts to make cloning a human being possible.

The headquarters church of Christian Science, the First Church of Christ, Scientist, in Boston

Another UFO group was the small Heaven's Gate movement founded in Texas in the 1970s by Marshall Applewhite. Applewhite (who called himself "Do") claimed that he and his wife ("Ti") were beings from another world, which he said was at an "evolutionary level above human." Claiming to have already come to earth as Jesus, Applewhite argued that the "kingdom of heaven" that Jesus taught wasn't symbolic, but an actual place inhabited by highly evolved beings. Earth was the "Garden of Eden" in which human beings had been "planted" by the otherworldly beings. Applewhite organized communal living for his group of "plants" in a new "garden." He taught that the "plants" could evolve into "members of the level above human," but only if they shed their humanity, including sexuality; in response, some members of the group castrated themselves. This self-mutilation foreshadowed worse violence to come. In 1996, the group settled near San Diego, California, where it supported itself by creating websites for Internet users. Most people who came in contact with the group thought they were harmless eccentrics, but in March of 1997 Applewhite declared that the coming of the Hale-Bopp comet meant the arrival of a spaceship in its tail, sent to gather up the "mature plants" before the "garden was spaded over" and the Earth was destroyed. Led by Applewhite, the thirty-nine members of the group committed suicide together in order to free their spirits and be transported to the aliens' spaceship. The Heaven's Gate movement perished with them.

Explore the 1997 Heaven's Gate website.

As we've seen from the example above, these UFO-oriented NRMs can express traditional religious themes in the language of science, science fiction, and biological evolution. As space-alien fervor has waned in North America with the ending of the Cold War, other types of scientific NRMs have become popular. Most prominently, the Church of Scientology expresses religion in the language of modern psychology. We'll consider the Scientology movement more fully below.

NATURE NRMs: NEO-PAGANISM, WICCA, AND DRUIDRY

A variety of neo-pagan NRMs, of which the Wicca movement is one example, are antiscientific. They oppose the alienation of humans from nature that they see science as promoting, and advance the "re-enchantment" of

A Closer Look:

Druidry Gains Official Status

Druidry, the pagan worship that its current practitioners claim has existed for thousands of years, in 2010 gained recognition by the British government as a bona fide religion after a four-year process. The Charity Commission, established to oversee charities in England and Wales and the body that determines whether movements qualify under British law as religions, ruled that the Druids' worship of spirits in nature is a religious activity. The Charity Commission didn't have to rule on how ancient this movement actually is, only its present status as a religion.

Current membership in the Druid Network totals about 350 dues-paying members, although the BBC claimed in 2005 that Druidry is practiced by as many as 10,000 people in the United Kingdom. Druidry has

Modern Druids carry out a summer solstice ceremony at Stonehenge in England.

ANNIEGREENSPRINGS

eight annual festivals, including rites at the summer solstice amid the ancient stone monoliths at Stonehenge.

Wicca [WIHK-kuh] NRM of modern witchcraft

Qi Gong [chee gong] "Energy Working," the ancient Chinese tradition of spiritual and physical exercise

New Religions Characteristic name in scholarship for NRMs in Japan

nature. They offer a way to return to and participate in the meaningful rhythms of the natural world. Their use of magic, spells, potions, and the rest to help pursue their personal goals in everyday life intentionally opposes some of the basic tenets of modern science. Neo-pagan groups are found particularly in Europe, but can be found in North America as well.

Some neo-pagan groups claim to revive the pre-Christian pagan traditions of Europe. They understand themselves as an attempt to reclaim their "roots." Other groups go collectively under the name **Wicca**, the NRM of modern witchcraft. Wicca draws on religious articulations of ideas and sentiments in the modern ecology movement and feminism. Wiccan NRMs, mostly but not exclusively composed of women, tend to center on the figure of a Goddess and the "female principle," which they see as the leading force of nature. Like other neo-pagan groups, they attempt to re-enchant and re-personalize the natural world, a world they believe that science has wrongly objectified.

Watch a BBC report on current Wicca.

NRMs in Asia

Religious movements that emerged in Asia after 1850 reflect the colonial impact of the West on that region. The NRMs that evolved in this sociopolitical and cultural environment were either in opposition to Western religion and culture or in some sort of blended agreement with it. When they were against Western imperialism, these NRMs reinvented older Chinese traditions; when they agreed with parts of it, they blended Western and Asian religions. Both types of NRMs helped Asian cultures adapt to growing Westernization there.

NRMs in China arose soon after the first Opium War (1839–1842). Western imperialism, poverty in southern China, and the work of the first Protestant missionaries were a part of the mix that occasioned Chinese NRMs. The most important of these NRMs was the Taiping Tianguo (tigh-BING tee-ahn-GWOH), the Heavenly Kingdom of the Great Peace. This NRM was a mixture of evangelical Christianity, Confucianism, and various popular Daoist traditions. Guided by its powerful leader, Hong Xiuquan (hong zyoo-KWAHN), the Heavenly Kingdom of the Great Peace established a religious state, which its follower saw as a kingdom on

earth and in heaven. It controlled several provinces at first in southern China, and then moved into the center of the country. It threatened the stability of China until it was finally put down in 1865.

The Emperor legalized Christian missionary work in China in 1858, and many types of Protestant messages and churches then spread through China. One effect of this was the rise of indigenous churches that were independent of foreign control. Most of these were Pentecostal or evangelical groups; mainline Christianity didn't spawn independent churches so readily.

Some of China's later NRMs grew out of popular Daoism that predated the Opium Wars. New Daoist groups had been arising regularly for almost two thousand years, and the coming of Westerners didn't change this. One such major new body, which evolved out of the White Lotus millenarian tradition and the related tradition of spirit writing done in a shamanic trance, is the highly syncretistic Yiguan (yee-GWAHN) Dao, the Unity Sect. This spirit writing provides moral direction for the group. Another spirit-writing group, the Zhihui (ZHEE-hwee) Tang, the Compassion Sect, began in Taiwan in 1949.

By far the most significant type of NRM to arise recently in China relates to **Qi Gong**, or "Energy Working," the ancient tradition of spiritual and physical exercise. In the 1980s and 1990s, China experienced a rebirth of traditional exercise practices with a religious basis. These promote health by energizing the flow of *qi* ("matter energy" or "vital force") through the body. Qi Gong masters developed followings throughout China by demonstrating their extraordinary powers. Many NRMs arose from these Qi Gong activities. The most controversial and best-known Qi Gong group is Falun Gong, which began in 1992; we'll consider this more fully below. Religion in China today is growing rapidly, and NRMs are playing a significant part.

Read a 2011 report on the resurgence of religion in officially atheist China.

Japan has proportionately more NRMs and people in them than any other nation today.

In Japan, the rapid political, economic, social, and cultural changes that took place during the 1800s contributed to the formation of a large number of new religious entities that scholars of Japan have termed **New Religions**. In the wider field of international religious studies, they are usually seen as NRMs. Most Japanese new religions have their roots in Buddhism, some in Shinto, and a few in Neo-Confucianism; they tend to be eclectic, blending these three in unique ways. The perceived empty formalism and lack of vitality in the older traditions, particularly Shinto and traditional Buddhism, has given space for new Japanese religions to arise, with their vitality and dynamism. Like most NRMs worldwide, the new religions of Japan draw on high levels of popular participation, with followers running day-to-day operations and converting new adherents. It's safe to say that Japan, despite its modern, increasingly secular society, has proportionately more NRMs and people in them than does any other nation today. Here, of course, we can mention only a few.

The earliest of the Japanese NRMs include Tenrikyo (ten-REEK-yoh) and Konkokyo (kon-KOHK-yoh). The years between the world wars saw the development of Gedatsu-kai (geh-DAHT-suh-kai), a blend of Shinto, Buddhism, and Confucianism. The postwar period saw further development of some earlier groups, such as the Perfect Liberty Church. New sects also appeared, including the Dancing Religion, and Johrei (JOH-ray), a Christian-based self-help movement. The most notorious of the Japanese NRMs, the radical doomsday religion Aum Shinrikyo (ohm shin-REEK-yoh), was founded in 1987 by Chizuo Matsumoto (chih-ZOO-oh maht-soo-MOH-toh), whose teachings were a mixture of Asian traditions and Christianity. The group fell into disgrace after it launched a 1995 nerve-gas attack on the Tokyo subway system in which twelve people died and more than fifty were seriously injured. The group later renamed itself Aleph, the first letter of the Hebrew alphabet, and tried to rehabilitate itself without its founder. Three of its members are still being sought by the police for this attack.

The most successful of the Japanese NRMs is Soka-Gakkai (SOH-kah GAHK-ai), the Value Creation Society. This lay Buddhist group claims more than 6 million members today. Founded originally in 1930, it was repressed and disbanded during World War II for its opposition to the war, but it was refounded in 1946. It grew rapidly in the 1950s, and in 1964 it founded the Clean Government political party. Its teachings are rooted in the tradition of Nichiren, a thirteenth-century Japanese Buddhist, but it is independent enough from Buddhism to merit standing as an NRM. Soka-Gakkai stresses the values of beauty and goodness, as well as the saving benefits of chanting an invocation to its chief scripture, the *Lotus Sutra*.

The largest NRM to emerge from Korea is the Unification Church, the short name of the Holy Spirit Association for the Unification of World Christianity. The Unification Church was founded in Pusan, South Korea, by Sun Myung Moon in 1954. The church has generated much controversy, and its members are commonly derided as "Moonies."

Born in 1920 and raised in a Korean Presbyterian church, Moon relates a vision while a teenager in which he was charged with completing Jesus's unfinished work. Because of Adam and Eve's failure to obey God, their selfish love has dominated human existence, and God tried to restore his original plan in the life of Jesus Christ. Although Jesus was the First Messiah and should have brought full salvation to humanity, he didn't marry and have children, so he failed to complete God's plan. The Unification Church now openly identifies Moon as the Second Messiah who will complete the mission of Jesus.

Having married and become the True Parents of an ideal family, Moon and his wife Hak Ja Han called on members of the church to follow his example in marriage and thereby participate in God's plan for restoration. This invests special significance in the mass wedding ceremonies for which the church became well known. The emphasis on family originates in Confucianism, where marriage and family are central to religion and life. Moon's own task as "Lord of the Second Coming" is to continue the unfinished work of

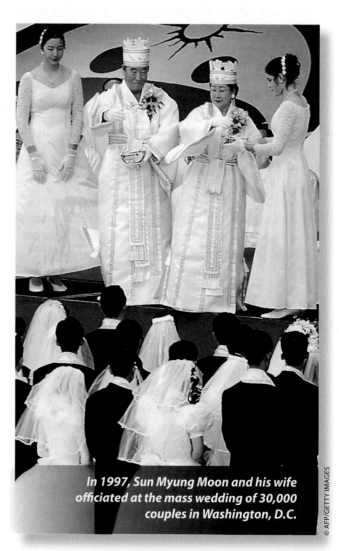

In 1997, Sun Myung Moon and his wife officiated at the mass wedding of 30,000 couples in Washington, D.C.

Jesus Christ and, in a perfect marriage and family, to fulfill God's original plan of creation. Moon's second marriage marks the beginning of a new age. The **True Parents**, Moon and his wife, can realize perfection and lead humanity to a perfect state, in order to build God's ideal world on earth.

Watch a brief statement of basic Unification beliefs.

Read an excerpt from the Divine Principle on salvation through the True Family.

In the late 1950s, the church spread to the West, and in the 1970s, it worked especially for the conversion of college students and used means that proved controversial. Some parents protested their children's membership in the communal-living group, which usually meant severing family ties. Controversy surrounding the church led to congressional hearings, and in 1982 Moon was convicted of evasion of his personal taxes and spent a few years in federal prison. His supporters, including many mainline Protestant church leaders, saw his prosecution as persecution, even if most Protestants disagreed with his adaptation of Christianity. The Unification Church emerged from these troubles in the 1990s with a more international base. The church now has a presence in more than one hundred countries, but reliable membership figures are hard to come by. Its influence is extended by a variety of church-funded organizations that embody Unification ideals but without its name, such as the Professor's World Peace Academy, the International Conference on the Unity of the Sciences, and the International Federation for World Peace. The church also owns media companies such as the conservative *Washington Times* newspaper and the Associated Press, a leading news-gathering company.

In Vietnam, Cao Dai (cow digh), a syncretistic religion, became a military and political force with considerable power during the final years of World War II and in the First Indochina War (1945–1954). Its political power is reduced in now-Communist Vietnam, but as a religion it is still strong. Cao Dai attempts to create a perfect synthesis of world religions, combining Christianity, Buddhism, Islam, Confucianism, Hinduism, Daoism, and shamanism. The Cao Dai faithful are expected to renounce materialism in order to cultivate their spiritual growth. They worship

True Parents Sun Myung Moon and his wife, who can realize perfection and lead humanity to a perfect state

Falun Gong [FAH-loon gong] "Practice of the Wheel of Dharma," a Chinese NRM founded by Li Hongzhi in 1992.

Cao Dai monks inside Holy See Temple, Tay Ninh, Vietnam

STEVE TAYLOR

one God, the most prominent spirits, and ancestors. Cao Dai also uses spiritual mediums in its worship. These mediums offer guidance from those in the spirit world, departed family members, and other wise individuals.

LO4 An NRM from Asia: Falun Gong

Falun Gong, "the Practice of the Wheel of Dharma," is a controversial Chinese spiritual movement founded by Li Hongzhi (lee hong-ZHER) in 1992. *Falun Gong* is the common name in the West and in China, but its adherents more frequently call it *Falun Dafa*. The essence of this NRM is to achieve mental and spiritual renewal by way of physical and mental exercises, as well as some mystical teachings. The teachings of Falun Gong tap into Buddhism, popular and religious Daoism, Confucianism, and even Western New Age movements. Li taught meditation techniques and ritual exercises designed to provide a means of obtaining spiritual and mental renewal. The group exploded on the scene in 1999 with a dramatic demonstration in Beijing against the Chinese government, which

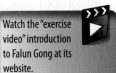

Watch the "exercise video" introduction to Falun Gong at its website.

had denounced Falun Gong as a "teaching falsehood" or "cult." The government continues to suppress the group through today.

HISTORY

The origins of the movement are found both in long-standing Chinese practices and in recent events. Qi Gong—the use of meditation techniques and physical exercise to achieve both good health, peace of mind, and religious blessing—has a long history in Chinese culture and religion. However, practitioners in modern China present these techniques as purely secular in an effort to evade the government prohibition of independent, unapproved religious activity. Nevertheless, in the late twentieth century, new masters appeared who taught forms of Qi Gong more clearly rooted in religion. The most influential of these, Li Hongzhi (1951–present), worked in law enforcement and corporate security before becoming the full-time spiritual leader of Falun Gong in 1992.

Li, a Qi Gong practitioner who had studied under Buddhist and Daoist masters, promoted his own version of Qi Gong techniques. He synthesized these techniques with Buddhist and Daoist concepts about self-cultivation. In his book, *Zhuan Falun*, or *Turning the Wheel of the Law*, he called for spiritual enlightenment through meditation and the striving toward a high moral standard of living. Shortly after publishing *Zhuan Falun*, Li announced that he had completed his teachings in China. He began to travel extensively, making appearances at conferences in support of his movement and its teachings. Li became a U.S. citizen in 1997 and moved to New York City in 1998.

Falun Gong became popular in the 1990s largely because many followers claimed to have been healed of diseases that modern Western medicine or traditional Chinese remedies couldn't cure. Membership in the new movement grew rapidly. By 1999, Li estimated there were around 100 million Falun Gong practitioners throughout the world; this is no doubt an exaggeration, but practitioners do number in the millions. Their public meditation sessions raise Falun Gong's visibility.

> Falun Gong members outside China have tried to keep up pressure on the Chinese government.

The Chinese government, however, became increasingly nervous about Falun Gong's popularity. Li, a charismatic teacher, developed a New Age theory of the end of time that he revealed only to followers. Government officials feared that Li's movement could inspire a revolutionary challenge to public order and Communist Party rule. On April 25, 1999, more than ten thousand Falun Gong practitioners protested in Beijing against being labelled a "superstitious cult" by the Chinese government. This massive sit-in somehow caught the Chinese government by surprise. Saying later that he was unaware of this upcoming event, Li had left China just one day before the protest. Three months later, Chinese president Jiang Zemin (zhahng zheh-MIHN) declared the practitioners of Falun Gong a threat to the government and issued a warrant for Li's arrest. He detained thousands of Li's followers, some of whom were officials in the Chinese Communist Party. Li's books and cassette tapes were destroyed by the millions in the crackdown. Hundreds of Falun Gong leaders are imprisoned in China today. Falun Gong members outside China have tried to keep up pressure on the Chinese government, and have even accused prison authorities of harvesting vital organs for transplant from live Falun Gong prisoners.

The Chinese government's actions against Falun Gong are rooted in concerns about the recent revival of independent religious activities in China and fears of the revolutionary nature of religious movements in Chinese history, for example, the Taiping Rebellion. Its concern also derives in no small part from the Communist Party's unwillingness to give up power. These measures are driving Falun Gong in China underground, but its beliefs and practices are surviving there.

Living now in the United States, Li has called for dialogue with the Chinese government to resolve the crisis that resulted over his system. His teachings continue to be spread around the world by a variety of methods: in books and on audiotapes; a free newspaper, *The Epoch Times*, which has an online version; Chinese-language television and radio networks; and a Chinese New Year entertainment held in major cities around the world.

TEACHING AND PRACTICE

Falun Gong's scripture, *Zhuan Falun,* is the main book of its founder. It contains a series of lectures, indicating the origin of the book in Li's efforts to spread his teaching beginning in the 1990s. It was first published in 1995, soon after the founding of the movement. Most of the chapters in the book preserve the feel of lectures to live audiences. *Zhuan Falun* has already been translated into forty languages. Although the Falun Gong movement doesn't explicitly describe *Zhuan Falun* as scripture—for example, by calling it a *sutra*, the formal Buddhist name for a scriptural writing, or venerating it in ceremonies—it is clear nonetheless that the movement regards it as such. *Zhuan Falun* is organized into nine "lectures" or "talks." These nine teachings discuss all the basics of Falun Gong theory and practice. A good deal of treatment is given to the relationship of Falun Gong practice with other traditional Buddhist teachings and with Daoism.

In Chinese Buddhism, *wheel* means the "wheel of law" or "wheel of dharma," as it does widely in Buddhism, but Li uses "wheel" for the center of one's spiritual energy. He locates it in the lower abdomen and believes it can be awakened through a set of exercises called "Cultivating and Practicing." Unlike other Qi Gong groups, which are inclusive in spirit, Falun Gong maintains that Li alone has established the correct exercises. The spiritual discipline he teaches, the "cultivation Mind-Nature," is essential to the success of the exercises.

In a teaching reminiscent of UFO NRMs, Li has said that demonic space aliens are now actively trying to undermine life on earth. He claims that since their arrival in 1900, these aliens have controlled scientists and world leaders. Critics of the movement ridicule this as bizarre, and they regard reliance on Falun Gong as a hazard to health. Indeed, the Chinese government claims that 1,400 Falun Gong devotees have died as a result of this alleged rejection of modern medicine. The controversy between the

Read a short excerpt from *Zhuan Falun* on Falun Gong teaching.

Chinese government and Falun Gong looks to continue for at least the near future, especially if this movement keeps gaining strength and stature in the world.

LO5 A North American NRM: The Church of Jesus Christ of Latter-day Saints

The Church of Jesus Christ of Latter-day Saints is one of several churches that originate in a movement begun by Joseph Smith Jr. (1805–1844) in New York State in 1830. The name **Mormon**, often used for these churches, is from the *Book of Mormon*, which was published by Smith. Now an international movement, Mormonism differs from the Christianity it separated from by its understanding of God, emphasis on family life, belief in continuing revelation, and its system of missionary work. This mission work has been largely effective in making the LDS church one of the fastest-growing religious movements in the world, perhaps the fastest, with 14 million members. Most of them are outside North America, with about a third in Latin America.

HISTORY

Mormons believe that in 1827 an angel named Moroni (moh-ROHN-igh) appeared to Smith and told him about engraved golden plates. Using what he called "seer stones," Smith translated them from their "Reformed Egyptian" language into English as the *Book of Mormon*. The Mormon after whom this book is named was an ancient American prophet who, according to Smith, authored the text recorded on the plates. The *Book of Mormon* tells the story of a family of Israelites that migrated to America centuries before Jesus Christ and were taught by prophets similar to those in the Bible. The religion Smith founded originated amid the great fervor of competing Protestant denominations in early nineteenth-century America; the area of upstate New York where he lived was known as the "burned-over district" for its frequent emotional revivals. Mormonism departed from them in its proclamation that, through Smith, God had restored the "true church" by

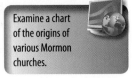
Examine a chart of the origins of various Mormon churches.

A Falun Gong meditation session in Warsaw, Poland. The sign gives the three key concepts of Falun Gong: truth, compassion, and tolerance.

LONGTREKHOME

Joseph Smith's boyhood home in Manchester, New York, where some of the translation of the Book of Mormon *was done.*

reestablishing the true faith from which all Christianity had strayed since the first century C.E.

This new church was millennialist, and Smith hoped to establish God's kingdom in the western United States. Smith received revelations of new teachings and traditional teachings in the *Book of Mormon*, and also received practical help from Moroni. Smith and most of his followers soon began their westward trek by moving to Kirtland, Ohio, then to Jackson County, Missouri. There it was revealed that Zion was to be established, Smith instituted a communalistic society. Tensions with slave-owning Missourians, who thought that the Mormons' religious idealism cloaked abolitionism, escalated to armed skirmishes that forced fifteen thousand Mormons to leave Missouri for western Illinois in 1839, where Smith built a new city, Nauvoo. The Mormons' commercial success and growing political power once again provoked hostility. A new complication in Missouri and Illinois was increasing rumors about Mormon polygamy. Smith's repression of some Mormon dissidents in 1844 intensified non-Mormon resentment and led to his arrest. While Joseph Smith and his brother Hyrum were in jail in Carthage, Illinois, near Nauvoo, they were killed by a mob on June 27, 1844.

After Joseph Smith's death, the Council of the Twelve Apostles assumed the leadership of the church. Most Mormons favored Brigham Young's appointment as Smith's successor. Increasing violence made the Mormons' continued presence in Nauvoo impossible, and Young led a 1,100-mile migration to Utah in 1846 to 1847. There the Mormons hoped to establish a commonwealth where they could live by themselves and practice their religion without opposition. Young established more than three hundred communities in Utah and neighboring territories. To build the population, he sent missionaries across North America and to Europe. Converts were urged to migrate to the new Mormon land, and it is estimated that about eighty thousand Mormon pioneers traveling by wagon trains, by handcarts, or on foot reached Salt Lake City by 1869.

Despite the difficulties of life around Salt Lake, the pioneers made steady progress in farming and trade. Their request for statehood in 1849 was denied by the U.S. government, which instead organized the area as a territory, with Young as its first governor. Future efforts to gain statehood were blocked by the church's announcement in 1852 of its practice of polygamy, which Mormons call "plural marriage." It had been practiced secretly by Smith himself and by most leading Mormons since the church's time in Nauvoo, but at this time it became a key doctrine and practice of most Mormons. Young and federal officials disputed this practice, and Mormons continued to press for their own church-directed government during the 1850s. In 1857, a group of Mormons murdered all the men, women and children of a wagon train attempting to move through the Mountain Meadows, Utah area. In response to continued conflicts with federal officials, U.S. president James Buchanan threatened to dispatch a military expedition to Utah to suppress the Mormon "rebellion" and impose a non-Mormon governor on the territory.

Troubles over polygamy continued until 1890, when the president of the LDS church, Wilford Woodruff, announced with great anguish the church's abandonment of the practice. This and other changes led to the 1896 admission of Utah into the Union as the forty-fifth state. However, Woodruff's pronouncement forbade polygamy only in the United States, and for more than a decade it continued in the LDS settlements in Mexico and in remote places in the American West. The LDS church's finally-effective renunciation of plural marriage is probably a main cause of its increasing strength during the 1900s; those Mormon groups that kept to it have had smaller growth. The church grew rapidly through the traditionally large families that Mormons have, and after World War II the practice of sending young Mormons out as missionaries led to exponential growth. At any given moment, the LDS church has around forty thousand missionaries active around the world. The church's appeal throughout the world was greatly enhanced when in 1978 it dropped its racist teachings of the 1800s and allowed Africans and members of the African diaspora to become full-fledged members of the LDS Church.

In the fractured history of Mormonism, more than 150 different independent groups have formed to follow new prophets, to practice polygamy, or to continue other practices that were discarded by the mainstream LDS church. For example, some Mormons rejected Brigham Young's leadership and remained in the Midwest after the death of Joseph Smith. The largest of these groups, which Smith's widow Emma and his son Joseph Smith III joined, formed the Reorganized Church of Jesus Christ of Latter Day Saints in 1852 to 1860. The Reorganized Church eventually settled in Independence, Missouri, which Joseph Smith, Jr. had designated as the location of Zion. For many decades they were led by the descendants of Joseph Smith. In the 1990s, they renamed themselves by the more mainstream Christian name the "Community of Christ." They number around 250,000 members and keep only the *Book of Mormon* as their scripture besides the Bible. Another faction moved to Independence and purchased the so-called Temple Lot, the site chosen by Smith for the new temple. The possession of this valued property embittered relations with the Reorganized Church, whose headquarters were on land immediately to the south. David Whitmer and Martin Harris, two of Smith's first converts who claimed to have seen the golden plates and talked to the angel Moroni, eventually left the church in Kirtland, Ohio. In 1847, James Strang established a polygamous community of about three thousand people on Beaver Island in northern Lake Michigan, proclaiming himself its king. Despite these splits, the LDS church has always been far larger than all other Mormon groups combined.

Among the most significant of Latter-day Saints factions to emerge in the twentieth century were groups that kept openly to polygamy. The first such group was established at Short Creek (now Colorado City), Arizona, in 1902, shortly after the Church of Jesus Christ of Latter-day Saints prohibited entering into or officiating over a plural marriage. Additional polygamist colonies were later founded in Mexico and near Salt Lake City. Church and federal authorities have attempted to stamp out the polygamy-practicing groups, which nevertheless claim a membership of more than thirty thousand. The largest single group committed to the continuation of plural marriage calls itself the Fundamentalist Church of Jesus Christ of Latter-day Saints.

SCRIPTURE

The Church of Jesus Christ of Latter-day Saints has a four-part scripture. The *Book of Mormon* is the leading part, and it is from this title that the followers of the movement came to be known as "Mormons." (This is the only instance among world religions of a faith being named, or in this case nicknamed, from the name of its scripture.) It was first published in 1830 at Grandin Press in Palmyra, New York. A second, shorter scripture is the *Pearl of Great Price*, and the third scripture is *Doctrine and Covenants*, which contains the continuing revelation of God's word through Latter-day Saints prophets, especially Joseph Smith. In addition to this "second canon" of scripture, the Latter-day Saints church has a "first canon" of the Christian Bible—the King James Version of 1611. The *Book of Mormon*, but

Book of Mormon *first edition (1830) with a printing plate.*
It was published with a large initial print run of 5,000 copies.

© ISTOCKPHOTO.COM/ANDREW RICH

not the other two Mormon books, is also considered scriptural by the Community of Christ.

The contents of the scriptures of the Church of Jesus Christ of Latter-day Saints are fairly complex. They record a story of ancient American peoples descended from ancient Hebrews who left Judah and sailed to North America around 600 B.C.E., and the appearance in the first century C.E. of the resurrected Jesus Christ to these Americans. This purported record ends around 400 C.E. The *Book of Mormon* has fifteen main parts, known, with one exception, as books. Like the Bible, these books are subdivided into chapters and verses. Mormons believe that these texts are based on writings appearing on four groups of metal plates: gold plates of Nephi (NEE-figh), Mormon, and Ether, and brass plates that, according to founder Joseph Smith, people fleeing Jerusalem in 600 B.C.E. brought to the Americas. In 421 C.E., Moroni, the last of the Nephite prophets, is believed to have sealed the sacred plates and hidden them by divine instruction. Smith said that in 1823 this same Moroni visited him as a resurrected prophet and directed him to these sacred plates. He reported that he translated the writing on the plates into English, and he published the text in 1830 as the *Book of Mormon*. The plates themselves, Mormons believe, were returned to Moroni and then hidden away for all time.

The second Latter-day Saint scripture, *Pearl of Great Price*, was first compiled in 1851 by Franklin Richards, then a member of the church's Council of the Twelve Apostles and in charge of the church's missions in Great Britain. Richards intended this book to increase circulation of Joseph Smith's testimony among Latter-day Saints. *Pearl of Great Price* quickly received wide acceptance, especially in mission fields, and became a scripture of the church by the action of its First Presidency (highest official body) in 1880.

The third Latter-day Saint Scripture, *Doctrine and Covenants*, has 138 sections, plus two "official declarations." It contains revelations on doctrines and community life, some narrative, some theological, and some legal, from 1823 until 1978. The declarations deal with two controversial topics—the ending of polygamy and the admission of blacks to the priesthood. Although the LDS Church has an "open" canon, and thus could add an entirely new scriptural book if it decided to do so, its well-established practice is to add any new material to *Doctrine and Covenants*.

Ironically, the *Book of Mormon* tends to be more similar than later official church writings and teachings to mainstream Protestant Christianity.

This is even true about the controversial doctrines that have set the Latter-day Saints apart from other Christians. For example, the *Book of Mormon* promotes monogamy and discourages (but does not forbid) polygamy (see Jacob 2:27, 30), but the *Doctrine and Covenants* preserves both the approval of polygamy (section 132.37–38, 52, 61–62) and the official disapproval of it ("Official Declaration 1"). Although opponents of the church point to more than three thousand alleged changes to the *Book of Mormon* since its initial publication, the majority of them are corrections and updates of spelling and grammar. In essence, this important book remains as Joseph Smith Jr. wrote it.

DOCTRINES

LDS beliefs are in many ways similar to those of mainline Christian churches, but its distinctive doctrines make it an NRM in its beliefs as well as its organization. Latter-day Saints believe that their religion restores true teaching as well as organization and practices. Their doctrinal statement, the "Articles of Faith," affirms belief in God, the eternal Father; in his Son, Jesus Christ; and in the Holy Spirit. But the three are considered to be distinct divine beings rather than united in a single deity, as in orthodox Christian teaching. God was once similar to a human but became divine, as all righteous Mormons also hope to do after death. Although Mormons believe that Christ came to Earth to bring salvation, they maintain that salvation comes by one's own actions as well as by the grace of God in Christ. Mormon belief reflects American optimism in the 1800s on humanity's basic goodness and potential for progress. Mormons also stress faith, repentance, and acceptance of the key practices of the church, including baptism by immersion. They administer the sacrament of the Lord's Supper as a memorial of Christ's death, but use water instead of wine. They attend Sunday services regularly, and tithe (give one-tenth of their income) faithfully.

As stated above, Mormons believe that faithful members of the church may receive God's fullness and thus become gods themselves. Everyone who ever lived, except for a few who reject God after coming to know him, will receive a blessed afterlife. At Christ's return, he will establish a millennial kingdom. After this millennium, Earth will become a celestial sphere and the inheritance of the righteous. Others will be assigned to lesser kingdoms.

Read the Articles of Faith of the LDS church.

INSTITUTIONS, PRACTICES, AND STRUCTURE OF THE LDS CHURCH

The LDS church dissolves the distinctions between the clergy and the laity that are found in most branches of Christianity. At age twelve, all worthy males (a category that until 1978 did not include black men) become deacons in the Aaronic priesthood; they become teachers at age fourteen and priests at age sixteen. About two years later, they can enter the Melchizedek priesthood as elders and may then enter the lower, local ranks of church office. In general, middle-aged LDS men have local and regional authority; national and international authority goes to men in their retirement years. In addition to service in the priesthood, many Latter-day Saints do missionary work. Young men, generally between the ages of 19 and 21, undertake a twenty-four-month proselytizing mission. Young women of age 21 and older serve for eighteen months. This is voluntary, but many young "Saints" participate in it. They may serve in this country or in a foreign land. Many older married couples also serve as missionaries for eighteen months. This missionary work has helped to make the LDS church one of the fastest-growing religions in the world. It has also helped to give young Saints a remarkably important role in the church.

Baptism, a rite of initiation, repentance, and obedience, is considered essential for salvation. Baptism is administered to children at age eight and to adult converts, and may be undertaken by proxy for those who died without knowledge of the truth. The Mormons' commitment to compiling genealogies springs from their concern to bring their ancestors who have died into the fullness of blessing. This information is used to identify candidates for baptism by proxy. In 2010, after some Jewish groups protested, the LDS Church changed its procedure for collecting genealogical information, especially to prevent the names of Jews who had died in the Holocaust from being baptized by proxy.

> *The LDS church dissolves the distinctions between the clergy and the laity that are found in most branches of Christianity.*

© ISTOCKPHOTO.COM/JASON LUGO

LDS missionary in typical clothing

Baptism for the dead, **endowment**, a rite of adult initiation in which blessings and knowledge are imparted to the initiate, and the **sealing** of families to assure their unity in time and through eternity are essential ceremonies that take place in the temple. During the endowment, the person is ritually washed and anointed with oil. This is followed by a dramatic performance of the story of creation, the fall of humanity into sin, and God's bringing of salvation to the world.

In general, Mormon ethics flows from the New Testament and is much the same as in mainstream Christian churches. In addition, Mormons have moral commands particular to them. The use of alcohol and tobacco is forbidden, as is caffeine in coffee, tea, and other drinks. Mormons promote education and have a strong work ethic. Their outer clothing must always be modest. A **temple garment**, more commonly called simply *garments*, is a type of white underwear worn by members of the LDS church after they have gone through the endowment ceremony in the temple. LDS members receive their first temple garments during the washing and anointing part of this ceremony. An observant Mormon wears garments day

endowment Mormon temple rite of adult initiation in which blessings and knowledge are imparted to the initiate

sealing Mormon temple rite uniting families for time and eternity

temple garment Type of white underwear worn by members of the Latter Day Saints church after they have taken part in the endowment ceremony in the temple

342 CHAPTER 13 ENCOUNTERING NEW RELIGIOUS MOVEMENTS: MODERN WAYS TO ALTERNATIVE MEANINGS

and night; any endowed adult must wear them to enter an LDS temple. The undergarments remind those who wear them of the sacred covenants made in temple ceremonies. Today, the temple garment is worn by LDS members and by members of most Mormon fundamentalist churches, but not by more liberal Mormon groups.

The LDS Church is structured as follows. The "General Authorities" of the church are the First Presidency (the church president and two councilors), the Council of the Twelve Apostles from which the president is elected, and the First Quorum of Seventy. These men have primary spiritual and ecclesiastical leadership in the LDS church. They also manage the church's extensive properties, businesses, and relief programs. All these are "sustained in office" by a vote of confidence at the twice-yearly General Conference, which is open to all LDS members and to outside observers.

At the regional level, individual churches are gathered into **stakes** of four thousand to five thousand members under the leadership of a stake president. The **ward** is the local church, each with no more than a few hundred members, under a bishop. Stakes and presidents are filled by men who hold the Melchizedek priesthood, but they are not "clergy" in the wider Christian sense, nor do they have a theological education. The religious life of each member is focused on the ward, through which weekly worship, economic, and social activities; tithing; and the operation of the church's elaborate welfare plan are organized. With this focus on ward activity, Mormons do their part to make the Church of Jesus Christ of Latter-day Saints one of the fastest-growing religious movements in the world.

Read about Mormon clothing expectations on a church website.

LO6 The Church of Scientology

Scientology is the international movement that emerged in the 1950s from the thoughts of L. Ronald Hubbard (1911–1986), a writer who introduced his ideas to the general public in *Dianetics: The Modern Science of Mental Health* (1950). Hubbard's stated goal was to analyze humankind's mental and emotional problems and to offer a means for overcoming them. He eventually broadened Dianetics's focus on the mind to a more explicitly religious approach to the human condition, which he called **Scientology**. The Church of Scientology was founded in 1954, and today is perhaps the most controversial—and one of the most powerful—NRMs in the world.

Visit the sophisticated official website of the Church of Scientology.

L. Ron Hubbard

AP PHOTO

stake Regional body of Mormon churches under a president

ward Local Mormon church under a bishop

Scientology Psychologically-oriented new religious movement founded by L. Ron Hubbard

L. RON HUBBARD'S LIFE AND TEACHINGS

Hubbard attended George Washington University from 1930 to 1932 but dropped out to pursue other interests. He married in 1933 and settled down to a career as a writer. His writing included western fiction, horror stories, and especially science fiction, and he was a frequent contributor to pulp magazines. Hubbard had also developed an interest in exploring and seafaring. In 1940 and 1941, he was awarded licenses as a master of power and sailing vessels. Ships would later play a role in the operation of the Scientology church.

engram In Scientology, image of past experience stored in the mind that hinders full mental and emotional functioning

auditing In Scientology, a one-on-one counseling process in which a client is helped to deal with his or her engrams

E-meter Electrical instrument used in Scientology auditing, allowing the identification of engrams

clear In Scientology, the fully functioning state of the mind when it is rid of engrams

thetan [THEE-tan, with *th* pronounced as in *the*] In Scientology, spiritual entity that can exist apart from the body, the true self of every person

During World War II, Hubbard didn't see combat but served in naval intelligence in Australia and aboard several vessels off the U.S. coast. He ended the war as a patient at a naval hospital in Oakland, California. This seems to have been the catalyst for his considerations on the human problem, and he began a personal quest for a "science of the mind." His initial conclusions appeared in his book *The Original Thesis* (1948), followed by a more developed presentation in *Dianetics*. These and all Hubbard's writings on what would become Scientology, both published and unpublished, are considered scriptures by the church.

Hubbard believed that the world is overall a good place and that the basic principle and goal of human existence is survival in this good world and enjoyment of it. He wrote, "Life, all life, is trying to survive." Actions that lead to survival are good and yield pleasure, he argued. Actions that go against survival are destructive, and they "perpetuate negative mental states." Each individual's mind in a normal state makes correct survival-oriented judgments. However, when one's normal mind isn't fully functioning, the "reactive mind" takes over. This part of the mind contains memories called **engrams**, which have strong negative emotional content. Later experiences may call forth negative emotions from the stored engrams, leading to actions that hinder pleasure and survival.

To help people bring engrams to their consciousness, confront them, and eliminate them, Hubbard developed **auditing**. This is a one-on-one counseling process in which

an "auditor," or therapist, helps the client deal with his or her engrams. A key part of this process is the **E-meter**, an instrument that measures a very small electrical current as it passes through a person undergoing auditing. According to church teachings, E-meter readings allow the identification of engrams. The goal of auditing is to rid the mind of engrams; when that is accomplished, the individual is said to be **clear**. Much of the income of Scientology comes from fees for these auditing sessions.

What moved Hubbard from Dianetics as a psychological system to Scientology as a religion was, among other things, his experience of what he called "exteriorization." This is the separation of individual consciousness from the body. His own exteriorization allowed Hubbard to see the real spiritual self, what he called the **thetan**, as an entity that can exist apart from the body. The thetan is the true self of every person, but most people never know this. Thetans had inhabited many other bodies before their present one, a concept similar to reincarnation. This focus on the thetan led Hubbard to construct a worldview that has much in common with Eastern faiths and the Western Gnostic tradition, without embracing them. But it was incompatible with the teaching of Christian churches associated, at least by implication, with his "Church" of Scientology. Even though Scientology is a church and has some of trappings of Christianity such as crosses and church services adapted for Scientology, it has never claimed to be Christian. In other words, for Hubbard and most Scientologists today *church* means simply "religious organization."

A Scientology recruiter (left) demonstrates the use of an E-meter to a man taking a free "stress test."

TOM HARPEL

Hubbard wrote that thetans originated billions of years ago with the original Cause (loosely understood as God), whose entire purpose was the creation of effect. The Cause created thetans first, and their interaction with each other led to the creation of MEST (matter, energy, space, and time), and the visible universe was born. Over time, the thetans fell into MEST and were trapped. Eventually, the thetans experienced events that stripped them of both their creative abilities and the memories of who they were. Their movements through the MEST universe eventually brought them to Earth.

The Church of Scientology asserts that, through its efforts, its members come to understand themselves as spiritual beings and how engrams as energy clusters inhibit them from functioning freely as thetans. Hubbard believed that the process of freeing the individual from mental error is the fundamental purpose of religion. Thus, a main goal of religion has been the salvation of the human spirit. The most sacred and secret teachings of Scientology are about the **Operating Thetan** (OT) levels, when the individual lives as a fully conscious, well-functioning thetan. In the Operating Thetan, the spirit controls the body and can act independently of it.

Hubbard then developed a more extensive worldview by identifying larger realities than the individual thetan. He named these *dynamics*. At the earliest stage of auditing, the individual learns the dynamic of individual survival, but goes on to learn three other dynamics of survival: the family, the tribe or nation, and all humankind. It is from these other dynamics that much of the extensive social-service efforts of Scientology flow. These first four realms of survival were expanded in Scientology to include four greater units—the animal kingdom, the physical universe of MEST, the spiritual universe composed largely of thetans, and finally infinity or God. These eight dynamics are symbolized in the eight-pointed cross of the Scientology movement.

As individual Scientologists experience God, the highest dynamic, they must reach their own conclusions as to God's nature. This freedom does not mean that belief in God is irrelevant or unimportant. As Hubbard wrote, "No culture in the history of the world . . . has failed to affirm the existence of a Supreme

Artist's depiction of the human spirit or soul, in Scientology understood as the thetan

© ISTOCKPHOTO.COM/CHRISTOS GEORGHIOU

Being. It is an empirical observation that men without a strong and lasting faith in a Supreme Being are less capable, less ethical and less valuable to themselves and society." Despite this affirmation, Scientology does not specify any teachings about God, but concentrates on helping its members to realize their personal essence and abilities. Scientology is a psychological, not a theological, religion.

ORGANIZATION OF THE CHURCH

Hubbard resigned from his leadership of the church in 1966 in order to develop the OT levels. Much of this was done aboard a seagoing vessel. During this period, Hubbard also formed a society of highly dedicated church members who were entrusted with the teachings he was developing. He called this society the Flag Service Organization. Now headquartered in Clearwater, Florida, at the Fort Harrison Hotel owned by the church, it is responsible for providing instruction for OT levels VI and VII. The related Flag Ship Service Organization, quartered on the ship *Freewinds*, provides on board the highest level of OT training, stage VIII. Contents of the OT training is only for church members who pay for the courses to rid themselves of the engrams acquired through the millennia, thus perfecting their abilities as Operating Thetans.

The most well-known part of Scientology is the Sea Organization (or Sea Org for short), established in 1968. Its members are found in the central offices of the Church of Scientology as well as in individual churches; they are considered the most dedicated of Scientologists. Initially created when Hubbard was at sea, maritime customs and traditions persist today even in the land-based branches of the organization. The Sea Organization itself is a fraternal religious order. Sea Org members do not actually work for the Sea Org, but for the local church or regional Scientology office where they are employed and receive their weekly allowance.

Scientology operates mainly through its local churches and missions. They are local, autonomous corporations franchised to use Scientology materials, teach the basics of the religion, and conduct auditing procedures and counseling. A church member who has attained "clear" by auditing and wishes to become an Operating Thetan can attend one of the Advanced Organization centers at which training for the OT levels is offered. As stated above, much of the church's income comes from auditing sessions and instruction to reach OT levels.

Oversight of the local Scientology churches and organizations is done by the Church of Scientology International (CSI), which coordinates the activities of the movement and promotes the church internationally. The Religious Technology Center (RTC) has ultimate authority for the teachings of Scientology. It owns and cares for the manuscripts, recordings, and publications of L. Ron Hubbard—the Scientology scriptures. It also grants legal permission to operate to local Scientology churches and regional organizations. The RTC is also charged with ensuring that the church's procedures are followed fully and that its "spiritual technology" such as E-meters is used properly.

Examine an interactive Scientology timeline.

In the 1970s, the Church of Scientology spread across Europe and began translating Hubbard's writings into many languages. Its growth continued through the 1980s, and, following the fall of Communist governments in Eastern Europe, it spread quickly there. Today, the Church of Scientology operates in more than 150 countries, but it remains a subject of controversy, to which we now turn.

CONTROVERSY AND PRESENT STATUS

Scientology has been embroiled in controversy from its beginning. When Dianetics was introduced as a "mental therapy," physicians and psychiatrists claimed that it involved practicing medicine without a license and disputed Dianetics's understanding of the human mind. Church leaders in turn charged psychiatry with denying the spiritual side of man's nature. Thus began what would prove to be a long conflict with the medical and psychiatric establishment, especially the American Psychiatric Association (APA). The church developed a strong opposition to the use of any medicines to treat mental illness, claiming they did more harm than good. Conflict with the APA, including a crusade against the popular drug Prozac, has been pursued by a special organization in the church, its Citizens Commission on Human Rights.

In 1958, the U.S. Internal Revenue Service began taking action against local Scientology churches for their practice of selling counseling services. Agents of the Food and Drug Administration raided the church in Washington, D.C., in 1963 and seized its E-meters on the grounds that they were unauthorized devices for the diagnosis and treatment of disease. These actions by the U.S. government also led to action against the church in both Australia and the United Kingdom. In response, the church created the Guardian's Office in 1966 and assigned it the task of vigorously defending the church, at times by going on the offensive against its opponents. (Scientology does not "turn the other cheek.") The

Guardian's Office brought legal actions against publications it deemed libelous, and in the 1970s it launched an extensive operation to gather information about attacks on the church around the world. Frustrated at the lack of response to their requests for documents from the U.S. government, some leaders in the Guardian's Office approved a plan to infiltrate or break into various government agencies in the United States. As a result, agents of the Guardian's Office were arrested and convicted for a variety of crimes in 1979. Following the church's internal investigation, several people associated with it were fired or expelled from the church and the office was disbanded. However, the church can still take an active role in dealing with its opponents, especially those who have left the church and are publically critical of it.

> In recent years, many protests and demonstrations have been held at Scientology locations by anti-Scientology groups.

Over the years, the church has argued many lawsuits in court. In 1993 it gained tax-exempt status with the IRS in court, ending a long battle. The church saw this as vindication of the many criticisms it has faced over the years and recognition that it is a genuine religion. Nevertheless, problems remain for Scientology. Several former members have become intense critics of the church, alleging financial fraud, illegal practice of medicine, harassment of journalists critical of the church, and vindictive actions against its former members. The rejects these charges. Scientology is under pressure in Germany and France. In 1997 and again in 2007, Germany's domestic intelligence agency investigated the church. Some Germans hold that Scientology is a totalitarian organization, forbidden under the postwar constitution. The German government even proposed in the 1990s that a symbol of Scientology be put on Scientologists' identity papers, which understandably raised a storm of protest because of the use of identity symbols during the Hitler era. In 2009, a French court convicted church officials of fraud but did not order the church to suspend its activities. Scientologists regard these government actions as a violation of their religious liberty.

Some former Scientologists have taken to the Internet, posting copyrighted Scientology material. Especially harmful to the church has been the posting of materials for the OT levels. In recent years, hundreds of protests and demonstrations have been held at Scientology locations by anti-Scientology groups. Despite all this controversy, Scientology continues to do its work and spread its message.

In conclusion, NRMs, for all their wide diversity, are a religious response to modern life: religious and cultural pluralism; the influence of science, especially the rise of psychology and psychotherapy; and secularization. They are also attempts to find new spiritual alternatives to the mainstream religious traditions. Although a few NRMs have led their adherents to tragic ends and some have faded away quickly, many have provided religious solace to those who feel they cannot obtain it elsewhere. Some of them will undoubtedly become, over time, part of tomorrow's "mainstream" religions. Even now, NRMs increase the diversity and vitality of the world's religions.

Read one of the most hard-hitting press articles against Scientology, from *Time* magazine.

Watch the statement of a woman who left the Sea Organization of Scientology.

Watch a statement by Scientologists explaining the appeal of their beliefs.

Anti-Scientology protesters approach the Fort Harrison Hotel in Clearwater, Florida, the headquarters of Scientology.

ANONYMOUS9000

Index

Entries in boldface are key terms.

Not For Sale

To help you take your reading outside the covers of RELG, each new text comes with access to the exciting learning environment of a robust eBook.

Working with Your eBook

You can read RELG wherever and whenever you're online by paging through the eBook on your computer. But you can do more than just read. Your eBook also contains hundreds of live links to

 Videos from YouTube, BBC, National Geographic, and others

 Google Earth™ explorations

 Interactive maps

 Sound clips

 Readings and articles

 Image galleries

 Websites

Each link takes you to an introduction, the link itself, and a series of questions about it. Your eBook also features easy page navigation, different page views, highlighting, note taking, a search engine, a print function, and a user's manual (at top right, under the "Help" question mark).

To access the eBook and many other resources, visit CourseMate at www.cengagebrain.com or by using the access card provided with this book.

What's Inside

Key topics in this chapter: Defining *religion*; why we study religion; six different dimensions of religion: cognitive, ethical, ritual, institutional, aesthetic, and emotional; the branches in the study of religion: theology and religious studies; the other academic disciplines involved in the study of religion: history, psychology, sociology, cultural anthropology, women's studies, and biology; special issues in the study of religion today: tolerance and intolerance, violence, pluralism, ecology, and new religious movements; "preunderstanding" and the study of religion.

Learning Outcomes

LO1 State and explain the definition of *religion* used in this book.

LO2 Give your own answer to the question "Why study religion?"

LO3 List and describe the six different dimensions of religion.

LO4 Discuss how the various academic disciplines contribute to the study of religion.

LO5 Explain the special issues in the study of religion today.

LO6 State and explain your own "preunderstanding" of religion.

Chapter 1 Outline

Discussion Questions

1. The "What Do You Think?" at the beginning of this chapter asked your opinion about the statement, "Religion is mostly about finding one's way to eternal life, however that is understood." In what ways is this statement true, and in what ways is it not? Explain your answer.

2. Explain and critique this statement by Peter Berger: "The process of comparing multiple conflicting beliefs in world religions requires a 'methodological atheism.'"

3. Some have labeled Andrew Newberg's work not neuroscience, but "neurotheology." Taking into account what this chapter says about the difference between theology and religious studies, do you think this is an accurate or helpful term?

4. Which one of the definitions on page 5 is the most appealing to you? The least appealing? Why?

5. Assess this provocative declaration by University of Chicago religion professor Jonathan Z. Smith: "Religion is solely the creation of the scholar's study."

6. In his book *Religious Literacy*, Stephen Prothero suggests that every American high school should teach a required course on the Christian Bible and another one on world religions. What to you are the pros and cons of this suggestion?

7. What way of studying religion seems the most important to you? The least important? Why?

8. The ancient Roman philosopher Terrence once wrote, "I am a human, and nothing human is alien to me." What might this proverb mean for your study of world religions?

Religion in Film: Suggestions for Viewing and Discussion Questions

Religulous, directed by Larry Charles, written by and starring Bill Maher, is rated R. It is a scathing attack on all religion in general, particularly religion that is politically to the right of Maher. Although it contains some scurrilous statements and ad hominem arguments, his film is a good summary of current popular critiques of religious belief and practice. It might not be easy for you to watch if you are religious. Watch it with an open mind, and then consider these questions: What are the main objections to religion in this film? In your opinion, is it fair overall?

Beyond the Class

A selection of materials is in the Instructor's Manual and PowerLecture.

Terms

religion *5*

monotheism *6*

polytheism *6*

private religion *6*

secularism *7*

ritual *10*

**new religious movements
(NRMs)** *11*

theology *12*

religious studies *13*

civil religion *16*

shaman *17*

atheism *20*

agnosticism *20*

tolerance *20*

pluralism *23*

preunderstanding *27*

What's Inside

Key topics in this chapter: the different names used for this type of religion; the special challenges students and scholars alike face in studying indigenous religions; the common features of indigenous religions; the main features of Lakota (North America), Yoruba (west Africa) and Vodou (Haiti) religions.

Learning Outcomes

LO1 State and evaluate the different names for indigenous religions.

LO2 Explain in your own words the challenges to the study of indigenous religions.

LO3 Discuss the common features of indigenous religions.

LO4 State and explain the main features of Lakota religion.

LO5 State and explain the main features of Yoruba religion.

LO6 State and explain the main features of Vodou religion.

Chapter 2 Outline

Your Visit to the Polynesian Cultural Center, Hawaii

Names for This Type of Religion
Traditional Religion
Primitive Religion
Animism and Totemism
Manaism
Shamanism
Small-Scale Religions
Nature Religion
Indigenous Religions

Challenges to Study
Lack of Written Sources
Difficulty Discerning Continuity and Discontinuity
Mainstream Guilt
Misrepresentations in Popular Culture
Misuse of Indigenous Rituals

Common Features of Indigenous Religions
The Importance of Place
Global Distribution
Many Gods and Spirits
Influenced by Other Cultures
Based on Orality, Story, and Myth

Discussion Questions

1. The "What Do You Think?" at the beginning of this chapter asked your opinion about the statement "Native American religions still have something significant to offer people of other religions or people of no religion." In what ways is this statement true, and in what ways is it not? Explain your answer.

2. In what sense are indigenous religions "world religions," and in what sense are they not?

3. Rank in order, beginning with the best, the names for this type of religion. Then answer the question: Why did I put them in this order?

4. What is the most difficult challenge to you in studying this type of religion?

5. What is the present state of Lakota culture and religion, in terms of strengths and weaknesses?

6. What, in your estimation, are the most important things to know about Yoruba religion and culture?

7. How might the recent interest in "zombies" reflect a continuing North American mainstream fascination with Vodou?

Indigenous Religions in Film: Suggestions for Viewing and Discussion Questions

Avatar (2009, rated PG-13), written and directed by James Cameron, is the story of struggle between natives on another planet and American corporate interests. Its visual appeal was more widely praised than its story line. *Avatar* gives a rich treatment of indigenous religion.

Questions: How does this film understand and explain the notion of an "avatar"? Why is the main character so attracted to indigenous culture that he becomes a part of it? How are the main parts of the indigenous religion depicted here similar to the main parts studied in this chapter? What happens at the end of the film that is strikingly different from the way other stories of this type, in real life in North America and Africa, typically end?

Dances with Wolves, 1990, directed by and starring Kevin Costner, is the fictional story of a U.S. Army officer who becomes a Lakota Indian. This film won the Academy Award for Best Picture of the year.

Questions: Why is the main character so attracted to indigenous culture that he becomes a part of it? What in this picture of Lakota life is, in your opinion, idealized? What is realistic? Explain your responses. How are the main parts of the indigenous religion depicted here similar to the main parts studied in this chapter?

Chapter 2 Prep Card

The Mission (1986, rated PG), directed by Roland Joffe: This is a study in indigenous-colonial interaction, as eighteenth-century Spanish Jesuit missionaries protect a remote South American Indian tribe in danger of falling under the rule of pro-slavery Portugal.

Questions: When the emissary says, "Sometimes a surgeon has to cut off a limb to save the patient," what does he mean by it? Do you agree with this statement? Had you been one of the Jesuit priests, what would have been your choice? What does the sad ending of this film say about what happens overall in interactions between indigenous peoples and colonists?

Apocalypto (2006, rated R), written and directed by Mel Gibson: Like many films by Gibson, it is drenched in bloody violence. As the Mayan kingdom in Central America faces its decline, its rulers insist that the key to survival is to build more temples and offer more human sacrifices. Jaguar Paw, a young man captured for sacrifice, flees to avoid his fate.

Questions: What to you is the meaning of the title of this film, drawn as it is from Jewish and Christian religions? How does this film portray the interaction of a large-scale Native American empire and small-scale tribes? How might the portrayal of violence in this film distort ancient Central American religion, as some film critics have said? Discuss in particular the depiction of human sacrifice in this film.

Terms

What's Inside

Key topics in this chapter: the diversity and unity of Hinduism; the history of Hinduism as it explains its diversity today; key Hindu teachings on gods and religious concepts; Hindu ethics and ways of life; Hindu worship and ritual; Hindu life in North America today.

Learning Outcomes

LO1 Explain what *Hinduism* means and its strengths and weaknesses as a name.

LO2 Explain how the main periods of Hinduism's history have shaped its present, especially its unity and diversity.

LO3 Outline the essentials of Hindu teachings in your own words.

LO4 Relate Hindu ethics to the essential Hindu teachings.

LO5 Outline the ways Hindus worship, at home and in temples.

LO6 State the main aspects of Hindu life in North America today.

Chapter 3 Outline

Your Visit to Varanasi, India
The Name *Hinduism*
The Hindu Present as Shaped by Its Past
The Vedic Period (1500–600 B.C.E.)
The Upanishadic Period (600–400 B.C.E.)
The Classical Period (400 B.C.E–600 C.E.)
The Devotional Period (600 C.E.–present)
Essential Hindu Teachings
Main Deities in the Three Devotional Movements
Hindu Doctrinal Concepts
Hindu Ethics and Ways of Life
The Caste System
The Four Stages of a Man's Life
The Four Goals of Life

Discussion Questions

1. The "What Do You Think?" at the beginning of this chapter asked your opinion about the statement "Hinduism is mostly about escaping this material world." In what ways is this statement true, and in what ways is it not? Explain your answer.

2. What makes it possible for Hinduism to tolerate, and even celebrate, so much internal diversity?

3. Give in your own words a statement of the "essence/essentials of Hinduism."

4. Radhakrishnan, a former president of India, said that "Hinduism is more a culture than a creed." What are the strengths and weaknesses of this understanding of Hinduism?

5. Give in your own words a critique of Sharon Stone's comments about karma given in the box on page 74.

6. How does the caste system undergird the main teachings of Hinduism? What is your take on the rightness of this system, first from a Hindu and then a non-Hindu point of view?

7. Reflect on this statement by Louis Dumont: "The secret of Hinduism may be found in the dialogue between the renouncer and the man-in-the-world [the householder]."

8. How was Mohandas Gandhi's movement similar to the Hindu reform movements before his, and how was his different?

9. Explain how this definition of happiness by Mohandas Gandhi is related to Hinduism: "Happiness is when what you think, what you say, and what you do are in harmony."

10. What do you find to be the major strengths and weaknesses of the Hindu notion of karma and reincarnation? How might a Hindu reply to your answer?

11. Explain the essential points of Hindu life in North American today, and then give your opinion of the future of Hinduism in North America.

Hinduism in Film: Suggestions for Viewing and Discussion Questions

The Indian film industry is second in size only to the film industry of the United States. However, it has not produced many English-language films that deal with Hinduism. *The Mahabharata* (1989, not rated), directed by Peter Brooks, is a short version of the lengthy stage play done by the Brooklyn Academy of Music and has a short section on the *Bhagavad Gita*. It is available on YouTube.

Questions: How is the teaching of the *Gita* summarized in this film? How effectively, in your opinion, is the enlightenment of the main character portrayed?

Sita Sings the Blues by Nina Paley (2008, not rated) is an animated retelling of parts of the *Ramayana* from a woman's perspective; it is available free of charge on the web.

Questions: Does the filmmaker protect the original intent of the story, or has she changed the story and themes? How effectively does this film adapt the story of the original *Ramayana* by adding the filmmaker's personal story?

For a treatment of the history and culture of modern India, see *Gandhi* (1982, rated PG), directed by Richard Attenborough and starring Ben Kingsley; this excellent film won eight Academy Awards.

Questions: How did Gandhi motivate people to follow him, and would these same techniques work today in India and elsewhere? Some people have said that Gandhi's type of nonresistance only works if the governments one resists have a conscience. What do you think? Explain the following saying by Gandhi and relate it to situations today: "An eye for an eye only makes the whole world blind."

Set in the time of Gandhi is *Water* (2005, not rated, in Hindi with English subtitles) by Deepa Mehta, the riveting story of widowed women and widowed girls confined to an ashram for the rest of their lives.

Questions: The lead character in the film asks, "What happens when our conscience conflicts with our faith?" What do her faith and conscience say, and how does she answer that question? Has the United States had any similar problems regarding widows in the past? Have these problems been fully corrected?

For a contemporary treatment of stages of life, marriage, and role relationships in a modern Western context, see *Monsoon Wedding* (2001, rated R) or *The Namesake* (2007, rated PG-13), both directed by Mira Nair.

Questions for *Monsoon Wedding*: How does this movie portray cultural differences? What is ironic about Aditi's choice to agree to an arranged marriage? Do you think that Lalit Verma is more concerned that his daughter is married properly and traditionally than if his daughter is happy in her marriage? How does the film portray class issues? What does Lalit and Pimmi's marriage show you about arranged marriages?

Questions for *The Namesake*: Why are names and naming practices important in Indian culture, and how might they be important for you in North American cultures? What surprised you about the Ganguli family's immigrant experiences? What questions does the film raise for you about real-life experiences of immigrants? At the conclusion of the film, has Gogol successfully reconciled both of the worlds he inhabits? Where is "home" for each of the characters at the conclusion of film, and what defines home or family for you?

Finally, *Slumdog Millionaire*, directed by Danny Boyle, is a 2008 blockbuster with several Academy Awards. It tells the story of a Muslim boy in Mumbai, India, who "strikes it rich" with the Indian version of the television show *Who Wants to Be a Millionaire*.

Questions: What does the title mean? How do the contrasts within it provide a summary of the film? Compare and contrast the pivotal choices or decisions made by Jamal and Salim; how do their choices affect their respective paths in life or "destinies"? How are those who have money and power glamorized and criticized in this film?

Beyond the Class

A selection of materials is in the Instructor's Manual and PowerLecture.

The Lives of Hindu Women
Hindu Rituals
  Images
  Worship in the Temple and the Home
  Pilgrimage
  Funerals
  Yoga
Hinduism in North America Today
  Hindu Movements in North America
  Hindu Migration and Life in North
    America

Terms

What's Inside

Key topics in this chapter: the meaning of *Jainism* and related words; how the history of Jainism has shaped its present form; basic Jain teachings; the main ethical precepts for lay people as well as monks and nuns; Jain worship and meditation; Jain life in North America today.

Learning Outcomes

LO1 Explain the meaning of *Jainism* and related terms.

LO2 Summarize how the main periods of Jainism's history have shaped its present.

LO3 Outline the essential Jain teachings in your own words.

LO4 State the main ethical precepts of Jainism for monks/nuns and laity, and relate them to Jain teachings.

LO5 Outline the way Jains worship and practice other rituals.

LO6 Explain the main aspects of Jain life in North America today.

Chapter 4 Outline

Your Visit with Jain Nuns
The Name *Jainism*
The Jain Present as Shaped by Its Past
　Founding and the First Thousand Years
　(600 B.C.E.–c. 400 C.E.)
　The Next Thousand Years (600–1600)
　Early Modern Times Through Today
　(1600–present)
Essential Jain Teachings
　No Gods
　Time and the World
　Jiva and Ajiva
　Karma and Liberation
　Theories of Knowledge
Ethics: The Five Cardinal Virtues
　Do No Harm; Speak the Truth
　Do Not Steal; Do Not Be Possessive

Discussion Questions

1. The "What Do You Think?" at the beginning of this chapter asked your opinion about the statement "The most important Jain teaching in the world today is nonviolence as a way of life." In what ways is this statement true, and in what ways is it not? Explain your answer.

2. Why and how has ahimsa played such a large role in Jainism?

3. What are some of the basic similarities and differences between Jainism and Buddhism?

4. Explain the rise of different Jain groups and sects, and how Jainism is now working to overcome some of these differences.

5. What are some of the main features of Jainism in North America today?

6. Give a reflection on this statement: "When Jainism's large contribution to the world is compared to its relatively small numbers, it may not be an exaggeration to say that person for person Jainism is one of the most powerful religions in the world."

7. Explain this irony, that the same religious principles and practices that help to detach Jains from attachment to the world are the same things that have brought them material success.

Beyond the Class

A selection of materials is in the Instructor's Manual and PowerLecture.

What's Inside

Key topics in this chapter: the meaning of *Buddhism* and related terms; how the history of Buddhism's founding and growth has shaped its present form; basic Buddhist teachings such as the Four Noble Truths and Eightfold Path; the main ethical precepts for laypeople, and for monks and nuns; Buddhist ritual and meditation; Buddhist life in North America today.

Learning Outcomes

LO1 Explain the meaning of *Buddhism* and related terms.

LO2 Summarize how Buddhism developed into what it is today, especially its diversity and geographic spread.

LO3 Outline the essential Buddhist teachings.

LO4 State the main ethical precepts of Buddhism for both monastics and laypeople.

LO5 Discuss the way Buddhists worship and meditate.

LO6 State the main features of Buddhist life in North America today.

Chapter 5 Outline

Your Visit to a Zen Retreat Center
The Name *Buddhism*
Buddhism Today as Shaped by Its Past
  Gautama's Road to Enlightenment
  Achievement of Enlightenment
  India, Sri Lanka, and Theravada
  The Rise of Mahayana: China and Japan
  Tibet and the Diamond Vehicle
  Buddhism in Modern Asia
Essential Buddhist Teachings
  The Four Noble Truths
  The Noble Eightfold Path
  The Three Characteristics of Existence
Buddhist Ethics for Monastics and Laypeople
  General Buddhist Morality
  The Five Precepts
  Other Precepts and Moral Rules

Discussion Questions

1. The "What Do You Think?" question at the beginning of this chapter asked your opinion about the statement, "The most important aspect of Buddhism today is meditation to bring inner peace." Now that you have encountered Buddhism in this chapter, what is your opinion on this statement, and why?

2. Explain why the life and experience of Siddhartha Gautama is exemplary for Buddhists today.

3. What are the differences and similarities between the lives of Buddhist monks and nuns, and those of laypeople?

4. Explain the Four Noble Truths and the Eightfold Path as much as possible in your own words.

5. Explain the Dalai Lama's often-repeated statement: "My religion is very simple— my religion is kindness."

6. Some claim that Buddhism is a "world-denying" religion, too negative about the human condition and the future. To what extent might that be accurate?

7. What are some of the main features of Buddhism in North America today?

8. Why and how did Zen become the most influential form of Buddhism in North America? Discuss both religious and cultural factors.

9. Do you think that "celebrity Buddhism" is a fair name for what it claims to describe? Why or why not?

Buddhism in Film: Suggestions for Viewing and Discussion Questions

Although the life of Gautama Buddha has great meaning as a narrative for Buddhists and for many other people, no feature film has been made of his life. Martin Meissonier's 2001 film *Life of Buddha* is a blend of documentary and drama.

Questions: How effective do you think this film's blend of drama and documentary is? What did viewing this film contribute to your knowledge of the life of Gautama Buddha?

Little Buddha (1993, rated PG), directed by Bernardo Bertolucci and starring Keanu Reeves in the title role, tells the story of the Buddha in tandem with a search for a new Tibetan leader that leads to the United States.

Questions: How effective in your opinion is the tandem narration of the story of Buddha and that of a new Tibetan lama? What did you learn about the Buddha and Tibetan Buddhism that you didn't know before?

Two films made in 1997 and rated PG-13 tell the story of the current Dalai Lama. The better one, from both cinematic and religious studies points of view, is *Kundun*, directed by Martin Scorsese. The other is *Seven Years in Tibet*, directed by Jean-Jacque Annaud.

Questions for *Kundun*: In the meeting between Chairman Mao and the Dalai Lama, Mao says, "Religion is poison"; what does he mean by this?

What compelled the Dalai Lama to flee Tibet for India? Explain this statement given as advice to the Dalai Lama: "Nonviolence means cooperation when possible, resistance when not."

Questions for *Seven Years in Tibet*: What is the European political context for the main character spending seven years in Tibet? What perspective do you get on Tibetan Buddhism? How does this film compare with *Kundun*, in your opinion?

What's Love Got to Do with It (1993, directed by Brian Gibson, starring Angela Bassett and Laurence Fishburne, rated R) is the story of singer Tina Turner and her conversion to the Soka Gakkai sect of Nichiren Buddhism.

Questions: What leads Tina Turner to convert to Buddhism, according to this film? How does Buddhism help her to cope with the problems in her life, particularly spousal abuse?

Beyond the Class

A selection of materials is in the Instructor's Manual and PowerLecture.

Buddhist Ritual and Meditation
Temples
Images of the Buddha
Prayer and Meditation
Protective Rituals
Funeral Rituals
Buddhism in North America
Buddhism Comes to the Western World
Early Buddhist Immigration to North America
The Next Wave of Buddhist Immigration
Conclusion

Terms

What's Inside

Key topics in this chapter: the meaning of *Sikhism* and related terms *Sikh*, *Gurmat*, and *Panth*; key formative events in Sikhism, especially the ten founding gurus, formation of the Khalsa, and Sikh life in the British Empire and in independent India; essential Sikh teaching of monotheism, devotion to the one God, and release from reincarnation; the main ethical principals in Sikhism, especially equality in caste and personal moral rules; the way Sikhs worship in the gurdwara; and Sikh life in North America today, especially the challenges of discrimination and diversity.

Learning Outcomes

LO1 Explain the meaning of *Sikhism* and related terms.

LO2 Summarize how Sikhism developed over time into what it is today, especially its founding by the ten gurus and its life in the British Empire through the present.

LO3 Explain the essential Sikh teachings.

LO4 State and discuss the main ethical precepts of Sikhism.

LO5 Outline the way Sikhs worship and practice other rituals, especially life-cycle rituals.

LO6 Summarize the main features of Sikh life in North America today.

Chapter 6 Outline

Your Visit to a Sikh Temple
The Name *Sikhism*
Sikhism Today as Shaped by Its Past: Two Key Periods
The Ten Gurus
Sikhism from British Rule until Today
Essential Sikh Teachings
The One God
Devotion to God
Key Sikh Ethics
Rejection of Hindu Caste
Other Moral Rules

Discussion Questions

1. In the "What Do You Think" section at the beginning of this chapter, you were asked to give your opinion on the statement, "Sikhism is just a combination of Hinduism and Islam." Now that you have finished reading this chapter, what is your opinion of this statement?

2. Discuss this statement: "Sikhism is perhaps more than any other religion in the world a 'religion of the book.'"

3. How is Sikhism similar to Hinduism and Islam? How is it distinct?

4. Explain how and why Sikhism went from a pacifistic religion to a militant one.

5. What effects have the events of 1984 in Amritsar had on Sikhism, then and now?

6. State and explain the Five Ks—with "kudos" to you if you can give the Sikh terms!

7. What is the layout of the typical gurdwara, and what are the main parts of the service?

Sikhism in Film: Suggestions for Viewing and Discussion Questions

One recent film giving good insight into contemporary Sikhs in the Western world is *Bend It Like Beckham* (2002, directed by Gurinder Chadra, rated PG-13), the story of how the daughter (played by Parminder Nagra) of strict Sikhs living in London is attracted to soccer (football).

Questions: How well is this serious topic treated as comedy? What are the differences, if any, between Sikh religious practices and Punjabi cultural practices? What does this film say about the challenges and opportunities of living in the Sikh diaspora, especially for young females?

More serious is the 2008 drama *Ocean of Pearls*, directed by Sarab Neelam. When Amrit Singh, played by Omid Abtahi, sees his dreams of becoming chief of surgery at a prestigious transplant center disappear because of his traditional Sikh appearance, he cuts his hair. When his other compromises result in the death of a patient, Amrit reexamines Sikh traditions.

Questions: Why is Amrit so driven to achieve professional success? Why and how do people misunderstand his Sikh religion? How does his religious and cultural assimilation lead to a personal crisis, and how does he resolve it? What does this film say about the challenges and opportunities of living in the Sikh diaspora?

Beyond the Class

A selection of materials is in the Instructor's Manual and PowerLecture.

Sikh Ritual and Worship
The Gurdwara
The Langar
Sikh Life-Cycle Rituals
Other Festivals
Sikhism in North America
The First Wave (1900–1940)
Second and Third Waves
(1965–Present)
Sikhism in Post-9/11America

Terms

What's Inside

Key topics in this chapter: the meaning of *Daoism* and *Confucianism*; how Daoism and Confucianism developed over time into what they are today; the essential teachings of Daoism and Confucianism; the main ethical precepts of Daoism and Confucianism; the way Daoists and Confucianists worship and practice other rituals; Daoist and Confucian life in North America today.

Learning Outcomes

LO1 Explain the names *Daoism*, *Confucianism*, and related terms.

LO2 Outline how Daoism and Confucianism developed over time into what they are today, especially in relationship to each other.

LO3 Explain the essential teachings of Daoism and Confucianism, especially their similarities and differences.

LO4 Paraphrase in your own words the main ethical principles of Daoism and Confucianism.

LO5 Outline the way Daoists and Confucianists worship and practice other rituals.

LO6 Summarize the main features of Daoism and Confucianism in North America today.

Chapter 7 Outline

Your Visit to the Forbidden City in Beijing, China
The Names *Daoism* and *Confucianism*
Daoism and Confucianism Today as Shaped by Their Past
China before the Birth of Confucianism and Daoism (ca. 3000–500 B.C.E.)
The Origins of Daoism (ca. 500 B.C.E.–200 C.E.)
Daoism from 200 C.E. to 1664 C.E.
The Near-Destruction of Daoism (1644–1980)
Confucius and the Origins of Confucianism (551–479 B.C.E.)
The Rise of Confucianism and Neo-Confucianism (ca. 350 B.C.E.–1200 C.E.)

Discussion Questions

1. The "What Do You Think?" at the beginning of this chapter asked your opinion about the statement "The two main religious and ethical systems of China, Daoism and Confucianism, are trying to reach the same goal by different means." Now that you have studied this chapter, in what ways is this statement true, and in what ways is it not? Explain your answer.

2. How well does Wayne Dyer's advice "Stop striving, start arriving," explain the Daoist concept of wu wei?

3. Give your critique of the following statement: "In Chinese religion, Confucianism is the yang, and Daoism the yin."

4. Critique this statement: "In Daoism, following the Way entails becoming more like nature; in Confucianism, it entails becoming more human."

5. Discuss the possible futures of Daoism and Confucianism in Asia and the West.

6. Explain why Confucius would probably not have wanted what we call "Confucianism" to be named after him.

7. Suppose someone said to you, "Confucianism isn't a religion—it's just a cultural and ethical heritage." How could you answer this statement, based on what you have learned in this chapter?

Daoism and Confucianism in Film

Confucius (2010, rated PG-13; in Mandarin, with English subtitles), directed by Mei Hu and starring action-film star Chow Yun-fat, is a retelling of the story of Confucius.

Question: Why was this film controversial, in both the casting of Chow Yun-fat as Confucius and in the portrayal of the life of Confucius? What insights do you get on Confucius and his times from this film?

The Last Emperor (1987, rated PG-13), directed by Bernardo Bertolucci, tells the story of Pu Yi, China's final monarch; it was filmed in part in the Forbidden City in Beijing. See the "director's cut" DVD for a fuller story that carries the life of Pu Yi through Communist "reeducation" camps.

Questions: How does this film show Confucian ideas of government? What might this film have to say about the possible transition from Communist rule to another form of government?

Raise the Red Lantern (1998, rated PG), directed by Zhang Yimou, deals with the life of a traditional Chinese family in 1920.

Questions: How does this film portray the difficulties posed by second and third marriages in China? How are the "family values" of Confucianism reflected here?

The Joy Luck Club (1993, rated R), based on the novel by Amy Tan, tells the story of challenging relationships between Chinese immigrant mothers and their adult Chinese American daughters.

Questions: What relational "issues" do mothers and daughters have with each other? How might this illustrate not just the first and second generations of Chinese immigrants, but those of all immigrants?

Crouching Tiger, Hidden Dragon (2000, directed by Ang Lee; in Mandarin, with English subtitles), shows the connection between Daoism and martial arts. This film, which won four Academy Awards including Best Foreign Film, draws on the Wudang Daoist School of meditation and martial arts, although this is not made explicit in the film.

Questions: How much of the portrayal of martial arts is realistic, in your opinion, and how much is not? How do Daoism and Buddhism relate to these martial arts?

Koyaanisqatsi ("Life Out of Balance," 1982, directed by Godfrey Reggio), has a more avant-garde presentation of Daoist themes. Without any characters or conventional plot, this film uses music and film photography to depict the balance in nature that humans should study and adapt to—a key Daoist teaching.

Questions: What impressions do you get about the Dao from this film? How does it present the balance of human life and nature?

Beyond the Class

A selection of materials is in the Instructor's Manual and PowerLecture.

What's Inside

Key topics in this chapter: the meaning of *Shinto* and related words; how the history of Shinto has shaped its present form; basic Shinto teachings; the main ethical precepts; Shinto worship and meditation; Shinto life in North America today.

Learning Outcomes

LO1 Explain the meaning of *Shinto* and *Kami no michi*.

LO2 Summarize how the four main periods of Shinto's history have shaped its present.

LO3 Outline essential Shinto teachings in your own words.

LO4 Describe the main features of Shinto ethics.

LO5 Outline Shinto worship and other rituals, and explain why they play a leading role in Shinto.

LO6 Explain why the practice of Shinto in North America today is so small.

Chapter 8 Outline

Your Visit to the Tsubaki Shinto Shrine in Granite Falls, Washington
Names
The Shinto Present As Shaped by Its Past
Before the Arrival of Buddhism (to 600 C.E.)
Shinto and Buddhism together in Japan (600–1850)
The Meiji Period (1850–1945)
Shinto in Recent Times (1945–present)
Shinto Teachings
The Kami
Characteristics of Other Shinto Teachings
Shinto Ethics
General Characteristics
Purity

Discussion Questions

1. The "What Do You Think?" question at the beginning of this chapter asked your opinion about the statement, "The Shinto religion explains the Japanese 'love affair' with robots and robotics." Now that you have finished this chapter, what do you think about this?

2. How do the basic Shinto teachings as outlined above illustrate that ritual is more important in Shinto than doctrine?

3. Explain why a better understanding of *Shinto* might be "the way of the kami" rather than "the way of the gods."

4. Why do Japanese myths place so much emphasis on the creation of Japan and so little on the creation of the world?

5. Why is the Shinto ritual performed at the Yasukuni Shrine controversial in Japan and even more controversial in China and South Korea?

6. In your opinion, what might the future of Shinto be?

Shinto in Film: Suggestions for Viewing and Discussion Questions

The best recent film that portrays Japan's religion and culture is *The Last Samurai* (2003, rated R), directed by Edward Zwick. Tom Cruise plays an eighteenth-century American military adviser who, after being captured in battle, embraces the samurai culture he was hired to destroy. The film begins with a brief retelling of the creation myth from the *Kojiki* and reflects its feeling for the land and peoples of Japan. The film also illustrates well the interplay between Buddhist tendencies to pacifism and Shinto militarism.

Questions: How does Buddhism relate in this film to its traditional pacificism? What Shinto "spin" is put on this film by its opening citation of the *Kojiki* creation myth? How can Shinto be seen in the traditional Japanese cultural elements shown in the film? How might the samurai-warrior ethic, portrayed sympathetically here, have had a resurgence in the twentieth century?

Beyond the Class

A selection of materials is in the Instructor's Manual and PowerLecture.

Shinto Ritual
 The Shinto Shrine
 The Shinto Priesthood
 Wish Plaques and Fortunes
 The Wedding Ceremony
 The Home Shrine
 The Shinto Funeral
Shinto in North America Today

Terms

What's Inside

Key topics in this chapter: the meaning of *Zoroastrianism* and related words; key formative events in the history of Zoroastrianism; essential Zoroastrian teachings of monotheism and moral dualism; the main ethical principles in Zoroastrianism; the way Zoroastrians worship; and Zoroastrian life in North America today.

Learning Outcomes

LO1 Explain the meaning of *Zoroastrianism* and related terms.

LO2 Outline how Zoroastrianism developed over time into what it is today.

LO3 Explain the essential Zoroastrian teachings of monotheism and moral dualism.

LO4 State the main ethical precepts of Zoroastrianism.

LO5 Outline the way Zoroastrians worship and observe rituals.

LO6 State the main features of Zoroastrian life in North America today.

Chapter 9 Outline

Your Visit to Yazd, Iran

Names for Zoroastrianism and Zoroastrians

Zoroastrianism As Shaped by Its Past

The Birth of Zoroastrianism (ca. 630–550 B.C.E.)

The Spread of Zoroastrianism in the Persian and Sassanian Empires (550 B.C.E.–650 C.E.)

The Coming of Islam and the Zoroastrian Dispersion (650 C.E.–present)

Essential Zoroastrian Teachings: Monotheism and Moral Dualism

The One God, Ahura Mazda

The Spirit of Destruction, Angra Mainyu

Moral Dualism

Supernatural Intermediaries

Judgment and the Final Victory of Ahura Mazda

Discussion Questions

1. In the "What Do You Think?" feature at the beginning of this chapter, you were asked to consider the statement "The belief that the world is locked in a cosmic struggle between good and evil, as Zoroastrianism believes, makes for a powerful faith." Now that you've finished the chapter, what do you think about this, and why?

2. In what sense can the Zoroastrian belief in many supernatural beings but only one God be compared to Christian and Islamic belief in one God and many angels, archangels, and demons, and the devil?

3. How does Zoroastrianism answer one of the perennial questions of many religions: How can one reconcile the imperfections of the world with the existence of a good God who created and sustains it?

4. The Parsis are often called "the Jews of India." Explain this expression.

5. What might Zoroastrian monotheism and the heritage of tolerance toward other religions and ethnic groups say about the belief today, commonly held by some, that monotheism is intolerant?

Beyond the Class

A selection of materials is in the Instructor's Manual and PowerLecture.

Zoroastrian Ethics
Zoroastrian General Morality
A Current Ethical and Social Issue:
Marriage and Children
Zoroastrian Rituals
Fires in the Fire Temple
Interior Plan of the Fire Temple
Worship
Priesthood
Other Rituals
Funeral Rituals
Zoroastrianism in North America

Terms

What's Inside

Key topics in this chapter: The meaning of *Judaism* and related words; key formative events in the history of Judaism, especially the rise of Jewish diversity; essential Jewish teachings of monotheism, creation, the chosen people, and life after death; the main ethics of Judaism, especially the commands of the Torah and more-general ethical principles; the ways Jews worship, celebrate festivals and the Sabbath, and observe life-cycle rituals; Jewish life in North America today.

Learning Outcomes

LO1 Explain the meaning of *Judaism* and related words.

LO2 Summarize how the main periods of Judaism's history have shaped its present.

LO3 Outline the essential teachings of Judaism in your own words.

LO4 Describe the main features of Jewish ethics.

LO5 Summarize Jewish worship, the Sabbath and major festivals, life-cycle rituals, and the Kabbalah.

LO6 Outline the main features of Judaism in North America today.

Chapter 10 Outline

Your Visit to the Western Wall in Jerusalem
The Name *Judaism* and Related Terms
The Jewish Present As Shaped by Its Past
From the Creation to Abraham (ca. 2000 B.C.E.)
The Emergence of Israel (ca. 1200–950 B.C.E.)
The First Temple Period (950–586 B.C.E.)
The Second Temple Period (539 B.C.E.–70 C.E.)
Revolts and Rabbis (70 C.E.–ca. 650)
Jews under Islamic and Christian Rule (ca. 650–1800)

Discussion Questions

1. In the "What Do You Think?" at the beginning of this chapter, you were asked to consider the statement "Judaism is the best example in world religions of 'ethical monotheism.'" Now that you've finished the chapter, what do you think about this, and why?

2. What are the main commonalities of the three major Jewish movements (Orthodox, Conservative, and Reform)? What are their main differences?

3. What is accurate and inaccurate in the term "ultra-Orthodox"?

4. How does keeping the law of God relate to being a member of the chosen people of God?

5. How does the term *ethical monotheism* relate to the teachings and practices of Judaism?

6. What does it mean to be "Jewish but not religious"?

7. Describe the situation of Judaism in the modern state of Israel.

Judaism in Film: Suggestions for Viewing and Discussion Questions

Hollywood hasn't made major films based directly on the Hebrew Jewish Bible/Old Testament for more than fifty years, despite the grand narratives of the Bible that are seemingly tailor-made for film. One exception is the acclaimed animated film *Prince of Egypt* (1998, directed by Brenda Chapman), the story of Moses and the Exodus.

Questions: How closely does the *Prince of Egypt* film follow the biblical account, in your opinion?

The Holocaust has so shaped recent Jewish life that it and other contemporary Jewish events have received the lion's share of attention in film (*Schindler's List, Sophie's Choice, A Beautiful Life,* and other movies).

Questions on *Schindler's List*: How realistically does this film present the motives of Oskar Schindler? Some have called him a "saint"; would you? Why do you think actions such as his were comparatively rare in the Holocaust?

A more recent treatment of a contemporary topic is *Trembling Before G-d [God]*, directed by Simcha Dubowski (2001). This prize-winning documentary film deals with Jews from Orthodox backgrounds who are dealing with their same-sex orientation and with the traditional biblical reaction to it by other Orthodox Jews.

Questions: How sensitive is this film to the concerns of same-sex Jews? To heterosexual Jews maintaining the traditional Jewish view on this topic?

Beyond the Class

A selection of materials is in the Instructor's Manual and PowerLecture.

Emancipation and Diversity
(1800–1932)
The Holocaust and Its Aftermath
(1932–present)
Essential Teachings of Judaism
Foundation of Jewish Teachings:
The Tanak
One God
The Jews As God's Chosen People
Life after Death?
Essential Jewish Ethics
Ethics in the Image of God
The Torah
General Jewish Ethics
Modern Jewish Ethics
Jewish Worship and Ritual
Worship in the Synagogue
The Sabbath
Jewish Annual Festivals
Kosher Food
Circumcision, the Sign
of the Covenant
Bar Mitzvah and Bat Mitzvah
Marriage
Funeral Rituals
The Kabbalah
Judaism in North America Today

Terms

Judaism 226

Hebrews 227

Israelites 227

Israelis 227

menorah 227

patriarchs 228

covenant 228

circumcision 228

Torah 229

Ark of the Covenant 229

First Temple Period 229

prophets 230

Second Temple Period 231

Diaspora 231

Pharisees 232

Maccabean Revolt 232

Hanukkah 232

rabbis 233

synagogue 233

anti-Semitism 233

Babylonian Talmud 234

Sephardic 234

Ashkenazi 234

emancipation 235

Zionism 236

Holocaust 238

Tanak 239

Shema 240

halakhah 245

kosher 248

mohel 249

bar mitzvah 249

bat (bas) mitzvah 249

Hasidism 251

What's Inside

Key topics in this chapter: the meaning of *Christianity* and related words; how the history of Christianity has shaped its present form; basic Christian teachings; the main ethical teachings of Christianity; Christian worship and ritual; Christian life in North America today, especially its diversity.

Learning Outcomes

LO1 Explain the meaning of *Christianity* and related terms.

LO2 Trace how the main periods of Christianity's history have shaped its present.

LO3 Outline in your own words essential Christian teachings as found in the Nicene Creed.

LO4 Describe the main features of Christian ethics.

LO5 Summarize Christian worship and other rituals.

LO6 Explain the variety of Christianity in North America today.

Chapter 11 Outline

Your Visit to St. Peter's in Rome
Names
The Christian Present As Shaped by Its Past
The Life, Death, and Resurrection of Jesus Christ (ca. 4 B.C.E.–33 C.E.)
The Earliest Church (30 C.E.–100 C.E.)
The Ancient Period (100–500 C.E.)
Byzantine, Medieval, and Renaissance Christianity (500–1500)
Reformation in the Western Church (1500–1600)
The Early Modern Period (1600–1900)
Modern Christianity (1900–present)
Christian Teachings As Reflected in the Nicene Creed
God the Father
God the Son
God the Holy Spirit
The Conclusion of the Nicene Creed: Church, Baptism, and Christian Hope

Discussion Questions

1. In the "What Do You Think?" feature at the beginning of this chapter, you were asked your opinion about the statement "Its universal spread shows that Christianity is the most culturally adaptable religion in the world." In what ways is this statement true, and in what ways is it not? Explain your answer.

2. Discuss this provocative comment by a Jewish scholar on the relationship of Judaism and Christianity: "Christianity is Judaism's gift to the non-Jewish world."

3. Aside from the life of Jesus, what period of the church discussed here do you think is most important for Christianity? Why?

4. What were the main issues that the Protestant Reformers were concerned about?

5. How different is the Jewish conception of God different from the Christian teaching about God the Father?

6. Explain why Jesus Christ is thought by Christians to be Lord and Savior.

7. Explain the similarities and differences between Christian ethics and Jewish ethics.

8. Despite obvious differences in music style, level of formality, and so on, how is most Christian worship similar? What are the deeper differences?

9. Is Christianity more internally fractured than other major religions such as Buddhism or Islam? Explain your answer.

Christianity in Film: Suggestions for Viewing and Discussion Questions

Of all major world religions, Christianity is the most fully, if not always the most artistically, represented in feature films. *The Gospel According to St. Matthew* (1964, unrated), directed by Pier Paolo Pasolini, is the most cinematically artistic.

Questions: What view of Jesus comes through in this film? How accurate is it as a retelling of the Gospel of Matthew?

The Passion of the Christ (2004, rated R), directed by Mel Gibson, is a controversial, thought-provoking depiction of the death of Jesus.

Questions: What do you think caused such a stir about this film? Do you think it is accurate as a retelling of the death of Jesus? How does this film suggest his resurrection?

For a taste of apocalyptic style in the New Testament and in modern film, see *The Seventh Seal* (1958, unrated), one of the classics of world cinema, directed by Ingmar Bergman.

Questions: What are the apocalyptic elements of this film? How does it draw on Christian themes?

Also of interest to students of Christianity is *Jesus of Montreal* (1989, rated R), directed by Denys Arcand, in which a Montreal theater troupe puts on a controversial passion play and begins to experience suffering akin to that of Jesus.

Question: How does this film relate Jesus' suffering to the troubles of the modern actors?

Babette's Feast (1987, not rated but suitable for all audiences, in Danish with English subtitles), directed by Gabriel Axel, is a story of frugality and prodigality that won the 1987 Academy Award for best foreign film.

Questions: How does this film show the beauty of God's grace in the Christian view? The extravagance?

Beyond the Class

A selection of materials is in the Instructor's Manual and PowerLecture.

Christian Ethics: Following the Way of Jesus Christ
Foundations in the Ten Commandments, the Sermon on the Mount, and the Letters of Paul
The Enactment of Moral Life in the Church
Christian Worship and Ritual
Christian Worship before Constantine
Worship after Constantine
Christianity in North America Today
Overview
The Different Churches: Roman Catholic and Protestant

Terms

What's Inside

Key topics in this chapter: the name "Islam"; the growth of Islam; the different groups in Islam; the essential teachings of Islam; Islam as a way of life; the Five Pillars of Muslim worship; Muslim life in North America today.

Learning Outcomes

LO1 Explain the names *Islam* and *Muslim*.

LO2 Know how the main periods of Islamic history have shaped its present, especially the different Muslim groups.

LO3 Give the essential elements of Islamic teachings in your own words.

LO4 Explain Muslim ethics, especially in diet, dress, and marriage.

LO5 Explain the ways Muslims worship, especially the Five Pillars.

LO6 Explain the main aspects of Muslim life in North America today.

Chapter 12 Outline

Your Visit to Mecca
The Name *Islam*
Islam Today As Shaped by Its Past
Arabia at the Time of Muhammad (500s C.E.)
The Life and Work of Muhammad (ca. 570–632)
Islam Immediately Following the Death of Muhammad (632–661)
Islam from the Ummayads until Today (661–present)
Diverse Muslim Groups Today: Mainstream, Zealous, and Moderate
Essential Teachings
God Is One
Angels and Spirits
The Qur'an
Prophets

Discussion Questions

1. In the "What Do You Think?" feature at the beginning of this chapter, you were asked your opinion about the statement "Islam is mostly a religion of peace." In what ways is this statement true, and in what ways is it not? Explain your answer.

2. How did the Sunni and Shi'a groups arise, and how do their differences today relate to their origins?

3. How did Islam come to Africa and south Asia?

4. Name the main Muslim groups today and the issues on which they both agree and disagree.

5. What special opportunities and difficulties do you see in studying Islam in our post-9/11 situation?

6. In what ways is Islam especially Arabic, and in what ways is it not?

7. Explain the statement "Islam is a religion of the book."

8. How does Islamic monotheism relate to monotheism in Judaism and Christianity?

9. How, and how well, does almsgiving function to promote compassion and social justice in Islam?

10. Give your choice of a term for modern militant Islam, and explain why.

11. Why do you think the remake of the 1976 film *The Message* is now titled *The Messenger of Peace*?

12. Comment on the 2008 statement by Madeline Albright, U.S. secretary of state in the 1990s: "I know there are some who would like to engage with Muslim communities without bringing religion into the conversation. But to them I say, 'Good luck.'"

Islam in Film: Suggestions for Viewing and Discussion Questions

Significant but of mixed cinematic value is *The Message* (1976, rated PG), directed by Moustapha Akkad, the story of Muhammad (without depicting him directly) and early Islam. Production work began in 2008 for a remake of this film, tentatively entitled *The Messenger of Peace.*

Questions: How well does this film depict Muhammad without depicting his face? *Messenger of Peace* is not a common Muslim title for Muhammad. Why do you think the film makers are using it for the remake? What overall portrait of the birth of Islam emerges from this film?

An excellent film on the history of Islam in America is *Malcolm X* (1992, rated PG-13), directed by Spike Lee and starring Denzel Washington.

Questions: How does this film show the "conversion" of Malcolm X to mainstream Islam during his pilgrimage to Mecca? What is the appeal of both mainstream Islam and the Nation of Islam to African Americans, according to this film?

Persepolis (2007, rated PG-13), an animated film directed and written by Vincent Paronnaud and Marjane Satrapi, is an acclaimed coming-of-age story about an outspoken Iranian girl. It begins near the time of the Islamic Revolution in Iran, which it presents unfavorably.

Questions: How do the personality and views of the main character in this film shape her view of Islam in Iran? What is the meaning of the film's title? How does this film express the unhappiness of many young Iranians with religious and social conditions in their country?

Kite Runner (2007, rated PG-13), directed by Marc Foster and based on a novel by Kaled Hosseini, is the powerful story of an Afghani expatriate who goes back to Taliban-controlled Afghanistan to bring out the child of a friend.

Questions: How does this film portray the strength of mind and courage of the main character? How accurate is the depiction of Taliban rule, in your opinion?

Arusi Persian Wedding (2008), directed by Marjan Tehrani, is a documentary about Iranian Americans who travel back to Iran to be married, with good treatment of the social, political, and religious contexts of modern Iran.

Questions: What are the challenges facing Iranian Americans who go back to Iran for marriage? How might this film illumine the experiences of people of other religions who go back to their homelands for engagement and//or marriage?

"People of the Book": Jews, Christians, and Zoroastrians
Final Judgment
Islamic Ethics
The Hadith
Shari'a
Diet and Other Regulations
Marriage and the Status of Women
Jihad
Worship: The Five Pillars of Islam
Confession of Faith
Prayer
Fasting
Almsgiving
Pilgrimage
Islam in North America
The Nation of Islam and the American Muslim Mission
Muslim Migration to North America
Muslim Life in the United States after 9/11

Terms

What's Inside

Key topics in this chapter: the different names used for this type of religion; the common features of new religious movements; the spread of new religious movements in the world today; the main features of Falun Gong, the Church of Jesus Christ of Latter-day Saints, and the Church of Scientology.

Learning Outcomes

LO1 Evaluate the different names for new religious movements.

LO2 Summarize the common features of new religious movements.

LO3 Survey the distribution of new religious movements in the world today.

LO4 State and explain the teachings and practices of Falun Gong.

LO5 State and explain the history, teachings, and practices of the Church of Jesus Christ of Latter-day Saints.

LO6 State and explain the teachings and practices of Scientology.

Chapter 13 Outline

Your Visit to Temple Square, Salt Lake City, Utah
Names for This Type of Religion
Common Features of New Religious Movements
New Religious Movements in the World Today: A Survey
NRMs in the Western World
Asian NRMs in the West
"Scientific" NRMs: Christian Science, UFO Groups, and Scientology
Nature NRMs: Neo-Paganism, Wicca, and Druidry
NRMs in Asia
An NRM from Asia: Falun Gong
History
Teaching and Practice
A North American NRM: The Church of Jesus Christ of Latter-day Saints
History
Scripture

Discussion Questions

1. In the "What Do You Think?" feature at the beginning of this chapter, you were asked your opinion about the statement "New religious movements are often dangerous organizations." In what ways is this statement true, and in what ways is it not? Explain your answer.

2. How adequate is the term *new religious movement*, in your view? What are its strengths and weaknesses?

3. What similarities and differences can you draw between Falun Gong and Buddhism?

4. Critique this statement: "The LDS church is, among all world religions or NRMs, the most American."

5. The Church of Jesus Christ of Latter-day Saints has given the *Book of Mormon* an unofficial subtitle: "Another Testament of Jesus Christ." What do you think was the church's reason for doing so?

6. Would you say that the Unification Church is a Christian church? Why or why not?

7. At what point do NRMs cease being "new religious movements" and begin being "religions"? Explain your answer, using the example of a traditional religion such as Christianity, Islam, or Buddhism.

8. What is the most difficult challenge to you in studying this type of religion? Why?

New Religious Movements in Film: Suggestions for Viewing and Discussion Questions

Perhaps because of their controversial nature, the stories of new religious movements are not often captured in feature films. One exception can be found in connection with the Latter-day Saints church, which has a motion-picture operation loosely related to the church (nicknamed "Molly-wood").

God's Army (2000, rated PG), directed by Richard Dutcher, tells the story of four young LDS missionaries as they encounter various problems and opportunities in their work and their lives.

Questions: What are some of the main LDS teachings and practices highlighted in this film? What did you learn about the work of Mormon missionaries? What are some of the challenges facing Mormon missionaries today?

The Book of Mormon Movie (part 1; 2004, rated PG), directed by Gary Rogers, tells of roughly the first half of the Book of Mormon. The portrayal of this book is selective but literal. Viewers—including Mormons—accustomed to typical Hollywood production values may be disappointed with the cinematic quality of this film, but it is worthwhile watching as an example of Mormons explaining their scriptures through the medium of film. Part 2 of the *Book of Mormon Movie*, titled *Zarahemia*, was released in 2008.

Questions: What key insights into Mormonism can be derived from these films? Why do you think the LDS church has invested so much money and effort into making these films? What is your own conclusion about the "production values" in these films? Do they help or hinder your own viewing?

Beyond the Class

A selection of materials is in the Instructor's Manual and PowerLecture.